MORE THAN JUST
THE CLIMB
Life's Lessons Well Learned

MORE THAN JUST THE CLIMB

Life's Lessons Well Learned

Martyn Bould

UNICORN

Published in 2025 by
Unicorn, an imprint of Unicorn Publishing Group
Charleston Studio
Meadow Business Centre
Lewes BN8 5RW
www.unicornpublishing.org

Text copyright © 2025 Martyn Bould

All rights reserved. No part of the contents of this book may be reproduced, stored in or introduced into a retrieval system, or transmitted, in any form or by any means (electronic, mechanical, photocopying, recording or otherwise), without the prior written permission of the copyright holder and the above publisher of this book.

Every effort has been made to trace copyright holders and to obtain their permission for the use of copyrighted material. The publisher apologises for any errors or omissions and would be grateful to be notified of any corrections that should be incorporated in future reprints or editions of this book.

ISBN 978 1 917458 41 2
10 9 8 7 6 5 4 3 2 1

Design by newtonworks.uk
Printed in Glasgow by Bell & Bain Ltd.

Acknowledgements

With thanks to Eva Menuhin who edited it, Lord Ian Strathcarron and Ryan Gearing of Unicorn Publishing who published it. Jonathan Dingle for his introductions and unflagging support and ideas, Patricia Bradley for her guidance and review and of course for my 'teenager' and wife Vivian for her unwavering support, particularly as writing is a somewhat selfish endeavour, taking up a lot of free time over some 4 years of drafting. And, of course, to all those people who have so enriched the journey of my life to date and to those who will continue to do so.

'To appreciate "More Than Just The Climb" is to appreciate a crucial chapter in the modern history of the Cayman Islands – and Martyn Bould's unique contribution to it.

'It is a story not of a single event, but of a quiet, humble, steady force who helped shape our country's infrastructure; whilst demonstrating how, skill, integrity and a deep sense of community can lay the foundation for lasting success.

'As an integral figure in the construction industry, his influence extended far beyond the buildings he helped erect. He is, in essence, a master builder of trust.

'"More Than Just The Climb" offers more than a chronicle of professional achievements. It paints a portrait of a person who is deeply committed to his adopted home. Martyn's story is a testament to the power of a life lived with purpose. It reveals his dedication to his profession, his unwavering support for the arts and culture, and his profound belief in the potential of the Caymanian people.

'The pages that follow convey a rich and detailed account of Martyn's journey. It is a story of life lessons learned, of meticulous work, and of a commitment to the highest standards.

'Martyn's legacy is therefore etched not only in the structures that dot our landscape, but also in the principles of honesty, dedication, and Caymanian community spirit that he championed throughout his life. It is an inspiring read, reminding us that true success is measured not just by what we build, but by the character we bring to the task.

'I am honoured to make this small contribution to Martyn's book, as his Member of Parliament – but more importantly as a fan and friend.'

Hon. Andre Ebanks MP, Premier Cayman Islands 2025

'I have read the content on which your book will be based – congratulations on a remarkable record of a remarkable life – what energy, insight, kindness and achievements! I am proud to know such a man, and to be counted in his friends.

'VIVA!! Alan.'

Alan James Scott CVO CBE, Governor of the Cayman Islands 1987–1992

'From pirates to penalties and big mountains to big machines, this careful and considered autobiography spans eight decades of compassion and charity that define a remarkable individual. Martyn Bould's insightful yet always kind writing takes the inspired reader across continents and deep into the Caribbean as it develops from a postcolonial backwater into the thriving centre of trade finance and tourism that it has become. The characters the story introduces, the at times absurd contractual problems of building in a climate of ever shifting foundations, and the cultural heritage with which the narrative is imbued make this an excellent guide to the development of the region in the second half of the 20th century. The work is of course a tribute to the author's own authenticity and the support his remarkable "teenage" life partner has given him, but it is far more than simply a paeon of praise. The author encounters hard truths, steep climbs and the reified atmosphere of mountain ranges and the largest business deals the region has seen. It should be essential reading for all those who want to know how things came to this point and how they can be taken forward. warmly recommended with joy and delight.'

Jonathan Dingle FRSA FSOM, Mediator, International Arbitrator

'A colourful, panoramic narrative of a life well lived in the rapidly changing post war era.'

Duncan Taylor CBE, Governor of the Cayman Islands 2010–2013

'As a young boy, I first heard of Mr Bould long before I had the privilege of meeting him. My uncle, Jimmy Powell – widely known as the "Condo King of Cayman" – often spoke of him with the greatest respect and admiration. Together, they worked on the very first condominium developments along Seven Mile Beach, projects that would set the course for the Island's future growth. My uncle frequently described Mr Bould's talent, integrity, and, above all, his genuine love for the Cayman Islands. When I later had the honor of meeting him myself, I immediately recognized the same qualities my uncle had spoken of so often.

'Mr Bould's contributions have been both pioneering and profound. As a quantity surveyor and developer, he helped shape Cayman's physical landscape through developments that remain milestones in our history. Yet his impact reaches far beyond construction. In his role as Chairman of the Cayman National Cultural Foundation (CNCF), he carried Cayman's name proudly onto the world stage, representing our Islands at major international forums while also fostering cultural preservation and creative expression at home.

'His life's work reflects a rare blend of professional vision and personal devotion. He has enriched Cayman not only through the structures he helped bring into being, but also through his steadfast commitment to our cultural identity and heritage. His memoir offers an invaluable record of that journey – a generous sharing of a life that has been intertwined with Cayman's own story of growth and development.

'While Mr Bould was not born in Cayman, it is clear to me, and to many others, that he is truly Caymanian at heart. His legacy is one of integrity, service, and inspiration – a legacy that will continue to guide and uplift generations to come.'

Hon. Franz Manderson Cert. Hon. JP, Deputy Governor & Head of Cayman Islands Civil Service

Contents

	Foreword	ix
	Introduction	1
CHAPTER 1	From Birmingham to Boldmere (1945–1969)	4
CHAPTER 2	Kingston Calling (1969–1971)	13
CHAPTER 3	Planes, Projects and Paradise (1972–1981)	33
CHAPTER 4	Crisis and Construction (1982–1987)	56
CHAPTER 5	Storm Clouds over the Tropics (1988–1992)	78
CHAPTER 6	Cayman Rising (1993–1997)	98
CHAPTER 7	Seven Mile Dreams (1998–2002)	125
CHAPTER 8	Global Ambitions, Island Roots (2003–2007)	168
CHAPTER 9	Shockwaves and Aftershocks (2008–2012)	217
CHAPTER 10	Baha Mar and the Impossible Question (2013–2017)	277
CHAPTER 11	Pandemics and Perspectives (2018–2021)	351
CHAPTER 12	Beyond the Summit (2022–2025)	411
	The Cayman Islands: Significant Dates	484
	Bibliography	488
	Index	490

Foreword

More Than Just The Climb chronicles the remarkable life and times of the author and his beloved wife, Vivian, as well as the colourful cast of dozens of people who have so far played a role in his journey. This memoir traces Martyn Bould's long and eventful life from his birth in Birmingham, England, shortly after the end of WWII right up to the eve of his recent conquest of Japan's tallest peak, Mt. Fuji, at the tender age of 80. It is the challenges, adventures, globetrotting, opportunities and the singular achievements of the years in between that make his an amazing life story. Regardless of how you define success, Martyn Bould's life story will meet that definition. Born into a family of modest means, he qualified as a chartered quantity surveyor and at age 24, took a leap of faith that would see him working first in Jamaica, and eventually setting up shop and settling in Cayman in the early 1970s.

Following the end of WWII in 1945, there was great agitation for independence in many of the British colonies and both Jamaica and Trinidad & Tobago declared independence in 1962. Prior to that, the Cayman Islands, which had been a dependency of Jamaica, had opted not to go with Jamaica and had been granted its own constitution in 1959, thereby becoming a crown colony in its own right, freed from the control of the Jamaican government. For the first time in its history, Cayman had its own Executive Council (Cabinet) which could make major policy decisions and promote the Islands' growth and development. Thus, when the independence honeymoon in Jamaica started to sour and foreign exchange restrictions were introduced, Cayman was viewed as an alternative place in which to invest and develop. This was similarly the case when Bahamas gained independence in 1973 and became less welcoming to foreign investors. Cayman became the beneficiary of both of these policy decisions.

Martyn was among that first cadre of professionals who arrived in Cayman on the cusp of the Islands' first development boom, bringing expertise and experience that was otherwise not readily available amongst the Islands' population. As such he was instrumental in helping lay the foundations for

Cayman's modern infrastructure, not just as a quantity surveyor, but also as entrepreneur and developer.

For me the memoir makes fascinating reading. It describes in accurate and vivid detail the Cayman I grew up in. I was a mere schoolboy when Martyn arrived in Cayman and the book is replete with anecdotes, circumstances, places, events and people that I recall with a rush of nostalgia. In my lifetime the Islands' population has grown from a mere 8,500 people to more than 85,000 and most people resident here now will not recognise the Cayman that Martyn writes about. It is thus a good history lesson.

I first met Martyn in 1984 when I was an articled clerk, articled to the late Colin Charles Adams at the law firm Charles Adams & Co. After qualifying as an attorney-at-law, I also served with Martyn on the Board of the Cayman National Cultural Foundation. CNCF was and indeed remains one of Martyn's passions and his work and involvement in the foundation feature often and prominently in the Memoir.

Martyn loves to climb. Whether Kilimanjaro or Mt. Fuji, it's the challenge that thrills him and drives him on. It is in meeting and surmounting the challenges that life's lessons are well learned. I am certain he feels a kinship with the legendary mountain climber Sir Edmund Percival Hillary who along with Tenzing Norgay in 1953 became the first to reach the summit of Mt. Everest. And that he like Sir Edmund will also affirm "It is not the mountain we conquer but ourselves."

Hon. Sir Alden McLaughlin KCMG MBE KC JP, Attorney-at-Law,
Premier Cayman Islands 2013–2021

Introduction

In the early eighteenth century Edward Teach, otherwise known as Blackbeard, set about transforming the north coast of Nassau into a den of iniquity, rife with gambling and piracy, slavery and smuggling, partying and drinking. He created a legend and, heedless of the cost to others, imposed on the Bahamas a new order which remained until suppressed by the Royal Navy in 1718.

Some three hundred years later, a new project arose to capture the imagination of all who came to glittering Nassau's northern shores. This was the Baha Mar resort development – a US$3.4 billion building scheme to create, if not iniquity, indisputably extraordinary venues for gambling and partying, hotels and holidays. This time, however, it was not the likes of Teach and his pirates bringing the changes, but funds from a Chinese lending institution that surpassed the World Bank in the monies it could command.

But, like Blackbeard, they had found some troubles on the coral coast. They needed careful handling – checks and balances rather than cannon and crossbows. In 2010, the Project Monitor appointed by the Export Import Bank of China (known as China Exim) to oversee the disbursement of their enormous loan to build the Baha Mar resort was, to my delight and at times deep concern, me.

At that time, the largest construction project in the Western Hemisphere was not going well. Some five years into construction and as mid-2015 approached, after various project delays the Baha Mar project was, at best, struggling to reach completion. Reservations had been accepted for the opening, though they were unlikely to be honoured, and the possibility of opening several floors in the high-rise towers was discussed, while construction would continue on the remaining areas.

Moreover, acceleration costs would require additional funding. Proposals were made that included partial funding from China Exim and China Construction America (CCA), the contractor, and from the developer, Baha Mar Ltd. Accordingly, a meeting was scheduled in Beijing for the second week in June.

I arrived there on the morning of 8th June, and the following day met with China Exim and Allen and Overy, their attorneys, to discuss the terms of the guarantees to cover the additional proposed borrowing.

On 10th June 2015, we were summoned to a 9am meeting in the boardroom of China Exim bank. A vast boardroom table accommodated over thirty participants, with many additional advisors positioned in rows behind them. I was seated at the table directly across from the Bank's President, Mr Lui. Around the table were various bank officials, Sarkis Izmirlian and his development team, as well as Tiger Wu and his contracting team. Behind me sat our site manager, Gordon Glen, and our attorney, Jerry Katz.

The discussions were conducted either in Mandarin with translations, or in English, also translated. The meeting commenced with representatives from each department of China Exim bank affirming they were an honourable institution and had acted appropriately. These statements took some time, and I found them puzzling. Later, I was advised that the two silent individuals seated in one corner had reportedly been from the Central Government. There followed a presentation by the Baha Mar development team, explaining the causes of the delays and cost overruns, and attributing these to the contractors. They proposed that with a further injection of some US$200 million, the hotel could be completed and opened within a matter of months.

The proposal called for a funding contribution of US$100 million from China Exim Bank, US$50 million from CCA, the contractor, and US$50 million from Baha Mar Ltd., the developer. CCA then responded, blaming the delays and cost overruns on Baha Mar, but ultimately agreeing that the additional funds would enable the development to be completed.

At this point, the President of the Bank looked directly at me, and asked in Mandarin if this was possible, to which I replied – perhaps too softly – 'impossible'. This was translated as *ke neng*, and I was surprised to see everyone smiling and thumbs-up.

I was then asked, again, if completion was possible within the claimed period, and I said a little more forcefully, 'not possible', which was then translated as *bu ke neng*, which understandably changed the mood of the entire meeting. After further discussions, we were all asked to reconvene to explore how we might progress and develop a mutual agreement on cost, timeline to completion, and the specifics of the guarantees. We worked for several days, arriving at various proposals before I left Beijing to return to Cayman on 13th June.

But on 29th June we were shocked by the following press release:

29th June 2015 PR Newswire – Sarkis Izmirlian Chairman and Chief Executive Officer of Baha Mar Ltd., the developer of the Baha Mar resort announces that in order to complete construction and open Baha Mar as soon as possible, Baha Mar Ltd., and entities associated with it, are voluntarily undertaking the process of Chapter 11 under the US Bankruptcy Code.

The Board of Directors has determined that due to the financial consequences of the repeated delays by the general contractor, and the resulting loss of revenue, the Chapter 11 process is the best path to provide the time to put in place a viable capital structure and working relationships to complete construction and successfully open Baha Mar. The voluntary Chapter 11 filing has been made in the US Bankruptcy Court for the District of Delaware. Baha Mar Ltd. will be filing an application in the Supreme Court of the Commonwealth of the Bahamas seeking approval of the US court orders.

As might be imagined, there followed a flurry of telephone calls discussing how to proceed, while I pondered to myself how it was that a mere quantity surveyor from a not-so-leafy suburb of Birmingham, should end up seated at the boardroom table, offering my opinion and playing a central role in resolving the completion of such a massive project.

Well, here is my story – written because, in retrospect, the journey so far has been hard to believe and because for years my dear wife Vivian (my eternal teenager) has been encouraging me to set down some of these stories. So, here we go.

> *'We shall not cease from exploration and the end of all our exploring will be to arrive where we started and know the place for the first time.'*
> 'Little Gidding', T.S. Elliot, 1885–1965

CHAPTER ONE

From Birmingham to Boldmere (1945–1969)

'Life is either a daring adventure or nothing at all.'   Helen Keller

I was conceived during the Second World War, but had the sense to pop out when it was safe to do so – after the shooting had stopped – on 10th December 1945 in Glendower Road, Perry Bar, a suburb of Birmingham.

My dad, Fredrick Charles Bould, was a joiner (a timber craftsman or finish carpenter) and from a Shropshire farming family. My mom, Phyllis Margaret Bould, was from a butchering family from Handsworth, another Birmingham suburb.

One of my earliest clear recollections was moving from Glendower Road to 102 Antrobus Road, Boldmere, Sutton Coldfield, in a more 'upmarket' suburb of Birmingham, when I was five. Another clear recollection of this time is an ambulance ride to hospital, with the bell ringing, with what was initially thought to be meningitis. I was there for two weeks and only one parent at a time was allowed to visit, and only one visit. The primary reason for the draconian restriction was, I was told, that healing would be quicker if one was not pining for home! I did not in fact have meningitis but remember finding it difficult to walk on release after lying in bed for two weeks. One lesson I did learn from my hospital stay was to frequently and thoroughly wash my hands, particularly before eating, which has stayed with me throughout life. Thus, during the COVID pandemic in 2020, this guideline was nothing new to me.

I attended Boldmere Primary School and joined the 1st Wylde Green Cub pack, led by Amy Hudson, and earned a number of badges, which were dutifully sewn on my uniform by my mom. I then graduated to the Scout troop and became patrol leader of the Peewit Patrol. The Scout leader was Jim Hudson, Amy's brother, whose day job was making and delivering Vesey cordial to people's homes. The Cub and Scout hall was in a large parcel of land behind the Hudsons' house where we would all attend camp and make twisters – flour dough twisted over a stick and cooked over the camp fire – and sing 'camp-fire' songs. It was excellent training for a young person, and I acquired skills such as cooking, navigation and astronomy that have stood me in good stead during later life.

In 1957, when I was eleven, the 9th World Scout Jamboree was held in Sutton Park over twelve days to celebrate the fiftieth anniversary of Scouting. It was attended by fifty thousand Scouts from around the world and opened by the Duke of Edinburgh. My job was to deliver the Jubilee Journal – the daily newspaper. Swapping badges was an enjoyable part of the daily round and I well recall getting a badge from a dark-skinned scout from Frankley Beeches and rushing home to tell my dad that I had a prize badge from an African scout. My dad burst out laughing, and explained that Frankley Beeches was a suburb of Handsworth not far from where we lived!

That same year I passed my 11+ examination, which meant I would go to a grammar school as opposed to a government secondary school. Bishop Vesey Grammar School, named after its founder, was established some five hundred years ago by Bishop Vesey, who served as Bishop to King Henry VIII. I found it enjoyable, and played second row forward for the school rugby team. The first time I played on a Saturday, I hadn't realised I was required to arrive at school in uniform. Having already cycled several miles from home on my Dawes Dalesman drop handlebar bike, I was told by the sports master to ride all the way back, change into my uniform, return to the school, and then change into rugby gear to play. It was worth it in the end – we won. Much later in life, BVGS became a common bond with Alan Scott, the Governor of the Cayman Islands. He had also attended BVGS to study Latin & Greek, as Geoffrey Cross, the headmaster, was acknowledged as an authority in teaching the Classics.

My older sister, Carole Patricia, was born six years before me, while my younger brother, Robert John, arrived nine years after I did. Carole was lively and fun-loving and enjoyed parties. She began working at the Dunlop tyre company as an electron microscopist, studying high-hysteresis rubber for racing tyres. At a Birmingham university dance she met Graeme Heldreich, a dental student; they married in 1963 and went on to have five children: Richard, Edward, Anne-Marie, Jonnie and Charlotte.

In 1962 my time at BVGS culminated in 'O' levels, with passes in Maths, English Language, Latin, French, Chemistry and Science. So, at sixteen, my dad suggested I consider a career as an estate agent or general surveyor. Coming from a farming background, his reasoning was simple: in his experience, even if things went wrong with the farm, the agent always made money. As we knew little about university life or entry requirements, we turned to Graeme, who had university experience. He identified the Royal Institution of Chartered Surveyors as the best qualification to aim for, with the recommended path being via the University of Reading College of Estate Management. My application was duly submitted to the college, and I eagerly awaited a response indicating when I could move to London (the college was situated in St Alban's Grove, South Kensington) and begin my university studies.

What we did not know, and what no one told us, was that to gain entry to the college as a full-time student one needed 'A' levels, even though the RICS only required 'O' levels, which I had.

In the interim, whilst waiting for a reply from the college, I was working at my dad's factory in Aston, where he made furniture and fitted out shops and bars in pubs. I had done this during holidays since I had been a small boy, as in my dad's opinion a week's holiday leisure was enough, the balance being most productively spent gainfully employed with him. My thought had been that I would eventually take over my dad's business, but he cautioned that I should gain a degree first to have a fallback position. This followed from his experience as the fourth of five brothers with only two farms to inherit, one being in my grandmother's family and the other in my grandfather's. Dad's farming upbringing also led to a lifelong tradition on his birthday, which was in May. Everyone else's in the family ranged from December to February, and as dad's special day was an outlier, the family would often forget it. On such occasions dad would come down to breakfast and, missing a birthday greeting, would always exclaim, 'Not even a new-laid egg!' – that being, as a farmer, the least present one could expect!

Whilst working at the factory, I decided to build a canoe. It was fourteen feet long and had plywood cross frames and ash stringers. The framework was then covered by canvas, stretched and tacked to the stringers. I was very lucky that dad employed a Welshman upholsterer called Len, who would take the dark blue metal tacks into his mouth and then one by one pick them out with a magnetic hammer and hammer them into the canvas and stringers. Perhaps understandably, Len liked his beer (who wouldn't after having your mouth full of tacks all day!) and typically, by Monday, Len's wages had gone and he would need a float until next Friday payday. The canvas was then painted, and on completion I named the vessel *Alma* after the street where my dad's factory was located. *Alma* was taken for a launch ceremony to Powell's pool in Sutton Park and we were delighted with its performance on its maiden voyage. There followed many exciting trips white water canoeing on rivers such as the Wye, particularly in the spring when the rivers surged with runoff from the winter melt.

By this time I had missed the start of school, where I could have returned to take 'A' levels, so an alternative plan was needed. My dad took his lunch each day at one of the pubs he had fitted out, and one day he asked me to join him. Sitting at the table was a quantity surveyor who invited me to visit a building site in Perry Bar, on which he was working and where he showed me what he did. It looked interesting, and so my career path took a slight deviation. Enquiries were made about where I might learn the profession, and one Gordon Britton, a professional quantity surveyor, became the pathway to my future life. His office was in Edmund Street in Birmingham, close to Snow Hill train station. It was accessed by a narrow flight of stairs that opened into a linoleum-floored reception area and several rooms warmed by gas fires, with very sticky brown paint to imitate woodwork on the walls.

I was advised that I would be an articled pupil and appropriate parchment papers were drawn up, these being an agreement between my dad and Mr Britton. I would be taught by Mr Britton and his staff, but with essentially no rights under the 'Articles of Pupilage'. The office team was Norman Mills, the 'taker off'; Roger Peyton, the 'worker up'; Miss Dot, a part time secretary; Mr Britton, 'the boss' and me, 'the pupil'.

Norman guided me in construction details and how a logical sequence of measurement and marking up the drawings being 'taken off' resulted in an accurate list of quantities. These then had to be 'billed' and like items collected together on a large sheet of paper, which was Roger's job. All entries were in fountain pen ink and if one made a mistake, one used a small bottle of bleach to eradicate the error on the paper, which once dry had to be rubbed with your fingernail to give a smooth surface so the corrected entry would not smudge.

My job was to open the office in the morning, put on the tea, and light the gas fires to warm the office, and my initial task was to learn how to multiply in 'duodecimals', essential for 'working up' measurements in a process known as 'squaring' to arrive at quantities in square or cubed amounts.

My pay was five pounds three shillings and sixpence per month. Despite this modest income, my dad – who always dressed impeccably for more formal occasions and had his suits custom-made by a tailor from Hector Powe who visited our home for measurements and fittings – kindly availed me of the same service, covering the cost himself. That early experience sparked a lifelong love for well-made suits and, as you will see later in this story, I would later be introduced to fine tailors in London to continue the tradition he began.

I enrolled as a student with the Royal Institution of Chartered Surveyors and also began a five-year correspondence course through the College of Estate Management, part of the University of Reading, which did not require 'A' levels if you were not attending full time. To further my skills, I also attended evening classes at Matthew Bolton Technical College. This being before email, each completed lesson had to be mailed in and it would take a couple of weeks before the marked papers were returned by the tutor.

After some eighteen months working at Gordon Britton, I considered I was becoming reasonably proficient and summoned up the courage to enter Mr Britton's office to request a raise. He looked shocked, and informed me that, in fact, my pay was to be reduced due to an increase in National Insurance deductions from my base salary. More importantly, my Articles were an agreement between him and my dad and I had no right to request a salary increase directly.

Accordingly, I asked dad to approach Mr Britton on my behalf, which he duly did. Net result? Mr Britton said I would never make a quantity surveyor, suggested I return to work full time at my dad's factory, and wrote a letter to that effect. My mother kept that letter in a black safekeeping box for the rest of her life.

So, I needed employment. I interviewed with one D.F.J. Henri & Partners, based in Erdington, which was much closer to our Antrobus Road home than Edmund Street, and got a job at five times my previous salary. Our offices were on the second floor above a row of shops and we often amused ourselves by throwing erasers out of the open window and then hiding, but peering to see the reaction of pedestrians on the sidewalk below as the rubber missiles bounced on the pavement before them.

An early assignment was a dormitory block under construction by Tarmac contractors at the RAF College at Cranwell in Lincolnshire. I had a Lambretta scooter for transport because my first car at that time – a 1947 MG TC roadster that leaked oil prodigiously – was in bits being slowly reassembled by a friend. No one else in the office had a scooter, so my expenses for the journey were paid at the same rate as for a car and often exceeded my salary, which was a nice bonus. I rode the several hundred miles from Erdington to Cranwell on my scooter in all weathers. One Friday night around Christmas / New Year, I had an accident on an icy road and took a good chunk out of my knee. The resulting scar is still clearly visible. My dad had signed me up for a residential course at the College of Estate Management on the Monday following the accident, and although I was hobbling on crutches he insisted I attend the course, which required travelling by train from Birmingham to London, to avoid forfeiting the fee. The MG TC was finally reassembled and sold, and I bought a blue Austin Healey Sprite which was far more reliable, soon followed by a red Triumph Spitfire – another two-seater roadster.

I had to wait for one year between my final Part 1 and final Part 2 exams as I had not attained the required age of twenty-one, but I fortunately passed all the RICS examinations at first attempt and was duly elected a 'Professional

Associate' of the Royal Institution of Chartered Surveyors, on 7th October 1968. My proud parents and I attended the ceremony, held at the wonderful Georgian building on Parliament Square, Westminster, that houses the Royal Institution, to receive my Diploma Certificate from the President. So much for Mr Britton's prediction that I would never make it as a quantity surveyor!

I fondly recall my twenty-first birthday celebration, which was a black-tie dinner held at Park House in Sutton Park, and where my mother gave me Rudyard Kipling's poem 'If—', which sits on the desk in my office and by which I have attempted to live my life since then:

IF— Rudyard Kipling

If you can keep your head when all about you
    Are losing theirs and blaming it on you,
If you can trust yourself when all men doubt you,
    But make allowance for their doubting too;
If you can wait and not be tired by waiting,
    Or being lied about, don't deal in lies,
Or being hated, don't give way to hating,
    And yet don't look too good, nor talk too wise:

If you can dream—and not make dreams your master;
    If you can think—and not make thoughts your aim;
If you can meet with Triumph and Disaster
    And treat those two impostors just the same;
If you can bear to hear the truth you've spoken
    Twisted by knaves to make a trap for fools,
Or watch the things you gave your life to, broken,
    And stoop and build 'em up with worn-out tools:

If you can make one heap of all your winnings
    And risk it on one turn of pitch-and-toss,
And lose, and start again at your beginnings
    And never breathe a word about your loss;
If you can force your heart and nerve and sinew
    To serve your turn long after they are gone
And so hold on when there is nothing in you
    Except the Will which says to them: 'Hold on!'

If you can talk with crowds and keep your virtue,
    Or walk with Kings—nor lose the common touch,

> If neither foes nor loving friends can hurt you,
>   If all men count with you, but none too much;
> If you can fill the unforgiving minute
>   With sixty seconds' worth of distance run,
> Yours is the Earth and everything that's in it,
>   And—which is more—you'll be a Man, my son!

Further career moves took me from D.F.J. Henri in Erdington to Hart Gilmore in Edgbaston and then on to Wills and Hingley in Wednesbury, both times quadrupling my salary. I secured my own office at Wills and Hingley, with a window that looked out onto a soot-stained brick wall – Wednesbury is in the heart of the so called 'black country', the manufacturing centre of the Midlands. As you will see, I have had so many supposedly spontaneous connections in my life, and in retrospect it is interesting that my secretary at Wills & Hingley came in one day with 'Jimmy' written on her hand, and when I asked who that was, she said, 'Jimmy Cliff, of course.'

'And who is he?'

'A reggae star', she replied.

I was now fully qualified as a chartered quantity surveyor, playing rugby for the Old Veseyans, enjoying my job, driving a fancy British Racing Green TR4A sports car (the successor to the red Spitfire) and living high on the hog.

In addition to my job, I enjoyed ventures into commerce by selling bri-nylon shirts and men's cosmetics under the brand name of '12 Bore – for men of the right calibre'. I would take orders in the pub for collar sizes and cosmetics and then place bulk orders from the wholesale market in Birmingham. The merchandise would be distributed back at the pub at a retail price. My partner in crime in this venture, Michael Johnson, remains a lifelong friend and his daughter Hannah is my wife Vivian's and my god-daughter. Michael and his wife Doreen eventually came to Cayman to live, but here I am getting ahead of myself.

During a business trip to London, I was invited to a newly opened boutique Chinese restaurant – Mr Chow's, in Knightsbridge, which was a restaurant with a difference: all the waiters were Spanish but all the cooks were Chinese. I was introduced to Michael Chow, whose passion was collecting Thunderbird cars. The décor of heart art pieces (it opened on Valentine's Day) was attractive and the menu was excellent, with many small tapas-size Chinese dishes. To this day, more than fifty years later, the menu remains essentially the same and I'm sure that Dino, the current maître d', gets tired of me saying I have been a regular customer for more than that long!

In mid-1968, I was sitting at my desk one day, idly perusing a copy of the RICS monthly journal *The Chartered Surveyor*, when I noticed an advertisement for the RICS Appointments Register – a form to fill in stating one's qualifications, experience, and where one would like to work. I thought I'd try this, just for fun, and filled it out, noting down my contact information and writing 'the Caribbean' as my desired work location – I have no idea why. I had not studied what the opportunities there were, whether it was safe, what the quality of life was, what the economy was like. But, I wasn't taking this seriously anyway and I soon forgot about it.

About three months had passed, when I received a telephone call at home. A gentlemen on the other end, Basil Cawston, said, 'I understand you want to work in Jamaica.'

I replied, 'I believe you have the wrong number; I don't know anything about working in Jamaica.'

He responded, 'This is the number I have on the Appointments Register in front of me, and Jamaica, in case you don't know, is in the Caribbean – which is where the Register states you want to work. You do remember filling out the Register?'

'Oh yes,' I said. 'I do remember.'

'You don't sound very keen – are you interested or not?' said he.

'Errrr – yes I am,' said I.

'In that case,' said Mr Cawston, 'are you available to attend an interview with me at the White House serviced apartments in London this Saturday at 10am?'

'Yes,' I said, 'I will be there.'

Saturday dawned overcast, and I arose early to make sure I had ample time to drive the one hundred and twenty miles from Sutton Coldfield to London for the interview. All went well until I reached the M1 motorway, where an impenetrable fog had descended and traffic moved at a snail's pace. It eventually cleared, but I only reached the White House apartments' front desk at 11.30am – a full hour and a half late for my appointment. I asked the concierge for the number of Mr Cawston's apartment, which was 5C on the fifth floor, and he directed me to the elevator.

I stepped out on the fifth floor, located 5C and knocked on the door, getting no response. In frustration I hammered on the door, but to no avail. Dejected and annoyed, I turned away and pushed the button for the elevator to descend. The elevator arrived, the door opened, and then there was a magic moment of serendipity – I heard a sound behind me in the corridor, turned, and there in the open apartment door stood a gentleman in a terrycloth robe, looking very much the worse for wear, who said, 'Were you the one banging on the door just now?'

'Yes,' I reply, 'are you Basil Cawston?'

'Yes,' he says, 'who the hell are you?'

'I am Martyn Bould here for a 10am interview – I'm terribly sorry I'm late.'

'Thank goodness you're late. I was out very late last night, and I feel like sh—. Please go downstairs and as soon as the bar opens order two Bloody Marys. In the interim I will have a shower and get dressed, and after the Bloody Marys we will both feel better.'

Little was I to know that my life had taken a major change of direction. Three months after the interview I was offered the job by Mr Cawston, and arrived in Jamaica on 1st March 1969.

CHAPTER TWO

Kingston Calling (1969–1971)

'Love the life you live – live the life you love.' Bob Marley

Preparations began for my departure from the UK, and many questions needed answering, especially about clothing and luggage. It seemed a white dinner jacket was considered essential attire and duly acquired (I only ever wore it once!) and I bought a large trunk made of plywood with an aluminium outer covering. My dad insisted on making a tray with a series of different sized compartments for the upper level of the trunk to help organize the contents. It would be sent ahead by ship, accompanied by a set of golf clubs bought for lessons dad and I had begun some months earlier. Dad had adopted the frugal approach in case we didn't enjoy the game and purchased a full set of irons, from which he took the even-numbered clubs and I the odd, while both of us purchased a driver and a putter.

When I boarded the flight from Heathrow to Kingston my Jamaican work permit had not yet been granted, so the intention was for me to overnight as a tourist in Kingston and continue on to George Town, Grand Cayman – where it was easier to get a permit – to wait until such time as my Jamaican work permit came through.

The trunk and golf clubs were duly dispatched to the Cayman Islands. The trunk was eventually transshipped back to Jamaica, but the clubs never turned up. On the bright side, the insurance settlement for their loss provided useful working capital for my new life in the Caribbean, since my only other funds were £500 from the sale of my TR4A car.

On stepping off the plane at Palisadoes Airport in Kingston, the heat at the aircraft door almost bowled me over. I was met by the smiling face of Ivor Spry, one of the partners at BGW Cawston & Partners. He announced my work permit for Jamaica had been granted and so I would be staying in Kingston, and drove me to the Four Seasons Hotel on Ruthven Road, where I fell straight into bed for a deep sleep.

Next morning, Ivor arrived to take me to the office and introduce me to the team on the second floor of the IBM building in New Kingston, up-town from the main area of Kingston on the waterfront.

My secretary was Alison Shervington, married to the famous musician Pluto Shervington, and one of my first assignments was to work on the extension to Medical Associates Hospital, owned by the gynecologist Jimmy Burrowes. Jimmy was a Rhodes scholar and, unbeknown to me at the time, was little impressed by expatriates who came to Jamaica to seek employment. I hasten to add he subsequently became a very good friend.

I visited the site as soon as I could, since the foundation work had started, and was looking around early one evening when I hear a tap on one of the office windows in the completed part of the hospital. A man inside beckons me over.

'What are you doing nosing around my site?' he says.

'I am Martyn Bould the new quantity surveyor assigned to manage this project.'

'In that case,' says Dr Jimmy 'come into my office,' which I did.

'What would you like to drink?' he asks.

I look a little uncertain as to what he is offering – maybe water?

'I have Red Stripe, rum or whisky,' says Dr Jimmy.

Coming from England, this young QS is more used to doctors being reticent about your ailments than offering you a drink! I updated Jimmy on the work progress, had two or three Red Stripes and we had an enjoyable time chatting.

The contractor on the Medical Associates project was L.D. 'Jenks' Jennings, who became a close friend until his death in 1973. Jenks was from Coventry in the UK and his wife, Brenda, always well dressed, was part of the 'St Andrew Housewives Set' who spent much of their time exchanging views about the difficulty of securing and managing good household staff. At that time it was considered normal in Kingston to have a nanny, a maid, and a gardener/yardman. Prior to starting his own company, Jenks had been the MD of Higgs & Hill (he affectionately nicknamed the company 'Pigs & Swill') an international UK contractor operating in Jamaica. He was also the representative for Frankipile, a foundation piling company, and Jenks would take great joy in the strapline he invented for them: 'Piles for the Poor but Hemorrhoids for the h'Aristocracy.' He was one of the world's true characters.

While at Higgs and Hill Jenks had built a hotel, later rebranded as the Jamaica Hilton, near Ocho Rios on Jamaica's north coast. The quantity surveyor was one C.T.R. (Terence) Kelly, who wrote a book titled *Carib Sands* about his experience, which vividly described the construction process in Jamaica and its many challenges. Jenks gave me a copy and insisted I immediately read it in detail to prepare me for the job I was to do in this part of the world – it was one of many life lessons I was to learn.

I have frequently described my arrival in Jamaica as 'dying and going to heaven – the girls are beautiful and partying an art form'. For example, Saturday lunchtime drinks at Basil Cawston's home on Millsborough Avenue in Barbican were a tradition, and generally continued into the late afternoon while the ladies went out shopping. Late one particular Saturday afternoon at Basil's, I suddenly felt a stabbing pain in my back that quickly had me curled up on the floor in agony. The assembled group, by then all well-oiled after an afternoon of imbibing, agreed I should be taken to Dr Jimmy's house just up the road. Jimmy took one look and sent me to Medical Associates for overnight observation. Basil drove me to the hospital where the nurse on duty admitted me with: 'Mr Bould, please fill out this form and pee into this tray for testing.' I'm on the bed, still doubled over in pain, so Basil fills out the form for me … and also donates the urine sample on my behalf!

His generosity caused some consternation, because Basil was a diabetic. He had already left for the night when the worried nurse returned from testing the sample and announced I needed to be on a special diet! The nursing shift changed overnight, and the morning nurse looks at my chart – and looks at me – looks at the chart again – and at me – and says, 'Mr Bould, there is something wrong here. Dr Burrowes admitted you last evening as Mrs Bould and about to deliver your baby!' Fortunately, my problem was merely a kidney stone, so less life-changing, but the incident taught me a cautionary life-lesson about remaining alert when with a group of fun-loving and inebriated friends and colleagues!

After about a week at the Four Seasons it was suggested I move to the Liguanea Club, a residential and squash, tennis & golf sports club. The institution was a remnant of Jamaica's colonial past, which was waning and would do so more rapidly some years later when the Manley PNP administration replaced the Shearer JLP government.

To become a resident at the Liguanea, an interview with the manager – one Colonel Figeroa – was required. I duly presented myself at his office, where I was rigorously questioned about my profession, my way of life, and, most pointedly, my morals (specifically, whether I would refrain from bringing ladies back to my room if admitted!) I must have passed inspection, because the Colonel summoned a smartly dressed young man – black shoes, pressed trousers, starched white jacket and a bow tie – and introduced him as Aston, my steward. I must have looked a little bewildered, because the Colonel rapidly added, 'Aston will bring you your morning tea or coffee, your daily newspaper and see to your laundry.' I thanked him politely, wondering at the serendipity of it all. Here I was, living a life of luxury – this very ordinary young man from the Midlands who had, just a few months earlier, been disconsolately waiting for the fifth floor lift in the White House apartments before turning around to see a hung-over Basil, clad in his terrycloth robe, demanding to know who the hell I was!

The Liguanea was within walking distance of our office at the IBM building on Knutsford Boulevard in New Kingston. We frequently lunched there but the service was typically slow, and an initial Red Stripe usually turned into several more while we waited in the bar or on the terrace overlooking the tennis courts for our sandwich orders. Tired of the interminable waits, the Athenaeum Club was set up on Oxford Road, at the rear of a former residence that had been converted into the offices of Chalmers Gibbs, an architectural firm. The club was a 'key' club; discreet and unmarked. No sign announced its presence, and only those with a key could unlock the black door set into an otherwise featureless wall. Aston, my steward from the Liguanea Club, was appointed as barman, with the promise of faster, more intimate service. Members had a 'tab' which was paid at the end of each month, so no cash changed hands.

The Athenaeum rejoiced in a cast of characters so colourful they could easily serve as the basis for a book of their own. I can offer only a brief vignette here, but among the key founding members were Dr Cliff Western, architect Ian Gibbs, Keith Fredricks and Basil Cawston. An initial hiccup concerned a favoured lunchtime drink: the bullshot. This concoction – vodka and beef consommé laced with Lea & Perrins sauce and black pepper – was served over ice and we could drink a surprising number with no evidence of inebriation. It was only sometime later we discovered that no one had thought to mention vodka as one of the ingredients when instructing Aston.

A game of darts known as cricket was popular in the lounge, and we spent many hours over lunchtime and early evening drinks enjoying the competition. On occasion, wives would suspect the presence of their wayward husbands inside the club. Memorable amongst these was Kitty Cawston, who would bang on the locked black door shouting, 'Basil I know you are in there – come out!'

Cliff Western was a UK doctor who had come to Jamaica and married Beverly, his stunning-looking Jamaican wife. He also trained and sponsored Bunny Grant, an aspiring boxer who eventually became the Jamaican light and welterweight champion. Sadly, Cliff drank a little too much whisky, though he disciplined himself at lunchtime. He would arrive at the Athenaeum at noon and order a 'doctors special': soda water, bitters and a squeeze of lime poured over ice – a drink I continue to thoroughly enjoy. Cliff would leave the Athenaeum at 1pm to go back to his surgery and then return to the Athenaeum at 3.30pm. At parties he could be seen standing up and fast asleep!

Other characters included Dossie Henriques and Willy Priestnell, both of whom had drivers who patiently waited whilst they enjoyed the camaraderie of the Athenaeum. Willy was driven around in a Rolls Royce of some vintage, which he always maintained was well serviced. This was checked, as the service manual recommended, by placing a thru'penny bit standing on its edge on the dashboard. If it did not fall over, the car was correctly balanced and tuned.

Another character I met was Bobby Nunes, who enjoyed giving parties at his home in Kingston, and who would subsequently become a great friend and business associate. At one of these, while still a nervous young Englishman newly arrived in Jamaica and who had not formally been invited, I politely introduced myself to the host, 'Thank you Mr Nunes for your hospitality.'

To this Bobby replied, 'What is your name?'

'Martyn Bould,' say I.

'The bold Mr Bould,' Bobby responded, 'Let me introduce you to some chicks!'

Bobby's politically incorrect classification for the fairer sex at the time would, during the course of his life, become subject to further sub-classification: Baby, Grannie, etc.

Alan Foster, a Jamaican architect, had qualified at the Architectural Association in London in 1967, married Jenny, and returned to Jamaica to work for Chalmers Gibbs. In 1969 Alan won the Governor General's Award for Architecture for the design of the Department of Psychiatry at the University Hospital of the West Indies, and he and Jenny remain very close friends of ours. In 1970 Alan Foster joined Dennis Chalmers and Ian Gibbs, the two principals of Chalmers Gibbs, along with John Martin, whom he had met in London at the Architectural Association, to form Chalmers Gibbs Martin Foster.

I was keen to learn as much as possible about Jamaica and purchased *Exploring Jamaica – A guide for Motorists*, published the year I arrived. This most useful book contained a series of routes covering the entirety of the wonderful Jamaican countryside. My white Vauxhall Viva company car, with red upholstery, subsequently travelled to more remote places in Jamaica than any car before it. One special trip I recall vividly was to Accompong in St Elizabeth, established in 1739. It is the principal Maroon village in the Cockpit Country of Jamaica, and where I was privileged to meet the Colonel of the Maroons. The Maroons were freed slaves from Africa who fought the British and won. The British subsequently signed a treaty granting them lands and freedom from taxation, a privilege they enjoy to this day. Bob Marley's mother was a Maroon who lived in St Ann's Bay on the north coast.

The Liguanea was convenient accommodation, but one day Basil announced in the office that his daughter Jackie was dating a young pilot, Robbie Hamaty, who was renting a two-bedroom townhouse at Sutton Place on Ruthven Road in New Kingston and was looking for a flat mate. I therefore moved in, and so was blessed to become immersed in Jamaican society and culture early on. Robbie's father, Munair Hamaty, was an attorney and also the Custos of Westmoreland. He flew a Cessna 172 from Sweet River in Westmoreland to Tinsen Pen in Kingston to conduct his daily business. The Hamaty's house in Savanna la Mar ('Sav la Mar') was spacious and I was soon invited to spend weekends there, flying down from Kingston on Friday evenings and returning early on Monday mornings. Days were spent on Bluefields beach with Robbie and his brother Freddie (later to become a Jamaican senator) and Freddie's wife Merle.

Flying in small planes quickly got into my blood and I decided to become a pilot myself. I joined the Jamaica Flying Club, located near the end of the Palisadoes Airport (now Norman Manley International Airport) runway in October 1969. My instructor was an extremely patient and relaxed Mike Came. I attempted my first solo flight after only five hours of instruction in a Piper Cherokee 140, and I clearly remember leaving the ground, looking at Port Royal in the distance and the Palisadoes runway far below me, and asking myself what the hell I was doing up there on my own. But by the time I turned onto the final approach and had clearance to land from the tower, I had calmed down sufficiently to land and taxi back to the flying club, where a time-honoured tradition awaited me: the back was cut out of my shirt, marking a successful first solo flight! I gained my first pilot's licence #289, dated 18th August 1970, which I still have.

One of the students in my group was a photographer who offered one evening to pick up his girlfriend, a Bunny at the Playboy Club in Oracabessa on the North Coast and fly her back to Kingston. Tragically, he became disorientated when flying over the Blue Mountain range in a cloud and crashed. Subsequently, all students were asked to secure a night rating to add to their licence. This involved flying under instruction with all instruments covered, except for the airspeed and turn-and-bank indicators. As Mike Came took the plane up, I wore a hood that blocked any view outside the cockpit and looked at the floor. He then put the plane into a spin and said, 'OK, now you sort this out.' At his cue I lifted my head to see the airspeed rapidly increasing and the turn and bank indicator spinning wildly. The response: pull the nose up and apply the opposite tail rudder to counter the spin, level off and return to safety. Finally, I had to plan a night flight from Kingston over Air Hill to Montego Bay ('Mobay'), land for a coffee, and fly back along the North Coast to Boscobel airfield (since renamed Ian Fleming International Airport) and then return to Palisadoes. I secured my night rating on 11th July 1972.

Willy Priestnell had significant experience as a private pilot, so I asked him one day if he ever felt frightened or concerned when he flew. He responded, 'Young man, on occasion I have been so frightened flying that only God and my laundry mistress knew how frightened I was!' Instead of driving along Jamaica's winding roads, which could take hours out of one's work day, flying quickly became my preferred mode of transport to conduct my QS work.

There was a drawback to the convenience of flying around Jamaica, which was that friends living 'Country' – i.e. away from Kingston – would ask for favours. These would usually be the quick delivery of key items they needed from the capital. One day, whilst I was working at my desk, such a request came from Patrick Marzouca, who lived in Sav la Mar in Westmoreland and whom I had met through Robbie Hamaty. Patrick said he was able to purchase a Volkswagen Variant station wagon from a Peace Corps worker at a very attractive price, but that it needed a new windscreen, and could I pick this up from the dealer in Kingston and fly it down to Frome, a sugar estate, which had a grass airstrip near where Patrick lived. I objected, saying I was busy, but after much cajoling I succumbed, collected the windscreen and flew it down to Westmoreland, where I was met by Patrick. He quickly installed it in the vehicle and said, 'Why don't we drive to Mobay for a night on the town, and then you can stay with me overnight and fly back to Kingston tomorrow morning?'

This sounded like a good idea and off we drove, visited several nightclubs in Mobay, drank many different beverages (none of them non-alcoholic) and did a good deal of dancing. Then came time to drive back to Sav la Mar. We climb in, Patrick starts the car and finds that when he presses the accelerator nothing happens. We open up the engine cover in the rear of the car and discover that the cable to the accelerator had broken. 'No problem,' says Patrick, 'I'll drive and you straddle the engine and work the accelerator lever.' The car had a stick shift, and Patrick shouted when to apply the gas and when to release so he could change gear. We drove this way over the mountains, surrounded by the evening mist – it created a surreal and slightly spooky atmosphere – to Sav la Mar, arriving at his house somewhat exhausted, but home safe. As we walked in, we were greeted by a terrifying sight for a couple of inebriated young men who had just driven through a horror-movie landscape: on the dining room table was a body, covered by a white sheet, which reared up on our entry! It turned out to be Patrick's aunt, who had a back problem and was sleeping on the hard surface of the table for relief. In our state it was more like being greeted by a duppy [ghost/spirit] at that very early hour of the morning. I flew back to Kingston the next morning to start a day's serious work.

I was a keen rugby and squash player, and soon after getting settled began playing squash at the open air courts of the Liguanea Club. Games tended to be rather sweaty affairs, and afterwards we would sit on the club's outside terrace and consume copious Red Stripe beers – hence our cautionary saying: 'Mind the Red Stripe don't get you', referring both to the red stripe on the side of the bottle and the similar stripe down the dark blue trousers of the police uniform, and the twin perils of a hangover or driving ticket.

I joined the Privateers Rugby Club, where I played second row along with Mervyn Cumber, who had arrived in Jamaica in 1968 to work for Barclays Bank DCO in St Ann's Bay. He drove to Kingston in his MGB for our Saturday rugby games and, as our friendship developed, he often invited me to stay at his wonderful home in Browns Town, in the hills overlooking the North Coast. Mervyn had recently married Penny, a schoolteacher, and both have remained lifelong friends. I learned to water ski at Discovery Bay during my visits to Mervyn and Penny's home, and we enjoyed long BBQ lunches at the Bauxite Company's beach club. Through rugby I also met John Ambrose, a contractor, who supplied me with work producing estimates for jobs he was bidding. John had a 50 percent share in a Piper Cherokee 235, and I eventually flew the plane more often than John or David Lue, the other partner, who operated an air conditioning business.

Mervyn's father, Sir John Cumber, had been Administrator in Cayman from 1964 to 1968, so Mervyn had long connections with the island. He saw huge potential in Cayman, and in 1970 Mervyn and Penny left Jamaica and bought a house on Melmac Avenue in George Town, Grand Cayman. Working for Scotia Trust, they also set up a maid service: 'Redi Maid' and a rental company: 'Cayman Rent a Villa' (now 'Cayman Villas'). The latter is now run by their daughter Juliet. Mervyn and Penny urged me to leave Jamaica too and come to Cayman to live and work. They invited me to stay with them for a week, which further whetted my appetite for these small but fascinating islands that 'time had forgot'. Cayman then had a population of only little over ten thousand inhabitants, and everyone waved in greeting as you passed on the road.

Also, what I was learning about Cayman and Caymanian society led me to believe that a key to Cayman's future success lay in its unique historical background, which set its people apart from those of other Caribbean islands.

The settlement of the Caribbean began with the Arawaks, a people who migrated north from the Amazon basin. They brought agriculture to the region and established the earliest communities. Later, they were followed by the Caribs, a more aggressive and warlike people, who would have likely been the inhabitants encountered by Columbus when he arrived searching for gold and a new route to India. Gold eventually was discovered in South America and the Caribbean became a centre for piracy, targeting the ships carrying gold and other treasure back to Europe.

By the 17th century, the growing demand for tea and coffee in Europe coincided with the expansion of sugar plantations in the Caribbean. This gave rise to the transatlantic slave trade to provide the labour needed to harvest and process the sugar cane. After the abolition of slavery, indentured labourers were brought in to maintain sugar production. This in turn led to the rise of labour unions and, eventually, independence movements, with the initial governments often led by former union leaders.

Cayman, however, followed a very different path. Although slavery existed – in fact, at one point there were more slaves than freemen in Cayman – the islands never supported large plantations. Instead, Caymanian men made their living at sea, initially hunting turtles, then subsequently working as merchant seamen. They were often away for six months or more and, in their absence, a matriarchal society developed at home, with women managing the households and making thatch rope to supplement family incomes. Homes were built gradually, on a piecemeal basis, funded by earnings from the men's work at sea; construction would begin, pause when money ran out, and resume after another voyage. Mortgages were unheard of – Cayman's first bank, Barclays, didn't open until 1953.

This self-reliance, combined with the men's exposure to different countries and cultures, shaped a kind of Caymanian very different to many of their Caribbean neighbours – pragmatic, independent, and aware of the wider world.

But against this tapestry of paradise, what was really happening in the Caribbean – particularly in Jamaica? After gaining independence from Britain in 1962, many Jamaicans hoped for a brighter future free from the island's colonial past. However, the JLP ruling party failed to deliver, and the music scene began to reflect the people's frustrations. The position is well described in John Masouri's excellent book *Wailing Blues - the Story of Bob Marley's Wailers*. It describes the rise in Rastafarianism, especially following Emperor Hailie Selassie I's visit to Jamaica on 21st April 1966, when he arrived at Palisadoes Airport to a tumultuous welcome by over one hundred thousand Rastas.

I have written a lot about the social side of life in Jamaica, but the truth is, while we certainly enjoyed ourselves, we worked very hard. BGW Cawston and Partners had set up a joint venture company with Wakeman Trower and Partners, a global QS practice headquartered in London. The new company was called Wakeman Trower, Cawston and Partners (WTC&P) and based in the Cayman Islands. WTC&P's Cayman attorney was Bruce Campbell and the local Partner / corporate secretary was Paul Harris of Pannell Fitzpatrick. Paul had arrived in Cayman in 1967 and was the first chartered accountant to reside here. David Martin was another Pannell Fitzpatrick partner residing in Jamaica.

Essentially, pre-contract work was done in London by the Wakeman Trower entity, and post-contract work on the ground was done by BGW Cawston & Partners in the Caribbean. The fee billing entity was Wakeman Trower Cawston & Partners in Cayman. Expenses were paid for work done by London and Jamaica and the balance remained in Cayman tax free. At this time there were no restrictions on the movement of monies between Cayman and London and Jamaica. This was to change dramatically in 1972–73.

During my first visit to Cayman, in 1969, I had been handed a small white booklet extolling the tax benefits of setting up companies and trusts in the Cayman Islands. It had been written by William (Bill) S. Walker, a visionary Guyanese barrister, and Marshall Langer, a US tax attorney. The booklet was commissioned by Jean Doucet, a Montreal banker who had learned of Cayman through Marshall Langer. Subsequently twenty thousand copies were mailed to potential investors around the world.

Bill Walker had been born in Guyana and discovered Cayman on a holiday visit while still working with Ramon Alberga in Jamaica. In January 1964 he decided to set up a Cayman office in the Rembro building. By 1968 he had been joined by Bruce Campbell, who only stayed with him briefly before joining Jim Bodden, a realtor, land developer and Cayman politician. In 1970 he set up his own practice, Bruce D. Campbell & Co. Today Walkers employs over a thousand staff in ten offices, and Campbells employs one hundred and fifty staff in three offices. Bill's wife, Janet, is an excellent artist whose depictions of typical Caymanian scenes helped lay the foundation for the appreciation and artistic representation of our culture. Many years later, her work, along with that of several others, provided the impetus for the formation of the National Gallery.

Doucet moved to Cayman in 1968 and formed the International Corp of the Cayman Islands – later known as Interbank. In 1970 he established Sterling Bank & Trust, which became the first bank to use a computerised system for managing accounts. In a sign of the times, female staff members were encouraged to wear hot pants, mini-skirts and knee-high boots to work!

Cayman was in many ways lucky, as key events happened in the right order – another factor contributing to Cayman's success: Marco Giglioli arrived to commence work on eradicating the mosquitos; Cable and Wireless came with a reliable overseas phone system in 1966; the British Government built the jet runway and then, in 1968, the Pindling Government in the Bahamas took full control of power and began moves towards independence and the revocation of expatriate work permits of those working in the offshore centre there, which resulted in some lawyers and accountants deciding to move to Cayman.

Following the introduction of the Banks and Trust Companies Law in 1966 and the Trust Law in 1967, more and more attorneys and accountants were making their base in Cayman. For example, Jim Macdonald, a colourful Canadian attorney already based here as a law agent (and who intelligently registered the name 'McDonalds' in Cayman) hired one John Maples in early 1969 to form Macdonald & Maples. Douglas Calder, a friend of Mervyn's, joined the company that same year. It is interesting to note that today the Maples Group comprises three thousand staff in sixteen offices around the world.

To jump forward briefly: by July 1974 Doucet was successful enough to host one thousand guests at the Holiday Inn to celebrate the launch of Cayman Mortgage Bank, which was offering home loans to Caymanians. But, on 16th September 1974, Doucet's $50m empire collapsed because of liquidity problems. Doucet had left on a private jet three days earlier, bound for Monaco.

Back to my own employment; WTC&P secured work building the Pegasus Hotel in Kingston and the Frigate Bay Infrastructure project in St Kitts, which involved building a road connecting Basseterre to the beaches of Frigate Bay to the south, a beach club to seed the beginning of development in this area, and a golf course some time in the future.

So, who to send to St Kitts to process the monthly payment certificates for contractor Higgs & Hill and liaise with architects/ engineers Covell Mathews? How about Martyn Bould, a single young man keen on travel? I first arrived at Golden Rock airport in St Kitts in October 1969 and stayed at the Ocean Terrace Inn overlooking the curve of the Caribbean Sea. It was owned by Colin Pereira, the local Phillips Electrical dealer and political activist, and each room had the best and latest tape and radio players.

The Kingston to St Kitts route via commercial airline offered some interesting variations, such as Kingston to St Kitts via Haiti or Santo Domingo. I took full advantage of these. On my first trip to Haiti I stayed at the extraordinary gingerbread palace known as the Grand Hotel Oloffson, named after a Swedish sea captain and the setting for Graeme Greene's 1966 novel *The Comedians*. A film of the book had also been shot there. At this time, Papa Doc Duvalier was ruling Haiti with an iron rod and using the threat of the infamous Tonton Macoute to suppress any political opposition. The visit sparked a fascination with this exotic but sad country that has remained with me since, and through many visits.

Following the above trip, on Boxing Day 1969, I was asked to fly to St Lucia to look at a hotel site at La Toc, leaving Jamaica on 27th December and arriving in Castries in St Lucia on the 28th. Trying to find detailed information on construction and development during the Christmas break anywhere in the world is not easy, but on a Caribbean island is nigh-on impossible. Be that as it may, my report was well received by the would-be English developers.

By this time, I had once again moved my residence in Kingston from Robbie's apartment in Ruthven Road to one half of a duplex in 19B Waterloo Avenue. I built a wonderful barbecue in the front, using the bricks from the construction site at Medical Associates. These bricks told a story, as they would have come to Jamaica as ballast in sailing ships outward bound from English and Scottish ports. The duplex was owned by one Dr H.D. Collins who had been the Medical Officer of Health in the Cayman Islands for a number of years.

Because I had flown to St Lucia right after Christmas, I had accumulated many bottles of Christmas booze in unopened presentation boxes. So, on my return home, I thought, 'Now I'll enjoy a nice rum and coke!' But as I lifted the gift box of a fine aged bottle of Appleton Estate it almost flew from the top of the cabinet – the gift box was there, but no bottle inside it! All the other gift boxes were the same. In my absence I'd been robbed, the thief cleverly leaving the boxes in place to cover his tracks.

Not long after my arrival, I had been introduced to an attractive blonde lady whose family had deep roots in Jamaican society. We began dating and I met many interesting people through her, including her uncle, who was Jim Paterson, the Custos of Portland on the north coast. She worked for Lufthansa as a travel agent and her job had its perks, which eventually led us to travel to Trinidad for Carnival, arriving on Sunday, 8th February 1970. Early Monday morning, at 4.30am, we arose, dressed in all-white cotton outfits and joined one of the groups for 'J'ouvert'. We chipped down the streets to Independence Square, surrounded by oil-covered 'mudders' attempting to brush up against us, all while following a loud band – and, yes, sipping rum at 5am! The celebration continued non-stop until midnight on Tuesday and included the colourful bands of Pretty Mas, many thousand strong, working their way across the Savannah in Port of Spain.

What a wonderful assemblage of people of every race and colour, all enjoying themselves! But this carefree atmosphere was to change dramatically with the growing Black Power movement, as on 6th April 1970 a protestor was shot by police. Prime Minister Eric Williams declared a state of emergency on 21st April 1970, at which both the Trinidad Defence Force and the Coast Guard mutinied and took hostages.

I have always struggled to understand prejudice of any kind, but particularly that relating to race. Hailie Selassie I encapsulated the issue magically in October 1963 during a speech to the United Nations in New York:

> ... on the question of racial discrimination, the Addis Ababa Conference taught to those who will learn this further lesson that until the philosophy which holds one race superior and another inferior is finally and permanently discredited and abandoned, that until there are no longer first-class and second-class citizens of any nation, that until the colour of a man's skin is of no more significance than the colour of his eyes, that until the basic human rights are equally guaranteed to all without regard to race, that until that day, the dream of lasting peace and world citizenship and the rule of international morality will remain but a fleeting illusion, to be pursued but never obtained.

In later years I would spend a lot of time working in Trinidad for both public and private clients, and this early introduction taught me a lesson about the background to its culture.

I toured South America after Carnival in Trinidad, though I'm not sure how I pulled off permission to do this after working at Cawston for less than one year. I arrived in Caracas, Venezuela, on Friday 14th February, then went on to Quito, Ecuador; La Paz in Bolivia; Buenos Aires, Argentina; Rio di Janeiro and Brasilia in Brazil; back to Venezuela, then Curaçao in the Dutch Antilles. I arrived back in Jamaica on 6th March after a month away from work!

Toward the end of March 1970, I was asked to go to Cayman, where WTC&P had secured an assignment to prepare renovation/expansion estimates for the Beach Club Colony. I was delighted, and proudly shared the news with my many friends and colleagues in Jamaica – many of whom joked that Cayman was where they sent people who had done something wrong. I asked why and received the response that there were only ten thousand people there, and that the mosquitoes would carry you away!

The club's owners were John Hatch (who had a profound knowledge of naval history) and his wife Andy. Their four children were called Chi Chi, Bug, Bird and Quatro, and Blue was a huge dog that always lay across the door as one tried to enter the office. It was a truly fascinating establishment with a very popular bar. Mosquitos were indeed very bad – at cocktail hour one had to run from the car to get inside relatively unbitten. Chi Chi was married to David Foster, who had the bar concession. David was so generous that his bar tab generally exceeded anyone else's, to the point that he needed to rent out his car to cover his monthly tab. Fortuitously, this led to the founding of CICO Rent-a-Car, which eventually grew to the point that David asked his brother Steve to relocate from Jamaica to run it.

As I've mentioned, Cable and Wireless provided telephone service to the island, and international calls were connected through their exchange by an operator called Christine. As part of our company was in the UK I had many international calls, and so got to know Christine quite well. If a call came in after working hours, Christine – bless her – would patch it through to the bar at Beach Club!

Regulars at the Beach Club included David Penaydo and Horace Duquesnay, whose party trick was to bet a round of drinks if he could eat a champagne glass – which he did! Others included the architect Pat Quinn; ex-commissioner of police Sandys Sherwood, who always wore a cravat, and Jamaican barrister Karl Brandon, whose party piece was reciting, in a wonderful booming voice, 'Invictus' by the Victorian poet William Henley, which concluded

> It matters not how strait the gate,
> How charged with punishments the scroll,
> I am the master of my fate,
> I am the captain of my soul

Perhaps it was these words that gave Karl the temerity to run in the George Town constituency during the 1968 Cayman elections, but he soon realised that Caymanians would not readily accept someone they viewed as a foreigner to be among their leaders.

The Cable & Wireless field team were led by Stan Green, who at a suitable point in the day's work would declare, 'Enough work for a day! We will repair to the Beach Club bar.' I have it on good authority that the reason Heineken beers are called 'Greenies' in Cayman is not because of the bottles' colour, but in deference to Stan Green's copious consumption thereof!

Ken Spraggon, a tall and very thin bookkeeper, was another champion Heineken drinker. He was practically a chain smoker, with an animated way of talking with lit cigarette in hand, with which he would regularly, albeit accidentally, burn holes in other drinkers' clothing. This became such a regular occurrence that it achieved its own name – 'getting spragged'! Occasionally the

Heineken supply would run short, brought on by high demand and shipping delays. However, Ken, resourceful as ever, always stockpiled many cases in the empty cistern of the duplex where he lived on South Church Street, so that became the place to stop when all other sources of supply failed.

In early May 1970 I visited St Kitts to prepare the contractors certificate for payment for the Frigate Bay project. I travelled via San Juan, Martinique, Dominica and Antigua, again taking advantage of the Caribbean islands' proximity to each other to discover more about each country's cultural and topographic differences.

My next Cayman visit was in late May, when I was accompanied by Blair Kay, one of WTC&P's partners, and Peter Moulton, another quantity surveyor, who had joined WTC&P in Jamaica earlier that month. He was to remain in Cayman to run the new office there. We searched for suitable office space, and were offered one to share with an engineering firm – Wallace Evans & Partners, whose representative was Brian Clarke – and architectural firm, Chalmers Gibbs Martin Foster Partnership (CGMFP), represented by Rod Clarke. The office was in a pink wattle and daub cottage next to the Lobster Pot restaurant, with a charming view of the ocean.

The Lobster Pot was run by Pat and Spencer Barnes, and a favourite game at the bar was liar's dice, which Spencer greatly enjoyed but played rather badly. As bets were normally for a round of drinks or even the amount of your bar tab (which Pat rendered monthly) the Pot's financial security could become precarious. Most conveniently, Saturday morning hangovers could be cured by personal delivery of an ice-cold Heineken from the Pot to the office.

We remained there until the end of 1970, when, after a visit from Colin Davis, one of WTC&P's London partners, it was decided that relocating to a newly completed four-story modern building (which qualified as a sky scraper in those days) would project a 'more professional image'. The building, recently completed by Jimmy Powell of Ranja Construction fame, also housed the Royal Bank of Canada. Whether the move was truly about a professional appearance, or a subtle attempt to wean us away from the delights of the Lobster Pot, we will never know!

At this time a developer called Freddie Mann had purchased a parcel of land on Seven Mile Beach on which to develop Caribartel Cayman. Purchasing an apartment there would entitle the buyer to access similar blocks of apartments in other locations. For example, if you bought apartment 122 in Caribartel Cayman, the same key would open a matching unit in a similar development Freddie Mann was developing in Antigua. It was an early concept that in some ways anticipated the modern idea of timeshare ownership. At the centre of the site he developed a clubhouse with a swimming pool and a BBQ area, run by Rudi Czeranka, which was very popular on Sundays. The development eventually changed its name to Harbour Heights.

In addition to my professional life, I have always been interested in development. Concerns about the security and safety situation in Jamaica had prompted the development of townhouses, which allowed for the integration of protective features. Many such projects were under construction at this time. The Athenaeum had an investment club, which enabled members to invest on the Jamaican stock market. I suggested to the club that they should consider investing in a townhouse development in Cayman, and Basil thought this an excellent idea.

We looked for a suitable parcel of land, and in June 1970 Paul Harris identified Portuguese Point as a likely area. He wrote with details and mentioned that John Maples was a good friend and had lots for sale at J$4,600 for 10,801 sq ft, and that beachfront lots in South Sound were selling for US$25,000.

Finally, in November 1970, realtor Jim Bodden wrote to inform us that a decision would be needed by 1st December regarding the purchase of land on Walkers Road. The property – half of a four-acre parcel – was being offered by Dr Freddie Mann (also behind Caribartel), but through a company called Foreign Portfolio Investment (FPI) (West Indies). The price was US$15,000, equivalent to J$12,525 at an exchange rate of .835, with a 10 per cent deposit and half stamp duty set at 7½ per cent. On 20th December 1970, an agreement was signed for the purchase of the southern 2.1 acres of land with 162 feet of road frontage. The agreement was subject to legal opinion on title, as property in those days was unregistered and held under common law title. It was also contingent upon receiving planning approval for twenty-four one- and two-bedroom apartments. As mortgage funds were limited at the time, an alternative development concept was also considered: sub-dividing the property into five separate lots. During the same month, CGMFP sought planning approval from Willie Hamilton, Government Town Planning Officer, for a project to be called Cayman Court.

On 4th March 1971, Cayman Court Limited was incorporated with intention of starting construction in 1972. The land was conveyed to Cayman Court Limited on 12th May 1971, and a new Trade & Business Licence and Local Companies Control Law licence was granted on 27th March 1972.

As there was no Strata Titles (Condominium) Law in place at the time (it was not introduced until 1973) Cayman Court Owners Association Limited (CCOA) was established. The land was then leased by Cayman Court Owners Association Limited for a term of 999 years

Funds for the purchase were advanced by Basil Cawston, Michael Carter and Michael Blake, who contributed J$8,806.00 (75 per cent) on behalf of the Athenaeum Investment Club, and Martyn Bould, who contributed J$2,935.24 (25 per cent). A deposit of J$1,250 had already been paid. And so, at the age of twenty-six, Martyn Bould became Cayman's youngest property developer – featured in London's *Investors Chronicle* and the publication *Personalities Caribbean*, amongst some significant Cayman personalities!

Now that we had secured the land, Cayman Court needed a logo and a sign to announce the development. Ed Oliver, an artist, had a shop on the George Town waterfront called Cayman Art Ventures. He sold postcards and art supplies, gave lessons in watercolour painting, and was also a graphic designer. We used the logo he designed on our site sign and promotional marketing materials. We also had sales interest from Jamaica through the Athenaeum Club, and by October 1971 had already sold two town houses at J$29,000 each.

Next came planning approval. One rather bizarre requirement was we drop two of the twenty town homes from the layout in the middle of the two front blocks because 'it looked better'. Because the blocks stepped back at each junction with the next house, the only position from which one could see the 'missing' house was directly in front of it. Naturally, we complied with the request in order to get underway on the project's first phase of six houses.

A construction contract was negotiated with West Bay Contractors Ltd., owned by Dalmain ('DD') Ebanks and Ed Dowsey. Dalmain was not only a builder, but a singer, politician and boxer, and trained many young people over the years. His son Gary was a talented musician and at lunch break would play saxophone at the site. What a rich tapestry! Construction was soon underway. Progress was rather slow but we eventually completed the first phase early in 1973.

In 1970, I flew solo in John Ambrose's Cherokee 235 to Cayman. These journeys were always an adventure – not only in their own right, but because of the preparations involved. The plane was kept at Tinsen Pen, Kingston's commuter airfield, and the evening before the flight we would gas up both main tanks and the tip tanks. Arising early, our plan would be to drive to Tinsen Pen, then fly to Palisadoes to clear with immigration and customs and obtain the winds aloft forecast to calculate and file our flight plan. However, we often found the gas would have been siphoned out of the plane's tank overnight, which meant we'd have to find someone to refill it – not easy in the early morning! Once at Palisadoes, there would often be no one to clear us through immigration and customs, or in the tower with whom we could file our flight plan, so we had to wait until the staff arrived.

In addition, Rudi Czeranka, who was now working at the Lobster Pot, would occasionally ask us to pick up some sausages made by Charles Hernod, the German owner of the Green Gables pub in Kingston. The first time we expected maybe a shopping bag full, but instead were given literally a crate of them, which we then had to strap into the rear seat of the plane. Its weight, added to the full fuel load and safety equipment, and would cause the stall warning device to sound alarmingly as we struggled to get airborne.

As WTC&P's business in Cayman grew, we purchased a Vauxhall Vega as the company car from Yorke Kirkconnell at Kirk Motors. I would frequently meet Yorke in the Jonkanoo Lounge at the Sheraton Hotel in New Kingston when he visited Jamaica. This was a very popular spot, with live music played by a trio led by Dennis Sindry, an Australian-born singer, songwriter and composer. One evening I joined Yorke for a drink there, and sitting at the other side of the 'U' shaped bar was a stunning-looking brown-skinned girl. Yorke knew her, introduced us, a romance flourished, and I moved into her apartment at Worthington Court.

Initially, all was smooth sailing. But, despite her beauty, the lady turned out to be extremely jealous. This manifested itself over an innocent misunderstanding. It was my birthday, and I was heading to Ocho Rios to carry out a payment inspection. I told her I would fly from Tinsen Pen airstrip, which meant turning left when leaving the car park of the apartment. However, on walking out the door, I remembered I had left some documents I would need in the office. This required turning right instead, leading her to believe I was going somewhere else, maybe to meet some fictitious lady. I thought nothing of it, carried out the inspection, flew back to Kingston, and on the way home stopped for a drink at the Athenaeum Club. Big mistake. I arrived home about two hours later than expected, to be greeted by the sight of all my clothes, cut to pieces, with a birthday cake sitting on top.

Needless to say, I moved my Jamaican abode again, this time to a house on Wireless Station Road, high in the Blue Mountain foothills in Old Stony Hill. I shared the accommodation with Rex Howieson, a gregarious salesman and squash player, affectionately known as 'sexy Rexy'. In the mornings the clouds would blow in through the windows and it was wonderfully cool and fresh. We had a fabulous maid called Ruby, who had the great knack of cooking meals for us that still tasted just-cooked and delicious when we got home in the evening.

Architect Bill Bissell and his wife Edna arrived in Cayman in 1971 to run the Cayman branch of the Onions Bouchard & McCulloch (OBM) architectural practice, headquartered in Bermuda and also active in the Turks & Caicos Islands. We soon formed a strong professional bond and friendship.

Bill and Edna moved to an apartment on the top floor of Merren's Apartments on South Church Street, and when in Cayman I would frequently stop by for a drink on the way home. John McCulloch, a Canadian, had lived in Bermuda for a number of years, and I once asked him where he stayed when he was visiting London. He introduced me to Jo Butcher, who managed lettings of central London homes for residents who also had country residences. I believe that under the terms of their leases subletting was not permitted, but for cash payment this was ignored. The homes were magnificent, with all the accoutrements such as cut glass and silver left in place. Thanks to this introduction we stayed at many fine homes in the centre of London over the years.

Work was increasing in Cayman and I was busy on a number of projects in Jamaica, so in 1971 I travelled frequently between the two islands. Around this time I was introduced to Charles Adams, a banker and attorney who became a lifelong professional associate and friend.

Charles had joined the Bank of Nova Scotia in Toronto in 1961 and was posted to Jamaica to establish BNS Trust Jamaica Ltd. in Kingston. Interestingly, during his time there he met Bill Walker – then working with Ramon Alberga in Jamaica – and encouraged him to come to Cayman and set up practice. In May 1964, Charles made his first visit to Cayman, where he met with Administrator John Cumber, who encouraged Charles to set up a trust company. In October 1965, Charles established the Bank of Nova Scotia Trust Cayman Ltd., in company with John Collins, who would go on to run the Trust Company. It took Charles a year to get permission for this from head office in Toronto, on the understanding that if the Trust Company survived for a year the retail bank would follow. Charles had wanted to move to Cayman at that time, but head office insisted he remain in Kingston, which he did until his resignation in 1968.

While at BNS Trust, in 1962, Charles met Peter Anninos who was seeking investments in Jamaica. Peter was later instrumental in uniting the unlikely co-investors – Crown Agents and the Chicago Bank Continental of Illinois – to form Crown Continental Merchant Bank Jamaica Ltd. in 1966, which acquired many properties in Jamaica. Simultaneously, the same co-investors established Caribbean Bank (Cayman). Architect Jerry Sibley designed Crown Continental's award-winning headquarters in Jamaica on Duke Street, and it was here that I met Charles in 1971. Charles had his law practice on one floor, while the bank occupied another. I was invited to lunch in the magnificent boardroom occupying the top floor, where the white carpet was kept pristine under dust sheets except during meetings and on special occasions.

I was also the quantity surveyor on the Turtle Towers Condominium being built by McAlpine in Ocho Rios. I would fly into Boscobel airport, take a taxi to the site and then climb four twelve-story towers on foot to inspect the progress on each apartment. This was good exercise. and I would be reward myself with a lunch of green pasta with a magnificent meat sauce served at the stunning Sans Souci resort, before flying back to Tinsen Pen.

Charles asked me to look at many of the Crown Continental properties including Carib Ocho Rios's, Sunset House in Montego Bay, and Silver Sands, and being able to fly made reviewing these projects much more efficient than driving. The architect for many of these Jamaican properties was Jim Mitchell, an American. He eventually came to Cayman to work on projects that included Charles's house, known as 'The Roost', in Frank Sound, Grand Cayman, on which I was the quantity surveyor.

When in Cayman I shared a house on Seven Mile Beach with Bruce Campbell. The house was owned by a Mr and Mrs Cox, had two master suites facing the ocean and a superbly equipped kitchen. Mrs Cox was one of three sisters who all persuaded their husbands to build houses in a beach-front complex. The other two sisters were Mrs Grimmer and Mrs Miller – the latter was married to Mitch Miller, the famous band leader of the 'Sing along with Mitch' US TV series. Mitch was always very relaxed when in Cayman and walked around the beachfront compound in his 'Y' fronts.

The compound's guest cottage was occupied by Reid Dennis and Rita Turen. Rita was the daughter of Mae and Teppo Turen from Finland, who wrote of their adventures escaping from Finland with seven other people in a book called *The Tuntsa*. After World War II, the Soviets did not permit the Finns to leave their economically devastated country. The Turens and their companions set out for the United States in an old 30-foot fishing boat converted into a ketch rig sailboat. They made it past all obstacles, despite being completely inexperienced sailors except for their colourful, alcoholic navigator. Teppo and Mae came to Cayman, where Teppo became a land developer. He dredged the Palm Heights canal and developed the Portuguese Point subdivision south of George Town.

In 1971 I was invited by WTC&P to become a partner in the practice, perhaps as the reward for having travelled so much to assist in building the practice both in Cayman and regionally. I was, of course, absolutely delighted!

Christmas 1971 saw my first visit back to the UK since leaving for the Caribbean. I visited my old haunts to see my friends, who said, 'We haven't seen you for a while.' I replied that I'd been in the Caribbean for three years! I started to relate stories of my adventures and the places I had visited, and it was a bit like a tennis match: 'I have been to Ecuador' – 'Well we were in Benidorm', and so on. I soon learnt that it was best to keep fairly subdued about what you had been doing, otherwise the listeners' eyes glazed over!

CHAPTER THREE

Planes, Projects and Paradise (1972–1981)

1972

'Life is a succession of lessons which must be lived to be understood.'
Ralph Waldo Emerson

In 1972, planning and construction began on the Bank of Nova Scotia Building on Cardinall Avenue in Georgetown, on the former site of Panton's gas station. In a major coup for the practice, WTC&P were appointed as quantity surveyors, working alongside Empire Realty's Toronto-based architects and Hadsphaltic, the contractors. Although by now I was spending more time in Cayman than Jamaica, I renewed my Jamaican work permit for a further three years, because I still had a lot of work there.

In Jamaica, major changes occurred when in March 1972 Michael Manley stormed to victory in the polls. During his popular rallies the PNP leader – like an Old Testament figure of Joshua – had promised much-needed social reforms while waving his ebony and ivory 'Rod of Correction', reputedly given him by Emperor Haile Selassie I during his 1966 visit. Manley had enlisted the assistance of increasingly popular Rastafarian Reggae stars as he turned the tide from JLP to PNP, using songs such as Bunny Livingston's *Better Must Come* and the tracks from the art house hit film *The Harder They Come*, directed by Perry Hensell and starring Jimmy Cliff – incidentally also the first English-language film with subtitles translating the Jamaican patois! Rastas typically were apolitical, but Manley's popularity with them had been enhanced by a government report that recommended the decriminalisation of ganja, their sacred herb.

That year I met Dave and Noreen Twiss. Dave was a land planner with Shankland Cox, who were preparing extensive planning studies of various sites in Jamaica, including the rugged Hellshire Hills, where Dave's associate, Steve Mendes (film director and Sam Mendes's uncle), had once been lost for a couple of days. The coastguard had to be sent out to find him. As it happened, they had been walking in circles, because the local guide had been holding his machete next to the compass, throwing off the readings the entire time! The Twisses lived at #12 Kingsway Town Homes in New Kingston, halfway along the road between downtown Kingston and the St Andrew foothills. Unfortunately for them, this meant their home was a natural stopping point because Jamaica, then and today, has an informal culture – you don't have to be invited to visit, people just stop by. And so it was for Noreen, with the patience of Job, whose home was pretty much invaded every night by a group of homeward-bound business people. Dave added a room at the end of the garden, which they were kind enough to let me use on my many visits to Kingston.

1972 also saw the founding of Design Collaborative, by Dave Twiss in partnership with Evan Williams, Steve Mendes and Patrick Stanigar. Evan had worked with McMorris Sibley Robinson, another esteemed architectural practice, but his outside commercial interests became a little too much for partner Jerry Sibley and so they parted ways. Alan Foster also joined Design Collaborative a few years later. As a practice, Design Collaborative would become prolific and their designs would sweep the prestigious Governor General's Awards. Projects like the National Cultural Training Centre, McIntyre Lands Development and Ward Theatre were but a few of their outstanding projects between 1975 to 1978.

Tourism was on the increase in Cayman. In August 1972, the first internationally branded hotel opened there: Holiday Inn, developed by Herbo Humphreys, whose cousin and part-owner Anderson (Andy) would play a big part in producing Cayman's full-length feature film: *The Cayman Triangle*, completed in 1977.

Basil Cawston's eldest daughter Sandra had met and married an architect, Arek Joseph, who arrived in Jamaica in July 1972 to work for Chalmers Gibbs. However, he encountered difficulties obtaining a work permit for Jamaica, and was asked to work from Cayman during the week, where obtaining a permit was no problem. Arek would return to Jamaica on weekends, and Basil asked me to assist him in any way I could, which I was delighted to do.

Arek's weekly flights lasted until September that year, when he decided his future lay in Cayman and moved there with Sandra and their young son Nick. Arek had identified a promising duplex located on Melody Lane close to the airport, built and owned by David Arch. In November he wrote to David offering to purchase it for $38,000 with a deposit of $2,000, on the condition he could obtain a mortgage. Ralph Coatsworth, a realtor and valuer, provided a valuation of $40,000. Arek asked me if I would purchase half the duplex, which I did. It was not easy to secure mortgage funding, but John Morgan of Royal Bank & Trust provided a loan of $12,500 over ten years at 10 per cent interest with a monthly payment of $167. Unbeknownst to me at the time, the funds I borrowed had been invested by a certain Phil Lustig, who later became a very good friend and neighbour.

So now I had my own home in Cayman, where I lived until 1978!

1973

'Creativity is intelligence having fun.' Albert Einstein

By February 1973, five units in Cayman Court had been sold, all purchased by Jamaicans. Many were looking for a safe haven for investments as they became increasingly concerned about the new politics in their homeland.

That same month I joined a group of architects and quantity surveyors who regularly met at the Galleon Beach Hotel to discuss matters of joint professional interest. The group was called the Cayman Society of Architects, Surveyors and Engineers (CASE). It was headed by Jack O'Connell, who worked for Rutowski Bradford and Partners, architects and engineers based in Kingston. I was to become President a few years later and was named an Honorary Fellow in June of 2012.

Although I frequently flew myself between Cayman and Jamaica, I also flew commercially with Cayman Airways or British West Indian Airways (BWIA). Cayman Airway's DC3 would occasionally stop in Cayman Brac ('the Brac') where Harriet Lott, Olice Yates and Isabell Thompson, the three flight attendants, would leave the passengers on board and drive to the Buccaneers Inn to fetch fresh ice to cool drinks during the remainder of the flight to Grand Cayman. On BWIA's BAC 1-11, the front seat #1C, closest to the galley, self-reclined and so was decidedly uncomfortable. However, it was Ian Gibbs's seat of choice as it was the only one that ensured he could be served three gin & tonics during the short journey!

On these flights I joined a group of 'regulars' all commuting between Cayman and Jamaica. One of these was Henry Propper, who had joined McAlpine's operation in Cayman after several years as an engineer with Nakash and Fong Yee in Jamaica. We spoke of development and construction in Cayman, and I told him of our Cayman Court development which I was keen to develop further as we had now sold all but one unit.

Foreign-exchange controls had been introduced by the Manley government, and the UK had decided to change the Sterling Area when it joined the EU in 1973, so moving funds between the UK and Jamaica or Cayman had become extremely difficult. Accordingly, my fellow shareholders in Cayman

Court could no longer participate in the venture. So, on one of the flights, I discussed the situation with Henry. He and a fellow engineer friend, Rick Murray, offered to purchase a portion of the shares held by the Jamaican shareholders. John Ambrose purchased the other portion in November 1973.

The exchange controls also impacted WTC&P's ability to manage the cash flows to Jamaica and the UK for the partners there, so I agreed with them that I would purchase their interests in the practice. I wanted to retain the company's name, as we had by now built an excellent reputation and had upcoming projects on the books. These included Kirk Motors; a new supermarket for the Merrens; a Cash & Carry store for the Kirkconnells and pricing work for a new building for CIBC, in addition to pioneering professional property market appraisals. The partners agreed to a name that really was far too long: 'Bould-in-succession to Wakeman Trower Cawston & Partners.' We continued using this mouthful until the late 1970s, thereby preserving the brand we had developed while simultaneously introducing the succession.

We then commenced work on Phase Two of the Cayman Court development on Walkers Road: six more townhouses. The contracting company was Island Contractors Ltd., whose shareholders were John Ambrose and Dalmain Ebanks, and the project was completed at the end of 1974. I had by then moved the WTC&P office from the Royal Bank building to Abacus House on Walkers Road, adjacent to the office of Island Contractors Ltd.

In pushing forward with the second phase of Cayman Court we had perhaps misread the global economic situation. The 1973–1975 oil crisis led to a three-day working week in the UK, which resulted in a slowdown in potential sales. The situation did, however, open my eyes to an alternative opportunity; on a visit to the UK, I noticed that the shortened working week had led to a greatly increased interest in sports, and in particular squash. Cinemas in the UK were being converted into squash courts by a company called County Squash Racquets.

As I've mentioned, I was a keen squash player, but there were no courts in Cayman. Although we had reserved a small piece of land at Cayman Court for a sports club, it wasn't really adequate, so I met with Jim Bodden, who was developing Omega Bay, and placed a deposit on a parcel of land there to develop a racquet club. I invited Evan Williams of Design Collaborative to design the facility.

Evan's commercial interests, which had led to his departure from McMorris Sibley Robinson, included a very popular night club called Epiphany, located in Spanish Court in New Kingston. It was jointly owned by Evan and his partners Claude Chung and Bernie Ruziewicz, and featured live music celebrating the burgeoning reggae scene. One group that showcased there was 'Third World', part-managed by Evan, and whose earnings from foreign tours were paid into a Cayman company that I had set up for him.

1974

'When nothing is sure, everything is possible.' Margaret Drabble

London's 1974 Notting Hill Carnival featured music by Bob Marley and the Wailers – reggae was becoming increasingly popular with UK audiences – but it was a tumultuous year in many other respects. The IRA bombed the Houses of Parliament and the Tower of London, US President Nixon resigned over Watergate, and a series of bank failures unsettled the international banking community.

In Cayman, Interbank and Sterling Bank collapsed, and Mike Austin and Keith Norman were appointed as joint liquidators. Many Caymanians had deposited their funds in the banks, which offered very attractive interest rates compared to other local banks, and the collapse led to significant hardships in the community.

With the downturn in the economy, I began looking for opportunities elsewhere in the Caribbean and flew with John Ambrose to scout out the Turks & Caicos in July 1974. We arrived in Grand Turk and stayed at the Turks Head Inne, where we were greeted at the bar by, John Houseman, a wonderful character who published the bi-weekly local newspaper, the Conch News.

The vision for our practice was established very early on and remains the same today. With small island economies, it was key for us to be able to offer a full range of services to clients throughout the Caribbean region (and later to include Central America) so multinationals did not need different professional advisors in different islands, and to iron out the occasional ups and downs in the economic climate.

To this end, with the idea of opening an office in the Turks and Caicos, we were introduced to Finbar Dempsey, an Irish attorney, who set up Bould Construction Economists Ltd. on our behalf. We then flew to Providenciales and purchased two lots in the Turtle Cove subdivision from realtor Bengt Soderqvist for $15,000 each – with just 1 per cent down and 1 per cent per month, if memory serves.

I was also interested in building a home, and early that year had purchased a lot in Whitehall Estates at the southern end of West Bay Road. Dave Twiss designed a magnificent house, and I applied to the Bank of Nova Scotia Trust for a mortgage. In the end, I did not build the house and sold the lot in 1976. I do, however, have a wonderful sketch of 'Martyn Bould's bathroom' from Dave's design that my dear wife Viv found rolled up in a closet, which hangs in my dressing room to this day. Dave Twiss had a great sense of humor and imagination!

1975

'Nature does not hurry, yet everything is accomplished.' Lao Tzu

In February 1975, I travelled to London to attend and exhibit at the International Home Show to promote both the Cayman Islands and our Cayman Court development. *The Economist* featured it in an article, but unfortunately this did not result in any sales. I joined my brother Rob at his 21st birthday celebration at Park House in Sutton Park, where nine years earlier I had celebrated my own 21st birthday. I also took the opportunity to meet with the Squash Racquets Association in Knightsbridge and then on 12th March flew to Halifax, in Nova Scotia, to discuss Cayman Court sales and possible investors for the Racquet Club with Rick Murray.

I had purchased a Mercedes S500, duty free, in 1974, intending to export it to Cayman. However, I decided to sell it in UK instead and advertised it in the UK papers for sale – again duty free. Little did I realise this was illegal, until one evening two raincoated gentlemen knocked on the door of my parents' house where I was staying, and enquired if said advert was mine. I nodded yes, and they said they were from Customs and Excise and had come to confiscate the car. This they did, and drove away in my lovely Benz! Negotiations took place and after paying the £1,400 duty, I duly licensed and sold it.

In early April 1975 I again moved office, this time from Abacus House to the top floor of the Barclays Bank building on Cardinal Avenue. W. S. Walker & Co were on the third floor below, and Cayhaven Corporate Services Ltd., Bill Walker's company registration arm, was adjacent to my office. Bill's practice was rapidly expanding, and I distinctly recall returning to work after one weekend to find Bill had 'captured' part of the corridor and made it into offices! Later that month, my brother Rob arrived in Cayman, and we visited Jamaica to continue celebrating his birthday and so he could see where I had been living for the previous six years. I was able to fly him around Jamaica in John Ambrose's Cherokee 235, and we had a great time.

John Ambrose was then building a town house development at Mona Great House in Kingston for Harold Ashwell, an architect turned developer. I introduce Harold here, because an amazing co-incidence would occur in South Africa years later, when, unscheduled, we knocked on the door of a homestay – to be greeted by Margaret Ashwell, Harold's wife!

I was working on several Jamaican projects. These included Hampshire House, and Carib Ocho Rios Condominiums for Crown Continental Merchant Bank Jamaica with Charles Adams. We had completed the new Merren's Supermarket in Cayman, and tenders had been secured for the new CIBC bank building in George Town. The Negril Beach Club, with Dave Twiss as architect, was also an ongoing project. We would fly from Tinsen Pen to the Negril airstrip, carry out our site visit and then fly back. The weather in Jamaica can change rapidly and I recall leaving Tinsen Pen on a beautiful sunny day and returning in a violent thunderstorm. To this day Dave thinks I am a great pilot – little did he know how frightened I was!

Another memorable flight to Negril was with Evan Williams, who asked if I would like crab backs for dinner, to which I replied, 'Fabulous!' I had not realised the crabs would be alive in a gunny sack, which as it turned out was not well tied at the top. During the flight they escaped and began crawling around my feet at the controls of the plane, which was somewhat distracting. On landing we managed to round up them up – not an easy task as they were land crabs with one large claw and could be quite vicious. Once cleaned and cooked they were delicious and well worth the drama.

Cicely ('Cissy') Delapenha and her husband Bunny arrived in Cayman from Jamaica that year with their two children, Cathy and Richard. Cissy opened a Chinese restaurant with Franklin Smith, called Twin Gates, located in Red Bay. To boost business, they utilised part of the restaurant for bridge games in the evenings. When it was time to close, Franklin's wife Elizabeth would place a broom upside down in the corner and sprinkle salt around it – and as if by magic the guests would leave. A well-known bit of Caymanian folklore! Later, Cissy moved the restaurant to West Bay Road, renaming it The Golden Pagoda. Bill Bissell and I became such regulars that I had a running tab – she'd send me the bill once a year. I called it 'Cissy's Christmas Club'. We became very good friends, and she affectionately referred to me as her second son. People would look at me, then at Cissy's Chinese features. and Cissy would dismiss the puzzled look with, 'same mother different father!'

Cissy was always at the Pagoda, and always had a new, fairly risqué but innocent joke to keep one entertained while waiting for one's Chinese meal (cooked, incidentally, by a Jamaican chef named Shakespeare). Occasionally, Cissy would read your tea leaves. Her readings were not only entertaining but on occasion uncannily accurate. Once, she told our skeptical Swiss friends about a property they had just acquired in Frank Sound – about which she had no way of knowing. Cissy claimed she learned the art from Aunt Gladys, who once read my tea leaves during one excellent Delapenha Sunday brunch, and pointed to Vivian, my future wife, and said we were an item! There is no way she could have known (as many of you know, Cissy catered our wedding!).

As regards the Racquet Club, we decided that Omega Bay was too far out of town. I had been introduced to Colin and Gurney Panton, who had a property in George Town called Partner Ground, where the Government Administration Building now stands. I had also secured part of the necessary finance we required from David Martin, a partner in Pannell Fitzpatrick.

Colin had been in discussion with Cayman quarry owner Bobby Butz about developing affordable housing using proprietary aluminium forms from a company called International Housing Limited, owned by Daniel Ludwig. He was also the owner of National Bulk Carriers, which employed many of our Caymanian merchant seamen. We decided to build a sample house on lot 20 in Portuguese Point, which I purchased. Bobby was another one of the world's wonderful characters and at school he had been told 'No buts Butz!'. He told stories about daily problems at his quarry that would always finish with, 'You have to live it, otherwise you wouldn't believe it could happen!'

On the music scene, Third World were the warm-up group for Bob Marley on 17th and 18th July 1975 at the Lyceum in London, and were so popular that Bob said he would not play after them again! In the meantime, Evan Williams was continuing with his adjacent commercial interests and opened a cocktail bar in New Kingston called 'Theophany', with Jenny Foster as manager. 'Dizzi', in Northland Plaza on Hope Road, featured similar music to Epiphany and we enjoyed going there too. Cindy Breakspeare worked there and would go on in November 1976 to become Miss World, as well as bearing a son, Damian, to Bob Marley.

10th December 1975 marked my 30th birthday, and to celebrate I chartered Captain Cadian's houseboat ('Cadie' was one of the last of the Turtlemen) and invited thirty of my best friends to join me on a North Sound excursion. Ron, Captain Cadian's son, dived for conch, lobster and fish, which were cleaned in the middle of the sound in the location that became today's Stingray City. Marinated conch, and lobster, and fish wrapped with peppers and onions and cooked over an open fire on Rum Point beach, were all washed down with copious amounts of Veuve Clicquot champagne. What a way to start a new decade of one's life! I still have the Swiss Army knife – the one with all those attachments including the hoof pick – gifted to me by Denny and Sue Diedrick.

Every time I use it (not on horse's hooves!) I'm reminded- of that wonderful day on the Sound – pure paradise.

1976

'Three things cannot long stay hidden: the sun, the moon and the truth.'
Buddha

Security in Jamaica had gone from bad to worse, and a State of Emergency was declared that lasted for the entire year. A Gun Court was established and a dedicated prison had been built, about which Michael Manley declared, 'It's painted Red to show it's Dread', and to which one could be committed for gun and financial crimes without bail or appeal. In the UK, Enoch Powell was in full flight with his racist policies, so in Cayman we felt blessed to live in such a wonderfully peaceful society.

The start of 1976 saw the Lobster Pot in receivership. Spencer's lack of prowess at liar dice finally appears to have taken its toll! Chris Johnson was appointed as Receiver, and John Benbow recalls flying in from the UK with Christine, his wife, to take up an accounting position with Coopers and Lybrand which Chris now headed, and immediately being transported to the Lobster Pot for drinks instead of to their hotel for a rest. Shortly thereafter Doug and Joanne Rollins took over running the Pot until they sold it to the Cumbers.

In Kingston, John Ambrose became overextended due to his construction company operations. He developed an interest in art instead, learned to paint, and befriended Valerie Bloomfield, an excellent artist whom he ended up marrying a year later. Around that time, I met a physical education teacher from the UK who engineered a major change in my life. I had smoked cigarettes from age sixteen and on certain days could consume up to three packs a day. This young woman hated the smell of cigarettes and before kissing her I would have to use breath freshener and clean my teeth. Eventually, I felt this was ridiculous and so quit smoking for good. My wife Vivian, knowing this story, always said she wanted to meet this girl and many years later, by sheer coincidence, when we were at Robbie Hamaty's 60th birthday party, she was also a guest. When I introduced them, Vivian thanked her with a big hug!

At this point I should probably mention that I have been blessed throughout my career with excellent secretaries, In fact, given the amount of time I spend travelling, I would have been lost without them. My first secretary in

Cayman was Betty Evans (now Baraud), who subsequently went on to build Cayman's largest recruitment business. My secretary in Cayman in 1975 and 1976 was Cathy Thorpe, the wife of a local school teacher, who was excellent in managing the office and I was sad to see her go. However, she recommended Ethyl Bodden, an older woman, on the strength that they played bridge together and anyone who could remember the cards as well as Mrs B (as we called her) had to have a sharp brain in spite of her age. Cathy was right, and Mrs B worked for me for many years, later to be joined by Jewel Bodden. In 1979, Amy Henning, from the Brac, joined Mrs B and Jewel, and stayed with me for many years. Amy was married to Glair, an excellent mechanic who tended my car, which was then a dark brown Cadillac.

In 1975, the liquidators of Interbank had been approached by Dwight Crater, who offered to purchase the part-completed Mitchells Creek condominium project. Dwight was a wonderful character: a big, cigar-smoking American with an attractive, petite, blonde wife called Judy. Dwight then approached us and asked if we could sort out the procurement of the part-completed project, inventory the large quantities of materials on site and negotiate with a contractor to complete construction, which, of course we were delighted to do.

I worked with McAlpine as the contractor, and by February 1976 we had completed the first phase of the development, which had been renamed to Lime Tree Bay. I had a briefcase full of Lime Tree Bay documents, and weeks later I would open it to be greeted by the smell of Dwight's cigars. If we couldn't negotiate a price for a particular item of work that met with Dwight's approval he would simply do it himself. I arrived one weekend to see him completing a kitchen cabinet installation with a wall-hung kitchen cabinet on his back, a hammer in his hand and a fixing nail in his mouth!

Shortly after Dwight's arrival in Cayman, a Canadian developer, Don Butler, arrived and purchased a parcel of land to the north of Seven Mile Beach for US$200,000. This was to be to be developed with twenty condominiums, and called Tarquynn Manor. Don wanted to speed up the construction process and visited Flowers Block factory to ask them to introduce a plate into the block machine that would cut though all but an inch of the concrete fin in the block, which could then serve as the bond beam at the top of the wall. That way, there would be no need for formwork – clean outs were introduced at the base of the vertical steel to ensure concrete had completely filled the vertical cores of the blockwork.

The construction contract was put out on competitive bid and won by Jimmy Powell of PRAG construction in September 1976. PRAG had been formed as a joint venture between Pioneer (David Arch), Ranja Construction

(Jimmy Powell and Ranburn Christian), and Arch & Godfrey (Heber Arch & Mike Godfrey) to compete with the somewhat larger contractors such as Hadsphaltic and McAlpine. Don's 'system' and Jimmy's determination paid dividends, as the roof was on in February 1977, only eight weeks after starting construction on the project.

The Racquet Club design was completed, and in early September, tenders for the project came in. PRAG was the successful contractor, and by October we were setting out the project on site. The club had one squash court, two floodlit tennis courts, changing rooms and a bar. The latter was a challenge, as it was not possible to secure an 'in principle' liquor licence based on drawings. The building had to be completed, health and fire inspections made of the completed structure, and then a licence might be granted provided you were further than a certain distance away from a church or school. Both of these would be a challenge and might significantly impact the viability of the project, but we decided to proceed.

Arek sold his half of the Melody Lane duplex for CAN$36,000 in April 1976, and I instructed Ralph Coatsworth and Tibbetts Realty (Art Davidson) to sell my half, which included some approved plans I had for an extension. In the event, it would take until December 1978 for me to sell my half.

1977

'In the end, it's not the years in your life that count. It's life in your years.' Abraham Lincoln

In 1977 I was honoured to be appointed President of the Cayman Society of Architects Surveyors and Engineers (CASE). One of my goals was to standardise construction contracts and tendering procedures to protect both clients and contractors through best practices. To this end I enlisted barrister Ramon Alberga, who had adapted the UK JCT Standard forms for use in Jamaica. He gave excellent advice on how we could tailor the Jamaican forms to Cayman's unique challenges, such as the reliance on imported building materials and the widespread need for work permits for imported labour. These and other risks required careful management during the procurement process. However, such things take time, and it was not until November 1983 that CASE, jointly with the Cayman Contractors Association, published *The Code of Procedure for Selective Tendering for Use in the Cayman Islands, Building Works Agreement Small Contracts* and *The Standard Form of Building Contract Private Edition with Quantities.*

The Cayman Triangle, a Cayman-made parody-satire movie about a fictional one-legged pirate called Durty Reid Walker, was released in 1977. Directed by Andy Humphries, it had taken several years to complete, but provided endless hours of fun for all, especially the local extras (paid in Heineken 'Greenies') and Reid Dennis, who played the protagonist. Memorable scenes included a Pirates' Feast at Pedro's Castle, and one in central George Town in which I played an English tourist dressed in a suit and bowler hat, complete with rolled umbrella! Filming for this scene began early one Sunday morning, with Reid Dennis in the role of a statue of Durty Reid on the traffic island by the central post office. Ed Oliver, the celebrated local artist, made up Reid in grey stone-coloured make up, and a Cable & Wireless cable drum was covered with a grey sheet to create a very convincing looking stone statue base. Professional cameramen set up a camera dolly to record the scene of the tourist group, headed by yours truly, looking up at the statue as the tourist guide related the story of Durty Reid. The scene required many takes, and the day got hotter and hotter. Poor Reid, like many of us, was suffering from a Saturday night hangover, and it wasn't long before he started to sway on his peg leg. If you watch the movie carefully, you will see the statue move slightly!

By May 1977 we had completed the Racquet Club. It was instantly hugely popular, and the squash courts were in use from early in the morning until midnight, when we closed. We had to close half an hour each day to clean the floor – players sweated profusely, as the court was not air-conditioned, and the floor would become quite slippery and dangerous. We were the first bar in Cayman to serve draught John Courage beer and we served a lot! I noticed, however, that around 7.30pm the bar would be packed and suddenly it would be empty. I wondered why, and was told 'We can only drink so much beer and then we need to eat.' All my customers had been abandoning the Club for the Cayman Arms on the waterfront.

We took action and installed a full kitchen and began serving both lunch and dinner. We would have daily specials such as leg of lamb or beef roast, which were popular, and I would instruct the cook to serve what was left as a salad or similar the next day. Cook would say, truthfully, there was none left – omitting to add that was because leftovers were disappearing out the back door! The bar was not much better, as the barman would bring in his own bottles of cheap 'well liquor' and sell that instead of our stock, pocketing the cash. Since then, whenever people ask me if I have an interest in a bar or restaurant business, I emphatically tell them I was cured of that years ago.

We decided to add a second court – this time with a glass back wall. To watch play on the first court one had to lean over the upper-level balcony and look down on the players. With a glass back wall the spectator area was increased significantly, and it meant we could bring in world class players like the Khan brothers to give exhibition matches and coaching. I flew to the UK in December and spent six weeks there holding meetings with Pilkington Glass, who had pioneered the development of these walls.

We were also looking into taping rugby and other sports in the UK and playing them at special evenings at the Club. At this time UK TV used the PAL format, which had a different number of lines in the screen than the NTSC format used in the US. We were able to find a VHS machine that could play PAL formatted tapes on a NTSC formatted TV, but also had to find someone who could record the tapes for us in the UK. We were able to do so, and these events became extremely popular at the Club, with the consequent increase in bar sales.

1978

'Life is a long lesson in humility.' James M. Barrie

Shortly after I returned to Cayman from the UK, on 2nd February, I had another kidney stone. An x-ray of my kidneys showed the stone clearly stuck there, and I was advised to drink as much coconut water as possible, so the staff at the Racquet Club would have a pint glass waiting for me on the bar every time I arrived. It was recommended that I fly to the UK to have the stone removed surgically. This I did, giving the Cayman X-rays to the doctor with whom I checked in. On the day of my surgery I arrived at the East Birmingham hospital, where the surgeon said they would take additional X-rays prior to surgery. These showed the stone had disappeared. Gallons of coconut water had obviously done the trick!

After surviving this ordeal, I felt I deserved a week driving through the Loire valley. I had always enjoyed jumping in the car and, with no particular plan, driving to see where one finished up. I had also found a rental firm in London that hired out Rolls-Royces, and for many years I was one of Guy Salmon's best customers.

Before the interruption, I had been preparing quantities for a project called Christopher Columbus, developed by Don Butler's brother Brian, just north of his brother's Tarquynn Manor development. We were also advising on other developments, including Villas of the Galleon, located south of the Galleon Beach Hotel and owned by a group of Canadian investors that included Ray McLean, Keith Baldwin and Arnie Armstrong. Ray's son, Rod, led the development team working with architect Bill Bissell and Jimmy Powell of PRAG Construction. Jimmy was also building Brian Butler's Christopher Columbus and by then had deservedly earned the title 'Condo King of Cayman'.

By April the glass wall had arrived for the Racquet Club and by June we were able to host teams from visiting British warships on patrol in the Caribbean to play our national side, as well as visits from World Champions, the Kahn brothers, and the UK and Caribbean squash teams.

Shortly after this, Raymond Legge, founder of the Hash House Harriers – a non-competitive running club patterned after the British game of 'hare and hounds' – arrived in Cayman from Hong Kong and asked to base the Hash House Harriers at the club. Broadly, the concept was for one runner to set a marked course each week, and the lead pursuing runner would call out 'ON, ON!' when he found the correct trail. Eventually it became an evening run without a marked course, but bar sales went up nevertheless after the strenuous activity!

Don Butler had now also found a new site to develop, called Beachcomber. We negotiated the contract with Jimmy Powell (of course) and the contract was signed on 30th June 1978. By this time I enjoyed an excellent working relationship with Don, and as a gesture of appreciation for the projects we had successfully completed together, he invited me to join him in early August 1978 at Roche Harbor, in the Pacific Northwest. We sailed all through the San Juan Islands aboard his beautiful 65-foot motor sailor, *Tarquynnarian*. During the trip, I took the opportunity to share my ambition with Don: that I was very keen to build a condominium on Seven Mile Beach for my own account. Bill Bissell and I had prepared a comprehensive drawing of the entire Seven Mile Beach, detailing each beachfront plot, including dimensions, area, ownership and development capacity of each vacant lot. Don offered to assist in any way he could, even encouraging me to approach his bankers, Northland, with his blessing.

In September 1978 I was able to sell the half duplex in Melody Lane to Eversley Bodden for CI$20,500. He took possession on 1st December 1978 and Ethyl Bodden (Mrs B), my long-time secretary, went to live there. I was able to pay off the balance of my CI$7,058 mortgage to Roywest Banking Corporation, and went to live in a rented apartment on Walkers Road.

Don Butler had offered to sell me unit #13 at the Beachcomber for US$78,000, which I gladly accepted, and Haydyn Rutter of Bruce Campbell & Co. formed a company to own the apartment. That Christmas, in the UK, I bought my mother a beautiful maroon-coloured Triumph 1500, with burled walnut trim and beige leather seats – she was in tears. We picked it up from the car showroom, where it waited with a bow tied on top! This was the happy finale to many years of driving lessons, and many attempts at getting a license. She had finally passed, which was as well because by then my dad had had a stroke and for a while she had to run the business on her own, as well as do the accounts, payroll and typing as usual. Notwithstanding her new freedom of movement, after a lifetime of taking the 107 bus, she still always followed that same route when delivering workmen to various job sites, to their considerable mystification.

1979

'If you are not willing to risk the unusual, you will have to settle for the ordinary.' Jim Rohn

Shortly after the Second World War, Olney Webster, a Jamaican businessman of Caymanian heritage, had come to Cayman and purchased significant portions of Seven Mile Beach for one pound a front foot. The parcels generally stretched from the high watermark on the beach to the water on the North Sound, i.e., right across the West Bay Road. I had met Olney's brother Burnett and his son Desmond, and I expressed my interest in acquiring one of their parcels for my own condominium development.

Don Butler had acquired the Beachcomber land for CI$800 per front foot – the highest price paid for land at the time – and Charles's advice was, if we were to be successful in having the Websters sell (they were notoriously indecisive) we should offer an amount that would knock them off their feet. We looked at the numbers and Bill Bissell came up with a great 'X' design of units on the site of the 400-foot frontage. I could see that at a price of $3,000 per front foot, we could still make a feasible development. Problem was, I didn't have $1.2 million!

While pondering this problem, I happened to be invited to my good friend Mikol Dise's Easter Sunday, April 1979, drinks party. Mikol and his dad were the developers of Cayman Kai, which they had pioneered in 1962. Mikol had just completed a house at Cayman Kai for Don Messick, an American grain trader based in Geneva. Don was at Mikol's party, and serendipity stepped in once again. Don mentioned he was scouting investment opportunities for himself and two friends, Dietmar Volker and Tom Berna. I told him about the Webster land and my idea for development. He responded, 'I will come to your office, and we can talk further.' At the time, I assumed this was just typical cocktail party chat.

After the Easter holiday long weekend, I arrived early at my office to find Don Messick already waiting there. He warmed immediately to the idea that the 'cost of land element' was not as key to overall success as good design, and, given Charles Adam's relationship with the Websters, agreed we should proceed to assemble a viable project. John Rudolph and his wife Kay, who were in the oil business and based in Denver, joined the team. In anticipation of being able to proceed, we visited Arthur Hunter's office to describe what we wanted to achieve and set up a company. But what to call it? As we pondered, Sandra (Don Messick's wife and a keen gardener) said, 'As we were driving here, I saw a lantana plant. How about Plantana?' And so it was.

Charles said we needed to act decisively to demonstrate our commitment. His suggestion was to charter a plane to Jamaica, meet with the Webster patriarch, Burnett, and their personal attorney, complete with a purchase agreement, and present the deposit cheque. Taking his advice we duly chartered a plane from Jack and Jill Bodden and headed to Owen Roberts International Airport at the appointed time to board the charter flight to Jamaica. Several drinks later, while waiting at the Hungry Horse Bar, we learned that the plane – returning from Honduras – wouldn't be available until the next morning.

The next day, the development team – Charles Adams, Don Messick and Sandra, John Barnett and his wife Kay, and myself – returned to the airport. To ease the tension from the previous day's frustrations, Kay had made a jug of Bloody Marys for the flight to Kingston. On arrival, we took a taxi to the Webster Estate on Seaview Avenue, where we were greeted by Burnett's butler offering glasses of freshly squeezed grapefruit juice on a silver tray. After pleasantries, the attorneys got down to business on the details of our property acquisition. Much discussion followed and finally the deal was done and the contract signed, to everyone's relief, and we proceeded back to the airport and our charter plane for our return home.

Back in Cayman, with the land secured, work commenced in earnest on the design. OBM's design guru at the time, Mitch Stuart, spent significant time with me finessing the unique 'X' format of Plantana, frequently making superb design breakthroughs half-way through a bottle of Johnnie Walker Black Label whisky at my apartment at the Beachcomber. To this day I am of the opinion that Plantana remains unique as a condominium design by offering a maximum density development of forty-nine apartments, all with maximum sea views.

The market for Seven Mile Beach apartments was hot at this time. We prepared a very modest brochure and presales commenced. These required stage payments through the construction process, which part-funded the costs.

But, we still needed additional funding, and approached international contractor McAlpine Ltd., with whom we had worked extensively both in Jamaica and Cayman, who graciously offered bridge funding.

Through the Villas of the Galleon project I had met Whitey Bozman and his wife Ruthie; and Whitey could sell the proverbial ice to Eskimos! One day he was having lunch at the Petroleum Club in Denver, and returned with twenty signed contracts for Plantana Units.

So, we had our design, our planning approval and a great team, and we built a great development. My fellow shareholders asked me to purchase an apartment, which I did, once more through a company with nominee shareholders.

All in all, 1979 had been an eventful year. Mrs Thatcher became the UK's Prime Minister, the Shah of Iran was overthrown, the socialist exile Maurice Bishop took control in Grenada after a coup, and Martyn Bould not only began a unique Seven Mile Beach development, but also began dating a young lady who owned a duty free business in Cayman. She was also one of the chaperones for Jennifer Jackson, Cayman's entry, to the Miss World competition, so I joined her for the event, held at the Royal Albert Hall in London. The competition was just being acquired by Eric and Julia Morley from Grand Metropolitan, with the assistance of Billy Butlin, of holiday camp fame. It was great fun seeing the build-up to the big night on 15th November, when Gina Swainson, Miss Bermuda, won the competition. Afterwards we enjoyed a driving trip through the Loire valley, delighting in the pleasures of the table.

At the end of 1979, Bould Chartered Quantity Surveyors moved office from the Barclays Bank Building to the offices formally occupied by Chalmers Gibbs Martin Joseph Partnership (CGMJP) on the second floor of the CITCO office building on Albert Panton Street in George Town.

With so much development activity going on, the Racquet Club was taking up a little too much of my time. So, when we were approached by Joseph Turnaretcher, a talented chef and maître d', with an offer to lease the club we grabbed the opportunity with both hands. Joseph ran the club until early 1981 when we sold it to Keith Baldwin, one of the owners of Galleon Beach Hotel.

Planning permissions, sales, and negotiations for Plantana took the rest of 1979 and part of 1980. We were also challenged by the ground conditions of the Plantana site. Seven Mile Beach is a hurricane ridge built up over many years. This consists of hurricane-driven sand deposited over mangrove swamps, with a layer of semi-desiccated peat lying approximately twelve to twenty feet beneath the surface. This needs to be removed to avoid subsidence of multi-storied buildings. It can be dug out, but we wanted to see if there was a more economical solution. We discovered G.K.N. Keller, a firm that used a system of ground stabilization called 'vibro-floatation', where a hollow probe is jetted into the ground with water under high pressure which then, in conjunction with horizontal vibration, compacts the ground and blows out the peat. Afterwards, stone is poured into the remaining cavity to form a stable column on which we could safely place our foundations. It worked – as of now, more than forty-five years later, we have never had a settlement crack in the development!

1980

'Life has no limitations; except the ones you make.' Les Brown

On 1st July 1980, I was honoured and privileged to be granted Caymanian Status. Given my peripatetic background, I had to prove I had been resident in Cayman for a certain number of years. Fortunately, from the day I arrived I had paid the annual Head Tax of CI$10 required of all males living in Cayman and had the receipts to prove it. Bill Bissell had encouraged me to apply for status at the same time he did. We studied the little Red Book, *The History of the Cayman Islands*, sat the required written examination, but then it all almost came unstuck at the interview with Mr Ormond Panton. Initially, Ormond Panton thought Bill was Martyn Bould. This caused Bill to go cold – as a happily married man, he feared that being mistaken for one of the island's most notoriously fun-loving bachelors might affect his chances. However, after the small matter of the mistaken identity was cleared up, he and I both were awarded the honour of Caymanian Status.

That year Raymond Legge, who had established the Hash House Harriers at the Racquet Club, arranged for the famed American runner Bill Rodgers to come to Cayman in September. He started what was to be an annual 10K run bearing his name (and which he won five times in the first six years of its running). 10k is a distance that I really enjoyed running, and I participated in the event for many years. In fact, Bould Chartered Quantity Surveyors (later BCQS) sponsored many running events over the years. These included the BCQS Turtle Run around a Walkers Road South Sound course with teams of five, including one female runner, and divided into financial and non-financial groups. We were also regular participants in the cross-island relay in which teams of six ran four miles each from East End to George Town.

Famous amongst Cayman's watering holes was the Seaview, where for many years Miss Mona patiently served lunchtime Heinekens to a regular crew that included Bill Gunner, Chris Johnson, Jim Walker, Ken Spraggon and Rodrick

Donaldson. Rodrick was the legal draftsman for the government, and a highly intelligent man who could complete crosswords faster than anyone else I knew. Each day Rodrick would take his dog Swamp (he had rescued the lucky creature from one) to his office, which was decorated with centrefold pictures from *Playboy*! Sadly, he died in 1980 and had requested in his will that he be buried at sea. This being a first for Cayman – to the best of my knowledge – the simple request caused some logistical head scratching. However, after a suitable number of holes had been drilled in his coffin and appropriate weight added, it was sunk off the west coast. And that was that – until the next day when it floated up close to the Seaview bar. It was widely reported that Rodrick had returned for a final Heineken with his friends! Many years later I was at a dinner in the Middle Temple in London, sitting at one of the trestle tables amongst a group of soon-to-be barristers. Somehow the subject of Cayman and burials at sea came up, and I regaled the assembled group with the Rodrick story, after which the gentleman sitting opposite me said, 'I know that to be true – I am Rodrick's grandson.' Talk about an amazing coincidence!

1980 was also the year Mikol Dise and I became interested in the concept of small storage units. At this time the Foster family had purchased vast areas of land at the airport to form Airport Industrial Park, and so, in June Mikol and I met with Steve Foster at the Cayman Arms to set out our plan to build twelve single and four double garage-size units for sale. These could be built on one of the industrial land plots that the Fosters and their partners owned. Dave & Steve Foster agreed to put in the land at a value of $26,000, and Mikol and I would contribute $26,000 each as working capital. And so Mini Warehouse Ltd. came into being. The Strata Titles Registration Law did not come into effect until 1973, and even then did not permit the sale of commercial strata lots until 1983, so we sold shares in the company with a right to use the designated space in perpetuity.

The concept proved to be wildly successful, so after completing and selling the Mini Warehouse development and the development company itself, we wanted to continue building on the success of this new concept of storage space and small business premises under one roof. So, in October 1981, we formed Mini Warehouse Two Ltd. Initially, we sold these units both to owner-occupiers and investors. For around $25,000, investors could acquire an asset in Cayman showing a 15 per cent tax free return, with the added benefit of keeping the funds in Cayman to use for holidays here. We sold buildings in the first five blocks we developed, but then asked ourselves, 'Why are we selling these highly profitable units?' Instead of selling, we retained ownership, and today we manage a portfolio of almost one thousand rental units.

One of the purchasers in Plantana was an Indianapolis engineer whose daughter was an aspiring actress living in Hollywood whom I dated on a long-distance basis. The family were avid skiers, and I was invited to visit them at Boyne Highlands, in Michigan, to ski during the 1980 Christmas holidays. I had always wanted to try skiing, but the appropriate opportunity had never presented itself, so I greeted this invitation with open arms. It was bitterly cold, and the icy East Coast snow conditions meant I spent a lot of time falling, but by the time the five-day trip was over I was hooked. Over the years, the sport has taken me to many North and South American and European resorts, meeting great people and enjoying the outdoor and gourmet camaraderie of this activity.

1981

'You define your own life. Don't let other people write your script.'

Oprah Winfrey

January 1981 began with some significant changes: Richard Jones, who had come to work for Bould Chartered Quantity Surveyors in April 1980, joined the practice as a partner as our workload continued to expand. Don Messick and I also flew to Chicago to meet with Don Dise, as Don Messick had an idea that we should purchase the entire Cayman Kai property. This did not materialise but serves to illustrate that he had become bitten by the 'development bug'!

Of sad note, Bob Marley died on 11th May 1981, and I mention this because he and his music provided a running commentary on the regional and cultural events which would become part of my life a few years hence.

Plantana introduced me to some truly great people. One couple who really stand out and became close friends, are René and Claudine Meister. René worked for the Panchaud Brothers – Swiss grain traders – and he travelled all over the world on their behalf. Dietmar Volker, one of our Plantana development partners, introduced me to René, who subsequently purchased an apartment at Plantana. Both René and Dietmar had a love for Ferraris and enjoyed racing them at meets around Europe, often held in the grounds of beautiful chateaux. René was a gourmand of no mean order and Claudine an outstanding cook. At the Great Chefs' restaurants, obtaining a reservation typically requires booking months in advance – unless you were René Meister. Thanks to his significant patronage, he was able to secure bookings with just a few days' notice.

Over the years René arranged some fabulous trips for us. We visited the very best locations, with his recommendations of the best items on the menu.

René was also a linguist and had a keen interest in all languages – illustrated by one amusing exchange when my loyal housekeeper for many years, Maureen Coley, who was Jamaican, said in René's presence, as she was leaving one day, 'If ya doon't see me I'm not eer.' René queried what she had said. I replied, 'She said she was leaving for the day,' and 'If you don't see me I am not here.' 'Ahhh', René replied, 'so I can say to Claudine, "If you don't hear me snoring, I am not sleeping"!'

René and Claudine were the Swiss couple I mentioned previously in connection with Cissy's uncanny talent for reading tea leaves. The incident came about one evening when they had joined us for dinner at the Pagoda shortly after René had purchased some land in Frank Sound. After the meal, I asked René if he would like Cissy to read his tea leaves, and, though clearly sceptical, he agreed. Cissy took his cup, emptied most of the remaining liquid, swirled the leaves, and began to read. She said she saw a piece of oceanfront land René had just purchased – something she could not possibly have known. Intrigued, René asked if she saw anything else. Cissy replied, 'There's a large vehicle parked on the land.' There was, in fact, an abandoned school bus on the site. After that, René became a little more of a believer.

In early June I flew to the UK with my aspiring actress lady-friend, and once again toured the Loire Valley, this time with a Rolls Royce that succeeded in dropping its drive shaft on the road. What to do? I called my wonderful Plantana purchasers, René and Claudine Meister, and asked for advice. In a flash, René said, 'I am watching the Grand Prix, but there is a wonderful restaurant close to where you are. I will make a reservation. Enjoy their duck and a fine bottle of Margaux, and I will be there to pick you up in two hours and organise another car for you.' All of which he did, and the meal was indeed magnificent!

Later that month, my brother Rob married his beautiful wife Jenna, and at the reception my aspiring actress surprised the somewhat staid guests by leaving the table, changing into her singing telegram outfit, and re-appearing singing a live congratulatory telegram to the newly married couple and their assembled guests. I was informed this is what aspiring actresses do to gain acting confidence! The next day Rob and Jenna flew to Cayman and stayed at #13 Beachcomber to enjoy Seven Mile Beach for a couple of weeks. I know Jenna found our summer Cayman weather warm, to say the least, after the UK's temperate climate.

As I mentioned, Don Messick and his partners had become enamored with the property development business. Buoyed by the early and immediate success of Plantana, Don, while playing tennis one day with Bruce Parker, owner of the

Rum Point Club, casually asked if he could buy it. Bruce replied, 'Of course,' and so we formed a new company, RP Developments Ltd., and began planning the development, although I wasn't entirely convinced this project would meet with the almost instant success we had enjoyed with Plantana.

The Rum Point Club had originally been developed by Ralph Coatsworth and built by a crew that included Jimmy Powell. At the time, the only way to reach the site was by boat – meaning all labour and materials had to be transported in by water. Talk about a logistical challenge! As part of due diligence in acquiring the property, we discovered that the sliver of land forming the actual 'Point' did not belong to Bruce Parker but to one mysterious Amy Green, with an address in New York. We managed to track her down, purchase the land, and then were able to assemble a complete site.

The development at Rum Point Club was named The Retreat and its tag line was: 'The Private World for the Privileged Few'. We put out a Request for Proposal (RFP) competition to select an architect, and a Barry Sugarman emerged as the lead contender, although Bill Bissell of OBM was also in the running. In the event, Barry designed a house for Don Messick in Big Sky, Montana, but OBM went on to design The Retreat and McAlpine built it. The development also included another innovation for Cayman – it had Cayman's first Racquet Ball Court with – yes – a glass back wall!

The site of the first phase of The Retreat was located just north of the Rum Point Club, which we continued to operate for several years with Joey Ebanks of North Side as the manager and lessee. Ironically, after my experience with the Racquet Club, which I thought had cured me of the bar and restaurant business, I had found myself right back in it!

During 1981 the idea of developing my own condominium office building in George Town had begun to germinate, and I identified and took out an option on a half-acre plot owned by Jim Bodden just off what is now named Dr Roy's Drive. As with the Mini Warehouse development, commercial condominiums were not catered for under the original Strata Titles Registration Law. So, we set in motion changes that would enable such commercial stratas to be registered. My good friend Harvey Stephenson, who was an insurance guru, wanted to develop a similar building and this he subsequently did.

By early December 1981 we had completed the development of Plantana but were awaiting Certificates of Occupancy from the Central Planning Office. Somewhat earlier, I had read of a cooking course, 'The Great Chefs of France', that was to take place from 1st–6th December in Napa Valley, California. It was being organised by Billy James and Michael Cross at the Robert Mondavi vineyard there – the thrust of the promotion being to move away from the idea of California 'jug' wines to those that could compete with the best France could offer. The course would include blind tastings of French versus Mondavi's wines.

Robert's Swiss-born wife Margrit Biever was a brilliant promoter, and I joined the weeklong course preparing and cooking French-style dinners with Michel Guérard and lunches with a range of chefs including the amazing Indian chef, Madhur Jaffrey. Peter Allen (Liza Minelli's husband) played piano whilst the waiters and staff served drinks and the final lunch while wearing roller skates. It was an impressive and most enjoyable event. I recall reading an article about it in *Newsweek* magazine, which described it as 'How to do the Napa Valley on $1,000 a day – before lunch!' In addition, Robert Mondavi, as part of his reputation-building promotion, had formed an association with Baron Philippe de Rothschild of Château Mouton Rothschild, in Bordeaux, to produce a very distinctive up-market wine called Opus One, made from Cabernet Sauvignon, Cabernet Franc, Petit Verdot and Merlot grapes, which we had the unique opportunity of tasting.

As you will by now have gathered, I travel very frequently. Luckily, I have been blessed with outstanding travel agents throughout my career. The first of these was Cayman Tours and Travel, owned and run by Catherine Coxe, who managed most of my travel until the early 1990s. Catherine's husband was Hugh Coxe, who also happened to be an excellent trumpet player. Catherine would not only find the most convenient and economical flights but, when last-minute changes were required on the road, a telephone call to her would solve any issues.

During the trip to Chicago with Don Messick, we had met one of his trading partners from the Chicago Mercantile Exchange. I had mentioned my interest in skiing and asked where he suggested I go. Without hesitation, he replied 'Snowmass in Colorado and stay at the Top of the Village', and kindly offered an introduction to the manager. So, I skied there the entire second week of December 1981. I sought out an instructor, because I wanted to improve my technique, and was introduced to Rob Tiernan, a mountain man from Montana who was a park ranger when he wasn't teaching skiing. Rob was a fabulous teacher and always had several ways of getting across how to make a turn. For many, many years we would ski together, to the point that the other instructors said I was a clone of Rob, and that when we came down the mountain, they could not tell who was who, as we are about the same size and build.

After spending Christmas in the UK, I returned to Cayman and began closing on the Plantana apartments and discussed the setting up the office development company with Charles Adams.

CHAPTER FOUR

Crisis and Construction (1982–1987)

1982

'There is a force of exultation, a celebration of luck, when a writer finds himself a witness to the early morning of a culture that is defining itself, branch by branch, leaf by leaf, in that self-defining dawn, which is why, especially at the edge of the sea, it is good to make a ritual of the sunrise.' Derek Walcott

Unexpectedly, a new interest – soon to become a life-long passion – was about take hold of me. In some ways it seems natural that in the multicultural society and region where I had become so much at home, this passion would take root. It still resonates in the way so eloquently expressed by Nobel Prize winner Sir Derek Walcott, whom I would have the privilege to meet many years later.

It began with a chance meeting – or was it truly chance? Perhaps it was life's synchronicity at play. So many seemingly coincidental events have enriched my life, that I do not believe them to have happened by mere chance.

In January 1982 I met Geoff Cresswell, a drama teacher at the local High School, who had introduced students to West Indian drama as a change from the previous Eurocentric curriculum. Geoff and his talented team – Anita Ebanks, Frank McField, Bendel Hydes and others – had been putting on a series of plays as 'The Inn Theatre' in various hotel conference spaces. Geoff greatly desired his own dedicated theatre, to avoid having to dismantle and reassemble sets daily, and had tenaciously sought funding from private sources with some success. Steve McTaggart, a local businessman, had offered to fund a new theatre and Mr Lawrence Thompson agreed to provide the land. A further anonymous benefactor offered CI$500,000 to fund construction.

Geoff and I were standing at the bar of the Royal Palms Hotel during the interval of one of his shows, when he asked if I knew anything about costing theatres. I said not, but that I could find out, although first we would need

Crisis and Construction (1982-1987)

some idea of size and scope. I ventured that there must be some type of magazine in which we could advertise and solicit interest from designers. This was done, and from among the applicants we chose a company called Theatre Projects. Little did I know then that this marked the beginning of what would become a major part of my life, dedicated to the preservation of heritage and the development of culture. It was an awareness that had perhaps started with my involvement with the Third World (though I didn't recognise it at the time) which has continued to this day.

In mid-February I met with David Staples of Theatre Projects in London, invited them to Cayman, and during the same visit took the opportunity to interview Pete Widmer to join our growing quantity surveying practice. I was staying in one of Jo Butcher's managed residences on Hasker Street, and the day of the interview was bitterly cold. Pete knocked on the door, dressed in only a suit with no overcoat, and came in for an interview that lasted about an hour and a half. We had been chatting for some forty-five minutes when Pete somewhat nervously asked if he could invite his wife in, as she wasn't wearing a coat either. It took her some time to thaw out! Pete and Sue arrived in Cayman that April, to a rather more welcoming climate!

After the London interviews I went skiing for two weeks in St Moritz. I stayed at Suvretta House, which had been recommended by the mother of Tom Berna, one of the Plantana shareholders. It offered a level of hospitality, cuisine and service that made the typical American ski resort look very down market! On arrival, you were greeted by the General Manager, Rudolph Muller, and invited for an aperitif at the famous Carousel Bar. After a day on the slopes, you skied into the *porte cochère*, where a valet took your skis. The food was superb, and we received a Christmas card from Herr Muller for many years.

Jeremy Spencer, whom I'd also interviewed in London, joined the practice in July 1982. At the time, we had been retained by the Bank of Nova Scotia to carry out an audit on a hotel and condominium development they were financing, and which was in financial trouble. So, I sent Jeremy together with Pete Widmer to measure and count the rooms on site – Jeremy, of course, still jet-lagged from his previous day's transatlantic flight. I handed him my prized wooden measuring rod, which I had had since I was a trainee and which needed to be folded in a specific way, with strict instructions to be careful about folding it correctly. We all met at the Cayman Arms for lunch and my first question to Jeremy was if had they done a count of the rooms. Jeremy replied, 'Yes, indeed, there are 290 rooms.' I told him there were supposed to be 360 rooms, and that he must be jet-lagged. He counted again, and again there were 290 rooms, although the bank was financing 360. He then, ruefully, said he had broken my measuring rod! He subsequently admitted to being so notoriously clumsy and absentminded that his friends would lock away the cut glass when he came to visit and preferred he stand with his back to the wall with his hands folded behind him.

In August that year I visited Haiti again, this time to stay in Petit Goâve, at the Relais de L'Empereur, owned by the somewhat notorious French businessman Olivier Coquelin. It was quite an experience. Coquelin, formerly the owner of the Pink Elephant night club in New York, had arrived in Haiti and set up this unique hotel, where leopards roamed the property and there was a beach club which you reached by canoe, and the swim-up bar dispensed Veuve Clicquot champagne.

Mid-1982 saw my move from #13 Beachcomber to #26 Plantana. On the first morning in my new home, I awoke early and opened the drapes to the sight of an extremely attractive bikini-clad lady sitting by the pool, being photographed by a gentleman who looked to be a professional photographer. I donned a pair of shorts, went down to the pool, and asked them if they were guests. They replied that they had been given permission to shoot for a magazine. I asked their names, and learned the attractive lady was the famous model Christie Brinkley. I, of course, said go right ahead, thinking this was a great start to life in my new home!

I rented #13 Beachcomber to an American couple, Bob & Sue Mitchem, who had wanted an unfurnished property. My Roche Bobois furniture, including a marble dining room table and soft comfortable modular sitting area chairs, fitted well with the new layout in Plantana and it is still there today – buying quality pays off!

On 26th May 1982, Office Developments Ltd. had signed the purchase agreement on the land registered as OPY 45 in central George Town, Bill Bissell designed a building of some 30,000 square feet over five floors, and Neil Cruickshank and Denny Diedrick (a good friend from Jamaica days) joined me as co-investors in the project. We secured planning approval in principle, valid until February 1983.

We had spoken with various people who might be interested in purchasing space in the completed building. These included accountants Peat Marwick Mitchell (as they then were named), attorney, Casey Gill, Neil Cruickshank, and Quatro Hatch, who might open a deli to anchor the ground floor. Denny Diedrick, who owned an office supply store called Hampstead, also purchased space on the ground floor. Later, Neil, Denny and I formed Equal Investments Ltd. and purchased the top floor and rented it out.

Casey carried out a lot of legal work for me and also helped Bobby Butz, who nicknamed him 'Two Gun', and claimed that in resolving issues for Bobby, Casey had to fire both guns during his legal representations. Casey is still across the corridor from my office in the Genesis building, and I always greet him as 'Two Gun'. Such nicknames stick around for decades in Cayman!

Key, however, was to find a marketing company that could come up with a promotional theme for this entirely new concept of a condominium office building – the first of its kind in Cayman. We scoured the lists of companies in Miami, but none had any idea how to address a community of 17,500 people. Serendipity once again stepped in when I was introduced to a company called Slaughter Hanson and Partners out of Dothan, Alabama, which was a small American town associated with a US Air Force base. I met with Terry Slaughter there, and he immediately grasped what we were trying to do. He advised that what we needed was a hard slipcover case book with original art. As we had nothing to show but a piece of land, the original art had to be very good and different. To that end, Genevieve Meeks came to Cayman in July and prepared some wonderful images of what we were to create.

Once the hard cover brochures were completed, we had a launch cocktail party, for which the invitations were a piece of heavy 5" × 8" clear plastic, with the message 'To give you a clear view into the birth of a new concept, Martyn Bould, on behalf of Office Developments Ltd. invites you to attend an evening of splendid food, cocktails and celebration, Friday September 24, 1982 6.30pm at the Caribbean Club.' It was a fabulous evening, and we got the message out. Moreover, I saw the invitations on people's desks for several years after the event. The name of the development, as at this time we did not have an anchor buyer, was 'Genesis', as it was the birth of a new concept.

Terry Slaughter won an Addy Award for his stylish and effective campaign, and as thanks invited me to a college homecoming American football game between the Dothan and Rutgers College teams. I had never seen an American football game before and all I knew were the rules of rugby, which I was quickly to discover vary significantly from those of American football. We duly set off from Terry's house in a van with swivel captain's chairs in it and an ice chest full of cold beers. We parked in the lot at the stadium and enjoyed hot dogs and beer at a 'tailgate' party – another novel experience for me. During the game, my questions to Terry and his partner about the proceedings on the field elicited some puzzled looks from adjacent spectators. They must have thought I was from Mars, not to know the rules of such an institution as American Football!

I wanted to thank the McAlpine family for the support they had offered for the construction and financing of Plantana, and invited the patriarch, Sir

Robin McAlpine, for dinner in November. Henry Propper, who managed their office in Cayman, had seen my completed apartment and was familiar with its informal Roche Bobois furniture. He said somewhat sheepishly, 'Martyn you will need to buy a more upright chair for Sir Robin.' We have the chair to this day, and it is still called Sir Robin's chair. We were also advised that Sir Robin only drank Piper Heidsieck champagne, so a suitable supply was purchased and chilled. A thank-you letter the next day from Sir Robin noted, 'I was most interested to see a completed flat and thought your interior design used the space well. The bath is certainly very unusual.' I had installed a huge jacuzzi in the master bathroom, with a jaw-dropping view that looks north along the stretch of Seven Mile Beach.

1983

'A problem is a chance for you to do your best.' Duke Ellington

Her Majesty Queen Elizabeth II visited Cayman in February 1983 – the first visit of a monarch to our islands, and a notable event.

Following my meeting with David Staples in London, Theatre Projects had sent a team to carry out a feasibility study to see what size theatre a small community such as Cayman could support. Theatre Projects met with more than a hundred people during 1982, and by March 1983 had produced their study. It recommended the creation of a cultural campus, which would include not only a theatre but a heritage village, a series of meeting rooms for use by Cayman's many groups and associations, arts and crafts workshops, and the establishment of an organisation to record, document and preserve the cultural heritage of the islands. The organisation should also encourage story tellers, dancers, musicians and singers to perform their traditional works. This concept required a much larger site than originally planned. The previously anonymous donor revealed herself as Mrs Helen Harquail, who generously agreed to not only donate twelve acres of land adjacent to Mr Lawrence's, but also to subscribe some CI$2.5 million for the construction of the theatre, which was to be named in memory of Frank J. Harquail, her late husband. The Cayman National Cultural Foundation (CNCF) was formed, with Mr Oswell Rankine as Chairman and yours truly as Deputy Chairman. Given the much larger concept, it was agreed to hold a competition to design a temporary or studio theatre to house the Inn Theatre Company in the interim, because they were about to lose their home due to the sale and redevelopment of the Galleon Beach Hotel.

John Doak, of Onions Bouchard & McCulloch, won the competition and was also retained to design the various components of the Cultural Centre. The studio theatre was completed and opened in November 1983, the Inn Theatre Company was renamed the Cayman National Theatre Company, and they completed a full season of productions in their new temporary home.

Since 1982, I had been dating an architect who worked in Bill Bissell's office and who shared my love of cooking. She decided to write a cookbook, *A Taste of Cayman*, and for the best part of a year we had to sample the menus included therein. The book was launched at a cocktail party at #26 Plantana on 27th November 1983. I remember the precise date, because it was at this party that my future wife Vivian and I got to know a little more about each other. We had been acquainted since the Racquet Club days, and during our conversation we reminisced about those times, and about some of the members who had since left. We also discussed some business and Vivian, adept at bookkeeping and accounting, was available to look at some accounting matters I needed help with. We had so much in common it was uncanny, and our business relationship developed into an affair of the heart. The fire that was ignited at that party still burns to this day!

When we finally let the world know that we were in a relationship, we had lived separately for about a year, alternating between Lime Tree Bay and Plantana. We both loved to cook and, coincidentally, had the same French cookbooks in our libraries. It was always an adventure when we got together as we both loved to travel. Viv bought me a leather-bound travel journal for my birthday, which I religiously filled in at every destination. That journal became the foundation for much of this book's content, and re-reading it while writing was not only a source of pleasure but most cathartic. Viv took to skiing like a duck to water, and in the summer months we hiked through mountains in the US and Europe – often with a picnic. We continued our picnics even in winter while skiing. We would stash our rucksacks under a tree in the snow and then sit on our skis to enjoy a feast of hot stew and a good bottle of red wine. Viv, ever-fascinated by bears, once asked me during the first of our winter picnics, 'What do we do if a bear comes along?'

'Well, we give him lunch!' I said. 'After all, in a forest all sorts of things can happen!'

In early December I flew to Aspen to ski for a week, staying at a new condominium in Snowmass, called the Enclave. After some excellent lessons with Rob Tiernan, I flew on to Edmonton to meet with Hal Walker, who had purchased a parcel of land on the east side of West Bay Road in Grand Cayman and wanted to develop a golf course, condominiums, and a hotel.

On the 19th December 1983, I was a passenger on Cayman Airways's inaugural flight from Grand Cayman to Grand Turk. This was wonderfully convenient, avoiding the need to fly via Miami with its attendant immigration and customs delays. Chris Johnston was a fellow passenger, and by this time was in charge of both Coopers & Lybrand's Cayman and Turks & Caicos offices, as well as his other Caribbean duties.

I left Grand Turk on the 21st and flew on to London, where I met my sister Carole at Heathrow early the next morning. She had driven dad down from Sutton Coldfield so I could bring him back to Cayman for a long overdue visit. Despite my fourteen years living in the Caribbean, my parents had never visited – mainly due to dad's health and their general reluctance to travel. Dad was dressed in true British style in a three-piece suit and tie. While he waited, Carole handed me a cold pack containing three months' worth of insulin injections, announced that dad now needed these to control his diabetes, and – right then and there – she proceeded to give her jet-lagged brother a crash course in how to administer them as dad hadn't yet got the hang of it! I don't recall why I didn't spend the night in London recovering from the flight over. Suffice it to say, that shortly thereafter we were back on the same plane I had arrived on, heading to Cayman. I handed the bag of insulin to the flight attendant who promised to keep it on ice for me until the first injection was required just before lunch.

When it was time, I escorted dad to the bathroom for some privacy. Getting two six-foot, 200-pound men into a tiny airplane lavatory and closing the bifold door was no mean feat in itself. Undressing him layer by layer – jacket, tie, shirt, long-sleeved vest – and administering the injection while mid-flight turbulence rocked the plane was quite another kind of challenge. Injection completed, we reassembled his wardrobe and emerged to an audience of puzzled passengers, who no doubt wondered what had just taken place behind that door.

We finally arrived in Cayman, exhausted and jetlagged, and settled in at #26 Plantana. Dad was hungry, so I cooked him a meal, but first – following Carole's instructions – gave him another insulin shot. After that, we ate dinner and shortly thereafter we both fell into bed exhausted. The next morning jetlag woke me early, and I found dad drenched in sweat and feeling unwell. We headed to the emergency room, where I explained the recent events to the doctor. It turned out dad was hyperglycemic, because the insulin schedule we'd been following hadn't accounted for the time difference between the UK and Cayman. After a couple of days in hospital, dad was discharged and was finally able to begin his holiday.

1984

'Don't be afraid to give up the good to go for the great.' John D. Rockefeller

The next three months with dad were a truly special time. A keen photographer, he wanted to make a photographic record of the many buildings I had been involved with. He had lost a lot of weight, so building him back up became a priority. Luckily, with his farming background, he had an excellent appetite. Before his arrival, living on my own meant I could travel to New York or Miami for meetings at the drop of a hat. Suddenly, I had someone else to think about. I'd find myself mid-meeting, then remember – dad needed his lunch on time for his insulin schedule. More than once, I had to excuse myself with an, 'Oops, I've got to go feed my dad!'

As I mentioned earlier, Hal Walker, whom I met in Edmonton, had purchased ninety acres of land on the east side of West Bay Road to develop a golf course and a hotel. The site already had an abandoned condominium project built using blocks of Haitian bagasse – the waste fibres remaining after sugar cane is crushed – which had stalled due to planning issues. It had been financed by Northland Bank from Canada, a somewhat 'go-go' bank funded by oil revenues, that had also funded a number of other failed projects in the region. Hal and his partner, the accountant Wieland Wettstein, were asked by Northland to review these stalled projects and advise how best to extricate them. In Hal Walker's ninety acres, Hal and Wieland had seen an opportunity: at the time, Cayman had no golf course, so they decided to develop the property with a golf course as the centrepiece. Jack Nicklaus was brought in to design a course on just forty-five acres – about half the space typically needed. He designed a links-style course that was a masterpiece, with extra tees and greens, allowing it to function as either a 9-hole full length course, or an 18-hole par three course. Then Jack came up with a brilliant idea: Japan was golf crazy at the time, and available land areas there were generally limited, so MacGregor – Jack's golf manufacturing company – introduced the 'Cayman' ball, specially designed for space-constrained courses. The dimples on the Cayman ball protruded instead of being indented, and although it had the flight characteristics of a normal ball, the Cayman ball only travelled half the distance. Subsequently, many a trick was played amongst golfers, as they occasionally swapped a Cayman ball with their opponents' regular one. Hal appointed Maurice Cullen as general manager and Chalmers Gibbs designed the clubhouse, which was put out to tender and awarded to McAlpine. The course was opened in early 1985 by Jack Nicklaus himself – golf was officially on its way in Cayman!

To help offset the cost of the course, plans were drawn up for approximately four hundred and fifty condominiums and housing lots around its perimeter. The property was bounded on the north by a canal, constructed by Teppo Turen, making it ideal for waterfront condominiums. At the heart of the development was an upmarket two hundred and thirty-bed hotel. We spoke to various hotel groups but ultimately selected Hyatt in Chicago, who would brand it under their Regency mark.

Although Northland bank was to be bought out eventually, additional funds were needed from investors in the interim, so Hal and Wieland created an investment package aimed at Canadian professionals – doctors, dentists, lawyers etc. – who were able to invest using tax-efficient structures. To make the investment attractive, Hal included a guaranteed return. He achieved this by convincing engineer/businessman Ben Torchinsky, whose company, Agra, was a significant engineering company in Canada, to provide the guarantee. Hal went on the road, and the necessary funds were raised.

Hyatt insisted on choosing a 'big name' American architect – RTKL Associates from Baltimore – to design the hotel. Their team was headed by Ed Haladay, and the interior designers were Hirsch Bedner from Atlanta, with Bould Chartered Quantity Surveyors as cost consultants. Hal, Weiland and I had warmed to each other almost immediately and Maurice was also a great character, so our initial role as cost consultants rapidly became more significant. We considered various methods of procurement, choosing Cementation from the UK provided they could meet our budget, and Hadsphaltic as subcontractors to carry out the main structural work. So, with a developer in Edmonton, architect in Baltimore, Interior Designer in Atlanta, hotel operator in Chicago, and contractor in London for a project in the Cayman Islands, we were a widely dispersed team.

This required contracts that addressed both American and English law. We engaged Whitman & Ransom, an American legal practice with offices in London. Hal, Maurice and I duly arrived at their Pall Mall offices, ascending to the second floor in a rickety, Dickens-era elevator to a rather sombre reception area with leather couches and walls lined with law books. We announced our arrival for a 9am appointment with Gordon Jaynes and were asked to wait. About ten minutes later, we were ushered into Gordon's office, where our mouths dropped open. Gordon sat, Buddha-like, on a Swedish style stool with his legs tucked underneath him, and the walls of his office were covered by extraordinary photographs of exotic scenes and remote tribes. Gordon was used to the reaction, and quickly explained that his partner, Lyle Lawson, was a freelance photographer who took photographs of interesting and remote destinations for the Insight travel guides.

During the meeting Gordon showed his clear expertise in dealing with complicated projects such as Hyatt Britannia. We then held meetings with Cementation and the negotiation continued over many weeks. Gordon was astonishing: we would meet over dinner, discuss the day's events, consume copious amounts of wine, and Gordon would leave, announcing he was going to stay at the RAC, his London club, on Pall Mall. By the next morning, the revised contracts would be ready. We frequented some fine restaurants in London, including Al Gallo D'Oro, on Kensington High Street, where – amid bowls of pasta – we signed the construction contract for the Hyatt Britannia.

I have been blessed throughout my life to meet people as part of my work, who go on to became very good friends as well as business acquaintances. This was certainly true of Gordon and Lyle, Hal and his wife Maddie, and Maurice Cullen, who eventually married Jo Butcher, our London accommodation guru.

Work on the Britannia project got underway in June, with Pete Widmer from the practice leading cost management. Well into construction, senior Hyatt executives arrived in Cayman to check on progress, walked the site and said, '… where's the beach?' There was none, because the property fronted the main West Bay Road. Fortunately, directly across the road was a private beach-front residence owned by Gary and Arden Shaw, with whom we had been working on a condominium project. Negotiations followed, and the property was acquired for a beachfront restaurant called Hemingway's. To connect it to the hotel, we built Cayman's first-ever pedestrian bridge over West Bay Road. The hotel opened for the first guests on 17th December 1986 – on schedule! Bould Chartered Quantity Surveyors's role was recognised in a feature article in the Royal Institution of Chartered Surveyors globally circulated magazine in May 1988, as well as in a subsequent feature article, 'Portrait of an Island Practice'.

In our warehousing business, Mikol had spotted a swampy, low-lying parcel of land slightly larger than an acre on West Bay Road, listed at $4 per square foot. When he urged the company to buy it, I said he must be crazy. But Cayman Kai, Mikol and his father Don's company, wanted an office on the West Bay Road and the idea was to build a small block of shops/offices in the centre of the strip, such as it was then. Don, who had been inducted into the Housing Hall of Fame for the many homes he had built in Boulder Hill, Aurora, a suburb of Chicago, also prepared the designs. That's how the Greenery Shopping Centre began – a 6,000 square foot development with tenants such as Patrick Broderick, a leading photographer, and Gary Callan, a hairdresser, as well as a small convenience store operated by the Fosters, alongside Cayman Kai's 'town' office. Foster's did so well that a 9,000 square foot expansion was later added.

In late March I flew back to the UK with my dad, this time at a reasonable tempo, and after giving him into the care of my sister, accepted a kind invitation from René and Claudine Meister to ski with them in Verbier. There, they owned a wonderful chalet that looked exactly like a Swiss musical box, complete with a natural 'frigo' for white wine on the external window cill.

Returning to Cayman in mid-April, by which time construction was well underway on the Rum Point Club's Retreat, I was caught speeding during one of my frequent trips between there and my office in town. When I was called to court, my attorney humbly apologised to the court on my behalf, and pleaded against confiscating my license because I had to drive between the two locations. The magistrate, unimpressed, said I could take the ferry instead. However, by pure luck, David Ritch, an attorney who was waiting in the court Room for another case, stood up and said, 'Excuse me, your Honour, but the ferry sank yesterday!' and I got off with a $200 fine!

RP Developments Ltd., the developers of The Retreat, commenced work on the second phase of the development at Rum Point, this time with Olsen Construction, led by Harry Olsen, as the main contractors; they finished their work in May 1985.

We were also completing a project at Cayman Kai for Don Dise, called the Gardens of the Kai; building a luxury house on Seven Mile Beach for Bill Tomasso; working on a new project for Brian Butler and on a low-cost housing scheme, so things were buzzing. For the sake of convenience, and to attract buyers to the Cayman Kai area, the Dises had started a company called the North Sound Ferry and ran a regular service from the George Town area to Cayman Kai. The ferry that had so providentially (for me) sunk was theirs, and they'd had to replace it.

On the 13th June I called my dad in UK and was told he was very ill. I immediately booked a flight for the next day, drove up to the Midlands to see him in hospital, and spent a week with him before returning to Cayman. My visit had appeared to greatly lift his spirits and by the time I left, he looked a lot better.

But on the 17th July I received the terrible news that my dad had passed away at the age of seventy-five. I was devastated. Yet, I couldn't help but feel the Good Lord had been watching over us, granting me the gift of those three months together in Cayman. I returned to UK for the funeral and did my best to console my mom, who was also by then in poor health. But, after my dad's passing, it was as though she lost the will go on, and she herself passed away on 19th January 1985 at the age of seventy-three.

1985

'Believe and act as if it were impossible to fail.' Charles Kettering

For some time, Don Messick had been in talks with Tino Gonzales, the MD of Cayman Airways, and an agreement was reached to launch a charter airline, Cayman Express, which would fly directly between Cayman and the East Coast gateway cities of New York, Chicago, and Detroit. Don's idea was, if occupancies for tourist rentals could be improved by direct flights, then sales at the Retreat would be improved due to higher returns. I was never very keen on the idea, as I felt that trying to push demand would be difficult, and so did not join the venture. Nevertheless, I enjoyed some good perks, such as flying with Don to New York, purchasing delicacies like smoked salmon, and returning the same day. We also put on fashion shows, with the flight attendants modelling the latest styles during the journey and with yours truly in the MC's role.

On 26th January 1985, the New Terminal at Owen Roberts airport opened. It was a huge change from the previous one and, although it was much more luxurious, many missed the warm conviviality of the old terminal and, in particular, the Hungry Horse bar, where many a happy hour had been spent waiting for flights or simply socialising with friends.

Mikol Dise was a very good friend as well as my business partner. He owned an eleventh-floor apartment in Yacht Harbour in the Coconut Grove area of Miami, and generously let me use it whenever I was in town. During one stay with Vivian, I asked her to see if there were any apartments for sale in the building. Sure enough, a one-bed and den unit was available on the floor below and we purchased it though the décor was pretty terrible. We had Bill Bissell rework the layout and, though the apartment contained little more than a sofa bed, for many months we used it in that spartan state anyway. At one point, the building Manager, Bill Schwab, enquired if we were short of cash after the purchase, and kindly offered to lend us some spare furniture he had in the basement until we got on our feet! Truth is, we had ordered furniture from the Italian company Saporitti, which had a long delivery time. We contracted a D.J. Stour to handle the interior work, and we were very pleased with the end result.

At Plantana, Ken Webb, one of the owners, told me about a course he had taken at Harvard Business School – the 'Owner President Management Programme' – and recommended it highly during a discussion we had about business planning. I was intrigued, especially given the rapid growth of our quantity surveying practice and my expanding real estate interests. I enquired how to apply, and with Ken's help and contacts, I duly submitted my application. To my amazement, I was accepted into Unit 1, scheduled for 11th–30th August 1985 at the Harvard Business School. There were to be some one hundred and twenty attendees from all around the world. The course consisted of three units, each taken at least one year apart, to allow participants to apply what they had learned in their own businesses and report back during the next session.

The faculty for Unit 1 was Louis Barnes, Professor of Organisational Behavior; John Bishop, Professor of Management Control; J. Keith Butters, Marty Marshall and Phil Thurston, Professors of Business Administration. We had been sent an informative brochure which described the course grandly as:

> The principal focus of Unit 1 of OPM is on formulating effective goals and strategies for a growing firm in its entirety, as well as for each of the major functional activities of the company. The risks and opportunities of a strategy of rapid growth are highlighted. Emphasis is also placed upon the interrelatedness of the various facets of business and the resulting need for multi-dimensional analysis of management decisions. Techniques that assist such analysis are stressed. In order to obtain these objectives, the curriculum of Unit 1 consists of five courses: Human Aspects of Business, Professor 'By' Barnes; Financial Policy, Professor Keith Butters; Management Control, Professor John Bishop; Marketing Strategy, Professor Marty Marshall; Strategy in Smaller Companies, Professor Phil Thurston.

So, what was it like arriving at this world-famous centre of learning? The Harvard Campus, set along the Charles River in Cambridge, a suburb of Boston, is truly beautiful in summer. The campus is built of low-rise, red brick buildings and is generously supported by its alumni.

Participants live on campus, and I was assigned to Suite 14 in Mellon Hall. Eight small bedrooms opened onto a large and commodious living room, with just two bathrooms shared among us. When I arrived, I was greeted by a blonde lady, Anne Toth, who introduced herself and announced – as she did to each of the other group members – that she would be claiming one of the two bathrooms, as her morning makeup routine took at least an hour. The remaining seven members of our group would have to make do with the other!

A promising start.

The small bedrooms are specifically designed to encourage you to spend the maximum amount of time in the shared living room, interacting with the others. These groups are informally known as 'can' groups – a name that stems from Harvard's use of case methodology in their study system. In this system, case writers visit real companies and create scenarios based on actual business challenges. The cases are distributed without revealing the outcomes, and the participants must analyse the situation and propose solutions. Each morning, the members in your group discuss the case informally – often while someone is in the bathroom – hence the name 'can' group. Following these discussions, we joined a larger session in a lecture hall with about sixty participants (the full cohort of one hundred and twenty was divided into two broad categories: Service and Manufacturing) to discuss the case further.

The lecture began with the professor introducing the case, after which students took turns presenting their views on how to solve the problem. Occasionally, the professor would have secretly invited the actual company owner to sit in on the lecture. This led to some embarrassing moments, such as when a student dismissed a particular strategy as crazy, only for the professor to reveal the owner's presence and invite him to explain why the 'crazy' solution had, in fact, been the correct one!

One particular incident I'll never forget involved a case study on Vlasic Pickles, where Robert J. Vlasic, the owner, was exploring how the shape of the jar and the colour and mixture of the pickles might encourage people to buy, and what factors would make his product the market leader. Unbeknown to anyone, a student named Glen Ellion decided to get the inside story. Posing as Professor Phil Thurston, he telephoned Robert Vlasic and explained he was teaching the case the next day and asked how Vlasic had solved the problem. Vlasic explained exactly how he had tapered the jar, adjusted the pickle mix and colour, and how that strategy had brought the product to the front of the supermarket shelves. Next day, as Professor Thurston began the classroom discussion, of course Glen had all the answers. What he didn't know, was that Vlasic had remembered something else and phoned the real Philip Thurston – only to discover he'd been speaking with an imposter. Realising what had happened, Phil cleverly steered the lecture with specific questions that gradually exposed Glen. Finally, he pointed at Glen and said, 'You are the one that pretended to be me!'

The university selected participants in each 'can' group based on their particular skills, so there would always be one person in the group that understood finance or accounting, to assist those who might not be so *au fait* with these skills. The constant reading required to keep up with the case studies made the workload intense. Professors were constantly encouraging us to get outside and try to relax, but that was easier said than done. Without an intimate familiarity with the material, it was difficult to contribute meaningfully in the lecture hall exchanges. I do recall once sitting on a rock in Harvard Square, immersed in a case study and feeling as though knowledge was literally coursing through my veins.

Running along the banks of the Charles River was a wonderful way to clear the head though. Some more enthusiastic students decided football would be a great way to relax, but this was not necessarily such a good idea, mid-life and out of shape. Within days, there were three or four students on crutches due to knee or ankle injuries!

Many of the people I met on the course have become lifelong friends, and during reunions held all over the world, hosted by local alumni, we have got to see places like true 'natives', in ways we would never have experienced as tourists. Jimmy Nowery is one of these – more about him and his wife Cynthia later! When we met in Unit 1, Jimmy, a contractor from Shreveport, Louisiana, bore a striking resemblance to Jack Nicolson and his accent marked him as coming from the Deep South. In his 'can' group was Edson Bueno, who owns a significant health insurance business in Brazil, and whose English was quite basic at the time. Jimmy helped Edson, whose spoken English improved significantly over the three years at Harvard – but is now spoken with a distinct Southern drawl!

Construction had by now commenced on Genesis, and we had a great team. OBM were the architects; the attorneys were C.S. Gill & Co, who were also taking space in the building, as were Bould Chartered Quantity Surveyors and Peat Marwick Mitchell. Washington International Bank & Trust, who funded our Mini Warehouse projects, were our bankers, with Arch & Godfrey as main contractors. Since our launch party in September 1982, it had taken much negotiation to find purchasers and tenants and secure the financing. We had considered possible export credits from Italy, where I visited steel frame manufacturers in Genoa, and ended up chasing a fraudster financier through the New Orleans courts – a challenge due to the French-based system of private law in Louisiana. He had come to Cayman on his Learjet, assuring me that funds were readily available. But now we were underway. The steel frame was on site in November and the frame was at the fourth floor level on my fortieth birthday.

On the CNCF front, work had also commenced. Jason Construction, who had built the Studio Theatre, were contracted for the Main Theatre and the extensive siteworks for a large water feature in the shape of Grand Cayman. The theatre procurement was divided into two parts: the main structure, and the interior frame and furnishings which were supplied by Theatre Projects from the UK.

The design was unique in its flexibility. While it could seat three hundred and fifty people for major productions, it allowed for a more intimate setting during smaller performances, which enhanced the connection between the actors and their audience. Partway through construction, Jason Construction ran into financial difficulties and McAlpine stepped in to complete the project. Despite this setback, Jeremy Spencer of Bould Chartered Quantity Surveyors provided excellent project management and cost control, with a variation in the final contract amount of only 3.9 per cent.

For my fortieth birthday, Vivian asked me what I wanted to do, to which I seem to recall responding, 'Nothing fancy.' She said, 'Then let's go out for a nice dinner, and because it's a special birthday why don't you put on your black tie dinner suit and we'll ask your good friend Mike Johnson (who was visiting Cayman at the time) and Cissy Delapenha, and we'll hire a limo to take us so we can have a couple of drinks and not be driving.' Well, I fell for it, and asked where we were going, to which I got, 'It's a surprise!' We drove to the Caribbean Club, my all-time favourite restaurant and the only one in Cayman where you had to wear a jacket and tie for dinner, and were directed upstairs by reception. There, forty of my very good friends greeted me, singing Happy Birthday. The band included Ed Oliver, Ed Solomon, Wil Steward, Jack Andressen, and Jeff Parker! It was an incredible evening and had been planned to perfection by Vivian over many months. I promised to 'get Vivian back' for this trick, which I did in May 1986 for her own fortieth birthday.

1986

'Always remember that you are absolutely unique. Just like everyone else.' Margaret Mead

Spurred on by my time at Harvard, and with a more focused view of business planning from that experience, my attention was caught by a press release in the *Caymanian Compass*. A representative from British Executive Services Overseas (BESO) was assisting a section of the Civil Service in Cayman in need of specific skills. I hadn't heard of this organisation before but when I learned more, it and the services it offered seemed to fit the bill for what we needed.

Generally speaking, the experts working with BESO were retirees who wanted to continue sharing their specialised knowledge with those who could benefit from it. I submitted an application asking for assistance from an expert in business planning to review our QS practice, which was now some seventeen years old but which had never had much formal planning. As has so often been the case in my life, serendipity intervened; Mortimer Raath had scarcely retired as Chairman of several of Lonrho's companies, when my application reached BESO. He was given our application and agreed to join us for a three-month assignment to assess our company and help us develop a structured business plan. Lonrho was a global conglomerate of companies owned by Tiny Rowlands, who finished up having a huge fight with Mohamed Al-Fayed over the purchase of Harrods – but that's another story. Tim (Mortimer) Raath arrived in June and commenced work. He went on to play a huge part in my personal and business life for more than thirty years.

Viv's fortieth birthday was in May, for which I had planned an appropriate 'revenge' surprise. We had purchased a maroon Mercedes 500S for European delivery, to be collected in Stuttgart. After a weary flight we collected 'Rosie', as the car came to be called, from the Mercedes factory and gingerly drove out onto the German autobahn to find the nearest hotel where we could to sleep off our transatlantic journey. The next day we left for Switzerland, as we had to exit Germany to a non-EU country in order to recover the VAT paid on the purchase. From there we drove around Europe for a week having a glorious time and stopping, like Mary and Joseph, wherever the Michelin guide recommended. Viv thanked me for making her fortieth birthday so wonderful, and we returned to London by ferry via Calais. When we arrived at Claridge's, our favourite hotel, the doorman took the car away and we went upstairs to our suite, where I said to Viv, 'Why don't you order a bottle of champagne, have a nice soak in the wonderful deep tub, and I will go downstairs and see if I can get some last minute tickets for a show,' and disappeared out the door.

Now, before leaving Cayman I had written to Ronald Jones, the general manager of Claridge's, to enlist his assistance with my surprise. I had also contacted Joe and Flo, Viv's parents, in Belfast and asked them to come to London to surprise her, but they were to stay in their room until someone called so they didn't accidentally meet Viv in the lobby. Bless them, they stayed in their room all day, but with ample room service, courtesy of Mr Jones. After letting them know 'the game was afoot', I returned to our suite and announced that I had managed to get seats for 'Starlight Express' and ordered a limo to take us there. Viv was delighted, dressed quickly, and we went down to the lobby and out through the front revolving door where Roman, the doorman, pointed out our car. Just before he opened the rear door for us to get in, Viv noticed that there someone was sitting in the back seat. I said, 'It's rush hour for the theatre so we have to share.' Viv got in – to be greeted by her parents sitting in the back seat! The tears flowed and the makeup ran, but it was such a happy moment none of that mattered.

'Starlight Express', with its roller-skating cast and vibrant music, was a great hit and we went on to have dinner at Inigo Jones, another of our favourite restaurants. After an excellent meal, I asked Joe if he would like a cigar, which he thought a great way to cap off a wonderful evening. Unbeknown to Joe, I had given the maître d' two Royal Jamaican cigars, each wrapped with a custom label reading *Specially selected and custom rolled for Joseph Brown*, a box of which I had purchased in Jamaica from Gore Brothers during my last visit there. The maître d' arrived with the cigars on a silver platter. Joe picked them up, read the label, and looked at me in astonishment. 'How did they know my name?' he asked. I laughed and replied, 'They know you are a good customer.'

The next day, I told Viv that we had been invited to a client's board meeting and lunch in Geneva followed by a black tie dinner, so we would need to dress in the appropriate clothes and take evening dress with us to Victoria station for the Gatwick Express. So, still somewhat hungover, we bade goodbye to Joe and Flo and took a taxi to Victoria, where I steered us to the check-in desk for the Orient Express to Venice. It was not until a Burberry-clad lady with a silk scarf asked Viv what luggage she required in her cabin, that a somewhat tired Vivian looked up and saw the gleaming livery of the carriages of this famous train. More happy tears ensued! We had lunch and cocktails while speeding through the English countryside and dinner on board near Paris. Overnight we sped across the continent and arrived in Venice the next day, where a Vaporetto took us from the airport to the wonderful Hotel Cipriani on its own island. A fabulous week in Venice followed, walking the narrow winding streets and visiting the art galleries and museums of this magical city. By the end of it, Viv agreed I had indeed 'got her back' for the wonderful birthday surprise she had prepared for me.

'Back to porridge' – as they say.

By June we were able to give Peter Lloyd, the then Governor of Cayman, and his wife, a tour of the Genesis building. We announced more new tenants and owners, including Ernst & Whinney, and confirmed Hampstead, an office supply company owned by Denny Diedrick, one of ODL's shareholders. Peat Marwick Mitchell took occupancy in August, Quatro Hatch opened a deli on the ground floor in September, and Vivian's employers, Tricon International Limited, eventually purchased space in the building.

The Harquail Theatre was completed in July at a total cost of $3m excluding the generous land donation, all provided by Mrs Harquail, and the formal opening was set for 1st December 1986, which was Mrs Harquail's birthday. The opening was expanded into a weeklong celebration, which included a production of the *Sound of Music* with a dance performance by Lorna Reid and troupe, who went on to found Dance Unlimited in 1988, as well as piano recitals and an art exhibition with works by Bendel Hydes lighting up the theatre's foyer with vivid colour and form.

A few weeks later, following completion of the theatre, I was back in Boston attending Harvard OPM Unit 2 from 10th–29th August with ninety-eight other attendees. This time we were housed in a newly refurbished Baker Hall in Suite #7, which was real luxury: each bedroom, while still tiny, had its own bathroom! My 'can' mates were Norm Brown, Hugo Burgos (from Mexico), Paul Haviland, Chuck Patterson (who owned a car dealership), Camilo Wilson, Lanre Towry-Coker (an architect from Nigeria), Dominico Costa of cruise line fame, and New York developer Daniele Bodini, who arrived complete with a red Ferrari and a beautiful, statuesque blonde girlfriend who would wait at the rear of the lecture hall until class was finished and then be driven away in the Ferrari to Daniele's power boat moored on the Charles River. Whilst Daniele's accoutrements might have been enough to make him stand out in any case, his real claim to fame came during an unexpected event. During our course of study, pretty much everyone except Daniele had answered or posed questions during the lecture hall sessions. He had gone through Unit 1 and part way through Unit 2 without uttering a sound until, suddenly, during Professor 'By' Barnes's 'Human Aspects of Business' lecture on how to motivate staff, Daniele raised his hand. Called upon to speak, he said,

'Professor Barnes I really do not like what you are teaching here.'

'Why is that?' By responded.

Daniele replied, 'Professor Barnes, there are only two ways to motivate staff – Fear & Cash!', which brought the house down.

The collective knowledge and experience of the ninety-eight attendees, all senior decision-making executives, was awesome from a business sense but was also notable in other areas. Kim Hatfield, an oil expert from Oklahoma, was an extremely talented musician. He took highlights from the course of study and turned them into a musical revue, which we performed at the end of each course and went on to do the same at each subsequent reunion. As you may imagine, the 'Fear and Cash' comment featured in the revue!

The end of August bought me back to Cayman and an office move to our new premises in the Genesis building.

1987

'Happiness often sneaks in through a door you didn't know you left open.' John Barrymore

In early 1987, I prepared a joint venture proposal for the property north of Plantana, which I had first discussed with Desmond Webster in late 1983. At the time, he had indicated that the Webster family – through the Grand Cayman Company – not only wanted to sell the land to secure funds but also participate in the profits from its development. I presented the proposal to Desmond in February 1987 and he expressed interest, promising to consult with other family members involved with the company.

Through Bould Chartered Quantity Surveyors, we carried out significant feasibility studies with Desmond to explore relocating West Bay Road eastward, which would deepen the beachfront lots and increase their development potential given the setback requirements, thereby also making the Webster holdings more valuable. Socially, Desmond and his uncle, Burnett were extremely entertaining. Vivian and I frequently joined Desmond and his relatives for drinks in Cayman, and had visited Burnett's Jamaican Great House in St Ann, Geddes. Burnett was a great expert in furniture, and was passionate about restoring and recreating period pieces.

Desmond's finances were largely managed by Charles Adams's office, where Mary Cooper, his long-suffering secretary, would be driven almost to insanity by Desmond's frequent demands. In Charles's office the famous call, 'Mary, where's the file?' arose all too frequently, to which she would always calmly reply, 'It's on your desk, under your elbow, Charles!' But, truth be known, Desmond was not known for being especially discreet and loved to trade information, so one always had to be cautious about discussing anything sensitive, particularly regarding development.

It is interesting to note that Charles, who had in large measure been responsible for the formation of the Cayman Islands Law School, had for several years been encouraging Alden McLaughlin, the Deputy Clerk of the Court, to join his practice as an articled clerk. Alden joined Charles's practice in 1984 and remained there until 2005. Alden, as you will see, went onto perform an outstanding role in Caymanian politics, and our paths would frequently cross.

At the end of March, Charles Adams, the attorney for Grand Cayman Company and the Webster family, telephoned me to discuss the joint venture proposal which had been circulated to the family. Three days later there was a meeting, attended by Burnett Webster, Desmond Webster, Carl Webster, Jeffrey

Parker, Edward Haladay, Whitey Bozman, Charles Adams, J.C. Calhoun and myself.

Jeffrey was the accountant for the Grand Cayman Company; Edward Haladay, the design architect who had drafted various sketches, preliminary plans and site layouts for a proposed development of twenty-six luxury residences on the property; Whitey was a friend and neighbour at Plantana, who had been assisting in the promotion of the proposed development, and J.C. Calhoun was a local real estate agent. Chalmers Gibbs Martin Joseph Partnership were the supervising architects.

The presentation was favourably received by the Webster family, and it was agreed that Charles Adams would draft a letter of intent on behalf of the Grand Cayman Company outlining how the joint venture would proceed. The letter, dated 27th April 1987, was signed on 8th May 1987 after outline planning permission had been granted on the 29th April. The development was to cost US$16,800,000 including all soft costs. Sales were to yield US$21,820,000 and generate a profit of US$5,020,000.

Two days, later a bleak call came from my brother Robert in the UK – my sister Carole had died suddenly of a brain aneurysm at the age of forty-eight, leaving her husband and five children ranging in age from nine to nineteen years. Vivian and I flew back for the funeral to try and do what we could.

During all these developments in the UK and Cayman, Unit 3, my final session of the OPM Programme, loomed large in my preoccupations. It would take place from the 9th–28th August, and this was the year we were to graduate. Even more exciting, this year our partners would be able to participate in five classes, to experience first-hand what we had been trying to explain to them – an almost impossible task. We returned to live in Baker Hall, this time in Suite 10. My 'can' mates for this session were Jim Bryson, Terry Davison, Ray Debenham, Alex Silva, Peter Stauffer, Camilo Wilson, Ax Wu and Daniele Bodini. As there was a high demand for this last Unit of the OPM programme, not only from our original group from 1985, but also from others who wanted to complete the course, there were one hundred and thirty-four students this time.

We fell back into our by now well-practiced routine: reading all the cases obsessively, getting minimal sleep, discussing the cases, and then trying to work out strategies to follow during the group lecture hall discussions. This mid-life educational experience (far from cheap!) taught us an interesting lesson about elective education. Unlike studying to qualify in a profession in order to follow a particular career, everyone in OPM worked as if our life depended on it. The professors said they much preferred teaching the OPM course over the

MBA programme, because MBA students asked many questions before giving an answer, while OPM participants gave answers based on the information to hand. This may be because one of the requirements for admission to the OPM course is that you are already a decision-maker in your company.

Our guests and partners arrived on Wednesday 26th August for the final five classes. They had been given three business cases to study for Thursday and two for Friday. Vivian, in her signature Irish style, relished the debates. We had all moved out of the student accommodation on Wednesday, and were now ensconced in the luxury of the Ritz Carlton overlooking the beautiful Boston Common. We did get to show our partners our student accommodation, but, as described earlier, the bedrooms were barely large enough for one person, let alone two!

Graduation followed on Friday, 28th August at 1.30pm in Burden Hall – we were now Harvard Business School Graduates! That evening we celebrated with a dinner dance at the Ritz Carlton, and then an exhausted sleep.

After more than three weeks away from the office, it was not easy to follow Harvard's parting advice: 'Take a week off before returning to work as you are now a graduate of one of the best Ivy League colleges in the world and everyone will be looking at you to produce miracles – so go somewhere very quiet and contemplate what you have learnt over three years and what you will say to your work colleagues and what plans you will implement.' However, I thought we might as well, and to that end Viv had already researched and settled upon a week at the wonderful Cotton House in Mustique. So, from Boston we flew via Barbados, landing in Mustique to begin a decade-long love affair with this island, which later became the setting for many stories to come.

CHAPTER FIVE

Storm Clouds over the Tropics (1988–1992)

1988

'Promise me you'll always remember: You're braver than you believe, and stronger than you seem, and smarter than you think.' A.A. Milne

On 1st January 1988, Jim Slattery and Pete Widmer joined me and Richard Jones as partners, and we changed the name of the practice from Bould Chartered Quantity Surveyors to BCQS. The name was changed because the partners were frequently asked if they were property developers because of my own development activities.

Reservations to purchase apartments in the Great House had begun in early 1987. Following the registration of the company these were formalised. By February 1988, prospective buyers had expressed sufficient interest to allow GH Ltd. to sign conditional sale agreements for the apartments. These agreements were subject to the land purchase option agreement, and the shareholders agreement; the latter was signed on 16th February 1988. The property, measuring 3.471 acres with a 416-foot frontage, was purchased for US$4,000,000 – half in cash, and half in preference shares. Part of my obligation under the agreement was to raise US$2,500,000: US$2,000,000 in cash payable to the Websters, and US$500,000 for working capital. In order to augment the funds I needed to participate; I sold Beachcomber #13 in December 1987.

An Offering Memorandum was completed on 8th February 1988 and sent, along with other documentation, to those interested in acquiring preference shares in GH Ltd. One investor was my neighbour at Plantana, who was insistent that I invest personally by purchasing ordinary shares, preference shares, and an apartment, to demonstrate that I had some 'real skin in the game' beyond my role as promoter of the development.

The investors were also apartment purchasers as well as investors in preference shares. One of the unique aspects of the Great House project was that purchasers were permitted to customise their apartments. By February 1988, the design drawings had advanced far enough to incorporate these customisations, which we frequently discussed with the investors over dinner at my apartment in Plantana.

The first agreement for sale was signed on 4th February 1988 for my initial choice of apartment #9, but in order to accommodate subsequent interest I shifted my choice on several occasions to help meet the sales threshold, on each occasion reselling the apartments at an increased price, however, always passing on any premium to GH Ltd., and finally settling on #21. I detail all of this, as a later dispute with certain investor preference shareholders led to legal action involving my purchasing company.

At the insistence of the investors, in addition to the apartment purchase, I personally agreed to purchase one block of preference shares for US$500,000. Bank of N.T. Butterfield (previously Washington International) were kind enough to lend me this sum, and a second block of preference shares was purchased by my good friend and fellow Plantana apartment owner, Al Hallock. With sufficient funds in place, the land deal closed on 16th June 1988. As a condition for proceeding with development, at least twelve condos had to be sold to mitigate risk. Construction financing was provided by the Bank of N.T. Butterfield, as well as McAlpine Ltd., who also contributed US$1 million – both of these had provided similar services on Plantana.

There were many meetings during the first half of 1988 in order to develop the design and arrive at an affordable budget, and the team at BCQS had their work cut out, but by mid-1988 we were close to where we needed to be. Vivian and I flew to London in July, rented a house at 62A Cadogan Square from Jo Butcher, and fell easily into London life.

While he was in London, Maurice Cullen had introduced me to his tailor, Benson & Clegg, located in the Piccadilly Arcade off Jermyn Street in a tiny shop with bow windows and with a bell that clinked distinctively to summon attention as you opened the shop door. Benson & Clegg had received the Royal Warrant as tailors to Prince Charles, and the atmosphere inside was calm and regal. Their tailoring is superb, and has accommodated my fluctuating weight over the years. My tailor, Kenneth Austin, always met these requests with aplomb and good humour. I still wear suits made there. Maurice always said – and he was right – that you could sleep through a transatlantic flight in a Benson & Clegg suit and arrive looking immaculate and ready for a business meeting!

Every day, real estate magazines would be delivered to the house, and it's a measure of how easily Vivian and I had fallen into the London lifestyle, that one day I suggested to her that she take a look at properties for sale while I was out working. So said, so done, and soon Viv had shortlisted some for us to view together.

The very smartly dressed young sales agent from Foxton's showed us several properties that were not very inspiring, and we were already beginning to tire of looking at houses – we were on holiday after all – when we said we really wanted a Mews house. No problem, there was one around the corner! Well, we looked at the house, and it was perfect. The living space was level with the cobbled Mews, with two bedrooms and two bathrooms on the lower floor. This meant we would be in the centre of London, yet have perfect peace and quiet. We were sold. We didn't have the funds to buy in cash, so needed to arrange a mortgage. There was also paperwork to be arranged and furniture to be bought, so what with everything going on back in Cayman, we agreed to return in September to complete the purchase, which we did. The 'Doll's House', as we nicknamed it, did not have a window onto the Mews at the living room street level, but only one that looked onto the rear lightwell. so Alan Foster kindly applied for planning approval to insert another on the Mews side, which was eventually granted. He also supervised the installation and redecoration. Given the significant activities in the Caribbean and the need to service the mortgage, we rented out the Doll's House for a number of years to a succession of tenants – some good, some not so good.

Alan Scott and his wife Joan had arrived in Cayman on 10th June 1987 to take up his posting as Governor of Cayman, and we had been introduced to them at a friend's luncheon party. Somehow the discussion got around to running, a passion of mine, and cross country running in Sutton Park was mentioned. His Excellency said he also used to run there, as he had been a student at Bishop Vesey Grammar School – where of course I had been as well – and a friendship began that remains to this day.

Shortly after her arrival, Joan – an enthusiastic community worker – became involved with the National Trust, along with her good friend Dace Ground. Between 1985 and 1987 Kearney Gomez, Patricia Bradley and Joe Parsons recognised the need to protect the natural and cultural environment through legislation. Working with a legal advisor sent from the UK National Trust, they drafted a bill to establish the National Trust for the Cayman Islands. The law was passed in 1987, and Dace Ground became the Trust's first director. Since then, the Trust has achieved extraordinary success in securing key land holdings and historical sites over the years.

I was delighted when His Excellency agreed to commence construction on the Great House, and he had his first shot at driving a JCB while leading the ground-breaking ceremony on 5th September 1988.

McAlpine's were the general contractor, with a contract figure of US$11,500,000 and started work under a letter of intent. The contract was signed on 11th November 1988, with a fifteen month construction period giving a contract completion date of 26th February 1990.

Preliminary site set-up had been carried out when Hurricane Gilbert hit Cayman on 13th September 1988 with gusts of 150mph and a pressure of 900mb. Decisions needed to be made about where to take refuge from the storm. Well, Genesis was well-built, and our offices were above the level of any projected storm surge, so a group of us including our good friends Bobby Nunes and his mother – affectionately known as 'Ma' – and Cissy and Bunny Delapenha, collected in the boardroom with appropriate supplies. It was a terrifying night and downbursts shook the building to the core but, amazingly, there was minimal damage to our building. This was the first time Ma had left her residence at Point Four since her arrival in Cayman many years earlier. She arrived with her own supplies, including her quilt, and Cissy decided it was best to sleep under the table in case the ceiling fell in.

We quickly got on with clean-up and registering the damage with the insurance company and loss adjusters. This slightly delayed a planned trip to Europe, at the start of which we picked up 'Rosie' from Mr Foitek's garage in Zurich, where René had arranged to store it alongside two of his Ferraris. René had also scheduled the most incredible gastronomic tour for us, beginning with lunch at their home in Lutry, where Claudine had prepared a pumpkin soup served in the hollowed-out pumpkin shell and delicious veal cutlets, washed down with a refreshing and slightly pétillant white Fendant and a full-bodied red Dôle. We then drove some 500km to spend three nights with Alan and Joan Scott at their summer home in Callas, enjoyed a magnificent lunch at Roger Vergé's Moulin de Mougins, and drove to Eugénie-les-Bains to become re-acquainted with Michel Guérard at Les Prés d'Eugénie. There, we once again enjoyed his Cuisine Minceur for three days and, at their wonderful spa, undid some of the damage wrought by the previous few days' indulgence. Then we went on to enjoy delicious food and wines at Domaine Les Hauts de Loire, a former hunting lodge built in 1860 and now a Relais and Châteaux hotel.

We took the Calais ferry back to the UK, where I made arrangements to ship Rosie back to Cayman and carried out staffing interviews for new quantity surveyors for both our Cayman and Turks and Caicos offices. We were staying at one of Jo Butcher's managed houses at Cadogan Square, and a few days before leaving we had a wonderful party there, with our guests merrily spilling out into the street to the amusement of passersby.

We moved to Claridge's for a few days to stay until our departure on the 11th, booking our usual mews-facing double corner suite on the fourth floor – much quieter than the rooms facing Davis Street. At times this suite was let as two separate bedrooms and so had telephones in both rooms, each with a different number. Shortly after we arrived, I made a business call from what was currently the living room, and left that number for them to call back. When we awoke the next morning, I asked if Viv would order breakfast – the drill being that you press a button beside the bed for the floor butler, who arrives dressed in a tailcoat and takes your breakfast order. Viv pressed the appropriate button, and a short while later the telephone rang in the living room. I jumped out of bed to answer it, not bothering with a dressing gown, just as the butler began to open the bedroom door. The only refuge I can think of is behind the opening door! Viv is lying in bed, and while the butler asks Madam what she would like for breakfast, she can barely contain her laughter as the door slowly begins to close on its own, revealing yours truly standing there in his birthday suit, hands strategically covering his vital parts. Having taken the order, the butler turns round to see me standing there like an idiot. 'Good morning, sir,' he says with magnificent composure. 'How is your day so far?'

When our cohort graduated from Harvard, we had decided to organise yearly get-togethers to keep alive the camaraderie we had established over the last three years. I suggested everyone come to Cayman during 1988. Hal Walker was delighted at the thought of increased business at the newly completed Hyatt, so we had arranged to assemble in Cayman from 20th–24th October, which would encompass Pirates Week, and eighty-five Alumni and their wives attended.

I had contacted Alan Scott and Joan to ask if they would be kind enough to host a cocktail party for our group at Government House, to which they graciously agreed. With about one hundred and twenty people, the first logistical challenge was transportation. Rollin Ebanks, of Tropicana Tours, said he had plenty of twenty-seater buses to shuttle guests from the Hyatt to Government House, and later to Grand Old House for dinner.

The evening of the cocktail party, I stood next to Alan and Joan and introduced the guests one by one. When I introduced Giorgio Sermoneta from Rome, he surprised Joan by saying, 'I know you.' Joan looked a little puzzled, until Giorgio added, 'You buy your white gloves from my shop at the foot of the Spanish Steps in Rome.' Joan laughed and replied, 'Yes, indeed, I do!' Small world!

The evening was a great success. Around 8.30pm, Alan asked me when I would like to close the bar. Our dinner reservations were for 9pm. I saw a

Storm Clouds over the Tropics (1988-1992)

Tropicana bus waiting at the end of the long driveway and suggested we wrap things up to get the guests moving. I directed everyone towards the waiting bus, which filled and departed. But I noticed a large group still waiting at the end of the driveway. Curious, I walked over – to find only one bus. The driver casually explained they'd just taken another job at the airport and would be back soon!

In the end, everything worked out. We enjoyed an excellent dinner at the Grand Old House, followed on Saturday by an address to the alumni by Professor Bruce Scott from Harvard, and remarks from local business and government leaders. That afternoon we joined the excitement of the Pirates Landing in Hog Sty Bay. Sunday ended with cocktails on the beach at Plantana, and on Monday morning our group winged their way home.

A tradition began that weekend that continues to this day. Jimmy and Cynthia Nowery were our house guests at Plantana, and had kindly brought with them a magnum of Dom Perignon. What would be the best way to compliment this fine wine on a Sunday morning? Caviar eggs, of course! I had learnt to cook this delicacy with Michel Guérard and although it takes some preparation and presentation, it is quite stunning. You take a raw egg and carefully remove the top, pouring the egg into a mixing bowl. Then you wash out both the empty eggshell and its top and set them to one side. The egg is beaten with butter and milk and chopped chives are added. You cook the egg until it is creamy but still soft, then put it back into the cleaned eggshell, topped with a healthy pile of caviar. The top of the eggshell is placed over the caviar, with a very small piece of chive peeping out the top, and the dish is served with a glass – or several – of champagne. We have stayed many times with Jimmy and Cynthia and we always have caviar eggs.

In early December I was humbled to receive an award from the Cayman National Cultural Foundation for my work with them. On the award plaque was written, 'In grateful appreciation for your wisdom, patience, strength and understanding during the formative years of the Cayman National Cultural Foundation and whose devotion and dedicated efforts made this dream come true.'

Changes were about to occur in the composition of CNCF's board and senior management. Oswell Rankine, who had served as Chairman from the Foundation's inception with myself as Deputy Chairman, was preparing to step down. As I noted earlier, the management of the foundation had fallen to Geoff Cresswell and the Cayman National Theatre Company. However, following some personal life changes, Geoff had left. In his absence, Mrs Harquail introduced a friend of hers, John Calvert, a magician with a touring show known as the 'Magic Castle', who, along with his wife, managed the theatre for a time.

This arrangement proved unsatisfactory, and we advertised for new leadership. In February 1989 we were fortunate to secure the services of Henry and Marcia Muttoo as Artistic Director and Managing Director respectively. Oswell stepped down as Chairman, and his role was taken up by Dave Martins, a talented and well-known Guyanese musician and leader of the band 'The Tradewinds', who had found fame and fortune in Canada.

My birthday falls on 10th December and that year Ruthie Bozman, who lived downstairs from us in Plantana, invited us to use her apartment in Big Sky, Montana, for a ski holiday. This extraordinarily beautiful part of Montana had been developed by Chet Huntley of TV fame. So on the 8th December we flew to Bozeman, Montana, and then went on to Big Sky, where we had a great holiday and met many of Ruthie's friends. We returned to Cayman on the 19th, in time to enjoy Christmas with René and Claudine.

After Christmas, I suggested we celebrate the New Year in Jamaica. René and Claudine had not been before, and instantly loved the idea. Bookings were quickly made, and we flew into Montego Bay on the evening of 30th December. Upon arriving, we enquired for a rental car but, because it was holiday season, options were scarce. However, a gentleman in a hoodie approached us, claiming he had a car available. We followed him and finished up at a rental shop behind the airport. 'Where's the car?' we asked. 'Just fixing the starter motor,' was the reply. Some forty-five minutes later, we were finally on our way to Ocho Rios where we had miraculously secured two rooms at Sans Souci. En route we discovered the car's headliner was loose, and its flapping noise accompanied us for the next two days.

On the way to Ocho Rios, René said they were starving. No problem. I took a detour from the main road into St Ann's Bay High Street and spied a jerk pork vendor. 'What's that?' René, the super European gourmand, asked. 'The national dish,' I replied. The vendor obligingly chopped up the jerk with great gusto using a machete on a sawn-off tree trunk, placed the chopped pieces in newspaper, splashed on additional scotch bonnet sauce, and handed it over. 'Welcome to Jamaica!' René and Claudine did enjoy it – or so they said.

1989

'Always do your best. What you plant now, you will harvest later.'

Og Mandino

The next morning we drove along the magnificent North Coast to Port Antonio and the Trident Hotel for lunch. After exploring the area, including the famous

Titchfield Hotel and Errol Flynn's Navy Island, we drove back through the Blue Mountain foothills via Highgate, as the road along Annotto Bay had been washed away by Hurricane Gilbert. Glancing at the gas gauge, I saw it was nearly empty. 'Not to worry,' I said, 'I know a gas station run by a Chinaman at the bottom of the hill running down into Port Maria which is sure to be open, even on New Year's Day.' It was closed! Now what? We cautiously drove on, with the A/C off, windows open, and coasting wherever possible to conserve fuel. Suddenly, in a narrow residential street in Port Maria, Claudine shouted, 'I just saw a man with a gas can coming out of one of the houses!' I was sceptical, but she insisted, so more to humour her than out of conviction, we turned around. Claudine identified the house, I walked up through a tiny gate, calling out to see if anyone was home. A gentleman appeared and I asked, 'Do you sell gas?' To my utter amazement he replied, 'No problem, mon – how much you want?'

True Jamaican resourcefulness! Tank filled, we made it back for a wonderful dinner at Sans Souci.

Later in January I met with Ed Haladay in Baltimore to further develop the Great House details and then visited Atlanta for the Home Builders' Show to see the latest developments in construction techniques and materials. We wanted the Great House to employ the very best and latest innovations the industry had to offer.

The BCQS practice was growing significantly in Turks & Caicos under Jim Slattery's leadership, and in February we added another QS, one Simon McGrail. We also celebrated Jimmy Burrowes's 75th birthday that month, at the Grand Pavilion Hotel, as he had by then moved to Cayman.

An opportunity to engage in a Caviar Egg breakfast soon presented itself as Jimmy and Cynthia Nowery invited us to Aspen, where we stayed at Sardy House, a delightful Victorian-style bed and breakfast on Main Street. We skied with them for four days and then flew on to Vancouver to ski with Hal and Maddie at Whistler/Blackcomb. On one memorable day, the weather at Blackcomb was miserable – snowing at the summit but raining at the base. We donned plastic garbage bags over our ski suits to keep dry, but to no avail. So we gave up and repaired to a restaurant at mid-station where, in a corner, was a bistro style section with table cloths. For Viv, tablecloths have always been a sign of better food, so we seated ourselves. Most serendipitously, the winemaker from the Inniskillin Winery had set up shop in that section of the restaurant to sample their finest wines. These were excellent and seemed to get better by the glass, particularly given the miserable weather outside. By the end of the tasting, Inniskillin were to be the featured wines back at the Hyatt

Regency in Grand Cayman! Quite a coup for the winemaker, from a really chance meeting on the slopes.

On 15th March, Viv and I left for Cayman for the UK, via Miami, where we caught British Airways Concorde. We flew subsonic to Washington DC, and supersonic on to Heathrow. Although the plane was small inside and smelled strongly of fuel on takeoff, the experience was exhilarating, and the sky is a deep and extraordinary blue at the higher altitudes. We spent a couple of nights in Claridge's and then travelled to Verbier to stay with René and Claudine in their chalet. As always, Claudine's cooking was outstanding and René made the Dôle and Fendant flow. The latter was cooled in the 'natural frigo', as René referred the windowsill where he left the bottles to chill in winter. Naturally, the neighbours always knew when guests were in town by the number of bottles ranged outside. Our days skiing were pleasantly interrupted by long lunches at a mountainside restaurant where the Meisters were well known as regular customers – a status Vivian and I were happy to share as honorary family members.

Viv was still relatively new to skiing when René suggested we should go heli-skiing on the Petit Combin. She loaded her skis into the helicopter's side basket and climbed aboard with some trepidation. We soon landed at the summit and, after some cautionary advice about avoiding the crevasses which lined our descent route, we set off. We made it down safely and celebrated with a wonderful lunch at an excellent restaurant.

From Verbier, we drove back to Geneva and continued on to Rome – and the Hotel d'Inghilterra on Via Boca di Leone – to meet with our Harvard friend Giorgio Sermoneta. The next day we met Giorgio at his famous shop, eponymously named 'Sermoneta', at the foot of the Spanish steps. After exchanging greetings, Giorgio told us to wait a minute and he would secure our transportation around Rome. He returned with a Vespa scooter which he had 'captured' from his fellow merchant next door for a few hours. Off we drove, following Giorgio on a whistle-stop tour of Rome's most interesting sites, though we later had to buy a guide book to identify all the sights we had seen.

Lunch at a fine restaurant followed, in company with Giorgio and Pino and his wife – friends of his that had accompanied him to Cayman for the Harvard reunion. Giorgio had to leave early to take care of some business matters, and when we called for the bill, we found he had already paid it. After lunch Pino and his wife invited us to their shop and asked Viv to look around. Viv found a belt she really liked but, as she offered her credit card to pay, Pino insisted it was a gift. We protested, and he appeared to accept the payment, but we later learned he had torn up the charge slip. What great and generous friends!

We flew back to London on 26th March, dropped off some film of our adventures during the previous couple of weeks for developing overnight and checked into Claridge's. On our departure the next morning for the airport we asked the driver to pass by the photo shop on Regent Street to collect our photos, and from there proceeded to Heathrow to catch Concorde back to Miami. We were unexpectedly greeted by a tailcoated footman from Claridge's who looked after the luggage and accompanied us to the counter to check in, where the British Airways agent said. 'Mr and Mrs Bould you are very late and I am not sure you will make it to the gate on time.' Whereupon the footman said, 'Not to worry – I will come with you to the gate.' So we ran full tilt through the airport, the footman pushing our luggage cart with his tails flying, while I jokingly asked if we could stop for Duty Free! As we arrived at the departure gate, the door to the plane was just being closed, but we persuaded them to let us aboard, where once seated we asked for a towel to wipe the sweat off our faces – not the usual way the Concorde passengers boarded!

On 7th May, we were invited to the Lacovia condominiums on Seven Mile Beach to have drinks with Baron Jean-Louis de Gunzburg and his wife Dagmar. Vivian and I had met Jean-Louis in slightly unusual circumstances. We had rented, once again through Jo Butcher, 20 Clabon Mews, a wonderful two-story house with a basement just off Cadogan Square. I vividly recall the staircase, which had a wrought iron balustrade which rattled as you held it going up and down the stairs. The house was occasionally used as a movie set, and this unusual feature made the house instantly recognisable.

Jo had asked if we would be kind enough vacate the house by 10am on the day we were to leave, as the next renter, one Jean-Louis de Gunzburg, was due to arrive at 11am. Now, as was typical of gravity-fed water systems in UK homes, the best shower was in the basement. On the day in question, Vivian was downstairs showering at around 9am when there was a knock at the door. I answered, and there stood Jean-Louis. I welcomed him in with the offer of a cup of coffee and the newspaper, quite forgetting Vivian was downstairs. Well, Vivian emerges from the depths, fetchingly clad only in a towel and meets Baron Jean-Louis, who politely asks Vivian what she does for a living, to which Vivian replies, 'I am a banker in the Cayman Islands.' Jean-Louis replies, 'Well, I am a director of a bank in Cayman – what a coincidence!' In fact, Jean-Louis's bank had a stellar board which included the Marquess of Tavistock, the Duke of Bedford's son. Vivian made her way upstairs to dress and after further polite conversation with John-Louis we agreed to meet up when he was next in Cayman.

In early May, Mortimer Raath came out to Cayman to continue working on the business plan for BCQS, and on the 25th we flew to Providenciales and stayed with Jim Slattery and his wife Margaret in an octagonally-shaped house they had rented. Unusually, the partitions in this house stopped short of the ceiling, with the result that Mort's thunderous snores after one sumptuous dinner made it difficult to carry on a conversation in the living room. Jim came up with a great idea: we should record his snoring, as the next day Mort would not believe it had been so loud. Jim's daughter Kate had a toy tape recorder with which to secure evidence of the event. It's a testimony to our state of inebriation that instead of simply opening the bedroom door and placing the recorder in the room, we decided to tie a rope on the handle of the recorder, stand on a chair, and then lower the instrument into the bedroom! All for naught. On hearing the playback the next day, Mort simply denied it was him.

We memorialised the trip with a photograph taken of Mort on Grace Bay beach. Dressed in his trunks with his more-than-adequate corporation (belly) on full display, and with an empty Heineken bottle on each finger, he stands looking imperiously down the beach. The photograph was printed and framed, and a title added: 'Lord Mortimer surveys the Colonies'. Lord Mortimer he was from then on! The picture was hung behind the bar in the 'City Pipe', a Davy's wine bar in the City of London that Mortimer frequented.

On the 27th June we heard the wonderful news from my brother Rob and his wife Jenna that a healthy, bouncy 7lbs 8oz daughter, Annabelle, had been born on 25th June 1989.

In late October, I received a call from Jean-Louis de Gunzburg asking if Vivian and I would entertain Andrew Howland, asking us to keep the fact that he was Lord Howland, grandson of the Duke of Bedford and heir to Woburn Abbey, strictly under wraps. We were of course delighted, and duly invited him to drinks at #26 Plantana to meet our friends. Andrew was really enjoying himself and was an easy-going fun guy, so we asked if he would like to join us for a BBQ on the beach the next day, Saturday, as a precursor to the Pirates Week landing downtown later. He was delighted and joined us, along with many other guests, one of whom was Bobby Nunes. Bobby, the son of a Jamaican lawyer who was the first ever captain of the West Indies cricket team from 1928 to 1932, was a gregarious character who, following his education at Dulwich College, went on to study law at Cambridge. Bobby was fond of many pastimes, including cricket and horse racing and mixing with 'society' in London. Bobby talked of horses (he claimed he was both the youngest and oldest racehorse owner in Jamaica) and racing with Andrew; and Andrew announced he was in charge of the Tavistock stables. Bobby then said, 'You must know Lady Henrietta Tiarks, who I met at her 'coming out' ball.' Andrew replied, 'Henrietta is my mother' – and so much for keeping his visit 'low key'!

1990

Without the darkness you would never know the light.

The customisation of apartments by individual owners at the Great House led to significant delays, ultimately pushing the official completion to 4.30pm on 31st August 1990. At that moment, His Excellency the Governor, Alan Scott, and his wife Joan once again performed the honours at the Grand Opening, followed by a celebratory dinner at our home at Plantana, next door to the Great House. It had been a long and complicated journey, but one well worth the effort. The Great House remains unique in its distinctive style and sophisticated grandeur on the finest stretch of Seven Mile Beach and set the standard to achieve for future developments on the beach.

Bobby Nunes's 'Ma', a poet of no small talent, captured her view of the achievement in the following verse:

THE GREAT HOUSE

> Martyn, I've heard from everyone
> What The Great House has become
> Everyone will indeed be proud
> Grace and Beauty much endowed
> The Proud Owners when they come
> Will be the envy of everyone
> Comfort & Beauty will be theirs
> No distress and no fears
> The sparkling sea, the white sands
> All will clap their happy hands
> Great luck be theirs, no doubt
> For Martyn knew this and went about
> Comfort & luxury too
> He knew just what to do
> So happiness lies ahead
> With never any harm or dread
> May the future years to come
> Please and comfort everyone
> For there will always be success
> And never any signs of distress.

A few days later, I flew to Providenciales for meetings about BCQS's expanding practice there, and then to London for Annabelle's christening, which was truly a joyous occasion. Afterwards there followed a memorable dinner with my brother Rob at Tante Claire, a three-star Michelin restaurant in Chelsea owned and operated by Pierre Koffman. I had a number of business meetings with Lord Mortimer and Cullum McAlpine to discuss the Great House and a number of other development opportunities, and on the 15th September interviewed a potential new quantity surveyor for BCQS, Liam Day, who came to lunch at the Doll's House with his wife Helen. Little were we to know that Liam would go on to lead BCQS International, which has become the largest Construction Advisory practice in the Caribbean and Central and South America.

On the 16th September, Vivian and I returned to Cayman and within a few days received some shocking news: the board of GH Ltd. clearly had not read Ma's beautiful poem because they suddenly advised, following my successful completion of the project, that the contract for purchase of Apartment #21 – signed on 3rd June 1988 and intended as Vivian's and my dream home – had never been formally presented to an independent board. On 28th September 1990, they rescinded the purchase agreement. We were dumbfounded to say the least. For over two years, we'd attended many long board meetings where the contract for the purchase of Apartment #21 was never questioned, and we had frequently discussed customising our apartment, just as other shareholders had, with no objections raised.

Vivian and I were advised by several leading members of the legal fraternity to sue GH Ltd. for specific performance of the purchase contract, but by this time, after completing such a complex landmark development project and enduring years of litigation, we were simply ready to move on and focus our energy on new opportunities.

The wonderful quote by Vivian Greene, *'Life isn't about waiting for the storm to pass. It's about learning to dance in the rain'*, taught me a wonderful lesson about this experience, and particularly about who can be trusted when large sums of money are involved.

We spent Christmas Day 1990 with Alan and Joan Scott at Government House. They had become really good friends, and we were frequent guests of theirs, as indeed they were at our home. Alan and Joan had started a Christmas Day tradition they referred to as 'Waifs and Strays', of inviting people with limited or no family to their home to celebrate. Vivian and I have continued the tradition since their departure from Cayman.

1991

'Wisdom is not a product of schooling but of the lifelong attempt to acquire it.' Einstein

As I mentioned earlier, BCQS's vision was to be a Caribbean-wide practice. With the Turks and Caicos office now operating successfully, we had for some time been exploring the possibility of opening another branch in the British Virgin Islands. To this end I met Jim Slattery in Miami in mid-April 1991, and flew from there to San Juan and on to Tortola. This was our first time travelling this route, but in the years to come it would be travelled hundreds of times more. We had a number of good meetings with architects, realtors and government officials, and laid the groundwork for opening an office there, but it would not be until 1995 that our fully operational office would be open. The greatest challenge was to be securing our business licence, the interview for which became quite a story in itself.

Another potential area of service expansion for the practice had first been mooted in November 1988. The idea was to form a professional Property Management company, for which I developed an outline feasibility study. At the time, property management in the Cayman Islands was largely being handled as a sideline by the Island's realtors. Our goal was to offer a professional service, using chartered surveyors and following the RICS professional guidelines. The idea had been thoroughly discussed amongst the BCQS partners, and we also sought advice from Charles Adams. Although the idea was raised again in mid-June 1991, other commitments delayed its execution. Eventually, BCQS Property Management Limited was registered on 7th June 1995. Today, the company has grown to become the largest property management practice in the Cayman Islands.

Our first chartered property manager, Stephen Pedrick-Moyle, joined us in August 1996. Stephen will always be remembered for two things: his enthusiastic response of 'Absolutely!' to most questions, and his distinctive 'bowling arm' gesture when discussing business. He was followed by a series of colourful managers, including Mark Jeff-Herbert, who disliked the sun. Vivian stepped in for a time after his departure – though she claims 'never again!' – and finally Tim Hepburn, who today runs the business.

In August, Vivian and I flew to London and then took a train to Birmingham for Hannah Johnson's christening. Mike and Doreen had graciously asked us to be godparents, an honour we were delighted to accept. To date we have twelve godchildren, and we just keep our fingers crossed they do not all need us at the same time! From there we flew to Belfast to celebrate Jo and Flo's 50th anniversary. For this we drove to Lough Erne, where we rented a motor yacht and had great fun cruising around the Lough for a week, stopping at a different marina every night. We visited Ardhowen theatre in Enniskillen for a show by Clubsound, preceded by dinner at a charming country inn with great home cooking, and finally we enjoyed coffees and a digestif on board. One day a fierce storm blew up out of nowhere, severely rocking the boat, while in the galley the plates and cutlery were crashing around inside the cupboards and I did my best to keep the boat on an even keel. Afterwards Flo announced she was not in the least bit scared, as she had looked at me and I had not shown any concern – little did she know!

We returned to London on the 21st August and stayed at Charlie and Lori Adams apartment in Walton-on-Thames, as our Queen's Gate Mews home was still rented out. Over the years Charlie and Lori were extremely generous with the loan of their home, which is located on the Thames towpath, along which walking and running was a wonderful way to exercise and enjoy the fresh air. I met with Gordon Jaynes (the only person I know who comes from Walla Walla, Washington State), who was assisting with some construction claims issues, and with Cullum McAlpine, about some exciting projects. These included the redevelopment of San Salvador Island (the reputed landfall for Columbus's first journey to the West Indies) as well as a potential office building on land, owned by McAlpine's in central George Town Grand Cayman.

On the 27th August we were back in Cayman, but not for long. On the 13th September we were off again, this time to Calgary for Hal Walker's 40th surprise birthday party on the 14th, returning to Cayman on the 16th.

I mentioned earlier that key to maintaining a rigorous travel schedule is having an excellent travel agent! By the early 1990s we had moved our business from Cayman Tours & Travel to International Travel. This is owned by Faye Davidson, whose husband Art had been the real estate agent acting on the sale of my half of the Melody Lane duplex. Angela Morgan, who worked with Faye, looked after our business. Angela was exceptional at her job and remains a great friend. No change in our travel plans, especially those made on the road, was ever a problem for her. Faye and Art were seasoned travellers themselves, and had visited many of the destinations we planned to explore, so they could provide first-class intelligence on sights to see, the quality of hotels and other key travel tips.

Another person who made our travelling experience vastly more pleasant was Mr Kelly, the manager of Pan Am's Clipper Club Lounge at Miami Airport. As club members, we always waited for our flights there and Mr Kelly would routinely check the available seating in Business Class and upgrade us from Economy when possible. Over many years, he treated us and our guests with the greatest hospitality, and we always returned the favour at Christmas with the finest bottle of Scotch – his favourite tipple!

On one memorable occasion, we phoned Mr Kelly from Cayman to let him know that our house guest, 'Lord' Mortimer, would be passing through Miami en route to London. We asked if Mr Kelly if he might extend him the usual courtesies. 'No problem', came the reply. Mortimer duly arrived, and was greeted by Mr Kelly, who mentioned that there was another Lord of the Realm in the club lounge that day – none other than Lord Snowden – and offered to introduce them. Mortimer quickly responded that wouldn't be necessary, as he already knew Lord Snowden. That was in fact the truth as they had met through Rotary projects!

Vivian and I had made a tradition of skiing on my birthday, and so in early December we flew to Bozeman to ski at Big Sky. And, once again, we stayed at Ruthie's Silver Bow #20 condo and reacquainted ourselves with her friends, including Sarah Bickerstaff who lived upstairs and who always welcomed us with open arms. Big Sky's natural beauty was immortalised in the 1992 film *A River Runs Through It* directed by Robert Redford and starring Brad Pitt. Big landowners in the area included Ted Turner and Jane Fonda.

1992

> *'When we are no longer able to change a situation, we are challenged to change ourselves.'*   Viktor E. Frankl

Early in 1992, Dave Martins, Chairman of CNCF, presented the idea for a yearly satirical musical revue called *Rundown*, encouraging Caymanians to laugh at themselves and the events of the year. Its debut on 6th March 1992 was accompanied by some trepidation – would Caymanians enjoy self-deprecating humour? They did, and enthusiastically, and *Rundown* went on to become CNCF's most popular annual event for many years. The talents of some wonderful actors were featured, including Leroy Holness, Harwell McCoy, Frankie Flowers, Alan Ebanks, Consuelo Ebanks and Morgan DaCosta, to name but a few.

Around the same time I was approached by Wiley Samuels, an enterprising young man, who proposed using a Great House apartment for an Artists in Residence programme. He introduced me to John Broad, who, with a team of other enthusiastic artists, set up a temporary studio in a vacant unit. This led to an exhibition at the West Indian Club on 5th June, and initiated the process of identifying five leading Caymanian artists for inclusion in Carib Art, an ambitious UNESCO-backed travelling exhibition of contemporary Caribbean Art to open in Curaçao in August 1993. The exhibition would be organised by the National Commission for UNESCO of the Netherlands Antilles, and feature one hundred and forty works by artists from thirty-two Caribbean nations, including sculpture, painting and mixed media.

Funding the logistics of moving this exhibition – including packing, shipping and insurance – was a major undertaking. Henry Muttoo and Leslie Bigelman, a CNCF board member, headed up Cayman's bid to host the show in the Cayman Islands from 12th January to 12th February 1995, and asked me to head the fundraising committee, which I gladly accepted. The five artists eventually selected to represent the Cayman Islands were Bendel Hydes, Terry Grimes, David Bridgeman, Joanne Sibley and Gladwyn K. Bush – affectionately known as 'Miss Lassie'.

Miss Lassie lived in South Sound at the end of Walkers Road, in a traditional Caymanian home on the beach built by her father using ironwood posts and wattle-and-daub lime plaster. She was a self-taught artist, and began painting at the age of seventy-two. Her work being selected for the Carib Art Exhibition took her off Cayman for the very first time in her life, at the age of seventy-nine, to see it as part of the exhibition. I asked her when she returned if she had been frightened flying for the first time. She looked at me and said. 'No, my chile, I was closer to God.' In 1994, CNCF went on to publish a book of her paintings titled *My Markings*. I was delighted to serve as fundraising chairman for the project, and we proudly continue to give the book as a gift as we travel the world, as it truly represents all good and authentic things Caymanian.

On 19th May 1992, I received a telephone call from Margaret Dise advising me that Mikol had been admitted to the intensive care unit at Mercy Hospital in Miami with acute pancreatitis. We had become extremely close over many years, and had both worked and played hard, but in Mikol's case this had unfortunately caught up with him. I flew to Miami and found him in a bad way indeed – hooked up to bleeping machines and unconscious – so encouragement by conversation was out of the question. Only family could stay after visiting hours, so I said I was Mikol's brother, which seemed to convince the nurse, and spent the night in the easy chair in the room, holding his hand a good part of the time. Miraculously, Mikol recovered, and afterwards said he had been able to feel it. No more alcohol or cigarettes for Mikol thereafter! I had stopped drinking in 1989 during the stressful Great House saga, and so in some ways bonded further with Mikol as there was no temptation to drink when we were together. Cigarettes were more of a challenge for him, and I remember him trying patches, an alarm system, hypnosis and other methods before finally quitting.

One never knows when a meeting will be the start of a major development in one's life or career. So, it was on 22nd April 1992, when I met with Alan Burland of BCM Cape Ltd., who wanted to discuss the disputed cost of a hotel in St Thomas. I was familiar with the company. In the early 1980s I had held discussions with their John Morton about building and possibly financing the Genesis Building, which did not materialise, and I had been invited to a cocktail reception they hosted in Cayman.

Burland, Conyers and Marirea of Bermuda and EGM Cape, in Toronto, Canada, were both long-established family-run companies, and it was due to these 'family' connections that I eventually introduced BCM to McAlpine, who went on to form what turned out to be a very successful alliance – but I am getting ahead of myself.

Following Alan Burland's initial request, David Cape contacted me on 27th May and asked me to attend a meeting on 18th and 19th June in Washington DC to discuss the dispute with Katz and Stone, their attorneys there. Ed Haladay kindly put me up at his home in Baltimore and I drove to the initial meeting at Katz and Stone's office, attended by Jerry Katz, Louis Degas and Martin Bellamy. The St Thomas hotel in question was named the Grand Palazzo, and BCM Cape's contract had been terminated under the guise of poor performance. The developer believed that because the construction contract was in a 'Guaranteed Maximum Price' format, it could be changed more or less at will on site, and the 'price' was still guaranteed not to increase, Furthermore, he had convinced his bankers that this was the case.

So why, you might ask, were BCQS involved as a quantity surveying company?

Simply, BCM Cape needed an expert witness to assess whether, given the same information they had been given prior to signing the contract, we would have arrived at a similar price. Once that was established, we were to give our opinion of the cost implications of the many subsequent changes, both in terms of actual expense and of the impact and cost of any delay caused to the regular progress of the works.

I was given the same information BCM Cape had received: approximately six drawings and a site visit to the Royal Pavilion Hotel in Barbados, a similar development by the same developer. I was to review the specification based on a physical inspection of the rooms and common areas, and use this information to calculate a 'Not to Exceed' price based on the rates current at the time BCM Cape did their original costing. When I suggested to Vivian that she might enjoy staying in a luxury hotel whilst I was busy noting finishes and studying pricing, she didn't hesitate to join me on this arduous assignment!

We departed Cayman on 12th August and flew through Miami (I am convinced, whether going to heaven or hell, we will need to transit through Miami!) to Barbados and duly checked into the Royal Pavilion. The next day I gathered the information I needed, then held meetings in Bridgetown at the Business Advisory Service and British Development Division about other projects we were chasing in the region. These included the Mariner's Hotel in Anguilla and the Police Barracks in Turks and Caicos. Then Viv and I had the unusual pleasure of sightseeing, followed by dinner at the Bagatelle restaurant, which was to become a firm favourite of ours over the years.

Then Vivian suggested we spend a little time in Mustique, as it was so close. This we did, staying at the delightful Cotton House Hotel. Mustique as a development was a dream canvas for a developer, and Colin Tennant, later Lord Glenconner, had taken full advantage of this opportunity by creating large lots, each several acres in area, and then permitting only sufficient land to be cleared to accommodate a dwelling, the remainder of each lot to be left in a natural state. In order to 'seed' the development of the island, Mr Tennant secured the services of Oliver Messel, Lord Snowden's uncle and a celebrated British theatre and stage set designer, whose designs were drawn on graph paper as opposed to using a scale rule. The charming result was that proportionally the homes exhibited wonderful symmetry, but were not always entirely practical. One owner of a two-story house complained that the staircase to the second floor was outside, which meant they would sometimes get wet. Messel replied that it did not rain often, and that to move the staircase inside would result in loss of symmetry and view!

Vivian and I returned to Cayman on 21st August, but just ten days later I was back on a plane, this time to St Thomas, to evaluate the Grand Palazzo Hotel. I spent five days there, studying how the plans from the Royal Pavilion in Barbados had been reflected in the rooms and common areas of the Grand Palazzo. Given the hotel's steeply sloping site, part of my task involved examining the foundations to assess their impact on the construction costs. More than once, I was asked why a guest was crawling under the building!

Later in September, I flew with Mortimer to Providenciales for a four-day trip to update BCQS's five-year business plan, originally completed after my Harvard course graduation in 1987. At the time, we were working on the rebuild of the historic Government House in Grand Turk, known as 'Waterloo'. On the strength of this project, the Foreign and Commonwealth Office (FCO) had asked us to assess a number of their other properties in the Caribbean including on Montserrat, Tortola and Barbados, and subsequently Trafalgar House in Jamaica for rebuild/renovation as well. So, business was certainly expanding, and we needed careful planning of resources going forward.

On the 2nd October 1992, I flew to Baltimore/Washington for an initial presentation on the Grand Palazzo costs, and then to Bermuda to present our findings to BCM Cape. The stakes were quite high – if our estimated figure aligned closely with BCM's, they would feel vindicated and this could potentially open the door to future collaboration. Well, we were within 5 per cent of BCM's figure, which, given the paucity of information, was a pretty impressive result.

Although we had arrived at similar cost estimates, the impact of the multiple design changes still required careful analysis. This meant frequent meetings in Washington as autumn turned into winter. One trip in particular stands out: a heavy snowfall had blanketed the city, and the snowplows had left deep banks of snow that we had to cross on foot to reach Jerry's office. We stepped out of our hire car and into a snowbank, only to discover an icy stream running underneath it. We arrived at the office with frozen feet. One of the secretaries, ever practical, said, 'No problem – take off your socks.' She placed them in the office microwave, turned it on … and our socks melted into one solid lump. So, it was shoes and no socks for the rest of the day – in the middle of a Washington winter!

1992 was to finish with a ski trip to Big Sky for ten days, where fresh new snow fell every day and we celebrated my forty-seventh birthday.

CHAPTER SIX

Cayman Rising (1993–1997)

1993

'Always go with your passions. Never ask yourself if it's realistic or not.'
Deepak Chopra

1993 kicked off with frequent trips to Washington DC to continue developing the strategy for the Grand Palazzo project. A pleasant interlude, and a highlight in the CNCF calendar, was the visit of the Jamaican Folk Singers to Cayman, generously funded by Blanche Blackwell, mother of Chris Blackwell, who was then living in Cayman.

Skiing also provided a pleasant distraction from the arbitration paperwork, and once again Al Hallock and family hosted us at both their main home in Evergreen and their condo in Keystone, where we took full advantage of the Colorado ski resorts. These included Copper Mountain, Breckenridge and, of course, the three great mountains at Keystone including the back bowls and Al's favourite run, 'The Griz', where the only way you can check your progress along the tight course is by using the numbers affixed to the trees to either side. A morning's hard skiing would be followed by the reward of lunch at the Alpenglo Stube, where excellent food was served on white table cloths, and sheepskin slippers were provided for tired feet.

Viv had not yet joined me on any of my visits to Washington, and so, in May, we changed this. We enjoyed some great meals with Jerry and Sheila Katz, and became tourists for a day. We visited the Smithsonian, the National Gallery of Art, the Barnes Foundation with some eighty wonderful works from the Masters: Picasso, Matisse, Cezanne, as well as the Phillips Collection. We saw the Lincoln Memorial, the Washington Monument and the Vietnam Memorial, followed by a dim sum lunch at Mr Yang's and dinner with Ed and Elspeth Haladay at Paolo's in Baltimore's Inner Harbour. We topped off this marathon with a visit to Mount Vernon the next day.

Our successful projection for the Grand Palazzo arbitration led to an amazing eighteen-month assignment with some forty-eight days of hearings held in Miami. These began on 7th June 1993 at the Miami Headquarters of the American Arbitration Association on Brickell Avenue. Hearings took place before three Arbitrators, with attorneys and expert witnesses facing each other. We began early each day with preparations for that day's hearing in our 'war room' at the Holiday Inn on Brickell Avenue. Then we walked across the road to the AAA, pushing a trolley laden with papers, for eight hours of hearings, after which we returned to analyse that day's events. In total, we worked for fifteen to seventeen hours each day.

To distract ourselves occasionally, we visited the movies. One of these was *The Firm*, based on the novel by John Grisham and starring Tom Cruise and Gene Hackman. The movie had been partly shot in Cayman and many local people had applied for and been hired as extras. We pointed these out to each other, causing some annoyance to the other movie-goers judging by their frequent exclamations of 'Shush!'

The movie had been shot partly at the Hyatt and partly at the Great House, where we had come to an arrangement with Paramount Pictures, who paid $50,000 to rent one of our apartments for a month. To achieve the right camera angle for a scene where Tom Cruise takes various papers from the wine cellar, Paramount, who had their own tradespeople, had taken out the fridge and cut a doorway into the wine cellar. The scene was shot, the door removed, and the wall to the wine cellar repaired. I had been away for a scene where Tom Cruise is romancing a Caymanian girl. Viv, walking over from Plantana next door, tells the security guard that her husband is the developer of Great House and asks if she might watch the filming. The answer was a firm 'No', which goes to show how much clout a property developer has in the film industry!

In July 1993 we were contacted by Keith Copper, of Davis Langdon & Copper, and asked if we could conduct a survey of luxury hotels in the Caribbean as part of a due diligence exercise for a $110 million resort to be built in Union Island in the Grenadines. Now, this was a really tough job, as it involved staying in each of the selected hotels in Anguilla, Antigua, Nevis, Barbados and St Vincent, among others. At the Four Seasons Hotel in Nevis, I had on my dinner table a *buerrière*, a butter dish with a cover and a compartment for ice below, ideal for patio lunches at Plantana. Having first seen one during a visit to France, Vivian and I had been fruitlessly looking for another for a long time. Good chance here for some serious brownie points! I enquired from the waiter if I could purchase one and he said he would check. The next morning, when I went to check out, there was a gift-wrapped package containing one *buerrière*. Now that is what I call service!

For some time Vivian and I had been discussing with Ed Haladay the development of single-family homes in the Cayman Islands Yacht Club. These were to reflect the light and airy vernacular architecture of the West Indies, using pavilions to contain specific living elements, and would be in direct contrast to what we call 'Florida homes' transposed to Cayman. We had been in discussions with the Japanese developers of CIYC about purchasing a finger of some twenty lots on which to build a number of homes, but the developers were somewhat intransigent as to price. So, we just acquired the very end lot which looks onto the marina and has an almost 270-degree view of the water.

The arbitration hearings continued through August, and I had other business in London, so I spent even more time on airplanes than usual. I know I was in Miami on 8th October as Mike Johnson, his wife Doreen and our god-daughter Hannah came to visit us at Yacht Harbour. I recall this so clearly, because I had commissioned an engagement ring from jewellers in Coco Walk near our apartment, and Mike came with me to collect it. This was to be a complete surprise to Vivian, who knew nothing about the upcoming event.

On 10th October, Viv and I flew to Mustique to stay at Cotton House, in one of their beautiful Grenadine cottages. For a couple of days we relaxed, but on the 13th I went for a seven-mile run on my own to suss out a suitable place to ask for Vivian's hand. The big day arrived, and I asked for a picnic lunch to be made up and for the driver, Snakie, to drive us to the beach I had decided would be a suitable location. But, damn it – there was another couple already there! This happened several more times, and finally Snakie said, 'I know the staff at Princess Margaret's house, and no one is in residence at the moment so you will have your privacy there.' So that's where we went, and the beach below her house was deserted, and had chairs and cabanas as well! We unpacked the picnic, and then I got down on one knee and asked Vivian if she would marry me. Completely astounded, Vivian squealed, 'What?! Ask me again!!' Overjoyed, she said it was her dream come true. Back at Cotton House, Vivian announced the good news to all the waiters and hotel staff and proceeded to call all our friends. I think our overseas phone bill came close to matching the entire rest of the hotel bill by the time we left! Romance notwithstanding, from Miami airport, Vivian returned to Cayman and I went on to Washington DC to prepare final arguments for the arbitration with Jerry.

That year, we spent Christmas with Viv's mom and dad in Belfast. This was the first UK Christmas in six years, and also gave Viv the wonderful opportunity to show friends and neighbours her engagement ring. It was a cold, snowy winter in Northern Ireland, and I noticed Viv's parents' house was the only one in their cul-de-sac without snow on the roof – a clear sign of heat escaping. Sure enough, a quick check revealed there was no insulation. We dashed off to the local B&Q store, packed Joe's small car full of insulation (Viv could barely find space to sit), and installed it in record time before rushing to catch the flight back to London. We spent New Year's Eve at the Blue Elephant Thai restaurant in London with Alan and Jenny Foster. They had decided to return to live in Jamaica – fortunately for me, as you will see later.

1994

'Success is stumbling from failure to failure with no loss of enthusiasm.'
Winston Churchill

I was considering building a number of one-bedroom apartments, to be designed by Bill Bissell, on the land in front of Cayman Court which had originally been reserved for a squash court. But before planning permission was given we had to show that the eight units proposed would be no denser than the squash club originally proposed.

It was only in late June 1996 that we finally overcame the planning objections to the eight-unit apartment complex now called Gingerbread. Gingerbread Ltd. had been registered earlier that year, and we had negotiated a contract with Harry Olsen of Olsen Construction Ltd. to build them, so construction could start where my developer's journey had commenced some twenty-five years earlier!

In January, as part of BCQS's continuing promotion efforts, we began publishing a newsletter called *Building Confidence*, which continued to come out regularly until June 2003. We also began hosting lunches in our boardroom for a cross-section of the business community. These proved to be a very successful way of promoting our services, as our guests felt comfortable in the confidential setting of our office. In a small community such as Cayman, any kind of meeting in a public setting, such as a restaurant, would elicit comments about why one might be meeting or what one might be up to. Excellent menus from Vivian and a few glasses of wine didn't hurt either!

Some weeks later in Washington DC, Jerry Katz and I spent three days preparing for our first construction claims seminar: 'Construction Claims – How to Avoid Them, Defend Them and Pursue Them.' The seminar was held on 14th March 1994 in the Marriott Hotel in Cayman. It was opened by The Hon Thomas Jefferson, Minister of Tourism, Planning and the Environment, and was enthusiastically received by contractors, building professionals, government officials, attorneys and bankers.

10th February was my brother Rob's 40th birthday, for which a big weekend 'Country House' party was planned at Periton Park estate on Exmoor. Dinner was black tie, and Rob, having once seen my white dinner jacket, had begged me not to wear it. I didn't. Instead, I came down in a T-shirt with a dinner suit painted on to it. Rob's stunned expression at this newest antic perpetrated by his mad brother led me to quickly say, 'only joking' and retreat back upstairs to put on more conventional attire.

As we were already in Europe, we took the opportunity to go skiing. This time we went to Val d'Isère, staying at Hotel Le Parc just across from the slopes. One day, high on a pass getting ready to ski down to the neighbouring resort of Tignes, Viv mentioned what fun the tandem paragliding looked. I didn't say anything, but during lunch I excused myself for a moment – and came back with a paragliding ticket I had just purchased for her. So, before she knew it, Viv was airborne, fortified by the wine from lunch. Another day, there was an excellent layer of new snow as we set off down a trail. We set off a minor avalanche and the snow, which a second earlier had been the lightest, fluffiest powder, set like cement around our ankles. Fortunately, we were high enough up the slope that nothing serious happened, but the instant change in texture was frightening to say the least.

Back in Cayman, a meeting was called for the ushers at Elmslie Church, where Vivian and I had attended services for several years. We had important guests coming to worship on Sunday 27th February – Her Majesty the Queen and Prince Philip – and all the correct protocol had to be clearly understood and followed.

Her Majesty arrived in George Town Harbour aboard the Royal Yacht Britannia. It was her second visit to Cayman, and I was honored to be one of the ushers when she came to worship at Elmslie. She had her arm in a sling – the result of a riding accident – which must have been uncomfortable for her, but which would provide a useful topic of conversation when I next met her at Buckingham Palace in 2012.

I had become involved in a project supported by Elmslie Church called 'Ministries in Action', which developed various projects in Haiti while trying to ensure donated funds and materials reached the correct hands. We joined a trip to Flamand, in southwest Haiti, near Les Cayes, over Easter. After tetanus shots and with an ample supply of malaria pills, we flew to Port au Prince on Good Friday and took a long, dusty truck ride over the mountains to Flamand, where over the years Ministries have built a clinic, a school and a chapel. Dr

Edlin Merren, a dentist, came with us and was kept busy with extractions. On clinic day, the normally empty track would be congested with the donkeys transporting patients. Part of my team's assignment was to build a classroom block for the school, the first task being to lay the blocks. Now, this was an interesting task for a quantity surveyor; I had counted many blocks in my career to this point, but had never physically laid any. Perhaps inevitably, as soon as I put down the trowel a Haitian labourer next to me picked it up and laid the block perfectly. So, why were we here? Truth is, our presence ensured the materials we had donated weren't diverted. It was a very rewarding and educational experience, but, sadly, since my visits to Haiti in the seventies during the dictatorship of Papa Doc, the country had certainly declined.

The end of May found me in London, meeting with Mortimer in the Institute of Directors on Pall Mall, one of his favourite watering holes. This is a fine Georgian building and much of our business planning was carried out here from well-stuffed leather arm chairs. The conversion of BCQS from a partnership into a limited liability company was now scheduled for early 1995, with Richard Jones, Jim Slattery, Pete Widmer and myself purchasing shares. Jim was in London again in early June, and over lunches with the senior members in the FCO in Croydon, we discussed the renovations to Waterloo in Grand Turk, the Governor's Residence, and the exciting new project rebuilding Trafalgar House in Kingston, Jamaica.

During this time BCQS also secured a fabulous assignment for Barclays Property Holdings, working with their senior project manager, Dave Scott ('Scottie'), on the refurbishment of some fifty Barclays Bank branches throughout the Caribbean, including an entirely new building in Tortola. Dave, incidentally, became a very good friend.

Time had flown, and by July 1994 we were celebrating the 25th Anniversary of the founding of BCQS as well as CNCF's publication of Miss Lassie's book *My Markings* – I treasure the copy she signed for me on 7th July 1994. I should mention that in Turks, I had been in ongoing discussions with Joe Zahm – a property manager, realtor, and keen songwriter – about the release of a debut CD by Everyman, a talented group he was promoting. Drawing on my experience working with Third World, I had been helping Joe with industry contacts. By July 1994, Everyman had completed their first CD and taken it to Miami for final mixing in Chris Blackwell's studio.

I went to Kingston in early September to interview potential contractors for the Trafalgar House rebuild, and stayed with Alan and Jenny Foster at their town house in Norbrook Mews. I popped in and out so often, that Jen christened me Mr Pim (as in the A.A. Milne play *Mr. Pim Passes By*). After a couple of days interviewing contractors, I made my way to the Chinese Embassy on Seaview Avenue, and secured a visa for Vivian and myself for our first visit to China later that month. Little did I know, that I would be working on a major project with the Chinese some years later.

And so, to China. We left Cayman on 16th September, arriving in Hong Kong on the 18th at 6.30am. We didn't do much harbour viewing from our 'harbour view' room at the Shangri La Hotel, but slept most of the day instead. Rested, we had a wonderful dinner with Brian and Sylvie Kieran at China Max, where we celebrated the tradition of 'dotting the eye of the dragon', as it was a newly opened restaurant. Brian and Sylvie were good friends from Cayman, where Brian had written *The Lawless Caymanas*, a fascinating book detailing the relationship between the Cayman Islands and the West India Regiment. The next day began with a typical Chinese breakfast of congee (a kind of savoury rice porridge), a workout at the gym and a ferry ride across the harbour to the Jade market on Kowloon side to buy a jade pendant for Cissy Delapenha.

For all keen shoppers – Viv chief among them – there can never be enough shopping in Hong Kong. So we caught the bus to Stanley Market where, as Viv noted, 'Shopping was terrific, and Martyn all patience!' That afternoon, on our way to the funicular to the Peak, we were walking along an elevated walkway and were stopped by a Trevor and Hannah Shakeshaft, who said to us 'You are from Cayman!' I had dealt with Trevor for several years on a real estate transaction in Cayman, but never met him face to face, and here we were on the other side of the world and had bumped into them. This kind of coincidence has happened to us time and again over the years, but never ceases to astonish us.

On the 24th, we boarded the three-hour Dragonair flight from Hong Kong to Beijing. Outside the terminal, we were accosted by eager drivers offering us a ride into the city. I would discover only during subsequent visits that it is best to take a metered taxi. I felt really smart negotiating the fare to take us to the Shangri La Hotel from 580 yuan down to 300 yuan. I vividly recall feeling uneasy during the ride, with the driver and his entrepreneurial assistant up front, and Vivian and I in the back. Playing it safe, I hid all my cash in my shoe – clever, I thought. We arrived at the hotel, and I once again pulled what I thought was a smart move: leaving Vivian in the car to guard the luggage (very chivalrous!) to 'get cash' to pay the driver. Turned out we had not only been seriously overcharged, even at 300 yuan, but we'd been dropped off at the wrong Shangri La. We needed the China World Shangri La, close to Tiananmen Square. A new car and driver took us to the correct hotel, which felt like any one of the business hotels I had spent so much time in over the years. We checked in and spent the rest of the day sleeping, coupled with room service, recovering from the excitement of the travel and our not-quite-cured jet lag.

The following day, we visited the Forbidden City bordering on Tiananmen Square, guided by a headphone narration featuring – of all people – Roger Moore. Incongruous as it was, it described in detail the wonders of this incredible historical site.

The next morning, we'd had enough of the business hotel and moved into the Beijing Hotel, an exotic location that connected via a walkway with several others. In the afternoons, an orchestra played in the lobby while guests enjoyed jasmine tea, taken with jam- and cream-filled cornetto pastries – not very Chinese, but great for people-watching.

We toured the Summer Palace, enjoyed some excellent dinners at the nearby Grand Hotel, and made an unforgettable trip to the Great Wall which, compared with photos we have seen recently, was not at all crowded.

The next day, we rented bicycles to explore the city. The main street outside our hotel had four lanes for cars and ten lanes for bicycles! Given my height, the bicycle man struggled unsuccessfully to adjust the seat for me, and I rode off regardless, with my knees splayed wide and my head and shoulders towering above the sea of surrounding cyclists. Conveniently, this made me easy for Viv to spot when we got separated. We cycled to Beihai Park, built in the 11th century, which contains numerous architectural replicas of famous buildings from other parts of China, magnificent gardens and lakes. Of course, we visited the adjacent market area, where Viv, always thinking of others first, stocked up on unusual presents for friends' Christmas stockings.

There was a wonderful painter with a long flowing white beard plying his trade in the Beijing Hotel, and we sat and talked with him about a typically Chinese painting of an elegant man with a captivating expression and wearing a long flowing robe, sitting beside a jasmine tree. Although we tried to negotiate the price, the painter could see we loved the painting, and so were hooked. We bought it and it hangs with pride in our Miami apartment, an enduring reminder of the Beijing Hotel, jasmine tea, cornettoes, and the wonderful artist.

All good things come to an end and so on 30th September we flew back, crossing the International Date Line en route and becoming a day younger.

Shortly after returning to Cayman I left again for Bermuda. There, Caribbean Construction Advisory Services (CCAS), as we called the joint venture between Katz and Stone and BCQS, presented their second seminar on construction claims to the Bermuda Society of Architects and the Bermuda Contractors Association. BCM Cape had incurred considerable expense during the Grand Palazzo arbitration, and on that basis, Jerry Katz and I felt we should develop a 'road show' highlighting all the pitfalls of incomplete contract documentation, record keeping, and failing to comply with required notices. Charles Leonard, our star programmer, was a key speaker. His graphic illustrations, which so ably depicted complex timing and contractual matters, became known as Charlie's Charts. Jerry explained the finer points of contracts with great clarity, and yours truly detailed record-keeping and measurement requirements. For many years we presented these seminars throughout the Caribbean to a wide audience of both private and government clients. According to our feedback, a lot of people saved a lot of money by applying the principles we had taught.

I subsequently spent a week in Tortola, where our attorney, Sheila George, had applied for our Business Licence for the British Virgin Islands so we could set up an office there to manage our assignments for Barclays and the FCO, and also follow our corporate philosophy of training local people wherever we were based. The licence had been issued but was limited to carrying out services only for Barclays and the Governor's House for the FCO. This was, of course, a severe setback to BCQS's expansion plans, and I asked with whom could I talk to explain our objectives and have the restriction lifted. I was advised to consult the Minister of Trade, The Hon Lavity Stoutt. Although I tried to arrange a meeting over the next six months, he died suddenly at the age of sixty-six in May 1995. I did eventually get to meet with his successor, The Hon Ralph O'Neal, two years later.

On the 3rd November, ground was broken on the old Galleon Beach Hotel site for the new three hundred and fifty room Westin Casuarina Hotel, for which BCQS were the QS. The loss of this location as the performance space for the Inn Theatre had been the catalyst for the establishment of CNCF, so life was turning full circle! A few days later, the 10k Corporate Cup took place, for which BCQS had shorts and T-shirts in the purple corporate colour and printed with our logo to best promote the company. The Holiday Inn 10k followed on the 19th November, and our team was out there keeping fit, promoting worthy causes, and promoting our product. Harvard was paying off!

A particularly interesting project that year was the construction of a 12,000 sq ft house in Vista del Mar facing the North Sound. I had been approached by the owner's representative to monitor the costing of the construction, which was being carried out by Tommy Bodden. There was significant secrecy about the owner, whose name was initially not revealed. Eventually he visited with his wife, Pru, and prior to his arrival the representative cautioned, 'Whatever you do, please do not call him Mike but use Michael instead.' When we met, he introduced himself as Michael Hammer, and the reason for the caution became clear – he disliked the reference to the brawling, brutal private detective 'Mike Hammer' of pulp fiction.

Michael and Pru were pleased with their home, and one evening we invited them to Plantana for dinner and gave them a welcoming gift of a signed copy of Miss Lassie's book *My Markings*. They asked if I was interested in art, and I gave them the background of CNCF, Carib Art and the 'discovery' of Miss Lassie. Michael said his family had an interest in collecting art and had a gallery. No more was said at this point, but they asked if they could meet Miss Lassie, and I replied that she would be delighted. Miss Lassie was as gracious as ever, and as we left her home, Michael gave Vivian and me one of the most beautifully presented books I have ever seen. *The Armand Hammer Collection* contained very fine prints of the paintings owned by the Hammer Galleries, their history and how they had been acquired. It was only then that the penny dropped, and I realised this was Armand Hammer's grandson. Michael and Pru lived in Cayman for several years, establishing a school and a Christian radio station. I believe it was a book called *Dossier – The Secret History of Armand Hammer*, which described his grandfather in not very flattering terms, that led to their eventual departure.

The then Governor's wife, Monica Gore, was a keen artist and very supportive of the fundraising efforts for Carib Art. Monica, along with Leslie Bigelman, were in many ways key to the subsequent establishment of the National Gallery, but Monica left before this came to fruition. On leaving, she handed a coconut to the incoming first lady, Carol Owen, saying, 'This is the seed for Cayman's National Gallery – nurture it well!'

CNCF was continuing to produce plays, and on 17th November presented *Moonshine Tonight* at the Harquail Theatre.

1995

'You only live once, but if you do it right, once is enough.'   Mae West

We finally managed to assemble all the funds we needed, and Carib Art opened at the Harquail Theatre on 12th January 1995 to a tremendous reception. This was understandable, being the first time such a large collection of contemporary art, from such a wide range of Caribbean countries, had been exhibited. I must admit one of my favourite pieces was a bronze sculpture of a very large West Indian lady riding a surfboard, entitled 'Playing with Nature' by Aruban artist Maritza Erasmus. I think it must have been the inspiration for M.F. Gazer's sculpture of a lady with a similar size 'bunkie' riding a bicycle, that Vivian and I subsequently purchased and have at our home today.

Early February 1995 we had agreed the contract terms for the rebuilding of Trafalgar House, and I flew to Kingston to sign the contract with John Miles, the FCO representative. The project was exciting, because it would restore the High Commissioner's residence back to its former glory. The house had been built following the 1907 earthquake that devastated Kingston and killed over one thousand people. Over the years, additions had been made to the traditional West Indian architecture with its cooling balconies and large airy rooms, and its classical look had been somewhat diminished. As project manager, I was assigned a Clerk of Works, called Bill Southwick, by the FCO. He was to be my eyes and ears on site, as he lived close by in a staff apartment.

That same month, Al Hallock asked if I would like to invest in a vineyard project his son Mike was putting together in the Willamette Valley in Oregon. Both Al and Mike were geologists, and Mike had been experimenting with winemaking at his home in Denver for several years. The plan was to grow primarily Pinot Noir with some Pinot Gris and Chardonnay on sixty-six acres, in an area southwest of Mt Hood. The idea was appealing, even though I was not drinking at the time. Also, Al and his family had not only been great friends, but also, as a shareholder in the Great House, most supportive of the decisions I had made. And so, in short order, we became investors in a vineyard that came to be called Carabella, bringing us not only the pleasure of producing exceptional wines, but also the delight of wonderful new friendships in this beautiful part of the world.

As I mentioned earlier, Foster's Food Fair was located at the Greenery. By now it had become so successful they had outgrown their space there. We looked for land close by to build a larger development that could house them, and located a parcel immediately north of the parcel adjacent to the Greenery, which had been developed by Mervyn Cumber and which was owned by a Bill Becker, who lived in Denver. So it was that in mid-1995 I spent a lot of time flying back and forth to discuss terms with Bill, and how we could acquire the property. I was also very active as Chairman of the Historic Advisory Committee of the National Trust, and we had a plaque programme to recognise buildings of historic significance, including Elmslie church, the town hall and library in George Town and the Mission House in Bodden Town.

At around this time, Burland Conyers and Marirea (BCM) and McAlpine announced their association. Sometime after the completion of the Grand Palazzo arbitration, Alan Burland asked me if I knew of a construction company that shared the same 'family' type principles that BCM did. I replied that I had enjoyed a great working relationship for many years with the McAlpine company and its family owners, and I felt that they would be ideal. I asked my good friend Henry Propper to contact Alan and discuss possible business opportunities, which he did, and so a very successful business partnership was formed.

I believe it was around June 1995 when Vivian and I agreed we should set the wedding date. We liked the symmetry of '50 years single, 50 years married', and so chose the 10th December 1995 – only to realise that was a Sunday, so we brought it forward to Saturday 9th December. I considered it only proper to formally ask Joe for his daughter's hand, so we arranged a visit to Northern Ireland to coincide with Joe and Flo's wedding anniversary on 13th August.

Before that, I had some business in London, meeting with both the FCO and Barclays regarding major work on their Caribbean properties, and so we flew to London on 6th August. During that trip we were also recruiting for BCQS, and I interviewed Neil Purton, who would become an important addition to the team.

Business done, I flew to Belfast on 12th August – later than planned – but we still set off on our driving tour of Ireland's beautiful country houses, chosen as a fitting backdrop to ask Joe for Vivian's hand. Our first stop was Rathmullen House, Donegal, but we arrived too late for serious conversation. The next night, at Markree Castle in Collooney, we had a grand meal to celebrate Joe and Flo's anniversary, but Flo felt sick afterwards. The following evening, at Coopers Hill in Riverstown, I was struck by a migraine. By then, Vivian was beginning to lose hope.

Finally, at Enniscoe House in Castle Hill, County Mayo, over brandies in the lounge, I asked Joe for his blessing. He was delighted – provided I could keep her in the manner to which she had become accustomed! Joe had, by this time, become a little forgetful. This was demonstrated the next morning when Flo had to remind him of the engagement, which prompted him to toast the news with champagne all over again!

Shortly after that, we shared the news with Gordon and Lyle at Faircross, their home in Wentworth, and were joined by Alan and Jenny Foster. Champagne was produced to celebrate the occasion, served in elegant flutes. When Vivian admired them, Lyle said they were from Tiffany. At our wedding on 9th December, Gordon and Lyle presented us with a beautiful turquoise box tied with ribbon and containing a dozen Tiffany champagne flutes, which we use at home to this day.

At the end of August in Cayman we were in the wedding planning mode, but not for long. On 8th September we travelled to Istanbul for another Harvard OPM XII reunion, this time hosted by Hasan and Handan Saraç. We stayed at the beautifully restored Ottoman Çırağan Palace on the Bosphorus, and they had organised a magnificent programme taking in all the exotic sights of this city – one of the few cities in the world spanning two continents. Hasan had thoughtfully asked a number of his friends to each host a few couples to dine in their homes, so we experienced one-on-one interaction with locals. After one fine dinner, I was asked if I would like a coffee, which I gratefully accepted. Turkish coffee is very strong, which I really enjoy. After three coffees, our hosts gifted me the small porcelain cup, contained by beautiful silver holder, to take home, which we continue to use at Callaloo.

A visit to Turkey would not be complete without experiencing a traditional hammam, so Viv and I visited the Cağaloğlu Hammam near the Grand Bazaar. The baths are strictly separated by gender, so I made sure I was entering the men's side. I chose a mid-range treatment from the menu displayed. The layout of the hammam has three distinct areas: the camekan – the reception and changing room where you undress and leave your clothes and sip tea afterwards; the soğukluk – a passageway between the camekan and the hararet – the hot steam room where the massaging and actual washing takes place, with marble walls and floor, and marble basins and brass taps all around. In the centre is a large marble slab, heated by a wood fire below. This is the 'bellystone' where you lie to sweat, relax and be massaged, all the while gazing up at the patterned light that pours through the domed ceiling. I really enjoyed the experience.

Afterwards, I had a glass of tea and then re-entered the outside world looking for Vivian … and waited. After some time, and a brief detour to a carpet shop opposite (complete with offers of tea, lunch and sales pitch), I began to worry she had been whisked away to some harem! Eventually Vivian turned up. She had opted for the deluxe 'Sultan's Special' on the female side of the hammam, which had taken far longer than my treatment. The carpet shop proprietor became the beneficiary of the delay, as we purchased a carpet from him.

We wandered the Blue Mosque and the Grand Bazaar, with its multitude of shops where everything is for sale. All prices are subject to negotiation, and I gave Vivian a crash course in bargaining: show mild interest, halve the asking price, and be prepared to walk away if you do not agree on a price of, say, 75 per cent of the original one. The merchant will chase you. Viv tested the method on some small, beautifully hand-painted cocktail plates for hors d'oeuvres. Viv halves the merchant's stated price, he looks shocked, Viv walks away. No chase ensued. We bought similar plates at the hotel for twice the price. If you want my QS services, I promise I can give better advice!

From Istanbul we visited the capital, Ankara, to visit Atatürk's museum and watch whirling dervishes, and then went on to Izmir. The highlight of the trip was a visit to Cappadocia, the extraordinary region of Central Anatolia famous for its weird volcanic landscapes and painted churches, and the joy of a sunrise balloon ride over apple orchards, where the captain swooped down and allowed us to pick apples from the trees – doubtless to the annoyance of the farmer! We ended the reunion with a tour of Efes (Ephesus) on the Aegean coast and the remains of the Temple of Artemis, one of the seven wonders of the Ancient World, and one of the modern world's most extensive archaeological sites.

At our farewell dinner, the Harvard alumni decided we should have a practice wedding (an example of sound planning) and set up the ceremony right then and there, so we were married before we were married!

On the 22nd September, we flew to Jamaica for one of the regular site meetings on Trafalgar House. This gave Viv and me the opportunity to undertake an adventure we had been talking about for some time: climbing Blue Mountain Peak, at 7,402 feet one of the highest in the Caribbean. Alan Foster was to accompany us, having climbed it before.

We set off from Alan and Jenny's home in Norbrook Mews in his truck, with rucksacks of food and a thermos of hot coffee. We drove up through the foothills to Mavis Bank – said to produce the best coffee in the world – but because recent heavy rainfall had damaged the roads, we were forced to park the truck and start walking. It was pitch black, with no moon, and we had forgotten to bring a flashlight, so we used our camera flash to check signposts. At one point, we found ourselves in the middle of a coffee field, turned the flash on a sign, and read: 'Trespassers will be shot on sight'. This was a little more adventure than we had bargained for!

Some hours later we reached Whitfield Hall, just below the trail head. We had planned to rest there for a while, but it was still too early, so the gates were locked. We decided to keep walking, climbing up through Portland Gap and reaching the summit just as dawn broke. It was raining and we sheltered in a dilapidated hut, sitting on a bed frame as we ate our sandwiches. Hot coffee would have been welcome but the thermos had been dropped, breaking the glass liner. There were huge hydrangeas at the summit, and the rainforest through which we had travelled contained giant tree ferns. In fact, much of the vegetation in the Blue Mountains is endemic, and seen nowhere else. We descended and made our way to Whitfield Hall, now open, where we had many cups of hot coffee, wrapping our chilled hands around our cups for warmth. Revived, we continued our walk back to the truck and returned to Norbrook Mews at around 5pm. Jenny had prepared a wonderful curry, but we badly needed a shower first after some fourteen hours walking non-stop. The hot water felt wonderful, and we lay down for a quick rest afterwards. That was a mistake, because we slept through until the next morning – and the curry was duly enjoyed for Sunday lunch.

Back to Cayman and wedding plans. The reception was to be held on the beach at Plantana, and my good friend Henry Propper, head of McAlpine, kindly agreed to build the stage. CNCF generously offered to provide entertainment, with Dave Martins reassembling his group, the Tradewinds, to provide music. Paul Keens Douglas would tell stories, there would be quadrille dance performances, and of course there was the food – Cissy's Chinese prepared by Chef Shakespeare, Jerk Pork, many assorted sundries – and many tables and chairs for our two hundred and fifty guests. We wanted the invitation to be unusual, and Simon Barwick of BB & P, who had prepared all our promotional material for The Great House, obliged. He suggested we needed a painting by a local artist, and Chris Mann was the ideal person; he painted a picture of Viv and me walking along the beach, yet also through a window into a new world of marriage. Neil Cruickshank would be the Master of Ceremonies, René was to give the toast to the Bride and Groom, Bill Bissell, a toast to the Groom, and Mortimer, a toast to the bride.

Most important, of course, was the service. We asked Chris Baillie, the minister at Elmslie, to marry us. He agreed on the condition that we attended counselling regularly before the wedding. It was good advice and is something we now pass on to others: a successful marriage requires you to look after your partner's needs before your own. Counselling sessions were always scheduled for around 5pm and Vivian, who is always punctual, did a fair bit of nail-biting when, as often happened, I was still trying to complete more tasks than I had time for by the end of the day and turned up late.

On 21st October 1995, I was surprised and delighted to receive the Joy Brandon award for my outstanding contribution to the work of the Cayman National Cultural Foundation at the annual CNCF Gala.

November saw me back in Tortola for meetings on Barclays, and then to Antigua to look at the Barclays branch there with local representative George Bernard 'Monty' St John. Barclays had assigned Monty to provide local overview for the Caribbean projects, and we established a close friendship while visiting the refurbishment projects and addressing the challenges presented by their many different locations. One of Monty's favourite sayings, penned by Theodore Roosevelt, was 'The credit goes to the Man in the Arena' and we were spending a lot of time in the arena! Monty was from Grenada and had worked for Barclays for more than forty years – from the time he'd left school – holding senior posts in Grenada, Barbados, St Vincent and St

Lucia as well as the UK. The rest of that month was a blur of travel: visiting Antigua, Kingston, Tortola and Miami, all while fitting in the requisite number of marriage counselling meetings with Chris Baillie in Cayman.

On 4th December, the guests began arriving from overseas. The 8th saw the rehearsal and stag night, then came the big day – at the age of forty-nine years, three hundred and sixty-four days, Martyn Bould was getting married to this fabulous lady, Vivian.

When Rob arrived at Plantana before the ceremony, I said we needed a drink and opened a bottle of Dom Perignon – my first drink in some seven years! We then drove to the church and waited for Viv, who arrived late due to traffic on West Bay Road. She looked radiant coming up the aisle to join Rob and me at the altar. When Chris asked, 'Who giveth this lady …?' it had been agreed both Joe and Flo would say 'we do'. In the event, Joe forgot and said, 'I do' while Flo said, 'we do'. When Chris presented Mr and Mrs Bould to the congregation, the entire church erupted with cheers and applause. René had made it to the church just as the service was taking place, arriving at Elmslie straight off the plane from Switzerland, where he had been attending a good friend's funeral. So, he was able to toast the bride and groom at the reception, as planned.

I drove back to Plantana in the limo with my new bride (and the balance of the Dom Perignon) to a cheering group of friends. It was a magnificent evening on the beach, surrounded by our friends and family, with great food, wonderful entertainment, and a speech by Bill Bissell describing my bachelor's life. Quite unbeknown to me, he had previously cleared it with Viv. Towards its end, he walked over to Neil Cruickshank as Master of Ceremonies, and then returned to the mike saying, 'My apologies, I checked with Neil – I thought I was to roast Martyn, not toast him!'

Gordon, being the character he was, decided after dancing that he was too hot and walked into the pool fully clothed! We were blessed to have Lyle in attendance. As a professional photographer, she took some wonderful pictures which we did not see until about a year later. Our 'official' photographer took rather disappointing shots, so we didn't have a good photographic record of this wonderful day. We enjoyed ourselves late into the night and the next day, on my 50th birthday, we left for our honeymoon. No prizes for guessing where – Mustique, of course – for an idyllic eight days at Cotton House. One day we were on the beach and Viv asked one of the waiters about lunch, and if anyone was at the pool café. It seemed Mick Jagger was there, and Viv said 'Let's go.' I protested, 'He is not troubling me so I won't trouble him.' We went to the pool café anyway, and Mick was indeed there with Jerry Hall and family.

En route back to Cayman, I had to leave my new bride when we passed through Miami. I had a Trafalgar House meeting in Kingston on the 19th but was back in Cayman that same evening for the BCQS Christmas party on the Genesis roof terrace and Christmas dinner with René and Claudine at Plantana.

I should mention here, that on a visit to the UK I had given Gordon and Lyle a copy of Miss Lassie's book *My Markings*. While visiting for the wedding, they met Miss Lassie at her house and purchased three wonderful paintings from her for the significant sum of $50,000. These paintings adorned the entry into their home 'Faircross' on the Wentworth Golf course in Virginia Water for some twenty-five years, until they gifted them back to CNCF in 2021.

1996

'Experience is not what happens to a man; it is what a man does with what happens to him.' Aldous Huxley

The New Year, 1996, commenced with another trip to Kingston and then to London to carry out interviews for staff for Cayman, Turks & Caicos, Tortola and our property management company. Neil Purton had agreed to join us, and I interviewed a Sanjay Amin for our Tortola office, Russell Alwell for Turks & Caicos, and Stephen Pedrick–Moyle for BCQS Property Management. All these individuals would play significant roles as we expanded the business. I lunched at the Foreign and Commonwealth Office (FCO) in Croydon with Derek Evans, who had replaced John Miles as the FCO Caribbean region representative. As I've mentioned before, most of my work colleagues become friends. Derek and his wife Dawn fall very much into this category.

A key task during this London visit was to find a suitable location for the UK reception to celebrate our wedding for guests who had been unable to join us for the reception in the Cayman Islands. We settled on Cannizaro House in Wimbledon after looking at several others, including an island in the Thames.

On the 20th January I met Vivian at Terminal 3 at Heathrow, and we flew to Geneva then drove to Meribel for eight wonderful days of skiing, during which we covered 142,000 vertical feet of descent. Much to Vivian's horror, Basil Behrman had given me a watch for my 50th birthday that counted runs and vertical feet. I say horror because, as a good QS, I love to count things, so once I had it, when Viv would say, 'Let's call it a day' after a hard day's skiing, I was more than likely to suggest, 'Let's make it an Everest Day – 29,000 ft!' But what a wonderful wife! Since we always carry our own skis and other equipment, Viv had lugged all this from Cayman to Heathrow where we met up.

In February I met with Evelyn Rockett, who, together with Gerry Harper, organised many of the sporting events in Cayman. As part of BCQS's marketing, we promoted what would become known as the Turtle Run around South Sound. Teams of five would complete a two-mile circuit, which provided great spectator involvement. Our first run took place on 25th May 1996. Our T-shirt was magnificent, with a running turtle chasing the RICS Rampant Lion, designed by Wray Banker who was to form part of the Native Sons Art Collective formalised later in the year. We held these runs annually for many years.

That month we also held another Claims Seminar at the Radisson. Gordon Jaynes flew out to present the legal sections of the seminar and I once again presented the record-keeping and claim calculations section.

At the end of March, I met Dave Martins to discuss Cayfest, especially the wide range of plans we had for a cultural extravaganza that ended up growing over the years to include a traditional boat launch – the first of which we held in South Sound that August – Photography, Fashion, Dance, Film Making, Music and Theatre, all celebrating Cayman's rich heritage.

On 9th April 1996 I flew to Kingston for the official opening of Trafalgar House by Sir Malcolm Rifkind, the Secretary of State for Foreign Commonwealth and Development Affairs in John Major's government. The project had not been easy, but the end result was well worth the effort, and Sir Malcolm paid the project great compliments, as did the High Commissioner and Ainsley Henriques, head of the National Trust for Jamaica, who noted the building had been restored to its original glory as originally anticipated.

Vivian and I celebrated our wedding with our UK friends and family at Cannizaro House, on Sunday 5th May. It was a beautiful, sunny day, perfect for outdoor photographs and a lavish, joyful lunch complete with speeches and toasts. Viv's 50th birthday on 7th May was appropriately celebrated at Tante Claire.

Back in Cayman, in May I was privileged to meet John Owen, our new Governor. Since becoming chairman of CNCF, I had made a point of meeting with each arriving Governor to introduce him to CNCF's work and seek his support. I would also present him with copies of our publications to provide background. Unbeknown to me at the time, John's wife Carol was a keen and accomplished artist, and this fortuitous meeting would lead, as you will see below, to the founding of our National Gallery.

On the development front; in June, construction started on Building 11 of our Mini Warehouse project at the Airport Industrial Park. When this was completed, we would have run out of land on which to continue our expansion of this venture. However, we were fortunate to meet with Jerry and Cathy

Frasier, who owned the two acres or so of land adjacent to us. Although they did not want to sell it outright, they agreed to lease it to us for three periods of thirty years, and so our expansion looked set for a long time. In the end, by 2005 we had completely developed this new property as well.

We had final numbers from Harry Olsen of Olsen Construction for Callaloo, the pavilion residence Viv and I had discussed with Ed Haladay and that Classic Homes were building on the end lot of the yacht club. We signed the contract on 23rd May and commenced construction.

After making many, many attempts to meet with the Chief Minister in Tortola to resolve the restrictions on our business licence in BVI, I finally received an appointment to meet with the Hon Ralph O'Neal on 5th September 1996 at 10am. I arrived at his office early, and was asked to take a seat facing the clerical staff in what I assumed was his outer office. I waited patiently for some twenty minutes or so. I heard a sound behind me, a deep voice said, 'Good morning', there was a sound of shuffling feet and a large gentleman in a suit passed by me. I waited another ten minutes or so and a secretary asked me to enter the Chief's office.

To my greeting he responded, 'I do not like you!' Startled, I enquired why, and got, 'You did not say good morning when I entered my office a while ago.' This was a good start to sorting out our restricted licence to operate! I explained I had not seen him coming as my back had been to him. I then clarified that BCQS as a company were not an 'airline ticket and briefcase' type of consultancy and wanted to be a full-service company in the BVI. Mr O'Neal countered by saying he felt we would only give work to companies owned by white people. I responded by saying that I would have to think hard to remember the colour of the owners of those companies with whom we worked throughout the Caribbean and named several of them. These, of course, were companies owned by people with a broad range of skin colour. I also noted that work assignment was based on skill, not pigmentation. Mr O'Neal said he would think about it. Maybe it was the Caymanian Tortuga rum cake I presented to him, or perhaps I did indeed convince him we were there to stay in the BVI, because a few weeks later we received our unrestricted licence!

Meetings then followed with Dancia Penn, the attorney general and a most gracious lady who became a good friend, and with Governor David Mackilligin, to discuss the new residence planned for him.

As noted earlier, I sat on the board of the National Trust and was chairman of the Historic Advisory Committee, where one of our projects was recognising structures and sites of significant historic interest and confirming their recognition by erecting a plaque to that effect. It is of particular interest that there was resistance in some quarters to this recognition, as certain property owners felt it might restrict their ability to subsequently develop a recognised property with an alternative use. However, this was not the case for Elmslie Church, which we 'plaqued' on 11th September 1996, much to my delight.

Viv and I had planned to visit India for some time, and so, on a trip to Kingston in mid-June 1995, I had gone to the Indian High Commission in Retreat Avenue and secured visas for the proposed visit. Viv and I left Cayman on 1st October, arriving in Mumbai, very jetlagged, at 11.25pm. We decided to catch the first Air India flight to Delhi, which left at 3.45am, and after a two hour flight and hotel transfer we checked into the Taj Mahal and slept round the clock until the next morning, when we woke early and went out for some exercise.

We were truly astonished at the surreal sight of large packs of monkeys patrolling the streets of this large Indian city. We tried to keep out of their way as they ran diagonally across the road, the baby monkeys clinging to their mothers' backs. We were then absorbed by the magic of this continent. We visited the Red Fort, Jama Masjid, the Presidential Palace, Qutab Minar, Raj Ghat, India Gate and Humayun's Tomb – phew! The next day we flew to Katmandu for more sightseeing and the following day to Maghuli, to stay at Tiger Tops Lodge. To reach this we travelled by Land Rover, canoe and finally elephant! I speculated that there must be a rear entrance to bring in supplies, but no – everything there arrived by the same route. Our room was nestled high in the trees and lit only by oil lamps. Very early next morning we ventured out on elephants, looking for tigers. We were seated in a large basket-type saddle called a howdah, with the mahout on the elephant's back, and were amazed at how the elephant used his trunk to carefully check the depth of the water before venturing into lakes.

On 8th October we left Tiger Tops by the same route and flew back to Katmandu, where we arranged a change to our itinerary with our guide, Hilary, an immaculately dressed Nepalese gentleman wearing shirt, tie, jacket and Gucci loafers. We wanted to overnight in Nagarkot to witness the sunrise over Everest and then walk down from there to Katmandu. We drove to Nagarkot, and Hilary arranged for a Sherpa to come to our hotel after sunrise the next day and walk with us on the trail. The sunrise was magnificent, breakfast enjoyable, and we waited for the Sherpa to appear, and waited, and waited, but no Sherpa! Hilary apologised and insisted on accompanying us himself. The trail back to Katmandu included some wonderful scenery, monks, monasteries and insights into daily village life. Viv and I were dressed for the trail but Hilary, who was very keen to be in as many photographs as possible, was still immaculately dressed as he had been the day before, complete with those Gucci loafers, which made for some oddly incongruous images!

We left Katmandu the next day and flew to Varanasi. As we were checking into our hotel, Viv noticed a man dressed in white, sitting behind a notice advertising yoga lessons. In reply to her questions, he said he taught Ashtanga yoga and could come to our room to give us a class. Our room had just enough space for me to practice on the floor with Viv sitting on the bed and with the yogi sitting in a corner. The yogi demonstrated various positions and poses and after we had the hang of these, he said, 'Now we will meditate. Please close your eyes and breathe deeply. Do not let the noise outside distract you. Let those sounds go.' We practiced this for a while and I suddenly thought, here we are, with someone we do not know, with our eyes closed, and our wallets and passports sitting on the dresser! Viv must have thought the same thing at the same time, because as I opened my eyes slightly to see, Viv opened hers slightly too, and we both burst out laughing! There was, of course, no problem.

Our yoga lesson over, we visited Sarnath, where the Dhamek Stupa marks the location where the Buddha preached his first discourse to his first five disciples and where all five eventually became fully liberated. On the 11th we were woken very early, before sunrise, and were taken for a boat ride on the Ganges. Many funeral pyres were being lit, candles floated on the water, and a shaman seated high on a rock was beating a large drum. The sense of peace and wonder in the early morning scene, illuminated by a huge, rising sun, was palpable. That afternoon we flew from Varanasi to the Khajuraho Monuments, a group of intricately carved Hindu and Jain temples and now an UNESCO World Heritage Site. Originally there had been some eighty-five in number, of which approximately twenty-five remain. The site had been abandoned, forgotten, and engulfed by the jungle until it was rediscovered by a British engineer in 1838. It is claimed that the graphic carvings on the temples helped the young men who lived there learn about the ways of the world!

We were then due to leave Khajuraho on the 13th to fly to Agra, but our tour guide arrived to announce the flight had been cancelled – but not to worry, we could travel to Agra by train. Not wanting to miss the Taj Mahal at sunrise, we readily agreed and were driven to the train station in an Ambassador, the wonderful classic Indian car whose design was based on the UK Morris Oxford. The train was late, so we were advised to wait in the comfort of the car's air conditioning. This we did, surrounded by a mass of humanity – eating, drinking, sitting, waiting, sacred cows wandering through the crowd at will. The scene had a surreal feel to it. After a few hours we were told that the train for Agra had been diverted for the use of a senior government official, and we were taken to a local hotel to sleep in comfort until the next train arrived. We eventually arrived in Agra before daybreak, and from our hotel window saw the incredible sight of the Taj Mahal illuminated by the brightening sky. Of course, we visited this beautiful Islamic mausoleum made of white marble, a true monument to Shah Jahan's love of his favourite wife, and where his tomb joined hers. The serene reflecting pool leading up to the entrance must be one of the most photographed sites in India, visited by some seven million people a year.

We then drove from Agra to Jaipur, visiting the Bharatpur Bird Sanctuary en route. We took a rickshaw ride through this wonderful park, where in the 1930s birds were slaughtered en masse during shooting parties put on by the then maharajah. Now, it has become a place for them to grow and thrive, and the branches of the trees laden with so many birds were a sight to behold.

In Jaipur, we stayed at the Jaimahal Palace and visited the Maharaja's Palace and Observatory, and then flew to Udaipur for a 3-day stay at the Lake Palace. This is a truly exotic and fascinating location situated in the middle of a large lake, and the only access was by boat. We arrived back home in Cayman on 23rd October, with vivid memories of this wonderful country. The trip gave us the taste for many more enlightening and educational travels.

At this time, there was a growing interest in, and recognition of, Cayman's artistic expression, and in November 1996 a respected and prolific group of Caymanian artists that included Al Ebanks, Bendel Hydes, Wray Banker, Randy Cholette, Chris Christian, and Horatio Esteban established the 'Native Sons'. They held their first exhibition at the Harquail on 2nd November 1996.

The day after our return I was on a plane once more, this time to London for business meetings with Barclays about their branch in Nassau, and then on the Eurostar to Brussels with Mortimer, where we met with representatives from the European Union to discuss various projects the EU were financing in the Caribbean. We also met with Adrianus Koetsenruijter to establish BCQS's listing as an approved monitor for such projects. Not forgetting the ladies, we purchased some Bruges lace doilies, which we still use at Callaloo. The next stop was Providenciales. As I've mentioned before, part of our business plan for BCQS was to offer our regional clients services tailored to their specific needs, both geographically and as regards the services they required. This approach would allow them to rely on our understanding of cross-border due diligence requirements, and our ability to 'iron out' economic fluctuations in different countries. We would also be able to offer a wider range of complementary services than our competitors. In essence, we would be offering a 'one-stop-shop' to make our customers' lives easier. To this end, we wanted to form a civil and structural engineering company and had entered into talks with a local Providenciales engineer, Rolf Annonsen.

In early December, Viv and I enjoyed a couple of weeks' skiing in Big Sky, Montana, and then travelled to Belfast to spend Christmas with Viv's parents. On 3rd January we spent a week in Edna and Bill Bissell's apartment in Villars – the wonderful wedding present they had given us – and racked up 134,000 vertical feet and almost ninety runs. That pesky watch again!

1997

Serenity Prayer: 'God grant me the SERENITY to accept the things I cannot change, COURAGE to change the things I can, WISDOM to know the difference.'

Possibly related to the Native Sons' emergence, in January I was summoned to Government House to meet with Carol Owen and Leslie Bigelman, where we discussed the formation of an 'Art Institute' or National Gallery to fulfill the promise made to Monica Gore a few years earlier. The ever-generous Mrs Harquail had offered some three and a half acres of land adjoining the CNCF property to accommodate a potential new building. The project almost came undone when, at CNCF's invitation, the Jamaican National Dance Theatre headed by the multi-talented Rex Nettleford performed at the Harquail on the 1st February. Mrs Harquail, as guest of honour, departed part-way through the performance as she considered the tight leotards and modern ballet performance 'pornographic'.

However, with McKeeva Bush as the Minister in charge of Culture, articles for the formation of the National Gallery were drawn up for review by the Attorney General, and these were approved by the board, including yours truly, on 4th April 1997. I remain a board member, being the only founding board member still serving.

On 5th February a meeting was held at Government House to assemble various parties interested in recognising Cayman's cultural expression, and the potential for linking up with the Museum and the National Trust to review future growth, the establishment of a Heritage Law, and most importantly, how all of this could be funded.

What's fascinating is that, as I wrote this in February 2023, at CNCF we had just set up the structure for a Strategic Planning Exercise – first set in motion in 2016 – to guide the overall development of our cultural organisations. In 2023, it was ready for its final review and implementation. That's twenty-six years in gestation – even an elephant would lose patience with that kind of progress!

I travelled to Turks and Caicos to continue developing our new engineering venture and then to London to interview staff for our property management company and for meetings with Mortimer. Another one of his favourite watering holes at that time was the Dock Blida, a Davy's wine bar in a cellar just off Chiltern Street. It was dark, with sawdust on the floor, and we were barely able to see the paperwork we were perusing in connection with our accounts and business plan! While spending two days in Belfast with Flo and Jo, Charlie Nicol, a neighbour of theirs who was a plain clothes policeman, invited me to his station and a tour of the troubled areas in his standard-looking Rover saloon. I commented that it felt oddly tight inside given its outside dimensions, to be told it was an armored car! I was to pretend to be a plain clothes policeman, but while we were visiting the new performing arts centre, situated on Belfast Lough, I almost blew my cover by asking questions related to Cayman's cultural work – hardly the typical questions of a policeman.

In May, Viv's parents came to Cayman to stay with us for her birthday, and as a surprise we took them on a 'magical mystery tour'. We boarded a Cayman Airways flight without telling them where we were headed, and it wasn't until we landed in Havana and they realised people were speaking a different language, that they realised where they were. We had a wonderful time staying at the Hotel Inglaterra, full of colonial charm. We took rickshaw rides in the old town, had drinks in Hemingway's hangout, El Floridita, and visited the National Theatre to see a striking ballet with the dancers all on their toes complete with castanets. The theatre building was disfigured with external graffiti but immaculate on the inside, with plush velvet seating and starched white antimacassars, and all the young people in the audience were immaculately dressed.

At this time the CNCF board comprised Roger Ebanks, Consuelo Ebanks, George McCarthy, Mrs Harquail, and yours truly as Chairman (Alden McLaughlin had resigned as Deputy Chairman and board member of CNCF on 27th November 1996) and we were delighted to hear Miss Lassie had been awarded an MBE in the Queen's Birthday Honours on 12th June 1997.

In late July, after four days in Oregon during which we attended a Carabella partners meeting, we assembled four cases of our Pinot Noir and Pinot Gris, and loaded them into our car for transport back to Cayman. We had originally booked at a Holiday Inn close to the airport for the last night as our flight left very early but decided a more upmarket last night would be appropriate. Driving through downtown Portland, we saw an elegantly attired doorman in a top hat standing in front of the Heathman Hotel and decided this looked more like it. Viv jumped out and confirmed they had rooms, and the doorman said he would take the car and park it. I agreed but said we would need to leave at 4am to catch our flight and asked if our car would be available. Reassured that it would be, we checked in and had a magnificent dinner complete with two bottles of very fine wine. We slept well until the alarm woke us at 3.30am. I phoned down to reception and asked for the car to be brought up, we showered and dressed, packed, and went down to the front desk to check out. An embarrassed concierge at the front desk said, 'We are very sorry sir, but the code on the garage door has malfunctioned, and your car is locked in.' The hotel quickly arranged for a car to take us to the airport and waived the bill not only for the stay, our magnificent meal and the wine, but also paid to ship the wine to Cayman. That is what I call service!

I left Cayman again on 3rd August, this time for Trinidad, to represent Cayman at a five-day creative arts conference at the St Augustine campus of the University of the West Indies. Back in Cayman, Foster's Food Fair opened in their new location in the Strand. Foster's had been a great tenant of ours for many years at the Greenery and we were sorry to see them go, but the space they vacated would soon be repurposed as a bowling alley – another first for Cayman. Also, on our development front, we had completed Callaloo in the Cayman Islands Yacht Club and received the CO on 18th August 1997.

BCQS was at this time continuing research into tying up with larger UK market leaders and worldwide practices, so in late August I held meetings in London with several international QS and PM firms. BCQS was seeking to grow its network and offer bespoke Caribbean wide services, with specific local knowledge, to clients seeking international-size companies that had such detailed knowledge and expertise. In late November, we would have more meetings in London with Cyril Sweet, Beard Dove, Handscomb, and Gardiner & Theobald, in which I was ably accompanied by Mortimer, who was continuing to update our business plan.

Cayfest was in full swing when I returned, including a presentation of 'Pass it On' where senior community members, such as Ira Walton, passed on the skills of boatbuilding, including demonstrations of the tools used and sourcing of materials. This was very topical, as two days later we had a typical boat launch in South Sound with the boat on rollers, an anchor out to sea and a winch to pull the boat into the water, accompanied by festivities and much music. This was followed, a few days later, with an art show at the Harquail with Miss Lassie's work on display, and 'Praise', a wonderful selection of church choirs giving thanks through song. All keeping the culture alive!

On 23rd September, Viv and I were travelling again, this time to Stuttgart, where we collected a new Mercedes from the factory. We stayed the first night in Fribourg, and drove on through the Alsace and then to Lugano to meet our good friends René and Claudine, who also assisted with culinary recommendations for our planned trip through northern Italy. I had always been fascinated by Palladian architecture, and we wanted to view first-hand the many masterpieces the stonemason and architect Andrea Palladio had created in this part of the world. Palladio was born in 1508 (I always like to compare dates with what was happening in Cayman at that time – we had been discovered by Columbus only five years before!), right on the cusp of the architectural transition from the Renaissance to the Baroque. We were privileged to be able to explore Villa Barbaro, Palazzo Chiericati, Villa Emo, Villa Cornaro and the masterpiece of La Rotonda.

We then travelled to Florence, taking in Michaelangelo's David, then on to Sienna, in whose town centre the annual Palio takes place. This is one of the world's oldest horse races, dating back to 1656. In Pisa we saw the famous leaning tower, and finally drove to Callas, where we were hosted royally by Alan and Joan Scott from Cayman. They had draped the Cayman Island flag over the entrance, so knew we were in the right place!

We drove back through France and through the channel tunnel (which had opened in May 1994) to England. It was fun to drive onto a railcar and remain in your car during the journey. Well prepared with some great French cheese, a baguette, and, of course, a nice bottle of French wine, the journey was most enjoyable. Back in the UK we had established a great working relationship with Mathew Lines, who would collect the car from us at the airport, take it to be serviced, then keep it for us in a secure air-conditioned storage facility that had once been his mother's indoor riding ring. On our return, Mathew would be there waiting with our car ready for the next adventure, of which there were many.

Meetings followed in London with the Barclays team handling Caribbean projects, and, at around this time, we received our first enquiry for our services to manage the rebuilding of key facilities for a new town in Little Bay, Montserrat. This was to replace the original capital, Plymouth, that had been buried by volcanic ash during the eruption of the Soufrière Hills volcano on 18th July 1995. This enquiry developed into a significant assignment for us, with many interesting challenges, not the least of which was getting there as the airport had also been destroyed in the eruption.

Many more meetings followed in Cayman, including with the National Trust's Mission House project in my role as head of the Historic Advisory

Committee, with the Elmslie Property Committee and with the National Gallery and the Visual Arts Society. Carol Owen, John Doak and Meg Patterson and others were trying to bring these organisations together to collaborate in a closer working relationship. At CNCF we were privileged to have a visit from Dominican playwright Alwin Bully, a good friend of Henry Muttoo, who delivered a thought-provoking dissertation on 'Our Cultural Diversity' based on the 1996 UNESCO-published paper. Alwin had designed the Dominica national flag for that country's independence in 1978.

We also held a joint board meeting of the National Gallery and CNCF on 7th November, coupled with the joint meetings being held with the Visual Arts Society, to help align the somewhat disparate efforts of many people with common interests. Our current work with CNCF – to act as an Arts Council, and to develop a strategic plan for the overall preservation and development of culture – continues many years later to accomplish a similar goal.

Our Barclays rebuilding work, and that for the Foreign Office, were focused on Tortola, in the BVI, at this time. Both the new Governor's Residence and the new Barclays Bank building on Wickham's Cay were on site, and Mortimer and I flew there on 9th November for meetings with our team. We then went on to Providenciales for discussions with Jim Slattery about the sale of L'Oasis, his home there, which I had part-financed back in 1983.

On 3rd December we were graced with a further visit from Rex Nettleford at the Harquail – this time not to dance and frighten the wits out of Mrs Harquail, but to deliver an inspiring lecture about his life. Rex had received a Rhodes scholarship to Oxford, was a respected social commentator and choreographer, and had founded the National Dance Theatre Company of Jamaica, which did so much to incorporate traditional Jamaican music and dance into the formal balletic repertoire.

We spent December skiing in Bozeman, celebrated Christmas with Joe and Flo and, early in the new year, enjoyed a celebratory dinner with René and Claudine, their daughter Michèle and her husband Ray, and Bobby Nunes and his 'chick', Sharon.

CHAPTER SEVEN

Seven Mile Dreams (1998–2002)

1998

'We are born, and the human drama plays out around us and inside us, with each breath we get the opportunity to choose our role and play our part, writing the story of our life.' Prem Rawat

Of course we did not miss David and Chi-Chi Foster's traditional New Year's Day bash, during which they entertained a huge crowd of friends at their home on Melmac Avenue and where we would always catch up with many friends whom we might have seen little of during the year.

On 9th January, we flew to New York to meet with Peter and Sonia Coster about a house they were building at Cayman Kai and on the 17th, in Amsterdam, I met with NACO, the airport specialists, with whom we were working on several airport developments. Since we never missed an opportunity for a European ski trip, we then flew to Verbier, where we met Ray and Michèle. We spent three wonderful days skiing together at Mont Fort, Gentianes, Super Nendaz, Tortin and La Chaux, accompanied by sumptuous meals and copious amounts of delicious Dôle and Fendant at the Fer à Cheval.

The 8th February saw me flying to Barbados for meetings and then to Grenada, Antigua, St Kitts and Nevis to inspect progress on the many branches we were repurposing for Barclays. Culturally, this work was extremely interesting. The bank intended to create a contemporary atmosphere in its branches, with more open and non-secure spaces as opposed to the existing model where some 70 per cent of the space was closed off behind a screen. Customers could thus sit at a desk in the open with their banking representative and discuss their requirements. The problem was that in our small-town, gossipy Caribbean environment, local people seen talking to their banker were automatically assumed to have a cash flow issue and would immediately be questioned by friends, 'Saw you in the bank today talking to a bank representative – do you have a problem?' Moreover, for economic reasons, head office in London had decided offices were to be smaller. However, many bank managers now working in the Caribbean were from African postings where they were used to very large private offices, so much diplomacy and cajoling was required to sell the downsized space!

On 13th February we were off skiing again, this time for ten days in Keystone, staying with Al and Jane Hallock. Robin and Christine, their grandchildren, were there too. As avid snowboarders, they persuaded us to give it a try, promising it would be easy. So, on the 16th we set off for a lesson and then onto the slopes for my one and only snowboarding experience. I lost count of the number of times I fell on my bum and by lunchtime we had repaired to the Alpenglow Stuben for a well-deserved lunch and a glass or two to repair the damaged ego (and backside). By this time, Viv had had enough, so took the lift down. Meanwhile, yours truly 'boarded down' (or more correctly, slid down) taking some four and a half hours to accomplish what on skis would have taken me about seven minutes.

Arriving back at the condo, it was suggested a jacuzzi would ease the pain in my rear end – to no avail, as turned out I had a cracked coccyx. A donut pillow of the kind favoured by post-partum women to take pressure off the pelvic area could provide the only relief, and for this I had to go to the maternity ward at the local hospital. Once home, I would take my pillow to the office and blow it up to sit on during the day, then deflate it to take it home. Quickly tiring of all this blowing up and deflating, I simply kept it inflated and hung it over my arm. Ovaine, the son of our Jamaican housekeeper, Maureen, and who worked for us as a book-keeper, had acquired a particularly dry English sense of humour. He would innocently comment, 'Mr Bould, are you learning to swim?' when I came into the office.

Rundown opened on 27th February at the Harquail. By now, the show had become hugely popular and was in its seventh year. We attended with our Governor, John Owen, and his wife Carol, which was a bit nerve-wracking. We hadn't seen the script beforehand, and since the Governor was usually the target of a few light-hearted jabs about the past year's events, there was always the chance he might take offence. But John had a great sense of humour, and because of the work we were doing with Carole on the National Gallery, I was a frequent visitor to Government House – almost 'one of the family' in a way. Indeed, the following evening there was a 50th birthday celebration at Government House, to which we were invited.

At CNCF we were truly busy, as on the 2nd March Peter Minshall, the 'MasMan' of Carnival from Trinidad, brought alive his creative talent in Cayman. For more than twenty-five years, he and his Callaloo Company had presented large scale spectacles involving hundreds of people in bands during

Trinidad Carnival. As I have said throughout this book, I have led a truly blessed life when it comes to the people I have met, and Peter is one of those outstanding, truly unique people. When he speaks it is pure theatre, script and music that dance in the drama of his voice and eyes.

March saw the start of an exciting project: Vision 2008, a ten-year National Strategic Plan, based on the belief that the Cayman Islands can continue to develop in harmony and prosperity if we implement the plan's recommendations, guided by the principles of balanced growth and integrated policy development. The project, headed by Mrs Joy Basdeo, included a foreword noting that,

> This National Strategic Plan was created through a strategic planning process. Strategic Planning is a means by which an organization, and in our case, a country, continually recreates itself. This process deals with people and the way they see themselves. It is based on aspirations. It is proactive; it allows us as a people to celebrate our uniqueness and enables us to choose the future we desire. The design of the planning process invited participation and created a climate that produced real change champions. This type of strategic planning is based on our core beliefs and values, the things we, the people of the Cayman Islands hold most dear.

As Chairman of CNCF, I was privileged to be invited to head one of sixteen Round Tables – each aligned with a strategic area – and we met regularly throughout 1998 to establish action plans. Several meetings, appropriately, were held at Pedro's Castle, which formally reopened in November 1998 after its refurbishment. I felt my time developing strategic planning at Harvard continued to prove its worth, not only in my business but also in my community work. The Round Tables submitted two hundred and thirty action plans, and these were reviewed in detail by the planning team during several day-long sessions. The Vision 2008 Plan was published, together with a companion 'Priority' document, in April 1999. As Mrs Basdeo wrote in the foreword, 'We wanted wide political ownership to ensure a lasting commitment to successful implementation. We feel that we have fulfilled our planning objectives, and that the way forward being offered to the policy makers of government is realistic and achievable. Vision 2008 has been built on a tremendous amount of good will, interest and expertise from thousands of individuals.'

Like many such plans, Vision 2008 may not have been implemented in full or within the expected timeframe, but in my view it remains a magnificent document, created by a group of people who expressed the true principles of what makes us Caymanian, and it underpins many of the positive developments we see today.

Early March saw me flying to Providenciales to review the activities in our office and then to Tortola, where I secured my work permit for the BVI and was invited to Sanjay's house for a wonderful Indian meal he prepared himself. The Chief Minister, Ralph O'Neal and his wife Edris, were surprise guests – in far more relaxed and convivial circumstances than my first meeting with him. It spoke volumes for Sanjay's networking skills that, having been in the BVI for just a few months, he was able to secure the head of government as his dinner guest. It's a skill that Sanjay uses to this day with much success.

Despite our best efforts to sell Callaloo we had been unable to do so. Ed Haladay, Viv and I met with realtors John and Gloria May, who suggested naming a house after a modest West Indian staple vegetable might be holding up its successful sale. Wanting to get out of the mortgage which had us tied down, we thought, 'nothing ventured/nothing gained' and reluctantly changed the name to 'Villa Sorrento'.

Early April required a quick visit to the UK to meet with John Elgie and Peter Griffin to discuss the work we were doing on the new Governor's Residence in Tortola. I stayed at the Adams's flat in Walton-on-Thames and commuted with the suburban masses into London on the train, often on days damped by a wet, cold drizzle. It was a really sobering experience seeing these people, some travelling up to ninety minutes in each direction daily, with their heads buried in their newspapers and no-one speaking or even looking at each other. It was a stark contrast to the joys of our wonderful Caribbean life.

I was back in Cayman for Easter and Cayfest celebrations and Seaside, then flew to Tortola for a progress review in our offices there. These were in a wonderful location, with our front entrance on Main Street and an eclectic Italian restaurant called Capriccio di Mare at the rear, from which we would secure our excellent morning espresso and homemade pasta and fresh fish for lunch. Capriccio's had an amusing T-shirt printed with the owner's view of heaven and hell:

> Heaven is where the police are British, the cooks Italian, the mechanics German, the lovers French and it is all organized by the Swiss.
>
> Hell is where the chefs are British, the mechanics French, the lovers Swiss, the police German and it is all organized by the Italians.

The trip to Tortola enabled me to reconnect with Harvard Alumnus John Robertson and his wife Barbara. They lived in a house on Great Camanoe, an island north of, and close to, Beef Island in the BVI, and accessible only by small boat, which Barb skillfully piloted. John was an inventor – the first I had ever met – and an interesting character, who joined us on many of our reunions over the years.

Back in London on 1st May, I had a suit fitting with David Clegg, met with Barclays regarding the tender for their new office building in Tortola, and with the FCO about the new Governor's Residence there. From London, we set off on a drive around Europe, stopping to hike in some stunning locations, especially in Provence, inspired by Viv's gift of *Walking in Provence* by Janette Norton. Each day brought a new trail, a fresh baguette and, of course, a chilled bottle of the local rosé for lunch. Using the red Michelin guide, we chose our hotels like Mary and Joseph seeking an inn – I stayed in the car while Viv dashed inside to inspect the rooms, returning with either a thumbs-up or down, depending on the state of the sheets and bathroom.

We drove more than four thousand miles in three weeks before returning to the UK to stay at Gravetye Manor and have dinner with Michael Whitelock. Before the meal, Michael invited us to his house for drinks and proudly showed off his latest acquisition: a massive, hand-carved elephant he had brought back from a recent trip to Thailand, which he had converted into an outdoor bar. This was located in a field next to his daughter Sky's pony, which seemed perturbed by its new, oversized neighbour and huddled nervously in one corner of the paddock.

Back in Cayman, space had kindly been donated in Alexandria Place, close to the airport, to accommodate the National Gallery; Leslie Bigelman, the director, was already planning exhibitions there and classes were well underway. Carol Owen announced the formal opening of the National Gallery on this site on 12th June, with an exhibition of Miguel Powery's work made possible by the generosity of Dick Christiansen, Andreas Ugland and Naul Bodden. At the same time, Mrs Harquail announced she would donate more land adjacent to CNCF's property to house the Gallery, the museum and a crafts village.

CNCF had long been lobbying government to raise the funds needed to acquire Miss Lassie's entire collection of paintings, and on 4th June we succeeded – acquiring some one hundred and fifty of her works in perpetuity. Although Miss Lassie was considered a national treasure, very few of her paintings had been sold, and the opportunity to preserve almost her entire body of work for the people was simply too important to pass up.

This acquisition, and the National Gallery's efforts to raise awareness of local artists, such as exhibiting Miguel Powery's work, somehow seemed to give

Caymanian artists the confidence and legitimacy they needed. From that point on, true Caymanian art began to emerge more freely, and it has continued to flourish ever since.

Of considerable interest during this time was my appointment as a mediator for a hearing scheduled on 22nd and 23rd July, concerning a dispute over a generator installation for an electric utility company. The case was very much aligned with my interest in alternate forms of dispute resolution, methods far less costly and time-consuming than litigation or even arbitration, as I had seen firsthand during the experience with the Grand Palazzo in St Thomas from 1992 to 1994.

The mediation took eighteen hours over two days to reach agreement. It was a true exercise in 'shuttle diplomacy' with three separate rooms – one for each party and a shared meeting room. I moved between them, discussing one party's position, then the other's, before bringing everyone together in the common room. Given the significant sum at stake, the process' efficiency, leaving both parties satisfied with the outcome, illustrated the clear advantages of mediation over other forms of dispute resolution. Moreover, it allowed senior executives to continue running their businesses rather than being tied up in litigation or arbitration for months.

We were invited to Garth Bevan's 4th of July wedding in Canada and left Cayman on 2nd July, flying to Buffalo and then driving to the event by way of the Niagara Falls, which were absolutely stunning. We couldn't possibly have missed the event, as Garth was the foreman in charge of all the glazing work to the Genesis office building. We called on him for any aluminum work we needed – including the very large assignment to repair my aluminum ski poles after a very aggressive black diamond ski trip! Garth was one of the world's true characters. His extremely dry wit enabled him to deal with the many labour and materials supply-side challenges of his job, and he did not suffer fools gladly.

On 9th of July I was off again, this time to visit Tortola for the grand opening of the new Barclays Bank building, where I met with Dave Scott 'Scottie', and also with the Governor Frank Savage to deal with issues pertaining to the access road for the new Government House we were managing. Then we went on to Antigua to look at Halcyon Cove Hotel, which, ironically, we are currently monitoring during its redevelopment as a Royalton CHIC hotel. Life does indeed go full circle!

In July we were retained to advise on a dispute concerning a house in Jumby Bay, an exclusive island just off the coast of Antigua, where the most popular sport was croquet in the afternoon. We have taken up this game at our home Callaloo, particularly prior to our traditional Christmas lunch. Also in Antigua, we were introduced to Asian Village, a large property including several offshore islands, and to which the government had granted significant concessions under the Asian Village Act 1997. Since then, we have been involved with this project, under various iterations and owners, to the present day.

As I've mentioned before, at BCQS the key view of our business plan was that to be successful and to enable our talented team, it was essential to cover the entire Caribbean region both geographically and in terms of the services we offered. The rationale for regional coverage was obvious: the economies of the thirty four Caribbean countries tend to fluctuate independently, and several of our clients, such as Cable & Wireless, Barclays, CIBC, Scotia, RBC, the FCO and the hotel chains, operate on a pan-Caribbean basis. These clients preferred to work with a single professional advisor to carry out their work across the entire region, rather than engage with separate consultants in each country.

Travel times were key to covering all of these countries efficiently. From Cayman we could cover the northern Caribbean; from BVI, the Leeward islands – Puerto Rico, US Virgins, St Martin, St Kitts, and others – often as day trips. From Barbados we could cover the southern Caribbean including St Lucia, Antigua, and Trinidad. We used our regional airline LIAT, sometimes referred to as 'Luggage In Another Terminal' or 'Leave Island Any Time', but seriously, without this key link between the islands, doing business there would have been close on impossible.

During 1998 we continued to develop our service diversity, allowing different disciplines to generate contacts for one another. A very important consideration was to avoid possible conflicts of interest – seen in earlier decades when architects and quantity surveyors had formed joint practices, undermining the 'checks and balances' between costing and developing a design, and making it difficult to challenge design errors.

We did not see such a conflict in establishing a structural engineering company. We successfully developed Civil & Structural Engineering Limited in Turks & Caicos, and although we explored developing a similar venture in Cayman, it ultimately did not materialise.

Construction of Mini Warehouse buildings 14 & 15 began in late August. They had been designed by George Serrant, who had handled the majority of the projects for Mini Warehouse Two at the airport industrial park. There seemed to be an almost limitless demand for our product, which offered units of 5×5 feet, 5×10 feet, and 10×20 feet. Interestingly, although many others entered the storage business over the years, very few focused on units this small, so we continued to expand the business on this basis, and today we are the island's largest provider of mini self-storage.

In late August, I met with one Neil Rustin, the general manager for Mike Bell, who had developed a subdivision called Heron Harbour. This included a 29,000 sq ft supermarket for Hurleys and a shopping centre of approximately 80,000 sq ft. There were plans to add a water park in the near future, and Neil wanted advice on costing and development for the ongoing project as well as how to resolve some issues on the works to date.

On 12th September 1998, Vivian and I flew to London to collect 'Goldie' for a gastronomic tour of Europe that René Meister had arranged for us. We reacquainted ourselves with the 'Cuisine of the Sun' of Roger Vergé at Moulin de Mougins, whose recipes we frequently cook in Cayman. We then revisited St Paul de Vence and tried to find the shop where we had first seen Paul Pacotto's shadow sculpture *Le Baiser*. The wonderful piece rotates, illuminated by a projector, and its shadow on the wall takes the shape of two bodies that morph into two people kissing. The shop had moved, but we located it and purchased the sculpture, which continues to fascinate people visiting Callaloo.

We spent a wonderful month touring Europe and were particularly impressed by our stay at Torre Del Remi in Puigcerdà at the foot of the Cadi Mountain range on the Spanish/French border. This incredible twenty-four-room hotel had been built at the turn of the century and was frequented by the King of Spain. It offered tremendous service and food. We returned to it frequently to enjoy the walks in the mountains, and it was where Vivian persuaded me to take up sketching as a form of relaxation. We would sit on the hotel lawn sketching its façade and, quite unbidden, a waiter would arrive with a glass of champagne and nibbles (to get the creative juices flowing)! It did take some time to get used to the Spanish custom of very late dinners – at 9.30pm we would find ourselves the only guests in the dining room, and as we were finishing, we would see the other hotel guests arriving.

We were back in Cayman on 8th October, where good news awaited that the ever-generous Mrs Harquail had confirmed her donation of three and a half acres of land adjacent to the Harquail Cultural Centre, on which to develop a purpose-built National Gallery. The growing recognition of the cultural importance of Miss Lassie's work was reflected in the Post Office's decision to issue an Easter stamp series featuring her paintings.

For many years I had served on the board of the National Trust and as head of its Historic Advisory Committee. I was honoured and privileged to be elected Chairman for two successive terms from 1998 to 2002, during which time we developed the first five-year business plan for the Trust. We enlisted the services of an extremely talented and giving lady, Judith Gates, who had also helped me with plans related to my business activities. The committee developed five programmes to promote awareness and appreciation of Cayman's heritage, one of which was the Historic Plaque programme, and as I mentioned earlier, this last faced occasional challenges because some recipients feared the recognition might negatively affect their property value or restrict future development.

In late November, representing the Trust, I met with the developer of the Ritz Carlton in relation to the clearance of a large area of mangrove to construct a golf course. It was an amicable meeting, during which I expressed the Trust's concerns, but in spite of the fact that no planning approval had been granted, the developer cleared the land with no one's knowledge – a strip of mangrove forest paralleling West Bay Road had been left in place while the clearing took place! Thankfully, this kind of thing rarely happened.

On a more positive note, the exciting process of creating the purpose-built Gallery was gaining momentum, and an architectural competition had been launched to see who would come up with the best design.

1999

Trust is the union of intelligence and integrity.

Early in January, while I was in the UK interviewing property managers for BCQS Property Management Ltd., I felt the call of Verbier. Staying at the Relais de Pachou, I skied for three days with Roger and Jill Bailey, friends of Ray and Michèle. Roger had worked for most of his career on CERN's Large Hadron Collider (LHC) which is the world's largest and most powerful particle accelerator. The LHC consists of a twenty-seven kilometre ring of superconducting magnets with a number of accelerating structures to boost the energy of the particles along the way. Inside, two high-energy particle beams travel at close to the speed of light before they are made to collide, and various experiments at the point of collision are carried out. For many years, while sitting next to me on ski lifts, Roger would explain to me what he did, which I never did fully understand, but Vivian and I were privileged to be able to enter the LHC just before it started up in 2008.

In late January, back in Cayman, I was appointed arbitrator on a stormwater outfall dispute in Montego Bay and flew there for a preliminary hearing on 24th January.

The Native Sons exhibition opened on 2nd February. The group, comprising Wray Banker, Al Ebanks, Horacio Esteban, Miquel Powery, Randy Chollette, Nasaria Suckoo, and later Gordon Solomon, were all initially managed by Morgan DaCosta, and reflected the growing recognition of the nascent talent of Caymanian artists. On the same note, *Rundown* opened on 26th February to sold out performances, as this CNCF production had by now become an eagerly anticipated staple of Cayman's annual theatre scene.

In 1999, we celebrated the 30th anniversary of the founding of BCQS, which had now grown to three offices with a staff of sixteen. We held an anniversary party in June, which was followed by an appearance on CITN TV and by several office lunches also attended by senior management from Butterfield, our bankers. They had provided unwavering support for BCQS's operations as well as for our Mini Warehouse developments over many years. This was topped off by a beach BBQ at Plantana with Sanjay cooking a magnificent curry. He left his mark not only as a great chef, but also on the Formica kitchen top, in the form of a scorch mark from the very hot pan!

Our first business plan had covered the period from 1989 to 1994, the second 1994 to 1999, and the third 1999 to 2004, and our progress was manifesting the direction and detail of these plans. The driving overall philosophy of BCQS's business plan had always been to offer a regionally and professionally diverse Caribbean-wide service to our clients. In addition to the core QS service, this included civil and structural engineering and property management services. The company was expanding on so many fronts, and because ownership was becoming more widely spread amongst the shareholders, as part of our business planning we had begun discussing both how to value the company and my longer term plans to gradually sell my interest.

In early March, Vivian and I left for Cape Town and a Harvard Alumni reunion hosted by Alastair and Frances Moodie. Soon after arriving, we took the cable car to the summit of Table Mountain. Having ascended in comfort, we purchased a trail map and decided to walk down, not appreciating the size of some of the boulders we would have to climb over. The next day, it took a Herculean effort to step up into the tour bus as our extremely sore quads protested – our bodies' revenge for the long climb down! Alastair and Fran entertained us at their farm in Elgin where Alastair showed us around his operation. Typical of the Harvard alumni, when we were in Boston Alastair had been very modest about what he did, simply stating his occupation as an 'apple grower'. Seeing the operation on-site revealed a vastly different story. He employed several thousand workers, providing them with housing, schools and medical facilities, and his operation exported a significant supply of fruit to UK supermarkets.

Then came our first safari at Sabi Sabi, in Kruger National Park. We went on early morning and late evening game drives, seeing the 'big five' game animals – lion, leopard, rhinoceros, elephant, and African buffalo – and experienced a *braai* at night in the middle of the jungle, where a sixty-strong choir serenaded us. Just as we were finishing dinner, news came of a 'kill' and we drove out in the dark to witness a female lion with six or seven cubs eating a kudu. It was surreal sitting in the pitch-blackness of the African night, smelling the blood and hearing the crunch of bones, and the lions a mere few feet away. Elliot, our tracker, reminded us in a whisper from the front seat, 'Whatever you do, don't stand up to take pictures.' Jimmy and Cynthia Nowery were in the seat behind us, and Jimmy, in an equally hushed whisper, replied 'I wouldn't stand up if my arse was on fire,' followed by 'Cynthia, I want to sit in the middle' to which Cynthia replied, 'Jimmy, there is no middle, there is only you and I on this seat!' Lions, apparently, perceive seated passengers as part of the Land Rover's overall bulk, so you are safe. Once you stand up, they see you as separate to the vehicle and a potential meal.

On another evening game drive, we came upon a leopard with a bloated belly sleeping in a tree, having gorged itself on its kill – a kudu balanced high off the ground on an adjacent branch. Vivian and I were the only people in our Land Rover, with another couple in an adjacent Land Rover, as we all marvelled at life in the wild in its rawest form.

Our reunion came to a close with a farewell dinner in The Castle (the oldest building in South Africa), and then Viv and I decided to drive along the Garden Route. We stayed in private homes that took guests, with each host calling forward to our next destination to secure our accommodation. We got as far as Knysna and decided to return to Stellenbosch to visit the vineyards and taste some wonderful South African wines. Our host duly phoned suitable accommodation in the area, but every place she tried was full. After this went on for a while, our host said, 'I know a great place to stay, the Rome Homestead Great House – it is in Somerset West, a little way from Stellenbosch, but you have a car so it should not be a problem.'

We readily agreed and drove to the property and were greeted by the hostess, who asked us where we were from. When we said Cayman, she replied that she and her husband had owned land in Little Cayman and then introduced herself as Margaret Ashwell, saying that her husband, who had passed away, was Harold Ashwell, an architect. I replied that I had known Harold and worked on a project in Jamaica that he designed and owned, called Mona Great House! Margaret was delighted and asked us to join her for dinner to catch up on all things Caribbean. She had also invited two other guests, and as we got chatting, they said they had been on safari in Sabi Sabi, to which we replied, 'So were we!' and told the story of the leopard in the tree with the kudu. It turned out they had been the couple next to us in the second Land Rover! What are the odds? Over dinner, Margaret entertained us with stories: of how she left England with five shillings and a bicycle, sailing on a banana boat to Jamaica; how she played piano in hotels to earn extra money to supplement her teaching income, and how she met and subsequently married Harold. Before we left she presented us with a copy of her life story – titled, fittingly, *Five Shillings and a Bicycle*.

We arrived back in Cayman on 29th March and the following day the Governor entertained everyone involved in the preparation of Vision 2008 at his residence. He was busy preparing for the momentous occasion the next day: the groundbreaking ceremony for the new National Gallery next to the Harquail. At about the same time, the Miss Lassie stamp was released on the first day of Easter as part of Cayfest.

On 14th April CNCF presented *Sitting in Limbo*, a play written by the Jamaican playwrights Dawn Penso and Judith Hepburn, who lived in London, about the murder of Maurice Bishop, the Grenadian Prime Minister in 1983, which led to the subsequent US invasion of Grenada. The play is a two-hander about the imprisonment of Phyllis Coard, a Jamaican and the wife of Bernard Coard, one of Maurice Bishop's Ministers. He, it was claimed, following a challenge to Bishop's leadership, ordered his execution. Her only contact is Nita, her jailer. As the play commences, Phyllis's manner is imperious. She treats Nita more like a maid than a warder, insisting her imprisonment is a mistake which would soon be resolved. But as time passes, Phyllis's confidence erodes and she becomes increasingly reliant on Nita, especially as her health deteriorates. It was an excellent and very powerful play, and especially the way in which the two actors conveyed the evolution of their relationship.

Two weeks later Vivian and I were invited to dinner at their home by Alex Wood, the local Barclays manager, and his wife Jill, in honour of Monty St John who was visiting Cayman with his wife, Maureen. I recall Monty saying she was from Grenada. Before dinner, I found myself in conversation with Maureen and, making the Grenada connection, brought up *Sitting in Limbo*. I commented on how the play stirred sympathy for Phyllis Coard by the end. Maureen replied, 'Sorry for her? She should be shot – she took part in the murder of my brother. I am Maurice Bishop's sister.' Talk about opening your mouth and putting your foot in it. I quickly slipped over to Vivian and said, 'Do not mention the play!'

In early May, at the National Trust's AGM, we were graced with a visit by the new Governor, Peter Smith, accompanied by McKeeva Bush, the Leader of Government Business. During this visit I had to field questions about the National Trust being anti-development, and how I intended to go about using my expertise as a property developer to buttress environmentally sensitive development without destroying Cayman's natural habitat. These questions arose, of course, from the stance the National Trust had taken under my leadership over clearing a vast area of North Sound mangroves to create the new Ritz Carlton golf course! This was followed by the presentation of the Historic Awards at Pedro's Castle.

On 23rd May, Viv and I travelled to Denver to meet with Al Hallock and his family to keep a promise made years earlier: to ski with Al on his seventieth birthday – 24th May 1999, a milestone date when lift passes became free for him. We drove to Chateau d' Mont in Keystone and, the next morning, we headed up to Arapahoe Basin, at a higher elevation than Keystone. Al proudly walked up to the ticket booth, presented his driver's licence to verify his age, and was rewarded with a free lift pass. We then enjoyed a few runs in rather heavy snow, but Al was thrilled – he had made it and was delighted with the newfound economy for an expensive sport. In fact, he was so delighted that he changed his email address to 'ARHskifree'. Sadly, when the 1999–2000 skiing season began that December, the age to qualify for a free pass was raised to seventy-five. No more free skiing for Al, though he kept the email address out of nostalgia! Today, the age limit is eighty for a free pass in Alta, Utah, and so I am hoping to follow in Al's tracks and ski free there myself this December.

The BCQS 30th Anniversary party in Turks and Caicos Islands followed, as well as ongoing meetings on the make-up of our structural engineering business there. The Barclays branch we had refurbished in Providenciales opened, and we established an office in St Thomas to carry out work in the BVI's neighbouring islands. On 4th June we celebrated BCQS's thirtieth anniversary in BVI at The Moorings and the next day flew back to Cayman for Dance Unlimited's performance at the Harquail.

In early June I paid a traditional courtesy visit to His Excellency the Governor Mr Peter Smith, this time in my capacity as Chairman of CNCF, to acquaint him with our work and also to present him with copies of CNCF's publications for his further review. These included copies of plays, poetry and publications, including Miss Lassie's book, all carried in a Caymanian thatched basket, and with an invitation to join us at our productions and to support our work.

The next day, well immunised, Viv and I left for Port au Prince. The lorry drive to Guishard was long and very dusty, and we spent a week there. I joined the men painting and carrying out electrical work and Viv joined the ladies, who taught the young children. Viv and I were privileged to have the luxury of our own separate room, the 'honeymoon suite', as opposed to the bunk bed accommodation that housed everyone else – that said, the tarantulas paid no respect whatsoever to our exalted status. As usual on these trips, Elizabeth Hurlstone (Bobby Nunes's aunt), affectionately known as 'Aunt Libber', led the team. This wonderful lady spoke Creole, and her boundless energy and enthusiasm belied her diminutive size and senior years. The resident nurse, Joan Bain, from Jamaica, likewise put us all to shame with her calm temperament and unselfish commitment to the hard work needed to support this bush community. Since then, the situation in Haiti has become increasingly dangerous. There has been a complete breakdown in the rule of law, with anarchy reigning, and gangs controlling Port au Prince and essential fuel supplies. In spite of this, Joan remains there, working to help the Haitian people she loves.

On 22nd July I travelled to the UK for meetings with Scottie on the Barclays projects and to interview staff for our QS practice, our property management practice, the structural engineering business in Turks & Caicos, and for a new financial controller for our head office in Cayman. I also met with the Department for International Development and the Overseas Estate Department of the British Government, after which Mortimer and I took the Eurostar to Brussels, where we met with representatives from the European Union, who were funding projects in the Caribbean, and with NACO, the airport designers who were working on the Tortola airport. Back in Cayman via New York on 31st July, there followed meetings with Mike Bell on the Heron Harbour development and his bankers, Barclays, as well as work with Mortimer continuing the development of the five-year business plan for the National Trust – the first that had been completed on a formal basis.

3rd October was a sad day, as it was Don Dise's funeral, with a service at North Side United Church. I was honoured to have been asked to deliver a celebration of this extraordinary man's life and his huge contribution to Cayman and, in particular, to the Northside district. I fondly recall referring to an incident involving Don's Rolls Royce, whose vinyl roof had become detached from its frame. Don drove past a trucker on CB radio, who saw the flapping roof and radioed others on his frequency saying, 'Look at that high-dollar vehicle with the detached roof – must be short of money!'

In Cayman, on 25th November, CNCF's Gimistory, the Caymanian festival celebrating the tradition of storytelling as entertainment before the advent of radio and television, was launched at the Crow's Nest and Harquail. Performances took place in districts throughout Cayman until the 27th – it was fabulously entertaining event which cost nothing to attend. That month also saw CNCF's annual awards ceremony, as well as an exhibition of Miss Lassie's work at Kennedy Gallery.

The UBS building on which BCQS had acted as Project Managers and Quantity Surveyors opened in early December. Commercial development was obviously in the air, as Captain Charles confirmed the plans for the Gibbons'-led development of a 40,000 sq ft four-story office building opposite the Kirk Home Centre on Eastern Avenue, which was to become the BritCay building.

Viv and I departed for what had now become our annual skiing trip on 8th December. However, our enquiries about the snowpack in Big Sky had revealed that it was minimal. So, what to do? Somewhere I must have heard that Utah was a great place to ski. Their licence plates certainly feature the slogan 'The Greatest Snow on Earth'. So, we left for Salt Lake City, with absolutely no idea where we were going to stay. Arriving at the Salt Lake City airport we saw a bank of courtesy phones and picked up one that was labelled 'The Cliff Hotel, Snowbird' and booked a room. Then we hired a car and drove up Little Cottonwood Canyon to arrive at a huge hotel. Having been spoilt over the years by superbly generous friends who had lent us apartments in ski areas around the globe, the hotel environment felt strange and impersonal. The following day we set about trying to find a condominium we could rent and revert to our own routine of meals and the relaxed informality of being in our own space.

We ended up renting a condominium in Sugarplum, a small town-house development located between Snowbird, a large very modern resort, and Alta, a picturesque, very European resort with lodges, which had opened in 1939. The condo even had a wood-burning fireplace, which we loved. Exploring the area, we skied at Snowbird and the very posh Deer Valley, where a valet would come to take your skis and store them until the next day! But we spent most of our time in Alta and even managed to overcome the challenge of finding a lunchtime glass of wine in the 'dry' State of Utah. We accomplished this by having lunch in the Alta Lodge, where food had to be ordered prior to ordering anything alcoholic, and the first glass had to be empty before a second was ordered. The super friendly maître d', Mikey even admitted us to the Sitzmark Club as his guest, where we could enjoy après-ski wine upstairs in the lodge.

One day on the Alta ski lift I overheard someone talk about the Mormon Tabernacle Choir Christmas Concert, which I vividly recall seeing on the TV as a child and had thoroughly enjoyed. I asked how one obtained tickets, and was told that they were free, but would have been widely distributed earlier in the year. I was advised there was a very slim chance that tickets might be available if one went to the Tabernacle in Salt Lake City and queued. 'Nothing ventured, nothing gained', so Viv and I drove into Salt Lake City and joined the queue. It certainly didn't look very promising, and after some time I went to one of the trenchcoated ushers and produced from my pocket one of my CNCF Chairman business cards and explained we had come from the Cayman Islands to see the performance! The usher asked me to wait and disappeared for what seemed ages but then returned and asked us to follow him – much to the disgust of the many other hopefuls in the queue. He led us to front row seats in the Tabernacle to witness a genuinely incredible performance of the huge Mormon Tabernacle Choir and Orchestra.

We have returned to Alta and stayed at Sugarplum for my birthday and our wedding anniversary in December almost every year since, so it has become pretty much our second home for winter skiing and we have made friends with many wonderful people there.

Back in Cayman on 19th December, we were joined by Flo and Joe along with René and Claudine Meister to celebrate both Christmas and the New Millenium. The turn of the century had been met with a fair degree of concern, due primarily to our increasing dependence on information technology. Fears of system failures – dubbed the Y2K bug – focused on potential disruption to worldwide infrastructures in computer-driven industries, including tourism, reservations systems, flight scheduling, ticketing and so on. In fact, the issue generated a notable amount of work for our business, as we were engaged in preparing reports on the readiness of building systems such as air conditioning, fire and security alarms, and lighting.

As the New Year was welcomed in, the feared chaos never materialised. Systems seemed unaffected by passing into a year containing three zeroes. We spent part of New Year's Day at David and Chi Chi's house on Melmac Avenue for their traditional party, where we saw people we had not otherwise seen all year. Cayman had certainly changed from the island of ten thousand people that I had first seen thirty-one years before, when everyone waved at you when passing by on the street, taking genuine delight in meeting a new face.

2000

'As we reflect on where we are and look toward what's next, let's remember: "The future depends on what we do in the present."'

Mahatma Gandhi.

During the second week in January, I made a quick trip to the UK for meetings with Rodger Fidgin at Gardiner and Theobold, the London international practice for whom Sanjay had previously worked, to discuss a possible tie up with BCQS. I then returned to Cayman via a quick detour to Verbier to ski for three days with Ray and Michèle. I also stocked up on viande séchée and raclette cheese from La Chaumière on the Rue de Médran. The convenience of skiing in Verbier was, if I caught the early flight out of Geneva to London, I could connect with the Miami flight and be back in Cayman the evening of the same day I had left.

Once home, we were graced by a visit of the Jamaican National Dance Theatre Company at the Harquail Theatre. On this occasion, after her previous dismay at the costumes, the redoubtable Mrs Harquail did not join us!

On the 19th March I was invited to represent CNCF at a dinner for Prince Andrew, who was visiting Grand Cayman, and whom I had seen earlier at Elmslie church where I was an usher when he came to worship. Tables in Government House were set for eight persons with one place set for the Prince, who changed tables at each course. I was able to discuss CNCF's work with him and also ask about assistance he might be able to provide with the work the National Trust was doing. He offered to see what he could do, but I am afraid nothing really materialised from the conversation. Given subsequent revelations perhaps his thoughts were elsewhere.

Meetings took up a good part of my time during the first months of the year. The National Trust met several times to continue discussions about the five-year Business Plan, and there were strategic planning meetings and conference calls with fellow arbitrators over a dispute on the construction of an underwater exploration institute facility in Bermuda. In Antigua, we were working on several projects including an appraisal of Mill Reef Club, the brainchild of the talented and prolific architect Robertson 'Happy' Ward, whom I had the privilege of meeting. Other projects were the costing and project management of Asian Village, a large planned community on the north of the island; a dispute on a house in Jumby Bay, mentioned earlier, together with the preparation of Bills of Quantities for the Prime Minister's office. As a consequence, I met with Asot Michael, Minister of Public Works in the Antigua Government, to research the possibility of setting up an office there.

In Barbados there were meetings with Windy St Agarth and Monty St John to discuss progress on the Barclays Bank refurbishments, and I joined the fourth annual Caribbean Hotel and Tourism Investment Conference attended by some four hundred and thirty-seven delegates from thirty-six countries. This occasion brought together governments, investors, hotel operators, professional advisors, bankers, and everyone involved in the industry in the

Caribbean, and was a very efficient way of networking. Its efficacy might be reflected by the fact that the two most popular sessions were 'Meet the Opportunity' and 'Meet the Money'. The Caribbean Hotel Association had for many years held an annual conference, but prior to the Investment Conference it had been less focussed on the investment aspect of our industry, and more on hospitality supplies and equipment.

On the Mini Warehouse development front, after constructing fifteen buildings, we had now developed almost all the available land at the airport industrial park. However, we had on a long-term lease on some space at the rear part of the land, and this became the site for Building 16, which also became the company's entry into the world of climate-controlled space.

To learn more climate-controlled warehousing, I flew from Barbados to Atlanta to meet up with Otis Blake and his wonderful wife, Nancy, who lived in Griffin just outside of Atlanta. Otis was one of my fellow Harvard Alumni and at that time had been in the building supply business. Perhaps benefiting from what he learnt there, he had sold his building supply business and developed a most successful mini self-storage business. There was an annual convention for self-storage owners being held in Atlanta, and so Mikol Dise and I became Otis and Nancy's house guests and attended the convention to see what we could learn for our operations in Cayman. You will note I have referred to both self-storage and mini warehousing. In the US 'warehousing' implies a legal responsibility for the goods that are stored and hence the term 'self-storage', to ensure that the goods inside the warehouse are the responsibility of the tenant/persons storing the goods and not the owner of the warehouse in which they are stored. We also held a meeting with Mike Bell in downtown Atlanta to discuss the ongoing development of Heron Harbour / Cayman Grand Harbour.

In Cayman, we began exploring the opportunities of expanding our warehouse business to West Bay Road. The Fosters owned a parcel on Canal Point Drive that was vacant and which we had initially looked at to create an office complex, but a two-story climate-controlled warehouse seemed just as feasible, or better. Accordingly, we asked George Serrant to redraw the plans for the office complex into a warehouse facility.

I returned to Cayman and held meetings with Leslie Bigelman, director of the National Gallery, who advised that Andreas Ugland had been appointed Chairman of the board of directors with John Hurlstone as Deputy Chair.

On 27th April, Viv and I left for the UK and picked up Goldie, courtesy of Mathew, at the airport and drove north. We crossed by ferry to Northern Ireland and collected Joe and Flo for a driving trip through Ireland to celebrate

Viv's 54th birthday. We began at Marfield House, a Relais & Châteaux hotel in Wexford to commence our exploration of the southeast of Ireland, then drove on to Glanleam House on Valentia island, which has amazing subtropical plants. It is one of the most westerly points in Ireland, and the eastern terminus of the transatlantic cable. We finally stayed at Coopershill House, in Sligo, which had become a favourite of ours and where we made good friends with the owners Brian and Lindy O'Hara. We then drove back to Joe and Flo's house in Belfast, where we celebrated Viv's birthday. The next day Viv and I drove via the Calais ferry to Ribeauvillé, near Strasbourg, for some wine tasting and then to Metz. Crossing the Austrian border, we were stopped by the police and asked for documents including our car insurance. Although the car was properly insured, the documents we had were out of date, so there was a minor kerfuffle which was solved after we paid a fine for not having the correct ones, and then we were on our way to Vienna.

There, at the State Opera House, we saw a risqué production of the modern opera *Lulu* – the equally risqué story of a femme fatale set at the turn of the 20th century. We were staying in the Schönbrunn Palace Hotel and were able to enjoy a wonderful Mozart performance there. On 16th May we drove to St Wolfgang on Lake Wolfgangsee and discovered a charming guesthouse called Gasthof Hupfmühle, located by the stream feeding a mill and adjacent to the Schafberg Cog Railway. The host made us most welcome and asked Viv what she would like for dinner and Viv replied, 'Trout'. 'Come with me,' says the host and takes Viv to a pond and asks which one she would like. Viv points to one and the host catches it a net and then hits it on the head with a mallet. Fish doesn't come any fresher than that!

The next day we took the cog railway to the summit and walked down back to the hotel – a long seven-hour journey from Schafberg Pitz, negotiating some very steep descents, to a welcome reward of dinner in the romantic hotel 'Im Weissen Rössl', made famous in a UK TV series.

We drove from St Wolfgang to Liechtenstein and on to Mont-sur-Rolle to meet up with Ray and Michèle. There, we enjoyed a wine tasting, wandering through the village with our glass and stopping at various wineries to sample their wares. We left after lunch the next day to drive to Reims to once again enjoy the champagne capital and, of course, taste their wares, and then it was back to London for business meetings.

In July I received the sad news that in October, Wendy Moore (nee Daykin) would be leaving her position as director of the National Trust. Wendy was an outstanding director, who supported me and the board as we steered the Trust toward a sounder business footing and managed changes as we began implementing the first five-year business plan.

22nd July was the day of the memorial service for Richard Delapenha, Cissy's son. Richard had been doing what he loved most, scuba diving, and had gone on a deep dive on the north wall, from which, sadly, he had never returned. A very sad day indeed.

In July, I met with Henry Muttoo to arrange Cayman's team to represent us at Carifesta VII, to be held in St Kitts and Nevis from 17th–27th August. We had arranged for a dance troupe and a play to present Cayman's talent to the wider Caribbean, and for our team to see the standards set by other Caribbean islands. The conversations with our team members were always fruitful, in the sense that they almost always answered, 'Now we know what it means to be Caymanian' when I asked what they had learnt, in particular, from the opportunity to represent their country.

Montserrat was a Department for International Development (DFID) project that we were working on, and in July we were asked for a fee proposal to work on the airport. This was being relocated to the safe zone but, on such a mountainous volcanic island, finding a suitable level parcel of land on which to build it was no mean feat. We had the privilege of working alongside NACO, one of the world's foremost airport designers, who did indeed locate a suitable parcel for its development.

I caught the ferry to Montserrat from Antigua, to determine true and accurate construction costs on this remote island. This was particularly important, because since the destruction of the airport, it could only be accessed by ferry and helicopter service. Once the costs were established, we met with local contractors to discuss both these and potential forms of procurement documentation. There was a degree of tension between the islanders and DFID which had resulted from an initial UK request for islanders to resettle in the UK on payment of a certain sum of money. Islanders had responded that the monies offered were insufficient, and the situation had been exacerbated by the infamous comment by the outspoken Clare Short, Tony Blair's International Development Secretary, that 'They will be wanting golden elephants next.'

This led the islanders to feel that perhaps DFID were not really going to invest the rebuilding money, and DFID obviously needed to see that what they were spending was a reasonable price for what was received. Our costing approach went back to basics: materials costs, what it cost to get materials to the island, what labour costs were, to which were added the contractors' profit and overhead costs. This approach solved the problem, which enabled the rebuild of the essential government buildings and facilities including the

Volcano Observatory, Nursery School, Fire Station, Police Headquarters, and a sheltered housing scheme for the elderly.

During September work continued with meetings of the Wetlands Committee, ably chaired by Atlee Bodden, on which I served as a member. We were attempting to secure the protection of this national asset – key to storm surge protection during a hurricane – which was not being appropriately taken into account in the ongoing development of Cayman – and we were to meet with the Central Planning Authority on 28th November.

In 1984 we had met Gordon Jaynes and his partner Lyle Lawson and over the years we had become very good friends. Gordon, a specialist construction attorney, provided sage and highly experienced advice to me on many topics, and never failed to promote me to his significant circle of professionals within the construction industry and particularly in the area of dispute resolution, including the Dispute Resolution Board Foundation and the London Court of International Arbitration. I became a member of the latter and remain so to this day. Gordon was also one of the advisory board members to the FIDIC Contract, a globally-used standard form of construction contract. Both he and Lyle had travelled to more exotic places than I have probably had breakfasts and were always encouraging Viv and me to visit certain countries before they became spoilt by over-tourism.

A particular favourite of theirs was Bhutan, and so in October 1999 we had commenced researching itineraries, visas and general advice on the country. We came into contact with Marie Brown of Bhutan Travel, based in New York, whom we decided to visit and chat with face-to-face, as we were keen undertake a trek as well as go sightseeing. That November, after making an appointment with her to discuss our trip, Viv and I flew to New York and stayed at The Lotos Club on E 66th Street, one of the oldest literary clubs in the USA, courtesy of our stockbroker George Repper.

By May 2000, we were confirming the final numbers for the Jomolhari trek. Jomolhari is a part of the Himalayas that straddles the border between the Paro district of Bhutan, China and Tibet, and rises to an elevation of 24,035 feet. Our base camp would only be at around 13,000 feet, but we would go over several passes of sixteen thousand feet.

On 26th September we left for our trip to Bhutan. We began in Bangkok, where we checked into the Oriental Hotel located on the Chao Phraya River, followed by an outstanding breakfast by the river and incredible room service. This hotel has some of the best service in the world, as no sooner have you checked in than the doorman at the elevator greets you by your name! A hotel boat took guests to the other side of the river, to the part of the Oriental containing the spa and gym. We explored Bangkok and mastered the water taxi service – many of these had a very long pole-type rudder with an exposed engine that looked like it had been lifted from a car.

We had arranged a cooking course to acquaint ourselves with the finer points of Thai cuisine and left the Oriental by a series of water taxis for an overnight stay at a private homestay. As we ventured deeper into the city's waterways, we transferred from the larger boat into a smaller one, proceeding for some distance along a tributary, and eventually arriving at a flimsy jetty in front of what appeared to be a garage. There, we were met by our hostess, Pip.

In Bangkok, the waterfront land is subdivided into long, narrow parcels, with the waterfront being prime real estate, as it offers the easiest access to transportation and trade. Pip led us through the 'garage' – actually a boatshed – along a pathway past her parent's home, and into her own: a beautiful two-story mahogany Thai house. Our bedroom was upstairs, with a bed mat rolled out on the polished floor.

Once we were settled, our cooking lessons began on the ground floor terrace. My first task was to sit on a low stool with a pointed metal scraper affixed to its front, where I was handed a split coconut and instructed to grate its flesh into a bowl. Whilst I was so engaged, Viv chatted with Pip and asked if she was married. Pip nodded and pointed upward. Viv assumed this meant Pip's husband was asleep upstairs and suggested we speak quietly – not realising that, sadly, Pip's husband had passed away!

We discussed the menus for the meals and their ingredients, and Pip then took us to the local market to see the freshest of fish – many were still alive and jumping in the baskets which held them – and vegetables of every colour and description. Back at her house we began cooking dinner in a large wok on the gas stove. We were short of a few ingredients, so Pip simply hoisted a flag at the riverfront. A few minutes later we heard a bell, went down to the river, and there was a lady in a small boat with the freshest of ingredients so we could successfully complete our meal – which was delicious, even if I say it myself. That evening we had a great sleep on the floor and after breakfast, sad to leave Pip, we took water taxis back to the Oriental. There, we left our 'town' clothes for safekeeping, put on our hiking gear and left for Bhutan.

We flew on Druk Air via Kolkata in West Bengal, India, to Paro. Paro airport, at an elevation of seven thousand three hundred feet, is amongst the highest commercial airports in the world and, due to the strong crosswinds, there are only eight pilots in the world qualified to fly in and out. Tshering, our guide, was there to greet us along with the other four climbers: Reinhard, a German doctor and Jackie, his Canadian wife, and Richard and Stan from

California. We then drove to Thimphu, the capital, and checked into our hotel. Bhutan had been closed to tourists until the 1970s in order to preserve their culture, and even when we visited only a very limited number of visas were being issued. Almost everyone was dressed in traditional costume: a *Gho* for men and a *Kira* for ladies, and the success of the country was measured in a Gross National Happiness index as opposed to GNP. Tshering was wearing his *Gho*, which is a full-length, highly embroidered robe, tied at the waist and bloused out so it is worn knee-length, long sleeves that end in wide white cuffs, and it is worn with knee-length socks and polished shoes. The folds of the robe at the waist are used for carrying all the items one would normally carry in one's pockets. The *Kira*, for ladies, is a full-length embroidered dress and separate top.

We visited many *Dzong*s, or temples, fascinated by their scale and the way the Buddhist religion dominated life in Bhutan. One night, Tshering announced he had a special treat for us: the unfurling of a large religious tapestry, known as a *Thongdrel*, in the Wangdue Phodrang Dzong monastery. We went to bed and were awakened at around 2am and walked to the monastery with Tshering to witness a surreal scene in darkness. Some fires had been lit, and both monks and children were walking around, and then the beautiful *Thongdrel* was unrolled for all to see, accompanied by the chanting of the monks. It was hard to go back to sleep, given the excitement of the evening's activities!

One day, while driving to do some sightseeing, we were directed to pull to the side of the road and, lo and behold, we were passed by a motorcade in which the King of Bhutan was being driven. The four men in our group were somewhat in awe of the King, who happens to be married to three sisters. Now, that could be a lot of trouble!

After visiting various religious sites and hanging our own prayer flags in auspicious locations to protect us, we commenced our Jomolhari trek, walking about twelve to fourteen miles a day carrying only day packs, while Chinese ponies carried the camping equipment we needed. We soon learned to take one warning very seriously: when the ponies were coming up the narrow mountain track, we were to step off the track completely on the uphill side, as the loads the ponies carried were very wide and if we had been on the downhill side of the track we could easily have been knocked over the edge. The porters would race ahead and when we had finished walking for the day, we would round the bend and, just like magic, the camp had been set up, the fires lit and food would be cooking.

The food was excellent for our Caribbean tastes, as chillies feature in Bhutanese cuisine, and can be seen drying on the roof tops of the houses. Viv and I had decided a double sleeping bag would be a good idea, made up by zipping the two single sleeping bags together, inside which would be a nice double sheet sewn into a liner. We tried it the first night, and I almost choked Vivian every time I turned onto my side. That was it for the double bag! On waking, we were served 'bed tea' which was followed by 'wash water' – a small bowl of hot water that one could splash under the arms and on the face and which I used for shaving. Breakfast followed, and then we were back on the trail, walking through absolutely majestic scenery, passing stupas on the way and always walking around them in a clockwise direction in accordance with Buddhist custom. And then would come lunch. Once again we would round a corner and the porters, who had taken down the camp after we started hiking and who had cooked lunch whilst we were having breakfast, had packed it into stackable 'Tiffin' tins which they had carried, ready for us to eat. Likewise for dinner and the camp at night.

On day three we reached Jangothang, the Jomolhari base camp at 12,920 feet. We continued upwards on day four to the ridge north of base camp at 15,280 feet, and on day five to Tshophu lake and Bhonte La, at an elevation of 16,039 feet, which was festooned with Buddhist prayer flags.

The vegetation had changed dramatically as we climbed, with beautiful trees and rivers for the first three days and then barren, rocky scenery as we climbed higher, where of course it also got colder. One evening there was ice on the tent, and I was cold. Viv, however, said she felt not at all chilly, because a yak was lying against the tent canvas on her side and keeping her warm. Never thought I would be replaced by a yak!

After about eight days on the trail, and with only wash water in the mornings to bathe, Tshering announced a treat: we were going to arrive at Sharna Zampa and be able to have a stone bath. We all imagined a large stone bath filled with water we could soak in, but found out the bath was a very large hollowed-out tree trunk by the side of the river, filled with water and in the centre of a small village. Next to the 'bath' was a fire in which large stones were heating. Calipers were then used to lift the hot stones and drop them sizzling into the water – all this activity being watched attentively by the curious villagers. One problem: there was only one bath and six hikers, so we all drew straws to establish the bathing order. I pulled the longest one and was first and Viv was number three, but Jackie, who was number two, chickened out and gave her place to Viv.

At the start of the trek, we discussed what we might take for drinks at dinner, and it was generally agreed that, given the altitude, we would stick to tea. But after the first night, what should mysteriously emerge from the hikers' packs but various brands of flavoured vodka, which was consumed in small quantities after dinner. In Thimpu, before the trek started, Tshering noticed I enjoyed my wine – not an easy libation to find in Bhutan – and we discussed our interest in Carabella and winemaking. I thought nothing more of this conversation until the evening after we had taken our stone bath and were nicely refreshed and cleaned up. Tshering reached inside the folds of his *Gho* and produced a bottle of wine to accompany our dinner! As I said, all necessities are carried in this commodious garment.

At the end of our trek, we came up with a poem which summed up all the day's activities:

> A group of six went out to trek,
> With Tshering our guide to bring us back,
> We hiked by streams, in forests too,
> At one with nature, we could renew.
>
> The first class camp sites had beautiful views,
> So no-one missed the daily news,
> Evening camp fires touched our soul,
> And we finished the evening 'down the hole'.
>
> Sir Richard loved his baby blue,
> Lord Acton wanted to avoid the loo,
> Saint Noodle established a record of eight,
> And 'mazing' Martyn tried not to be late.
>
> We awoke each morn to bed tea,
> Which Norbu presented on bended knee,
> Breakfast of porridge, flakes and eggs,
> Gave us strength – especially in the legs.
>
> Each mountain pass was quite a test,
> But our team of trekkers gave it their best,
> New techniques became the norm,
> And no-one finished at all forlorn.
>
> Jackie and Vivian, life's stories did share,
> They talked on the flat, when not out of air,
> Miss Plum was asked is this the camp of the 'Anns'?
> But all she found was the lens cap of Stan's.
>
> This beautiful country of Bhutan,
> Has captured our hearts like no other can,

> We have wined and dined, laughed and opined,
> And all will return if God is so kind.

We had a final treat in store. This was to visit the Paro Taktsang, 'Tiger's Nest' monastery, perched on the side of a cliff. This is where Buddhism holds that Guru Padma Sambhava brought Buddhism to Bhutan in the eighth century, flying on the back of a tigress to the modern-day location of the monastery, where he meditated for three years, three months, three weeks, three days, and three hours. The majesty of it captured our attention for a long time – but not that long!

After a wonderful twelve days we left Bhutan and flew back to Bangkok and overnighted at the Oriental before leaving for a pre-booked and paid-for trip to Cambodia to visit Angkor Wat. We took the hotel car from the Oriental and were dropped off at the airport where we went to check in. We handed our passports to the airline representative who looked at them and said 'Mrs Bould you can fly but Mr Bould cannot travel'. I asked why not, and was told, 'You do not have a full clean page in your passport for the Cambodian Immigration to insert your visa and if we allow you on the plane we will be fined, and the Cambodian Immigration will send you back to Bangkok.' I asked what I could do, and the airline lady said we could contact the British Embassy but would have to be quick because it was a public holiday in Thailand after 12 noon. I asked if she would call the Embassy, and she readily agreed. I asked the receptionist at the Embassy if I could speak to the Ambassador and was surprised that she connected me. I explained my predicament, and he said, 'Today we are only working a half day.' I thought I might impress him by saying we had done extensive work for the FCO/DFID and knew senior people there, including John Elgie, Peter Griffen and Derek Evans, to which the Ambassador replied 'I don't care if you know Tony Blair, you are not able to get a new passport today', which certainly put me in my place!

So, we slept at the Shangri La – not a patch on the Oriental, which was fully occupied that night, though the next day we had our old room back. On 23rd October we left Bangkok and flew to Chang Mai for a four-night stay at the beautiful Regent Hotel, located in the middle of a working rice plantation and managed by Michael Kemp, a cousin of Irene Garbut from Cayman. We spent four wonderful days there visiting the incredible Sainamphung Orchid Nursery and the working elephant camp at Mae Taman, followed by lunch on a bamboo raft while being poled down the river. Leaving Chang Mai, we returned to Bangkok for a final night in the Oriental and flew back home via Singapore and Los Angeles, which gave us a great opportunity to overnight with Basil and Sammy Behrman.

In Cayman, Gimistory was in full swing. The 25th November was Duppy night at Smiths Cove, and on the evening of 28th November CITN televised the CNCF Arts Awards, where I was both surprised and honoured to receive the CNCF Award for outstanding support for arts in the Cayman Islands.

Late November, I flew to Ottawa to represent CNCF and Cayman at the inaugural meeting of the International Federation of Arts Councils and Cultural Agencies (IFACCA). This wonderful organisation brings together a global network of arts councils, ministries of culture and government cultural agencies from over seventy countries. The presentations and lectures were informative, and the artistic performances were outstanding. Canada clearly wanted to show all of the member countries the very best it had to offer. More importantly, it was eye-opening to be among much larger, more sophisticated and developed cultural institutions, and to see how others had resolved challenges common to us in Cayman. The networking and contacts I made there were invaluable for our work in Cayman. I went on to attend IFACCA summits in Newcastle, Johannesburg, Melbourne, Santiago and Kuala Lumpur. During these visits I strengthened our connections with influential organisations and individuals involved with cultural management on an international scale.

On the National Trust front, Barrie Quappe had joined us as director following Wendy Moore's resignation, and in time for December's Annual General Meeting. A few weeks later, in the new year, we toured all the Trust properties with the new post-AGM board, followed by a ferry trip across the North Sound to René and Claudine's apartment at the Retreat.

Viv and I topped off an exciting and eventful first year of the new Millenium in appropriate style by skiing in Alta, staying at the Sugarplum condominium which by now felt like a second home. We celebrated Christmas lunch with René and Claudine Meister and Gui Passos in Cayman, and this year David and Chi Chi Foster's New Year's Day celebration was held at Pedro's Castle, because by now they had so many friends that their home on Melmac Avenue could no longer hold them all!

2001

'Each moment is fragile and fleeting
The moment of the past cannot be kept, however beautiful
The moment of the present cannot be held, however enjoyable
The moment of the future cannot be caught, however desirable
But the mind is desperate to fix the river in place:

> *Possessed by ideas of the past, preoccupied with images of the future, it overlooks the plain truth of the moment.'* Lao Tzu

As we continued to expand BCQS, travel started early that year. I met with Johnston Construction, based in Turks and Caicos, about projects in St Lucia, and from there travelled to Montserrat to see how Ian Barnard, our man on the ground, was coping being based there, to meet with contractors on the Police Station project, and to look at potential sites for the new airport, about which we had been in conversations with NACO, the Netherlands based airport consultants.

My discussions with Mike Bell continued as he needed assistance with the finance package. He'd had to repay some of the debt, and one solution was to offer a parcel of land in lieu of cash to a contractor to whom he owed money. We were also looking at the development of a Professional Village where businesses could own their own space, as opposed to renting it. This would follow the model we had used successfully in the Genesis building in George Town, and McAlpine Ltd., with whom I had built both Plantana and the Great House, were interested in participating.

After a trip to London for more meetings, I took the opportunity for a three-day ski trip to Verbier. Viv called me while I was there and said we had received an offer on our spec house, Villa Sorrento, which was great news. When I asked Viv for more details about the offer, she said an attorney was willing to place a non-refundable deposit of US $10,000 to secure the property, whilst his feng shui consultant flew to Cayman and inspected the house to ensure it was appropriately compliant. If so, he would purchase the property. After a series of problem tenants who had rented the house while we were trying to sell it, this was truly manna from heaven. I, of course, said 'Absolutely, grab it!' So, the stars were shining down! The sale of Villa Sorrento was finalised in March, when we held a celebratory cocktail party at the house. It was a relief, to say the least.

In February the National Trust launched *Fish Tea*, a children's book of Caymanian tales with historical and environmental themes, at the Savannah Schoolhouse, a property we had restored, and where children took great delight in sitting at the desks to experience what school had been like for their compatriots in bygone days. The book saw a reprint and relaunch some nine years later. On Saturday 24th February, we held an open house to announce the Trust's restoration plans at the site of the Mission House in Bodden Town, initially built in the 1700s, and which had housed Presbyterian missionaries through the late 1800s. It had been donated to the National Trust, and for several years we had been working on a plan to restore it. We had finally received a generous offer from one of Cayman's leading law firms to fund its reconstruction. Sadly – or maybe fortuitously – the reconstruction did not proceed as the house was destroyed by Hurricane Ivan in 2004. But it was rebuilt later using traditional construction methods, again generously funded by the same law firm, and today provides a great insight into Cayman's life in earlier times.

Meetings in late February took me to Tortola, where we were looking at a site to house our own Main Street office building adjacent to where our rented premises were located, and to catch up on the claim we were mediating for the house on Jumby Bay, Antigua. In Turks and Caicos we were also looking for an office site, and in discussions with a firm of attorneys as potential tenants. Mortimer joined me there, continuing to provide his sage advice on our continuing business planning for BCQS and we stayed with Michael Whitelock, who welcomed us to his house with his usual superbly eccentric hospitality. We were also advertising for a new engineer to manage our structural engineering company, as the incumbent manager, Peter Kerrigan, had announced he was leaving. We were subsequently fortunate to interview and secure an excellent replacement, Chris Conway, who I believe still works with the company.

Returning to Cayman on 3rd March, I heard the good news that BCQS PML, our property management company, had secured the management of the Cayman Grand Harbour shopping centre for Mike Bell.

I had been working on an arbitration pertaining to the construction of a stadium in Grenada for a Trinidadian contractor and in early March I flew to Trinidad for the arbitration hearing. In Barbados I met with attorneys about the formation of our company there and then returned to Cayman for National Trust retreats to discuss the implementation of the National Trust Business Plan and meetings with Barrie about the National Trust fund-raising gala which was to take place on 23rd March.

CNCF's Cayfest was in full swing. We were graced by a visit from Rex Nettleford and enjoyed a series of cultural events: we held an art show on 3rd April, the National Gallery joined with us to present a slide show at Pedro's Castle on 5th April, alongside 'Granny Back Yard', and a meeting of the Cayman Maritime Heritage Foundation earlier the same evening. Butterfield, as generous as ever, hosted their own art show in their premises, bringing local art into the business place. A new event, Café Cayman, debuted on 10th April, focusing on local food and drinks as part of our cultural identity.

Later in April, in Providenciales, I dined with Washington Misick – Chief Minister from 1991 to 1995, and a very active realtor and developer. He returned as Premier in 2021, and I had the honour of reconnecting with him at an event at the House of Lords in 2023.

I was back in Cayman on 19th April for National Trust meetings on the five-year business plan and the Mission House renovation. Around the same time, CNCF launched its playwriting competition, introduced to develop local talent by providing tutors for entrants. The winning plays would then be staged at the Harquail. This competition ran for many years, funded through the generosity of Caribbean Utilities Company (CUC).

On 22nd April Viv and I began a long-planned trip to Moscow, where we were met by Derek Evans of the Foreign and Commonwealth Office, who by this time had taken up the role of property managing the estate there. Derek and his wife Dawn hosted us at their apartment, which was located away from the estate, I imagine so Derek could at least have some free time away from the complex he was managing. Moreover, the older architecture of his apartment building induced mental images of cameras and listening devices! We got used to the subway system, which was characterised by very deep access escalators so the stations could be used as shelters in the event of any attack, and managed to decipher the various colours of the lines. We saw Gorky Park and visited the Bolshoi Ballet. To get there, we simply went out into the street where Derek flagged down a passing car. This happened to be driven by an army officer, who drove us to the Bolshoi in return for a fare which Derek negotiated with him. The ballet had several intervals, each accompanied by a glass of champagne and a very varied supply of hors d'oeuvres, after which we enjoyed an excellent dinner. Derek had kindly arranged for us to fly to St Petersburg, which we thoroughly enjoyed. We spent hours in the Hermitage's incredible art collections and went by water taxi to the Grand Peterhof Palace.

We then flew back to London, picked up Goldie, and commenced a four-week tour driving around Europe, with some wonderful stays and gastronomic meals, including Madam Point's La Pyramide in Vienne and Côte Saint-Jacques in Joigny. We stayed with our good friends Alan and Joan Scott, and spent four nights at Torre del Remei, hiking each day in the Serra del Cadi mountain range with packed lunches and an excellent bottle of Spanish wine, and had a great celebration for Viv's 55th birthday. We then drove to Bilbao, where we visited the Guggenheim Museum, designed by Frank Gehry, which I had always wanted to see both for its design and the art it housed. Then we went on to stay at the Château de Curzay and back to the UK via Brittany, where we visited with Pierre Marais at his home, Château de la Seilleraye. This historical monument was built beginning in 1671 and completed in 1730. We had met Pierre in Mustique in 1986, where he was building a home. His task of renovating Seilleraye was significantly greater, and he had established a trade school on site to teach students the technique of replicating the finer points of this Baroque structure, designed by the classical architect François Mansart.

It is around this time that I was introduced to Dottie Rau, a personal trainer. For several years I had been working out at the World Gym in Cayman and, like many others, simply attempted to push or lift as much weight as possible on the Cybex machines, without a lot of thought as to technique. Once I began working out with Dottie, I soon found out that my technique was rubbish, and that when using the correct technique I need only lift half the weight that I had before!

Dottie, in truth, did not like the gym environment and encouraged me to try Pilates to further refine my technique. This, I found, appealed to my engineering mindset, because of the way various muscle groups were identified and isolated. Dottie had also trained and qualified as a master instructor in a programme developed by Igor Burdenko, which combined working out both on land and in the water. The water work requires you to wear a vest to keep you afloat, with the water at chin level while you exercise. The pool exercises use the resistance of the water to provide a workout, totally free of any joint impact that might occur on land. We carried out the water part of the programme in the pool at her apartment complex, which was a little challenging given my height and the depth of Dottie's pool. We had to ensure the water was well topped-up to prevent my feet from hitting the bottom. Igor's programme combines the essential qualities of strength, flexibility, speed, balance, co-ordination and endurance, and his clients include many well-known people including figure skaters Nancy Kerrigan and Paul Wylie, ballet dancer Sarah Lamb and economist Lester Thurow. Over the years, Igor and his beautiful wife Irina and daughter Nellie have become very good friends. To this day I work out almost every day with Dottie, incorporating the Burdenko method.

In late June, the National Trust held a meeting with representatives of Kenneth Dart, a new developer in Cayman, and they presented their plans to develop in a sustainable manner. One of Mr Dart's first investments was to establish a large nursery, which endorsed the claims made at the presentation.

At about the same time we decided the National Trust should host a wine tasting and auction. This provided the opportunity to donate some of Carabella's wines, and we were delighted that Grant Stein, a retired attorney and fellow wine producer, who owned the Piedra winery near Salamanca, Spain which he had started in 1998, followed suit. Given the size of Cayman, it is interesting that there are today probably eight or so vineyard owners in the Cayman

Islands. Other National Trust fundraising events at this time included a five-a-side cricket competition which we held on 7th July, and which attracted a large number of teams providing fast paced action.

In July, I also flew to Miami to have some work done by Wayne Bassett, my dentist, whose practice was in Fort Lauderdale. This involved a forty-five-minute drive from Miami, but Wayne had been my dentist for more than twenty-five years and I was reluctant to change as he was both a good dentist and, given our long association, graciously accommodated me with after-hours and weekend treatment to suit my peripatetic flight and work schedules. Viv and I took the opportunity to hear the Florida Symphony during this trip, then I went on to Montserrat to review progress on our projects. During this visit I was asked, based on my experience with CNCF, about establishing a Cultural Centre there, which was to be funded in part by George Martin, the record producer, who had a recording studio on the island where Elton John, the Rolling Stones and the Beatles had all recorded.

In Barbados, I had Barclays meetings and also met with John Murphy to visit the Elegant Hotels chain that he was managing. We stopped at each hotel to view rooms, food and beverage operations, and plans for various changes involving construction. As is so often the case, life came full circle when Marriott, who had purchased the Elegant Hotels chain in 2019, appointed us to manage their refurbishment in 2022–2023.

Vivian had grown to relish living in Villa Sorrento, particularly the garden, which she loved, and had asked me to promise we would build a new home after it had been sold. So said, so done, even though I had sworn I would never leave the beach front location we had at Plantana where, while shaving in the morning, I could gaze out from our bathroom window and see Seven Mile Beach stretching both to the north and south.

We began looking at other sites in the Cayman Islands Yacht Club and found one on Las Brisas Drive, for which Ed Haladay developed various plans, none of which we particularly liked. We were also talking with Gil Freytag, the developer of Vista del Mar, a subdivision within the CIYC. He owned several lots in the CIYC but outside the gates of Vista del Mar. Gil looked at the Las Brisas lot with us, then showed us two adjacent waterfront lots overlooking the canal adjacent to the Vista del Mar entrance. He generously offered us both lots for the same price as the single Las Brisas lot. We snapped up this offer and began thinking about the home we would build there. We commenced discussions with architect John Doak about possibly designing it, and how a 'pavilion' style house like Villa Sorrento would be laid out on our two new lots.

It was now late July, and Cathy Delapenha was getting married and called me to ask if I would propose a toast to the bride's parents. I was honoured and delighted, and Viv and I flew to Mobay, hired a car and drove to Jake's Hotel at Treasure Beach where the wedding was to take place. Jake's was a magical and eclectic hotel that had formerly been the home of Jake's mother's parents, now reimagined as a private getaway in St Elizabeth on Jamaica's south coast. Sally Hensel, Jake's mother, was married to Perry Hensel who produced the 1972 cult film classic *The Harder They Come*, starring Jimmy Cliff. Cathy's wedding was on 28th July and a large contingent from Cayman were in attendance for the ceremony and the party which followed.

In mid-August I flew to Providenciales for meetings about the new management of Civil and Structural Engineering, with architect Jeff Lee about several new projects that were on the boards, and about potential work for BCQS. In Cayman, I also met with Jim Lammers from the Dart organisation and discussed the services BCQS could provide for their development, which was to be considered by the Central Planning Authority on 26th September.

Viv and I then left for Belfast, where a party to celebrate Joe and Flo's sixtieth wedding anniversary was taking place on 27th August. Afterwards, we all drove to Ballinamore to collect a 40-foot-long barge from the Riversdale Marina we had chartered for a few days to cruise on the Shannon River. The pace of travel on the barge, which moved at a speed slightly slower than a walking pace, was a wonderful change to the fast-paced life of flying around the world on business and a great time was had by all.

Dave and Denise Scott soon came to stay with us in Cayman, and I vividly recall Dave arriving at a solution to a staircase issue with one of the designs of the new Callaloo house while sitting at our dining table.

This was also the time when we first heard of the merger of Barclays with CIBC to form First Caribbean International Bank (FCIB), which was of interest given that both banks had been significant clients of ours over many years.

On 27th September we held the reception for the launch of CNCF's culture magazine *Foundation*, which had as its stated purpose:

> This magazine is but one more instrument in the crusade by Cayman's cultural organisations to establish a cultural voice for Caymanians.
> It is a response to the repeated cries, particularly by concerned Caymanians, privately as well as in the media, that their society is becoming unrecognizable to them; and that the cultural heritage and value systems upon which their society was founded is fast eroding.

The first volume contained a wealth of articles about Cayman and its cultural recognition under the guidance of CNCF. This was then followed by a CNCF Retreat on the 29th and 30th September to plan the coming activities and direction for 2002.

On my work front, the seminars which CCAS had been presenting across the Caribbean had heightened general awareness of the need for professional advice in dealing with contractual issues. As a result, Jerry and I were working on a series of complex assignments for contractors, architects, governments and utility suppliers across the Caribbean region. These included a hotel project in Tobago for my good friend and architect Steve Mendes of Design Collaborative, whom I had first met back in Jamaica in 1972 and who was now based in his home island of Trinidad. Steve had a wonderful habit of calling up and saying he had a quick question about a contractual matter and about an hour later we would still be on the telephone discussing it! We were also working on a large construction claim for one of Barbados's leading contractors over a dispute about repaving Grantley Adams airport.

During the first week of October, Jerry and I flew to Puerto Rico for meetings in connection with CCAS's advisory services and on to Tortola for similar meetings, and then on to Antigua for meetings dealing with the Jumby Bay house dispute. Barbados was next, for meetings about BCQS's registration with the Caribbean Development Bank so that we would be able to bid on projects they were funding, at which time we also provided them with CCAS's advisory portfolio.

Whilst on the road, Jerry and I would have a pretty hectic time identifying possible clients. Typically, we would pick up the Yellow Pages from our hotel room, yours truly would drive (Jerry, by his own admission, is a terrible driver) and Jerry would be on the telephone, cold-calling contractors, architects, engineers, and government departments with whom we could meet. Jerry's tenacity frequently managed to secure us appointments at very short notice. After a long day of such activity, we always treated ourselves to a fine dinner and wine, and whilst in Barbados we booked at the newly renovated Villa Nova Hotel for dinner. The hotel had once been the Caribbean home of Sir Anthony Eden, the British Prime Minister, and had seen guests like Sir Winston Churchill, Her Majesty Queen Elizabeth II, Noel Coward, and Tony Blair.

At the end of October, Tim Raath arrived in Cayman, and on 1st November we held the first ever opera at the Harquail Theatre. The 23rd November brought dance to the Harquail, when Jackie Balls presented an annual smorgasbord of dance form, featuring performances by her dance school, covering all the age groups that she taught. Each year, the greatest delight was Tiny Tots – the youngest dancers on a large stage for the first time. Each took their cue from the child beside them, who would hopefully be making the right move. Jackie's school provided so many children in Cayman with their start in dance, which has led to today's plethora of talented dancers.

The 24th saw the first day of Gimistory, with Sir Colville Young, Governor General of Belize, headlining the event. He had developed his interest in Caribbean linguistics at the Mona Campus of the University of the West Indies and was himself a multi-talented educator, poet and musician, who had introduced the steel pan into Belize schools.

In November there was also a National Gallery Exhibition at DJ's, a popular eatery in Coconut Place, as we wanted to spread the word about art in both the work and entertainment spaces on the island. To ensure perspective on a broad scale at the National Gallery, from time to time we would bring in exhibitions of foreign artists and, in this vein, we opened a Keith Haring show at the Gallery on 3rd December. Keith Haring, who died in 1990, was an American artist whose pop art emerged from the New York City graffiti subculture of the 1980s. His animated imagery has 'become a widely recognized visual language'.

On 6th December we held the CNCF Awards ceremony, and the next day Viv and I flew to Salt Lake City for our annual Alta ski fix, to celebrate my birthday, and enjoy the Mormon Tabernacle Christmas Show at the Convention Centre in downtown Salt Lake City. We attended the Telluride Mountain Film Festival, which was on tour, and marvelled at some of the footage. It was hard to imagine how, for example, fish cleaning a hippo's teeth had been filmed or, for that matter, the front hooves of a Kudu running in front of tribesmen chasing it.

The ski days gave us time to think about our new house in CIYC, and we sat down in the evenings and mapped out exactly how we lived and used which rooms, and when we used them. We did not want a residence with 'trophy rooms' that were rarely used. We developed these ideas into a written brief, and I then drew out floor plans to see how the house interconnected. We finished up with a house that had a main building with the master bedroom, with his and hers bathrooms, and four cottages, one for guests, one as a gym, one for staff and one garage – a 6,500 sq ft home with a one-bedroom main house! We then faxed the brief to John Doak to use when developing the design but did not send him the plan I had sketched out. It was interesting that the plan John developed from the brief was almost identical to the one I had drawn. The house was to be called Callaloo – we retrieved the name from its reincarnation as Villa Sorrento. Callaloo as a house name always amuses our good friend Jimmy Nowery. Once I had described Callaloo as a spinach-like plant, at which he thought for a second and then said, 'You mean like Poke Salad?' This is a Southern dish made using the invasive pokeweed. 'Why on earth would you want to call your house after a weed?'

2002

I have always claimed that in life there are players and spectators. Theodore Roosevelt stated this far more eloquently:

> *'It is not the critic who counts, nor the man who points out how the strong man stumbled or where the doer of deeds could have done them better. The credit belongs to the man who is actually in the arena, whose face is marred by dust and sweat and blood, who strives valiantly, who errs and comes up short again and again, who knows the great enthusiasm, the great devotion and spends himself in a worthy cause, who at the best knows in the end the triumph of high achievement and who at worst, if he fails while daring greatly, so that his place shall never be with those cold and timid souls who knew neither victory nor defeat.'*

In mid-January Viv and I met with John Doak and reviewed his progress with the plans for Callaloo, for which he had developed a 'mood book'. This was very useful, because it allowed us to see not only the technical plans but also thoughts as to finishes, furniture, landscaping, and so on.

The 16th January was a significant day, as we held a meeting at Pedro's Castle for a discussion on the development of a National Cultural Policy. A very large and enthusiastic crowd had gathered to exchange ideas about where we had come from in Cayman and where we intended to go. It's worth noting that despite the enthusiasm expressed in 2002, it took more than fifteen years for such a policy to be published – again, talk about an elephantine gestation period!

The next day I met with John Papesh, Bob Dart and Jim Lammers to discuss their proposed development of eighty-five acres behind Galleria Plaza – now developed as Camana Bay. On the 20th I flew to Provo and then on to Tortola for meetings, followed by a visit to Montserrat to see progress on the buildings we were managing there, and back to Cayman after a few days. There, the Governor, Peter Smith, had kindly permitted the National Gallery to use the grounds at Government House for what was to become an annual event known as 'Art at Governors', drawing both visual artists, thatch exponents, practitioners of traditional cuisine and all things Caymanian.

In February, I met Jerry in Puerto Rico, as we were making a marketing swing for CCAS through the Caribbean, visiting St Kitts, Antigua, St Lucia and Trinidad. I recall one day vividly, as we had a meeting with Trinidad Contractors, one of our clients in San Fernando in the south of the island, followed by a meeting back in Port of Spain with the Solicitor General. I should explain that Jerry was always immaculately dressed, with a white monogrammed shirt, double cuffs with gold cufflinks, neatly knotted tie, and blazer with the requisite top pocket kerchief. Following our meeting with Trinidad Contractors, we left their offices through pouring rain. Jerry said he was starving because breakfast had been a long time ago, and we also needed gas, so I pulled into a gas station beside which was a roti shop. Perfect! I said we would fill up and then stop to get a roti and eat it on the way, because time was short to get back to the meeting in Port of Spain with the Solicitor General.

We walked into the roti shop and perused the offerings on the chalk board. Jerry spied a 'buss up shut' and asked what it was. I said, 'Jerry, you don't want that; it is very liquid inside the folded roti wrapper.' However, Jerry insisted, and we carried our meal back to the car and started driving. Jerry took a ravenous bite of his roti, and, of course, the curry sauce shot out all over his white shirt! Try as he might, he could not remove the yellow stain. We arrived just in time for our meeting and the charming lady Solicitor General immediately spotted Jerry's dilemma and said, 'I can see you have really become immersed in our Trini culture!' It was a great icebreaker and I believe it led to a number of government contracts we were to work on subsequently.

By 2002 we had definitely outgrown the space for the National Gallery at Alexandria Place and on 21st March we celebrated the opening of the National Gallery at its new premises at Harbour Place, thanks to the generosity of Andreas Ugland and Naul Bodden. We subsequently opened with a show by Al Ebanks on 25th April.

Two days later, on 23rd March, we celebrated the joyful wedding of Nancy Kirkaldy – formerly a secretary with BCQS – and Ian Barnard, who as you will recall was our man on the ground for the Montserrat rebuild projects. I think there may have been a few trysts in Antigua that flew under the radar of the Cayman office!

Viv and I flew to Kingston on 5th April to once again climb Blue Mountain peak with Alan Foster, although this time we were much better organised and completed the climb in three and a half hours for the ascent and the same time for the descent, and without drifting into the coffee fields to read threats of being shot for trespassing!

Later that month CNCF were approached to move Sunbeam Thompson's house on North Church Street, as a development was planned for the site. This was a traditionally built Caymanian house, which we were able to support on large steel beams and jack up onto a trailer to move it to the CNCF Cultural Centre. As the house moved along Seven Mile Beach, we had to walk in front to ensure that all power lines were lifted to make the passage of the moving house safe. We were excited by being able to save this house and followed the move with a lunch with Mrs Harquail on 20th April at the Thai Orchid restaurant. There, Mrs Harquail, a passionate gardener herself, gave Viv, the ever-keen gardener, a Neem tree in a pot, promising this would ward off mosquitoes. We have the tree at our home Callaloo today, along with a wonderful Naseberry tree that Mrs Harquail also gave us. Of course, these are now very large, mature trees. As the Greek playwright Aeschylus said, 'from a small seed a mighty trunk may grow.'

Jerry and I flew to Port of Spain, Trinidad in June to present a CCAS seminar, 'Caribbean Construction Claims – Suffer Not,' for the Joint Consultative Committee for the construction industry in Trinidad and Tobago. The seminar dealt with to how to avoid construction claims, which cost the construction industry vast amounts of money each year, and the eighty attendees included attorneys, contractors, sub-contractors, quantity surveyors, architects, engineers and government employees. They listened to talks covering the general background of the construction process and how claims arise, the legal implications of various forms of procurement, scheduling, performance-related issues, construction and disputes, including the importance of thorough record-keeping to link cause and effect. The attendees rated the seminar as excellent and asked for a repeat in the near future. Leaving Trinidad on 25th June, Jerry and I travelled to Barbados, Grenada, St Thomas and Tortola to promote CCAS and our services.

I was back in Tortola in July for meetings with Sheila George, our attorney there, in particular to finalise the removal of the protective clauses of the B-class shares of BCQS Ltd., the majority of which I owned. (When BCQS Limited had been formed, two classes of shares were created: A and B. Both shared dividend rights equally, except the B-class shares had approval rights to increase salaries or to change the company's place of business.) Board meetings followed, and a BCQS celebration party with our clients, as our office there was expanding rapidly.

Back in Cayman, on 24th July I met with His Excellency Bruce Dunwiddy, the new Governor, at his office to welcome him on behalf of CNCF and to present him with a 'gift basket' of CNCF publications to introduce him to our work and to seek his support. He was genuinely interested in our work and spent much longer asking questions than usually was the case. I saw him looking at my CNCF business card and he then said, 'Bould', that is an unusual spelling of that name, and I now recall my brother Charles wife, Sylvia's, maiden name was Bould. You wouldn't have any connection to a family of that name that came from Bristol?' I replied that my father's youngest brother Cyril had worked at the Long Ashton research station near Bristol and was a specialist in growing coffee. I said I had a cousin called Sylvia, who I'd not seen since I was fifteen. It was an amazing coincidence that my uncle Cyril had spent time in Kenya advising on the cultivation of coffee, and that is where Charles had met Sylvia.

Issue #2 of CNCF's *Foundation* magazine was published in August and again featured a wide-ranging perspective highlighting the richness and variety of our Caymanian Culture. It contained articles on Pedro St James, thatch plaiting styles, Radley Gourzong's music, Bendel Hyde's art, Leonard Dilbert's poetry, and other key commentary on who we are as Caymanians.

On 14th August, Tim Hepburn, who had joined us as manager of BCQS Property Management, announced he wanted to return to the UK and set up a business called BCQS Hepburn, as property managers there. Viv and I became their first client when we appointed them to manage our home in Queen's Gate Mews. In the event he did not stay long, deciding in 2003 that England was not so great after all, and we were delighted to have him back to continue his great work with us in Cayman.

The 17th August saw the National Trust cricket competition during the day, followed by the McCoy prize exhibition at the museum. This had been established by the McCoy family from Northside, with the aim of encouraging and rewarding excellence in Caymanian art. The family, represented by Harris McCoy, stated that they felt more should be done to encourage exhibitions of Caymanian-made things by Caymanian artists and, although there had been a standard of excellence in the past, it was felt that a cash prize and also money for further education would encourage all Caymanians to strive for that same excellence in the art and craftwork being produced today. The exhibition was a huge success and endorsed the fact that it is Caymanian artists who are the transmitters of our culture, and they must therefore be supported in every way possible.

The next day I flew to London for many meetings: with Gibb, to discuss the airport expansion of Norman Manley International Airport in Kingston, Jamaica; with Dave Scott about the Barclays projects, and also with Guy

Rockingham, who represented George Martin, on the proposed Cultural Centre in Montserrat. I also met with Chris Conway, who was set to join Civil and Structural Engineering in Turks and Caicos, before returning to Cayman on 27th August, where plans for the renovation of the Mission House for the National Trust continued and where Theresa Broderick was joining us as the Trust's Director after Barrie Quappe's resignation earlier in the year.

On 30th August, Vivian and I left for Kingston to attend the wedding of Saffron, Alan and Jenny Foster's daughter, to Lauren, held in Irish Town at a beautiful setting high in the foothills of Blue Mountain, after which I used the opportunity to meet with the Gibb representatives on the NMIA airport expansion.

Mid-September we held a two-day CNCF retreat to review what we had achieved, how we could continue to improve on the programmes we were presenting, and in what other key ways we could continue to preserve our Caymanian heritage and develop our Caymanian culture.

At the end of the month I flew to Port of Spain and met with Russell Sampath at Damus in San Fernando. Damus, founded in 1973, is the largest infrastructure contractor to the oil and gas industry in Trinidad and the Caribbean and they wanted CCAS to present a claims seminar to their senior management team. This we readily agreed to do and then returned to Cayman on 3rd October. We had by now incorporated BCQS in St Lucia, and Sanjay was following up with our registration with Caribbean Development Bank to ensure our ability to bid on any projects that required financing.

The next day, Viv and I left for Portland, Oregon to hike Mount Hood, on what is known as Boy Scouts Ridge. That provided a three and a half hour workout with an altitude gain of 1,800 feet – yes, Basil's pesky ski watch also doubled as a climbing watch and measured altitude gained as well as feet descended. On 9th October we were in the Carabella vineyard at 6am to assist with the vendage.

A large square bin was set up alongside a 4ft × 4ft plywood sorting table braced on legs. The grape pickers used five-gallon 'mud buckets' into which they cut the mature bunches of grapes, then carried the full buckets to the sorting table where we waited to spread out the grapes, toss out any affected by 'royal rot', then push the good grapes into the adjacent bin. Each picker was given a token to confirm their delivery of every full bucket. Initially, the pace was slow but soon speeded up as pickers began dumping grapes onto our sorting table as fast as they could. For them it was a backbreaking task, as the grapes hung low on the vines. For us, it wasn't long before our arms were sticky with grape juice, and we were plagued by yellow jacket wasps drawn to the sweetness. After our shift, our winemaker, Mike, rewarded us with a bottle of wine and treated us to lunch!

The process of deciding when to harvest is interesting, as it depends on when the sugar level measured in degrees 'brix' has reached the correct level. If it's too low, the wine will be low in alcohol and high in acidity; too high, the wine becomes too alcoholic and thereby loses its flavour. This balance is managed during the growing season by the quantity of grapes we cut off or 'drop' to thin the crop during the growing season.

Once picked and sorted, the grapes are taken to the winery for de-stemming and then crushing in a large vat. As the grapes ferment, they begin to expand and rise to the top of the liquid and have to be 'punched down'. The new wine is then put into barrels to mature. Our Pinot Noir is aged in oak barrels for two years before we taste, and then blend, the six varietals we grow to achieve the right balance of fruit and tannin, then bottle the wine for consumption. We also produce Chardonnay and Pinot Gris as our white wines.

Back in Cayman, we were working on the bid to be selected as the project managers for FCIB to rationalise all their properties throughout the Caribbean following the merger of Barclays and CIBC. I am delighted to say we eventually won the assignment, beating out stiff competition from both regional and global competitors.

Joe, Viv's dad, passed away on 20th October. He had been in an assisted living facility for about a year, but nevertheless it was a huge shock to us. Two days later I heard my godmother and aunt, Jessie Bould, had also died at the age of 89, as well as another aunt, Doris, at exactly the same age. Viv and I left for London on 23rd October and then for Belfast to be with Flo and attend Joe's funeral on 28th October. It was, of course, a very sad occasion, but we gave Joe a good send-off at his wake, as he would have wanted, and Viv and I walked along the Lagan tow path close to their home to reflect on Joe's life and the wonderful and colourful character he had been. Viv stayed on in Belfast and I returned to Cayman via London on 29th October for CNCF and National Trust meetings. Only back for a few days, I flew to Trinidad with Jerry to present the CCAS in-house seminar to Damus.

21st November was the National Trust AGM, bringing my four-year term as Chairman to an end. I feel we had accomplished a lot during this period, carrying out its mandate to preserve the history and biodiversity of the Cayman Islands and working to protect environmentally sensitive and historically significant sites through education and conservation across all three Cayman Islands.

The next day, Viv and I flew to Miami, where we had been invited to an art exhibition of Lisa Remony's work at the Dharma Studio on Commodore Plaza in Coconut Grove, close to our apartment in Yacht Harbour. We arrived and were walking around, admiring Lisa's work, when I felt a tap on my shoulder, and it was John and Val Ambrose who we had not seen for years. By coincidence we had been discussing commissioning a bust of Mr Harquail with Mrs Harquail and were looking for a sculptor. Lo and behold – here was Val Ambrose, a highly talented sculptress. I discussed a possible commission with Val, who invited us to their home in Pembroke Pines to discuss the details. She gave me directions and said we could not miss their house, which was at the end of the road and would have a statue of a man at one and a half times life size sitting in the garage. It was a statue of Sir Philip Sherlock, the vice chancellor of the University of the West Indies, who had died a few years earlier. Val had been commissioned to sculpt a statute of him to be placed at UWI in Jamaica. We discussed the commission of Mr Harquail's bust over dinner, and then Val came to Cayman to meet with Mrs Harquail, looked at photos of him and completed the sculpture. The bust was placed in the lobby of the theatre that bears his name. It remained there for a number of years until one evening, when Mrs Harquail was in the theatre, she saw someone place a drink on Mr Harquail's head. The next day the bust was gone. It was not until after Mrs Harquail's death, that I tracked down its whereabouts from the Executors of Mrs Harquail's Estate, and found it covered in dust in a warehouse. I placed it in the back of my car (with some significant effort as it was very heavy) and carried it back to the theatre and had it reinstalled in its rightful place in the lobby, where it sits to this day.

On 28th November, Jackie Balls would be putting on one of her wonderful dance performances and I was delighted to be asked to write the foreword for the programme. The next evening *The Cayman Triangle* movie was showing at the Grand Pavilion complex on West Bay Road, but before attending that event, Mrs Harquail summoned me to meet her at the Harquail Theatre, where she complained about our CNCF groundsman who lived on the property. He had grown bananas and corn and was raising chickens. 'He has turned the grounds of the theatre into a Jamaican farm house!' She was understandably upset, and I did the best to explain that his garden and fowl would be contained, but that we needed the security of someone living on-site.

On 6th December, Viv and I left for our annual ski pilgrimage to Alta. We stayed at Sugarplum G, as usual, which had the cheery wood burning fireplace in the living room, which we enjoyed every day. We reacquainted ourselves with our favourite lunch places, including the Rustler and, of course, the Alta

Lodge. Several of the guests at Alta Lodge were real characters, some of whom had probably skied there since it opened its doors for guests in 1940. One gentleman wore a stylish cravat and took one run before lunch, then stayed in for tea and cakes in front of the fireplace all afternoon. Another guest, Ruth Altman, whose family had invented the sewing machine that made the expanding spandex material that was popular for ski pants, also took only one run every day and then retired to her room to paint. Ruth would be in residence for a month or more, and during that time would paint mountain scenes and then hold a party in her room and sell the paintings to guests staying in the hotel, to assist in paying her tab. We were lucky enough to obtain tickets for the Mormon Tabernacle Choir Christmas performance with journalist Walter Cronkite as the featured headliner.

During 2001, I had had many meetings with the other shareholders about sale of my BCQS shares and about how BCQS would be run afterwards. 2002 had also been a busy year in that regard, with a lot of travel and business planning for BCQS and changes in the shareholding. These required the agreement of an equitable price for those shares, as well as additions to the board of directors. We discussed the new company structure and value, and how I would sell the balance of my shares in the company, over what period of time, and each director's other interests. On 17th December I had a meeting with my fellow directors in BCQS, and they announced that they wanted to acquire all of my shares, as by this time they felt they could run the company as well as I could. It took some time to finalise details, but we eventually came to an agreement, and so, after thirty-three years in one role, I had a totally open book about what to do next.

CHAPTER EIGHT

Global Ambitions, Island Roots (2003–2007)

2003

'If you change the way you look at things, the things you look at change.' Wayne Dyer

The year 2003 marked a significant milestone for Cayman, as it was the 500th anniversary of the year Christopher Columbus sighted Cayman Brac and Little Cayman, naming them Las Tortugas, presumably for the many turtles in the water. A series of quincentennial events celebrated this significant marker in Cayman's history.

At the end of January 2003, I stepped down as Chairman and Director of BCQS. The Building Confidence Newsletter noted that: 'Martyn had founded the company in 1969 and was instrumental in the company's geographical expansion into the Turks and Caicos Islands during the eighties and the British Virgin Islands in the mid-nineties. Martyn will be spending his time concentrating his efforts on his other business interests and will remain resident in Grand Cayman.'

I briefly considered attending Law School and consulted with Bobby Nunes, who advised that my skills were better suited to entrepreneurship than to the structured practice of advising others on the law. Upon reflection, I found myself more drawn to the idea of further developing Caribbean Construction Advisory Services (CCAS) with Jerry, and also to the growing opportunities of our warehouse business, which maintained close to 100 per cent occupancy. We also saw potential in the climate-controlled storage market, which we had not yet explored for our Airport Industrial location. And there was promise in expanding to the West Bay Road area, near the Greenery, where a multitude of condominiums created a demand for conveniently located storage space.

Viv and I flew to Las Vegas that month for the National Association of Homebuilders Conference, where we wanted to see the displays of the very latest materials on offer that we might want to use in the construction of

Callaloo. We had an amusing exchange with a shopkeeper along the route from our hotel to the conference centre, where there was another hotel displaying a live-action stage set for *Pirates of the Caribbean* in which cannons were set off and pirates swung through the rigging of galleons on a lake several times a day. We asked the shopkeeper opposite if he didn't get bored seeing the same show over and over again, to which he replied, 'Oh no, sir, last week the sails of the galleon accidentally caught on fire and the pirates had to jump into the lake to cool off.' We returned from Las Vegas on 24th January in time for Art at Governors, which the National Gallery was now presenting on an annual basis.

In January we heard that Joan Bain, the nurse from Ministries in Action in Haiti, had cancer and would require six months of chemotherapy in Jamaica. We called to see if we could assist with anything she needed, and I'm glad to say she recovered fully and is back in Haiti, married to a Haitian, and still running the clinic there despite the ever-increasing hardships and natural disasters that plague that country.

At CNCF, February saw us in discussions with Donna Myrie about Batabano, Cayman's annual street parade carnival that had initially been launched by the Rotary Club in 1983. Some say the festival was named after the tracks left in the sand by turtles coming onshore to lay their eggs. Also that month, and in significant contrast, CNCF hosted the performance of the Welsh Choir at the Harquail, demonstrating the diverse cultural influences from the hundred-plus different nationalities living in Cayman. In February we were also continuing our discussions with Steve and David Foster about the West Bay Road climate-controlled storage facility on Canal Point Drive, while for Cayman Grand Harbour I was looking at boat storage with Mike Bell. To that end I flew to Miami and then drove up to Jacksonville, and then to Marco Island and Pelican Bay to examine the details of the Naples Bay Yacht Storage facility to use when designing a similar facility in Grand Cayman.

Switching the subject from boats to cars, I had become intrigued by the new Smart car, and had looked at one during a visit to the UK. In Cayman, Andreas Ugland – a car aficionado – had one, which I had seen him driving in the Yacht Club. He agreed to let me take a test drive, and I was delighted with this wonderfully engineered vehicle. I would go on to buy one from the Smart dealer in Mayfair, using my credit card to pay for it after a fine lunch.

In early March Viv and I travelled to Aspen to ski with Jimmy and Cynthia Nowery, staying with them at their apartment on East Cooper just steps from the gondola, and complete with underground parking which was at a premium in Aspen. The Nowerys have been very close friends for many years and their hospitality extends to collecting us from the airport, lending us a car, accommodating us and, as Jimmy is fond of saying, it is a super-inclusive service – we have now stayed with them so often that Jimmy is threatening to place a brass plaque on the door to the bedroom we stay in, announcing it as the 'Bould Suite'. We skied in Aspen and also in nearby Steamboat, accomplishing some 150,000 vertical feet in eight days.

When we flew back, Viv went on to Cayman from Miami while I continued to Port of Spain for meetings with Jerry and then up to Barbados, where he was advising the contractor on various issues on the construction of the Barbados Hilton. From there we went to St Lucia, where we were talking with contractors, the government, and Carilec, the regional electricity organisation, about presenting a CCAS seminar. From St Lucia Jerry and I travelled to Grenada, meeting similar groups of potential clients, and back to Cayman.

On 3rd April Viv and I flew to London to take Flo back to UK, as she had been staying with us since January and wanted to return home to Belfast. I had meetings in London on business planning with Mortimer at his favourite abode, the Institute of Directors on Pall Mall, and made final shipping arrangements with John Walsh at Smart Mayfair to ship my new Smart car out to Cayman.

Viv and I had by now become totally enamoured of Igor Burdenko's programme and so we arranged to visit him in Boston, for a one-on-one week with him in April and get his feedback on how we were progressing. As time went by, this became an annual occurrence. I would work for an hour with Igor and Viv would take a video of the workout, then I would return the favour for Viv's one hour workout. We would take these videos back to Cayman and Dottie would view them and make a spreadsheet with the exercise, the equipment required, and cues as to correct form. The exercises would be specifically focussed when we had some form of injury to, say, our knees or back, and we both firmly believe that such exercises have kept us away from the surgeon's knife to this day, when so many of our friends are having knee and hip replacements.

We returned to Cayman from London on 29th April, just in time to have lunch with Derek Walcott and discuss his presentation the next day. Derek was a Nobel Laureate in Literature, and one of his most celebrated works was *Omeros*, which resets the Trojan war as a fight between Caribbean fishermen. He mesmerised the Harquail audience, reciting pieces from it and kindly answering questions about this and his other works. As with so many other Caribbean luminaries I have had the privilege of meeting, I was introduced to Derek by Henry Muttoo, CNCF's wonderful Artistic Director. I remain eternally grateful to him for his knowledge of West Indian culture and for graciously introducing me, over the past thirty-plus years, to an extraordinary array of the region's finest poets, authors, painters, storytellers and cultural icons – each of whom has enriched my life beyond measure.

Viv and I travelled to Havana at the beginning of May to represent CNCF at a photographic exhibition called 'Dos Visiones' which opened at Fototeca de Cuba on 7th May and ran to 3rd June before moving to Cayman at the National Gallery from 4th–28th June and then on to Santiago de Cuba and London. The Honourable Roy Bodden, Minister of Education, Human Resources and Culture, represented the Cayman Islands Government at the opening of this fascinating photographic examination of life in these two historically closely-linked countries described in the opening brochure as follows:

> Entitled Dos Visiones or Two Visions, this exhibition featured the work of photographers Patrick Broderick and Roberto Salas – both challenged to learn about and document each other's respective homelands through a series of black and white photographs. Sharing a rich cultural heritage, men from the Cayman Islands and Cuba fished and hunted turtles for over 300 years in the waters that separate and surround the two landmasses. Dos Visiones / Two Visions was subsequently intended to draw attention to the commonalities and differences between the two island nations – challenging preconceptions about life in both countries while fostering dialogue across the regional community.

On 10th May, HE Governor Dinwiddy kindly invited us to dinner at Government House, where the guest of honour was Prince Edward. He was visiting Cayman as part of the quincentennial celebrations, and would be unveiling the Wall of History created by John Broad. We had anticipated a similar table arrangement to the earlier dinner for Prince Andrew, with the Prince moving from table to table after each course, but Prince Edward remained at our table. We had a good conversation about his interest in acting, and he was keenly interested in the work CNCF was doing in preserving and developing Cayman's culture. Prince Edward's wife, Sophie, did not accompany him as she was pregnant with their first child, and Viv had thoughtfully purchased a Halcyon Days miniature porcelain box for her as a memento of Cayman. She gave it to the Prince to carry back to Sophie, and a few months later Viv received a thank-you letter from Buckingham Palace.

On the National Trust front that month, I met with Henry Propper, of McAlpine, and Henry Harford to discuss the rebuild of the Mission House in

Bodden Town, and in late May I met with The Hon Roy Bodden, to discuss CNCF's contingent to Carifesta in Suriname from 25th–30th August.

In late May, Viv and I held a dinner at Plantana for Robbie and Carlene Hamaty, and Robbie's mom, Tatiana. She and her husband, Munair, had been so kind to me when I arrived in Jamaica, frequently inviting me to stay at their commodious home in Sav la Mar in Westmoreland, and we had a great time catching up on all the good old times in Jamaica.

Early July saw two very sad occasions: Marjorie Panton's funeral on the 5th and Colin Whitelock's on the 7th. Both had been good friends of ours. Marjorie's name and that of her husband, Stanley, had been combined for StaMar Enterprises Ltd., a company that had looked after the shipping and customs clearances for my development projects for more than three decades. Colin had been manager at Barclays Bank for many years, had a great sense of humour, and one was of the two remaining pipe smokers I knew – Don Dise being the other.

CCAS was busy at this time with several projects, and I was liaising with Jerry on the BVI airport airside works. These were being managed by NACO and there had been several delays for our client, Trinidad Contractors, mainly because the airport remained in full operation throughout the works. We were also advising Damus about delays on a major infrastructure project they had with an Austrian contractor in Trinidad, as well as the arbitration in Bermuda. In addition, we were preparing an opinion on a dispute over construction at the Rendezvous Hotel in St Lucia.

CCAS had also been asked to look at a claim for Bob Mahabir of Trinidad Contractors in Grenada involving a seawall in Gouyave, and so on 1st August I met Bob in Kingston, where he was visiting. I took the opportunity to also meet with Alan Foster, who had kindly arranged with a local woodworking shop he knew to manufacture some mahogany serpentine louvres which we wanted to add to the sidelights of our front door at Callaloo to add some true 'West Indian' finishing touches to our new home.

A few weeks later, I received a call from Roberts Construction's QS, Michael Johnson, telling me they had reached a settlement on the Jumby Bay residence dispute Jerry and I been advising him on. It had been $600,000 over the contracted amount, and CCAS was, of course, delighted that our advice had such positive results for our client. So, Jerry and my promotional trips with the Yellow Pages and cell phone were paying off!

During July, I continued the meetings I was having on behalf of Henry Mutto in connection with his application for Caymanian Status, and we also celebrated Leonard Dilbert's book launch of *Grown from this Ground*, a collection of poems of 'love, doubt, surrender, dismay, despair, and hope'.

On 28th July my Smart Car arrived in Cayman from the UK, to my delight. Apart from Andreas', mine was the only other one on the island, which really turned heads when people saw this 6'3" man stepping out of it.

We had by this time prepared detailed quantities for the construction of Callaloo and commenced negotiation with the contractors, McAlpine. I had an excellent working relationship with them, developed over many years of friendship with Henry Propper, their Managing Director, and Sir Robin and Cullum McAlpine, and during the construction of both Plantana and The Great House. We were still some way from arriving at a price we could afford, so I travelled with a priced Bills of Quantities, knowing that the only way we could stay within budget was to examine every element and price in the Bills, scrutinising where we could save even a cent or two, exploring alternative materials and procurement methods for each item.

On 22nd August I flew via Trinidad to Suriname – for which we had needed yellow fever and Hepatitis A immunisations – to join our Minister of Culture, The Hon Roy Bodden, heading the Cayman contingent at Carifesta VIII. The Grand Opening Parade was held on 24th August and was, as always, a magnificent spectacle – a vibrant tapestry of colour and a crescendo of the multicultural richness of the broad Caribbean in which we live. The performances, lectures, interaction, music, art, fun and enjoyment of simply being alive, stamped itself forever in my mind. I can still see and feel them as I write this. This was followed by a reception in the garden of the Presidential Palace, to meet the President of the Republic of Suriname, Runaldo Venetiaan, and his wife Liesbeth, and several of the country's members of government and, most importantly, a contingent of their cultural icons.

The next day there was a little drama, as I suddenly developed a skin rash and a high temperature. I was whisked off to a mobile hospital, where I received an injection and a pile of pills. I don't know what had caused the rash – it may have been a reaction to the malaria pills I was taking – but I was able to rejoin the festivities after a couple of days. I used the time in isolation to work on the construction price for Callaloo, which was now getting closer to where it needed to be.

Henry Muttoo had seen some great sculptures and encouraged me to view the work of Jhunry Udenhout, being shown as part of one of the Carifesta exhibitions. I did so, and was taken with a magnificent mahogany piece about three feet tall called 'Dream Lover', with a man and woman intertwined, the space in between them forming the shape of a heart. Jhunry told me he had seen the tree when it being was cut down and, seeing the division in the branches, immediately knew what he was going to create. We agreed a price, and he wrapped the extremely heavy piece for transporting back home. Question was, how was I going to get it back to Cayman from Suriname as I was leaving from here on a trip throughout the Caribbean on CCAS business? 'No problem,' said our Cayman team, 'as long as someone can clear it through customs when we arrive, we can take it back to Cayman for you along with the props for our performance'. I called Viv, who was delighted with the purchase for our new home but had the slightly embarrassing assignment of explaining to the customs officer on its arrival that her 'Dream Lover' was inside the package!

I left Suriname on 31st August and met Jerry at the 'Upside Down' Hilton in Port of Spain (you enter at roof level and then go down into the hotel) for a couple of days' meetings with clients, which included Bob Mahabir on the Grenada and BVI projects. We flew from there to St Lucia, St Kitts, and through Miami to the Bahamas, networking with potential clients for our construction advisory and procurement services, and back home on 7th September.

Ed Haladay kindly introduced us to Rebecca Hoffberger, the founder, primary curator, and director emeritus of the American Visionary Art Museum, the country's official national museum for visionary art, located in Baltimore, Maryland. Ed had given her a copy of Miss Lassie's book, *My Markings*. Rebecca was overjoyed at the quality of Miss Lassie's work, and came to Cayman to visit her and meet with us, and we shared an informative enjoyable dinner.

For Callaloo, we met with Joe De Phillipo about the details for the swimming pool. To meet the very specific requirements of our Burdenko work, this needed to be some eight feet deep in the middle and sloping to approximately three feet at either end so that we could use it both for exercise and fun.

In September Viv and I were invited by our good friend Sallie Naylor, to stay on her ranch in Tucson. We enjoyed three days there, only to discover that, having bought the ranch, Sallie now wished to sell it. She asked our advice as to the best way to accomplish this, and we contacted Joe Zahm who undertook to make contact with potential groups of buyers and to see how he could best assist.

On 2nd October we were treated to a sterling performance by the Randy James Dance troupe at the Harquail, and a week later an exhibition of Charles Long's work opened at the National Gallery. Some years later, when Sallie was downsizing, she gifted us some of her art collection, which included pieces of Charles's work, and which are proudly displayed, and enjoyed every day, in Callaloo.

We flew from Tucson to Portland for a partners' meeting for Carabella, staying at a charming bed and breakfast called the Falconcrest Inn. We took advantage of Mount Hood's proximity to hike several trails, including Tamanawas Falls and Romano Falls. The partners' meetings were always great fun and once the business was over, we were able to enjoy the fruits of our labour – or more correctly, the fruits of our wine maker, Mike Hallock's, labour – to accompany the excellent cuisine found throughout the Willamette Valley.

The next day we flew to Nice for a five-day hiking trip in Provence, ticking off many more of the wonderful trails detailed in Janette Norton's book. We finished up at Joan and Alan Scott's house to enjoy Joan's wonderful cooking and Alan's hospitality with copious amounts of fine Provence rosé, which he purchased by the barrel and decanted into bottles.

We flew from Nice to Belfast for Flo's 85th birthday, which also gave me the opportunity to meet with the contractors, Lagan International, who were based there. They had large road-building contracts in Jamaica, for which CCAS were looking to provide construction and contract advice. We took Flo to London, where we went on the London Eye and then to the Oxo building for a sumptuous celebratory lunch. The next day we had Dim Sum at Yauatcha and listened to a symphony at the Royal Albert Hall, which is just around the corner from our London home. After Flo left us to return to Belfast we flew back to Cayman.

At the end of October, CNCF met with the Seafarer's Association to see how we could best ensure the preservation of their heritage which had very much shaped the development of Cayman. The CNCF eventually published a book called *The Southwell Years. Recollections of Caymanian Seamen and Those Who Served at Home*, compiled by Carole Winker and Consuelo Ebanks, one of CNCF's board members. We held our annual CNCF Retreat to plan our programmes and direction for the coming year on 1st and 2nd November.

We had been invited by Edson Bueno, one of our Harvard Alumni, to visit him in Rio. You will recall he finished up graduating from Harvard with an OPM qualification, and with Jimmy Nowery's Southern drawl. We arrived in Rio on 6th November after an overnight flight from Miami, and were met by Cupello, a colleague of Edson's, and two cars – one was for us to travel in and the second for our luggage, just in case we came with a lot! We then had lunch with Edson and Cupello and were introduced to his extensive office team. During lunch, Edson asked if we wanted to play tennis, to which we replied we would love to but had not brought any suitable clothing with us. Edson simply asked what size we were and left it at that.

Cupello then took us on a sightseeing tour of the city and up the Corcovado Mountain to the Statue of Christ the Redeemer that overlooks the city of Rio. He took photographs the whole time, which we thought somewhat strange but didn't comment on. When we returned to the apartment which Edson had kindly provided, the maid had ironed and laid out all our clothes and sewn on a missing button from one of my shirts – *service extraordinaire*! The next day Edson asked us to join him at his weekend home in the resort town of Armação dos Búzios, and we were driven there in a car he provided, complete with cushions so we could sleep on the long journey. We were greeted by the house manager when we arrived, asked if we wanted a massage, and we found in our room a set of tennis clothes and shoes for each of us. Edson and his wife Solange arrived and asked if we were ready for tennis, and whether we would prefer to play on a hard court, grass court or clay court. I said the last, not having played on one before, and we walked across the road from his house to the tennis complex where there was a resident pro and started playing.

Unfortunately, my enthusiasm got the better of me and I succeeded in pulling my Achilles tendon. Edson arranged for it to be iced, and later we went to an excellent restaurant in Búzios. Viv and I travelled there in one car and Edson and Solange travelled in another. When we reached the restaurant, Edson and Solange were in a different car to the one in which they had left the house. We asked if the first had broken down, and Edson explained that there were security reasons requiring them to change cars several times on any journey. The next day we went out in a boat, enjoyed a beach BBQ, and on our return to Edson's house he announced that on Sunday evenings the traffic back to Rio was appalling, so he provided a helicopter to take us back to the apartment.

On 10th November Cupello drove us to the airport for our onward journey to Iguazú. As we were leaving, he handed us a photo album, filled with his photos of all the things we had done during our whirlwind visit to Rio! What great memories. We spent three days visiting the area of Iguazú Falls, also seeing where the Iguazú and Paraná rivers join Brazil, Argentina and Paraguay into a triple frontier. There we purchased a driftwood-type sculpture that closely resembles the face of Christ, and which hangs in our gym today. We then flew to Buenos Aires, staying in the Claridge Hotel there – not, alas, any connection whatsoever with our favourite hotel of the same name in London. At a Buenos Aires *vinoteca* we bought some wonderful Cabernet Malbec from the Rutini winery from the Uco Valley in Mendoza for our cellar, and then flew on to Trelew, a town settled in the 1880s by Welsh immigrants. While walking along the town's main street, we met a lady who initially spoke Spanish but switched to English with a very distinct Welsh lilt.

After Trelew, we flew to Ushuaia and Tierra del Fuego, where the ships leave for tours to Antarctica, and then visited the Perito Moreno Glacier. While walking on it, outfitted with crampons, we were treated to a scotch on the rocks poured over lumps of ice chipped from the glacier itself. From there, we went on a trek to Torres del Paine National Park, where I could only walk part of the trip due to my Achilles problem, which I managed to relieve by soaking my foot in an ice-cold stream. Viv carried on and came back with outstanding and dramatic pictures of the Paine Massif for me to enjoy.

As we arrived home on 25th November, tired from the trip, both Viv and I wanted to crash and catch up on sleep, but something made me look at the answering machine. On it was a message asking me to make a speech at Miss Lassie's funeral, which was taking place at her home that afternoon at 4pm. We rapidly showered, dressed, and attended the funeral of this outstanding lady, knowing that the Good Lord had certainly been looking down to make me check for messages. As we had been off-island, we had no idea that Miss Lassie had passed.

On 28th November, CNCF launched the Quincentennial issue of *Foundation* magazine, featuring an interview with Lorna Reid about the founding of Dance Unlimited in 1988. The article reflects on her early dance performances and teaching after she arrived in Cayman from Jamaica in 1981, encouraged by Geoff Cresswell and the Inn Theatre, then based at the Royal Palms. The issue also featured John Broad's work on the creation of the tiles for the Quincentennial Wall of Caymanian history, Martin Keeley's efforts in teaching students an environmental Code of Ethics – especially relevant given these issues in today's global landscape – and an outstanding article by Rex Nettleford on Multiculturalism, the Arts and Nation-Building, still relevant today.

After a significant time spent negotiating the construction contract for Callaloo with McAlpine, we finally broke ground on 29th November. We celebrated the occasion by inviting the thirty or so people who had been instrumental during the team's effort in reaching this auspicious occasion. Almost immediately we needed information from Viv, in charge of the landscaping, about where the hose bibs for irrigation were to be located. Viv asked why we needed to know this so soon, and it was explained the supply pipes were in the ground. This pattern repeated itself throughout the construction, with Viv always coming up trumps with the information. That week, we had also broken ground on the Canal Point storage facility being developed by Mini Warehouse Two.

Flo arrived on 3rd December to spend Christmas and New Year with us, and Igor arrived shortly thereafter to conduct training sessions with Viv and me on our home turf. We all celebrated Irena's birthday on the 7th.

Viv had organised a party in celebration of my 58th birthday at the Hyatt, and we then flew to Miami to choose more materials for Callaloo, including tiles from Iberia Tile and Neff & Wolf appliances. We also visited George Sternberg at Causeway Lumber. We were blessed in finding George, who patiently dealt with all our enquiries and sourced many hard-to-find items. He also often helped us achieve the architectural effects we were looking for by modifying a stock item, such as taking a door, and adding mouldings to it. George continued to do this for us throughout the construction of Callaloo. We wanted the house to have traditional-looking louvered shutters which could be closed to provide hurricane protection, and located a company called Weather Guard Building Products, in West Palm Beach, whose brand Poma made traditional louvered shutters of aluminium, but which had a solid back. These could be closed and a reinforcing bar attached to fully protect the windows and doors. We also investigated options for the sauna and steam for the gym, and, most importantly, the fitting out of the wine cellar.

We returned to Cayman in time for a carol service on the lawn at Government House, and after Christmas and New Year celebrations in Cayman, we returned to Miami for a week of selecting materials, including the Spanish roof tiles. We researched the available selection of pots, urns, fountains and birdbaths for the garden and landscaping, eventually deciding to use a company called Haddonstone that manufactures classic pieces from reconstituted cast limestone and for which my good friend Charles Adams had an excellent contact, particularly given it provided a discount! Returning to Cayman, we met with interior designer Gina Hew to review the potential colour scheme for the house, which needed subtle changes of colour to highlight the transitions between the separate pavilions connected by corridors.

2004

Whatever is flexible and flowing will tend to grow. Whatever is rigid and blocked will wither and die.

The year began badly when, on 14th January, Flo fell and fractured her hip while walking back from the beach. She would require surgery which couldn't be performed in Cayman, but after complex negotiations with the insurance company, and thanks to the tenacious efforts of nurse Hazel Brown, she was flown to Mount Sinai hospital in Miami Beach. Luckily, the surgery was successful, and we were all able to return to Cayman and Plantana on the 25th.

A few days later I was back in Miami for a meeting with Bob Mahabir to finalise the claims for Gouyave in Grenada, while Viv was taking Flo to stay with her sister Pat, in Sebring, Florida. We then flew to London to celebrate my brother Rob's 50th birthday, after which Viv and I flew to Geneva and drove to Meribel. We skied there for four wonderful days, acquiring a taste for the Grand Marnier crêpes suzettes sold by a roadside vendor on the route from the ski lift to our guesthouse. This was run by a warm and welcoming hostess who had a striking resemblance to Mrs Doubtfire, the character in the Robin Williams 1993 movie of the same name.

On the Mini Warehouse front, I developed the feasibility for the climate-controlled Building #16 at our remaining site at the airport industrial park for presentation to our board and Butterfield Bank, our lenders.

On 28th February we celebrated our good friend Nita Wheaton's 90th birthday. Nita was a wonderful character, whose husband had developed Victoria House on Seven Mile Beach, where she lived and swam every day without fail. She would also walk each day to the Cayman Islands Yacht Club and past the site trailer at Callaloo. As she walked past the trailer window one day, I asked Graham Day, the foreman, how old he thought she was. Graham guessed around sixty-five, given the pace at which she was moving. When I told him she was ninety, his jaw dropped in disbelief. Just goes to show what regular exercise will do for you – one of life's lessons well learned.

The next day Viv and I were invited to dinner at Government House by Bruce and Emma Dinwiddy and I was reunited with Sylvia, my cousin who, as I mentioned earlier, I had not seen since I was fifteen years of age. Sylvia produced a photo of the occasion, to the great amusement of the assembled group.

On 5th March CNCF's annual *Rundown*, staged at the Harquail, was once again sold out as it had become Cayman's must-see annual event. A week later we were in Miami again to select materials for Callaloo and on 19th March we flew to Denver, collected a hire car and drove to Steamboat, where our good friend Al Hallock had now developed a condominium called Eagle Ridge. Given we stayed with them so often, he had combined a two-bed condominium with a one-bed condominium, to ensure we had somewhere to stay even if the Hallock family were in town. Talk about a good friend!

Shortly after we got back, Cayfest began with a revitalised 'Granny Back Yard' and 'Jonkanoo', as had been the tradition in Bodden Town. There was 'Praise' at Government House; the Jamaican actor, film director and stage director Lloyd Reckord at the Harquail and, also at the Harquail, Trinidadian Earl Lovelace, the author of *Dragon Can't Dance*, a novel set in Port of Spain, centred on the life of Aldrick Prospect, a man who spends the entire year recreating his dragon costume for Carnival. The book is most notable for the insight it provides into the passion which Trinis afford to this annual celebration.

It was in April that my discussions with Mike Bell about a waterfront development on a narrow parcel of land, created by moving the access roadway in Cayman Grand Harbour closer to the boundary and away from the water, were conceptualised. I wanted to develop units that were compact, similar to the Gingerbread apartments I had developed earlier, but now including one-, two- and three-bedroom units, all entered on the side in order to minimise circulation space, and that could be sold for less than $250,000 to first-time Caymanian buyers, who could benefit from no stamp duty on the transfer. I contacted John Doak, who developed a great layout, keeping the two-bed unit under 1,000 square feet, and creating a very pleasing aesthetic in Caribbean pastel colours with steep gabled pitched roofs.

In April, I also flew to Barbados to meet with Jerry and the contractor for the Barbados Hilton to discuss the claim which had now gone to arbitration – centred, as usual on delay, disruption, and changes in scope. From Barbados we went to St Vincent for meetings with the government and contractors, and then on to St Lucia, where we presented a two-day seminar titled 'Managing Construction Risk in the Caribbean' to the Ministry of Communications, Works and Public Utilities of the Government of St Lucia. This was most enthusiastically received and rated as excellent by the attendees, and the question and answer sessions at the completion of each talk demonstrated their keen interest in the range of topics we covered.

With the continuing buildup of work throughout the Caribbean, I was receiving multiple requests to provide Project Management and Quantity Surveying services from clients that CCAS had assisted with dispute resolution services. Whilst in Barbados I had met with Miles Weekes, who said that Tower Consultants, a local practice, had formed an alliance with Bucknall Austin, a firm I knew from my time in the UK Midlands. I also knew David Bucknall, one of its principals. Accordingly, I cold-called David on 6th May. I advised him I was connecting through Heathrow on 10th May en route to Rome where we were holding a Harvard Reunion, and asked if he had time to meet. To my surprise, David readily agreed, and we sat discussing opportunities in the wider Caribbean area for several hours. We left with an understanding to continue exploring possibilities, including David's joint venture in Barbados.

Viv and I then continued to Rome, where an exciting reunion had been planned by Giorgio Sermoneta and George Klopfer. After checking into the Hotel d'Inghilterra, we held a familiarisation meeting and enjoyed catching up with all the alumni news over dinner at the roof top restaurant La Terrazza. The wonderful thing about meeting with this group, is that within seconds we picked up where we left off at the previous reunion, in a most easy and relaxed fashion.

Giorgio Sermoneta had incredible connections in Rome, which became obvious as the visit unfolded. On 11th May, after breakfast, we met Walter Veltroni, the Mayor of Rome, at his office in the Palazzo del Campidoglio. This was followed by a tour of the Roman Ghetto and the Synagogue, taking in lunch at Da Giggetto, a restaurant serving typical Roman/Jewish cooking. We toured the Pantheon and the Piazza Navona, and enjoyed cocktails at Bulgari – where, no, we didn't buy anything! The next day began with a fashion show at Fendi, presented by Anna Fendi, and lunch at one of Giorgio's restaurants, La Barcaccia, and then the afternoon was left free for shopping. After the heavy lunch I was ready for an afternoon nap, as were several of my male colleagues, and so we retired while the ladies hit the shops. Viv returned following a successful expedition, and presented me with a most attractive, one-of-a-kind, silk tie from Giorgio's shop.

That evening we were to have dinner at the Roof Garden at the Hotel Hassler, at the top of the Spanish steps, and Viv said, 'Are you going to wear your new tie?' to which I replied, 'Of course!' Tie duly tied, we descended to the lobby and greeted our fellow alumni – of which four others were wearing the identical, one-of-a-kind, handmade tie! At first the gentlemen thought the ladies had all gone shopping there at the same time, but no, they had all been shopping at different times and had selected the identical tie for their husbands. We arrived at the Hassler where Giorgio, when confronted with this amazing coincidence, was embarrassed and said it would be sorted out. We enjoyed a magnificent dinner followed by our alumni group's tradition of making up a musical skit to illustrate the events taking place during the reunion. As might be imagined, the 'tie incident' featured prominently in the entertainment. The next morning we were taken on an archaeological tour of Rome, followed by a private visit to the Sistine chapel, where we were marvelling at Michelangelo's ceiling frescoes when Giorgio appeared with a bag containing five ties, each different, and gave one to each of the 'one-of-a-kind' brigade.

The following day the group left for a cruise on the Royal Clipper to Capri, Agrigento, Siracusa, Taormina and Positano. Viv and I decided we would rather fly to Nice and enjoy hiking in Provence, where in four days we completed the circuits of Lacs de Prals, Circuit de la Couletta, Tête du Garnier and Cime de Corvo, guided by Viv's copy of *Walking in Provence*. We then drove from Saint-Martin-Vésubie to spend the night with Alan and Joan Scott, and then flew back to Cayman.

June saw the annual graduation ceremony at John Gray High School, with yours truly presenting the successful students with the CNCF Award for Outstanding Achievements in Drama and The Arts. That month we also attended a retirement party for Chris Johnson, the managing partner for Price Waterhouse Coopers. It seemed strange to be celebrating the retirement of someone who had commenced his Cayman journey at the same time I had.

Mikol and I had continued our discussions about climate-controlled warehousing and I proposed a further visit to Griffin, Georgia, to meet with Otis Blake. I had spoken with Otis about such a facility during our Rome reunion. So, in July, Mikol and I flew out to meet with Otis and Nancy and review their storage operation. We were particularly interested in the climate-controlled aspect of their business, and Otis graciously lent me the plans for his development. Using them as a basis, I drew up the layout for Building #16, which was to be our entry into the climate-controlled mini self-storage business. I then passed these plans to George Serrant, who prepared the final drawings and subsequently submitted them to the Central Planning Authority for approval.

We were completing the outside paving and landscaping for the Canal Point Drive building, and we had managed to rent the ground floor to Mr Hung. He had a budget clothing business with the Foster family, named 'J. Michael' after David's oldest son, and he was busy fitting out the ground floor as a retail store to open in September, with storage for the inventory to be located on the upper floor.

On 26th July, Gingerbread Limited and Mike Bell's company, Cayman Grand Harbour Development Company Ltd., signed a joint venture agreement to develop the waterfront property at Cayman Grand Harbour. In addition to the planned apartments, this was scheduled to include boat docks that were for sale – another first for Cayman – and hence the name of the development: 'Careenage'. We met with John Doak to lay out the site, to be developed in three separate phases, and with land surveyor Eric Cronier to work out the challenges of establishing theoretical boundary markers on the seabed in order to sell the docks on a stratified basis. On the same day we signed a lease for the Bowling Alley at the Greenery on West Bay Road.

In August, the finishing works were well underway on Callaloo. The coloured exterior finish was being applied, and Viv and I toured the island looking at plants to complete the landscaping. We visited Mike Simmons's land in George Town to tag a series of matched Malayan Dwarf coconut trees that were to be transplanted to the west of the property to form a grove and shield Callaloo from the setting sun. John Doak had designed a series of external 'rooms' in the garden, each with its own personality, and Viv was working with

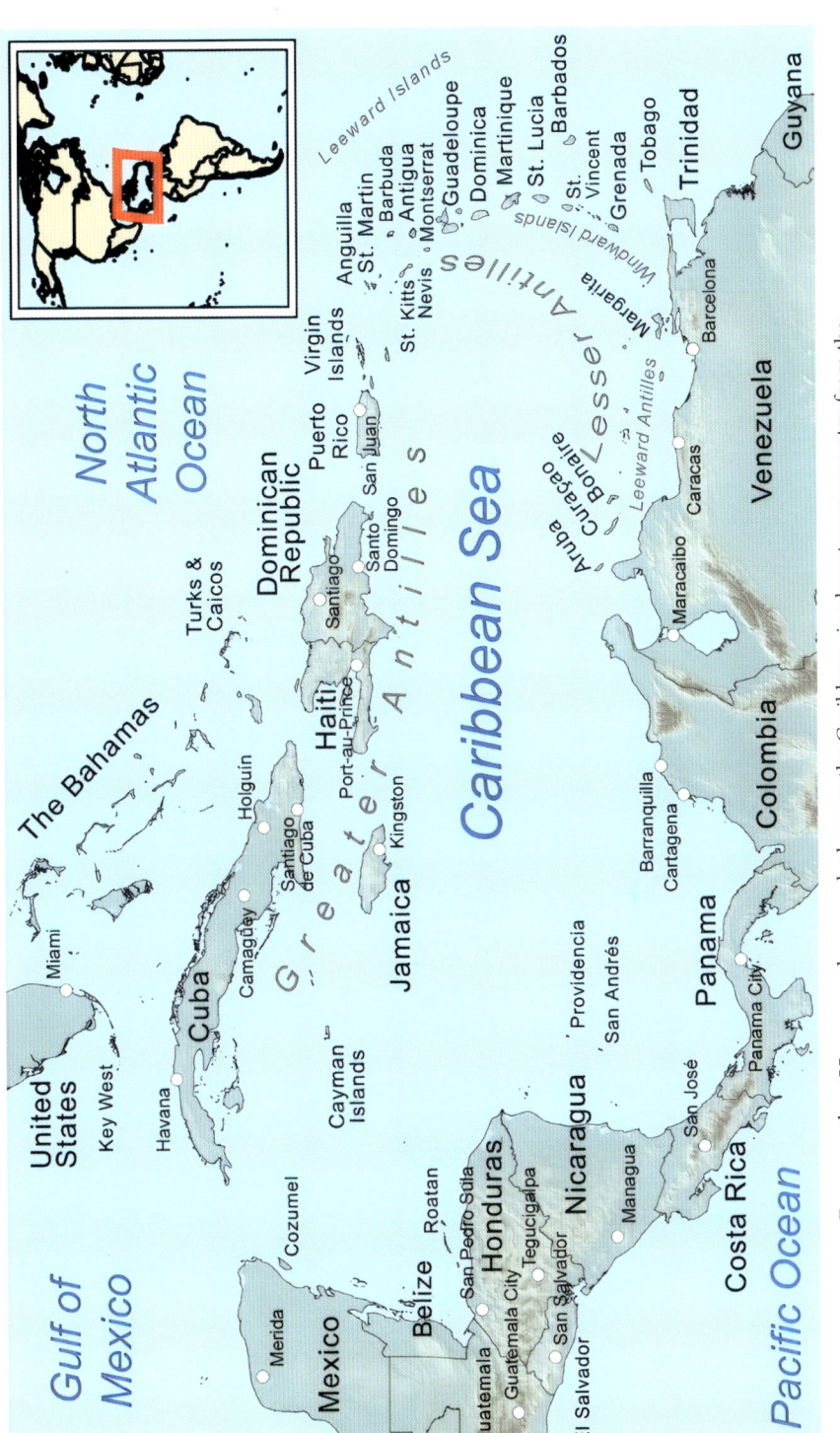

For more than 55 years we have worked across the Caribbean, in almost every country from the Bahamas in the north to Suriname in the south, and as far west as Panama.

My dad, Frederick Charles Bould, and my mom, Phyllis Margaret Bould, at my brother Rob's wedding in June 1981.

Yours truly at about 5 years of age.

BVGS 2nd XV Team 1961–62, with me in the centre of the back row.

Yours truly and my sister Carole who was 6 years older than me.

White water canoeing in *Alma* on the river Wye.

Beach Club Colony in 1970 on Seven Mile Beach, one of my early projects for WTC&P.

The Piper Cherokee 6Y-JDX that provided efficient transport around Jamaica and over to Cayman.

INVESTORS CHRONICLE

February 11, 1972/20p/445 to 536

Property: the quietest boom

Peter Wood

Martyn Bould, at 26 possibly Cayman's youngest property developer

Martyn Bould at 26 is one of the Cayman's latest and youngest property developers. He first recognised the potential in building private dwellings in Grand Cayman when on a routine visit for his firm he was asked to find accommodation for an expatriate employee. Bould, a Birmingham-born chartered quantity surveyor, was impressed by the number of new office blocks being erected in Grand Cayman and immediately realised the need for additional residential accommodation. He found a two-acre plot less than a mile south of Georgetown in early 1970.

The purchase price was at that time considered a bargain and Bould estimates the value of his plot to have doubled since then. In partnership with two colleagues, he formed a small company, Cayman Court.

Bould had first wanted to build apartment style homes but when he discovered the construction costs, boosted by labour intensive work such as concrete flooring, he opted for a small estate of 18 town houses. Here he could utilise timber floors and pre-engineered fitments and still preserve the same environmental conditions as before. The Development Control Board granted him building permission the actual site coverage which worked out at a density of 12·5 per cent.

In general, planning consent follows fairly liberal lines. There are no rigid standards in construction and the maximum density permitted by the planning authorities is 40 per cent, depending on zoning and type of construction.

Bould has arranged with a Miami building supplies exporter to have the bulk of the fittings shipped in special containers direct to the Caymans. He saves through bulk purchases of building materials and on freight costs and it also lessens the chances of material omissions.

Exterior construction of the town houses will be of locally made hollow concrete blocks rendered and painted on the outside. The interior consists of a living/dining room, patio, fitted kitchen, two bedrooms and a bathroom. Vinyl tiles will be used on the ground floors while the upstairs bedrooms will be completely carpeted. Console-type air-conditioners will be installed in the bedrooms.

Like most developers in the Caymans, Bould was faced with two elementary problems—water supply and drainage facilities.

So Bould asked his architects to design the roofs as a catchment area, with rain water fed into a 77,000 gallon central underground reservoir and pumped to the houses. This installation has added almost £12,000 to his construction costs.

Total cost of the construction is estimated to be £230,000 and take fifteen months to complete, and the 18 houses will sell on a 999-year lease for an average of £16,000.

So far Martyn Bould has sold six of his homes and this has convinced him that demand for private homes in the Caymans is bound to increase. He is already beginning negotiations for another site where he intends to build executive-style luxury apartments. He has also formed his own property management company which apart from looking after Cayman Court, will take on other management assignments.

Bould expects his town houses will be bought as an investment and rented by their owners on twelve-month leases for around £160 month, representing an attractive tax-free return.

Property development in the Caymans is very much an individualistic enterprise: The lack of previous example, the care taken over planning permission and the Caymanians' own approach to new developments are all hidden factors which only first hand experience can reveal. As one experienced property man put it, "we wouldn't try to enter the European market, it requires a very special knowledge—we would say the same about the Caymans."

The UK magazine *Investors Chronicle* published an article on the Cayman Court Town House development in February 1972.

of God. *Recreation:* Swimming. *Address:* P.O. Box 11, Grand Cayman.

BOULD, Martyn Charles William, A.R.I.C.S., A.I.Q.S., A.I. Arb., chartered quantity surveyor & property developer; Mng Dir.,Cayman Court Ltd. *Born* Birmingham, Eng., Dec. 10, 1945, son of Frederick Charles Bould and Phyliss *nee* Rowbotham his wife. *Educated* Bishop Vesey's Gram. Sch.; College of Estate Management. Unmarried. *Career:* Articled to firm of quantity surveyors, 1962, after qualifying as chartered quantity surveyor; senior asst., Midland firm; Sr. Asst., B.G.W. Cawston & Partners Ja., 1969; formed Cayman comp. (property dev.) 1971. *Religion:* C. of E. *Affiliations:* Prof. Assoc., Roy. Institution of Chartered Surveyors; Assoc., Inst. of Quantity Surveyor's, Assoc., Inst. of Arbitrators. *Club:* Liguanea (Jamaica). *Recreations:* Flying, squash. *Address:* P.O. Box 268, Grand Cayman, Cayman Islds, B.W.I., and P.O. Box 29, Kgn 6, Jamaica.

BOXALL, Ian Llewelyn, attorney-at-law; partner in Messrs. Hunter & Hunter. *Born* Dec. 22, 1943, son of Arthur Llewelyn Boxall and Molly Evelyn *nee* Radford his wife. *Educated* Exeter Sch., Devon, Eng.; College of Law, Guildford, Eng. *Married* Oct. 22, 1966, Elizabeth Beaufort *nee* Grimaldi; 1 son (Simon),

CALDER, Douglas Walter George, M.A. (Cantab), attorney-at-law (Cayman Islds.); solicitor (Eng.); partner, firm of Macdonald & Maples, attorneys-at-law, George Town, Gd. Cayman. *Born* Plymouth, Eng., June 6, 1939, son of late Rev. A. Calder, D.S.O., M.A., Mus. Bac. (Cantab), and Mrs. D. E. Calder, L.R.A.M. *Educated* St. Paul's Sch., London; St. Catherine's Coll., Cambridge. *Married* Aug. 1, 1970, Deborah June *nee* Slater. *Career:* With Eland Horse Patersons, solicitors, London, 1963-67; Gordon, Dadds & Co., solicitors, London, 1967-69; Rowing Correspondent, "The Times", 1967-69. *Religion:* C. of E. *Affiliation:* Law Socy. of Eng. *Clubs:* Leander; Hawks; Wig & Pen. *Interests:* Law, singing. *Recreations:* Rowing, sculling (rowed for Cambridge Univ. in Oxford & Cambridge Boat Race, 1961). *Motto:* "Vigilans non cadet". *Address:* P.O. Box 307, Gd. Cayman, Cayman Islds.

CAMPBELL, Bruce, LL.B., M.I.C.M., solicitor. *Born* Harrogate, Eng., Oct. 20, 1938, son of late Colin Campbell and Monica, his wife. *Educated* Rossall, Eng.; Leeds Univ. *Unmarried. Religion:* C. of E. *Speaks* French, Spanish. *Address:* P.O. Box 268, George Town, Grand Cayman.

COHEN, John Alexander, B.A. (Oxon.), solicitor & attorney-at-law; *Born* Southport, England, April 14, 1947, son of Albert Cohen and Nancy his wife. *Educated* King George V. Sch., Southport; St. Catherine's Coll., Oxford (B.A. 1968). *Speaks* French. *Married* Heather. *Affiliations:* Cayman Islds. Law Socy.; Cayman Islds. Divers (Secy. 1971). *Recreations:*

At 26, I was named 'Cayman's Youngest Property Developer' for building Cayman Court, which led to my inclusion in the 1972 Edition of 'Personalities Caribbean', alongside several esteemed attorneys.

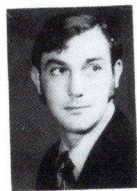

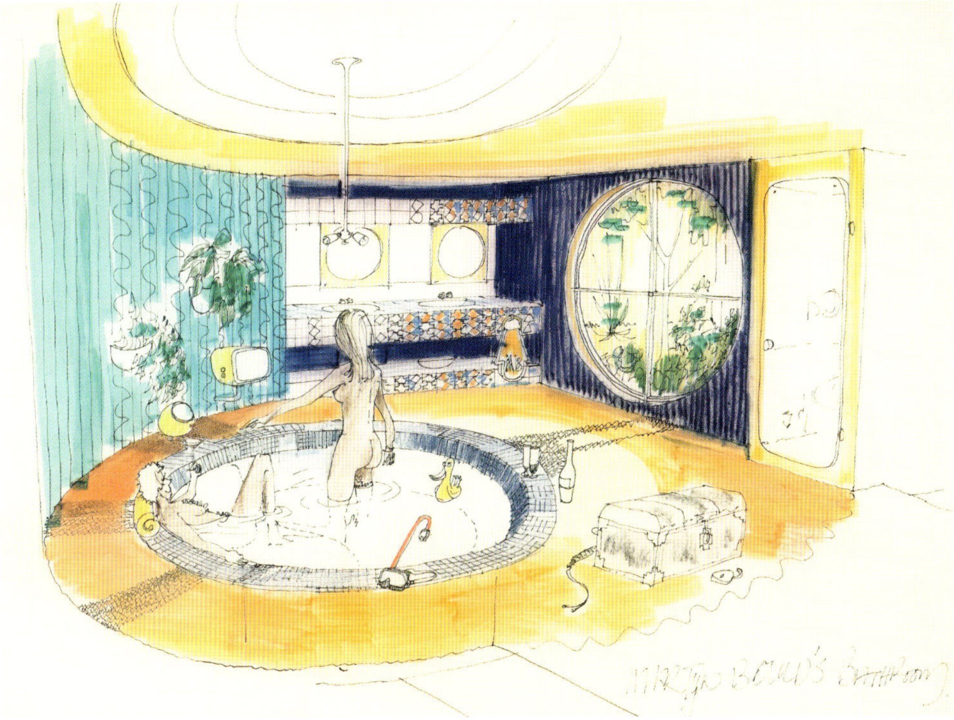

Architect Dave Twiss had a great sense of humour, which he demonstrated when designing my proposed house in Whitehall Estates.

Yours truly piloting Delta Xray into Negril airstrip, where we were building a beach club, and where we picked up the crabs for dinner that escaped their gunny sack during flight.

'Condo King' Jimmy Powell and I on the roof of Tarquynn Manor on Seven Mile Beach, 8 weeks into construction.

I introduced squash to the Cayman Islands when I developed the Racquet Club in 1977.

A Sunday in the centre of George Town, during the filming of *The Cayman Triangle*. I played an English gentleman tourist complete with bowler hat and rolled umbrella.

I quickly grew to love driving through France, particularly the Loire with its fine food and wine.

Me, Carole, and Rob at his wedding in June 1981.

I was best man for my brother Rob's wedding to Jenna in June 1981.

The Plantana property north of the Governor's Residence, is one of the finest locations on Seven Mile Beach.

The 'X' format of Plantana allowed us to maximise the direct sea view for all condos.

Mono skiing in front of Plantana on Seven Mile Beach.

The FJ Harquail Cultural Campus with the 'temporary' theatre in the lower left and the main theatre next to the lake representing Grand Cayman. The National Gallery is now located to the far left.

Dad and me on the Roche Bobois furniture at Plantana.

Top members of the Society of Architects, Surveyors and Engineers after recent elections. L-R: Jerry Sibley [President], Chris Evans [Secretary], Heber Arch [Outgoing Treasurer], Martyn Bould [Outgoing President], John Douk [Member], and Richard Jones [Treasurer].

I was President of CASE from 1980 to 1984, during which time we established standard forms of contract to meet our unique procurement requirements and tendering procedures.

The living room of our apartment at Yacht Harbour in Coconut Grove, Miami.

The Baker Library at Harvard University in Boston where I graduated from the Owner President Management Programme in 1987 after three summer semesters.

Viv's Mum and Dad on the beach at Plantana, which they loved.

We introduced condominium ownership to commercial spaces in Cayman, with the development of the Genesis building – another first for the island.

A great promotional piece when we made the front cover of the Royal Institution of Chartered Surveyors' globally distributed magazine.

A Michel Guérard recipe that I learned whilst attending the Great Chefs of France Course with him in 1981 and which became a tradition with Jimmy & Cynthia Nowery.

Our Doll's House in the heart of South Kensington, London, complete with Viv's urban garden.

The Great House setting new standards for development on Seven Mile Beach.

THE GREAT HOUSE
The Development that Stands Up to its Name

Martyn Bould presently lives in Plantana, a condominium complex he developed in 1979. It sits next door to Cayman's newest and most luxurious complex, The Great House. He is the property developer behind the Great House project and each morning, as he shaves, he sees through his window the many people who, taking a stroll on the beach, stop and look with admiration at the imposing and graceful lines of the buildings.

It is this simple yet telling reaction that gives him a sense of satisfaction, a feeling that The Great House is right.

The idea for the Great House was conceived in 1987. Having lived in the Caribbean for the past 22 years and having travelled to many of the islands, Mr Bould thought of building a true West Indian plantation great house, a house that stood at the centre of vast properties. The Great House was designed by architect Edward Haladay, a leading American designer, and incorporates the various architectural styles of the region: French, Spanish, English and African. The working drawings and project supervision were done by Chalmers Gibbs Martin Joseph Architects of Grand Cayman. "So much of the architecture here in recent years has been simply styles transplanted from elsewhere that I wanted to do something exciting and original," Mr Bould says. "I wanted to develop a property that didn't look like a block of apartments but like a house that complemented the magnificent location and I consider the end result most at-

Martyn Bould (top) developer of the Great House project

The *Real Estate* magazine provided comprehensive coverage for the Great House in their December 1990 feature.

It was a fabulous compliment to be the cover feature in the *Real Estate* magazine.

Our wedding invitation was conceived by Simon Barwick and painted by Chris Mann. It pictures Viv and me walking down the beach and through a window to a new beginning.

Viv and I outside Elmslie church on our wedding day with Jenny Foster showering us with flowers.

Miss Lassie wishing us a happy life together outside Elmslie Church on our wedding day in December 1995.

Miss Lassie's paintings reflected scenes from the Bible. Viv, who was a Brownies leader had taken her Brownies to meet Miss Lassie. This inspired her painting 'Suffer all the children to come unto me'

As part of our South Africa Harvard OPM reunion in March 1999 we visited Sabi Sabi Game Reserve in the Kruger National Park and saw the 'Big Five'.

The Tiger's Lair in Bhutan, where the 8th-century Buddhist master Guru Rinpoche meditated for 3 years, 3 months, 3 days and 3 hours. We visited it as part of our Chomolhari trek in October 2000.

Working with Igor in Boston, in April 2003, using his 'Burdenko Belt' with tethers attached to feet and arms to work on flexibility, coordination, alignment and strength.

Viv working with Igor on the bench for alignment, flexibility and strength.

At CNCF the Board and Staff regularly conducted two day planning retreats to review our programmes and direction.

Skiing is Viv's and my passion. Here we are in March 2005, in Steamboat, Colorado, with a 'Camp Robber'.

Viv's Mum, Flo, and I in Kensington Gardens in London.

The recently erected stadium in Grenada which was no match for hurricane Ivan in September 2004, which went on the devastate Cayman.

Mr Birungi was my travelling companion for many years.

Viv and I trekked the circuit around Mont Blanc in September 2005, passing through 3 countries en route.

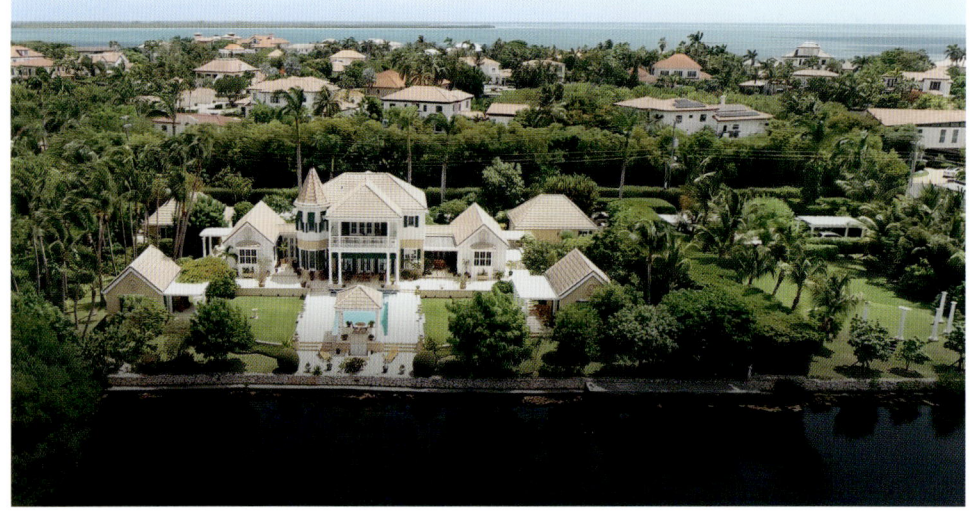

An ariel view of Callaloo with the performance space in the Orchard to the right.

Michele, Jill, Roger, Ray, me and Viv at lunch at La Croix Blanche in Étroubles after skiing down Grand St Bernard.

The bars from the Rooswijk in safe storage.

Viv, me, Sheila and Jerry Katz at the French Embassy in Washington at a CARE fundraising Ball.

Three Old Veseyans: Alan Scott, Rob and me in St Paul de Vence.

Rob Bennett to ensure we used all local plants, in keeping with our Great House concept. As part of the finishing works, we needed the serpentine louvres for the front door sidelights that Alan Foster in Jamaica was sourcing for me. Sadly, the woodwork shop had been robbed, and not only had our louvres been stolen, but also the shop's machinery to make them. True Jamaican style, Fos says, 'No Problem, Mon – we will find someone else to make them again.' By early September we had our electrical inspection and we were getting closer to finishing.

On 12th August, Cayman was brushed by Hurricane Charley. It subsequently caused major damage in Florida as a Category 4 hurricane with 240km/hr winds but, fortunately, did little damage in Cayman.

The 4th September saw the grand opening of the J. Michael store at our Canal Point building, and all guests were amazed by the vast selection of goods and budget prices that were displayed.

On 7th September, our nephew and godson, Edward, arrived to stay with us for a week, along with his girlfriend, Ewa, who was a charming, pretty girl who had not yet travelled very much and was delighted to be staying with us at Plantana with all the beauty of Seven Mile Beach on the doorstep.

Saturday 11th September started out as a peaceful, sunny day with a visit to Callaloo to check on progress. While speaking with the carpenters on site we discussed the possibility that a hurricane named Ivan might hit Cayman, and made the decision to close all the shutters on the doors and windows and, for the first time, put the locking bars in place. By the afternoon the shutters were firmly in place and the carpenters asked if we would like plywood fixed over the windows in our Plantana apartment as we had spare plywood on site. In all the years we had lived at Plantana we had never taken this precaution. However, with both the materials and labour to hand, I said we might as well, and so the windows were secured, sealing out all the light from what had been a bright and sunny apartment. As the evening wore on, the wind speed increased and kept increasing to the point where the timber panelled front door was flexing with each violent gust and threatening to blow inwards. We placed an ice chest against the front door, on which both Edward and I sat as extra weight. Ewa was watching the television, which was by now broadcasting non-stop news about Ivan and about the worst storms of the century, and how many people had died in them. Ewa would come into the hallway to relate the updates to Edward and me, sitting there on the ice chest. Viv was busy making sure we had all the supplies we needed. After about the tenth bad news update from Ewa we said to please turn the bloody TV off. No real need, however, as the power to the apartment and the complex went off as the power lines came down.

We remained at the front door pretty much all night as the violent downdrafts shook the entire building and the noise of the wind sounded like a dozen freight trains passing at once. By early morning, the wind had died down, and we looked outside into a scene of absolute devastation: all trees down and sand from the beach everywhere but, fortunately, the roofs were for the most part intact. We sat down and tried to plan a series of actions. First, we went out to check Viv's car. I had stored my Smart car in a Mini Warehouse, but Viv's Toyota was in Plantana's parking lot. We went out to it, took off some tree branches and got in, only then realising that the seat was soaking wet. We tried to start it and only then understood the car had been engulfed in water and was a write-off.

We then went out into West Bay Road, where we saw people wandering around in stunned disbelief at the damage. Edward and I decided to walk into town to see what damage had occurred to the office at Genesis and arrived with feet absolutely soaked from the water we'd had to wade through. Over the next weeks, keeping a dry pair of shoes at home was a terrific challenge. Fortuitously, whilst some windows were broken in the Genesis building, our offices there had been spared major damage.

We then walked to the Mini Warehouse complex to see if we could get the Smart car to work. We only found out later that the storm surge had come down the runway close to the Mini Warehouse and, although I had driven the Smart car onto some wooden pallets to raise it off the ground, it had still been soaked by the flood waters. We tried pushing to start it but to no avail, and we subsequently found out it was a write-off. So now we were on the proverbial 'Shank's Mare' for transportation.

We then walked back to Plantana, passing many dazed people looking totally lost. Viv had walked up to Callaloo, which appeared to have suffered little damage apart from some Spanish tiles blown off the roof, but could not get in because the bars across the shutters had been torsioned by the force of the wind and were difficult to unscrew. Our stove at Plantana was electric, and useless without power. The gardener at Plantana came by, however, and lent us a single gas ring with a tank of propane gas, which we set up and were now able to heat food.

Over the next few months, we became quite adept at timing the cooking on this single ring so that meat and vegetables were 'done' at the same time. The second major issue was that we had no water other than what we had filled into the bathtubs and a five-gallon bucket in the hallway. Our freezer contained a good selection of frozen supplies and meals, but without electricity the door to the fridge had to be opened quickly, items removed, and the door closed as fast as possible. Having Edward and Ewa staying with us was great from the point of view of assistance but was putting a strain on the available supplies, and they agreed to leave on the 15th if they could find a seat on a plane. No bookings were being accepted; one simply went to the airport and joined the queue.

By 14th September, we were becoming better organised, and had a meeting with Ron Shaw, who was head of the Exco at Plantana, to organise a review of the damage sustained throughout the complex. Then we tried to see who was available to carry out temporary repairs. Suddenly, of course, 'experts' in many fields were turning up at the complex offering assistance. I vividly recall a 'roofer' who had a six-foot ladder, a hammer and no nails (Plantana is a three-storey complex)! The same day I walked across West Bay Road to Governor's Harbour and met with Alastair Paterson to discuss how we could assist potential clients with their insurance claims. He had already managed to secure the use of a boardroom at a friend's office. This, being in the heart of George Town's Central Business District, was scheduled to have the power restored more quickly than areas away from the centre. The key requirement was a lot of paper, which we had from our office in town that was without power.

On 15th September we bid farewell to Edward and Ewa, who went out onto West Bay Road and succeeded in hitching a lift with their luggage to the airport. Viv and I walked back to the Cayman Islands Yacht Club with the appropriate tools to open the shutters and see inside Callaloo's main house. We were delighted to find the inside dry except for the entry hall, though the swimming pool had a small baby shark in it! We walked to George Town and collected the computer equipment from the office, and then to the airport, where we cleaned up our storage unit at the Mini Warehouse, throwing out wet boxes of files. Mikol came by Plantana (cell phones were not working) and when we told him we had no cars, he said one of his owners at Cayman Kai had a brand-new Ford Explorer that was undamaged and which we could borrow. However, as no gas was available due to its potential contamination from the storm surge, we would need to meet him halfway between Plantana and Cayman Kai to save on gas, and so Viv and I managed to hitch a lift and collected the car.

When we arrived back at Plantana, Viv walked over to see Ron Shaw and I walked back to our apartment, to be greeted by a complete stranger sitting on the steps outside our apartment who asked 'Are you Uncle Martyn?' I said 'Yes, indeed I am', and the stranger simply stood up and left, only to quickly return with Edward and Ewa in tow. Edward rapidly explained that they had queued all day waiting for a seat on the plane, and the couple standing behind them in the queue had been on their honeymoon in Cayman when Hurricane Ivan hit. Since none of them had been successful in securing a seat, he had kindly offered the couple lodging for the night with his Uncle Martyn and Auntie Vivian. Already short of supplies, we were now even shorter, but made the best of it, finishing all the food in the freezer, which was almost completely thawed out anyway, and making a heavy dent in the wine cellar. The next day, they all went out to the West Bay Road again, hitching rides to the airport. The honeymoon story would be repeated many times in the future, we were sure.

Bless Edward, he remained in Miami for a day or so and went to the hardware store and purchased a generator, chain saw and other essential tools, packed them and had them airfreighted to us in Cayman.

By this time, we came to the realisation that we would possibly be without water and electricity for several months. So Viv went each day to Cayman Water Company in Governor's Harbour and queued to fill the five-gallon mud bucket with fresh water. For showers, Viv and I would wait for a rainstorm and go outside and stand under the broken downpipe, soap up and shower off. When it wasn't raining, I would sit in the bathtub, soap up and Viv would rinse me off with water poured from a saucepan. Mobile coverage was also very limited as many of the cell towers had their storage batteries located at ground level and the storm surge had damaged them. As a result, it was difficult to use credit cards and so cash was once again king. But supplies of this commodity were very limited, and each day Viv would queue in the hot sun outside the bank to draw approximately $50 each time. Likewise, supermarkets limited the number of shoppers inside at any one time, and the quantity of goods one could purchase was limited to avoid hoarding. With so much standing in the sun, Viv developed a unique pattern on her feet from the straps on her open sandals.

Given the damage at home, I cancelled my CCAS trip to Trinidad and St Lucia, which Jerry and Charlie most ably and successfully completed without me. Instead, I focused on the huge potential workload of insurance claims, meeting with the insurance companies and brokers to offer our services to assist in assessing the loss reserve, all the time cognisant of the time limit for making claims.

On 22nd September I was able to meet with our team at CNCF. We examined the damage at the theatre, considered alternative accommodation for our offices, and planned how we could contribute to the country's needs in this most stressful time for all.

The next day, at his restaurant, I held the first of several meetings with Mr Hung, who had opened his new store in our Canal Point property only one week before Ivan hit. One of the benefits of these meetings was having great Chinese food to sustain us! Of course, out of great adversity can come great opportunity. Mr Hung had seen the extensive damage to the Bowling Alley at our Greenery property, and envisioned taking over the entire space to expand his fledgling store, returning the Canal Point property to us to revert back to its original planned use as climate-controlled storage.

For the next few months, we spent twelve-hour days carrying out property inspections; preparing reports; having meetings with home and business owners, insurance companies and loss adjusters; preparing claims for our own properties, including both physical damage and loss of rent; relocating the CNCF office to Elizabethan Square in George Town, and organising the rebuild of damaged properties. During those months, what stood out more than anything was the resilience of all Cayman's inhabitants, and almost everyone's unselfish contributions to helping others before taking care of themselves.

At the beginning of September, CCAS received an enquiry to review a contractor's claim on the Vieux Fort Police Station in St Lucia, meaning we needed to plan a trip to carry out a site inspection there. Given our ever-increasing workload, I resumed my conversations with David Bucknall in the UK. He remained keen to continue the dialogue we had started earlier in the year about planning a Caribbean-wide entity to service the region, and we began putting in place the foundations of a business plan to set this endeavour on the right track.

By 12th November, Viv and I were in need of a break and we flew to Miami. On arriving at our apartment, we stood under the shower for at least half an hour, delighting in the luxury of water not poured from a saucepan over our heads. Then we were off to Dadeland to purchase supplies and enjoy a lazy meal in a restaurant. Diane, Mikol's partner, was kindly assisting us with introductions to furniture suppliers in Miami so we could finalise our purchases for Callaloo, so we did a lot of driving from one supplier to the next. The owner of the Ford Explorer that Mikol had lent us wanted us to replace it with a new one, so we visited the Ford dealer to organise its purchase and shipping. We also visited various marinas, carrying out due diligence for our proposed facility for dock sales at Careenage.

We were fortunate that the Dresden Philharmonic was in town, and so in addition to lavish showers, delicious food cooked by someone else, and shopping, we were able to soothe our souls with some wonderful classical music after the trauma of a major hurricane and a very busy visit. Viv and I even went for our annual two-day physical at Cedars hospital. After the required pre-test fasting, and being declared totally fit, we indulged in a great meal and a bottle of wine.

Whilst in Miami we had been invited to Government House on 17th November for drinks with Prince Edward, who was visiting Cayman for the second time, but sadly had to decline due to previous commitments. We returned to Cayman on the 24th, and at CNCF we wanted to 'lift the spirits' after all Cayman had suffered from 'Ivan the Terrible'. So, on 27th November, CNCF presented Gimistory in the courtyard of our offices at Elizabethan Square. This was rapturously received by a huge crowd, happy to enjoy some light relief after months of difficulties. This was followed, as was the tradition, by a story tellers' party at Gaston Maloney's residence.

The Christmas season was now upon us, and the simultaneous opening of a Charles Long exhibition and one of Avril Ward's work at Grand Old House, was evidence of the Caymanians' ever-increasing interest in local art.

On my birthday Viv and I flew to Kingston and drove to Ocho Rios for the wedding of Dave and Noreen Twiss's daughter Vanessa 'Nessie' to Richie, held at Sans Souci. It was a wonderful opportunity to catch up with friends of many years' standing. While on the North Coast Viv and I drove to Harmony Hall, an eclectic restaurant and art gallery owned by Annabella and Peter Proudlock, and were much taken with a clay sculpture by Gene Pearson called 'Ashanti Lady', which we purchased to greet guests when Callaloo was completed. Annabella kindly packed the sculpture so we could carry it by hand, but when we boarded the plane, we placed it in the overhead luggage space and somehow it became damaged. When we told Henry Muttoo of our dilemma he immediately said 'No problem I will fix it', which he did, so that when you look at it today in Callaloo there is no sign that it had ever been damaged.

We celebrated the approaching Christmas season with a carol service at Government House, and on 20th December flew to Belfast to spend Christmas with Flo and visit family and friends. Returning via Heathrow, I had another meeting with David Bucknall in the airport terminal, followed by a meeting with Tim Raath to progress the business plan for the new Caribbean practice.

In many buildings damaged by Ivan, mould became a significant problem due to the damp conditions and prolonged power outage. During inspections of the affected buildings its presence was unmistakable – you could smell it, feel it, and even taste it on the back of your throat. Treating it required hazmat-suited workers to seal off the affected areas, remove the contaminated materials, and thoroughly deep-clean all surfaces. After this, air scrubbing was used to eliminate floating toxic particles. This process was expensive, and we had many arguments with the loss adjusters about whether the cost of such treatment was covered under the terms of the policy or not. Genesis was one building so affected, so we had to have the spaces treated. I am delighted to say we recovered the cost under the terms of our policy.

2005

'Experience is a hard teacher because she gives the test first, the lesson afterward.' Vernon Sanders Law

In January, Mark Green joined us. Mark had previously been employed with a marketing and public relations agency and so was able to design our corporate stationery and signs for the new office, which we had moved to the Commerce House building in central George Town. The volume of work CCAS was undertaking, and the seminars we were presenting, required more formal materials, and Mark Green developed a most professional brochure and marketing materials for us. More importantly, he quickly assimilated the requirements of reviewing claims and measuring site issues.

My Smart car had been written off, similar to approximately ten thousand other people's cars, due to its immersion by Ivan's storm surge. However, most owners were allowed to buy the cars back from their insurance company, which I did. I took it to my long-time mechanic and garage owner, Chris Van Der Bol, who rebuilt it and put it back on the road, and it served me well until I purchased a replacement in 2016.

Early in January, Jerry and I began planning our CCAS trips. They were to begin in April and include marketing trips to Trinidad and Tobago, Barbados, St Vincent and Grenada, followed by a FIDIC contract-focused seminar in Trinidad in September.

I met with Stanley Scott, who had provided fill for numerous development projects of mine over the years, and with Dave Champoux of Structural Engineers, Apec, at the site of Building #16 at the airport industrial park, to discuss the construction challenges on that development.

In late January I flew to Miami for an appointment at Cleveland Clinic to have an MRI scan of my back, which was giving me some trouble. I was diagnosed with a compressed spinal disc, and surgery was discussed. I was not keen on surgery so instead I consulted with Igor, who developed a water-based programme to elongate my spine and strengthen the muscles either side, with the result that to this day I have no issues with my back. It has been the same with any physical problem I have – just consult with Igor and he comes up with a solution.

Doreen Scott, Viv's childhood friend, who is an excellent seamstress, arrived in Cayman during February, and kindly spent the next five days at Callaloo, painstakingly making the drapes and sheers for the multitude of windows and French doors in our home.

Ray Morton, of Bucknall Austin in UK, arrived in Cayman on 8th February to progress the development of the business plan for our new company, which was to be called Bucknall Austin Caribbean Limited. In March, I travelled to Birmingham with Tim Raath, checked into the Hilton on Broad Street near my old 'stomping ground' night club, the Opposite Lock, and we then walked over to Bucknall Austin's head office for meetings with David Bucknall, John Morgan, Ann Bentley, and their other directors. We spent a week working through the business plan for the Caribbean company, which was enthusiastically received by all present, after which I returned to Cayman.

After catching up with a backlog of work for a few days, I left for Trinidad with Jerry, where we met with a wide variety of potential clients, including contractors, architects, engineers, insurance companies and government departments to whom we could present educational training seminars. Then we went to Grenada on 6th April, where we met more potential clients and also took the opportunity to inspect the damage from Hurricane Ivan, which had first devastated that island before moving on to Cayman. Looking at the stadium, with its concrete columns snapped in two, and the church with a gaping hole in its concrete floor, provided stark visual evidence of the hurricane's ferocity.

In St Vincent we met with a similar group of potential clients, after which, in Barbados, I met with Rupert Spencer, Tower Bucknall Austin's principal, and with Colin Brewer, a representative of the Airports Authority, about construction issues for which they wanted us to provide an opinion. In Miami I joined Viv to consult with a company called Mountain Travel Sobek about organising a hiking tour around Mont Blanc. We returned to Cayman on the 13th, in time for a Cayfest Benefit concert which we held in the Baptist Church Gym, followed by our Distinguished Lecture, held at UCCI.

There was increasing interest in our Careenage development, and several young Caymanian professionals were early preconstruction purchasers. This provided them with desirable waterfront locations and linear layouts that meant neighbours could not overlook their apartments. We were also talking to contractors about pricing the construction works.

On 5th May Viv and I flew to Washington DC at Jerry and Sheila Katz's kind invitation, to attend one of the CARE Dinners and Balls that Sheila helped organise. Small groups were invited for drinks and dinner at one of the Washington embassies. This was followed by dessert, coffee and dancing at a larger venue where all the guests were able to congregate. Over the years that we attended these most enjoyable black-tie functions, we were guests at the Indian, French and Maltese Embassies and the British Ambassador's Residence, the latter designed by Edwin Lutyens. In view of our work on the FCO's Caribbean properties, it was most informative to see this particular American property. During one evening at the French Embassy, there was an amusing incident during a performance by Eartha Kitt, when she sang 'My Heart Belongs to Daddy' while focusing her attention on Jerry all the while! While in Washington, I received a call from David Bucknall, which in retrospect was somewhat prophetic. He stressed that while Ann Bentley was the key director for financial matters, and David very much headed Bucknall Austin's external focus, John Morgan was meant to provide action, but that the board were somewhat disappointed in the results.

On 22nd May I flew to Barbados for Bucknall Austin Caribbean meetings with John Morgan and Rupert Spencer. Rupert had met John when they both worked at Silk & Frazier, a Birmingham-based QS practice, and then continued their association at Bucknall Austin, also based in Birmingham. On Rupert's return to Barbados, his current company, Tower Consultants, teamed up with Bucknall Austin to form Tower Bucknall Austin. While in Barbados I had a most enjoyable dinner with Robin Hunte and his wife Daphne. Robin was a member of the very popular Merrymen band, and Daphne ran a successful retail enterprise – Shellections – selling artifacts made from seashells with outlets in Barbados, Grand Cayman, BVI and other Caribbean locations.

I left Barbados two days later for Tortola to meet with Sheila George, our attorney, to discuss the operation of Bucknall Austin Caribbean in the BVI, and also to consult with potential partners in our future operation there.

From Tortola I flew to Kingston, to renew my US visa. The procedure was to arrive early and join the queue on the pavement outside the visa office on Oxford Road. Phones weren't allowed inside, so in true, enterprising Jamaican style, a local vendor walked along the queue collecting them in ziplock bags, giving handwritten receipts. With some trepidation I surrendered mine, hoping I would get it back. Inside, after a security search and a wait in another line, I was interviewed, asked why I needed a B1/B2 visa, and handed over my passport. I was told to return after lunch to collect it, properly stamped inside with the requisite visa. Viv had flown over to spend the weekend with Alan and Jenny at one of our favourite cottages – 'Highgate' at Strawberry Hill – and while waiting we had lunch at Norma's on the Patio at Devon House. Returning to the visa office, I was handed my passport and was about to leave after thanking the visa officer when she asked me to check it. I opened it – to see someone else's photo. Alfred Jack Birungi from Uganda, now a storeroom manager on a Carnival cruise liner, was to be my companion until my current passport was filled up or expired. The error was corrected of course: Mr Birungi's visa was stamped 'Cancelled Without Prejudice' and mine was properly inserted, but for years afterward immigration and airline officials would ask how that had happened! The only answer was, 'Even the US Embassy can make mistakes.'

In May, Scotiabank provided a term sheet for financing the Careenage Apartments construction, and the Careenage joint venture between Gingerbread Limited and Cayman Grand Harbour Development Ltd. would be signed on 25th July, moving the project one step closer to starting.

Viv and I spent five days in Miami finalising the Tour de Mont Blanc hike with Mountain Travel Sobek. It was to start in Chamonix on 3rd September, but we were cutting the hike short on the 9th, as we had been invited to René and Claudine's fiftieth wedding anniversary in Lugano. This would begin on the 11th and last for several days, and could certainly not be missed!

In July, I attended a seminar in London on the benefits of using the FIDIC construction contract. I also met with John Morgan to discuss details of the business plan for Bucknall Austin Caribbean. He and Rupert Spencer would visit Cayman in early August for more meetings. While in the UK, I received a telephone call from Cayman with the devasting news that David Foster had died. I arranged to return to Cayman for the memorial ceremony, held on 13th July at Pedro's Castle. It was hard to take in that David was no longer with us, after all the fun we'd had together since my arrival in Cayman.

Remedial works to the Genesis building to repair the hurricane damage were progressing well, and so was the work to rebuild the Anchorage and the George Town Villas, which we were managing. Negotiations with the adjusters about the hurricane damage continued. These included claims about loss of rent, and losses suffered as a result of mould. These were, in many cases, specifically excluded from the policy. The timing of when water damage resulted in mould development, and its subsequent remediation, was a fine balance point in negotiations.

In Trinidad we were assisting Chris De Verteuil of Pres-T-Con, the piling sub-contractor, with a claim against the main contractor concerning the construction of the jetty for Atlantic LNG Company. The amount of piling needed had grown exponentially from an earlier jetty they had constructed, due to revisions to the construction codes. As with so many claims, how changes in scope had caused delay were key, and we solicited the assistance of Charles Leonard to work on the scheduling aspects of the claim.

We were fine-tuning the content for a CCAS seminar to be sponsored by the Institute of Surveyors of Trinidad and Tobago. Its title was to be 'FIDIC 1999 and TTIA 82 – Perfect Contracts or Perfectly Awful', to be held in October 2005. Jerry and I were to be joined by Peter Morris, a Trinidad-based Quantity Surveyor and Project Manager for this event. At the same time, on the Mini Warehouse development front, we had received a financing offer from Andrew Hulse, our ever-friendly banker at Bank of Butterfield, who were now financing our sixteenth building with them.

I visited Barbados twice in August for meetings with the Grantley Adams Airport Authority, who had claims against the contractor building their new airport. During the second, I was at least able to entertain Robin and Daphne Hunte for dinner at our favourite restaurant, The Cliff, which not only had superb food and service but had a dramatic location on a cliff above the deep blue Caribbean Sea.

In September, Viv and I began our Tour de Mont Blanc trek, a spectacular climb that winds around the Mont Blanc massif through France, Italy and Switzerland. Between climbing and descending, we accumulated some 14,500 vertical feet in four days. We trekked through Les Houches, Les Contamines over the Col de Voza, and then to Les Chapieux. From La Ville Des Glaziers we hiked to Courmayeur in Italy's Aosta valley, finishing in Ferret in Switzerland. On most days we hiked for around six hours, but had the luxury of carrying only a day pack on our backs while a van brought our main luggage to a hostel each evening. Our guide on this trip was memorable because he did not change his shirt the whole time, and we soon did our best to stay upwind of him!

René and Claudine's fiftieth wedding anniversary in Lugano was quite a party! It lasted all weekend as lunches were followed by dinners and boat trips, one of which included an on-board tango demonstration by René and Claudine, of which they are master performers. We had not been able to find a suitable present for them before we arrived, and were racking our brains as to what we could get the couple that had everything. At dinner one evening, a very fine bottle of Barolo, by a maker called Luigi Baudana, was served and we said 'That's it!' We would drive the two hundred and forty kilometres to Serralunga d'Alba – a commune of Barolo – to collect a case of this excellent wine and be back in double-quick time. We reached Serralunga d'Alba at lunchtime, with no idea where to find Mr Baudana. The streets were empty except for one lone man walking down the street. So we stopped and asked him if he knew where to find our winemaker. As fate would have it, he was Luigi Baudana himself, and he invited us to his house for a tasting. We purchased two cases of this magnificent wine – one for René and Claudine, and one for our cellar back in Cayman.

On the 14th we drove to Draguignan to spend two wonderful days catching up on all the news with Joan and Alan Scott, and then to Morzine, where we spent three days hiking with Alan and Doreen Scott from their holiday home. During the visit I offered to cook chicken paillard, for which I hammered the chicken breasts flat, marinated them in olive oil, white wine, lemon and oregano and placed them on a very hot barbecue grill to sear them rapidly on each side and to leave grill marks in an attractive grid pattern on the meat. It was a new grill, and although the heat level was perfect, I may have used too much olive oil. Flames burst from the grill, threatening to set fire to the wooden structure of the holiday home! All's well that ends well, and the flames were extinguished, a fine glass of wine drunk, and a tasty dinner enjoyed by all.

Finally back in Cayman on the 21st, it felt good to return to a more normal, pre-hurricane routine. It was also pleasant to deal with 'new build' projects, as opposed to rebuilding hurricane-damaged buildings. Initial work began on Mini Warehouse's site for Building #16, which included meetings with the filling contractors – Paul Bodden, Stanley Scott and Justin Wood – to obtain competitive bids to fill the low-lying site. With lessons learnt from the flooding of adjacent buildings during Hurricane Ivan, we not only filled the site but also revised the plans to raise the floor level. The updated plans were developed by B.G. Serrant, and negotiations continued with Phoenix Group as general contractors for the build. Works were also continuing apace on the George Town Villas renovation project, and the owners held a thank-you BBQ poolside on 26th September, preceded by the Strata Corporation's AGM, where we were able to provide details to all on both the construction progress and the settlement negotiations with the insurers.

Viv and I flew to Miami for a wonderful performance by Pavarotti on 1st October, followed by dinner with our good friend and next-door neighbour at Plantana, John Davies. I left Miami the next day and flew to Port of Spain, where I met Mike Samms of the Institute of Surveyors of Trinidad and Tobago (ISTT). They had sponsored the CCAS seminar, 'FIDIC 1999 and TTIA 82 – Perfect Contracts or Perfectly Awful', which Jerry Katz, Peter Morris and I presented to a capacity crowd at the Normandie Hotel on 5th October. We took the opportunity to cover the cultural front, and met with Louis McWilliams, a talented drummer who frequently visited Cayman with dancers and storytellers. We also visited the Trinidadian artist, Leroy Clarke, at his home. There, upon meeting us, he enquired (to our embarrassment) where was the requisite bottle of duty-free Johnnie Walker Black Label whisky?

The 25th October saw the welcome party for Stuart Jack, our new Governor, who would go on to dispense with the ceremonial gubernatorial white uniform and hat and to finalise the modernised Constitution in 2009, his final year in Cayman.

John Doak submitted the plans for Careenage to the planning department for approval, and we had several meetings with Steve Ryder from Bellingham Marine to progress our ideas for stratified docks for sale as part of the development. In Trinidad, Jerry and I had meetings with Pres-T-Con to discuss their claim with Bechtel on the ALNG jetty, making a site visit to 'South', as they refer to this area of Trinidad. We also visited with Leroy Clarke again, this time accompanied by Johnnie Walker Black Label! We also met with Petrotrin and planned a CCAS educational seminar for their engineers to be held in February 2006

Callaloo was rapidly nearing completion by now. I met with Iberia tiles in Miami to source replacement tiles for those damaged during Ivan, and visited our good friend Leo Rodriquez at South Dade Lighting to source landscape lights. Back in Cayman, I met with McAlpine's project manager, Dave Hoptroff, to go over the list of outstanding defects. Completing these items would allow the project, so close to being finalised before Hurricane Ivan struck over a year earlier, to finally be concluded.

Viv and I were going through an interesting time. In many ways, I was holding on to the life we had enjoyed at Plantana and the 'beach scene', whereas Viv could see the private garden and expansive home space at Callaloo. So the move from one home to another might be best described as gradual, with me shifting my possessions one Smart car load at a time to our new, spacious home.

We had persuaded the bankers, Coutts, to sponsor a National Gallery exhibition at Pedro's Castle that year and also the 'Dancing to Art' exhibition at the National Gallery that followed on 24th November. CNCF Gimistory took place at Dart Park in South Sound, with its Sunday night closing celebration held at Gaston Maloney's house on 27th November.

Our tenth wedding anniversary and my sixtieth birthday were fast approaching and we had planned a black-tie event to be our first party at Callaloo. Mark Green was preparing the invitations and dinner menus, and we were delighted to secure the services of Eugenio Leon, 'Cayman Islands King of Romance', to serenade us with his harp during dinner, and Ed Solomon to play for dancing by the pool. Not all our furniture had arrived yet and we borrowed several round tables to accommodate our dinner guests in Callaloo's Great Room.

Ever since our wedding ten years earlier, we had always turned to Joanne Brown of Celebrations to help with the organisation of putting on a seamless event. So, we met with her and her team on 5th December to plan the celebration, which was to set the standard for many similar gatherings to come. Victor from Imperial Cabinets, the finish carpentry company, was fitting out the library and Great Room cabinets at Callaloo as the party celebrations were being discussed, and was frequently around during photo calls. He obviously felt it important to join the family and friends photo op, and so there's a stranger in the family album!

The festivities began with a large party for many friends on Friday the 9th, followed by a black-tie dinner on Saturday, a boat trip on the North Sound to visit our world-famous Stingray City during the day on Sunday, finishing with a relaxed, informal dinner on Sunday evening.

We were blessed with the presence of so many of our friends from both overseas and locally, including Basil and Sammy Behrman, Jerry and Sheila Katz, Sallie Naylor, our nephews Jonnie and Edward, and my brother, Rob. My brother has been a cigar aficionado for many years, and wanted to take the opportunity of Cayman's proximity to Cuba to fly over and purchase some of the world's finest. So, he duly departed after the event, appropriately dressed in a linen jacket and Panama hat, and arrived in Havana, where he was rapidly relieved of his wallet by a pickpocket. Thus being rendered penniless, he reported to the British Embassy, where he was provided with spending money and a roof over his head for the night before returning to Cayman.

After all the fun and the pleasure of seeing friends, came the sad news from Sacha Propper that on the 12th my long-time friend Henry Propper had suffered a stroke which had affected his speech and comprehension, and that he was being treated in the Baptist hospital in Miami.

Igor Burdenko had been able to join us for the celebrations, and was able to come to Callaloo with Dottie for a 7am workout session in the pool to repair some of ravages caused by the previous days' indulgence. For Christmas we went to see Viv's parents in Belfast and had a grand time, which even included a white Christmas.

2006

'Yesterday I was clever, so I wanted to change the world. Today I am wise, so I am changing myself.' Rumi

Viv and I wanted to thank all the workers that had created our wonderful dream home, so we hosted a party for them all on 20th January. During the party, one of the masons – the son of Mr Harvey, who had for years been a gardener at Plantana – presented us with a gunny sack. We opened it, and inside was an offcut from one of the lower sections of the columns we had installed in the house, which he had beautifully carved with the finely detailed face of a cat, which as you will see was prophetic, and which graces our entry hallway. All of the workers thanked us for thinking of them and said this was the first occasion where the owners of a house had given them a party of thanks.

During January I was occupied with several development projects. These included the Careenage apartments and docks; a Professional Village at Cayman Grand Harbour; the completion of Building #16 at the Mini Warehouse airport site, and finalising the details with John Morgan and David Bucknall for Bucknall Austin Caribbean.

I had been asking Mike Bell about contractors for the Careenage project and he suggested that I contact a construction manager he knew called Alan Veeran. Mike gave me Alan's cell phone number, and I gave him a call. We met on 26th January, when I gave him a copy of the plans. This initial meeting would be the start of a lasting business association and deep friendship.

In mid-February I met with Jerry in Port of Spain, where we presented a two-day risk management seminar to some thirty-six senior managers of the Petroleum Company of Trinidad & Tobago (Petrotrin). We were delighted by the lively exchange of questions and answers, indicating the attendees' comprehensive grasp of the issues they faced with the use of their chosen EPC form of contract. From Trinidad we flew to Barbados for meetings with Rupert Spencer, and from Barbados to St Vincent to meet with Trevor Thompson of TVA Consultants, whom we were advising in regard to their performance on design consulting services for the National Stadium project.

I stopped off in Miami for the weekend of 24th February and had discussions with John Morgan about producing Caribbean Intelligence for Bucknall Austin Caribbean. The idea was to share information about what was happening in the Caribbean through publications, seminars and cocktail parties. Over the years this developed into a major marketing promotion for the company. We would hold events in London, Miami, Toronto, Cayman and the Caribbean, and published economic data and construction cost information annually.

Returning to Cayman at the end of the month, I met with land surveyor Roland Bodden and the Lands & Survey department. We were working to resolve the positioning of theoretical boundary points on the canal bed in front of Careenage – an important step in being able to sell stratified boat slips as part of the development. By March, things were moving forward. We had negotiated a construction agreement with Alan's company, Smart Construction Management Limited, at an acceptable price and the start date for commencing to build the first sixteen apartments at Careenage was set for 10th April 2006.

At CNCF we were seeking bids to repair the significant hurricane damage to the Harquail Theatre so we could negotiate a settlement with the insurers. On 6th March I viewed the progress on site and shortly thereafter was asked by the Governor, Stuart Jack, to provide an update on how we were progressing.

During a visit to London at the end of March, I was advised that John Morgan was leaving Bucknall Austin. Given the work involved in setting up Bucknall Austin Caribbean, this was a blow, but I was advised that Simon Birchall, previously of Hanscomb's, was assuming John's position and had all of the joint venture paperwork for the company. I arranged to meet with Simon on Monday 27th March. Simon's initial comments about Bucknall Austin Caribbean were not very encouraging, as he began our meeting by saying he did not understand what Bucknall Austin, a UK company, were doing in the Caribbean. He felt that John Morgan's ownership of an apartment at the Crane in Barbados might have been more of a driving factor than the Caribbean's business opportunities. This view was to change rapidly due to events that took place a year later, but that was yet to happen. In the meantime, I left the meeting with the uncomfortable feeling that all the effort to get us to that point may have been in vain. However, David Bucknall assured me this was not the case, and that he would step back in and follow through with what we had agreed.

I was back in Cayman on the 28th, in time for the launch of the third edition of CNCF's culture magazine *Foundation* at the Brasserie restaurant. Highlighting the richness and breadth of CNCF's work, this edition featured an interview with Miss Lassie on her eighty-seventh birthday, interviews with actors and artists, with Frankie Flowers who was making a big impression in film-making, and an article on Dance Cayman, which had exploded onto the dance scene at the Aberdeen International Youth Festival in the summer of 2005.

In Trinidad we were invited by Udecott, the Urban Development Corporation headed by their MD, Calder Hart, to advise on construction issues for a wide range of projects, with a total value in excess of US$1 billion. These included delays on the five new buildings in downtown Port of Spain, known as Government Campus Plaza, as well as the Brian Lara Cricket Academy.

For a number of years, I had been asking Charlie Adams (attorney Charles Adam's son), from Artifacts antiques, to let me know if he came across any particular item that looked to be a good investment. Charlie demurred, saying he really didn't like making recommendations to friends because if they didn't work out it might cause a rift in their friendship. However, he called me on 18th April saying his good friend Rex Cowan, engaged in salvage, had acquired the rights to a treasure ship called the *Rooswijk*, which had sunk off the Goodwin Sands on 9th January 1740. The cargo had included silver bars that were being sent from the Amsterdam Mint to the Dutch East Indies to be melted down and made into coins for the various governments there. Charlie felt they would be an excellent investment, and so I asked him to buy twenty of these bars for me, costing £33,000. This Charlie did, then asked where I wanted them stored. I had to admit I hadn't thought about the implications of physical acquisition – each ingot weighed about 5lbs! Charlie was in the UK, and I asked if he could locate a safe storage facility. Being the great friend that he is, he said that wouldn't be a problem and duly deposited them in a very safe facility in his own name, protected by iris-secured technology. This remained the state of affairs for a little over a year, until one day Charlie called me and said, 'I don't know how to tell you this, but the police have seized the safe storage facility as it was reputed to contain stolen goods!' But he also said not to worry, because he had appropriate certification to show the silver bars had been acquired legally. The bars were indeed safe, but we could not get access to them until the police had completed their investigation. We eventually did, and moved them across north London on a set of luggage wheels to another facility in my own name. I'm pleased to say they have been an excellent investment in spite of their 'romantic' nature.

All the while Cayfest was well underway, and with a new event called 'Culture 360', which was held at the Westin Hotel, Praise, and a Coutts-sponsored event at Grand Old House.

After a meeting in Barbados with Rupert Spencer and Miles Weekes, I again met Jerry in Port of Spain to give a seminar on 3rd May to more than seventy attendees from the ISTT. The seminar was entitled 'Understanding Construction Claims', and included a workshop devoted to managing claims for delay, variations, disruption, price escalation and other common construction problems. The next day we presented the same seminar to the procurement team of the Educational Facilities Company, after which I returned to Cayman to be home with Viv for her birthday on 7th May.

There were, of course, hurdles with regard to the Careenage project. By the early May we were facing a three-month delay in sourcing fill – and we needed a substantial amount to fill the Careenage site: 10,000 cubic yards. But progress continued nonetheless. By August we received our planning approval letter, and construction queries would keep us busy throughout that month even as sales activity picked up. By the end of August the site would be visibly transformed, with excavation complete and steel fixed.

Towards the end of May we were approached again by the contractor in Vieux Fort in St Lucia who had built a new police station and was having problems with collecting his final monies due. Jerry and I agreed to fly down and meet with him, which we did, flying via Barbados and staying overnight at the Accra Beach on the south coast, before flying on to St Lucia and then back to Cayman on 5th June.

Our new Mini Warehouse climate-controlled project, 'affectionately' known as Building #16, was nearing completion and we gave the interior circulation corridors some personality by naming them 'Bould Boulevard', 'Foster Freeway', and 'Dise Drive', after the three shareholder groups.

In mid-June I left Cayman to represent Cayman and the CNCF at the third global IFACCA summit held in Newcastle. I returned to London on 17th June and went on to Cliveden, where we celebrated Vivian's sixtieth birthday in style: a black-tie dinner with friends in the 'Blue Room', followed by a trip down the Thames on the *Suzy Ann* barge to the Waterside Inn for Sunday lunch. We had a wonderful table facing the river and a memorable meal rounded out with brandy and cigars. Eventually, loath as we were to end this magnificent event, I asked Diego, the maître d', for the bill. He replied, 'Mr Bould I trust you have had a wonderful meal with us, and you certainly would not want to spoil it with the bill. I will post it to you in Cayman and you can send us a cheque.' I have repeated this story on subsequent visits to Alain Roux, then the Waterside Inn's head chef and his father, Michael Roux, the owner, and I am not too sure that they approved – but they smiled anyway, in a true professional manner!

We left London on 19th June and flew to Nice for a walking tour around Provence, after which we visited St Paul de Vence for Rob and Jenna's twenty-fifth wedding anniversary. Rob had attended Bishop Vesey Grammar School, as had both I and Alan Scott, our former Governor, who had driven to St Paul de Vence with Joan to join us for lunch. We took a photograph of the three Old Veseyans, which we sent to the school magazine. I then returned to London for meetings with David Bucknall, who had stepped in to continue the development of Bucknall Austin Caribbean as he had promised, and then back to Cayman.

On 10th July, Viv and I flew to Lima for a Harvard reunion in Peru and Ecuador organised by our alumni hosts, Vincente and Evelyn Sanchez. After spending the night in Lima, we travelled to Cusco and took the train to Machu Picchu, the 15th century Inca citadel, considered to be one of the new Seven Wonders of the World. It was indeed spectacular, and we spent a long time walking around the complex and reading about the fascinating uses of the separate buildings.

We then flew from Lima to Bogota and on to Quito, where we were shown around the city by Vincente and Evelyn. The tour included a visit to Vincente's mother's chocolate store, where we were given a beautiful wooden box containing handmade chocolates. After eating these, which were delicious, we kept the box. It now accompanies Viv and me on all our travels, as we keep our daily vitamins in it to have with our breakfast.

Of course, we could not be so close to the Equator without straddling it – one foot in the northern and the other in the southern hemisphere!

On 18th July, we visited Latacunga in Ecuador to view Cotopaxi, one of the highest active volcanoes in the world – 19,347 feet at the summit – and one of the few equatorial glaciers. We followed this with an adventure travelling on the roof of the Devil's Nose train. This is a section of the Quito to Guayaquil railroad constructed in 1901 that passes through the rocky slopes of the Andes, and it travels through some of Ecuador's most breathtaking scenery. It is so named because out of 3,000 Jamaicans and 2,000 Puerto Ricans who were bought in to work on the project, approximately 2,000 of them died during its construction. After the project was completed, many of the workers decided to stay, including some three hundred Jamaicans. One of Ecuador's most famous singers of the past, Julio Jaramillo, was a descendant of one of these Jamaican workers who remained in the new land.

Subsequently, we travelled by boat through the Galapagos Islands, which are a UNESCO World Heritage Site. We observed many native birds and also visited Lonesome George, the hundred-year-old giant tortoise – and the last of his subspecies – at the Charles Darwin Station on the island of Santa Cruz. We returned to Cayman at the end of July.

On 12th and 13th September, CCAS presented a seminar sponsored by First Caribbean International Bank with the title 'Public Private Partnerships and Understanding Construction Claims', held at the Barbados Hilton. We increased our speaker roll to include David Cooper, Director of Barclays Private Finance Initiative Group in the UK; David Quirk from Bucknall Austin Project Management Group in the UK; Rupert Spencer from Tower Bucknall Austin, Barbados, and Jerry and myself. The first day we dealt with the intricacies of the financing package and the complex contractual arrangements of this form of procurement, and on the second day we focused on claims that may arise from the procurement process and gave insight into how to avoid or deal with such claims in an efficient manner. Judging by the exit poll, the seminar was considered to be most timely and appropriate, and the audience felt that learning from the experiences of others who had resolved the problems of Public Private Partnerships in other jurisdictions was invaluable. In addition to local attendees, many other professionals who had enjoyed CCAS's seminars in their home islands attended – so our fame was spreading!

In connection with the work I was doing with CCAS, and our attempts at resolving construction disputes in the most efficient manner possible, Gordon Jaynes had recommended me as the Caribbean representative of the Dispute Resolution Board Foundation. I attended their annual conference in Orlando, Florida from 5th–8th October, and it was great to meet with so many like-minded people, as well as having the opportunity to catch up with Gordon Jaynes, whom I had not seen for some time.

Once back in Cayman, as Head of Delegation, I needed to conclude the final stages of planning for our contingent to attend Carifesta IX from 22nd September to 1st October in Port of Spain, Trinidad. As usual, Carifesta was great exposure for our young Caymanian artists to see themselves in the wider Caribbean cultural context, which they thoroughly enjoyed. CNCF was also invited by Val Kempadoo of the Gayelle TV network to be interviewed live, which gave the Cayman team great exposure to share their experiences of participating in Carifesta. Later in October, we held a get-together for the team at Callaloo, so that, having had time to reflect on their Trinidad visit, they could reshare their experiences with various other artists who had not had the opportunity to attend in person.

We went on to host an associated event at Callaloo on 28th November, called 'Culture Meets Tourism', employing the multiple talents of the Gimistory team. We had discussed the plan with the Ministry of Culture, Ministry of Tourism, Cayman Islands Tourism Association, and various hotel staff, and I met with Mark Green at the beginning of October and asked him to prepare the marketing material for the event, which would require us to build a stage over the swimming pool. The celebrations kicked off with the arrival of the Tassa drummers organised by Henry Muttoo – a loud, lively and attention-grabbing start to the evening. This was followed by our own Swanky Kitchen Band, Dance Unlimited and Kirk Rowe dance performances, and storytelling, which included David Bereaux and Black Sage's unique delivery. Not only was the evening most entertaining, but it achieved its second objective of highlighting our local talent and how it could be used to promote tourism in our islands.

A visit to Trinidad had given me the opportunity to visit with my good friend, architect Dave Twiss, who yet again obliged with accommodation. We had initially met in Kingston in 1969, and it was good to catch up on all his news. I also got the chance to view Leroy Clarke's exhibition, on show in the National Museum in Port of Spain; meet with representatives of Udecott regarding the projects we were reviewing for them, on which Steve Mendes was also working, and with Pres T Con regarding the ALNG claim. During this visit a director of Barbados Investment and Development Corporation phoned to asked me to fly to Barbados for the day to see how we could assist on the Newton Business Park, a project they were developing on which they were suffering significant delays. This I did, incidentally missing an earthquake that shook Trinidad while I was airborne. Just as well. With the construction claims I was dealing with, my life contained enough turmoil without experiencing any natural additions!

Interestingly, following my meeting with Dave Twiss in Trinidad and the invitation from Val Kempadoo to appear on the Gayelle TV channel, Dave called me on 1st November and said he was designing a project that Val was developing on the slopes of Mount Liamuiga in St Kitts, called Kittitian Village, and asked if we would be interested in providing cost consulting services. We were, of course, delighted to do so, especially given our long-standing connection with St Kitts over the years and, in my case, with the Frigate Bay Infrastructure project, which dated back to 1969.

The Careenage project continued at a good pace. Alan was pushing for final selections: kitchens, plumbing fixtures, doors and floor tiles. Construction of the second block 'C' began on 28th November. Sales were also progressing well – so well, in fact, that we began looking for additional parcels of land to continue development based on Careenage's highly successful formula. Meanwhile, the strata dock component of the development was also progressing. We were in ongoing discussions with Bellingham Marine about the technical servicing of the docks – electricity, water and sewage – which needed to be integrated into the dock walkway system.

CCAS's involvement with the BIDC Newton Business Park in Barbados was gathering momentum. The main contractor was from Trinidad, and we would have significant additional involvement with them in connection with the UDeCOTT projects there in the future. Jerry and I flew to Barbados on 5th November for meetings with BIDC to discuss in detail the reasons for the extensive delays and lack of progress towards completion, the poor quality of the work to date, and what we could do to turn the project around. Subsequently, in Port of Spain, Jerry and I presented a seminar to UDeCOTT, highlighting how to do this.

As I mentioned, the educational seminars we were presenting had an excellent marketing effect. While in Barbados, I met with Angus Edghill, who was experiencing problems converting a building he owned into the new home for the American Embassy. He had heard we might be able to help. The work was complex, as it was being overseen by US security personnel. So, for example, materials such as windows had to be selected at random and could not be assigned to specific locations in advance. All services, particularly those running through the ceiling spaces, could only be installed under the direct supervision of security staff. The problem was that there weren't enough security personnel available to allow the work to proceed at the originally planned pace.

John Doak called me on 18th November, to say that the leading lifestyle magazine *MACO*, the coffee table publication that focussed on outstanding and unique architecture throughout the Caribbean, wanted to visit Callaloo. They were contemplating featuring our home as the 'Culture House'. This was indeed a compliment to the sensitivity with which we and John Doak had designed and built the house to reflect its West Indian heritage.

By late November fundraising for the National Gallery was continuing apace, and we came up with the idea of bricks for an outside patio, each embossed with the name of a donor. Fortunately, Roger Judd, one of my buyers in the Great House project, owned a brick-making company and so I was able to seek his assistance with getting the bricks made.

To close out the month on a positive note, Wil Steward of Chalmers Gibbs confirmed we had received planning approval for the Professional Village we were planning to develop at Cayman Grand Harbour.

In early December Viv and I left for Alta, to ski in what the licence plates of Utah cars describe as 'the greatest snow on earth', which indeed it is, and we enjoyed many great days of skiing in the featherlight powder.

At CCAS we were very busy as we approached the Christmas close-down, and Jerry called to confirm that one of our UDeCOTT projects, the construction of the Brian Lara Cricket Academy, needed to receive our opinion report no later than 12th January 2007. Given the time of year, this was indeed a tall order.

We enjoyed delicious Christmas lunch at Callaloo with Andrew and Felicity Jones, Mike and Donna Kelly and Sallie Naylor, during which we had a Carabella wine-tasting and fine Madeira, this being Andrew's specialty and which we have enjoyed with him on so many wonderful occasions. The next day Alan and Jenny Foster from Jamaica joined us for post-Christmas and New Year celebrations. From the comments in our guest book, it seems we had a wonderful party!

2007

'Be mindful of your ultimate purpose, which isn't to meet a deadline, but to create a day with happiness in it.' Deepak Chopra

On 4th January 2007, I flew to Barbados for meetings on the BIDC Newton Business Park. The next day I was called to a meeting with the Minister of

Economic Affairs and Development, together with the team of professional advisors who had engineered the project from its inception and monitored it to its present state of much-delayed and unsatisfactory completion. The Minister tore a strip off all the advisors, and I was very glad to be the consultant advising on how to solve the problems rather than one of those responsible for its current state. The Minister, Mia Mottley, had been the first ever female Attorney General in Barbados and was to become the first ever female Prime Minister. I would continue to cross her path, including with President Bill Clinton as part of the Clinton Global Initiative.

During the second week of January, I met up with Jerry at the Coblenz Inn, a small boutique hotel in Port of Spain that was a favourite of ours. We were there to present our second EDFAC two-day educational seminar called, 'Negotiating Construction Contracts' to some twenty-eight of their project managers. It featured an analysis of the different types of construction risks to be considered when a contract is negotiated, and how those risks are allocated. It also addressed matters such as performance issues, including scheduling, notice, and scope change management. The seminar almost immediately resulted in work for us with EDFAC, who asked us to assist them with various design and build projects they were considering for new schools.

After a quick hop to St Vincent to meet with the Attorney General on the Stadium claim there, Jerry and I returned to Port of Spain the same day to present a CCAS educational seminar, 'Managing Construction Risk' to the team of some forty UDeCOTT project managers, focusing on important contract clauses covering programming, record keeping and claims, disputes and their negotiation.

In Cayman, Viv and I attended the National Gallery's Art at Governor's exhibition on 27th January. For this event, the Governor graciously opened the grounds of Government House to local artists and artisans to display and sell their work in a daylong event. The Harquail Theatre rebuild following Hurricane Ivan was proceeding well, but we were waiting for the delivery of new carpet, drapes and seating.

On 1st February, Viv and I flew to London and on to ski in Verbier with Ray and Michèle, and Roger and Jill. Ray, like Roger, worked at CERN in Geneva, and they asked if we would like to go down inside the almost completed Collider to see what it was like before it was put into operation. We donned hard hats and descended in the lift into this massive machine, which was indeed fascinating. After that we drove to Morzine to ski with Doreen, Alan and Rachel for five days.

David Bucknall called me whilst I was skiing in Morzine, and enthusiastically endorsed the Bucknall Austin Caribbean practice. The work book now included several potential and current projects: one hundred and eighty-eight schools in Trinidad; the work we were doing for UDeCOTT, including Government Campus Plaza and the Brian Lara Cricket Academy; a potential Rapid Transit System, working with several major contractors including Bouygues, Carillion, Bechtel, Turner and China State; work in Barbados for World Cup Cricket; work for Peter de Savary on a Grenada hotel, and several proposed luxury hotels in Turks and Caicos for Ritz, Aman, and Four Seasons. Some weeks later, I received a request from Simon Birchall for the Capability Statement we had published. At the time, I attached no particular importance to the incident given he had not been overenthusiastic about Bucknall Austin Caribbean during our first meeting in London.

On 19th February, in my capacity as chairman of the CNCF, I was invited to attend a youth symposium at the Marriott hotel, along with youth and social workers, church leaders, and government representatives. We had been provided with a copy of an excellent government-commissioned report by Bajan criminologist Yolande Forde, entitled 'Pre-Disposing Factors to Criminality in the Cayman Islands'. The report was eye-opening in its analysis of how and why some of our youth end up becoming criminals rather than successful members of society. In its conclusion, the report notes:

> One can conclude that the determinants of crime are rooted in the life experiences of the individuals who have been arrested, convicted and incarcerated. Moreover, as the study reveals, the seeds of destruction were often sown early in their youth. However, it is critical to note that when criminal risk factors are present in the life of a child, there must be appropriate early intervention if one wishes to save that individual from drifting down the path of anti-social behaviour, delinquency and ultimately into the revolving doors of the criminal justice system.
>
> It is important to understand that there is a fundamental difference between controlling the incidents of crime and teaching people, from a young age, how to control themselves. Everything must be done to address the circumstances that are crime generative in nature so that the individual does not develop a criminal pre-disposition. It is unfortunate that, over the years, myopic and blinkered views about crime prevention have led to an emphasis on individual crime prevention and control (i.e. policing) much to the neglect of more primary forms of prevention which would ultimately mean less hassle for the police and also less expenditure. One approach needs to complement the other. Therefore, what is hoped for in the

Cayman Islands is a comprehensive and holistic crime prevention strategy, one that contains elements of situational crime prevention and dispositional crime prevention which has been the focus of this Report.

We spent the day discussing the report, and had a follow-up meeting on 14th March after having had time to consider the information we had received. With my quantity surveyor's mindset, I was particularly struck by Yolande's conclusion, drawn from her extensive and comprehensive analysis, that we needed to control both the incidents of crime and, most importantly, to teach self-control from a young age.

This led me to ask how many students were currently attending school. I was informed there were approximately seven thousand five hundred, of which three thousand were in private schools and four thousand five hundred in government schools. There was no reason to assume that students in one group were more susceptible to criminality than the other. However, focussing on the students in government schools, I estimated – based on the report's findings and factors such as latch key children and single-parent households – that perhaps 10 per cent of them might be particularly vulnerable. That gave us four hundred and fifty children to focus on.

Surely, I thought, teachers could identify these at-risk students and, on an island that was one of the world's leading financial centres, it seemed feasible that we could assign a mentor to each of these children, someone to guide them away from criminality. I even considered that, if needed, these mentors could be recruited by the draconian method of requiring applicants to take on a mentoring role to secure a work permit.

To prepare myself for advancing this idea, I re-read *Getting to Yes*, by Roger Fisher and William Ury, a book about effective negotiating strategies I had first encountered at Harvard. I recall meeting with the Governor, the Chief Minister, the Attorney General and the Solicitor General, as well as Joe Crawford, our pastor at Elmslie Church, to share my ideas. Although there were nods of support and general agreement, nothing sadly developed in this regard.

It was an interesting and serendipitous twist of fate, that some twelve years later, our company, Bould Consulting Limited, would be awarded the contract to prepare the Outline Business Case for the rebuilding of the HMCIPS prison estate, an assignment that would very much focus on the recommendations contained in Yolande's Report. In another coincidence, Yolande's brother, Mark Forde, would become our corporate lawyer for a company we would set up in Barbados.

Jeremy Delmar-Morgan, our stockbroker in London, was a good friend of Bobby Nunes and always entertained us royally when we were there. He came for dinner at Callaloo in early March, with Jeremy and Joanne Sibley, Andrew and Felicity Jones and, of course, Bobby. Little did we know, as we enjoyed wonderful food and Carabella wine, that in August the world would commence its plunge into the worst financial crisis in history, and that would lead to Lehman Brothers's bankruptcy a year later.

John Doak submitted the plans for the stratified docks at Careenage to the Planning department for approval on 12th March. He also told us that the journalists from *MACO* magazine were now in Cayman and were still interested in featuring Callaloo in the magazine. Viv and I were initially somewhat hesitant about this proposal. However, after some discussion, we agreed, particularly as such an article would provide an opportunity to focus on the events we held at our home to promote Caymanian culture and tourism. It would be some time before the article was actually published and, in addition to the interview, many days of photography were involved. The meticulous photographer, David Wolfe, changed many of our traditional on/off light switches to variable intensity controls, so that the evening lighting effect in the photographs was just right. The final result was appropriately fabulous.

Vivian and I flew to Denver on the 16th to ski for ten days. We enjoyed Snowmass, Ajax, and then Steamboat and Keystone, staying as Mike Bell's guests at his Lone Eagle condo right on the slopes. We were back in Cayman on 28th March, in time to visit the Brac for the opening of CNCF's Bracfest. While there, I took the opportunity to meet with Conroy Ebanks, Tennyson and Simone Scott, to solicit their support as potential members of the Brac contingent of CNCF.

Cayfest began in April, with CNCF's distinguished lecture on 25th April, the Red Men performance at the Harquail on 27th April, and Roy Bodden's book launch of *The Cayman Islands in Transition – the politics, history and sociology of a changing society* at UCCI on the 28th. Cayman was indeed a much-changed society compared with what it had been when I'd first arrived, and Roy's laser insight reawakened at least some of us to the changes which were, of course, both good and bad. As part of the awakening of all things cultural, CNCF launched a new addition to the Cayfest lineup: a display of Caymanian fashion talent, called FRESH, on 29th April.

The National Trust's Mission House, in Bodden Town, opened on 4th May. For many years, and particularly during my chairmanship from 1998 to 2002, we had worked hard to reconstruct the house, which had been donated to the Trust by the Watler family in 1997. Sadly, it had been destroyed by Hurricane

Ivan in 2004. However, it was now rebuilt to highlight the traditional building techniques used during its original era. The garden represents a 19th century Caymanian yard, with ornamental and fruit trees, and a natural pond with wild birds and Cayman freshwater turtles, called 'hickatees'. It is believed this freshwater pond is what had originally made the site so popular with locals; not only did it have an abundance of waterfowl but also would have provided a supply of fresh water.

The CCAS wagon train was in full swing, and we flew to Port of Spain from Grenada, and on 10th May presented our third annual educational seminar 'Maximise Your Profit by Managing Construction Risk' to the Institute of Surveyors of Trinidad and Tobago. We had a packed audience, who by now were well versed in the value of our seminars and the considerable knowledge they acquired by attending them. The title to the seminar came from *Constructing the Team*, a report by Sir Michael Latham, in which he stated, 'No construction project is free from risk. Risk can be managed, minimised, shared, transferred or accepted. It cannot be ignored.'

Simon Birchall was in Barbados and had asked for a meeting with me. Simon's reticence and lukewarm attitude about Bucknall Austin's Caribbean operation had completely changed, and the reasons for his earlier request for a capability statement about our Caribbean operations were now revealed. Bucknall Austin had been invited to join in a company amalgamation to form a truly global practice with Rider Hunt, who were focussed on Australia, New Zealand and the United States, and Levett and Bailey, who were China and Asia based.

It is believed that Levett and Bailey and Rider Hunt wanted a new European partner after falling out with their former partner, Gardiner and Theobald. They had interviewed a number of potential candidates and settled on Bucknall Austin as their preferred choice. As Bucknall Austin had formed Bucknall Austin Caribbean with Bould Consulting Limited, we were being invited to join the global practice, and I was to become Caribbean chairman of the company. A significant amount of time and money had been spent deciding on a name for the global entity but, finally, simplicity and sensibility prevailed, and Rider Levett Bucknall, or simply RLB, was chosen. A caveat was included in my appointment as Chairman, which was that I could only serve for a period of ten years. I enquired about this requirement, and was told it had been introduced because David Bucknall never wanted to retire, and given my age and enthusiasm the shareholders were concerned that I would be there forever!

It was indeed a wonderful feeling at this stage of my career to be part of a global company and be able to make use of the resources now available to me from some two thousand five hundred staff and one hundred and twenty offices around the world. It meant I could offer a truly global reach in every aspect of the construction, development and advisory services, to the numerous clients and friends I had established across the Caribbean region. As you know, we had developed a five-year business plan for Bucknall Austin Caribbean, with Mortimer taking the lead, but we now commenced a refocus, taking into account the significantly increased resources we had available.

Jerry and I left Barbados on 7th June and flew to Trinidad for meetings with UDeCOTT about the various projects we were working on for them, returning to Cayman on 9th June. I was not acting as the best Callaloo 'super all-inclusive' host to Jimmy and Cynthia Nowery, who had arrived on the 8th whilst I was in Trinidad, so I now tried to take time off work to spend with them, and they had a great time, leaving us on 12th June.

With the formalisation of RLB, a considerable amount of information needed to be assembled for the website. These included Caribbean costings, experience, contract templates, staff CV's and so on. In this regard, Mark Green was an absolute godsend with his IT and marketing skills. Sadly for us, he gave his notice at the end of June, to go to live in Adelaide, Australia, where his wife Ali was from. They left Cayman in September. I am proud to say, that they have established a hugely successful loss adjusting company there, employing the skills he developed with us while working on loss adjusting in 2004, following Hurricane Ivan in Cayman.

On 1st July, Viv and I flew to Paris and spent two days with Derek and Dawn Evans at the British Embassy there, where Derek had been posted. We enjoyed great food, and caught up on all FCO happenings. From Paris we flew to Nice and had a wonderful time hiking for a few days in the beautiful Ubaye Valley and to the Refuge de Maljesset. We stayed in the unique town of Jausiers at the foot of the Mercantour National Park. As we drove through Barcelonette, we couldn't believe what we were seeing – we thought we were in Mexico. The large mansions showed a Mexican influence in their architecture, and the tourist office displayed posters of Mariachi bands. When we enquired, it transpired that there had been a thriving textile business in the area, destroyed by a world recession and Civil War. One Jacques Arnaud had crossed to Louisiana in 1805 and then moved to Mexico, where he was joined by many others from the Barcelonette area. There, they had thrived, but then returned to their homeland and built their mansions in the colonial style we could now see.

On 6th July we left this unique area and drove back towards the coast. I asked Viv to take out one of our trusty hotel books to see where we might stay for the night, and she found a really cosy-looking guest house called La Bouscatière (the wood cutter) in the hillside village of Moustiers-Sainte-Marie, and made a booking. We thought we would arrive in good time for dinner, but the drive across the mountains took a lot longer than we expected. When we arrived it was after 8.30pm. We introduced ourselves to the hotel's proprietors, Joel and Genevieve Callas, apologising profusely for our tardy arrival, and breathlessly asked if we were too late for dinner. Joel, in a very untypical French manner, said, 'Calm down. Go and take a shower as you have been travelling all day, and I will send down a bottle of cool white wine from the region with some Provençale marmalade – *tapenade* – and then cook you an elegant dinner.'

This was the start of a wonderful relationship that lasted for many years. La Bouscatière was indeed a unique hotel – a town house entered from the top floor via a courtyard, where Joel's office and the kitchen are located, from where a spiral staircase took guests down to their rooms. The building faced onto the main street, and a river ran through the very centre of the town. Genevieve was very slim and elegant, and an excellent seamstress, and it was hard to believe they had six children. When asked about the number, Joel replied that the quality of their TV signal was very bad! With so much work on my plate, I needed to keep in touch by internet even during our stay, and the only way to do this at that time was via a dial-up connection. Joel would kindly vacate his office so I could use the only phone line to connect to my office, catch up on emails and stay up to date. The Gorges du Verdon, one of the deepest and most beautiful canyons in Europe, lies very close to the village of Moustiers. The cliffs to the Gorges vary in height from 200m to 700m, and its landscapes are majestic. On a future visit, we were to hike down from the road at the top to the river level, and along the path to the lake of Sainte Croix.

We reluctantly departed from La Bouscatière after two nights, vowing to return soon, which we did in September. We drove to Draguignan and overnighted with Alan and Joan Scott, catching up with all their news, before leaving from Nice to return home via Heathrow and Miami.

Whilst dining at La Bouscatière, Joel introduced us to Bandol wines, a key appellation in southeastern Provence. These spicy and powerful red wines are made from a blend of Mourvèdre, Grenache, Cinsault, Carignan and Syrah grapes, and after leaving Draguignan I suggested to Viv that we stop by the Chateau de Pibarnon and pick up a case to take home, which we did. However, due to a long conversation with the winemaker at the vineyard, we almost missed our plane. Already pushing our luck, we drove along the single-lane road in front of the Nice air terminal where I stopped, leaving Viv in the car, ran up to the British Airways counter with the luggage and wine, dropped our passports on the desk, and ran out to the car, behind which by now there was a long queue of irate drivers. Viv went inside to continue our check in with BA, while I moved off and returned the car to the car hire company, sprinting back just in time to board the flight. We still have two bottles of the 2002 Chateau de Pibarnon Bandol in the cellar, kept for a special occasion.

On my return to Cayman things were hopping. We had been contacted by the National Housing Corporation in Barbados, to examine the contractual arrangements for four housing schemes that were being developed on lands that had previously been used as sugar plantations. In Trinidad, the government were considering forming a commission of enquiry to look into the construction practices of the private government-owned entities, and it was mooted that Professor John Uff would be heading it. It would be another three years, in March 2010, before the commission would issue its report, which endorsed the concerns about exactly those procurement methodologies that Jerry and I had been covering in our seminars and advisory work over several years. As we know, the Caribbean is a small community, and it was interesting that the contractor that had created so many problems on the Newton Business Park project for BIDC in Barbados, was the same contractor that had created similar problems on the Brian Lara Cricket Academy project in Trinidad, on which we were advising UDeCOTT. Back in Cayman, on the development front, some two thirds of all our completed units in the Careenage condominiums had already been sold.

On 26th July Viv and I flew to Portland to stay with Peter and Jill McDonald at Inchinnan Farm. There we enjoyed some great hikes off the Columbia River Gorge to Oneonta, Triple and Ponytail Falls, carrying with us a picnic lunch to be washed down with the latest vintage of Carabella wine. Then it was on to France where, in Bergerac, on 11th August, we celebrated Margaret Dise's seventieth birthday at an elegant chateau owned by one of the Dise's clients at Cayman Kai. Whilst there, we were able to meet up with Leslie Bigelman, who had retired from the National Gallery and moved to France. We had a splendid lunch while reminiscing about the journey we had both started as founding board members of CNCF in 1984, and the founding of the National Gallery, and Leslie's role as director. Viv and I returned via London to Cayman a few days later, in time for CNCF's Caribbean Film showcase on the 17th. This was closely followed by the edge of Hurricane Dean, which passed Cayman to the south as a Category 4 hurricane on the 20th. Luckily, Cayman was spared the worst of the storm, suffering only winds of 57mph, heavy rains, rough seas and storm surge.

On 30th August Viv and I were back in the air, flying to London and the next day to Belfast to see Flo, and back to Birmingham on 5th September for

Bucknall Austin / RLB meetings, leaving two days later from Birmingham to Nice, and driving up to La Bouscatière in Moustiers-Sainte-Marie as we had threatened to do earlier in the year. This time we carried with us some Carabella wine for Joel and Genevieve to enjoy!

We then spent three beautiful days of walking in Provence, completing the Sentier de la Chaîne, Circuit de Beaudet and the walk to Châteauneuf-lès-Moustiers. We returned to London on the 12th, where we dined with Tony Catchpole of Bucknall Austin, and interviewed staff for BCQS Property Management. Over lunch at Le Gavroche, David Bucknall introduced Viv and me to Mark Williamson, from Bucknall Austin's Bristol office. David apologised for the ups and downs of Bucknall Austin's involvement in the Caribbean business, and had assigned Mark to ensure that the business plan was put into full operation. Bucknall Austin's accountant in the UK, Stuart Stables, called me on 1st October to discuss the Caribbean's business plan. So David, true to his word, would now follow through to finally achieve the full launch of our joint business.

We stayed in London a few more days, during which I interviewed James Pollard, a valuation surveyor who would join Bould Consulting. He became a very talented head of valuations, and helped strengthen our reputation as one of the Caribbean's original and leading valuation practices.

On our home front, Viv and I had been viewing the adjacent lot in the Cayman Islands Yacht Club to the east of Callaloo, with the thought of building a tennis court. We called the owners on 8th October, asking if they wanted to sell and if so, what the price would be, whilst at the same time beginning discussions with John Doak about layouts and any key planning issues, particularly with regard to setbacks.

On 24th October we held a CNCF meeting at Callaloo to plan the programme for this year's Gimistory. Henry and I continued our discussions about the direction CNCF was taking, in particular addressing the fact that we had become a production entity as opposed to an Arts Council, which had been the original intention of the Foundation. These discussions would continue for many years before we could finally get traction on realigning the direction of the organisation.

On Saturday 3rd November, we attended the opening of the National Gallery's exhibition 'Casablanca' and then went on to the launch of Roy Bodden's second book, *Stories my Grandfather Never Told Me* at the Harquail. As noted, Roy was the former Education Minister, and the book contained nine short stories centred around Bodden Town life in the Cayman of the 1940s.

A few days later I flew to Montego Bay to speak at a RICS conference, after which Viv joined me and we drove to Strawberry Hill, in Irish Town, in the beautifully cool and lush foothills of Blue Mountain. We intended to spend four days with Alan and Jenny in 'Highgate', one of our favourite two-bedroom cottages there. We loved this cottage, because it had relaxing hammocks on the patios looking towards Newcastle and the JDF barracks. It also had a living room and a full kitchen, where we could cook up a storm. Alan drove up from Kingston with the food and wine, and we had arranged to meet them there. I said to Viv that we would drive via the north coast, turning inland at Buff Bay, and drive up to Irish Town via Cascade. We made good time from Mobay, but shortly after Ocho Rios there were lots of road works, and it had been raining heavily so it was muddy. We finally made it to Buff Bay and turned inland, but as we continued climbing, the vegetation on the verges became thicker, to the point that the car's wing mirrors were touching the branches on both sides. I began to think maybe we had missed a turn somewhere.

As we came into Cascade, we saw a lady sitting on a stone wall by the side of the road. We wound down the window, and asked her if we were on the right road to Irish Town. She replied that we were indeed on the right road, but that we would need a guide to make the journey. I confidently replied that I knew Jamaica well and certainly didn't need a guide. She said, 'But you do, as the road has fallen away'. She turned and called down to the rum shop below, and three men suddenly appeared and jumped into a Land Rover, which they pushed downhill in order to jump-start it. The lady told us to follow them. Here we were on a dark night, in the middle of the bush, following three men we didn't know, on a road that had fallen away. I asked Viv to call Alan and Jenny and tell them where we were, but there was no cell signal this high in the mountains.

It was a winding road, and suddenly, as we rounded a corner, the Land Rover was coming towards us. We stopped, and one of the men approached and said the road had fallen away round the next bend, and that we needed to turn 'up there', pointing uphill onto a steep mud track along the side of the hill, falling away precipitously on one side into the valley below. The man said, 'Let me drive your car up.' I told him no, thank you, that I could drive up myself, and stepped on the gas. I sped up the hill, with the wheels spinning and mud flying everywhere, until I got stuck about halfway up and had to reverse back down the hill to the road. The three men were there, smiling, their expressions saying, 'Told you so.' Viv then got into the back of our car, one of the men got into the driver's seat, and I sat in the front passenger seat. Off we sped up the steep mud track, fishtailing violently from side to side, but we eventually made it to the top before descending back onto the metalled road.

The man got out, and began walking away. We thanked him profusely, and although he did not want to accept any money for his kind assistance, we insisted. We drove to Strawberry Hill, arriving at reception with our car completely covered in mud, looking somewhat wild and completely unlike any of the other elegantly dressed, arriving guests. At our cottage we were greeted by Alan and Jenny, asking why we were so late. We said we had driven from Mobay via Buff Bay and Cascade, and they said that was impossible – the road had been closed for two years, ever since part of it fell away – hence the dense foliage we had experienced. We related the story, and had a good laugh over a glass of wine!

Joan Scott had written an excellent cookbook called *The Governor's Lady*, setting down the recipes she had gathered during her world travels. The book included a wonderful account of running Government House in Cayman, and stories about life there when Alan had been Governor. It was set to launch on 21st November, and we had the pleasure of having Joan stay with us at Callaloo. It was great to be able to return – in a small way – the hospitality that the Scotts had shown Viv and me on our many trips through Europe. Gimistory was also in full swing, and we hosted a performance at Callaloo on 25th November, once again building a stage over the pool to accommodate the performers and band.

At the end of the month I flew to Grenada to meet with Kerry, a Candy & Candy representative, who was looking at a development in the north of the island. The journey to view the site involved flying to Pearls Airfield, originally built in 1943, and used by the American Marines in October 1983 during the invasion of the island. It had been closed for many years, but was opened for our visit. The two Candy brothers were well-known developers, in particular for One Hyde Park, the luxury apartment block in London. This assignment was a good example of how the Rider Levett Bucknall Caribbean partnership brings together international developers and consultancies with local Caribbean knowledge, benefiting everyone involved.

I left Grenada on 30th November to return through Miami to Cayman, and as I landed in the airport I received a call from Edna that Bill Bissell was very ill and in hospital in Cayman, where he was being stabilised before being flown to Miami for further treatment. I told Edna I would wait in Miami to see if there was anything I could do to assist. Bill and I had shared so many great times together, both professionally and as friends. Shortly after he arrived by air ambulance, I went to see him, but he was not conscious, and after spending time with him and Edna, I went home to sleep. Shortly thereafter Edna called me and said Bill was gone. It was truly devastating. We held a celebration of his life on 4th December in Miami and then a funeral service in Cayman on 7th December, where I spoke with a huge lump in my throat. A wake at Callaloo for Bill's many friends followed.

Utah powder was calling, and Viv and I left on 8th December to stay at our favourite Sugarplum apartment complete with log burning fire, celebrate our wedding anniversary and my birthday, and to clock up some ten to fifteen runs per day during eight days of skiing. We were fortunate enough to secure tickets for the annual Christmas concert by the Mormon Tabernacle Orchestra and Choir, featuring one of the choir's most frequent guest artists – an English six-man a cappella vocal ensemble. I made a quick visit to Barbados on the 18th for meetings with BIDC on Newton Business Park, where we had appointed a new contractor to complete the buildings, and also with Angus on the US Embassy building, returning to Cayman on 20th December for the CNCF Christmas party.

For Christmas 2007, Len and Rona, Alan and Claudia Veeran's good friends that he worked with in Turks and Caicos, were visiting, and we all enjoyed Christmas lunch together then had a relaxing week after such a very well-travelled year.

CHAPTER NINE

Shockwaves and Aftershocks (2008–2012)

2008

Be still and let the wind speak. Hush, a World is talking.

The year began with a meeting in St Vincent with TVA on the stadium matter, and then a flight to Port of Spain to meet with Trinidad Contractors on the Toco bridges dispute, involving five bridges they were building in the north east corner of Trinidad. There were also a site visit and meetings pertaining to the Brian Lara Cricket Academy, and with EDFAC about the schools project.

I returned to Cayman on 12th January, where we began addressing the matter of Miss Lassie's House. Following Miss Lassie's death, her house and property had been inherited by her son Richard, and, after his death, by his partner, nurse Julie. She had now put the property up for sale, for a price in excess of $1 million. Given the beachfront location on South Sound, if the property were sold the house would most likely be demolished and the property redeveloped.

We therefore needed to quickly look at all alternatives to see how we could save the house and the treasures it contained. A typical wattle and daub house, built by Miss Lassie's father, it had survived numerous hurricanes, and over the years Miss Lassie had covered the walls with her artwork. We held a meeting with all interested parties on 17th January, and listed the potential ideas to save it. These included: bringing in a conservator to carry out a survey of the house, building a replica, seeing if there was a similar-sized and located Crown property we could exchange it for, and consulting with engineers to see if the house could be moved and relocated to another site. The timeline of any action would need to fall within the sale period, and we would approach Jim Lammers and Sandy Urquart to see if Darts might assist with funding. To this end, John Doak would complete a survey and Patrick Broderick would make a detailed photographic record of the house. So much to accomplish in a short space of time! On the same day we also met to discuss some issues on the rebuild of the National Trust Mission House, so preservation was very much the focus of early 2008.

On 21st January, Henry and I met with the Minister of Culture, Alden McLaughlin, (an Ex CNCF board member) to review the various options concerning Miss Lassie's House. The house in its current location epitomised the South Sound way of life that Miss Lassie had embodied, so the primary focus of our discussion was how to acquire the property, and where the funds to do so might come from. We had been informed that there was a Crown property north of Miss Lassie's House where a house had once stood. Formerly the home of the Director of Mosquito Research, Dr Marco Giglioli, it had been destroyed in Hurricane Ivan. A prominent attorney with a home on the neighbouring plot had expressed interest in purchasing the Crown parcel for the sum of $936,000, which would provide a good portion of the funds needed to pay Julie for Miss Lassie's House. Discussions were to continue for several months about this possible option but in the end the government were unwilling to sell any government land. Nevertheless, we continued with the negotiations to acquire Miss Lassie's House, and so we secured the services of Isabel Rigol, a Cuban expert on intuitive art and conservation, and Greg Howarth, a conservation specialist from the UK.

Some six months later, however, I would be asked to meet with Alden McLaughlin and the Leader of Government Business, Kurt Tibbetts, during a break in Parliament. I was told, with steely-eyed looks from both men, that government had raised the funds necessary to acquire Miss Lassie's House by charging each ministry a portion of the money required, and that we had now better make a success of developing it as a National Treasure. So, we had now saved the house, but had no money to renovate or maintain it. We immediately commenced a 'Save Miss Lassie's House' (SMLH) fundraising effort to ensure that we could not only own it, but also renovate and restore, and conserve and maintain it.

At the end of January, Viv and I left to join Jimmy and Cynthia Nowery on what had become an annual event: skiing in Aspen, while staying at their home in Aspen Glen. We skied in Aspen until the 31st, then drove to Keystone to ski there until 4th February.

Around this time, I was contacted by Jonathan Rowland and Simon Hill of Candy & Candy concerning the redevelopment of the Grenada project, and was asked to go to London to discuss RLB's involvement. I flew to London on 9th February, enjoyed dinner with Mortimer the following evening, and met with Candy & Candy on the 11th to review the feasibility study they had prepared for the Grenada project, while also examining the costs from a Caribbean perspective. After that, I had a meeting with Mark Williamson to discuss the RLB Business Plan. That evening, I dined with David Bucknall at Langan's restaurant on Stratton Street. He, as promised, was keeping the Caribbean part of the business to the fore. I noted that neither Cayman nor the Caribbean generally were currently shown on the RLB website, which he promised to rectify, and did.

I had been appointed as one of three arbitrators on a claim dispute about damage caused by Hurricane Ivan. I needed to meet with the other party-appointed arbitrator so we could agree over the appointment of the umpire, which we did in his London chambers. I then met with the RLB UK directors over a pleasant lunch at Luciano's, and then returned to Cayman on 13th February in time for Robbie Hamaty's sixtieth birthday party. Many of his friends from Jamaica days were present, including his brother Freddie and wife Merle, and we had a great catch-up about the days at Bluefields Beach in the early seventies. The former girlfriend for whom I had quit smoking was also there, and when I introduced her to Vivian, Viv went up to her and gave her a big hug, thanking her profusely!

On 21st February, we were in the air again, this time to Australia. We had decided to purchase an 'Around the World Ticket', which enabled us to fly to numerous destinations en route, as long as we travelled in one direction only. IFACCA was co-hosting an international summit in Adelaide, attended by thirty delegates from sixteen countries, to share their expertise on how governments support major performing arts organisations. I was attending to represent CNCF and the Cayman Islands. On the way through Los Angeles, we were able to meet with Basil and Sammy for a catch-up before leaving on the late night flight to Melbourne and then to Adelaide. After catching up on some sleep, I called Harley Hooper, a property developer and one of our Harvard alumni, who invited us to a BBQ on the 24th at a friend's house, adjacent to the track where the Clipsal 500 Supercars race was taking place. That evening we had dinner with Mark Green and Ali. Ali's brother, Russell Burns, is a wine maker in the Barossa Valley, and so on 25th February we drove out to the winery to taste and buy some bottles of his Cooper Burns Grenache for the Callaloo cellar.

RLB has a considerable presence in Australia, and Stephen Knight and Andrew Suttle in RLB's Adelaide office were able to provide useful insight into the company's activities in that part of the world. The IFACCA conference was held on 27th and 28th February, and covered a variety of ways governments could fund major performing arts organisations. These accommodated the wide range of countries' economies, as well as the need for major performing arts organisations and government funders to be able to undertake strategic planning to manage change. It was a rewarding and enlightening experience, and allowed me to make sure Cayman was keeping up with world trends in cultural development and management.

On the 29th, we flew to Melbourne and enjoyed the sights, including Captain Cook's Cottage. That had been built in England in 1755, and in 1934 was dismantled brick-by-brick, shipped to Australia and rebuilt. Viv and I were invited to the RLB office on St Kilda Road and Michael Kerr, the local director, kindly took us out to lunch. Michael shared our love of good wine and we had a very enjoyable and delicious wine tasting with him and his colleagues. We promised to send him some of our Carabella to compare with the fine Australian wines we had tasted, and did, only to learn some months later that although he had received the wine, the duty on it had been extortionate.

From Melbourne we flew to Sydney and drove up to Dubbo to spend time with Sally and George Falkiner. George and I had attended Harvard together, but Viv and I had not been able to attend the Alumni reunion he and Sally had hosted at Haddon Rig, their sheep station. It was fun to see where the event had taken place: the sheep shearers' bunk house had been 'tarted up' to accommodate guests, and some of the Alumni even tried their hand at shearing the sheep. Haddon Rig was founded as a 'Merino Stud' in 1882 and has been in George's family for almost one hundred years. It is vast, covering some sixty thousand acres. As George says, Grand Cayman, with an area of forty-eight thousand acres, could easily fit into Haddon Rig's property with space to spare. George also has cattle, and I drove out one morning to see him at work checking out which cattle were pregnant. At one point he asked me if I would I go back to the main house and ask them for 'smoko.' I asked what that was, and George replied they would know. I duly did, and found this was the mid-morning snack the workers enjoyed when they paused work to smoke a cigarette. Apparently, Sally had originally gone to Haddon Rig to work as a chef, and George fell for her. He proposed marriage when they were sitting in the living room – Sally asked for a cigarette, and George threw across a pack that contained the engagement ring. Sally said, 'What's this?' and George asked, 'Will you marry me?' Sally is a great girl, and a wonderful teller of jokes, and during reunions with our friends Jimmy and Cynthia, always competed with Jimmy to see who could come up with the best lines.

From Dubbo, we returned to Sydney on 6th March, and the next morning decided to climb the Sydney Harbour Bridge. I recall that before being allowed to climb the bridge you had to take a breathalyser test, and Viv had been so concerned the night before that she said we should limit our wine intake.

We arrived at the booking office, took the test, donned grey jump suits and, hooking our harness onto a wire that ran along the side rail, started the climb. The bridge has a span of 1,654 feet and is 440 feet above sea level and at the top we had a celebratory photo taken. Later that day we went to RLB's Sydney office, and met with Damian Judge, Stephen Moe and Stephen Ballestry, attended a Property Australia conference and lunch, and later that evening went out for drinks on the Sydney waterfront overlooking the iconic Opera House that was one of RLB Sydney's projects.

We then flew from Sydney to Bangkok, and stayed in the Oriental, which we had enjoyed so much during our pre-Bhutan visit in 2000. The Oriental has its own distinctive water craft to ferry its guests around, complete with the hotel's flag on the top. One day we caught this to travel downriver and into town. As we got off the boat, a tuktuk stopped and offered to take us into town for a very reasonable price, which we accepted. He asked where we wanted to go, and Viv mentioned a jewellery store, to which the driver duly took us. The only problem was, he parked so close to the curb that there was only one store we could enter, pretty much captured by the tuktuk-blocked entrance. Luckily for him, we did purchase some items on which I am sure he received a commission.

In Hong Kong next, we stayed at the Mandarin Oriental. We were greeted by the concierge on our arrival and shown upstairs to a harbour view suite, complete with a large bathtub overlooking the harbour. As we had booked a normal room, we had no idea why we were receiving such special service. However, when I met with Stephen Lai, RLB's Hong Kong director, and mentioned the service, he gave a wry smile and said nothing, but I believe our upgrade was linked to the fact that the hotel had been one of RLB's projects.

Of course, we took the bus to Stanley Market, where Viv once again enjoyed a shopping splurge, walking through the alleyways with stores either side packed with every kind of merchandise you can imagine. We took the ferry to the Kowloon side, where we did some more shopping and then had tea in the Peninsula Hotel. Back in Hong Kong, we took the Peak Tram funicular, which has been operational since 1888 and is in great working order, up to the summit for a sweeping view of the harbour and skyscrapers.

On 15th March we flew back to London, having thoroughly enjoyed the 'Around the World' experience, which we would go on to enjoy on many future occasions. Being able to meet RLB directors on the other side of the world, face to face, highlighted the global nature of our business and the unique advantages to our clients in the Caribbean of having extensive local knowledge backed by such global expertise on tap.

Two days later I met with Mark Williamson at Claridge's, where we were staying, to review the many meetings I had held. Lance Taylor, who had replaced Simon Birchall as RLB UK's CEO joined us. I was discovering that RLB UK is a fairly widely owned company, and so these changes in senior management happened with a greater frequency than I was accustomed to.

We returned to Cayman the next day, where CNCF had arranged a catboat race as part of our Cayfest celebration and I was asked to present the prizes. The handmade Cayman catboats, no two exactly the same, are unique to the island. They were first introduced in the early 1900s, as the primary mode of transportation from West Bay to George Town and everywhere else. They're slim, small, handcrafted boats of wood with a single sail, traditionally painted blue, without a fixed keel. Instead, a hiking plank is laid to extend from the side of the boat on which captain or crew sit at varying distances out over the water, to balance the boat while it's heeling. Viv and I had the pleasure of being taken out for one of the races, which made it easier to appreciate the skill required to sail these unique representations of Caymanian culture and tradition. Viv and I also were delighted to host Paul Keens Douglas, who was in Cayman for Cayfest, to dinner at Callaloo, particularly given the marvellous show he had put on for our wedding celebration on the beach at Plantana, some thirteen years before.

Cayfest events continued and included a sound bite about the events at the National Gallery, along with a photographic exhibition the same evening, with literary awards the next day at UCCI. So, our many and varied programmes were continuing to raise awareness across the heritage and cultural spectrum. As part of good strategic planning, we continued to develop our two-day retreats, during which we examined where we had got to and what we still needed to achieve. In particular, we knew we needed an overall Arts Council-style structure that could encompass the evolving entities and cultural groups. We made a plan to assemble them all at a meeting on 10th May. We also planned to create a performing group that would put on shows at various hotels and be paid for their efforts. We discussed this with the Ministers of Tourism and Culture and received a very favourable response.

While all these activities were happening, on 1st April, the arbitration case pertaining to the Hurricane Ivan damage, on which I was to act as one of three arbitrators, issued its preliminary directions. The case looked as though it was going to be an interesting one: the insurance policy had expired at midnight on the day Hurricane Ivan hit Cayman, and had not been renewed. Therefore, it would be key to prove at what time the wind reached hurricane strength, with reference to the anemometer located at Owen Roberts Airport.

As chairman of the National Gallery Building Committee, I had been busy working on what needed to be achieved to be able to build the National Gallery's new home. On the costing side, we had been very fortunate in securing the services of BCQS, led by Jeremy Superfine, in finalising our detailed budget, and Desmond Kinch and Henry Harford had been very active and successful in fundraising. We were, however, still short of the total necessary amount needed, so we liaised with Nancy Barnard, the Gallery's director, and came up with the idea of a play on words of the London Underground's 'Mind the Gap' motto as the theme of a fundraising dinner. We held the event, called 'Fill the Gap', at Callaloo on 18th April. It was very successful and got excellent press and TV coverage.

When Viv and I had decided to build a home, one of the key design requirements was that we would have a cottage so a couple could live on the property and manage it for us, since our plan was to travel to see as much of the world as we could in our lifetimes. Since completing the house we had been using a maid service agency, and were very pleased with the staff they had provided. Salvadora, from Honduras, whom we had assisted with a loan to build her home there, had now left us and had been replaced by Ingrid Swaby, a splendid lady. However, what we were really looking for was a couple to live in the cottage. When we told Ingrid this, she promptly replied that her husband Wayne, a carpenter, was 'looking a job' and they would be very happy to come and live as a couple on the property. As we say in Jamaica, 'So said – so done' and we applied for a permit for Wayne. He joined us in May 2008, and he is still with us as part of the Callaloo family to this day.

On 22nd April we held an RLB board meeting in Miami with a full agenda, including the matter of, and payment for, shares and share loan requirements, finalising the Memorandum and Articles, Due Diligence, change of secretary, and approval of accounts for 2006, 2007 and 2008 to date, and marketing and brochure production.

The owners of the lot we wanted to purchase on which to build a tennis court to the east of Callaloo, reverted to us on 28th April and, given there was no sales agent involved, agreed to sell the lot to us for CI$210,000 provided we could close in fourteen days. To this, we readily agreed. We began discussing the layout for the lot and tennis court with John Doak. We also discussed required setbacks with Gil Freytag, the Vista Del Mar developer and Great House apartment owner, and Burton Snyder at CPA. Gil agreed the reduced setback, and CPA said they would agree if adjacent land owners agreed, but Gil then said to Viv, 'Why do you want to build a tennis court when you can use the Vista del Mar tennis court across the road?' We thanked him for his great alternative suggestion, which we gratefully accepted.

We therefore re-envisioned the 'tennis court property' as an orchard facing the tranquil canal that leads to the North Sound. To ensure good growing conditions for some fourteen fruit trees, we dug out the existing marl fill and replaced it with good topsoil. We used the marl to create an elevated circular stage, complete with columns in a Romanesque style, and floodlights. We use the space for performances, philanthropic events and celebrations, and the adjacent croquet court is the venue for our traditional game of croquet before lunch every Christmas.

On 1st May we celebrated Bunny Delapenha's seventy-seventh birthday at Morgan's Harbour in Batabano. Bunny, as the unstoppable entrepreneur, had purchased a property there inclusive of a building with a restaurant, a boat dock and gas supply for boats.

I left Cayman on 5th May, overnighted in Miami and flew on to Port of Spain for the opening of the Caribbean Hotel Investment Conference. I stayed in our favoured Coblenz Inn, and met with Mike Samms to discuss the final arrangements for the next ISTT seminar on 13th May, while enjoying OBM's hospitality at a rooftop cocktail party at Zen. With Rupert, I also discussed the opening of a RLB office in St Lucia, as well as the July RLB launch party in St Lucia.

Next stop was St Lucia in mid-May, where I met with attorney Racquel DuBoulay to set up an RLB company so we could commence operations there. I then met with a long-established St Lucia quantity surveyor Brad Paul, to advise him of our intent to commence business on his 'patch' and to explore any interest he might have in joining with RLB, which he received enthusiastically. I also met with Mandish Singh of engineers Halcrow, and the Chief Engineer of the Ministry of Communications and Works, about presenting their managers with an educational seminar, and with the architect Claude Guillaume of NLBA Architects. I had first become acquainted with him through his work, exhibited in the classic Caribbean architecture book, *Caribbean Style*. The first line of that book expresses so much of what I have tried to cover in this memoir-cum-diary: 'The Caribbean offers a series of memorable, colorful, and ever-changing scenes in which the striking images of the idealised landscape are juxtaposed with the vibrancy of everyday life.'

On 15th June, Ken Corsbie, the multi-talented Guyanese storyteller, ably supported by his wife, Beth, was in Cayman to present a story-telling workshop at the CNCF studio theatre. On the 24th, I presented the Arts Awards at John Gray High School on behalf of CNCF, and the CNCF Arts Awards a couple of days later. I made the following comments in CNCF's Annual Report:

> At CNCF we have, with the efforts of our hardworking and dedicated staff, volunteers and the contribution of our Board, made tremendous

strides in the preservation and development of Caymanian culture and heritage as you will see from this report. Whilst we cannot and should not rest on our laurels as much remains to be done, it is useful as we travel forward to see where we have come from and see what we have achieved.

We have seen our cultural and art development move from new arrivals performing English drama to a vibrant cultural scene with it seems almost weekly art exhibitions displaying superb artwork in all mediums, a plethora of cultural education programmes, the use of culture in social programmes, including playwriting workshops in Northward Prison, world class dance and storytelling, a broad range of regional and international drama, our own annual satire, Rundown, a healthy publication of books, with such diversity as poetry, novels, cookery and those providing social commentary. We award grants to develop new and existing artists and art forms, run many workshops, and present film showcases.

Currently one of our most important and critical projects is the preservation of Miss Lassie's House, for which we have assembled a talented team of dedicated volunteers to make sure this iconic treasure remains for future generations to cherish and enjoy.

We take very seriously the responsibility of ensuring the development of our culture as an essential component of social stability, whilst at the same time carefully assessing and delivering value for money to our generous sponsors and benefactors. We are in the business of culture and remain on the cutting edge of local, regional and international developments in our business.

On 28th June Viv and I attended Graeme Day's wedding celebration. Graeme was McAlpine's foreman on the construction of Callaloo, and we were blessed to have had him. A foreman who was 'on the tools' to oversee the minute and essential details of quality when building a home, was invaluable. One does not necessarily notice such details on a cursory view, but one feels them nevertheless. It was a joyous occasion.

At RLB, we had been invited to look at a hotel project in Havana, Cuba. So, I contacted my good friend, Raglan Roper, who I knew not only through his janitorial business, but also from his reputation as a very talented dancer. He had business connections in Cuba, and I asked him to find out whom I could meet there to carry out due diligence on the costs to build a hotel.

On 2nd July, Viv and I flew to St Lucia for the official launch party of Rider Levett Bucknall Caribbean on 4th July, at the St Lucia Golf Club. What a journey it had been to arrive at this special day! But, like all good things, it was worth the wait. We would go on for the next ten years of my chairmanship to provide truly global expertise with all its advantages, coupled with detailed local Caribbean-wide knowledge, from which our clients benefited immensely. It was an offering which competitors attempted to copy, but with only limited success.

As part of RLBC's launch celebrations, on 8th July we presented a seminar on projects procured through a Private Finance Initiative. This kind of financing, given the global financial challenges at the time, enjoyed a high level of interest, but it was procured under a complicated legal framework which had to be taken into account. Again, the extensive resources and expertise of a global organisation became apparent, and we drew on RLB's UK expert in this field, David Quirk, and FCIB's Mark Young, to deliver an excellent and informative presentation.

On 10th July, back in Cayman, I liaised with Ballast Nedham-Per Arslaff on the cruise ship dock in St Maarten that we had just begun to monitor and which Brian Martin was managing for us. We were also holding meetings with the Met office in Cayman to look at the timing and strength of Hurricane Ivan's gusts – key evidence in the insurance arbitration. The insurance coverage had expired at midnight, as I've explained, but all damage would be covered under what is known as the 'single loss occurrence clause' under an insurance policy, where coverage remains in place for seventy-two hours, providing gusts in excess of hurricane force winds had begun damaging the structure before the policy expired.

Good news came on 17th July from Jeremy Superfine, who was cost-managing the potential build of the new National Gallery – he was able to announce that we had received four bids for the construction, and that all were within budget. We also continued to raise awareness of the importance of the Save Miss Lassie's House incentive, and on 18th July we had a television interview and held a reception at Callaloo for Isabel Rigol, who was visiting from Cuba.

2009's Havard OPM reunion began in Copenhagen, from where we would cruise around the Baltic on the *Amadeus*, the ship we had chartered. It was a great, fun time, and the crew said they had never had on board a group of people who took over the ship the way we did. There was Ken Lenoir, who woke everyone up with his morning 'breakfast show' at 7am, sponsored by Jim Hughes, with a sewage service offering a tag line of 'we do doodo better than you do doodo' and a marriage service song for a recently divorced alumnus, 'It's cheaper to keep her'.

Jim Nowery featured, of course, with the mouse and the giraffe joke, which was enacted by Doris and Wolfgang, all accompanied by what had become OPM's theme song 'Can't wait to be on the road again'. We cruised around the Baltic, stopping at Latvia, Estonia, Lithuania and finishing up in St Petersburg, where we visited Peterhof Palace with its wonderful gardens and water fountains, and had a private visit to Catherine the Great's Hermitage, where the ten-foot tall, 18th century Peacock Clock had been specially wound for us, and was 'set off' – what a spectacular way to tell the time! In St Petersburg, we decided we should have some Russian caviar washed down with a glass of champagne and so repaired to an appropriate vendor to order a bottle of Dom Perignon and the best Beluga caviar they had. Jimmy Nowery preferred sushi and ordered that instead. Well, the Dom Perignon was not chilled, but the caviar was excellent, and Jimmy to this day talks about the single piece of miniscule sushi he was served. For Russia, the total check was off the charts!

On 16th August CNCF presented a stage play, *One White, One Black* written by Frank McField. This was a two-hander starring Quincy Brown and Fritz McPherson, which we were showcasing prior to its performance at Carifesta, in Guyana. As the *Caymanian Compass* noted in reviewing a later performance:

> The play is an intriguing exchange between Bob, a past writer and George, once a musician, as they discuss their glory days and past romances. Eventually, they find themselves on a road to self-discovery, where they are forced to face their own personal shortcomings. Bob and George's arguments with each other and with themselves are thought-provoking. The conversations take the audience members on a journey, through moments of uncontrollable laughter, then anger and frustration with life and love, followed by moments of acceptance and the willingness to change.

On 21st August, I flew to Barbados for a RLBC meeting, and then to Guyana the next day to start the Carifesta X celebrations. As Head of Mission, I received the services of a security guard, who followed me everywhere like a shadow. As usual, for our contingent, exposure to the wider Caribbean culture was a massive benefit. We travelled on the ferry to Berbice, and then went to the upper floor of the town hall for the dress rehearsal of *One White. One Black*. Somehow, after the rehearsal, Quincy was able to join friends for a few libations, and during the evening's performance he managed to introduce some lines of his own instead of following the script, challenging Fritz to follow his lead while maintaining the story line! Fortunately it all worked out in the end. One advantage of my security 'shadow' was that when I left to fly back to Cayman, he escorted me though immigration to the foot of the steps to the plane, and I was first to board. I thought, *I could get used to this!*

Only back in Cayman a couple of days, I left for London and Geneva on 28th August, and then went to Villars, where Viv and I met up with Edna Bissell, to celebrate her and Bill's 40th wedding anniversary. Edna wanted each one of her guests to celebrate Bill's life by scattering some of his ashes on the mountainside where their Swiss home is located. This was followed by an excellent lunch, where we all shared stories of the great journey we had travelled together and of life's lessons well learned.

The Garden Club of Grand Cayman came to Miss Lassie's House on 13th September and replanted the yard in traditional Cayman style for the official launch of the 'Save Miss Lassie's House' campaign on the 17th. As always, multiple projects were underway and Nancy Barnard and I met with the Hon Kurt Tibbetts to finalise the contractual aspects of the construction of the National Gallery, and the same day we were setting out the final block of apartments at Careenage.

At CNCF, our 'Culture meets Tourism' programme was gaining momentum. On 18th September the *Caymanian Compass* reported that the Hon Alden McLaughlin, as Minister of Culture, and the Hon Charles Clifford, as Minister of Tourism, had agreed to fund the initiative following a motion introduced to the House by the Hon Alphonso Wright. He explained: 'My plan here is to see us organise a core group of entertainers whom the Ritz-Carlton could contract through the National Cultural Foundation and say, 'We want [the performance troupe] for three months and we are going to play them twice a week. You give us a price.'

At the end of September we held a SMLH fundraising event, with artists painting different views of Miss Lassie's House and then offering them for sale. Later the same day, Shayne Howe and his team from Phoenix Construction, with help from Steve Hawley and Alan Veeran, commenced the restoration work. The wooden shutters of the house, hand-painted by Miss Lassie, were works of art in themselves, so they were removed and put into climate-controlled storage. They were replaced with facsimiles of the original shutters, onto which Sue Howe had painstakingly copied the artwork from the originals. The crew from Phoenix worked over many weekends to stabilise the house.

On the 28th, I flew to Barbados for meetings, then continued to St Lucia the next day. We had been invited by Pascal Mahvi to manage the redevelopment of a $45m project called Jalousie Enclave, located on a four hundred and eighty-acre development facing St Lucia's iconic Twin Pitons. Mahvi is a descendant of Iranian royalty and author of *Deadly Secrets of Iranian Princes: Audacity to Act*, part of the former Shah's inner sanctum, and a most interesting man. The land had been purchased in 1982 by Lord Glenconner, who had left Mustique, disenchanted by what had now become a 'real business' of island management. Mustique was now ably run by Brian Alexander, and with many homeowners, but very different from the 'fun' paradise Lord Glenconner had originally created. Lord Glenconner and his wife Anne (Lady in Waiting to Princess Margaret) had lived for a time in St Lucia, in a small gingerbread house relocated from a nearby village to the Jalousie Plantation, overlooking the sea. He imported an elephant, Bupa, from the Dublin Zoo, to roam the estate, and – with architect, Lane Pettigrew – opened a restaurant called Bang (Between the Two Pitons) which opened only when Lord Glenconner felt like it. Our role in the Jalousie Enclave scheme was to prepare and monitor a project execution plan for the economic development of the infrastructure works, the clubhouse, the restaurant, and phased construction of the villas.

From St Lucia, I went on to Port of Spain for two days of meetings on the several projects we were working on. Of particular interest was Professor John Uff's appointment as chairman of a Commission of Enquiry into the Construction Sector in Trinidad & Tobago, which was to make such observations and recommendations as they deemed appropriate. The commission would not publish its report until March 2010, but it would highlight many of the issues addressed in our CCAS educational seminars. We would, in fact, focus specifically on the Uff report in a presentation we made to ISTT in May 2011, called 'Uff has Spoken – Practical Steps to Achieve Value for Money.'

Two days later I was flying again, this time to London to meet my fellow arbitrators for a hearing on the Cayman insurance claim related to Hurricane Ivan losses. While we were there, Viv and I experienced a very different kind of event – on 11th October we were invited to the Globe Theatre, in Southwark, for the performance of an opera directed by Derek Walcott and written by fellow Nobel Laureate Seamus Heaney, based on his poem *The Burial at Thebes*. The music was by the Trinidadian-born composer Dominique Le Gendre. It was Derek's debut as a director in the UK, and we sat at the bar with him after the performance. Sad to say, he was disappointed with the result, but truth be known, most hugely talented people that I have had the good fortune to meet and work with, like Derek, are perfectionists. As a result they are also frequently – and quite frankly – miserable!

The next evening we visited the Royal Albert Hall for a performance of Vivaldi, after a day spent finalising the refurbishment of our 'Doll's House' at 62 Queen's Gate Mews. We had rented it out, with only brief intervals, to a series of good and not-so-good tenants since the day we'd bought it. The interior was looking tired (and, as we say, 'mashed-up') after the last tenant had left, and needed a complete refurbishment.

On 20th October I applied to be naturalised as a British Overseas Dependent Territories Citizen, based on my Caymanian Status which had been awarded me on 1st July 1980. Mr Norman Bodden, who has been incredibly kind throughout our life in Cayman, generously offered to sponsor me. That same day I spoke with David Bucknall, who was in Beijing. The conversation was the seed of what was to become a huge project for us in the Bahamas.

In October, Viv and I flew to Miami and then drove up to Sebring, to celebrate Flo's 90th birthday at her sister Pat's house. We stayed for several days, returning to Miami for our annual physical checkup at Cedars. The stress test was always fun, as I would get onto the treadmill and, although the speed and inclination would be increased by the doctor, my heart rate would not increase quickly enough. The doctor would joke that he might as well go for his lunch whilst he waited for the requisite increase. We returned to Cayman for Cayman National Bank's cocktail party in their new premises at Camana Bay – one of the first banks to relocate there. We had been customers and shareholders of the bank since its founding in 1974.

On 7th November, Hurricane Paloma hit St Maarten and caused extensive damage to the cruise ship dock we were monitoring there. To increase the speed of completion, the precast deck slabs had been put in place but not yet secured. The storm swells had lifted and tossed the slabs like playing cards and they were now lying at the bottom of the sea. We needed to add additional staff to deal with the insurance claim aspects of this project.

A week later, we were back in London to meet with the contactor and our project manager about the refurbishment of 62 Queen's Gate Mews. It was going very well, but we needed to negotiate a final price for a few variations to the original brief. Having accomplished this, we enjoyed a wonderful lunch at Lucio's on the Fulham Road. Lucio, who for many years had been maître d' at San Lorenzo in Beacham Place, now had his own restaurant. One of his signature dishes was black truffles shaved over homemade pasta. The truffles were kept in a locked box, and only Lucio accessed them. Viv always kept him talking during the shaving process to ensure the most generous portion of this delectable dish.

The next day we returned to Mr Chow's to enjoy his green prawns and spicy beef – life is good with our favourite foods! On this trip to London, we hailed a taxi, and in the corner of the window was a notice that the driver did fixed-price journeys to the airport. We asked the driver, whose name was Frank Udall, what the fare was to Heathrow, and then booked him for our return journey. The relationship with Frank would continue for many years. We had lunch with Lance Taylor, and then Mark Williamson and his wife Adrienne, and discussed the expanding project list we were developing with the Caribbean business. We enjoyed another visit to the Royal Albert Hall to hear the Royal Philharmonic Orchestra play the 'Great Choral Classics', and then met with Paddy Dring, Head of Global Prime Sales at Knight Frank, at their offices in Baker Street to review joint Caribbean opportunities with RLBC.

It was the time of year when the Utah powder called out to us, and on 5th December Viv and I flew north to spend ten days at our favourite spot in the Sugarplum condo, where the wood fire burned brightly. We skied every day until 15th December, accumulating one hundred and thirty runs, and enjoyed dinner at the Rustler with George and Ellie Klopfer, who had a house in nearby Park City.

In mid-December I was contacted by René Hubert about the hotel construction contract in Havana I had discussed earlier with Raglan Roper. Now identified as Monte Barreto, it was being developed by René's company Bellavista. They wanted RLBC to verify the budget and schedule, for which we would visit the site early in the new year.

We had started a tradition of playing croquet at Callaloo on Christmas. We set up the course on the 'tennis court' lot that we had purchased, and enjoyed hors d'oeuvres and champagne during the game, followed by Christmas 'linner' – halfway between lunch and dinner – of turkey with all the trimmings. On Boxing Day, we went to Henry and Marcia's house, where Henry, ever the excellent cook, prepared delicious Guyanese food for all to enjoy.

2009

If you want to be strong, be gentle
If you want to be powerful, be kind
If you want to be rich, be generous
If you want to be smart, be simple
If you want to be free, be yourself.

On 4th January, I flew to Havana to meet with René Hubert, representing the developers of the two hundred and thirty-eight-room Monte Barreto hotel project. My primary goal at this initial stage, was to understand the parameters and complexities of operating in this communist country. First, the contractor, Bouygues, was required to 'partner' with a Cuban company at a 50 per cent level. For this project, the partner was the army! Secondly, pricing was based on standard rates, the logic of which seemed elusive. For example, if we were looking at the price for concrete blockwork, we expected a logical breakdown: the cost of the block; the cement, sand and water to make the mortar; the cost of labour to lay the block, and the cost of any equipment required, such as cement mixers, etc.

Despite asking many people for these basic prices, we got nowhere until we visited the offices of the Government Engineers, where we spoke with an obliging man who nodded his head wisely, left the room and returned with an elderly, dishevelled, grey-haired gentleman who looked a lot like the late Howard Hughes. We posed our questions about rates, and he explained in fine detail exactly what we were looking for – it was like finding the holy grail! When I asked him how many hotels he had built, he replied, 'Oh, around sixty.' His favourite? One on Varadero beach, because it was a great hotel, and its opening was attended by Fred Astaire and Ginger Rogers – which should give you some idea of how old this gentleman was.

When I returned to Cayman, Alan Veeran was setting out the site boundaries and batter boards for Block A, for the final phase of the twelve condominiums of the forty-four-unit Careenage development. I was home in Cayman until 11th January, when I left for Barbados. There, I stayed at my favourite south coast hotel, Accra Beach. In the early mornings I would walk for about a mile along the waterfront boardwalk to the Garrison, a UNESCO World Heritage site, where the jockeys would be exercising the horses on the racing track before the grooms took them down to the ocean for a sea bath. Each circuit around the track measured about one mile, so I would make three or four circuits, then walk back to the hotel. While walking, I was able to watch the vivid gamut of racing life – the grooms, jockeys and punters, all watching the horses and their form, and chat with the flagman – a colorful, jovial, dreadlocked Rasta named Richard Hart – who held up traffic so the horses could cross the road to the stables on the other side.

The clocktower on the main guard house chimes every fifteen minutes, and at 7am plays 'Morning has Broken' on its bells. What a great way to begin the day! From Barbados, I flew to St Lucia where RLBC were looking at assisting the build of a new national hospital. The project was being funded by the European Development Fund, and with an Italian contractor. In St Vincent next, I attended a preliminary arbitration hearing on some issues of the design of the stadium on 13th January. I was staying at the historic Cobblestone Inn, where Basil's Bar was owned by Basil Charles, well-known as a local celebrity because he had owned the famous Basil's Bar and General Store in Mustique, which had played host to both royalty and the rich and famous.

I returned to Havana some weeks later, this time with Alan Veeran, who had agreed to become part of the RLBC team to lead the cost aspect of our review of the project. We also visited many of the hotels on Varadero beach in order to gauge comparisons for the Monte Barreto project we were analysing in Miramar.

In 2008, we had reviewed the CNCF's 1992 version of our laws. We also met with Rod Wadell, a business plan facilitator, and Mary Elizabeth Rodrigues, a board member, to map out a revised business plan for the Foundation. Early in 2009 we had had a CNCF review meeting, asking board member and attorney Nick Holland to push the adoption of the revision to the CNCF Law which we had been pursuing for some time, Now, Rod Wadell had completed his report on CNCF, which we were able to review. To ensure CNCF's continued growth, it was key to ensure that we were efficiently using the government grant that formed a significant part of the organisation's funding. At the same time, we needed to ensure artistic freedom for the development of our culture.

On 15th February Viv and I left Cayman for New Zealand, arriving in Auckland on the 17th. After catching up on some sleep at the hotel, we were kindly invited to a delicious dinner at the Euro restaurant, on Princes Wharf, by Brian Dacres, head of the RLB office in Auckland. There, we were able to bring him up-to-date with first-hand information about all the projects RLBC were working on in the Caribbean, and he was able to provide expert information from his part of the world that might potentially be of use to us when bidding on projects. Karen Johnson, being from New Zealand, had told us of a splendid hike called the Tongariro Crossing, across the slopes of Mount Tongariro, an active, multi-cratered volcano on the North Island. We duly drove the four hundred kilometres from Auckland to the National Park, and checked into the Bayview Chateau, where we enjoyed a relaxing dinner. The next morning we arose, had breakfast, and asked for a map and directions to begin the hike, which is some seventeen kilometres in length. But we were firmly told, in no uncertain terms, that the crossing was closed due to bad weather and that any attempt to undertake it would be foolhardy.

We therefore left the Chateau early and drove to Napier, in the famous Hawkes Bay wine region, where we checked into the White House, a wonderful bed and breakfast located on the Marine Parade. There was a vintage car procession on at the time, with everyone dressed in the appropriate clothes to match the year their cars were manufactured, so it was quite a splendid welcome to this part of New Zealand. The town's centre was completely destroyed by a violent earthquake in 1931 and rebuilt in the then-popular Art Deco architectural style. Most of these buildings are still standing, and are now protected. The next day, 21st February, we visited the Sileni vineyard to taste their fine selection of Syrah and Chardonnay wines, followed by lunch. Afterwards, we climbed some 1,200 feet up a picturesque peak called Te Mata. Back at the White House, our host had arranged his party bus, complete with table, hors d'oeuvres and wine, and drove us to a concert by tenor Geoff Sewell at Church Road winery. I well remember sitting on a rug with Viv, who was dressed in white trousers, drinking red wine as we listened to this incredible tenor. As we applauded the performance, Viv's glass tipped over, splashing her trousers with a beautiful red design!

On 22nd February we left Napier and drove the three hundred and twenty kilometres to Martinborough, where we checked into the Martinborough Hotel, and fell to tasting some of the area's excellent Pinot Noirs. Before we left on this trip my brother Rob had been doing some research into our family's ancestry, during which he came across the fact that a Bould had emigrated to New Zealand and settled in Wellington. Out of curiosity, I asked the receptionist at the hotel if she had a Wellington telephone book, which she quickly provided. I looked to see if a Bould was listed and, sure enough, there was one Ann Bould.

I phoned the number and explained who I was to the somewhat surprised lady who answered the phone, and said that we might be related. By pure serendipity, she had retained her maiden name when she married. I asked if we might be able to meet in Wellington the next day, and suggested a coffee shop in the Johnsonville Shopping Centre. She agreed with this plan, and announced there was, in fact, a Bould Street just around the corner. The next day, we took photos beneath the street sign while waiting for Ann to arrive. She brought her father and mother with her, who were delighted to meet us and said the Bould family home was close, and hence the street name. We drove to see it, now situated in the middle of a suburban subdivision, and asked if we could go inside and view the house. This we did, and saw the original bathtub, sitting on cast-iron feet in the middle of the bathroom. It turned out that my ancestor had initially farmed sheep there but then built a horse racing track, which had subsequently been sold to create the subdivision – property development was clearly in the Bould genes!

From there, we drove to Wellington airport and caught a flight to Nelson, on the South Island, hired a car and then drove to the Resurgence Lodge, a beautiful eco-lodge in the Abel Tasman National Park. The next day we took a boat to the Abel Tasman Trail and hiked along the waterfront path. On 25th

February, we drove from Nelson to Hokitika, on the West Coast, and the next day, to beautiful Lake Matheson, which reflected the surrounding snowcapped mountains in its glass-like surface. We decided to take a helicopter flight to the Fox Glacier and landed on the top to check out the snow – but no skiing this time. We then drove to Te Anau, where we stayed at the Radford on the Lake Hotel, using it as a base to explore both Milford and Doubtful Sounds.

In Te Anau, the local bakery where we bought croissants for breakfast was run by the father of a friend from Cayman – it seemed strange to be talking with him, so far from the islands. On the 28th we took a cruise on Doubtful Sound, where we were surrounded by beautiful scenery and dolphins leaped before the boat's prow. On 5th May we flew from Christchurch to Auckland, Sydney, and on to Tokyo.

Our good friend, John Davies, had published a photographic masterpiece on the life of 'Kosen', whom he had followed and photographed over the five years of her 'apprenticeship' to become a geisha. So, when he heard we were going to visit Japan he had offered excellent advice about what to do and where to visit, and even had detailed recommendations about transportation.

On arriving in Tokyo, John's advice had been to take the bus to the train station where we were to catch the bullet train from Tokyo to Kyoto. It was a fancy bus with a concierge with white gloves who took our baggage and stored it in the locker underneath the comfortable seats. We drove to the station, the bus stopped, and we got off with our four large suitcases – to discover the station entrance was on the opposite side of a four-lane highway, and it was raining. We eventually managed to cross – umbrellas raised – without being run over by the fast moving traffic. We bought tickets and boarded the bullet train, depositing our luggage in the appropriate rack in the carriage. There were a couple of stops before Kyoto, so we practiced standing up and seeing how long it took us to pull the bags off the rack, and made note of how long it took for the doors to open so we could get out before the train moved off again. The trains in Japan operate to a very defined and efficient schedule.

Arriving in Kyoto, we took a taxi to the three hundred year-old Tawaraya Ryokan – the traditional inn John had recommended – and checked in. We were tired after so much recent travel, and I was ready for a sleep, but there was no bed in the room, just a futon on the floor. However, the service was impeccable, and a maid quickly came in and added further futons and pillows, so eventually we were able to have a sleep. There was a wooden tub in the bathroom, but once I had folded my 6'3" body into it I was doubled in two and had quite a job getting out again. The guest book at the inn contained a comment from Baron Hilton, stating, 'A lesson to hotelmen on what service is all about'.

On 7th March, John had arranged for Viv and me to enjoy a tea ceremony, and his driver, Katoh-san, came to collect us. He took us to a monastery where an aged and distinguished-looking monk invited us to join him on the floor. He was kneeling, sitting on his feet, but invited us to sit cross-legged as he felt we would be more comfortable that way. He then provided a most interesting discourse on Buddhism and made tea, clearly following a very formal ritual, and offered us a sweet, wrapped and placed in a beautiful ceramic container, which we treasure to this day as part of Viv's miniature box collection – I guess one day we may eat the sweet.

We then returned to the Tawaraya and enquired where we might go for a traditional Japanese meal. We were directed to a small upstairs restaurant with a long bar seating about ten people, with the chefs preparing the food behind it. No one spoke English and so, when offered the menu, we simply pointed to a list and the food started to arrive, all in small portions, exquisitely presented, with separate sauces in small bowls. A couple sitting beside us at the bar appeared to have ordered the same menu as we had, so we watched them to see which of the sauce selections they dipped their food into and followed suit. All went smoothly for the first several courses, but then the couple's selections began to diverge from ours and we were lost. Seeing our dilemma, they pointed to the appropriate dips to use. The food was delicious, with a very refined taste, and the courses kept coming. After a while, the couple ventured to try out their English and we managed to work out they were asking where we lived. I took a napkin and drew the United States, Florida, Cuba and then Cayman.

Then we got onto the subject of our respective jobs, and we managed to get across banker for Vivian, builder – well, close enough – for me, and architect for the gentleman. They then described how they had been shopping that day, and the lady presented us with a beautifully wrapped box of green tea chocolates. I thought of what we might have to give them, and remembered the Tortuga Rum cakes, such a typically Caymanian product, back at our hotel. So I ran back there, picked one up, and returned to the restaurant and presented it – to their delight. They then asked us, mainly through sign language, if we wanted to join them at their club for a drink. Somewhat nervously, given we had only just met, we agreed, and we drove to a club entrance where the gentlemen knocked on the door and it mysteriously opened.

We sat at a bar and were asked what we wanted to drink – I was a still a little nervous, thinking ungraciously we might possibly be drugged and robbed. Seeing an unopened bottle of wine, I thought that would be safest, and asked for a glass. The gentlemen then asked if we wanted our photographs taken with a geisha, and once again wondering if this was a ruse, I agreed, after which we returned to the bar for another drink. The gentlemen insisted on paying for everything and then drove us back to the Tawaraya, where we exchanged addresses. We had talked during the evening about cherry blossoms in Japan, and about three months after our return to Cayman, a beautiful wood-block print of cherry blossoms arrived in the post. In turn, we sent them a beautiful picture of Seven Mile Beach, while I felt really bad about having entertained such unpleasant suspicions of these kind people.

On 9th March we returned to Tokyo on the bullet train. We had asked the Peninsula, where we were staying, to send a driver to the station to pick us up. As the train pulled into the station, a liveried porter was waiting to take our bags, and we descended the stairs to discover a Rolls Royce with chauffeur standing by. The porter placed some of our luggage in the trunk of the car, but there was not enough room for all of it, so a cover was placed on the front leather seat, and our surplus luggage placed on that. Regrettably, there was now not enough space in the car for the porter, so he had to return by bus. As we arrived at the Peninsula we were greeted at the front door by a receptionist, who said we had been upgraded to a suite. She accompanied us there, and then spent about thirty minutes describing how all the switches worked, the special fan in the vanity for the drying of nail polish, the waterfall on the bathroom wall, how the drapes opened, and how we used the tablet to order food! All things considered, it was a pity we were only there for one night.

On 26th March, Viv and I were off again to Denver and Steamboat, where we skied until 4th April. When I first took up skiing, I bought a book by Billy Kidd, called *Ski in Six Days*, with a cover photo of him on his skis wearing his trademark Stetson. Sure enough, Billy was still teaching at Steamboat, and when he walked in for lunch, Stetson and all, I went over to thank him for the lessons from his book. Our good friend Al Hallock had sold his condo at Chateau D'Mont in Keystone, and developed a condominium complex called Eagles Nest in Steamboat. In order to be able to accommodate his family, as well as Viv and me, at the same time, he had knocked together a two-bedroom unit with a one bedroom unit. We stayed there many times – what a friend!

On 22nd April I was off to London for a RLBC meeting in Bruton Place and to meet with Nick Thomas, who was assisting us with the production of a report on Caribbean construction costs and development activities called *Caribbean Report – Construction Market Intelligence*, which we were intending to publish annually. I returned to Cayman on the 28th, in time for Dave Martin's Distinguished Lecture the following day, and on 1st May, 'Culture at Callaloo'. This opened with Steel Pan, drama by Izumi, storytelling with various tellers, kitchen music by Swanky, dance by Dance Unlimited and, of course, food and drink.

I attended the Chief Secretary's office in the Glass House, the Government Administration Building in George Town, on 8th May, where I had the privilege of becoming naturalised and given a Cayman Islands' passport, based on my having been granted Caymanian status on 1st July 1980. I was delighted to be greeted by the Chief Secretary asking me what I was doing there as he thought I was already a Caymanian!

On 13th May, Jerry and I presented the 5th annual ISTT seminar, titled 'Delays, Damages and Disputes – How to Manage in Troubled Times', to over sixty construction professionals at the Normandie Hotel in Port of Spain. We had changed to a totally new format for this presentation, using a fictious hotel as a working example. The 'Sunburn Resort', a luxury high rise project, was finally being built after years of effort to secure the necessary permits, but it was now some eleven months behind schedule. A cast of characters added realism to the example, and enabled attendees to more easily identify with the generic causes of delay, such as variations to the brief, changed conditions, disruption, material cost increases and labour shortages, all covered in the detailed set of hand-out notes and slides. Throughout the day-long presentation, the attendees engaged in lively question and answer sessions. The exit survey rated the seminar as excellent and the participants made several thoughtful suggestions for future seminars.

I was back in Cayman on 20th May for election day and meetings with Rod Wadell about how the fundraising Business Plan for the Save Miss Lassie's House programme was progressing. Mortimer arrived on the 24th, and on 5th June Emma and Bruce Dinwiddy visited Cayman and we caught up with everyone's news over dinner at Callaloo. Lisa Johnson, representing the *Caribbean Construction Magazine*, contacted me at about this time, to ask if I would write a series of articles about the Caribbean construction industry, to be published quarterly. The first of these, 'Common Problems in Caribbean Construction Contracts' was published in the first quarter of 2011. It addressed changes in scope and how these could be dealt with. The solutions included change orders/variations, effective record keeping for variations claims, providing timely notice, the impact on the schedule of such variations, and calculating and proving damages resulting from such variations. The second quarter publication was of particular interest as, in addition to my article, it also carried an article on the Marina Bay Sands hotel in Singapore, on which RLB were the quantity surveyors, which had won the 'Be Inspired' award for excellence.

On 7th June I travelled to Barbados for meetings with the Caribbean Development Bank in an attempt to secure monitoring work for RLBC on projects the bank were funding in the region. I then met with Butterfield Bank who had opened a branch in Barbados. Given our excellent and long-standing relationship with them in Cayman, we hoped to continue our work with their Barbados programmes.

On 23rd June, Jeremy Superfine confirmed that the plans for the new National Gallery had been submitted to BCU for approval, so there was good progress toward making our new home a reality. That evening, I presented the CNCF Award for drama at the John Gray High School graduation, held at the Agape church.

The next day, Viv and I left for London, to be collected by Frank who was given the requisite Tortuga Rum cake (as well as his fare, of course). He took us to 62 Queen's Gate Mews, where the renovations had been completed. We were so delighted with the result, that we decided we would no longer rent it out but keep it for our own use. On the 26th, Viv and I went to the Royal Albert Hall, where we saw a fine performance of *The King and I*. We had reserved a box, to which the concierge admits you with a large old-fashioned key. We had ordered wine and hors d'oeuvres to be delivered, and it was great fun being able to partake of a libation and titbit whilst enjoying the performance.

We had secured Debenture Holders tickets to see the ladies' finals at Wimbledon on 4th June, where Serena Williams defeated her sister Venus in a rematch of the previous year's final 7-6, 6-2. Then both Venus and Serena went on the win the ladies' doubles, beating the Australian pair of Samantha Stosur and Rennae Stubbs 7-6, 6-4. Naturally, we enjoyed the Wimbledon tradition of strawberries and cream and champagne. The next day, Charlie and Lori came to lunch at 62 QGM, and we then went to the safety deposit box facility in St John's Wood to reset the security settings for the silver bars stored there.

In June, I had met with Mark and Nick Thomas to work on the production of the Caribbean Market Intelligence publication, and by 7th August, Mark Green had completed the mockup. The work on the Monte Barreto costing continued, with extensive calls with René Hubert, and on 16th August I flew to Barbados. The flight from Miami arrived in the late evening, and by this time, we had established a great relationship with Anstead Coleman of Courtesy Rent-a-Car, based at the Grantley Adams terminal. They would leave a car for us to use, with the rental agreement and keys under the mat, and I would sign the agreement and deposit it in the box at their front door. We had a similar arrangement for early departures before their office opened. In a similar way, when staying at the Accra Hotel on the south coast, the hostess would seat me at breakfast, saying, 'Welcome back Mr Bould'. I would ask how she knew my name, to which she would reply, 'Mr Bould, this is the fortieth time you have stayed with us!'

On 27th of August, Viv and I travelled to Denver to celebrate the life of Jane Hallock, who had sadly passed away. She had become a wonderful friend after she and Al had purchased a condo in Plantana almost twenty-five years before. We returned to Cayman on 31st August but weren't there for long before flying to Portland for a Carabella partners' meeting. These meetings were great fun, as we only dealt briefly with accounts and budgets before going on to taste our recently bottled vintages and visit the latest trendy restaurants. The production of great wine in the area seemed to elevate the quality of the local restaurants – reasonable, if one thinks about it, as the two go together.

In early September, I was working on my speech to present at the 25th anniversary of CNCF. When tackling Caymanian culture, I noted:

> Our culture is integral to our own development, and for the past 25 years CNCF, with the efforts of our hardworking and dedicated staff, volunteers and the contribution of our board has carried out its mission of stimulating, facilitating and preserving artistic expression generally, particularly the preservation and exploration of Caymanian performing, visual and literary arts. The results – Miss Lassie's paintings, Swanky's music, Al Ebanks's sculpture, Bendel Hyde's art, Leonard Dilbert's poetry, Dance Unlimited's dance, Miss Julia's drumming, Cardinal DaCosta's singing, Dave Martin's Rundown, Frank McField's plays, Roy Bodden's writings, Radley Gurzong's fiddle, the Quadrille performed by our youth groups – and the list can go on and on. So here is Caymanian culture at its best.

Before these anniversary celebrations, I had travelled to IFACCA's world summit in Johannesburg to represent Cayman. I returned with an intensified sense of the critical nature of our work, particularly as it related to Cayman's social stability, to which I have always believed our cultural development was key. In Joburg, Viv and I stayed in the Rosebank area. While I attended the CEO's meeting on 22nd September, followed by the General Assembly in the evening at the Africa Museum, Viv decided to take a tour to Soweto. On the way there, she was shown the 'Bird's Nest Stadium' that had been built for the World Cup football celebrations. In Soweto she was shown Nelson Mandela's house and as she was standing outside, who should appear but Winnie Mandela. Viv asked her permission to take her photograph, to which Winnie replied, 'Only if you are in it with me!', which is what happened.

The next morning we received a call from Fred Walkup, Viv's sister Pat's husband, with the devastating news that Viv's mom Flo had passed away some days earlier. He had been unable to contact us before then due to our travels, and her funeral service was being held the next day in Florida. There was no way we could fly back in time to arrive for it, so we resolved to hold a Celebration of Life Service for her in Belfast. It was not easy to go on after receiving this sad news but on 25th September we left Joburg for Pretoria to take the Blue Train to Cape Town. Our steward greeted us as we boarded, and Viv was delighted to see that the bathroom in our cabin included a full-sized tub. She enquired if the water would overflow when the train was travelling rapidly. 'Absolutely not,' he replied. And to prove it, Viv ordered a bottle of champagne and hors d'oeuvres to enjoy whilst we luxuriated in the tub. We stopped along the route to explore the Kimberley diamond mines while the train was being serviced. In Cape Town, we met Alaistair and Fran for lunch before returning to Joburg again, from where we went on safari at Nagala Game Reserve in the Kruger National Park.

The Nagala Game Reserve is operated by a company called &Beyond, and they provide absolutely outstanding service. One morning while on a game drive, we struck up a conversation with the two young ladies seated in front of us in the Land Rover. They were both celebrating their 30th birthday, and they asked Viv and me about our travels and the people we had met. They were impressed by the number of places we had visited and people we knew. I replied that when they reached our ages, they too would have met a lot of people and travelled to many places. Minutes later, another Land Rover passed us, and the sole occupant said, 'Mr Bould, nice to see you; fancy meeting you here!' Our companions' jaws dropped – here we were, in the middle of the African wilderness, and we had just been greeted by the passenger of a random vehicle. I explained that she was Natasha Eves, a cultural researcher with IFACCA. We had no idea that Natasha would be at Nagala, and asked her to join us for dinner that evening. Little did we know that the staff had arranged a surprise for us. When we returned to our cottage, we found the staff had filled the tub and sprinkled it with flower petals, and organised for dinner to be served on our terrace. We learned that after dark, guests are only permitted to traverse the space between the accommodation cottages and the central dining area in the company of an armed guard. There was no one available that evening, so sadly we missed dinner with Natasha.

During the first weeks of October, we met with Clive Barclay, and had a meeting with Mary Chandler at the London office of Cayman Islands, on Albemarle Street, to discuss how our global and Caribbean presence could dovetail with the Cayman Islands' Government's promotion scheme. Later, we would meet with Camper and Nicholson about charter boat opportunities and marinas in the Caribbean. On the 9th, RLBC's Caribbean Intelligence held a lunchtime presentation at the Regatta Meeting room in Durrants Hotel. There, to a packed audience, we introduced our *Caribbean Construction Cost Commentary*, enabling UK based companies with common interests in the Caribbean to share our current market knowledge. We continued this interchange for many years. We were learning to merge our Caribbean expertise with our global approach, assisted by the collaboration between Tracy Highland – a most talented administrator and marketing guru based in our Barbados office – and our talented UK marketing team, led by Jenny in the UK office. Their communication was key to turning these efforts into tangible results. While in London we also had drinks with Jean Gooder, the owner of a villa in Tuscany – of which more later!

Wayne picked us up from the airport as usual on our return to Cayman, but when we arrived back at Callaloo, I heard a 'meow' as we got out of the car. I asked what that was all about, and Wayne replied, 'I have bought you a pussy cat.' Coming from a family that had never had cats or pets of any kind, I said OK, but that he could live in the garage. Viv named him 'Puddie', although he was a neutered male. As I am sure you've anticipated, his confinement to the garage lasted only for about a week. Then he was in the kitchen, and not long afterwards had the run of the house. Viv trained him very well – I am sure those of you who know Viv will not find it difficult to believe he stayed off the counters and chairs without covers. I, of course, also grew to love him, but called him Buster, which I felt far more appropriate. He was with us for fourteen years and it was a very tearful occasion when we had to have him put to sleep.

We were anxious to promote the UK incentive we had begun with the Caribbean Intelligence event in London. To that end, we liaised with the Caribbean Construction magazine, to which we were submitting articles for publication, to publish a press release highlighting the event, and the fact that it was to become a regular feature.

I had a meeting at Miss Lassie's House on 16th October to review progress on our plan to save the property in perpetuity and, on the CNCF front, I worked with Marcia on a press release to cover my attendance at the IFACCA World Summit in Joburg, and the key takeaways and benefits to us in Cayman.

We held a Careenage promotional party, featuring Steve Ryder from Bellingham Marine, who reported on the strata docks we were planning for the property, and on the 17th we hosted a lunch at Callaloo, in part to discuss the new contract we had secured to monitor progress on a new 150,000 sq ft national hospital, in St Lucia, for Italian contractors INSO. Brian Martin, who had now completed the cruise ship dock in St Maarten, agreed to relocate to St Lucia. On 19th October I was invited by Radio Cayman to make a presentation on RLBC's Caribbean Intelligence and *Caribbean Construction Cost Commentary*, how it related to the work we were doing in Cayman, and how our Caribbean clients could benefit from our global reach.

Geoff Cresswell arrived in Cayman shortly thereafter, to be part of CNCF's 25th anniversary celebrations. These were observed with a totally appropriate 'black-tie' affair at the Harquail Theatre. As I've explained above, attending the IFACCA World Summit had underlined and endorsed my views on the critical nature of our work, and I said in my speech:

> I have just returned from representing Cayman at the World Summit on culture in South Africa where some 400 representatives from 70 countries debated cultural diversity and its importance in society. So with cultural diversity, strangeness versus difference can result in opposite outcomes – strangeness can invite curiosity and engagement whereas difference can postpone engagement and lead to conflict. At the summit this was illustrated by a Danish cartoonist insulting Islam, a film maker from Slovenia showing the effect of a dramatic song on Serb war crimes, an actress from Pakistan showing how the partition from India and the motto of 'one country, one language and one religion' did not work, as it was clearly untrue and has in many ways led to the current Taliban problems in her country; a poet from Palestine showing the impact of the war with Israel being a result of their cultural differences, a cultural administrator from Chile speaking of the cultural revolution that led to Pinochet's downfall, a South African professor telling of the dark times of apartheid where music separated the students and, finally, the standing ovation that the Minister of Culture from Jamaica received after a presentation by her using Bob Marley's music and lyrics and its impact on Jamaica and the world.

Concluding:

> So, my friends, our culture is integral to our own development, and for the past 25 years CNCF, sponsored by our forward looking government, coupled with the efforts of our hardworking and dedicated staff, volunteers and the contribution of our board, has carried out its mission of stimulating, facilitating and preserving

artistic expression generally, particularly the preservation and exploration of Caymanian performing, visual and literary arts.

In Trinidad, at the end of October, I was introduced to Colin Barcant, who had significant expertise in the construction of docks, and who might be able to provide a competitive bid to that of Bellingham Marine for the proposed Careenage dock project. I then went to Grenada for a wide range of meetings, including with Keith Letton on the TVA stadium matter in St Vincent, with the Attorney General, about the possibility for CCAS to provide construction advisory and contract training services, Royston Hopkin on the potential expansion for his wonderful Spice Island hotel project, and contractor Mike Quin. While in Grenada, I received an email that would transform the next six years of my life and bring into sharp focus the benefits of the global entity that was RLB. The email was from the Export Import Bank of China (China Exim) and read:

> The project I mentioned is a world-class integrated tourism destination at the Cable Beach in Nassau, The Bahamas, with a total investment of over US$ 3.5 billion. This project comprises of four associated but separately branded hotels, a casino hotel with a 100,000 square foot destination casino, and other amenities, known as Baha Mar.
>
> We hope your good company can assist our financing for the following main tasks:
>
> - Verifying the project budget, focusing on measures to control or contain project costs.
> - Project monitor. Monitoring the project progress and assessing construction payment.
>
> If you need further project information, please feel free to contact me.

This was certainly the shortest scope assignment I had ever received, and for what was to become the largest construction project in the Western Hemisphere at the time. My first thought was that I'd need a new calculator – one capable of handling billions instead of millions!

Obviously, RLB's presence in China – with some twenty offices throughout the country and their head office in Beijing – was a significant advantage, particularly since China Exim's headquarters were also based there. We were also well supported by RLB's UK and global offices, who had significant prior expertise in monitoring projects and were able to provide samples of similar proposals from other major projects. We rapidly shifted into a resourcing role, and sought out key staff to fill the necessary positions. In this regard, our Caribbean expertise integrated perfectly with our global partners. Charles Leonard brought essential scheduling expertise, Jerry Katz covered legal matters, and Alan Veeran's construction management expertise would be essential. To round out our team we needed an on-site project manager, and asked our London office to suggest a suitable candidate. Our Beijing office kindly assigned a lender's liaison officer, Lo See Wing, who would manage the translation of our reports into Mandarin and field any questions from China Exim.

After this joyous shot in the arm, I got back to our somewhat more mundane daily operations, during which Jerry and I flew to Antigua for meetings and to catch up with old friends at OBM, including Mitch Stuart, who – as you will recall – had designed Plantana, inspired by a few glasses of Johnnie Walker Black Label. From Antigua we flew to Anguilla, on 29th October, to see what kind of foothold we could establish there.

Perhaps because of the size of the island, we were able to arrange a comprehensive list of people to see, including Larry Franklin, Principal Secretary in the Ministry of Works; the Attorney General, Dr Bourne; Aidan Harrigan, the Principal Secretary of Economy and Planning in the Ministry of Finance. We also visited the Viceroy Hotel, which was under construction but experiencing delays and claims issues with which CCAS could certainly assist. The airport in Anguilla could significantly benefit from an extension, but at its western end was restricted by existing properties and at its eastern end was controlled by a land-owning family that wanted to develop with a planned resort. As usual in our Caribbean society, politics came into play. We would continue over the years to be involved in this interplay.

I returned to Cayman on 31st October in time to volunteer for bar duty at the Harquail, and on 2nd November appeared on the *Talk Today* show. During the interview I discussed CNCF's twenty-fifth anniversary, what we had discovered during those twenty-five years, and how I viewed this progress as Chairman, particularly given what I had learnt from a global perspective by attending the IFACCA World Summits. I also expressed how I saw CNCF's role evolving in a changing Caymanian society during the next twenty-five years. I was honoured and humbled to be awarded the Gold Heritage Cross Award for my contributions to CNCF – along with Mrs Harquail, Dave Martins, Frank McField, Edmund Scott and Henry Muttoo. Later that month, I was invited onto the *Government Information Services* show to make a similar presentation.

We were still trying to settle a number of claims from the losses suffered by our clients in Hurricane Ivan and, during November, hearings commenced on the case mentioned earlier, where the insured's policy had expired at midnight on the day Hurricane Ivan hit, for which I was sitting as one of three arbitrators. Key to the claim, was that hurricane force winds had hit Cayman before midnight.

The weather office at Owen Roberts Airport maintains records, and the task of proving this key piece of evidence seemed easy, as a new anemometer had been installed on the side of the runway before the hurricane had hit. The records showed that hurricane force gusts had been experienced prior to midnight, so, under the '72-hour single loss occurrence' clause of the insurance policy, this meant that once the loss had commenced, further losses after midnight would be covered. However, it was found that debris could have caused the anemometer to malfunction, despite it being new, and so further evidence was presented by the insurance company. This came from the Co-operative Institute of Meteorological Satellite Studies Space Science and Engineering Center at the University of Wisconsin (that's a mouthful!), which records hurricane downbursts. Their records clearly showed that winds of hurricane force did not hit Cayman until after midnight. So, the claim was – very unfortunately for the insured – rejected.

Earlier in October, I had enlisted the gracious services of Nick Holland to review the construction agreement for the new National Gallery and Natalie Coleman's heads of terms for her upcoming employment at the Gallery. The 20th November would be the closing date for the contractors' tenders for the National Gallery building project, and we were eagerly anticipating the results.

Viv and I left for London on 27th November, and then went on to Belfast for Flo's memorial and celebration of her life. It was a good closing for Vivian and me, and family and friends who had also missed the funeral. While in Belfast I also had a productive meeting with the directors at Lagan Construction, who were active in the Caribbean, particularly on infrastructure projects, to discuss how RLBC could work with the company.

Back in London on 3rd December, I met with DFID (the UK Government's Department for International Development) to acquaint them with the services RLBC could offer on projects they were funding in the Caribbean. I also held a conference with the editors of *Building* magazine, to see if they would publish an article on RLBC. On the 7th I held a RLBC board meeting, followed by a dinner at Lucio's, where we had reserved a private room for some of our UK clients involved in Caribbean projects.

With my birthday fast approaching, we decided to fly to Nice and drive up to Moustiers-Sainte-Marie, to stay at La Bouscatière and hike the Gorges du Verdon. Genevieve had hand-embroidered a beautiful tray cloth with the inscription 'Bonne Année a Callaloo' for our upcoming New Year's celebration. We drove to Verbier on the 11th to ski with Ray and Michèle, where we enjoyed great mountainside lunches during our three-day visit, topped off with a Michelin-starred meal at Philippe Rochat in Crissier, at the Restaurant de L'Hôtel de Ville, formerly owned by Frédy Girardet.

It was around this time that International Travel was winding down, so we needed to find a new travel agent after having been served by them so well over many years. I asked Tim Peck, of OBM, for recommendations as he travelled frequently. He suggested Four Seasons Travel in Miami. So we met with them, and soon established an excellent relationship with Dean Hoffman, who has looked after us for our world travels ever since.

2010

Personal growth lies within the unknown – courage permits you to explore this space.

The new year began with the groundbreaking for Block A at Careenage on 8th January, and we began advertising for a new secretary / office administrator as Karen Johnson's departure for New Zealand drew nearer. We also needed an additional general surveyor for our growing appraisal/valuation practice. To this end I flew to London for a week on 12th January and interviewed six potential candidates at 62 Queen's Gate Mews.

Igor was visiting Cayman when I returned, so we were able to work out together at Callaloo and assess whether any adjustments to my programme with Dottie were necessary. On the RLBC front, we began reviewing a large resort project planned for Buccament Bay in St Vincent, and I received a request from China Exim to meet with their representatives and attorneys in Los Angeles.

On 24th January I arrived in LAX, then had a long and somewhat fraught ride from the airport to the hotel with a cabbie who got lost en route. He only admitted it was his first day on the job when I refused to pay the absurdly high fare he requested. The next morning, after breakfast, I met with Shao Di, Deng Yi and Li Yue of China Exim, and Cindy Lo and Yvonne Ho of Allen and Overy, China Exim's attorneys, to go through questions on the documentation we had been given. The Baha Mar project, which encompassed some thousand acres of land with three thousand feet of beachfront, had commenced some years earlier. Harrah's, the Las Vegas casino operator, was the planned major equity partner and operator. The global financial crisis of 2007–2008 had interrupted many real estate ventures, and Harrah's decided not to continue their involvement in the project

China State Construction and Engineering Corporation had entered the picture to negotiate a construction management agreement with the Baha Mar developers in 2009. As part of the negotiations, a financing package had been agreed with China Exim. The original budgets needed to be reviewed, and RLBC was asked to prepare an Initial Audit Report on both the costs and the procurement documentation. The meetings with China Exim and Allen and Overy went well, but we also needed to meet with China State as construction managers, Baha Mar as developers, and visit the site. I met with David Wang and Yan Wei of China State at their offices in New Jersey, to discuss the budget, schedule and quality aspects of the procurement documentation and on 30th January I flew from Newark to Nassau for meetings with John Pagano, President of Baha Mar and John Park, Senior Structural Design Manager of Baha Mar. The head of BML Properties was Sarkis Izmirlian, the son of Dikran Izmirlian who had made his fortune by creating a near monopoly on the world's supply of peanuts. Baha Mar with a total cost of $3.4 billion, was far from being peanuts!

The enabling works part of the contract alone were a major undertaking. They involved rerouting West Bay Street and demolishing five buildings. These included banks and fire and police stations, which then had to be rebuilt along the rerouted road. Back in Cayman, on 31st January, we had our work cut out for us to assign resources, and arrive at a fee proposal for this major assignment – one that would take several years to complete.

At the beginning of February, I appeared on the *Daybreak* show, making further funding appeals for CNCF's renovation of Miss Lassie's House. A few days later, CNCF presented a tribute to Rex Nettleford, who had sadly passed on 2nd February, in Washington DC. Again, I felt privileged to have met such a great man through the work and great staff at CNCF.

We interviewed several applicants for the position of secretary / office administrator for RLBC, including one Bernadine Murrain. Fortunately, she was working for an agency and was able to join us straight away. Karen Johnson was able to liaise with her before leaving for New Zealand on the 19th, and Bernadine remains with us to this day, running the office efficiently and with seasoned skill, good humour and extensive knowledge. She is also an absolute wonder at filling out forms, which is something I loathe doing.

Viv and I were invited to dinner at Andrew and Felicity Jones' home, to meet Duncan Taylor and his wife Marie Beatrice. Duncan had taken over from Stuart Jack as Governor, and I was able to discuss the work of CNCF with him.

We agreed I would meet with him again for a more in-depth engagement and to discover how he might assist in supporting our work. He graciously followed up on our discussion, and we subsequently met at the F.J. Harquail Cultural Centre on 4th March, where we presented him with a gift basket (appropriately made of thatch) of our publications over the years, for his further review.

Viv and I then flew to Denver, and went to Eagle Vail for a week's skiing at Winter Park, Loveland, Snowmass, and Aspen and Highlands. We returned from Eagle Vail to Cayman on 28th February. During this ski trip I had the opportunity to work on my agreement with RLBC. One of the terms had been that I would resign and ensure BCL's shares in RLBC were sold by 2017. As I mentioned earlier, David Bucknall never wanted to retire, but the shareholders of Bucknall Austin (now RLB UK) were of a different view – hence the condition built into my and BCL's arrangement with RLBC.

In early March we made an offer to one of the six candidates I had interviewed in January for the position of General Surveyor. On the same day, RLBC was instructed to prepare a Red Book valuation for the Buccament Bay project on St Vincent, so the timing was perfect. The Monte Barreto project in Havana, was moving forward, and we continued our negotiations with Bouygues on the construction bid. On the 6th I flew to London to meet Mortimer, and we both travelled by train to Birmingham to meet at the RLB UK headquarters there for a board meeting of RLBC. We held a Caribbean Intelligence Lunch at Durrants Hotel on the 9th, and at this lunch Peter Stokes, a QS with whom I had worked at DFJ Henri during my training and who was a great friend of my brother Rob's, mentioned a PFI project for the new Bermuda hospital. Earlier in the year we had been talking about PFI projects with Cullum McAlpine, and – for good or bad – this was a project that McAlpine's eventually built in Bermuda.

On 10th March Viv and I had an excellent lunch with accountant Nick Ross and his wife Annette. Nick had helped me value the interest in Wakeman Trower Cawston & Partners when I acquired the company back in 1973, and so was an excellent 'sounding board' regarding the terms of my RLBC agreement. On 11th March we were able to see Andrew Lloyd Webber's, *Love Never Dies*, the sequel to the *Phantom of the Opera*. The next day, over lunch with Mark Williamson, we discussed business development and the valuation we were preparing for Buccament Bay. I also met with Stuart Stables, RLB UK's financial director, about RLBC's valuation as part of my agreement.

I had to pick up my Chinese visa from the Chinese Embassy in Kingston on 15th March, as China Exim had requested a meeting in Beijing. I arrived in Beijing on the 18th, and met with Shao Di and Cindy Lo the next day to discuss our fee proposal and scope of work for Baha Mar. It can be very cold in Beijing in March, and I had brought my thermal ski underwear with me. I wore it for the walk to China Exim's offices, but the board room where we were to meet was super-heated. As I sat waiting, I became more and more uncomfortable until I was almost passing out. I got the underwear off in a bathroom, but had nowhere to store it except in my briefcase. The meeting began, and I soon needed to refer to some papers in my briefcase. These, of course, were under the clothing – so here I was, making a key presentation, and I had to take out my underwear to access my papers. Our clients were obviously not deterred, as we kept the job! The underwear was useful in the end as, after our meetings, despite the cold, I took the opportunity to visit the Olympic Park, site of the 2008 Olympics and to see the 'Birds Nest' stadium, where the layer of snow in the central arena was heavily discolored by the high level of pollution in the city.

On Easter Monday, 5th April, we had a catboat race from Seven Mile Public Beach as part of 2010s Cayfest. We also held a Distinguished Lecture on the subject of Miss Lassie's work, and 'Praise', a celebration with several church choirs, at Government House on 24th April. *Isabell*, a play CNCF had produced, was broadcast on Radio Cayman on 26th April.

On 9th April I flew to Nassau with Alan Veeran, who was to head up the costing aspect of our Interim Audit Report for Baha Mar, to meet with John Park and John Pagano to review various aspects of the documentation and inspect the site. We were back again for more site meetings at the end of April, then visited China State's offices in New Jersey on the 28th, and subsequently met with the design and construction document team, including engineers, in New York.

Both Viv and Mortimer's birthdays were coming up in May, and we had identified a beautiful Tuscan Manor house and farm, called Casa Berti, near Lucca in Tuscany, in which to spend them. It was described on its website as 'a lovely 18th century Tuscan Manor House, set amongst its own olive groves, and gardens. It has stunning views towards the Serchio river valley, the plain of Lucca, and the wild peaks of the Garfagnana.' It sounded ideal, as it could accommodate ten guests in the main house and had additional accommodation in the farmhouse.

We had previously met the owners of Casa Berti, Jean and Richard Gooder, in the UK some months earlier and invited them for drinks at 62 Queen's Gate Mews. They drove up to the front door, and we noticed that Richard had mobility issues and was wheelchair bound. Unfortunately, the front door was not quite wide enough to accommodate his wheelchair, so we had to serve hors d'oeuvres and wine through the front door to Richard, who remained in the car while Jean joined us in the lounge. As a result of Richard's mobility issue, Casa Berti had a stairlift. This greatly assisted Millie, Jan's mom, who joined one of the groups of guests that came to stay with us. Our guests began arriving on 2nd May, and included my brother Rob and his wife Jenna, Peter and Jill McDonald, Doreen and Alan Scott. They were followed on 5th May by Jonnie and Edward, arriving with Edward's new girlfriend, Gillian, all in time for Viv's most delicious birthday celebration dinner on 7th May, cooked by Paola da Patro, a chef recommended by Richard and Jean.

Edward's birthday was the following day, so we were able to celebrate a day early. Mortimer arrived in style in his BMW, with Jan and Millie, on 11th May. Unfortunately, they missed the turn to Casa Berti, and drove into the neighboring village. Attempting to turn around by backing into a field, the BMW got well stuck in the mud. Mortimer called me on my cell to tell me of their predicament, and by the time I arrived, pretty much the entire village had come to witness the action and were seated on various folding chairs around the edge of the field. The local farmer had started his tractor with the intention of pulling the car out of the mud. I suggested a simpler solution, which involved Mort, Jan and Millie leaving their comfortable seats in the car and unloading Millie's mobility scooter from the trunk. I jumped into the driver's seat, carefully applied pressure to the accelerator – and out came the car, to a rousing cheer from the many spectators.

Paul and Mary, Jan's brother and wife, then arrived along with Mikol, and we celebrated with another fine dinner on 14th May, catered by Paola, to celebrate Mortimer's 80th birthday. There was one book of particular interest at Casa Berti, because it included an entry from the second World War, when the house had been used as a base for the Allied forces. Mention was made of the Buffalo Soldiers, part of an African American regiment that had been based there – whose name subsequently became the title of a hit song by Bob Marley.

After a wonderful two weeks in the company of so many of our friends, and three birthday parties, we returned to London. There I took the opportunity to look at More London, a mixed-use development that had been completed by the same developers as Baha Mar. It was indeed impressive – well-conceived and built. During the next week Viv and I played a lot of tennis at our local courts in Hyde Park, and I had the opportunity to visit with Lance Taylor, RLB's UK CEO, at a local UK office in Wokingham, to see their operations there. On the 24th we were invited by Andrew Rosindell, the MP for Romford, to a party at the House of Commons. This was his kind way of returning our hospitality during his attendance at the Caribbean Intelligence lunch as the key Member of Parliament for Caribbean business development.

Garth Arch was providing significant assistance to CNCF with structural reviews of Miss Lassie's House and in return I was assisting him with a programme addressing leadership – it was indeed exciting to be working with the next generation of Caymanians, who were continuing the efforts to improve skills within our small island society. In similar fashion, the Cayman Islands Roads Law was gazetted on 24th May to assist the compensation process we were heavily involved with. The chair of such cases was Margaret Ramsay-Hale, whose father, Ian Ramsay, had been an outstanding jurist, and with whom I had worked with during my time in Jamaica. Our work was obviously continuing with Baha Mar budgeting and risk assessment, and around this time we were reaching an acceptable level of close to $2 billion.

I flew to Barbados in early June to carry out a site inspection of the stalled Four Seasons project being developed by the same developer as the Grand Pallazzo in St Thomas, and also to hold a RLBC board meeting, as well as enjoy a cocktail party reception for our clients. I returned to Cayman on 10th June, in time for Garth's Leadership seminar. We were working on several key CNCF projects at this time with Joel Francis, the Chief Officer in the Ministry. These included revisions to the CNCF Law, Miss Lassie's House renovation, and the formation of the National Folk Singers, with which Stephanie Williams and Lorna Bush were heavily involved.

On 10th July, Roy Bodden launched his most recent book at the University College of the Cayman Islands, where he was President. *Patronage, Personalities and Parties* is the second in his series on Caymanian political development, covering the period from 1950 to 2000. Roy's chronicles of Cayman politics and societal issues are without peer.

I left for Barbados on the 11th to meet with First Caribbean International Bank and Royal Bank of Canada to promote RLBC's Caribbean-wide services. I also met with contractors for whom we were providing claim consultancy services, and architects and realtors about our development advisory services in Barbados. Gordon Glen, from RLB's UK offices, confirmed that he was available to join us effective from 1st September, which was good news. Gordon would remain with us as a key member of our Baha Mar project team through the completion of our work. On the 13th Viv joined me and we were able to escape to Cotton House in Mustique for four days, where we enjoyed our traditional walks around this very hilly island, played tennis and relaxed completely.

The hurricane renovation works to the Genesis building had been completed, and we decided to move the office back there – our original home

– from Commerce House, where we had been based since 2005. We began redecorating and planned to move back to the 4th floor early in the new year, where we remain to this day.

On 25th July Viv and I left Cayman for Seattle, and then took a float plane to Salt Spring Island in British Columbia, with our luggage safely stored in the floats. We stayed with Jerry and Joanne Sibley at their home there. During the visit, we discovered by chance that Wieland and Sue Wettstein also had a home on Salt Spring Island (you may recall that Wieland was one of the original developers of the Hyatt hotel in Grand Cayman, on which we provided services) and they kindly invited Jerry and Joanne and Viv and me to a fine barbecue dinner at their home. We returned to Seattle for a RLBC directors meeting on 30th July, and then drove from Seattle to Inchinnan, to stay with Peter and Jill McDonald, play some tennis, eat some great food and enjoy the latest Carabella wine offerings.

Back in Cayman, we completed the subconsultants agreements on Baha Mar on 8th August. A few days later the Culture Minister, Mark Scotland, visited CNCF, where we were supporting Terri Merren, who was producing a book of Miss Olive Miller's poems: *Rhyme Time with Miss Olive*. We also had a visit to the National Gallery by HE Governor Duncan Taylor.

I flew to Nassau in mid-August for meetings with the new Baha Mar general manager, Tom Dunlap, who had taken over from John Pagano. There were also conferences with our Beijing office concerning the reporting format in Mandarin for the loan drawdowns. I also introduced Gordon Glen as our onsite manager. I met him again shortly thereafter in London, when he and his wife, Jude, came to 62 QGM for dinner. We were delighted that Gordon not only clearly possessed the key skills we needed for this extremely important position with our overall team, but that we instantly meshed socially as well.

On 1st September we had lunch with John Bowers, who was chairman of the Caribbean Council and with whom we had worked throughout the Caribbean when he was with Johnston Construction. I was now able to introduce him to Bruce Dinwiddy, who had kindly agreed to serve as Patron of RLBC's Caribbean Intelligence initiative. The next day, we took niece Anne Marie and nephews Jonnie and Edward to see The Enchanted Palace exhibition at Kensington Palace, where a number of leading clothes designers had taken over a maze of rooms in the Palace's state apartments. Inspired by stories of the seven princesses who had lived there, including the much-loved Princess Diana, they had created an exhibition space where fashion comfortably held its own at a crossroads with art and theatre. This was a wonderful opportunity for me to see the opportunities for our ever-expanding programmes at CNCF, where fashion was a key part of developing our cultural awareness by means of FRESH, our own programme that featured fashion.

Our work with the Caribbean Council continued in Cayman later that month when we met to discuss the Cuba Initiative with John Bowers, David Jessop, and the UK Government's All Party Working Group. In July we had convened a meeting of the National Gallery Building Committee, as we were making good progress toward planning the start of the new Gallery building's construction. In September, I met with Jeremy Superfine, Minister Scotland, and Chief Officer Joel Francis to discuss the development budget. At the same time, the Cayman Society of Architects, Surveyors and Engineers held its Governor's Award for Design event at Harbour Place, on 17th September. The award was given to acknowledge the talents of both architects and contractors, and encourage them to develop the best structures in the Cayman Islands. On Saturday the 18th, a CNCF sponsored play, *De Honeymoon Over* by Donna Tull-Cox, was shown at the Harquail Theatre. The play was interesting for many reasons, one of which was that almost all the actors had worked at CNCF.

Viv and I arrived in Athens on 1st October to join our OPM 12 group for our reunion. A visit to the Acropolis and a welcome dinner at the King George Hotel began the fun, where it was great to catch up on everyone's news. George Klopfer had chartered a magnificent sailing ship, *Star Clipper*, to tour the Greek Islands. We left Piraeus the next day, sailing to Delos, Mykonos, Turkey, Patmos, Rhodes, Santorini, Hydra and back to Athens on 9th October. From there, we flew to Cairo, visited the Valley of Kings and the pyramids, and then boarded a river boat for four-day trip along the Nile to Aswan. We experienced a most amusing and innovative commercial sales technique on board: vendors in passing dhows would throw djellabas up to the deck of our boat for us to try on and if we liked them we could throw cash in payment back to the waiting dhow.

On 27th October Viv and I began planning the party to celebrate our 15th wedding anniversary and my upcoming 65th birthday. We met with Greg from Hopscotch, who was doing the lighting and sound; Patrick Broderick, who was taking the photographs, and Henry who was directing the entertainment. This included a performance by the Cayman Islands Folk Singers, a Quadrille display by a young school group, and Sollie, whose band was to provide musical fun. Mise en Place would be supplying the bar and food, Joanne Brown and the team from Celebrations would be co-ordinating the events, all supported by Wayne and Ingrid, our wonderful staff at Callaloo. CNCF were particularly proud – and rightly so – of having ensured the dance steps of the Cayman Quadrille had been preserved, as until recently only a few seniors remembered them, and Viv and I were delighted to be able to provide this entertainment for our guests at Callaloo.

After yet another trip to Nassau for Baha Mar meetings, I returned on the 17th in time for the opening of the Guy Harvey art show in the evening and a Davin Ebanks exhibition some days later at the National Gallery, once again sponsored by Coutts. On 25th November we held a fundraiser for SMLH at Camana Bay with kitchen band Swanky, the Cayman Islands Folk Singers, and the George Town Primary Quadrille Dancers, where I welcomed the guests with the following:

> I am delighted to welcome you this evening to enjoy CNCF's presentation of the Cayman Islands Folk Singers together with the George Town Primary Quadrille Dancers and, of course, our very own kitchen band Swanky.
>
> For the past twenty-six years CNCF, with the efforts of our hardworking and dedicated staff, volunteers, and the contribution of our board has carried out its mission of stimulating, facilitating and preserving artistic expression generally, particularly the preservation and exploration of Caymanian performing, visual and literary arts.
>
> The results are becoming increasingly identified as part of our rich cultural heritage – Miss Lassie's paintings, Swanky's music, Al Ebanks's sculpture, Bendel Hydes's art, Leonard Dilbert's poetry, Dance Unlimited's dance, Aunt Julia's drumming, Cardinal DaCosta's singing, Dave Martin's Rundown, Frank McField's plays, Roy Bodden's writings, Radley Gurzong's fiddle, the Quadrille performed by our youth groups – and the list can go on and on.
>
> We have dedicated this evening's entertainment to assist in raising much needed funds for the restoration of Miss Lassie's House in South Sound.
>
> As many of you know, Gladwyn Klosking Bush MBE, affectionately known to all as 'Miss Lassie' was a Caymanian treasure who as a self-taught or intuitive artist started to paint at the tender age of 62 and continued passionately with her art until shortly before her death in 2003 at the age of 89.
>
> Through the generosity of our government and the unselfish work of numerous volunteers, the CNCF has acquired Miss Lassie's property, renovated the duplex into an educational centre for the temporary use by the National Gallery for its numerous outreach programmes, and is now working on the restoration of Miss Lassie's House proper.

We have come a long way but still have a distance to travel and any donation you are able to make will assist in ensuring Mind's Eye Cultural Centre (Miss Lassie favourite saying was 'I see it in my mind's eye' – and hence the name) continues as a centre that truly represents our Caymanian Heritage and Culture.

So now please enjoy our true Caymanian Culture through the Quadrille dancers, Swanky, and our Folk Singers.

I had been contacted by a cladding manufacturer and installer from Trinidad, who had a delay claim on the installation of their cladding on two twenty-five-storey towers which formed part of the Government Campus Plaza in Port of Spain, Trinidad. I carried out a site visit and met with them on 29th November. This project would result in a US$12m delay claim, and keep Jerry, Charles Leonard and myself busy for eighteen months, analysing the reasons why the projected contract period of some twenty months was turning into an actual period of sixty months. I returned to Miami on 3rd December, where I met up with Viv to see the Merce Cunningham Dance performance at the Adrienne Arsht Centre on the 4th. Back in Cayman the next day, we enjoyed Gaston Maloney's Gimistory wrap-up party at his home.

The 9th December arrived all too quickly, but the hours of planning for our 15th wedding anniversary paid off, and we were delighted to welcome so many of our friends from over the years. Many came from overseas, including Alan and Jenny Foster, Doreen and Alan Scott, Otis and Nancy Blake, Basil and Sammy Behrman, and Peter and Jill McDonald. We celebrated my sixty-fifth birthday on the 10th with a black-tie dinner, and then on 12th we had the *Cayman Illusion* luxury boat come to the Callaloo dock to take us all for a trip out to Stingray City and on to Starfish Point, where Alan and Claudia's son, Sasha, arrived on his jet ski. Jill, who had never been on one, was kindly taken for a high speed ride as his pillion passenger. We had started the tradition of having T-shirts printed for these Sunday boat rides, with an image of Callaloo and a saying printed on them; this year's saying was 'Life is Good', which it is indeed! After the boat ride, we returned to Callaloo, played croquet on the formal lawn, and then had dinner at the Calypso Grill – quite a day and weekend! Fos and Jen gave us a particularly great present – a hammock – which hangs in the gym garden, and on which Viv and I have spent many lazy Sunday afternoons since.

After all this partying, it was time to get back to work. We commenced the initial Roads Assessment Committee hearings on one of our substantial cases, had a visit from *MACO* magazine about an article they were preparing on Callaloo, followed on 14th December by the National Gallery Christmas party – which we were able to hold at the newly renovated Miss Lassie's House this year – and the CNCF Christmas dinner at the Grand Old House on 17th December.

2011

'Thought before Thought is Awareness.' Tao Te Ching

As we had missed our traditional early December ski trip to celebrate our wedding anniversary and my birthday, Viv and I left for London on 6th January. This time we stayed for a few days, indulging in a cultural whirlwind. On the 8th we went to a Cirque du Soliel performance of *Totem*, a breakneck take on the story of evolution with giddy acrobatics, at the Royal Albert Hall. On the 10th we saw a stage production of *The Rivals* at the Haymarket and *Isabell* at the Royal Opera House. We then flew to Geneva and drove to Verbier to ski with Ray and Michèle, enjoying some great snow well interspersed with delicious meals at Chez Odette, raclette with Ray and Michèle, and a ski excursion down to the Aosta Valley for traditional lunch at the Croix Blanche and, later, a *charbonnière* supper with René and Claudine in their delightful Swiss chalet.

Returning to Cayman on the 18th, we were busy planning BCL's office move back to our original home on the 4th floor of the Genesis building. We were also much excited by the groundbreaking ceremony for the National Gallery on 25th January, with Aunt Julia playing her drum. The next day, we gave a thank you party at Callaloo for all the sponsors whose generosity had made this possible.

An RLB Americas meeting in Phoenix followed on the 27th, and an RLBC board meeting in Miami on 3rd February, followed by a directors' dinner at Por Fin that evening. Viv and I left on another ski trip a week later. Initially we skied at Keystone, staying at the very traditional and cosy Ski Tip Lodge, and then went on to Aspen, chalking up a total of seventy-nine runs. In Aspen we stayed with Jimmy and Cynthia, whose hospitality knew no bounds. As a small token of appreciation for their generosity we always sent them a case of Carabella in advance of our arrival, and this time we had had Mark Green make up a certificate for them, reading 'Jimmy Nowery – the Carbondale Carabella Connoisseur', which we framed and presented to him. It now has pride of place in Jimmy's wine cellar. We left Eagle Vail on 20th February for Miami, and Viv returned to Cayman from there while I flew to Nassau for the groundbreaking ceremony for Baha Mar, which, as you might imagine, was a very grand affair indeed.

On 25th March, CASE held its AGM, and I made a presentation to the assembled building professionals entitled 'Project Procurement in the Caribbean – The Pros and Cons', relying heavily on the claims resolution work Jerry and I had performed throughout the Caribbean since 1992. I was back in Nassau for Baha Mar meetings at the beginning of April, and flew to Miami on the 5th, where I was joined by Viv for our annual physical at Cleveland Clinic. Whilst waiting for various appointments and test results, I was able to write my next article for the *Caribbean Construction* magazine and read the Uff Report and Conclusions to prepare for the upcoming ISTT seminar in Trinidad. On 8th April, we enjoyed the music of the Cleveland Orchestra, who were performing at the Adrienne Arsht Centre as part of their annual visit, which Viv and I always try to attend. On the strength of my chairmanship of CNCF, we were privileged to receive an invitation to meet the performers and conductor at a post-performance party, which gave me an opportunity to exchange ideas about the importance of music in a nation's cultural development.

Later that month, we received the excellent news that the Building Control Unit had granted a Red Card permit for the renovation works we had been carrying out on Miss Lassie's House. We had an official opening to celebrate, and a plaque ceremony on 29th April during which we were entertained by The Cayman Islands Folk Singers and Swanky Kitchen band.

Patricia Bradley, who from the very inception of the National Trust had been a most active proponent of all its aims, joined Viv and me for dinner on 7th May, during which we discussed the proposed overlay zones of the Wetlands Committee's Report, for which I had sat as a board member.

I flew to Montego Bay thereafter to attend a Caribbean Hotel Conference where we were fortunate to meet Dr Adam Wu, who spoke on Chinese interests in the Caribbean. We eventually established a close working relationship with Dr Wu, and he introduced us to many contractors and investors in the Caribbean region. The next day, we took advantage of having the directors of RLBC in one place to hold a board meeting and review the progress we were making in the region.

In Trinidad, Jerry and I presented our seminar 'Uff Has Spoken – Practical Steps to Achieve Value for Money' to a packed ISTT audience on the 17th. We subsequently met with RLBC's attorney in Barbados about corporate issues and, that evening, hosted the RLBC's Barbados team at dinner at Pices restaurant. In London, a RLBC shareholders meeting on 8th June was followed by drinks at 62 Queen's Gate Mews and a client dinner at the Chef's Office private dining room at Launceston Place, where I had arranged for Carabella wine to be served with dinner after organising appropriate corkage with Tara the sommelier. One interesting feature of the Chef's Office, was a TV screen live-streaming what was going on in the kitchen. On one occasion, we witnessed the head chef chasing one of the sous chefs around the kitchen with a knife. A waiter rapidly entered the Chef's Office and closed the curtain across the screen, murmuring something about a small altercation!

On 29th May, we had ordered Carabella wine for the UK celebration of our 15th wedding anniversary and Viv's 65th birthday at Ettington Park, in Stratford-upon-Avon on 11th June. It was a grand affair, and Viv had been tenacious about rounding up many family members we had not seen in years. Before leaving for Ettington Park, I and my brother Rob, who was Master of The Worshipful Company of Chartered Surveyors, had been fitted at Moss Bros with white tie and tails – a first for me, and the required attire for a dinner at Mansion House. There are one hundred and thirteen Livery companies in the City of London, and some of these ancient and modern guilds and trade associations date back to 1135. After driving back to London on the 12th we enjoyed a very fancy and formal evening at Mansion House as guests at Rob's family and friends' dinner, with the Lord & Lady Mayoress, Sir Michael and Barbara Bear, and the guest speaker Sir Philip Hampton, who was a fellow Old Veseyan, and who was, at the time, chairman of NatWest bank.

A few days later we flew to Nice for a week of hiking in Provence. While on the plane I realised, with a sinking feeling, that I had left my gold cufflinks, a treasured wedding gift from Viv, in the hired shirt from Moss Bros. I phoned them immediately upon landing, fearing the shirt may have been sent to the laundry with the cufflinks still in the cuffs. Not to fear, a charming lady called Christina, told me; Moss Bros had them stored safely and we could collect them on our return to the UK.

Panic over, we revelled in the solitude and beauty of Provence. We stayed at La Bouscatière and enjoyed many hikes, including to La Font D'Eilenc from the pretty village of Aiguines, located in the Verdon Regional Nature Park, followed by a pedalo ride on the Lake Sainte-Croix, complete with Bandol wine and sandwiches courtesy of Joel and Genevieve. A second hike, from Aiguines to the Ravine de Saint-Pierre and Col d'Illoire, offered magnificent panoramic views of Lake of Sainte-Croix and the Verdon Gorges and took us up to the lookout point of Saint-Pierre Chapel, now seen from a completely different vantage point. And, finally, we hiked the Lower Verdon Gorge. It was hard to tear ourselves away, but duty called, and we flew to London for a couple of days, and then back to Cayman on 22nd June.

Magic awaited us, as CNCF had invited the Trinidadian Carnival artist, Peter Minshall 'Man of Mas', to the Harquail Theatre. Peter was born in Guyana and moved to Trinidad as a small child, and had therefore been exposed to Carnival there from a very young age. He attended Queen's Royal College in Port of Spain, and then went on to study theatre design at the Central School of Art and Design in London. His journey to fame is said to have begun when his mother asked him to create a Carnival costume for his sister to wear at the 1974 Carnival. He called the costume 'From the Land of the Hummingbird', and claimed it took five weeks, twelve people, and one hundred and four feathers – each one made from one hundred and fifty different pieces of fabric – to assemble. From this debut, Peter went on to design full-size Carnival band costumes with themes that included Paradise Lost, and, close to Viv's and my heart (for obvious reasons), 'Callaloo' for a band at the 1984 Carnival. His talents were appreciated far beyond Trinidad, and his accomplishments included designing opening ceremonies for the Olympic Games, football and cricket World Cups, for which he received a well-deserved plethora of awards. And, once again, through Henry's contacts and friends in the Cayman Islands, we were able to learn about this great man's journey, his thoughts on the multitude of epic spectacles he created, and his view that Masquerade or 'Mas' is the 'living art that we make fresh every year'. And, again, as I often do, I wondered how I, as a mere quantity surveyor, became so lucky as to have my life enriched by the numerous people I have met and enjoyed conversing with for so many years.

At this time we were promoting BCL's valuation services and arranged meetings with the lending officers of several local banks, including FCIB, Credit Union, HSBC, Bank of Butterfield, where we staged Power Point presentations about the key issues of our work and the common misunderstandings about market and insurance valuations. These presentations were very well received, and the extensive question and answer sessions afterwards provided insight into what we were doing right, and how we could continue to improve our service offerings.

In April I had two days of Baha Mar meetings in Nassau, and 4th–6th May I had met with David Wang of China Construction Americas, to discuss progress on the Bahar Mar project. On 12th July I was off to Nassau again for meetings, this time with Tiger Wu of China Construction Americas at Baha Mar, and via conference calls with China Exim in Beijing.

On 3rd August Viv and I flew to Portland to attend RLB USA meetings for several days. As a result, sadly, we missed CNCF's presentation of the Young Image Makers films, shown at Camana Bay on 5th August. This is a most innovative and rewarding programme which came about because, with the advent of portable phones with built-in cameras and video capabilities, it had become possible for anyone to create a film using an everyday device, as opposed to expensive cameras and equipment. In fact, this new, completely democratic art form provides an opportunity for all people to express themselves, regardless of age or income.

Following the Portland meetings, we went to stay with the ever-accommodating Peter and Jill McDonald at Inchinnan, and from there drove to see Mount St Helens. We visited the observation centre, learned about the massive 1980s eruption, and looked at the various lava trails there. We followed this with a meeting with the Carabella accountants to review the financial operations of the vineyard that had provided so much fun and pleasure, and, by virtue of being an owner, the ability to enjoy the literal 'fruits of our labour' by serving Carabella wine at our many celebrations. We were back in Cayman on 14th August, from where I once again flew to Nassau, this time for a Baha Mar site visit to review progress. This was key given the magnitude of the project. With some five thousand men on site, deviation from the projected schedule could have disastrous effects on its ultimate cost and delay the ability to commence repayment of China Exim's huge loan.

In early September, Viv and I were in Santiago skiing for ten days. During our Caribbean journeys, Jerry had described his many visits to Portillo and the single hotel there, which he said had a very European atmosphere. We were not disappointed, and we met the USA ski team who train there, including Lindsay Vonn with whom Viv established a great relationship. During our visit we chalked up some 94,000 vertical feet in one hundred runs, and even tried out snow-shoeing for the first time. One unusual experience was being shaken in the middle of the night by an earthquake!

Back in Miami, I left on 19th September for an RLBC board meeting in Barbados, relying on my wonderful wife to lug the ski gear back to Cayman. I returned on 22nd September, in time for the Governor's Award for Architecture the same evening, followed by a cocktail party at Camana Bay to meet the new owners of the Caledonian Bank. Caledonian Bank had been set up by Bill Walker, and so we were seeing a changing of the guard in this long established institution.

Viv and I set off on another Around the World trip on 29th September. Our first flight was via Miami to Los Angeles, where we had dinner with Basil and Sammy. We then flew on to Melbourne, arriving in time to attend an IFACCA leadership conference on 2nd October, which was attended by some five hundred and twenty cultural attendees from seventy countries. I managed to fit in a lunch with RLB's local director, Michael Kerr, during which we had a good laugh about the bottle of Carabella I had sent him, which took so long to arrive and on which he had paid such a large sum in duty. As recompense, I covered the lunch tab!

On 7th October, we left Melbourne and flew to Singapore, where we enjoyed an excellent lunch with the local RLB director, Winston Hauw. One side benefit of being part of a global company was eating in wonderful restaurants, with or on the advice of people with local knowledge! On the 8th we flew from Singapore to Bali and stayed in Ubud, where, during a yoga session, we experienced another earthquake, during which the ground literally rolled beneath our feet. Less dramatic, but safer and more enjoyable, was a great cooking course, during which we prepared fish cooked in banana leaves. It's a recipe we have duplicated many times for lunch at Callaloo. From Bali we flew to Mumbai on 15th October and were met at the airport by the Cox and Kings representative, using one of their wonderful classic Ambassador cars, complete with starched headrest covers, to take us to check in at the Leela Kempinski Hotel. The next morning, after a sound sleep and hearty breakfast, we were walking through the gardens when we came upon a parked Rolls Royce with a gentleman sitting in the back and a chauffeur at the wheel. The gentleman greeted us and asked about our experience staying at the hotel. We said it had been excellent, which pleased him, and he explained he was the owner of the hotel and that he liked to carry out personal quality checks by asking guests about their stay.

From Mumbai we flew to Cochin, in Kerala, in southern India. We were staying in the Brunton Boatyard, in an ideal location on this fascinating city's harbour, which had once been the principal harbour of the Malabar Coast's spice trade. The rulers of Kochi (Cochin) had invited people of various religions to settle, attracting both Jews and Christians, who built places of worship and created their own communities. Today, there still remain traces of the influence of Portuguese, Dutch and British settlers, and even the Chinese, in the form of the famous fishing nets – huge contraptions that are still used to lift fish from the bay. After dinner we went to see a Kathakali dance performance. These highly ritualised performances, which still play an important role Kerala's cultural life, are based on three major Hindu epics, acted out with elaborate and precise hand gestures, facial expressions and choreographed movements.

The next day we drove to Alleppey for a cruise on a traditional rice barge through the canals and backwaters and saw a side of Keralan rural life that has remained unchanged for centuries. The next day, we drove from Alleppey to

Kumarakom to check into the Kumarakom Lake Resort, a tranquil hotel set on Lake Vembanad, where our accommodation was a relocated and restored illam (a typical Keralan homestead).

The next day we took a cruise on the lake and then enjoyed a delicious lunch at Philip Kutty's Homestay, where our hostess provided a most informative tour of their vegetable and herb garden. On 19th October we drove back to Cochin and visited the Paradesi synagogue, which was built in 1568 and has been recognised by World Monuments Watch of the World Monuments Fund – as has Miss Lassie's House. We then visited the St Francis church at Fort Kochi, the first European church in India, built in 1503 by the Portuguese.

We then flew to the garden city of Bangalore, staying in the Taj West End. The next day we drove to the island fortress of Srirangapatnam, the former capital of two of south India's most powerful rulers, Hyder Ali and his son Tipu Sultan 'The Lion of Mysore', which had been stormed twice by the British – once in 1782 and again in 1799.

We then drove to Mysore, known as 'The Jewel of Karnataka' because of the palaces and royal gardens of the Wodeyar Rajas, who were connoisseurs of art and architecture and who enjoyed a very lavish lifestyle. We visited the Maharajah's Palace, completed in 1912, which is a synthesis of Hindu and Saracenic architecture, with domes and turrets that give it a fairytale appearance. It was designed, interestingly enough, by Henry Irwin, a British architect.

From there we went on to the Nagarhole National Park on the Kabini River, where we were staying at Orange County Kabini, an environmentally sensitive resort of some thirty thatched cottages based on the design and construction of the dwellings of the Kuruba tribe. There, we enjoyed morning and afternoon game drives in the park, and on 22nd October took an early morning boat ride through the serene backwaters of the Kabini river looking for unique water birds and other wildlife.

After our river cruise we checked out and drove to Bylakuppe, the largest Tibetan settlement in south India and the second largest outside of Tibet. It is home to some six thousand monks and nuns, and during our visit we witnessed a prayer session of some four hundred monks chanting in unison. From there we drove to Orange County, Coorg, a beautiful hill country which retains much of its old-world charm. The Kodavas (Coorgs) are said to be descendants of Alexander the Great's Greek army and are both fiercely independent and were never conquered. They are ancestor worshippers, with each family maintaining an ancestral house called a 'Ainmane', and wear distinctive traditional dress for special occasions. Our resort was set within three hundred acres of coffee and spice plantation, and provided wonderful thatched cottage accommodation. We took early morning bird-watching walks with a Dr Selymaly, and over the course of our stay we saw some twenty-six different species. Dr Selymaly could imitate bird calls in an amazingly realistic manner, receiving answers from the birds on some occasions. We told him about our friendship with Patricia Bradley in Cayman and the books she has written on bird species in the islands. We later sent him some copies, for which he was most appreciative.

On 24th October we visited the Dubare Elephant Camp, where we enjoyed an elephant ride accompanied by a mahout. We left the Orange County Resort on the 25th and drove to Bangalore via Channapatna village, famous for its lacquered wooden toys. In Bangalore, we caught our flight to Mumbai, where we once again stayed at the Leela Kempinski before catching our flight back to London the next morning. There, we renewed our passports (and I was finally able to say goodbye to Mr Birungi's visa). We were back in Cayman on 1st November, in time for FRESH on 5th November. This fashion symposium highlights the true meaning of culture in our country. I have always espoused the idea that 'culture' encompasses the way we live, eat, talk, worship, dress, and interact with each other. Our recent experiences in southern India had embodied that country's rich and diverse culture. When I see the way our clothes designers have succeeded on the world stage, I appreciate how the early recognition of the nascent Caymanian talent for design was so encouraged by CNCF's early efforts.

Of particular note in November, was that I registered for a week-long mediation course run by Jonathan Dingle of the London School of Mediation. Given the work that CCAS had done since the early 1990s in resolving disputes by negotiation, it was interesting to be undertaking a course somewhat 'formalising' our work. Nevertheless, it was very rewarding, and J.D. became a close confidant and friend with whom we have solved numerous issues using mediation. As I write this, the Bould Foundation is funding free places for young Caymanians on a weeklong mediation course in Cayman, in the hope of boosting their competence in this essential life skill.

I flew to Nassau on 10th November to give a talk at the CHICOS conference on working with the Chinese as a Project Monitor for their funding and construction methodologies. The conference also allowed time for meetings with Andrew Miele of Four Seasons, and Patrick Freeman of Tropicalia. Following the conference I was able to meet with the Baha Mar team, continuing our review of progress. We were becoming increasingly concerned about this, and reported so to China Exim. On the 15th, I flew to Freeport to meet with Graham Torode of Hutchinson Whampoa, the owners of the Grand Bahama

Port Authority, to discuss a potential new airport terminal. The next day I flew back to Nassau for budget meetings on Baha Mar and then back to Cayman the same evening.

Back in Cayman, on 18th November, I had meetings with developer John Hare, who had sought our advice about contract terms for a development in Grenada that was potentially going to be funded and built by the Chinese. The same day, I met with National Gallery board chairman, Henry Harford, to discuss the new building budget and also met with Desmond Kinch, the fundraising lead, to discuss progress toward closing the gap between available funds and the cost of the new Gallery building, which was now under construction. The National Gallery had held a fundraising ball in March, and on 24th November we held a National Gallery Art Auction as part of our continuing efforts to raise funds. But in November we had received a report on the construction budget for the building, which was some CI$175,000 over budget – so either some value engineering or additional fundraising was urgently required!

On 2nd December we celebrated an early BCL staff Christmas lunch at Grand Old House. I needed to visit Barbados on the 4th for RLB directors meetings, and then Grenada to look at the hotel site for John Hare. I was back to Cayman on 8th December, turning round on the 9th to fly to Salt Lake City via Dallas for our annual dose of Utah powder.

During our time there we had a sobering call from Ingrid and Wayne, who had noticed water pouring out from under Callaloo's front door while they happened to be walking past. On entering the house, they found that the newly installed instantaneous gas water heater had burst its pipes and flooded the ground floor of the house. All our Persian rugs were soaked and needed to be replaced. This led to some interesting exchanges. We dealt with Mr Amini in Miami but, due to the embargo on Iranian goods coming into the United States, the rugs had to be shipped via Germany once they had been sourced. The rugs are unusual as they are square, and we realised how small the market is for rugs in this configuration when we went into an oriental rug store in Piccadilly, asking if they had any square carpets of a certain size, and the sales associate said, 'You must be the Boulds from Cayman. Mr Amini has been trying to source these rugs.' Right afterwards, we learned Margaret Dise had suddenly passed away, and we sadly returned early to Cayman to celebrate her life and to support Mikol for her funeral.

We brought 2011 to a close with a Christmas lunch with friends, a visit the National Gallery site from Governor Duncan Taylor, and our 'Do Drop In Party' at Callaloo on 31st December.

2012

'We make a living by what we get, but we make a life by what we give.'
Winston Churchill

January began with discussions with Shao Di, from China Exim (with whom I enjoyed an excellent relationship on the Baha Mar project) about the funding and construction of John Hare's Four Season's Hotel in Grenada, with Jerry reviewing the Chinese construction contract. Jerry and I were also continuing to work on the construction dispute relating to the Toco Bridges contract in Trinidad, and Viv and I were negotiating the insurance claim for the loss of our carpets and damage to the finishes of the house resulting from the flood at Callaloo. Alan Veeran was expertly managing the repairs, and it was he who came up with the brilliant idea of substituting the 12 inch-high softwood base boards, which had warped after being soaked in the flooded water, with a PVC material capped with the detailed top wooden moulding which, to this day, still looks brand new and with no warping at all.

It was about this time, perhaps spurred by the passing of so many friends, that Viv and I decided to draft our wills. As part of this exercise with the attorneys, the somewhat morbid subject of whether we wanted to be buried or cremated came up. I preferred the former and Viv the latter, Viv's intention being that if she died first, her ashes would be buried with me in my coffin, and if I died first, her ashes would be scattered over my grave. We had not discussed this somewhat sombre matter before but, in the context of cremation, I pointed out to her that unlike the UK, where cremations take place immediately and the ashes are handed to you after the service, when my good friend Bill was cremated in Miami, all cremations were held on one day of the week and the ashes are given to the families some days later. On reflection, Viv then said she had changed her mind and wanted to be buried like me. This time her rationale was that if there was a chance her ashes might be mixed up with someone else's, another woman's ashes might be in my coffin for the rest of time. This was an intolerable thought! So, then came the task of purchasing two suitable grave plots. We contacted Crighton's, who own the Garden of Reflection in Prospect, and we went there to locate two suitable plots, not wanting them to be too close to where the cars drove into the Garden due to exhaust fumes, which would disturb us. We received the two purchase contracts from Crighton's, and were about to sign them, when Viv noticed my gravesite was on the right-hand side. This would not work. said she. 'Why not?' I asked, to which Viv replied 'You always sleep on the left-hand side!', and so the contracts were revised accordingly. As part of our estate planning, Viv and I also discussed the formation of a foundation to be the recipient of our assets, and we instructed a Memorandum and Articles to be drawn up for this company, which is known as the Bould Foundation.

In mid-January we flew to London for a series of business meetings. These included one with Adam Wu, concerning Chinese funding of various Caribbean projects, and with several developers. I met with one of these at the splendid Royal Thames Yacht Club in Knightsbridge, with drinks at 62 QGM, followed by a RLBC dinner in the Chef's Office at Launceston Place. We enjoyed an excellent dinner with Jonathan Dingle at Middle Temple, followed on the 20th by my final mediation exam at the London School of Mediation at the Strand. I completed it successfully, and was awarded my certificate as an Accredited Mediator. On 21st January Viv and I tried 'Boris Bikes' for the first time. They had been introduced by Boris Johnson, the Mayor of London, and were all the rage. They were also great fun, but we were severely reprimanded in Hyde Park when we ventured off the designated riding paths. We returned to Cayman on 23rd January, in time to celebrate Aunt Julia's one hundred and third birthday at the Harquail. Aunt Julia and her drumming had been recognised by CNCF as a cultural treasure representing the strong matriarchal values of the Cayman Islands in a typically male-dominated musical world.

We flew to Eagle Vail to ski Aspen from 28th January to 6th February. We skied at Highlands, Snowmass, Aspen and Vail, and had a particularly enjoyable après ski meeting at the bar in the Ritz Carlton at Aspen Highlands with Matt Norton and his team from K&L Gates law firm. We usually met them at the CHICOS conferences, so this was a welcome change of venue in which to exchange ideas about hotel development, current issues and deals.

In Cayman, our good friend Crystal held an art exhibition at the Ritz Carlton at Grand Cayman, using the bridge over West Bay Road to maximum benefit as the exhibition space. Crystal had developed a signature style of painting, which focused on young people on the beach and highlighted the beauty of the sea and its movement. The following evening, CNCF held its annual Arts Awards. Each year the level of excellence in our cultural sector grew, but this year we were particularly proud of the recognition of Miss Lassie's House, and I commented in my Chairman's speech as follows:

> There is always a profound joy in recognising and celebrating achievement in any field, but particularly that of the Arts and Culture, as it lies at the true heart of who we really are as a people.

Tonight, as always, I am humbled by the expansive range of talent we identify and nurture in our comparatively small community.

CNCF's work covers a broad spectrum of activities of which we at CNCF are very proud and our Arts Awards recognise the efforts of a large number of people and organisations, without which our work would not be possible, both in front of our audiences and behind the scenes.

For the course of the last year, I would like to thank our hard working CNCF Board, our dedicated staff, volunteers and performers who together have made huge strides in continuing our mission.

As part of that mission CNCF recognised and has promoted for many years the talent of Caymanian cultural icon, Gladwyn K. Bush ('Miss Lassie'), representing as it does all that is good in the Cayman Islands. Of particular note, therefore, late in 2011 CNCF were delighted to receive the news that following on from the acquisition of Miss Lassie's House and property we have now secured international recognition and attention by having the property designated as a 2012 World Monuments Watch of the World Monument Fund. This in turn has led to a promise of additional financial support for this now internationally recognised heritage site, which will result in its enjoyment for locals and visitors alike.

Much, of course, remains to be done, but we are now well on the road to achieving this dream.

I flew to Kingston at the invitation of the Honourable Portia Simpson Miller, Prime Minister of Jamaica, to attend the Jamaica Investment Forum, held in Montego Bay on the 1st and 2nd March. I was there to highlight the consulting services we offered to a focussed group of leading business people. The forum assembled leaders of government, construction and development, tourism, banking and manufacturing industries for in-person discussion and networking and to review the many opportunities available in Jamaica for businesspersons and their advisers.

The event was divided into plenary and sectoral sessions, opening with 'Invest in Jamaica – Invest in a Global Brand', which examined why many of the world's leading investors and corporations have chosen to invest in the largest English-speaking island in the Caribbean, which also has the best infrastructure for foreign direct investment in the region. The Prime Minister led the opening session, which also included the Honourable Anthony Hylton,

Minister of Industry Investment and Commerce, and Mr Stephen Puig, the Vice President for the Private Sector at the Inter-American Investment Bank. A televised message from Hilary Clinton, Secretary of State of the United States, was delivered by Mr Kris Balderston, Special Representative for Global Partnerships at the US Department of State.

Arriving early, I was able to catch up with Alan and Jenny Foster over lunch and also fitted in a meeting in Kingston with China Harbour to discuss various potential projects they were considering, to be built using funding from China Exim. After the forum, Viv joined me and we drove to Port Antonio and stayed at Geejam, a wonderful recording studio with treetop accommodation, for a super relaxing few days in this beautiful part of Jamaica.

In March, we dealt with moisture testing at Callaloo following the renovations undertaken after the December flooding, and shortly thereafter I left for London to attend business meetings, including conference calls with Nassau and Beijing concerning delays in the construction schedule of Baha Mar. These calls essentially meant we were working round the clock as due to the twelve-hour time difference between the Caribbean and China, China was starting work as we were going to bed and, by the time we started work, China had already answered any questions we had raised.

On 21st March, Viv and I were in Manchester, UK, where I was to take part in a mediation demonstration at Manchester University led by Jonathan Dingle and the team from the London School of Mediation, of which I was now a fully-fledged member. I returned to London the next day, where RLBC hosted a Caribbean Intelligence lunch at Durrants Hotel. After a quick skiing trip to Verbier, I returned from Geneva to Heathrow on the morning of 2nd April, only to leave Heathrow again in the afternoon to fly to Beijing, where I arrived at 9.30 in the morning on the 3rd. In Beijing I met with Adam Wu, CEO of China Business Network, whom we had met at the May hotel conference in Jamaica, and then manned the RLBC booth at the Beijing Overseas Property & Investment Show, followed by an excellent dinner with the team from RLB's Beijing office. Over the next few days we had many meetings with China Harbour, other investors and contractors, and various Caribbean embassies who were interested in Chinese funding.

Key for these meetings, was to have our capability statements and business cards readily available, both in English and Chinese. It was an extremely busy week, during which carefully planning the location of meetings in the city and having a driver on hand were absolutely essential. I have a wonderful photograph of Adam organising meetings with three cell phones in hand, all being used at the same time! On Sunday the 8th I was, however, able to make time to visit the incredibly diverse 798 Cultural & Arts District created in a 1950s industrial factory area which was now a thriving artist's haven.

Back in London on 12th April, at 218 Strand, I attended a meeting to discuss and agree the Draft Constitution of the Property Mediation Council, a charitable body dedicated to advancing education, citizenship, community development, human rights, and diversity through the promotion and use of mediation in the UK and elsewhere.

After only being in Cayman for a day, I was asked to go to Nassau on 15th April to meet with the developers and China Exim and China State representatives, to review the budget and schedule for Baha Mar, exploring ways in which we could recover the lost time in the schedule. In Puerto Rico on 24th April, I made a presentation on Chinese Investment in the Caribbean at the 16th Annual Caribbean Hotel and Tourism Investment Conference, drawing for material on the meetings I had recently held in Beijing. The major challenge from the Caribbean point of view, was the use of Chinese contractors and labour at the expense of local Caribbean labour.

Back in Cayman on 26th April, I was able to attend CNCF's Young Film Makers Awards – an incentive to encourage and showcase film-making talent spurred on by the ease of capturing images using cellphones. This was followed by performance of Rundown on the 5th. Only two days later, I was back in Miami for the Caribbean Hotel & Resort Investment Summit at the J.W. Marriott Hotel, in downtown Miami, put on by the Burba Hotel Network. Jim Burba had initially arranged the Caribbean Hotel and Tourism Investment Conference, and had then gone on to present his own conference, which together with CHICOS, now meant we had three major hotel investment conferences every year.

Viv then joined me in Miami and we flew to Panama City, Florida to enjoy a long weekend with George and Boopie McInnis at their beautiful home on the bay. Back in Miami on 13th May, I had telephone discussions with Gordon Glen, who was on the Baha Mar site and in deep conversations with China State about how they were going to pull back the delay in progress on the site. Gordon sadly told me that there had been a fatality on site – one of the Chinese workers had fallen off the building – and this was now viewed as 'bad joss' on the project.

Viv and I then drove up to Sebring, to celebrate her sister Pat's birthday. While driving, I received a telephone call from Cayman Governor Duncan Taylor, who relayed the startling but amazing news that I had been nominated for an MBE (Member of the Most Excellent Order of the British Empire), for services to cultural preservation and development in the Cayman Islands. He was calling me in advance of the official gazettal to ask whether I would accept the honour, given that in the past some individuals had turned it down. I was momentarily stunned by the question but replied that I would be delighted to accept. Governor Taylor said the award would be announced on 16th June, the Queen's birthday, during an official ceremony on the streets of George Town to which Vivian and I were invited.

As if the pending award of an MBE was not enough, on 6th June, at a meeting of the Cayman Society of Architects Surveyors and Engineers (CASE), I was elected to the College of Fellows for the contributions I had made to the professions and the construction industry in general in the Cayman Islands. I was both humbled and delighted.

Saturday 16th June, Viv and I rose early. I dressed in suit and tie and Viv in a very smart dress, and we left in good time to be downtown by 8.30am for the Queen's birthday parade, where the Governor proclaimed the award of my MBE. Then we left at noon for Boston to stay with Igor and Irina for a week, so he could reassess both our training programmes and make any necessary adjustments to pass on to Dottie. Our friend, John Davies, was also being trained by Dottie. He had asked her to expand her repertoire by taking instruction to become a Thai massage specialist, and so we were fortunate to be able to benefit from this additional skill she now possessed. Frequently, on Sunday afternoons, Viv and I would enjoy the luxury of a most relaxing massage. After the week with Igor we made our usual journey to the Ritz Carlton, to slightly undo some of the good we had achieved.

I flew to Newark from Miami on the 24th to meet with China State / China Construction Americas, to discuss what had now been forecast as a four-month delay on Baha Mar. Charles Leonard, our scheduling expert, flew to Nassau, to physically inspect the work on site and to ascertain if he agreed with the projected delay.

Like most problems that arise this one began simply – but the dynamic was unusual. In a typical development format, the developer and lender metaphorically sit on one side of the table, with the contractor on the other. The developer and lender usually share a long-term interest in the project's success, whereas the contractor's focus is short-term: to maximise profit during construction. In this case, however, the roles were reversed. The contractor and lender aligned on one side, with the developer on the other. The contract spanned some fifty-four months. Each month, we issued progress reports confirming that delays were occurring and warning that the project was unlikely to finish on time, and that such delays could incur significant expense. China Exim, the lender, would then ask the contractor if there was indeed any delay. The contractor would deny this and suggest that I, as Project Monitor, simply didn't understand the Chinese. I would reply that while I might not fully understand Chinese culture, I did know what it took to complete a resort on time in the Caribbean – having completed many – and this one was going to be late.

Following the meetings with China State's senior team, I flew back to Cayman on 25th June. Gordon Glen and his wife Jude came to Cayman on 13th July to stay with us and discuss the way forward in a relaxed setting. We put on a cocktail party at Callaloo, and Alan and Claudia cooked a superb curry for a party at their home on the 16th to appropriately welcome the Glens.

At the end of July, I was contacted by Pieter de Bruijn of Ballast Nedam – with whom we had worked in 2008–2009 on the St Maarten Port expansion project – who asked if I could visit Suriname in August to look at an oil refinery project there. They were having problems with delayed information flow from the client/engineers. I confirmed that I certainly could, and he then asked if we would provide a proposal for our assistance. Once again, Charles Leonard, our scheduling guru, was brought into the frame, and we sent him the documentation for review.

I flew to Nassau for Baha Mar meetings at the beginning of August, and toured the site to review progress and to look at a new connector road to carry traffic from the airport to the site more directly than the original coast road. I stopped in Miami on my return to enjoy a performance of the New World Symphony, returning to Cayman on 6th August. A couple of days later we joined Alan and Claudia at ballroom dancing classes. They had invited Viv and me to join them in their new hobby, which we willingly did and repeated the exercise a week later. I'm not sure Viv's toes have recovered yet from having my size thirteen feet treading all over them!

On 23rd August I left Cayman for Trinidad and Paramaribo, Suriname, where I met with Oliver Cleghorn, who was to be part of our team on the oil refinery project there. We met with Ballast Nedam on Sunday 26th August to review the site and documentation. The site was challenging, as it was located in the river's flood plain, and the tankers were moored on the site's riverfront. The engineering was precise, with tight tolerances, and the piling required for the pipe racks was being carried out after the foundations had been poured. This resulted in movement of completed works, with consequent delays. I remained in Suriname until 30th August.

At the end of September we left Heathrow for Budapest, Hungary, to join thirty-two of our Harvard OPM friends at the Sofitel Budapest hotel to catch up with the news, followed by a river cruise on the Danube with Ama Waterways, on the Vessel *Amacerto*. We left Budapest on 27th September, stopping at Bratislava in Slovakia; Vienna, Austria; Linz and Passau; Regensburg in Germany,

Shockwaves and Aftershocks (2008–2012)

ending the journey at Prague and the Czech Republic on 4th October. We found this a most comfortable way to travel, because it allowed plenty of sightseeing in the different countries and cultures without requiring us to pack and unpack repeatedly. On 7th October we were met by our nephews, Jonnie and Edward, with Gill, and were taken to view the Pałac Włosień, the Heldreich family palace in Gorlitz, Poland. Then we took a tour through the Valley of the Palaces, which were outstanding and offered great food and luxury accommodation at an economical price, and returned to Prague, from where we returned to London.

I flew from London to Beijing on 14th October to meet with Adam Wu for more investor and contractor meetings, and to attend the sixth annual China – Latin America and Caribbean Business Summit in Hangzhou. The press reported as follows:

> With the growing Chinese investment in the Latin American & Caribbean areas coupled with RLBC's work on several projects in the Caribbean and South America including that of Project Monitor for the Export Import Bank of China on the Baha Mar resort in Nassau, RLBC were invited by the China Business Network to participate in the sixth annual China–Latin America & Caribbean Business Summit in Hangzhou China held on 17th & 18th October 2012. RLB Caribbean's Chairman, Martyn Bould, represented RLB at the event. The Summit hosted jointly by China Council for the Promotion of International Trade and the Inter-American Development Bank brought together Chinese businesses, lenders and Government Representatives with their counterparts from Latin American and Caribbean countries.

From Hangzhou, we travelled to Shenzhen and Shanghai, making additional potential contacts. While staying at the Swiss Hotel in Shanghai, I ordered room service, with a bottle of white wine, which was delivered while I was completing some work. When I opened the wine it was clearly corked, and so I called room service. The waiter came to the room, looked at the bottle and said now that it was open I could not return it. Accordingly, I called the food and beverage manager and asked him to come to the room with a glass, which he did. I said to him, 'If you will drink the bottle of corked wine, I will pay for it.' He took one sip, grimaced, and immediately agreed to replace it! I flew back to London on 23rd October where I met with Nick Holland to discuss potential revisions to a new CNCF law he was kindly reviewing for us,

We had been invited to provide project management services on a hospital in Trinidad that was being funded out of Austria, and responded to the RFP on 3rd November. At the same time, and in preparation for an upcoming Gimistory which we were hosting at Callaloo, we met with the organisers to discuss details of the evening.

On 6th November I was off again to Nassau for further discussions of the Baha Mar budget and schedule. Then I attended the annual CHICOS conference, which was held at Atlantis in Nassau, and presented a paper on Chinese Investment in the Caribbean, noting what funding options were available from China in the Caribbean.

On the award of my MBE, I had been asked where I would like the presentation of the medal to take place, and I requested that it be presented at Buckingham Palace. The date for the presentation was set for 16th November. Prior to the event, I was told I could have three guests attend the presentation, and was asked to send a photograph of each. I duly sent pictures of Viv, my brother Rob and Mortimer, who had offered so much invaluable advice as we built our various businesses over the years. Although I wasn't initially sure why the photographs were needed – other than security – I subsequently found out that, while photography was not permitted inside the Palace, a video was taken of each recipient and their guests as they moved through the Palace. The footage was then edited to include only the relevant scenes for each recipient and their party. Mortimer came to stay overnight with us in QGM, and both of us had hired morning suits from Moss Bros. A car picked us up, and we went first to Rob's office in Stratton Street, Mayfair, where we had a nerve-settling cup of coffee before driving to the Palace via the Mall. For security reasons, we had not been told who would be presenting the MBE beforehand, but as we drove down the Mall we were delighted to see the Royal Standard flying – a good sign it would be the Queen herself, which indeed turned out to be the case.

At the Palace gates, the guards opened the bonnet, checked the underside of the car with mirrors, and finally admitted us through to the inner courtyard. Inside, Viv, Rob and Mortimer were escorted to the Great Ballroom, while I and the other recipients were escorted to the Green Drawing Room, offered a glass of orange juice, and briefed on procedure, including how to address the Queen – 'Your Majesty' initially, then 'Ma'am' – and, most critically, how to leave – we were never to turn our backs to the Queen. After the investiture, we were to step backwards while facing her. We stood in a long line, and were instructed not to change position as the medals were laid out corresponding exactly to that sequence. Each recipient would have a one-minute conversation with the Queen, she would pin the medal on the hook pre-fitted to our lapels in the Green Room, then she would shake our hand, signalling it was time to back away and move on.

A big question at this point, was what to say. Fortunately, I had been an usher at Elmslie Memorial Church when the Queen had attended Sunday worship during a visit to Cayman. She had injured her arm falling from her horse and wore a sling – by Hermès, of course. As I approached the raised dais in the Great Ballroom, where the Queen was standing, she greeted me and thanked me for the work I had done in preserving and developing culture in Cayman, and pinned the MBE medal to my lapel. I said, 'Your Majesty, you look a lot better than the last time I saw you at Elmslie Church in Cayman and you had broken your arm and it was in a sling.' The Queen raised her arm and thumb and replied, 'No I had not; it was not broken it was simply sprained.' Viv, watching in the audience and unable to hear what was being said, and thought Her Majesty was giving a thumbs-up for my cultural efforts in Cayman. The Queen then shook my hand, and I backed away, turned to the side, and walked out of the side of the ballroom.

We then had photographs taken in the inner courtyard of the Palace and repaired to the Goring Hotel for a magnificent celebratory lunch, where I was congratulated by all the staff. The following day we went for a celebratory lunch at The Waterside Inn in Bray, and on Sunday 18th November had a lunch for some fifty family and friends at Great Fosters, with many heart-warming speeches from those assembled there. We realised that Alan Scott, our ex-Governor, my brother Rob, my friend Nick Ross, our nephew Richard Heldreich and myself, had all attended Bishop Vesey Grammar School and all were in attendance!

On 20th November, we had the pleasure of attending an art exhibition of work by Carole Owen in London and seeing many of our Caymanian friends there, as well as catching up with John and Carole, who had been so instrumental in getting the National Gallery of the Cayman Islands started. On the 21st it was back to work, when I attended a meeting of the Caribbean Council at the Caledonian Club in Belgravia.

On 28th November, we presented a film on the progress we were making with the renovation of Miss Lassie's House, and on the 30th, we held the Factory Ball to raise funds for the National Gallery, and attended a show of work by Charles Long the next day – we have several of his pieces in Callaloo.

During this time I made a presentation to CASE on the challenges of the Baha Mar project, and we were also very busy working on a 9,500-acre planned resort community in Belize, called Balam Escape, which I had visited and for which we had completed the costing for the significant initial works.

On Sunday 2nd December we held Gimistory at Callaloo, under the stars, to a packed audience, followed early the next morning by a workout with

Dottie and Igor, who was visiting Cayman for his annual stay. Two days later, Viv and I flew to Salt Lake City and on to Alta to ski for eight days, returning to Cayman on 13th December. While in Alta, we received an invitation to join George Klopfer and his wife on board *The World*, a floating condominium apartment ship which travelled the world, and on which George owned an apartment. I knew of this ship as I had seen a model of it in one of the London agencies offices when apartments on it were being sold. Ironically, we were in Utah, where George owned a house in Park City, and he was in Cayman, on board the ship, so for now we had to pass.

To top off a very busy and eventful year, we had a long and relaxing Christmas lunch and Boxing Day celebrations, and our 'Do Drop In' New Year's Eve celebration at Callaloo.

CHAPTER TEN

Baha Mar and the Impossible Question (2013–2017)

2013

'Gratitude makes sense of our past, brings peace for today, and creates a vision for tomorrow.' Melody Beattie

Although we had to decline George Klopfer's invitation to join him on *The World* over the Christmas period, he persuaded us, without much effort, to join him for a cruise to the British Virgin Islands in January. So, 4th January found us on a plane to San Juan with several cases of Carabella wine in our luggage. Once on board, we got ourselves settled in cabin 723, and then enjoyed dinner at the Pool Grill with George and Ellie. The next day we visited El Morro, the large citadel and fortress in the historic quarter of San Juan. While visiting, we made Ellie a lifetime member of the National Parks, so she could take four seniors with her to any National Park in the United States! We then enjoyed a delicious Puerto Rican lunch of grouper and yuca (aka cassava), followed by dinner at Rosa di Teriz, for an outstanding paella, where yours truly was gifted flamenco lessons!

The ship sailed at midnight for the island of Jost Van Dyke, in the BVI, where after breakfast we visited the bridge of the vessel then took a zodiac to Coral Beach for a picnic lunch. We dined at the Pool Grill again that evening, and learned the interesting fact that each owner on board was charged an annual fee for meals to ensure the viability of a multiple restaurant offering, and so each participant at the table vied to pay the bill!

On 7th January we once again sailed overnight, this time to Oil Nut Bay, where we enjoyed a breakfast of egg white omelette with black truffle and smoked salmon, with porcino bread and sambal sauce, at the Tides restaurant. We took the ship's tenders to Oil Nut Bay, a luxury residential development, where the developers saw the ship's passengers as potential wealthy customers. Hence, we were treated royally, with champagne on arrival, iced face clothes, and a delicious lunch. But, in truth, the ship's passengers were there precisely because they had wished to rid themselves of fixed real estate assets in favour of the freedom of their accommodation on a moving vessel. George, in fact, spent over two hundred and eighty days a year on board.

Richard Branson came on board at one point to sell tickets for Virgin Galactic's suborbital space flights. Some asked if tickets for the wife were one-way or return! Over dinner we met Colin and Anna Barrow, who were friends of Roch Hillenbrand and George and Ellie – a small world indeed, as Viv had worked with Roch at Commodities Corporation. On 8th January, we docked in Road Town, in BVI, and went to enjoy breakfast. We sat at what was known as the 'Tax Table', where George introduced us to Marshall Langer, now eighty-five years of age and who, with Bill Walker, had been one of the authors of the initial white paper publication about trusts in the Cayman Islands that I had been given on my arrival in Cayman more than forty years earlier. A colleague of Vivian's from Commodities Corporation, whom she had not seen for many years, also joined us at the table, so it was a day of coincidences.

It was also a day of travel: a trip with our luggage via taxi, ferry and Boston Whaler – ably captained by Barb Robinson – to their home on Great Camanoe, back to *The World* for dinner and goodbyes on board, then back to Great Camanoe in the dark. There, we finished a great day with Tortuga Rum cake and bottles of Carabella Chardonnay and Pinot Noir. After walking to the summit of Grand Camanoe the next morning, we took the Whaler back to Trellis Bay and the airport for our flight back to Cayman. We summed up our experience in our travel book as: '*The World* – fabulous ship owned by some 100 billionaires – different lifestyle – we loved the experience – but not for us. A 2-bed apartment costs USD 2.5m and an annual strata fee of USD 450k.'

Arriving back in Cayman, we got in touch with Mr Amini, who told us that the new carpets for Callaloo, replacing those damaged by the flooded hot water heater, were now in Hamburg. Carpet-less, we nevertheless hosted a dinner at Callaloo for Sir Peter Creswell, who was working with Jonathan Dingle on the Mediation School in the Caribbean. We also met with Lady Rabia, the storyteller; Michael Lemay, in charge of the entertainment, and Courtney Platt about photography for the celebration we would be holding at Callaloo on 6th February.

On 15th January I flew to Nassau to meet with David Wang and Tiger Wu, of China Construction Americas, to conduct a site tour of Baha Mar, then returned to Cayman on 17th January. These trips to Nassau would continue on a monthly basis (at least) for the duration of 2013 and 2014, as we carried out site inspections and met with all parties involved to discuss how we could bring this massive project back on schedule. The results of our inspections and discussions were set out in the Monthly Reports for China Exim.

At the end of January, we travelled to Verbier, where we checked into the Hotel Vanessa. The following four days were all wonderful bluebird days – bright sun, beautiful blue sky, still air and fresh snow – including 10cm of fresh powder at Savoleyres, all punctuated with excellent lunches and dinners. After skiing thirty one runs, I guessed (or hoped) we had skied off most of the damage done by the holiday overindulgence in food and drink! Afterwards, we held client meetings in London, and a Caribbean Intelligence lunch at Durrants to launch our Q4 2012 Caribbean Report to our clients and friends.

On 6th February, after an RLBC board meeting, we held the celebration party to announce the rebranding of Bould Consulting Limited to Rider Levett Bucknall. The change heralded the dawn of a new era with the global entity, which incorporated some three thousand employees in one hundred and seventeen offices worldwide. Our ethos of integrating local knowledge and expertise dovetailed perfectly with this new access to a global network. It would now be possible to provide even better and more up-to-date knowledge, with open communication and depth of interaction, and the ability to tap into a vast experience across a range of sectors. Quite a leap from RLB's roots as a small quantity surveying practice established in 1785, in Reading England – so somewhat older than BCL's founding in 1969.

On 21st February, we held the CNCF Arts Awards, and then left the next day to ski in Aspen, Snowmass and Beaver Creek. Jimmy and Cynthia Nowery kindly met us at Eagle Vail's airport, and we spent our first day skiing at Snowmass, after which George and Boopie McInnis joined us all at the Nowerys for dinner. The next day we skied Aspen, with lunch at Bonnie's and après ski at Little Nell, where George discovered the signature 'Passport' cocktail, which contains Tequila, Aperol and Grand Marnier, limes and rosemary – no wonder we were late for dinner!

On the 25th, we skied Aspen Highlands and lunched at Cloud Nine at the summit. This isolated restaurant is reputed to be the second-biggest seller of Veuve Clicquot champagne in America, and by 3pm it gets pretty wild, with people dancing on the tables and literally getting sprayed with champagne. How some people make it down the mountain in one piece is hard to believe.

The next day we skied Ajax Mountain in Aspen, and when we returned home that evening we discovered Jimmy and Cynthia had prepared a special party in honour of my MBE. A large Union Jack was draped at the top of the stairs, they had purchased bowler hats for the men to wear, and dinner included roast beef and Yorkshire pudding. Afterwards we watched the DVD of my inauguration at Buckingham Palace – what a fun evening!

We returned to Grand Cayman on 6th March, in time to attend a National Gallery exhibition of Shane Aquart's whimsical Dready paintings, followed by a visit to the Ritz Carlton exhibition space over the West Bay Road.

On the 13th I was back in the air again. I stopped in Miami for meetings with Hart Porsch and representatives from Four Seasons, with whom we were looking to brand the hotel at Balam Escape, and with my good friend, Robi Das, from Nemark Grubb Knight Frank, about various other hotel developments. We went on to London that same evening. On this flight we were well looked-after by Mark Welch, one of the attendants. Over the years, and with many Miami to London flights under our belts, we had got to know a number of the flight crew pretty well. They always looked after us, ensuring we had hangers at our seat on which to hang our clothes when changing into our sleeper suits for trans-Atlantic trips, a glass of champagne waiting, and cups of espresso coffee from first class if we were flying coach. We would return the favour by inviting them for drinks at 62 QGM. Mark Welch and Cathy Bennett were the crew members we knew best and, even if they were not on duty, we would let them know which flights we were on, and they would alert other crew members to look after us, which they always did.

Given the numerous flights we were taking at this time, we were blessed to see several frequent travellers on our flights. One was Emma Graham-Taylor, the daughter of friends from the early days in Cayman, who told us of a truly magical way of entering the United States. This became known as Global Entry, which was usually only available to USA citizens but for a trial period was being tested for non-citizens. She gave us the contact email for the person to whom we needed to apply. Emma, we are eternally grateful as it has truly lengthened our life by reducing immigration time from several hours to several minutes. Thank you from the bottom of our hearts!

On the 15th we took the train to Birmingham, where there was a reunion at Bishop Vesey's Grammar School the next day. It was the first time I had been back in fifty years. I chatted with many of my old school-mates, and in particular with Maurice Lea. He asked what I had been doing over the past decades, and I gave a very abridged account of my activities since leaving. He replied by saying, 'I was born 2 miles from here, married a girl from here, and have lived my whole life here.'

I then showed Viv Sutton Park, where I had enjoyed so many adventures, including the Boy Scout Jamboree, sailing and cross-country running, and then we drove to 102 Antrobus Road, where I had lived from age five to when I left the UK. The house looked the same, but the garage had been converted into an additional room. That evening, there was an Old Veseyans' dinner at

Moor Hall, where we sat with Pete Lucas, an old rugby team colleague, and Nick and Annette Ross.

Back in London, I applied for a Chinese visa for an upcoming visit but had to return the next day with a revised invitation letter, which worked, luckily. After an excellent lunch with Nick Holland in the City at L'Anima, we visited the Shard – a new, iconic tower on the London landscape, whose tip was engulfed in cloud that day.

We have always liked to exercise every morning wherever we travel, but I noted on this trip that the first opportunity to do so was on 21st March, when we walked on our favourite route through Kensington Gardens and Hyde Park. Viv has nurtured a garden in a collection of pots under the living room window of 62 Queen's Gate Mews, and we regularly walk along Kensington High Street to Rassells, a garden supply shop on Earls Court Road, to pick up plants, soil and pots (which are frequently broken by cars negotiating the turn in the Mews).

On 23rd March we had heavy snow, and so our walk was a true winter experience. After lunch with family and a trip to the Victoria Apollo theatre to see *Wicked*, we made an abortive attempt to view the Cutty Sark but gave up because it was too chilly. We returned home via Giorgio Sermoneta's shop in Knightsbridge to buy gloves for Viv.

We had been invited to tour One Hyde Park, a luxury apartment development connected to the Mandarin Oriental (formerly the Hyde Park Hotel, and a favourite of Maurice Cullen's), developed by the Candy brothers. So, given the Arctic temperature outside, we decided to present ourselves as potential purchasers. We viewed the completed apartments – with prices in the millions – and asked if we could change the floor finishes as they were not to our liking. We were told this was not possible, but that room service could be provided from the Mandarin next door by means of an underground tunnel. In some ways, the development reminded us of *The World* cruise ship – very luxurious, but not for us.

That evening, we enjoyed cocktails with Josianne, a good Swiss friend from the Mews, and met Neil and Fantana, who were from Sri Lanka and operated the travel agency on Gloucester Road, close to the end of the Mews. We would meet them again on a future visit to Sri Lanka.

In Cayman, delighted to be back in the warm climate which has by now become part of our DNA, we escorted the Governor to the Harquail for a CNCF show on 28th March. It was at this time I was introduced to a book by Ian Thomson, called *The Dead Yard* – tales of modern Jamaica which expertly describe the life there. In the words of one critic, Benjamin Zephaniah, 'If you are planning to go to Jamaica, don't buy a guide book, buy *The Dead Yard*, it takes you to the heart of Jamaica before you even get on the plane. Ian Thomson has captured the tension, the politics, the heat, the chaos, the beauty and the music of Jamaica. That's difficult to do, but in my opinion he did it because he got down with the people, he took risks, but Jamaicans do that every day.' I couldn't agree more, being fortunate to know many of the people in the book and the events that Ian describes.

In Miami for the CHRIS conference on 6th and 7th May, I left two days later for London. Viv had preceded me, flying in on the 5th to meet with Doreen, who flew over from Belfast. The two of them were to superbly manage the choice of new furniture and curtains for 62 QGM, and during this visit Viv treated Doreen to a wonderful musical performance at the Royal Albert Hall, which they really enjoyed – no husbands, just the two of them and so much to catch up on! On 10th May, we took the train to Sedlescombe for a weekend celebration of Mortimer's birthday, at his favourite Brickwall Hotel. It boasted a swimming pool, which I tried and almost froze to death. Instead, we visited Anne Boleyn's Hever Castle and enjoyed a hearty pub lunch.

On the 14th, Mort's birthday, we dined at L'Etranger in London, joined by Mikol, and on 16th Jonnie played host, cooking a delicious dinner for us all at his apartment. We held a belated birthday party for Viv on the 17th at Waterside Inn. We were always charmed by Waterside Inn's wine list, particularly when perusing the selection of champagnes for an aperitif. For Viv's favourite champagne, Bollinger, the menu quotes Lily Bollinger, who was asked at the launch of the 1959 vintage, 'When do you drink champagne?' She replied, 'I only drink champagne when I'm happy, and when I'm sad. Sometimes I drink it when I'm alone. When I have company, I consider it obligatory. I trifle with it if I am not hungry and drink it when I am. Otherwise I never touch it – unless I am thirsty.'

On 20th May, I made a presentation to British Expertise, the business development organisation, at Grosvenor Gardens, which was followed by cocktails at the House of Lords courtesy of the Caribbean Council, sponsored by RLBC, after which I held an RLBC client dinner at Mr Chows. The next day we held a Caribbean Council Advisory Committee meeting at the Caledonian Club, and the day after that I flew from Heathrow to Helsinki, and then Shanghai. We used this route, because we had found it had the most economical business class seats.

Adam Wu met me at Shanghai airport at 7.30am on the 23rd, and we boarded the Maglev train from the airport into the city, which reached 420 kph on the journey. By 11am, we were holding our first meeting with the Shanghai

Chamber of Commerce – obviously, if you snooze you lose! After lunch at the RLB Shanghai office, there were two further meetings with Chinese contractors who had interests in the Caribbean. Thereafter, meeting followed meeting with funding agencies and contractors until Sunday 26th May, when Adam and I boarded the bullet train to Beijing. This travelled at 320kph, covering the 1,300-plus km journey in five hours. Once again, we went straight into meetings to discuss the presentation I was to make at the China International Fair for Trade and Services (CIFTIS) and the various projects we were working on in the Caribbean that might benefit from connections made at the conference.

CFITIS was held at the China National Convention Centre in Beijing. It hosted some twenty-six thousand visitors and exhibitors from one hundred and seventeen different countries, and was supported by the World Trade Organisation, the United Nations Conference on Trade and Development, and the Organisation for Economic Co-operation and Development. My talk was on the 28th, and consisted of a twenty-minute presentation of six projects we were working on in the Caribbean, utilising green technology and promoting RLBC's services, with a request for investment in the subject projects.

Over the next several days there were numerous meetings with government departments, banks, investors and contractors, always followed by lengthy and delicious dinners, with hosts standing by your chair with a drink, greeting you with *Ganbei* (literally, 'dry cup'), and tossing back its contents in one gulp, while encouraging you to follow suit! On the 31st, I made a further presentation on Caribbean opportunities to the 'Go Global International Initiative', which led to some excellent networking prospects. Finally, I attended the Luxury Property Show, which promoted an interesting collection of overseas properties.

Investment by the Chinese outside of China was a hot topic at the time, as it spread the financial risk for Chinese investors. Of particular interest was property investment that included the potential for obtaining an alternate passport in countries that offered citizenship by investment programmes. There were several such countries in the Caribbean. It had been a tiring trip but most successful, and I flew back to London via Helsinki on 1st June. When in London, and in order to keep up with the water part of my Burdenko training programme, I enrolled at Ethos gym, part of Imperial College and located close to Queen's Gate Mews. They had a fabulous swimming pool, with an 8-foot deep end, as well as a steam room and sauna. This meant I could use a neck float and an elastic tether on my ankles, secured to the ladder, and 'run' for an hour without any joint impact. This facility became a daily 'go to' for me during visits to London from then on, whereas Viv generally preferred to walk in the Park and admire the change of seasons.

We had received notice that the face-to-face interview we needed to secure Global Entry was available in Tampa, and I asked Viv to jump on the opportunity and book flights. This she did, and we presented ourselves for the interview on 10th June, and passed.

We spent two days at home in Cayman, and then flew to London on 13th June. I met with the attorney, Sir Peter Creswell, to discuss mediation and arbitration, and how we could involve the RICS and the London Court of International Arbitration, of which we were both members. A couple of days later, we secured a chauffeur-driven car to carry Viv and me, together with our great friends, Andrew and Felix Jones, to Royal Ascot. Part way through the trip, we found we had left our entry tickets at home so had to turn around to pick them up before continuing on our way.

The Queen arrived in her carriage to open the event, driving into the Royal Enclosure. Looking at the race card, Viv decided to back two horses because they were ridden by Irish jockeys – and both won! The next day we returned, enjoyed an excellent seafood lunch with champagne, and Viv repeated her run of success by backing a further three winners – once again, all ridden by Irish jockeys! The proverbial 'luck of the Irish' was certainly with Viv both days. The next day Viv and I visited our safety deposit box at Metropolitan, and were delighted to see all nineteen silver bars were there. Then we went to a specialist bookbinders called Blissett (who hold a Royal Warrant) to have our huge family bible rebound. We had read this bible as kids, but one of its other key uses was to press wildflowers, due to its significant bulk, which probably didn't do it any good. I attended the Jamaican Think Tank, under Chatham House Rules, at Church House at the Palace of Westminster, and on 25th and 26th June, I delivered a presentation to British Expertise on funding opportunities from China, based on the numerous contacts I had made during my recent visits.

During the next few days we finally got to visit the Cutty Sark in Greenwich, enjoyed *La Vie Parisienne* at the Royal College of Music, and visited Kensington Palace for a lecture about the fashion designer Norman Hartnell, who was awarded a Royal Warrant as Dressmaker to The Queen Mother in 1940 and designed Queen Elizabeth II's wedding gown. We were also privileged to accompany Andrew and Felix to Henley, where we watched the rowing from the Stewards' Enclosure. We took a train to Gillingham in Dorset and were met at the station by Alan Scott, who drove us to their house for a wonderful Turkish lunch with much wine, after which I agreed to see which organisations in Cayman would like to receive copies of Joan's cookbook *The Governor's Lady*. So, on our return, I contacted the museum, Red Cross, NCVO and Humane Society, who ordered approximately seventy books.

At the end of July we held the CASE Governors Award and Reception at Government House. The next day was sad as we attended Bunny Delapenha's funeral. Bunny and his humour had been so integral to our life in Cayman, that we felt a key part of our life had now changed.

During the beginning of August I was flying back and forth to Nassau for Baha Mar quite regularly, and on the 4th I arranged a dinner at Luciano's for the Baha Mar crew with Viv as the guest of honour, because she had heard so much about them but had only met a few face to face.

Back in Cayman Viv interviewed our new housekeeper, Hyacinth Wilson, and commented she was a 'nice person'. She was, and remains, our housekeeper, and a sweeter, more cheerful and obliging person you will not meet. Six weeks later we met Hyacinth's husband, Canute (also known as Ken). Viv had considered bringing Ken to Callaloo to work for us alongside Hyacinth, but during the interview, it was clear he was keen to remain a roofer, and in any case, we wouldn't want to trade Wayne our house manager for anything.

In early August we also interviewed representatives from the four hotel brands that were to manage the four individual hotels in the Baha Mar, complex. These included the Mondrian (subsequently changed to SLS) which pitched their cutting-edge lifestyle-focussed facility aimed at the modern traveller; the Hyatt, positioned as a family-friendly and convention hotel, and the Rosewood, emphasising luxury, including a chauffeur who would phone reception from the airport to ensure the bathrobes in the guests' room would be the correct size. We also met with the casino operators, who so accurately embodied the classic image of the industry they might as well have been chewing on big cigars.

Mrs Harquail's funeral and celebration of life was held, most appropriately, at the Harquail Theatre on 24th August. During the occasion, I was honoured to be asked to speak of this great lady's significant and generous contribution to the arts and culture scene in the Cayman Islands.

Viv and I flew to London a few days later, and arrived in time to celebrate Daphne's 90th birthday at 62 QGM. Daphne lived across the Mews from our house and was a wonderful character. Her husband had connections with the All-England Lawn Tennis & Croquet Club, so she had many stories about Wimbledon, where they had been privileged to sit in the Royal Box during matches. On 2nd September, Jimmy and Cynthia Nowery arrived, finally giving us the opportunity to return some of their 'super all-inclusive' hospitality we had enjoyed over the years in Aspen. Jimmy arrived at QGM with a spectacular black eye, looking as if he had been in a serious boxing match. In fact, he had acquired it when he fell during a tour of the Omaha Beaches in celebration of the D-Day landings, prior to their arrival in London.

The next day we went to some of the great tourist attractions, such as the London Eye and Westminster Abbey, that one seldom visits unless guests are in town. The next day we visited the State Rooms in Buckingham Palace after an earlier hitch in the morning's routine. Cynthia had called out to me that Jimmy was stuck in the rather deep and narrow bathtub adjacent to the guest bedroom. Could I assist? Of course – and Jimmy, having covered his private parts with a washcloth, was ready to put his arms around my neck. As I straightened my back, I succeeded in extricating him from his wedged situation. We still laugh about the incident.

We proceeded to the Palace and then to the Goring Hotel opposite for lunch. After that we shopped at Trumpers for traditional men's toiletries; Caviar House, so I could make our caviar eggs for breakfast; Harrods for more shopping; and we visited Giorgio Sermoneta's glove shop in Burlington Arcade but, sadly, Giorgio was not in town. We topped off the day with an evening cocktail party so our family could meet Jimmy and Cynthia, as they had heard so much about him and his quintessential saying, 'Often wrong, but never in doubt' over the years.

After Jimmy and Cynthia departed, Viv and I had a few lazy days at home, entertained a few friends and business colleagues, and got ready to pack and close up the house. Before leaving, I managed to get to Blissett to collect the family bible, which had been beautifully restored.

We got back to Cayman on the 11th, and on the 16th I flew to Toronto for an RLBC board meeting and dinner, and then back to Miami two days later to attend a two-day Dispute Resolution Board Foundation Conference as the Caribbean area representative. Afterwards, I remained in Miami to attend the KPMG Infrastructure Conference, where I met with many colleagues from the Caribbean construction industry, including Robi Das from NGKF, and then returned to Cayman on the 24th.

During the end of September, we entertained Sir Peter Creswell at Callaloo to continue our discussions on mediation and to highlight some of the issues that had been raised at the DRBF conference in Miami, earlier in the month.

We were able to welcome our new Governor, Helen Kilpatrick, for a tour of CNCF, and enlighten her about the work we carried out in preserving and developing our culture. That evening she joined us at a photographic exhibition sponsored by our long-time supporters, Bank of Butterfield. The next day,

Henry Muttoo and I met with Moses Kirkconnell, then Minister of Tourism, to discuss ways to promote CNCF's work on cruise ships as a means of showcasing our heritage and culture. He welcomed the ideas enthusiastically, but pointed out the difficulties of getting such initiatives in front of cruise directors, who control the passengers' onshore activities and earn commissions from them. He also pointed out the long lead times required to secure listings in the cruise lines' schedules. We vowed to keep working on promoting the idea of giving small groups opportunities to experience Caymanian culture – such as visiting Miss Lassie's House to experience her unique artwork.

Back at the Factory Ball in November 2012, Viv had successfully bid on one of the items – a weekend at the Eco resort, Pico Bonito Lodge – but the visit needed to be completed within the year, and we were getting close to the deadline. I did mention to Viv that Honduras was one of the most dangerous places in the Caribbean to visit, but despite this caution we boarded Cayman Airways and flew to La Ceiba, Honduras, on 11th October. On board the flight was Lewie Ceato Hydes, from West Bay whom we had not seen for some time. Lewie was visiting Graham Thompson, who had developed an island resort in Honduras. We were able to relive some of the great old days of Galleon Beach and Holiday Inn night clubs, where Lewie was doorman and bouncer as an adjunct to his day job spraying mosquitos with Mosquito Research – memorialised in Andy Martin's song 'The Bugman'.

Arriving in La Ceiba, we drove to Pico Bonito Lodge, which was a wonderful Jamaican-style rain forest lodge. All things had turned out as they should be – we had time for the visit, the lodge was more than we had hoped for, lunch of grouper and local hot sauce was delicious, and we had helped the National Gallery, as Viv's bid for the weekend had been twice the rack rate!

The next morning, the lodge made up a picnic for us to take on our three and a half hour hike into the foothills of Pico Bonito, including a stop at Mermaid Falls for a swim in the crystal-clear water. We ate our picnic there, which included a chilled bottle of Chardonnay. On the 13th we rose at 6am for a birdwatching adventure, ably supported by Santos, our guide, who had a high-power telescope for viewing the birds and who was extremely knowledgeable about the region's other flora and fauna as well as bird species. In fact, the manager of the lodge, James Adams, knows our great friend and ornithologist Patricia Bradley, whom he met at a conference in the UK.

Close to Pico Bonito, our friend Mars Van Liefde had built a home. We had contacted her to let her know we would be visiting, and she had invited us to come to the house and see her garden. So, we left the Pico Bonito compound to walk the short distance to Mars's house, only to learn Santos and an armed guard would be following on a motorbike. We had not appreciated the level of security required in Honduras!

Back in Cayman, on 6th November, I flew to Punta Cana, in the Dominican Republic, to attend CHICOS at the Hard Rock resort there. I was there to discuss 'China's Interest in the Caribbean Hospitality and Tourism Sectors' with fellow panellists Adam Wu, Tiger Wu and Dennis Constanzo, the principal of USA Investment Advisers. With Tiger Wu of China State Construction, I flew by helicopter to Playa Grande resort to look at an Aman resort under development there. Coincidentally, Gary Hastings, who had previously worked for me and who had moved on to work at our office in Turks and Caicos, was working on an adjacent project in Playa Grande. On 9th November, I returned to Miami to connect with Hart Porsch for meetings on Balam Escape, and the next day travelled to Kingston to meet with Minister Phillips of the Jamaican Government about potential infrastructure projects that the Chinese were willing to fund.

Viv and I had met with Celebrations in late November to make plans to host Gimistory at Callaloo, which we did on 8th December, and a wonderful occasion it was! A week later we celebrated Miss Lassie's home by whitewashing it for Christmas and raking the yard with new white sand. This is a unique Caymanian tradition which involves bringing white sand from the beach and spreading it in front of the home to create a snowlike effect – a practice known as 'backing sand'. Families would collect sand in thatch baskets and then rake it into intricate patterns on Christmas Eve. This tradition, along with other festive decorations like Casuarina trees adorned with lights and garlands, helped to create a festive atmosphere even in the tropical climate of the islands.

Viv and I travelled to the UK where Mort and Jan came to QGM to spend Christmas with us, and we walked to the Royal Albert Hall on Christmas Eve for Christmas carols, which we enjoyed from our box, replete with wine and hors d'oeuvres. On Christmas day, Viv and I enjoyed a refreshing walk in Hyde Park, came back to cook an Ulster fry for Mort and Jan and then prepared for a wonderful Christmas lunch for the family, which included Anne Marie, Louis, Geena and Edward and Jonnie. On the menu were turkey crown, ham and pork stuffing, copious wine (of course), home-made cranberry sauce, Christmas pudding and brandy butter – all prepared by World Class Chefs Jonnie and Viv. Lunch started at 3pm and finished at midnight! We walked off the previous day's excesses in Hyde Park on Boxing Day, and Charlene joined us all for lunch.

We prepared the garden at QGM, pruning the roses and cleaning up, then flew back to Cayman on 29th December. Back in Cayman we enjoyed a 'Do

Drop In' party at Callaloo for New Year's Eve, rounded out with yours truly cooking duck breasts for Viv and myself, to enjoy while we sat in our pool cabana and watched the firework displays along the beach.

2014

'Trust the wait. Embrace the uncertainty. Enjoy the beauty of becoming. When nothing is certain, anything is possible.' Mandy Hale

As Chairman of CNCF, I had been invited to the sixth World Summit on Arts & Culture, with the theme of 'Creative Times: new models for creative development', which was to be held in Santiago, Chile, from 13th–16th January 2014. We always wanted to keep pace with what was happening globally, and IFACCA provided this opportunity in a most efficient way with its World Summits. Being part of the global community in this regard is particularly important to us because, in the wider Caribbean context, the cultural development of Caymanian society is unique, as I have described earlier. Accordingly, Viv and I left Cayman on 10th January, and took the overnight flight to Santiago, arriving in the early morning, and checking into the Sheraton Hotel, where we met Natasha Eves, and Sarah Gardner, the Executive Director of IFACCA, in the lobby.

On the 12th I attended the CEO's Rustic Retreat, and the formal AGM of IFACCA was held the next day, followed in the evening by the Grand Opening of the Summit at the Centro Cultural Estacio Mapocho (CCEM). Until 1994 the building had been a railway station, but was then converted into a cultural centre – a significant statement of Chile's return to democracy under the government of President Aylwin, and of the process of revitalising the cultural activity lost under the dictatorship. IFACCA sessions at CCEM took place during subsequent days, always followed by delicious meals of Chilean foods. Viv was introduced to Carménère, her favourite new red, and a leading grape variety originating in the Médoc region of France but now used primarily in Chile, which produces the majority of the world's Carménère wines.

After the conference we drove to the Undurraga winery, one of the oldest in the Maipo valley, with a history of some one hundred and thirty-five years. The next day we decided to try a little adventure using the public transport system. We took the subway to Pajarito from Pedro de Valdivia on the red line, and then the Pullman bus to Valparaiso, where we enjoyed a lunch of Spanish omelette at the Rotonda restaurant. Then we took the funicular from Plaza Sotomayor, to enjoy a spectacular view of this World Heritage city, with its amazing graffiti murals, and returned back to our hotel the way we'd come.

Viv and I decided to take a guided trek on the 18th. Alvaro, our guide, picked us up at the hotel and drove us to the trail head of Alto Maipo to hike to the San José Plantat Refugio, built in 1937. At first the weather was overcast, then it rained, and the 2,500-foot gain in elevation and return took almost eight hours. We felt in need of a little less strenuous activity the next day, so we took a limo to the Cousiño-Macul winery, which was founded in 1856 and is still in the founder's family. There, we purchased Carménère and Lota wines for the Callaloo cellar

Back in Cayman, Henry and I had a follow-up meeting with Moses Kirkconnell to discuss how to advance our culture-meets-tourism ideas, particularly those related to the cruise ship industry, and also to revisit earlier thoughts on performances in the hotels. Afterwards I met with Judith Gates, who had done such a sterling job facilitating the business plan for the National Trust in 1998, to discuss with her a similar planning exercise for CNCF.

Viv and I flew to Miami on 5th February to begin our next Around the World trip, and the next evening held an RLBC board meeting, with cocktails for our friends and clients on the rooftop of the Mayfair Hotel. By the 8th we were in London, where we enjoyed a bracing walk in Hyde Park and in the evening joined brother Rob and his guests to celebrate his sixtieth birthday in the Oliver Messel Suite at The Dorchester on Park Lane, complete with a performance by opera singers. The next day, we lunched at Yauatcha with Adam Wu, his wife Linda, and their two daughters, Sophie and Angelina. We also held meetings with our insurance company in the City, to explore how we could insure our house for all risks except named storms. Our friend, John Davies, had suggested doing this as it would reduce our premiums significantly each year, the difference of which we would then religiously place into a savings account as a contingency fund to cover any damage from a named storm. We were able to achieve this, and continue to do so.

We caught a Cathy Pacific flight to Hong Kong on 12th February, on which we received great food and service and were given new sleeper suits that remain my favourite for travel to this day. From Hong Kong, we flew on to meet our Harvard OPM reunion group in Ho Chi Minh City – formerly Saigon – the capital of the French Colony of Cochinchina and known as the 'Paris of the Orient'. We met Sally and George Falkiner in the lobby of the Sheraton where we were staying and had a quick catch up, then had an afternoon nap before meeting with our group of some thirty alumni and wives for dinner. The next day began with a city tour encompassing the Independence (formerly

Presidential) Palace, Central Post Office, Notre Dame Catholic Cathedral, and the War Museum. This last was fairly shocking to some of the Americans in our group as it told the story of the war from a Vietnamese point of view. We then visited the Chinese temple and lunched at the Lý Club Saigon, which was smart but not particularly Vietnamese.

In the afternoon we drove some 70km to visit the Củ Chi tunnel complex. This had housed some 10,000 Viet Kong, in approximately 200km of tunnels on three levels, and illustrated the tactics used in the war. Viv felt shopping in the famous Binh Tay market would be a better use of her time than looking at a few tunnels. Instead, she visited a lacquer factory and bought a stunning picture of a Vietnamese girl, made out of mother-of-pearl and duck eggshells covered with seven layers of lacquer, which now adorns the wall of the gym at Callaloo. Returning to Ho Chi Minh City, we had drinks with George, Sally, Franie (George's sister) and Frances Moodie from South Africa, on the rooftop bar at the Rex Hotel, which had been frequented during the Vietnam War by news correspondents. Then we left the hotel to board the Ama Lotus, moored at the My Tho port in the Mekong Delta, where we enjoyed the captain's welcome cocktail party and dinner at the Mekong restaurant.

On 18th February we took a junk trip around Cái Bè to see its famous floating market and visited a rice paper and candy-making workshop. Then we rejoined the Ama Lotus and cruised up to Sa Đéc, where we visited Maguerite Duras's lover's house, with its fusion of French, Vietnamese and Chinese architectural elements. It was a real evocation of a bygone era, and had become famous in 1984, when the French author wrote her novel *The Lover*, about her youthful affair with a wealthy Chinese/Vietnamese man in 1920s Saigon. Then we visited the Cao Dai temple, the home of a distinctive Vietnamese religion which fuses elements of Buddhism, Taoism, Christianity and Hinduism. After dinner on board, we enjoyed a late-night disco in the Saigon lounge on board the Ama Lotus.

On the 19th I had an early morning swim while Viv chose yoga, after which we visited Tân Châu, a traditional village on an island in the Mekong Delta, where we visited the house of an eighty-three-year-old Viet Kong veteran. It was a fascinating to briefly experience a local agricultural lifestyle, untouched by tourism. After a boat trip to a mat-making workshop and a silk factory, we returned by rickshaw to the boat, lunch and our OPM meeting while Viv did a cookery course, learning to make spring rolls and Tom Yum Gai soup. We arrived in Phnom Penh and docked on the 20th. As you may recall, Viv and I had tried, unsuccessfully, to visit Cambodia and Angkor Wat in October 2000, but were not allowed to board the plane as my passport was too full of stamps.

So it was great to have finally arrived – albeit almost fourteen years later – good things come to those who wait!

Cambodia's capital city is famous for its French colonial architecture. We visited the Royal Palace and the magnificent Silver Pagoda and Museum. We then toured the central market, where Viv spotted a 'Salomon' bag to carry our purchases, and which now doubles as Viv's ski gear bag for our ski trips. We enjoyed lunch on board and caught up with Vincente and Evelyn, and later had dinner with the Harvard group at the Chinese House, which is part owned by Evelyn's nephew. We then visited a local market, purchased school supplies, and took a tuktuk to visit a monastery school on Oukhty Island to distribute the supplies we had purchased and where the interaction with the children was an unforgettable experience.

We then visited a silk factory. Of course Viv could not leave empty handed, and purchased a most attractive blue silk scarf. We had dinner with the Harvard group, and enjoyed a show put on by a large number of the ship's crew. Edson Bueno and wife Solange, and Wolfgang and his wife Doris, felt the trip was not proceeding fast enough, and so had asked the travel agent, who was travelling with us, if she would charter a jet so that they could see the sights we were to see, but more quickly. She did this, so they left us at this point. Edson had the best suite on the Ama Lotus, and they suggested we move from our suite to enjoy the luxury of theirs, which we were delighted to do.

On the 23rd, we toured Phnom Srey and Phnom Pros, known as the 'Woman Hill' and 'Man Hill', where we visited the Buddha Garden and our guide, Moa, explained the 'mudras', the symbolic hand positions and meanings of the Buddha statues. We also learned that if the reclining Buddha is lying on his right side, he is dead; if he is lying on his left side, he is asleep. We disembarked at Tonlé Sap Lake, having travelled some two hundred and eighty miles on board the Ama Lotus.

A five-and-a-half-hour bus ride, during which we stopped at an eight hundred-year-old bridge, took us to Siem Reap, the gateway to Angkor, which had been the former capital city of the Khmer empire. We checked into the Sofitel Royal Angkor and began our sightseeing tour of Angkor Archaeological Park, which is a UNESCO World Heritage Site and one of the most renowned archaeological destinations in all of Southeast Asia. Our first visit was to the walled city of Angkor Thom, where we had our picture taken with a group of Apsara dancers, who symbolise spirituality, femininity, and the bond between humanity and the divine in Cambodian culture.

We then visited the temple, adorned with impressive temple carvings – all done in place by a reputed three hundred thousand workers on the orders of King Jayavarman VII during his reign between AD 1181–1218, during which he expanded the Khmer kingdom. As part of a grand programme of construction he also built the Terrace of the Elephants, the Temple of the Leper King, and the Bayon in Ankor Thom, and dedicated them to Buddhism. After lunch we visited the Banteay Srei temple, dedicated to the Hindu gods Shiva and Parvati. Because the pink sandstone of which it is made is soft, the decorative carvings are more detailed than those of some other Cambodian temples.

We then visited an orphanage, run by ODA (Opportunities for Development through Art) whose students put on a dance performance, showed us their accommodation, and then the artwork they had produced. We purchased a stilt house painting which hangs in the gym at Callaloo with many of our other travel memories – these may be why I feel so connected and calm when I am working out there. Viv and I then enjoyed dinner at the hotel, watched another Apsara dance performance, and went to bed early after our active, memory-filled day. The next morning we visited Angkor Wat, which reputedly took some thirty-seven years to build, and climbed to the upper level to admire an overall view of the complex. On the way down, now in the heat of the day, we enjoyed an ice-cold beer. We then went on to visit Ta Prohm, the temple famous for the intertwined Banyan trees growing out of and engulfing its ruins. It became famous after it was featured in the movie *Tomb Raider*.

We returned to the hotel for lunch, after which we took a short flight to Hanoi, where we checked into the Sofitel Metropole with its fabulous ambiance. We visited Ba Dinh Square, viewed Ho Chi Minh's body and the One Pillar Pagoda, the Temple of Literature, and went to the infamous 'Hanoi Hilton' – a prison during the French colonial era and which later held US POWs during the Vietnam War.

We lunched at the Press Club and then took a rickshaw 'cyclo' ride and walking tour of the Old Quarter, where we saw a traditional water puppet show. On the 28th we left the hotel at 7am and after a three and a half hour bus ride to Ha Long Bay, boarded our traditional wooden junk, which combined classic beauty with modern conveniences, for our overnight cruise. We had lunch on board whilst cruising and enjoying the magnificent scenery, set amidst stunning limestone cliffs. We then had great fun kayaking around a floating village. Rising early the next day, we practiced Tai Chi on the sloping deck and then visited the wonderful 'Surprise Cave', full of stalactites and stalagmites, which had been able to hide large numbers of soldiers during the war. We drove back to Hanoi and the Metropole after breakfast, where we discovered we had mislaid our passports somewhere. After the tour operator had checked with the junk operator, to no avail, someone suggested checking the safe in our old room at the Metropole itself – which is indeed where we'd left them the day before.

Panic over, we celebrated with drinks at the bar, followed by farewell dinner at the Lý Club with our OPM crew, enjoying a lesson in the Vietnamese alphabet followed by an excellent Vietnamese meal accompanied by Montes Alpha Merlot and Cordier white wine. On 2nd March we flew Dragonair to Hong Kong, where at the Hong Kong Club the next evening we had a pleasant dinner with RLB partners Philip Lo and wife Dorothy, and Stephen Lai and his wife Yolanda. At the time, Stephen was the Global Chairman of RLB, so there followed a press release to the effect that the RLB Global chairman and the Caribbean chairman had met in Hong Kong.

Friends in Cayman had told us about an excellent wilderness hike in Hong Kong, known as the Dragon's Back. It was hard to believe that a wilderness hike could exist in such a densely developed island. So, on the 5th, we ordered a picnic lunch from the Peninsula, which arrived in extremely fancy boxes tied in ribbons. These we managed to get into our rucksacks after some manoeuvring, and set off through the lobby of the Peninsula, where many elegantly dressed people were enjoying morning tea and sandwiches, looking somewhat incongruous in our hiking gear, which included boots, hiking poles, wide brimmed hats and L.L. Bean jackets. We walked to the underground station, took the train to Admiralty and changed lines to Shau Kei Wan station, where we picked up the #9 bus to take us to the trail head for Dragon's Back. We hiked up a narrow path, climbed some steps, and then made it onto the ridge, where we were literally in the clouds. Thank goodness we were appropriately dressed! The trail was fairly deserted, but when we came across other hikers, we exchanged pleasantries and took photographs. After the Dragon's Back we ended up on the Hong Kong trail and stopped to enjoy our picnic – there is nothing like a strenuous hike to work up a good appetite.

We returned to the Peninsula the way we came and retired to the spa, where yours truly luxuriated in the sauna and Viv in the steam room to ease our tired muscles, followed by a swim in the magnificent pool. We then dressed for a Peking duck dinner at the Spring Moon restaurant, and went back to pack for our next adventure – Hawaii, where Tony Smith, local RLB director, had been kind enough to arrange an early morning check-in to the Hilton Hawaiian Village. Tony and I then took a tour of RLB's projects, whilst Viv walked the beach. Tony's wife Martha, joined us for dinner at the Bali Grill, where we enjoyed an Oregon Willamette Valley Pinot Noir from Domaine Serene with our meal.

We flew to Kauai the next morning, arriving there at 2.30pm. At the airport we hired a Dodge minivan – necessary to accommodate all the luggage essential to our around the world journey. After a two-hour drive we reached Princeville and the St Regis Hotel, where we checked-in and had a relaxed evening and leisurely morning. After lunch the next day we went for an afternoon hike along the famous Na Pali coast hike of the Kalalau trail, starting at the beach trailhead at 4pm. The trail was very muddy, slippery and narrow, but the views were incredible. We continued on the trail to Hanakapiai beach, where a very fast-flowing waist-deep river discharged into a stony cove with big waves. We decided to return along the same route, arriving at the trailhead just as it was getting dark. We had walked for over three hours, covering a distance of four miles and one thousand two hundred vertical feet. We celebrated with a bottle of Sainsbury's Pinot Noir and steak frites, courtesy of room service, and a big clean-up of mud from our gear.

On 9th March we drove some two and a half hours to Waimea Canyon and Koke'e State Park, to enjoy the Awa'awapuhi trail in wonderful sunny weather. We descended some one thousand six hundred feet, inspired by trail markers every quarter mile and enjoyed our picnic lunch. We were joined by red-crested cardinals (Viv checked them out) with red heads, grey wings and white breasts, and a red jungle fowl, all of us enjoying the stunning views. Then Viv and I climbed back up the route we had descended, definitely helped psychologically on the way up by those quarter-mile markers, as Viv had a broken toe to contend with. Back in the St Regis, we lazed in the tub and ordered room service. Viv commented that for a sixty-seven and sixty-eight year old couple, we were not doing too badly! On the 10th we drove to Lihue airport and checked in, then went to view the Spouting Horn blowhole. But when we got there it was raining so hard that we drove through the Botanical Gardens instead, returning to Lihue airport for our flight to Honolulu, and on home. Our trip had taken thirty-five days – not as long as *Around the World in Eighty Days* but certainly equally enjoyable and informative.

After all our travels it was great to be back home and back into our Sunday morning routine with Tai Chi at Camana Bay on the 16th, followed the next day with a PPP seminar, hosted by the Chamber of Commerce. However, not home for long, I travelled to London on 26th March where, on the 31st, RLBC hosted a Caribbean Intelligence lunch at Durrants. On the following day we met with the partners of IGG – a Dutch company – to discuss a Euro Alliance, giving us more potential traction in the Caribbean with the Dutch, Spanish, and French speaking islands. That evening we sponsored the annual Caribbean Council cocktail event at the House of Lords, and on 2nd April I attended the Caribbean

Council Advisory board meeting, followed by drinks with James Burdess, Savills' Caribbean Director, at their head office in Margaret Street, London.

I flew back to Cayman on the 3rd, unpacked and then repacked with my ski clothes and left, accompanied by Viv, for Alta. Unfortunately, our usual accommodation at Sugarplum was not available, so we stayed in an apartment at Hell's Gate, so called because it is built in the direct line of a potential avalanche route! We were out on the slopes at noon the next day, with fresh powder, and enjoyed lunch at our favourite mountain restaurant: Collins Grill. The lunch was made doubly special as they served Viv's favourite new wine, Concha Toro Carménère. After skiing some more in the afternoon, we drove into Salt Lake City for supplies from Whole Foods, and then back to Hell's Gate for pasta aglio e olio.

For the next three days our routine was to do some administrative work in the mornings, be out on the slopes by about 11am, have lunch, and do some more skiing before returning home to Hell's Gate. The skiing was unusually good for spring, as it was always sunny with brilliant bluebird skies but the snow conditions were more like those we were accustomed to find in winter. We also had a new toy to play with: Basil Behrman had given us a most useful present the year before: a Go-Pro type video camera which could be mounted on our helmets and record our ski runs, to see if our techniques needed improvement.

There was a small hiccup to the routine on 9th April, when we were locked out of the apartment (the front doors are chained and locked) until 5.30pm due to avalanche risk after so many sunny days had followed significant amounts of fresh snow.

The same happened on the 11th, and as we were going to the theatre that evening we took our evening clothes with us so we could change at the Alta base. At the end of the day's skiing we went to change in the bathrooms at the Goldminer's Daughter Lodge. Getting our heavy ski boots and clothes off and changing in a tiny WC cubicle was a bit more of a challenge than we had expected, but we emerged looking respectably clad in street clothes. Off then to the Hotel Monaco and the Bambara restaurant, where we enjoyed a fine dinner and then saw the *Rite of Spring* – Ballet West's tribute to Igor Stravinsky's iconic score, at the Capitol Theatre opposite. This was a change for us, as typically the ballet is always the *The Nutcracker* in December. On 14th April, our wake-up alarm rang at the ungodly hour of 3.30am, and we drove to Salt Lake City to catch our 6am flight, via Dallas and Miami, to Cayman.

Back for only one day, I flew to Nassau for meetings with Tom Dunlap of Baha Mar, to discuss progress and the completion schedule, and to carry out a site inspection, returning to Cayman on the 18th. I was back in Nassau on 29th April, to meet with the China Exim team as well as the developers, to discuss progress and budget items, and on 28th May I met there with Tiger Wu, who undertook to add a further eight hundred workers to accelerate progress and attempt to make up the three months delay to completion. This, they claimed, was partly due to design changes, and to the need to respond to an outstanding five hundred RFI's (Requests for Information). The next day I met with Shao Di, from China Exim, to run through these proposals and their possible effects, returning to Cayman on 30th May.

The time had come to replace the Ford Explorer we had owned since Hurricane Ivan in 2004, and so I talked with Lee Foster, from Avis, about purchasing one of his used rental Ford Expeditions. We test drove a couple on 24th April, and bought one as our 'evening and airport' transportation, due to its commodious seven seats and lavish baggage space.

At the end of April, I attended the CHRIS conference in Miami, and a few days later met with clients of the Casi Cielo project in Punta Bocas in Panama, followed by a dinner with the Harvard Miami Chapter at the New World Centre on Miami Beach. After that I returned to Cayman on 2nd May, in time for our CNCF planning retreat, moderated by Judith Gates the next day.

At this time we were busy with several new projects at RLBC, holding frequent discussions about the Casi Cielo project in Panama, the Tropicalia project in Dominican Republic, and the hospital project in Trinidad. During the middle of the month I also met with Brent Woodson about the new airport in Anguilla, and a Haitian development called Île-à-Vache, which I had previously discussed with Stéphanie Villedrouin, the Minister of Tourism, whom I had met in 2013 at a CHICOS conference with Tiger Wu, of China State Construction, and Adam Wu.

The College of Science and Engineering in Beijing had asked RLBC to offer an overseas internship to a student on the Baha Mar project, to which we readily agreed. So, in early June, Chi Ho Law (George) joined us in Nassau. I was delighted to see him there during my visit to review the acceleration proposals on Baha Mar with Jerry Katz, Alan Veeran and Gordon Glen, and meet with China Exim and China Construction Americas.

On 15th June I left Cayman for a three-day visit to Panama to meet with the development team on the Casi Cielo project, arriving back to Cayman in time to attend the John Gray High School Graduation on the 19th, and to present the CNCF prizes for arts and culture to the successful winners.

Jerry Katz and I were in St Kitts on 1st July to look at the Park Hyatt development, on which RLBC had been asked to advise. Then we flew to Trinidad in connection with Abel's Government Campus Plaza claims, followed up by a conference call with Abel a few days later. On 11th July I met with Professor Lo, the intern's mentor from the college, to review George's progress and to receive a certificate of thanks from the college. There followed meetings with Tom Dunlap and Shao Di on Baha Mar.

I was back in Cayman in time for a 5pm ceremony at Miss Lassie's House to unveil the dedication plaque marking the success of the SMLH programme, attended by both the Premier, Sir Alden McLaughlin, and the Leader of the Opposition, McKeeva Bush. I was delighted to have reached this point, and to have both these important men attend the ceremony and celebration. Both, in their own way, had been pivotal in preserving this immensely important part of our heritage and culture.

On 18th July Viv and I flew to London so we could celebrate Jan's birthday at their home in Walthamstow, with a hog roast in the garden. It was a great party, and then Jonnie drove us back to QGM and provided some advice on a trellis *trompe l'oeil* I was painting on the wall of our downstairs patio.

We were collected by limo on 28th July, which took us to Luton and an EasyJet flight to Venice, where we collected a Mini rent-a-car, and drove into the Dolomites and to the Rosa Alpina, a classic mountain hotel in San Cassiano, where we checked into a most comfortable room, followed by a delicious dinner.

The next day we were off hiking to Bioch Pralongia, a climb of some one thousand four hundred feet. We stopped for lunch where we encountered Willie, who gave us a shot of Genziana, made from gentian root and wildflowers, reputed to be good for the digestion and joints, as well as a taste of Grappa. Back at the hotel, we luxuriated in the tub with a glass of Chardonnay, and then dined at the Armentarola Hotel, enjoying a perfectly cooked veal chop.

The next day we had intended to hike to the next village, La Ville, but we took the gondola to the top instead, and hiked down from Piz la Ila to Refugio La Fraina and had a great lunch outside, then took the Piz Sorega gondola home. The lift operator allowed us to go down on the gondola with the same ticket at no extra charge, which was pleasant. Dinner was at the Michelin-starred St Humberto's restaurant in Rosa Alpina, where we were also entertained by a delightful piano player.

We returned to Venice on 1st August and checked into the Hotel Danieli, where we had an alfresco lunch, and then walked around the surrounding maze of streets before dining in the hotel's rooftop restaurant with a magnificent view of the city and its canals. We planned our day over breakfast the next morning and began by taking the ferry to Murano, famous for its glassware, where we toured the glassblowing workshops and purchased some handbag hangers for Viv, Claudia and Dottie, for special dining-out occasions. I also bought Viv a beautiful pendant and earrings. We took the ferry back to the hotel, and that evening we listened to a wonderful concert of Vivaldi's *Four Seasons* in a church adjacent to St Mark's Square, followed by dinner and dancing.

On the 3rd we enjoyed breakfast in our room, with egg white omelettes and smoked salmon, and walked about during the day. Viv shopped for relatives, we took a boat back to the mainland, and then we were off back to Gatwick and home to QGM. There, I put the finishing touches to the painted trellis on the patio wall – Viv said it looked great – then we flew back to Cayman and Callaloo and a welcome home greeting from Puddie.

On 7th September I flew to Nassau for three days of meetings with China Exim and Ernst & Young about the Baha Mar schedule and China Construction Americas. Leaving Nassau on the 10th, I met up with Viv in Miami Beach, where I attended and spoke at the Urban Land Institute Conference in Miami Beach on 11th and 12th September, where the theme was 'Developing in the Caribbean Basin'. My fellow panel members were Fernando Garcia-Chacon, of JLL Hotels and Hospitality Group; Rodrigo Breton, of MIRA developers, and Benjamin Greenberg, of Deloitte Real Estate services.

Following a presentation about the Puerto Cancun development in Mexico, a lively debate and question and answer session ensued about the key issues of risk analysis and management, and the importance of thorough due diligence for developers. The importance of the comprehensive construction and development advisory services provided by RLBC throughout the Caribbean region for more than forty years featured significantly during the discussion. Key amongst these services was understanding the relationships in our diverse communities in the region.

Viv and I left for London after the ULI conference and, on 15th September, I met with a mirror installation company who were adding a smoked mirror to the centre part of the trellis I had painted on the patio wall. This was a great idea, as the reflection visually doubled the size of the patio and adjacent bedroom. I had meetings at QGM the next day with staff for the Casi Cielo project in Panama, followed by a further meeting with Caribbean Council managing director, Chris Bennett to see how we could further assist the Council through our Caribbean-wide contacts. This was followed by drinks on the newly decorated QGM patio with Mark and Cathy from American Airlines, as well as Daphne, Charlene and next door neighbour, Freddie.

After a lazy day at home on the 17th, we visited the Tower of London to view Blood Swept Lands and Seas of Red, a public art installation commemorating World War I, featuring a sea of scarlet ceramic poppies, one for each fallen Commonwealth soldier. We then had dim sum at Ping Pong before heading to the London Palladium for Michael Flatley's incredible Irish dance performance, *Lord of the Dance*.

After visits with family we flew back to Cayman, where we stayed for only a couple of days before leaving for Boston and our OPM Harvard reunion on the 24th. We were staying at the Charles Hotel in Cambridge, very convenient for walking along the Charles riverbank in the mornings, which always made me feel like a student. We met our good friend Evelyn from Quito over lunch, followed by leisurely stroll around Cambridge, and then met up with our alumni group for dinner at Legal Seafood. The 26th September began with a walk along the Charles River, after which we had lunch at the Harvard Club. This was followed by a lecture on a new type of currency, called Bitcoin, which few of us could understand, even though two undergraduates went to great lengths to explain its technicalities. Our group had dinner in a private room at the Harvest restaurant afterwards.

The Harvard and Cambridge rowing teams were practicing on the river during our walk the next morning, which was entertaining, and then we had lunch with our friend and fellow alumnus John Robertson and his wife Barbara. We surprised them with a gift of an album of photos that Viv had collated of our time together on *The World* and at their home in Great Camanoe. John is an inventor, as I've already described, and was currently working on a project to provide safe water for the world. Our group then gathered at the Charles Hotel for a tour of Lexington and Concord as part of an educational talk about the 1775 War of Independence. Boston residents and reunion organisers Gale and Ken Nill entertained us for dinner at their home, and we discussed plans for our next reunion in Chile.

On 28th September we drove to Newton to stay with Igor and Irina, where we always felt at home, and enjoyed Irina's Russian cooking for dinner. Whilst there, I began writing an article about CNCF's 30th anniversary. Our workout routines took place over the next few days, with Igor, as usual, modifying them to suit our current needs. On 2nd October, following our workout, we were invited by Igor's friend, Ben Zander, the conductor of the Boston Philharmonic Orchestra and of the Youth Orchestra, to a practice performance for an upcoming concert in November. It was a great experience to meet and talk with some of the orchestra's multi-talented musicians. Benjamin Zander's famous quote is applicable to more than just music: 'The conductor of an orchestra doesn't make a sound, he depends for his power on his ability to make other people powerful.'

A good part of October was spent away from home. By the 12th, I was off to Nassau for Baha Mar meetings with the developers and China Exim and contractors, and on the 14th I flew to Panama for meetings in Punta Bocas about the Casi Cielo project. I took advantage of being there on a Sunday, by taking a trip through the Panama Canal. I stayed in Miami until the 23rd, when I flew to Toronto for the Dispute Resolution Board Foundation AGM and awards. I took the opportunity to meet with RLB's Canada associate, Joe Pendlebury, and discussed the possibilities of co-operating on Caribbean projects together, particularly given the amount of funding coming to our region from the Canadian banks.

On 2nd November, in London once again, we had a dim sum lunch with Adam Wu at Ping Pong restaurant in Soho, where we exchanged gifts: we gave him a Tortuga Rum cake and he gave us some very refined green tea. On 3rd November, I attended the World Travel Market at the Excel Centre to experience what travel experts were promoting on a global basis, and to compare these promotions with the offerings from our Caribbean region. Back at 62 QGM, I interviewed Juan Soto for the role of Project Manager of the Casi Cielo project in Panama.

I flew to Punta Cana, in the Dominican Republic, for a RLBC board meeting on 11th November. This was followed by the CHICOS conference on 13th and 14th November, where I spoke on a panel about Public Private Partnerships and in what way they could assist, particularly with reference to infrastructure projects in the region. Tiger Wu, of China Construction Americas, was in attendance and still interested in looking at a hotel project in Playa Grande, so we took a helicopter from the Hard Rock hotel car park to the north coast, to view it. At the conference I was introduced to Michell Vargas by George Spence and we had a good discussion about projects, particularly those requiring Spanish speaking expertise. Although I didn't know it at the time, this was to be the start of a long-lasting relationship, with Michell becoming part owner and Managing Director of BCL, and an outstanding support and friend. I have indeed been blessed to have, as part of my life, introductions to people such as Michell and Alan Veeran, who possess unique qualities of calm, easy-going personalities, skill, knowledge, honesty and willingness to assist in any way, and at any time, without question. These are qualities that you come across only occasionally in life, and even more rarely in business.

On 17th November I was in Panama for meetings in Punta Bocas, and then for further meetings on Casi Cielo on the 19th and 20th. Juan Soto had come to Panama for a familiarisation tour, and Brian Martin had by this time also joined our Panama team. Brian, Juan and I enjoyed dinner together on 21st November and on the 23rd I flew to Nassau for two days of meetings with CCA and China Exim about progress issues. I returned to Cayman for the Gimistory storytelling festival, which we held in the Callaloo orchard on Sunday 30th November.

Viv, being the super keen and excellent gardener that she is, enjoys her membership in the Garden Club, and so we were able to begin celebrating the Christmas season by attending their Christmas dinner on 4th December before leaving to ski in Alta from 5th–15th December. On the 9th we celebrated our nineteenth wedding anniversary there, greeted by a bluebird day, great snow and lunch at Rustler Lodge of superbly cooked salmon and Argyle Pinot Noir 2012, which was delicious, and made more so as it was on the house! For dinner, we made spaghetti Bolognese, which we enjoyed with Côtes du Rhône and Andy Williams on the Decca Wi-Fi playing the anniversary waltz, to which we danced in the living room.

We celebrated my sixty-ninth birthday on the 10th with an egg white omelette and champagne for breakfast, followed by sorting out a few work issues in Panama, lunch at home, and then ten runs, after which we had dinner at the Shallow Shaft restaurant in Alta of kale salad and divers' scallops, roasted lamb, and iron-roasted chicken over a bed of polenta, with a 2009 Gigondas.

On the 11th we drove down to Salt Lake City after a day of skiing, to take our chances at securing tickets for the Morman Tabernacle Choir Christmas Concert at the new convention centre. We were queuing in the standby lane and Viv, in conversation with a member of the family next to us, once again happened to mention that I was the chairman of the Cayman National Cultural Foundation. Fortunately, I had a business card in my wallet. Viv gave this to him, he left our group, and – lo and behold – came back with two tickets! It was an incredible show, in which the Muppets took centre stage, and the Mormon Tabernacle Choir and Orchestra performed beautifully for the audience.

We returned to Cayman on 16th December, in time to welcome our niece, Anne-Marie, with her children, Geena and Louis, to join us for the Christmas season. A few days later we chartered a boat to take them to the world-famous Stingray City, which they thoroughly enjoyed. On the 19th we assembled the BCL team for Christmas lunch to thank them for a great 2014 and on the 22nd Angela Morgan arrived for our annual catch-up, bringing with her the sprig of Christmas holly which we looked forward to each year. Our link with Angela goes back a long way as she was our travel agent. One can image the hiccups we ran into with all the travelling we did. Angela was available 24/7 for our needs – just a wonderful person.

On 23rd December we entertained Bobby Nunes and sister Pat, and Cissy Delapenha for lunch at Callaloo, which was a wonderful opportunity for Anne-Marie and children to interact with some of our most colourful Caymanian friends. For Christmas lunch at Callaloo we enjoyed the company of Erik and Mary Monsen, along with Anne-Marie and Geena and Louis, playing the traditional game of croquet before sitting down to dine.

On Boxing Day, we were invited to Henry and Marcia's house at Caribbean Paradise for dinner, where we sampled some of Henry's delicious Guyanese food. It took him pretty much the whole day to prepare, but it was certainly worth the effort from our point of view.

We had enjoyed a fabulous time with Anne-Marie and her children, visiting all those places we rarely saw when there were no guests. But, sadly, all good things come to an end, and on the 27th they left our warm Caymanian sunshine to fly back to the cold UK winter. We had not had lunch with Patricia Bradley for some time, so she visited Callaloo for lunch with Sue Adams, and we rounded out a great year by holding our now traditional, 'Do Drop In', at Callaloo on New Year's Eve. Afterwards I cooked dinner, which we ate while enjoying the fireworks from the pool cabana.

2015

'Learn as if you will live forever, live like you will die tomorrow.'
Mahatma Gandhi

For Mini Warehouse Two, we began the year with plans for an exciting new development at the rear of our Greenery development on West Bay Road. As we had a large rear car-parking area, we'd had the idea of building over that space to provide two further stories of climate-controlled storage. We met with architect John Doak and Alan Veeran as construction manager, to discuss what the challenges of such a development might be. At the same time Viv and I had noted that in 2015 we would have what Viv calls 'one of those special functions' which happen every five years: in this case we would be celebrating our twentieth wedding anniversary and my seventieth birthday! So we wrote to Mark Green in Australia, asking him to begin working on the design for invitations, bookmarks, gift scrolls, menus, etc. I had come across a wonderful poem by Samuel Ullman, called *Youth is not a time of life – it is a state of mind*, and this formed the core message of the celebration.

On the RLBC work front, we were looking at issues pertaining to the delivery of the Park Hyatt Hotel in St Kitts, which had an interesting financing model: the provision of a St Kitts passport with the purchase of a room. On 13th January, Charles Leonard, Jerry Katz and I held a conference to determine the best way forward. I then flew to Nassau for a meeting with Shao Di, from China Exim, to discuss progress on the Baha Mar project. With the opening scheduled for 27th March 2015 and reservations having been taken, progress towards this date was now more critical than ever.

Viv and I flew to Phoenix on the 22nd for me to attend the RLB USA board meetings and update them about the work we were doing in the Caribbean. In the meantime, Viv made enquiries about local attractions and was fortunate enough to visit Paolo Soleri's studio (he had been a student of Frank Lloyd Wright) where she bought a wind chime bell with a beautiful sound that now hangs on the *Cordia* tree outside the kitchen window. She also found a lovely silver turtle pendant, which she wears often. People frequently comment on it, particularly given it is so representative of the Cayman Islands.

Following our board meeting we had a team dinner which was held al fresco, during which I found it interesting that, although we were in the middle of the Arizona desert, it was nevertheless cold at night. The outdoor overhead gas heaters used by restaurants are inherently unsatisfactory because they cook the top of one's head while leaving one's back chilly. Viv and I decided to visit Canyon Ranch Spa for four days, and so took the shuttle to Tucson and checked in. It was a fabulous experience, with very focussed heathy eating and cooking classes, water exercise utilising Igor's programmes – he is sometimes in residence at the ranch – as well as water colour painting, star gazing, drumming and yoga. As was to be expected, there was no wine, but we noticed that a supermarket just outside the spa had a superb collection of fine quality wines on the shelves. We assumed some guests must shop there! On 28th January, we checked out from Canyon Ranch and took their limo to stay with our good friend Sallie Naylor for a couple of days to catch up with all her news and see her two cats, which she took for walks in a baby pram.

We were back in Cayman on the 30th, and on 1st February I flew to Panama for meetings on Casi Cielo, and then to Nassau on the 7th, for Baha Mar meetings with Shao Di, Tom Dunlap, Tiger Wu and Daniel Liu of CCA to yet again discuss progress.

We left for our annual Aspen ski trip on 13th February, and were met at Eagle Vail airport by Jimmy and Cynthia Nowery. We stopped at their favourite store, Costco, on the way back to their home in Mariposa, where Jimmy once again threatened to put up a plaque identifying 'our' room because we had stayed there so often. We skied our favourite spots in Aspen until the 19th, including Snowmass, Ajax, and Aspen Highlands. On the 20th, we drove to Vail, and checked into the Sonnenalp, with a cosy log fire in our room, and skied the familiar Vail slopes until the 25th, when we returned to Cayman to meet up with Mort, Jan and Kay, who were visiting Cayman until 17th March.

Cayfest was underway when we got back, and on the 26th we held CNCF's Arts Awards celebration, 'Dress for Culture'. Subsequently our cultural extravaganza 'Red Sky at Night' was held in the grounds of the Harquail Theatre, with open-air performances and artisans displaying their wares at stalls set up throughout the property.

CNCF had just celebrated its thirtieth anniversary, and I said in the welcome programme for Cayfest:

> We at CNCF have just celebrated our thirtieth anniversary and what a rich and rewarding journey it has been, with witness to our work evident in so many activities and places throughout the Islands. And so it is with great pleasure that I welcome you to Cayfest, now in its twenty first year, showcasing the diversity of our cultural talents and demonstrating those things that make us uniquely Caymanian. Of course, any country's culture is not static or changeless. On the contrary, it is in a constant state of flux, influencing and being influenced by other cultures. A country's culture therefore reflects its history, mores, institutions and attitudes, its social movements, conflicts and struggles. At the same time, it is dynamic and continually evolving. And so the Cayfest line up this year mirrors the development of our multicultural community, which now includes more than 130 nationalities and to reflect this we are presenting the fourth year of Dress For Culture Day to raise awareness of the diversity of our society and, as importantly, to raise funds for CNCF's many youth programmes including Young At Arts, Young Image Makers, Summer Arts Camp and Grants for the Arts. Yet again the Red Sky at Night Festival will transform the Harquail centre stage into a celebration of music, dance, storytelling, arts & crafts, film, and of course, delicious Caymanian food! I wish to thank our hardworking and dedicated staff, our volunteers and particularly our sponsors for making Cayfest possible and continuing the tradition of showcasing all that is Caymanian for the enjoyment of all.
>
> Please enjoy!!!!

On 1st March, I flew to Anguilla to look at several projects there for our client, Brent Woodson, who kindly provided accommodation in a rather spectacular house there. As I had noted during an earlier visit, the Anguilla airport was somewhat constrained due to a sharp drop off at one end of the runway, with houses at the other end, so extending it presented some problems. These might potentially be resolved by the possible privatisation of its operation, which we were reviewing, particularly in light of the UK's privatisation of airports under the BAA. On 4th March I left Anguilla for Panama, where I had meetings on Casi Cielo and attended to staffing matters there. I then flew up to Nassau on the 7th for three days of meetings with Gordon Glen, Tiger Wu, Tom Dunlap and China Exim, as progress to completion was not looking any more promising. Leaving Nassau on the 10th, I flew to Montego Bay to attend the Jamaica Investment Forum for two days before getting back to Cayman.

Viv and I travelled to London a week later, where I went to get my passport renewed the next day. This happens rather more often than is normal, because I travel so much that the blank pages quickly fill with immigration stamps. In the evening, we had cocktails at QGM with the RLBC directors. The guest of honour was the Cayman Premier, Alden McLaughlin, who came with his team. Famously, as Viv often reminds me, I served him his favourite scotch in a crystal glass that had a big chip in it! We then all enjoyed dinner at Baglioni's restaurant, located at the top of Gloucester Road, so an easy walk from QGM.

The next day we held an RLBC board meeting and then enjoyed the annual Caribbean Council cocktail party at the House of Lords, followed by dinner with the RLBC directors at Mr Chow's. On 25th March, I attended a Caribbean Council advisory board meeting, and the next day my brother Rob and Jenna invited us to have lunch at Cliveden. There, Julia Fellowes gave a presentation – she is the daughter of Julian Fellowes, who wrote the script and was executive producer for the hit TV series *Downton Abbey*.

We were making good progress with the plans for the self-storage facility at the rear of the Greenery, and applied to Butterfield, our bankers, for construction and long-term finance. We have enjoyed a long, excellent relationship with them since our company was founded, and continue to do so to this day.

In early April there were more meetings in Nassau with CCA and China Exim, and with Casi Cielo after that. This time I took advantage of being in Panama to visit Colon, at the Caribbean end of the Panama Canal, which is a town very different and far less developed than Panama City on the Pacific end. I met with Juan Soto, RLBC's project manager on the Casi Cielo development a few weeks later in Miami, while I was there to attend the CHRIS

(Caribbean Hotel and Resort Investment Summit) conference on 'Emerging Markets'. Moses Kirkconnell, Cayman Islands Minister of Tourism, presented 'Opportunities in the Cayman Islands'. On 30th April we entertained Moshe Levy (one of the investors in Casi Cielo) and his wife Tela, for a most enjoyable lunch at Zuma, and then Viv and I returned to Cayman.

On 4th May, I flew to Punta Bocas for a Casi Cielo design charette with the architects, taking a boat to the project site the next day. On the 10th, I left Panama and once again flew to Nassau for meetings with China Exim, Tiger Wu from CCA, and Tom Dunlap for Baha Mar. Despite numerous promises to add additional resources and management, progress remained inadequate to meet the proposed completion date which would enable the resort to open. The contractor complained about design changes and tardy responses to information requests, while the developer quietly voiced concerns about a possible 'conspiracy' to delay completion. We completed a comprehensive site walk, before I flew back to Cayman for further discussions with Butterfield about our finance application for the Greenery, and to conduct annual reviews for the BCL staff.

Viv and I had long wanted to visit Napa Valley for a tasting tour for comparison with our own Carabella wine production, so we flew to San Francisco on 17th May and checked into the historic Fairmont Hotel. The next day we visited Fisherman's Wharf, lunching at a cosy Italian restaurant, where Viv struck up a conversation with the waiter, who was from Northern Ireland and who had sadly lost his family in the Pan Am Lockerbie plane crash. On 19th May, we visited Golden Gate Park – taking two buses to get there – and lunched at the Herzog & de Meuron designed De Young Museum, with an excellent dinner later at Acquerello, a restaurant with two Michelin stars.

On the 20th we rented a car and drove to Napa Valley, where we checked into the White House, a charming boutique Victorian building set in two acres of manicured grounds. We enjoyed lunch at the Ox Bow, and then took advantage of the White House's bonus of an evening wine and appetiser reception before going out to dinner at Angèle, which served simple but tasty French cuisine, on the banks of the Napa River. The next day we began our wine tasting. We first visited Domaine Carneros, to taste some excellent Pinots, followed by lunch at Bottega in Yountville, after which we went to a tasting at Opus One. They had built their own winery close to Mondavi, where I had initially tasted the Opus One wine whilst on the Great Chefs of France course back in 1981. The Winery's architecture was unique – essentially it is built into the earth – and the wines we tasted were rich and rounded. As the Opus One website states in the words of Baron Philippe de Rothschild: 'Wine is born, then it lives. But it never dies, in man it lives on.' The words of Robert Mondavi are also applicable: 'Wine to me is a passion. It's family and friends. It's warmth of heart and generosity of spirit' – though in this case, at $45 for a small taste, one needs to be very passionate about it!

On the 22nd we visited the Stags Leap winery and then went to Villa Ragazzi, one of the few wineries planting the Sangiovese grape varietal, where they produce a rich and intense red wine and also a good rosé. We purchased several bottles to bring back to Cayman, and took a bottle to one of our favourite restaurants, Ragazzi, for them to try. In Napa we lunched on excellent tapas at Zuzu, then boarded the Wine Train for dinner, which was unique and most enjoyable. We decided the next day that we would visit Calistoga for a mud bath, mineral tub and massage at the slightly sleazy-looking Golden Haven Spa. It was good for us, however, given our tasting routine of the previous few days.

We drove back into San Francisco on 24th May, and lunched on outstanding tapas at Coqueta, on the Embarcadero, before catching a flight to Los Angeles Airport to meet Basil and Sammy for dinner at the airport Hilton, before catching the flight to Tahiti. We arrived there at 5am and took a small plane to Raiatea, and then to Bora Bora, where a boat picked us up and delivered us to the Four Seasons Hotel. After checking in, we changed clothes and chilled on the beach after our long journey, then enjoyed lunch at the Sunset Bar, followed by a Polynesian dinner.

We easily drifted into a relaxed daily routine of late lunch, washed down with a well-chilled rosé. We were in Bora Bora, at this particular hotel, to investigate the construction of their overwater bungalows – and in particular the electrical and mechanical servicing – which we were researching for the Casi Cielo project in Punta Bocas. This involved getting into the water and taking photos of the underside of the bungalow floor. This was a seemingly simple task, except for the fact that the lagoon's fast-moving tidal flow meant I had to swim with one hand and hold the camera above my head with the other. The hotel provided a jet ski that patrolled the area around the bungalows to rescue honeymooning guests who would often decide to go for a swim, only to quickly find themselves tens of yards away from where they'd entered the water. Another interesting feature of the over-water bungalows' design, was the use of Perspex panels in the floor to provide daylight, which was reflected off the white sand sea floor. This design solution made up for the lack of windows in the walls. The use of these was restricted because over the water there was no possibility of providing privacy from neighbouring bungalows with screening vegetation.

Away from the currents of the main lagoon, Viv and I both tried paddle boarding – a first for both of us – with indifferent success. We were very well looked after by the staff, including Michael Volk, the manager, his HR assistant, Ewa, as well as the facilities manager who highlighted a number of specific maintenance challenges that we could review in the design of Casi Cielo. We were graciously invited to the manager's cocktail party, where he served fine Bollinger champagne. On 29th May, the boat carried us to the airport to catch our Air Tahiti flight to Tahiti, where we stayed at the Intercontinental, with dinner at Le Coco. On the 30th we took the ferry from Papeete to Mo'orea, Tahiti's sister island, and while talking with locals soon learnt about their Polynesian philosophy, *aita pea pea*, meaning 'not to worry' – or, as we say in the Caribbean, 'No problem mon'. Other words we learnt were, *māuruuru* – thank you, and *nana* – goodbye, which we said as we left on the Air Tahiti Nui flight to Los Angeles, and then home.

And so back to where this story started. The situation with the Baha Mar completion was not improving. Some five years into construction and as mid-2015 approached, after various project delays the project was, at best, struggling to reach completion. Reservations had been accepted for the opening, though they were unlikely to be honoured, and the possibility of opening several floors in the high-rise towers was discussed, while construction would continue on the remaining areas.

Moreover, acceleration costs would require additional funding. Proposals were made that included partial funding from China Exim and China Construction America (CCA), the contractor, and from the developer, Baha Mar Ltd. Accordingly, a meeting was scheduled in Beijing for the second week in June. I arrived there on the morning of the 8th, and the following day met with China Exim and Allen and Overy, their attorneys, to discuss the terms of the guarantees to cover the additional proposed borrowing.

On 10th June, we were summoned to a 9am meeting in the boardroom of China Exim bank. A vast boardroom table accommodated over thirty participants, with many additional advisors positioned in rows behind them. I was seated at the table directly across from the Bank's President, Mr Lui. Around the table were various bank officials, Sarkis Izmirlian and his development team, as well as Tiger Wu and his contracting team. Behind me sat our site manager, Gordon Glen, and our attorney, Jerry Katz.

The discussions were conducted either in Mandarin, with translation, or in English, also translated. The meeting commenced with representatives from each department of China Exim bank affirming they were an honourable institution and had acted appropriately – statements that took some time. I found this curious, until I was later advised that the two silent individuals seated in a corner were reportedly from the Central Government. There followed a presentation by the Baha Mar development team, explaining the causes of the delays and cost overruns and attributing these to the contractors. They proposed that, with a further injection of some US$200 million, the hotel could be completed and opened within a matter of months.

The proposal called for a funding contribution of US$100 million from China Exim Bank, US$50 million from CCA, the contractor, and US$50 million from Baha Mar Ltd., the developer. CCA then responded, blaming the delays and cost overruns on Baha Mar as the developer, but ultimately agreeing that the additional funds would enable the development's completion.

At this point, the President of the Bank looked directly at me, and asked in Mandarin if this was possible, to which I replied – perhaps too softly – 'impossible'. This was translated as *ke neng*, and I was surprised to see everyone smiling and thumbs up.

I was then asked, again, if completion was possible within the claimed period, and I said a little more forcefully, 'not possible', which was then translated as *bu ke neng*, which understandably changed the mood of the entire meeting. After further discussions we were all requested to convene again, to see how we could progress and develop a mutual agreement on cost and time to complete, and attempt to agree on the details of the guarantees. We worked for several days, arriving at various proposals, before I left Beijing to return to Cayman on 13th June.

Because of the Beijing meetings, I had sadly missed Jimmy and Cynthia Nowery, whom we had invited to Cayman to celebrate Cynthia's birthday and in some small way return their lavish hospitality over so many years. We were able to enjoy brunch together at the Ritz, on the 14th, for a belated celebration.

A few days later, I was contacted by Sharon Roulstone, one of the Executors of Mrs Harquail's Estate, and advised of a further donation to CNCF. Of course I was delighted, but first there were some complications about other bequests, and I undertook to assist Sharon in any way I could. The next day we held CNCF's Young Image Maker's awards at the Harquail.

On 21st June I travelled to Panama for several days' meetings on Casi Cielo with Alfredo, one of the principals, Colin Barcant from Trinidad, who was advising on some proposed docks, and my friend John Lancet, from HVS in Miami, who was preparing an appraisal of the property. We also discussed progress with Pablo, the owners' representative, and with Juan Soto and Nedson, from RLBC's team, before I returned to Cayman on the 25th.

On 29th June we were shocked by the following Press Release:

Me, Natalie Urquhart, Sir Alden McLaughlin, Minister of Culture, and Patrick Broderick at the IFACCA World Summit in Newcastle in June 2006.

Mort & Jan at Viv's 60th birthday celebration at the Waterside Inn in Bray in June 2006.

Viv and I on the roof of the Devil's Nose train in Ecuador in July 2006.

In the vineyard in August 2006 at the 10th anniversary celebration of Carabella.

Inchinnan Farm on the banks of the Willamette River where Jill and Peter McDonald have been such gracious hosts over many years – and "yes" as Peter said "Old McDonald really did have a farm".

Our great team of dancers and musicians outside our hotel in Port of Spain, Trinidad in September 2006 for Carifesta IX.

In my element in 'the greatest snow on earth' in Alta in December 2006.

For years we heard about the long construction of the CERN particle accelerator. We were finally able to descend into it in February 2007, right before it started operation.

Viv and I at the summit of Sydney Harbour Bridge in March 2008, after passing our breathalyser test.

The Haddon Rig shearing shed that was converted into bunk space for the Harvard OPM reunion in July 1990.

Mort and I at his birthday lunch. He was an incredible friend and mentor over so many years.

Swanky, Cayman's traditional kitchen band on the staircase at Callaloo in June 2008.

A play on London Underground's regular announcement to 'Mind The Gap'. The invitation was for our fundraising dinner at Callaloo to help fill the gap in the funds needed to complete the construction of the National Gallery.

Rasta Richard Hart at the Garrison Barbados horse track. A man whose face reveals his great character.

In February 2009 we tracked down my ancestors who had settled in Wellington New Zealand.

The Bould family home in Wellington.

On the Fox Glacier New Zealand, but no skiing this time!

Viv at the Bullet train station enroute to Kyoto, managing the luggage!

I'm in our tub at Tawaraya Ryokan, Kyoto, in March 2009. Folding 6'3" into it was hard but the unfolding to get out was even harder.

A mattress would have been nice after a 12-hour flight, but the floor had to do.

The 6 Musketeers, George & Boopie McInnis, Jimmy & Cynthia Nowery, and Viv and I.

Cissy Delapenha and I at Callaloo in August 2009.

Cissy with me in a pensive mood.

Viv with Winnie Mandela whilst I was at the IFACCA World Summit in JoBurg.

Morgan DaCosta receiving his award at the 25th Anniversary of CNCF in October 2009.

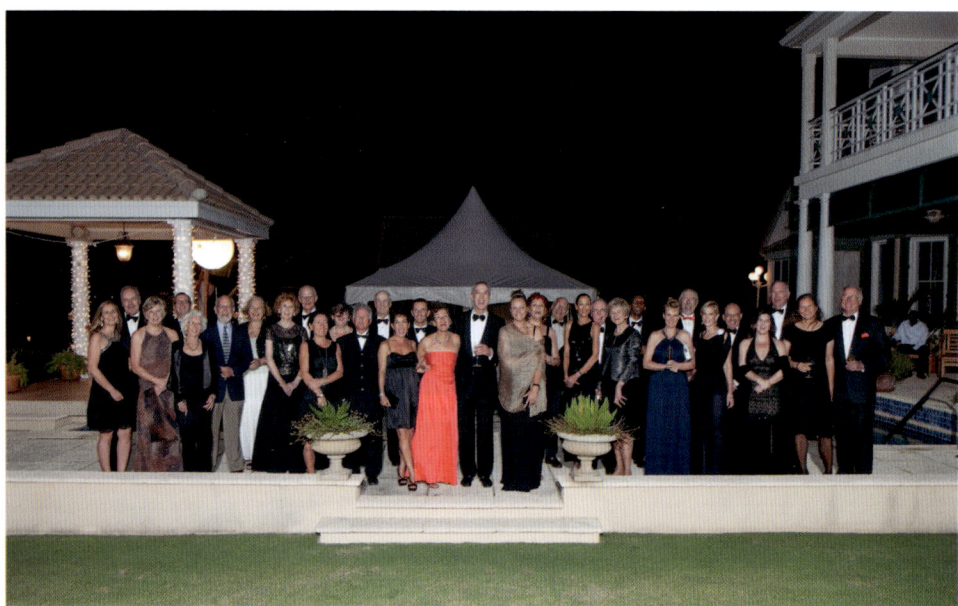

Our guests on the lawn at Callaloo for my 65th birthday and our 15th wedding anniversary.

Cayman's world-famous Stingray City.

During our extensive world travels we have seen Bob Marley everywhere. Here he is in India in October 2011.

Organising meetings in the heavy traffic in Beijing requires a lot of skill. Here Adam Wu deftly manages 3 telephones at once.

A typical delicious but lengthy dinner in Beijing in May 2013.

Igor and I during his birthday celebration at Callaloo.

Baha Mar in Nassau now that it has been completed.

What a hunbling experience being awarded my MBE for cultural preservation and development in Cayman by Her Majesty the Queen Elizabeth II in November 2012.

The staff at Da Mario around the corner from the Doll's House in South Kensington.

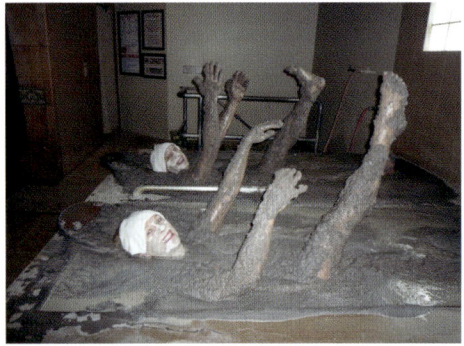

Viv and I in the mud bath in Calistoga, California in May 2015.

Me, Viv, Marcia & Henry Muttoo at an 'Arts in the Orchard' performance at Callaloo in November 2015.

Cayman Folk Singers on stage in the Orchard at Callaloo for my 70th birthday celebrations.

Viv's all time favourite ABBA song is Dancing Queen – here we are on stage at nephew Edward's 50th birthday party at Palac Wlosien with an ABBA lookalike group – Viv was in heaven.

The July 2017 running order for Carifesta.

At Nagala Game Reserve, stuck in the mud. We had to get out of the Land Rover, which is strictly forbidden, to free it.

Deepak Chopra signing a copy of *Ageless Body – Timeless Mind* in June 2018. Of his many books, it is one of my favourites.

Viv and I frequently host Girl Guiding at Callaloo for a wonderful evening of entertainment. Here we are on the lawn in front of Annahavil.

Sopris, near Aspen, which Viv and I climbed in July 2018.

On safari at Bateleur Camp.

A lion on the same safari.

The talking stick commands silence in the Masai village, but the one we have now in the Callaloo gym seems to have lost its potency.

Relaxing in front of the fire at Sugarplum in Alta, after a perfect day's skiing.

After the festivities for the 50-year celebration, we were set for an *Allura* trip to Stingray City.

In March 2019 we celebrated my 50 years in the Caribbean – following an amusing skit written by Henry Muttoo and Matt Brown about my arrival in Jamaica I was set to have a good time on the dance floor.

In Borneo, in April 2019 we spent the night with the headhunters in their longhouse, kept our heads on our shoulders, and by the time we were up, the ladies had already done the morning's laundry.

Viv shares a meal with the family in the headhunters' longhouse.

A welcome stop for lunch on the river after our headhunter experience.

Me on the summit of Kilimanjaro, in August 2019.

Kilimanjaro was followed by a climb in February 2020 to the summit of Pico Duarte, the Caribbean's highest mountain, with Michell and Beatrix. I descended on a mule, sparing my knees but not my rear end.

BCL's outstanding Managing Director Michell Vargas 'Reaching New Heights' for our clients on the summit of Pico Duarte with wife Beatrix and yours truly.

Jamaican ingenuity tackles anything, including COVID immunisation.

The humour of *Rundown* 2021 was a welcome relief after COVID.

Dance companies have continued to develop and flourish in Cayman. Here are the Dream Chasers in June 2021.

Alan Veeran, BCL's multi-talented director, with wife Claudia on the Camino di Compostela with Viv and me.

Sarah Lamb, one of Igor's clients, invited us backstage in the Royal Opera House after her lead performance in Mayerling in October 2022.

Our favourite of René's sayings – here with a Bajan twist.

After a rigorous early morning workout at the Garrison Horse Track in Barbados, the grooms bathe the horses in the sea.

Our beloved Puddie at Christmas 2022.

Viv's 77th birthday outing with friends on the *Allura*, to Stingray City.

A stay in Lady Astor's Suite at Cliveden was Viv's early birthday treat in April 2023.

Walkup Group photo at Callaloo, June 2023.

Patrick Stainton – BCL's ever improving talent.

During the Barrow canal trip in August 2023 with Alan and Jenny Foster. It needed plenty of muscle from Alan to work the manual locks.

From the Mountains to the Sea – me on the trail.

At the park entrance at the start of my Aconcagua ascent in January 2024 to raise money for the Red Cross.

With Cayman Island's Premier and Minister to receive my Legacy Builder Award in January 2025.

29th June 2015 PRNewswire – Sarkis Izmirlian Chairman and Chief Executive Officer of Baha Mar Ltd., the developer of the Baha Mar resort announces that in order to complete construction and open Baha Mar as soon as possible, Baha Mar Ltd., and entities associated with it, are voluntarily undertaking the process of Chapter 11 under the US Bankruptcy Code.

The Board of Directors has determined that due to the financial consequences of the repeated delays by the general contractor, and the resulting loss of revenue, the Chapter 11 process is the best path to provide the time to put in place a viable capital structure and working relationships to complete construction and successfully open Baha Mar. The voluntary Chapter 11 filing has been made in the US Bankruptcy Court for the District of Delaware. Baha Mar Ltd. will be filing an application in the Supreme Court of the Commonwealth of the Bahamas seeking approval of the US court orders.

As might be imagined, there followed a flurry of telephone calls discussing how to proceed.

On 2nd July, Viv and I left Cayman for Miami, where I met with Philip Parker about FF&E budgeting for the Casi Cielo project, then caught the evening flight on American to Heathrow, once again enjoying great service from the crew, who were friends of Mark Welch. Edward and Gillian drove us from the airport to the White Swan pub in Twickenham, where we knew Igor was going to be with Irina and Nellie, to surprise him for his birthday. He was delighted, though could hardly believe his eyes, and we had a fun evening with them and two of their Russian friends.

In London, through the Caribbean Council, we had the opportunity to meet the British Ambassador to Cuba to discuss potential opportunities for RLBC there, in the context of our experiences during the pre-contract work we had done on the Monte Baretto Hotel, back in 2009.

On 8th July the Caribbean Council held a meet and greet session with the new Prime Minister of St Kitts, Timothy Harris, who had been elected in February. I had the opportunity to discuss various projects we were reviewing, as well as talk about the Frigate Bay infrastructure project I had worked on back in 1969 – when Prime Minister Harris had been five years old!

Viv and I visited the Apollo theatre to see *The Audience*, an excellent play by British playwright Peter Morgan, about the weekly meetings between Queen Elizabeth II (superbly played by Kristin Scott Thomas) and her Prime Ministers. On 12th July, we watched the Wimbledon men's finals, and in the evening booked a box at the Royal Albert Hall to see Karl Jenkins's *The Armed Man* in a Mass for Peace, with a huge choir. We peeked around the corner of our box to see Josianne, our neighbour, in the adjoining one. What a coincidence, in such a huge theatre!

We had tried to contact Maurice and Jo on several occasions, and found out they were no longer in their house in Hasker Street, Chelsea, but in Acton Care Centre. So, on the 19th we went to visit them there. They were in good spirits, but it was somewhat sad to see them in this environment after the years of seeing them in so many fun settings. We then went to Mort and Jan's 'Chaucer House' with Kay, Edward and Gillian, for an excellent full roast lunch, with plenty of gravy for Mort – he typically emptied the whole gravy boat.

We had worked with John Doak, the architect of Callaloo, some years ago to create the orchard and performance space where we had originally intended to build a tennis court. John had produced some excellent plans of the proposals and we developed these further. We also called on the expert talent of the artistic director, Henry Muttoo, to make sure the sight lines and lighting were properly taken into account so we could make the very best use of this wonderful new facility for the events to be staged there. Eventually, we agreed a design for Callaloo Orchard's gates with the great artisan metal worker Karoly. Now, with the big 20/70 celebration coming up in December, and with the Callaloo Orchard nearing completion, we enlisted the help of Howie, who worked with Charles Gregory at Hopscotch Productions, to check out what equipment we needed for lights and sound, particularly given the exterior environment, about which he gave us excellent advice.

I had an upcoming trip to Panama planned for Casi Cielo and I wanted to celebrate the progress we had made on the project, so I ordered a case of Carabella for us to enjoy at an in-office party. Viv and I left Cayman on 6th August, and checked into my usual accommodation at the Hilton. The next day we walked four miles along the Costa Cintera, a beltway that runs along the Panama Bay and includes gardens, bike lanes, sports fields, exercise stations, lookouts and traditional restaurants.

That afternoon, at the offices of the Casi Cielo developer, Grupo Imalca, we held the party. There were many complimentary remarks about the quality of the Carabella, and afterwards we enjoyed dinner of veal stew and Rioja at Las Clementinas in Casco Viejo, the old town. We took the Panama Canal tour the next day, through the locks from Gatun Lake, with lunch on board. The boats passing through the locks on the Canal have minimal space and are pulled through using small locomotives on both sides of the canal.

On 9th August Nedson and Juan drove Viv and me to the San Blas Islands in the Caribbean, south of Panama towards Columbia, where we had a great time on the beach. Unfortunately, Juan drove on the way back and we were caught by a speed trap. The officer came up and started to issue Juan with a ticket. Nedson got out of the car, beckoned the policeman over and entered into a rigorous conversation with him. Then he returned to the car while the policeman simply walked away. We asked Nedson what had happened, and he just said it was solved. That evening, we returned to Casco Viejo and the Bistro Nani for dinner with Nedson, Juan, Pablo and Elia, his wife, and Alfredo and his wife, to feast on chicken brochettes, meat and vegetables, together with Mâcon Villages, and Cousiño Macul from the Maipo Valley in Chile. Viv returned to Cayman on the 10th while I stayed on until 13th August to complete further work on the project and meet with a second potential client, Verde Azul, who both developed and invested in a diverse range of market segments in Panama. Back in Cayman, we had now completed the plans for our Greenery self-storage project and submitted plans to the Central Planning Authority for approval.

At the end of August, Viv and I travelled to Aspen, once again staying with the Nowerys. On the 30th Viv and I hiked the Hunter Creek Smugglers Loop, with a start elevation of some eight thousand feet and a gain of one thousand one hundred feet. We stopped for our picnic lunch by the side of the river and as I got up afterwards, I unfortunately twisted my knee, which slowed us somewhat. As we passed several hikers on the way back, we noticed they had bells attached to their rucksacks. Viv stopped one lady to ask what they were for and got the answer that they kept bears away by warning them of the hiker's approach. Given Viv's horrible fascination with bears, I'm sure you don't need to be told that the next day we had bells fixed to our rucksacks! We had a rest day at Mariposa to give the knee a break, and on 1st September drove up to Maroon Bells for a picnic with Jimmy and Cynthia.

We were keeping our eye on the vendage time for Carabella, as we had not been for a number of years. Mike Hallock informed us that the vendage would be towards the end of September this year, so Viv and I left for Portland on the 27th. The next day we helped sort the grapes and then, as a special treat, enjoyed a great dinner hosted by Jill McDonald at the Inchinnan farm with Mike and his wife Cara, and our fellow investors, John and Judy Hammerstad.

On the 30th, we went for the crush at Union Wine, followed by a barrel tasting of our Pinot varietals. As the wine-making equipment is only used for very short periods of time, and each vendage takes place on a different date depending on the location of the vineyard, it is comparatively easy to use another winery's equipment to crush your own grapes. This is what we do at Carabella to avoid the significant expense of building our own facility. Typically, we barrel-age our Pinots for two years, keeping the different varietals separate, and then barrel-taste to determine what quantity of each varietal goes into each bottling to maintain a consistent quality and flavour profile. That is where the key skills of our winemaker come into play – and Mike is excellent in this key role. After our day of winemaking, Viv, Jill and I decided to do the Tamanawas Falls trail on Mount Hood, which is a beautiful hike of some four miles round trip along the side of the Cold Spring Creek and then to the spectacular waterfall, where we had our picnic lunch. After that we drove back to Inchinnan for a hearty steak dinner with Jamie, Jill's son, and a tasting of our current Carabella Pinot Noir.

We flew back to Miami through Dallas. After the success of the trellis *trompe l'oeil* painting in London, we had decided to paint another on the balcony wall of #10E Yacht Harbour. During this visit we continued the work, which we'd not been able to finish during our last visit. We also entertained Malcolm Butterfield at Ortanique, a Jamaican fusion restaurant in Miracle Mile owned by Norma, from Jamaica, whose cooking we had enjoyed at her restaurant, Norma's on the Patio, at Devon House. I attended KPMG's Infrastructure Conference, followed by cocktails at J.W. Marriott and dinner at Zuma, conveniently located across the street. On 6th October, Viv left Miami for Cayman, and I for Nassau – not, however, before discovering I had painted the trellis on the #10E patio out of square. This meant I had to paint over part of the design and then repaint it, which I did.

As usual, we were not home for long. Viv and I left for London on 15th October, and on the 20th we paid a visit to Maurice Cullen at the Acton retirement home, where we smuggled in a bottle of Carabella Pinot Noir for him to enjoy. Unfortunately Jo had passed away a few months before. That evening, we went to Royal Albert Hall to see the Welsh bass-baritone, Bryn Terfel, present an outstanding performance for his fiftieth birthday, accompanied by Sting and soprano Rebecca Evans, for a one-off gala.

I met with Pete Rose on the 21st to discuss a potential project to build a bridge across the Demerara River in Guyana, followed by a Caribbean Intelligence lunch at Durrants. The next day we launched our 2016 Caribbean Report, which provided key data on construction costs across the region, information and development intelligence about each island, as well as summaries of the projects RLBC were currently working on.

Viv and I then shopped at Fortnum and Mason for our traditional Christmas pudding to take back home for our 'dear friends' Christmas lunch at Callaloo. The 23rd October was a very sad day as my good friend David Bucknall had passed away. Viv and I took the train to Birmingham to attend his memorial service and then a celebration of his life at the International Convention Centre. It was good to see so many friends from over the years, including Norman Mills, who had mentored me so many years before at Gordon Britton, where I was articled. We stayed in the Copthorne Hotel and took advantage of being in Birmingham to have dinner with Mike and Doreen Johnson and their three children at the Pushkar Indian restaurant.

The official opening of Callaloo Orchard, commencing with a CNCF promotional event entitled 'Arts in the Orchard', was soon to take place, as was the big 20/70 celebration, so we met with Tom Balon, of Vigoro, to work out the timers on the landscape lights and the irrigation system. The next day we met with the performers for the 'Arts in the Orchard' production to work out schedules, and a week later we discussed music cues for the performance with Greg from Hopscotch, as well as Patrice Donalds. I also undertook a key inventory of the Carabella wines in the cellar, as these were to be featured at our 20/70 guest dinner.

On 3rd November, I met with Marcia Muttoo, together with the Premier and Deputy Governor, to discuss the formatting of 'Project Future', which was to be the National Cultural Policy for the Cayman Islands. On the 11th, I left Cayman for Puerto Rico, to participate as a speaker at CHICOS, where I moderated a panel of experts discussing the future of large scale developments in the Caribbean. This was appropriate as in some ways the focus was being led by the issues with Baha Mar and its completion. I returned to Miami on 13th November and held discussions with Parris Jordon, the Managing Director of HVS, on a large project in Antigua that we had been looking at for a number of years.

On 17th November, three days after getting back to Cayman, I left again, this time for Montego Bay, to make a presentation to the joint RICS/IPTI Summit Conference on Procurement Risks in the Caribbean. It was at this conference that I discovered that Allen and Overy, the law firm we were working with on Baha Mar, had provided advice on the Highway 2000 PPP project in Jamaica. Back in Cayman on the 20th, I met with Jennifer Ahearn and Nancy Barnard to discuss the proposed National Cultural Policy document for the Cayman Islands.

I then traveled to Panama and met with Natalia, with whom I had worked on Baha Mar and who was now advising CCA on projects in Panama. RLBC was advising Dolphin Capital, a London Stock Exchange quoted group, on various projects, one of which was Pearl Island, and so, on 26th November, we flew there to see the progress that had been made to date. I then returned to Cayman, where we held a National Gallery Board Retreat to review progress and plan the way forward.

The inaugural event at the Callaloo Orchard took place on 29th November. Some 100 guests enjoyed 'Arts in the Orchard', with performances by Ken Corsbie, Jevaughnie Ebanks, the Story Crafters telling traditional stories, Dance Unlimited, who entertained with stylistic dance moves, Matt Brown leading the fun, and Bernard McCoy – what a fabulous baptism for this celebration of our culture!

On 1st December, Henry Muttoo called to give me the sad news that Aunt Julia had passed away at the age of 106. Aunt Julia's oft-repeated saying was, 'Hard work killed no one', and she certainly lived by that adage. CNCF will always keep her memory and work alive through the work of the Cayman Islands Folk Singers and the Swanky Kitchen Band.

Our 20/70 celebration began on 3rd December with a formal black-tie dinner for eight guests at Callaloo. The following evening we hosted cocktails for some one hundred and fifteen guests, with steel pan, Tassa drummers, and dancing to Nathan's band. On 5th December, we set up a tent on the lawn for a formal dinner for thirty-nine guests, with Carabella wines, an entrée of duck breasts prepared by Sean Collins and his team from Mise en Place, and harp music by Eugenio Leon in the background. To encourage mingling, the male guests moved two places after each course, so despite the large table, everyone was able to interact with all the other guests at the table. Place cards included each guest's next seat on the back, to assist those who may have become a little confused after a few glasses of Carabella. It was great fun, and no one ended up on anyone's lap. On 6th December, we chartered the *Allura* catamaran, which sailed up to the Callaloo dock, where thirty guests were enjoying what we call a 'fizzy sharpener' and hors d'oeuvres on the lawn. We sailed out to Stingray City in the North Sound, and then to Starfish Point, for swimming, lunch and rosé. A perfect way to celebrate our twentieth year of marriage and my seventieth birthday!

We left for Salt Lake City on the 9th, picked up our rental car and drove to Little Cottonwood Canyon and Sugarplum. The day – my birthday – was cold and icy, and we skied only five runs before going in for lunch at Rustler to get warm and to catch up with the regular gang there. Afterwards, as we skied down to the rope tow, I turned on some ice and fell awkwardly onto my hip. It hurt, but I got up and was able to ski one more run before calling it a day. By the next morning my hip was very sore indeed, so we went to the Snowbird Clinic to get it X-rayed. The doctors there agreed it wasn't broken but that I should go to nearby Sandy to have an MRI, just to make sure, and get back to them on the 13th. What hurt the most was that we'd just had a perfect Alta powder snowfall, but I did not feel confident enough to ski it.

So, on 12th December, we spent the day resting at Sugarplum, with cosy log fires and a spaghetti Bolognese lunch. Back at the Snowbird Clinic on the 13th, Dr Nick announced that the MRI showed that my pelvis was fractured in two places, with a torn muscle to boot, and that there would be no more skiing for me this trip. So we returned to Sugarplum somewhat dejected, but spent the day planning an Around the World trip for February/March 2016 to console ourselves.

The next day there was more fabulous powder – twenty inches of it – which we could enjoy only vicariously, so we cooked frittata for breakfast, and spaghetti aglio e olio for lunch, and capitalised on the opportunity to research more hotels for our trip. Even more beautiful powder fell overnight, but for us there was only bacon and eggs for breakfast the next morning. Viv, most unusually, drove in the snow to replenish supplies and the cellar. On the 16th there was yet more snow, which we admired from inside until Jan, the manager of Sugarplum, kindly drove us to Rustler for dinner, where we had drinks at the bar, chatted with our friend Cathy the maître d', and met John, a nature photographer. On the 17th we called Igor for a conference to discuss the best treatment I could follow to help heal my pelvis. It has been a real blessing to have had Igor available over the years to provide the most natural solution to deal with any injury we have incurred.

That evening, Rustler kindly sent one of their guests, Matt, to pick us up for dinner there. Matt was a physicist who enjoyed British politics, so we had some lively dinner conversation. On the 18th we packed up at Sugarplum and drove to Salt Lake City, from where we left for Cayman the next day. It was good to be home, and the next day I was able to start the hip recuperation programme Igor had developed for me, directed by Dottie, in the Callaloo pool.

We held our BCL Christmas lunch on the 21st, and on the 23rd we were invited to make a proposal to cost-manage a project at Ocean Cay, in the Bahamas, for MSC Cruises. So, despite it being the festive season we were finishing the year with a bang. We enjoyed a fine Christmas lunch at Callaloo (with the Fortnum and Mason's pudding) with Erik and Mary, his son Justin and his wife Ivey, and Patricia Bradley. Angela and her mom came round to Callaloo on 29th December, and we rounded out the year on New Year's Eve with our traditional 'Do Drop In'.

2016

> *'Success is not final; failure is not fatal: It is the courage to continue that counts.'* Winston Churchill

The new year started with a flourish of activity: calls to Beijing regarding the next steps to be taken on Baha Mar; working on the proposal for the Ocean Cay project in the Bahamas; developing the business case for opening a fully-manned office in Panama in view of the work we were doing on the Casi Cielo project, and an additional assignment we were working on for China Construction Americas.

On 15th January, Viv and I left Cayman and flew to Tucson, to enjoy another few days at Canyon Ranch. We started the next day with egg white omelettes and banana bread for breakfast. The great thing about eating at Canyon Ranch was that the menus listed the calories and food values of all ingredients. This has, of course, become common in recent years. We then went to a drumming class, which was great fun, followed by a lecture from Michael Hewitt on how to keep your joints healthy. Lunch of Mongolian Salmon and Dal soup followed, and, as a complete contrast to the morning's lecture, we attended a class about Facebook for grandparents. Then at 3pm we had a workout in the pool, a stretch and relaxation class, followed at 5pm by an open 12-step recovery meeting for alcoholics – not because we needed it, but just to share with those who did.

Dinner was at Trattoria Locale at the UU bistro: white bean soup and kale, steak, mushroom, and arugula, with a desert of ice cream and blueberry tart. Time then for another lecture 'Health is in your hands', and to round out a busy day, a special Canyon Ranch massage at 9pm.

The next day, after breakfast, we entered into centring meditation, then practiced yoga for a healthy back and went to the pool for a workout using an underwater treadmill, followed by a swim. Viv then left for a private tennis lesson, and I went on to attend my Qi Gong yoga class. From 2pm to 4pm we participated in a hands-on cooking class with Michael, who gave us great tips on steaming food, and then we were able to enjoy the fruits of our labour at a late lunch. Viv and I then attended a lecture on making the most of massage, followed at 8pm by dinner at the clubhouse.

The 18th January commenced with our favourite egg white omelettes at 7am, followed by watercolour painting *en-plein-air*. Carrying on from our experience the year before, Viv painted the trees, and I tried painting the wagon in front of the UU bistro. We then participated in a two-mile walk around the Ranch, during which we learned about the different types of local cacti and birds. After lunch, we enjoyed a seaweed mask, which was something new, and then had a massage. I attended an excellent lecture entitled 'The real skinny on weight management' by Param Dedhia, while Viv attended a lecture on osteoporosis and exercise, after which we capped off the day with dinner at the clubhouse.

On the 19th, we took a two-hour bird-watching walk after breakfast, during which we spotted some thirteen varieties, then Viv left for her flight to Miami and Sebring, to visit her sister Pat. I went back to a drumming circle class, followed by an introduction to Ayurvedic yoga, where I discovered I am a Pita Dosha type. Then followed a lunch-and-learn session by chef Michael, where he demonstrated cooking Cajun shrimp with cheesy grits. After lunch I listened to an excellent lecture, 'Wake-up call: sleep for good health', again by Param Dedhia, at which I took plenty of notes to pass on to Viv. Having made the most of the day, I left Canyon Ranch and took a three-hour limo ride to Scottsdale, to prepare for a RLBC board meeting the following day. I also met up with fellow directors Mark Williamson and Stuart Stables, with his wife Gil, for an excellent dinner at the Old House in Old Scottsdale.

After getting back to Cayman, I left again on 24th January for Panama and three days of meetings on Casi Cielo, which included site visits to Punta Bocas. At the end of the month we completed and submitted the estimate for the Ocean Cay project and also finished the business case for the Panama office for submission to the global RLB board. I was back in Panama on 14th for meetings on the cost plan and market testing of our estimate for the Casi Cielo project, followed a few days later by a Casi Cielo Exco meeting. I also met with Davide Marianne about construction opportunities for his company. I got back to Cayman on 17th February, in time for a late evening call with China Exim about Baha Mar actions. We were also looking at the Viceroy Hotel construction issues in Anguilla that day.

On Saturday 20th February we met with Deanna Lookloy, at the cricket ground, to purchase some fruit trees for the Orchard at Callaloo, including a Sweetsop – this being my favourite Caribbean fruit.

I'd had an MRI of my pelvis at the end of January to see how my ski fractures were mending, and got a good report. So, on 24th February, Viv and I commenced another Around the World trip. Our first stop was Sydney, where, after catching a bit of sleep and stretching our legs in the Botanic Park, we had dinner with the RLB Sydney director, Stephen Mee, and his wife Kathryn, at Café Sydney, overlooking the Sydney Harbour Bridge. We went to the bar at the Opera House – which was one of RLB's iconic projects – finishing up at the

Garage Night Club. Our flight to Perth the next day got us in at noon – Perth is three hours behind Sydney time. We checked into the Hyatt, where we were upgraded to the Regency Club, once again caught up with some sleep, and enjoyed the hospitality of the club level facilities. We then had dinner at Coco's by the River, with Viv's cousin Peter, his wife Liz, their son Andrew and his wife Kim. Viv had not seen Peter for about thirty years, so there was a lot of catching up to do!

We walked through downtown Perth and the Swan waterfront the next day, then visited the Perth Mint to see their Million Dollar Coin. It's legal tender, with a face value of one million AUD, weighing one tonne of 99.99% pure gold. As we all know, Viv is worth much more than her weight in that precious metal, and here we were able to verify this: on weighing she clocked in at $3,925,822.64 – well undervalued, in my opinion!

On 2nd March, we walked three miles along the esplanade before catching our Qantas flight to Singapore, arriving at the Fullerton Hotel at 6pm. The Fullerton is a unique hotel, as it's been converted from the former general post office. The next morning we visited the fabulous orchid collection at the Singapore Botanic Gardens, after which we lunched with RLB's Singapore director, Winston Hauw, and his wife Margaret at the Pan Pacific Dim Sum. During our travels, it was great to connect face-to-face with the leaders of RLB's global practice. After lunch with Winston, Viv and I walked around the National Gallery – converted from the former Supreme Court building – and then visited another of RLB's iconic projects: Marina Bay Sands. Whenever the BBC transmits its Asia news feed, you see this three-towered building in the background, complete with roof top swimming pool.

On the 4th, we began organising our luggage in preparation for our trip on the Eastern and Oriental Express train. We walked to the Gardens by the Bay, which is a huge urban park that consists of an incredible series of structures and landscaping, then returned by foot to the Fullerton and checked out. Whilst in Singapore, we did not want to miss the famous Long Bar at the Raffles Hotel, so we took a taxi to enjoy lunch at their Grill, and then went to board the E & O to Bangkok – a 2,600km journey.

Once settled, we went to the bar car for a refreshing 'sharpener' of Pouilly-Fuissé. After a nap we had dinner and went to bed early. We were jolted several times during the night as the drivers changed during the trip, and yours truly slid down the mattress each time. Our Cabin Butler, Pasha, provided us with outstanding room service. We passed through Kuala Lumpur during the night, and Pasha greeted us with a *selamat datang* ('welcome' in Malay) as he brought our room service breakfast the next morning.

I am not sure what prompted me to do so, but I said to Pasha that I had always wanted to meet Sir James Sherwood, of Sea Containers fame, who had – together with his wife Shirley – revived the Venice Simplon Orient Express, and the Eastern and Oriental Express, and the Flying Scotsman in the UK. I then asked Pasha if he had ever met him. To this he replied 'Sir, he is on the train'. I asked how I could meet him, and Pasha replied, 'After dinner just look for a very large man.'

When the train stopped in Kuala Kangsar, we took an excursion to visit the Sultan's Ubudiah Royal Mosque, and then the Bamboo Palace (Istana Kenangan), built in 1926 of bamboo without a single metal nail. Then we viewed the Sultan Azlan Shah Gallery (or Istana Kata) housing the Sultan's collection of mementos and State regalia – an astonishing assemblage of personal items. Then it was back to the train for an early lunch of dim sum and fish, completed by Baron Ott rosé, followed by a civilised afternoon doze. Much refreshed, we were treated to a Thai dance performance before dinner, during which the dance forms from northeast and southern Thailand, which are markedly different both as to music and dance styles, were displayed.

Coming out from the dining room after dinner, I saw a very large man taking up the best part of a love seat. I went to him and asked if he was Sir James Sherwood, as I had always wanted to meet him. He replied that, yes, indeed he was, and introduced Viv and me to his wife, Shirley, sitting in adjacent love seat. He asked why I had wanted to meet him, to which I replied, 'Anyone who spends this amount of money refurbishing trains in such an opulent manner must have a lot of balls' – at which he laughed like a drain!

It always intrigues me, how life connects all of us as our paths cross. In 2025, I read Shirley Sherwood's autobiography *Shirley – The Life of a Botanical Adventurer* and learnt that her son, Simon, who had worked at Orient Express hotels left them and joined Elegant hotels in Barbados and engineered the sale of their chain to Marriott hotels, for whom BCL acted on their rebranding construction – small world once again!

We were woken with coffee and breakfast the next morning, and then the train took us to the 'Bridge over the River Kwai', made famous by the novel and movie. We visited the Railway Museum where the movie *The Railway Man* was made, starring Colin Firth.

We went back to the train for lunch, and reached Bangkok station some hours later, where we said goodbye to Sir James and Shirley and took a taxi to the Mandarin Oriental Hotel. I dealt with some business issues the next morning while Viv relaxed by the pool, reading *Stillness Speaks* by Eckhart Tolle, after which we enjoyed breakfast by the river. After lunch, the hotel

BMW drove us to the airport for our flight to Chang Rai, where we checked into Le Meridien.

In Chang Rai we took a boat ride to see Somluk Pantiboon, a ceramic artist, in north Chang Rai, and then went to studio Doy Din Dang to see Songdej Thipthong, famous for his temple paintings. Songdet gave us signed copies of his paintings as presents and we spent a great time chatting with him about CNCF's work in Cayman.

The next day, after breakfast, we visited Wat Rong Khun, the White Temple, which was simply incredible. At the Artbridge Gallery, an artist's collaborative, we met again with Songdet and his wife, and discussed ideas that might be useful for a similar venture in Cayman. This was followed by lunch of Pad Thai at Katiliya in the Golden Triangle – a beautiful resort, but we only saw one other person there.

We then drove on to the Mae Fah Luang Gardens Doi Tang-a, a most unusual and breathtaking temperate garden filled with flowers. On 11th March we flew to Yangon and were met by the Belmond representative, who took us to the Governors' Residence Hotel, to enjoy the manager's cocktail party, followed by a Burmese curry dinner accompanied by Burmese red and white wine, which was surprisingly good.

We made the 7am flight from Yangon to Bagan to join our Irrawaddy River cruise. From Nyaung U airport we were whisked off for a visit to a local, very bustling market, and then to the Ananda and Sulamani Pagodas – where it was strictly shoes off inside. We then travelled to Thung Be village near old Bagan to board Belmond's river cruiser *Road to Mandalay* for a safety briefing and lunch, followed by a tour of a lacquer house and the Minnanthu Monastic Complex, built in 1225. We were able to enjoy the sunset from the top of the pagoda, and then came back down to a candle-lighting ceremony at the pagoda and a grill dinner on the deck. We always try to learn some key words in the local language, and for Yangon we learned *Mingalar Par* – good morning and *Jay Zu Par* – thank you.

A 'Balloons Over Bagan' excursion the next day was fabulous, and well worth the 4am wake-up call for a 5am departure. After soaring over numerous pagodas set in the landscape below, we celebrated with a glass of champagne on landing. We were given blue-peaked baseball caps as souvenirs. These have the longest peak to shield one's eyes from the sun I've ever seen, and I still wear mine for trips around the Caribbean. Our boat left at 9.30am, en route to Mandalay (though we only reached Myin Mu due to the low water level) and Viv enjoyed a cookery demonstration along the way whilst yours truly worked out with a floatation collar in the pool.

Dr Hla Tun, the resident doctor, gave a most informative presentation on Belmond's social contribution project for typhoon relief, education, and medical projects, and after lunch there was a demonstration of how to tie a *longyi* – this is a fabric wrap similar to the man's *kikoi* or woman's *kanga* in Africa. Our guide, Yimong, provided insights into Myanmar's past, present and future, which was followed by dinner in the main restaurant and then a festival of lights floating on the river, which was a spectacular sight in the dark.

After arriving in Myin Mu, we drove two hours to Mandalay, where we visited Kuthodaw Pagoda, commissioned by King Mindon, where seven hundred and thirty marble slabs are inscribed with Buddhist texts, and Shwenandaw Monastery, erected by the last king of Burma, King Mindon's son, which has teak carvings of Buddhist myths adorning its walls and roofs. We purchased bells for Callaloo garden, so the wind in Cayman would remind us of this special place, as well as a miniature box for Viv's growing collection.

We then visited a silk weaving factory in Amanpura, the ancient capital and then Sagaing Hill, home to hundreds of pagodas and monasteries, nunneries and Buddhist learning centres, where we admired a panoramic view from the Penya Shin pagoda. Returning to the boat, we visited the bridge, chatted with the captain, and delighted in an acrobatic performance on the deck after dinner on board.

On 16th March, we bid farewell to *Road to Mandalay*, our home for the past week, and took a car to Mandalay airport for our 9-hour flight to Bangkok and then Tokyo. We received first class service from the Peninsula team when we arrived at 6am. They were inside immigration and customs to steer us through the formalities, then there was a soothing ride to the hotel in the Rolls Royce, where our suite was ready and awaiting us for a much-needed sleep.

Mary Monsen's friend, Kazuko, took us to enjoy a lunch of shabu-shabu – thinly sliced beef and vegetables briefly cooked in hot broth and served with dipping sauces – accompanied by refreshing green tea. Kazuko then took us to the Nezu Museum to view an exhibition of Buddhist paintings and teachings covering all eternity, and on a walk around the beautiful gardens surrounding the museum. Kazuko excelled in hospitality, taking us to her home – her father-in-law had been Prime Minister in 1948. On 18th March, Naoko, another friend of Mary's, came to accompany us for a very special treat that Mary had arranged: a traditional Japanese tea ceremony with Satsuko.

We were at first a little taken aback that her apartment was in a high rise tower, but as we arrived, after removing our shoes, we were taken into a room in the apartment that was a traditional Japanese tea house. We kneeled for the ceremony, then were invited to sit cross-legged for more comfort. Satsuko was assisted by a second lady in a kimono, and they performed the finely-tuned rituals of the tea ceremony, serving us while elegantly descending to their knees, then rising without effort even though they were probably more than eighty years of age.

Satsuko then gave us beautiful gifts of silk obi kimono wraps. One of these we hung in her honour in Callaloo, and the second in QGM, to always keep us focused on this magical ceremony. Satsuko also gave us a delicate bamboo spoon and said that, after making tea in Cayman, we were to write a message on it and return to her on our next visit to Japan. This was a hard act to follow, but Naoko took us to enjoy lunch of vegetable kaiseki at Nagami Ginza, which included many courses and two types of saké. We learnt that Naoko promotes the Japanese skating team – we felt we had been born lucky to be introduced to such warm and talented people.

After so much flying around, our luggage had suffered damage, so once we were in back in Miami on 30th March we took a trip to Kings Luggage – a great shop that fixes airline crews' luggage – to get it repaired. Viv and I then tested out the food at the National Hotel, on South Beach, for RLBC's Caribbean Intelligence event in April, and flew back that evening to Cayman, replete with memories of our wonderful five-week Around the World trip.

By this time, Deloitte had been appointed Receivers on Baha Mar, and at RLBC we were charged with establishing budgets and schedules to estimate the cost and time to complete the resort, so I had to get right to work the next morning. On 3rd April I flew from Cayman to Panama to meet with Alfredo, one of the Casi Cielo's principals, to discuss progress and budget costings, for a couple of days.

I flew back to Cayman on 6th April, from where Viv and I left for our annual Vail ski trip. During the next ten days we enjoyed some perfect skiing, wonderful meals and wines – with friends and by ourselves – and managed to catch our flight back to Miami in spite of a storm and a stuck elevator, though it was a close-run thing. Viv and I were in Miami again on 21st April to celebrate the tenth anniversary of the opening of the Adrienne Arsht Performing Arts Centre, where we had enjoyed so many great performances. That night there was a gala dance performance with the Alvin Ailey American Dance Theatre: pop, gospel, classical and jazz – a truly outstanding evening. The next day, we held our Caribbean Intelligence lunch at the National Hotel on Miami Beach for our clients and fellow professionals, which was very well received.

I had noticed a pain in my right thumb early that morning, which became gradually more painful as the day wore on, to the extent that I called my good friend Mikol for the contact number of his go-to doctor, Almeda, who said I should come to see him at the Baptist hospital. I arrived at the hospital, was given some pain killers and admitted to await a visit from Dr Miki, a specialist hand doctor, as well as a specialist doctor in tropical diseases. The latter arrived first and asked a lot of questions about where I had been over the previous weeks. Then Dr Miki arrived, quite late as he had had been operating on patients elsewhere, but he took one look at my thumb and said the nail had to be removed right away as there was a deep black line from the base to the top of the nail. This operation he proceeded to do then and there. Somewhere, he said, I had picked up an infection and I was very fortunate that the infection had not gone into my bone, as the thumb would have to be removed. I was then wheeled away to have an MRI done, after which I was returned to the hospital room, where Viv insisted on staying with me and had to sleep all night in a reclining chair. The next evening I was discharged and we returned to Yacht Harbour, where José, a male nurse, came to clean the thumb and redress it daily. Then Viv received detailed instructions as to what needed to be done until the thumb had healed.

Dr Miki is a great guy, and as we chatted, we discovered his daughter was an ice skating enthusiast. We told him of our friendship with Igor, and his work with ice skaters such as Nancy Kerrigan and Paul Wylie, and arranged to obtain autographed photos for his daughter, about which he was absolutely delighted. Whilst we were in Miami, we were able to go into Publix supermarket and purchase a portable freeway toll device that Cathy Bennett from American Airlines had told us about. Its great feature was that it had two suction cups, so when we rented a car we could simply stick this on the windscreen and the toll camera on the freeway would read it and charge our credit card, which was linked to the device. I carry it my briefcase at all times, and it has saved us from numerous fines over the years.

On 3rd May, Viv and I flew to Miami to meet with Dr Miki, who said the thumb was healing well, so that evening we flew on to London. There, in the evening, I attended a dinner at the National Liberal Club in Whitehall to bid farewell to Lord Foulkes as Chairman of the Caribbean Council, and welcome Lord Bruce as our new Chairman. The 7th was Viv's seventieth birthday, and we were chauffeured to the Waterside Inn to be greeted by maître d', Diego, for a sumptuous lunch of crab and caviar, and langoustine, followed by superb lamb, and their signature raspberry soufflé. These delights were bookended by Bollinger champagne, with Pouilly-Fuissé and Gigondas in between.

We then drove to Great Fosters, where we were overnighting in Charlie Chaplin's suite. We met up with Alan and Doreen, who helped us to tie yellow ribbons around the poem gifts we had brought for Viv's birthday lunch the next day, where we would see our family and some fifty-five friends who had not been able to join us in Cayman for the 20/70 celebration the previous December. We rounded the day out with battered fish and chips at the local pub, the Red Lion.

The 8th May was a beautiful day, with a classical guitarist adding to the wonderful atmosphere, and there was much catching up with friends we had not seen for some time. The food, of course, added to the celebration: smoked salmon, lamb, cheese, and white chocolate mousse and cardamon ice cream. The craic continued into the early evening, and we sat down with ski buddies from Verbier – Ray and Michèle, and Mike and Doreen Johnson, with open sandwiches and cocktails.

On the 9th it was back by chauffeur to QGM, a rainy four-mile walk in Hyde Park and Thai curry at home. We spent the next couple of days catching up with a backlog of emails and office matters that had been left unattended while we were having fun. We were able to have a picture from Myanmar framed, followed by a great dim sum lunch at Yauatcha and a visit to Daphne in her new home at Battersea Place assisted living residences.

On 14th May we flew to Split, where we picked up our rental car for a four-hour coastal road drive to Dubrovnik, passing briefly through Bosnia Herzegovina. There are no cars allowed in Dubrovnik's Old Town, so I parked the car at the outer wall of the city on a meter costing 40 Kuna/hour. Then we lugged our bags down so many steps I lost count, to the address of 'Simply Chic' – the apartment we had rented. Getting to the apartment required lugging the bags up many stairs, since it was on the top floor of the building, but we made it and then went out for a tasty dinner of local capon and sea bass, washed down with an excellent red Dingač.

We bought some supplies at the nearest supermarket the next morning, had breakfast in Libertas Plaza, near the Mala Onofrijeva Fontana, and then walked around the city walls looking down into the old town. We lunched on smoked ham, tuna tartare and seafood risotto, with a Pošip white wine, and walked back up the steps to feed the parking meter with 240 Kuna for twenty-four hours. In the early evening, we enjoyed a Trio Domine concert at the Domino Church, playing Handel, Haydn, Borodin, Mozart, Greig and Fauré, with flute, violin and cello. Afterwards we had an excellent late dinner of seabass and Pošip Cara from Korčula island, and Dingač Skaramuča. We had an early start the next morning, and drove from Dubrovnik to Kotor, in Montenegro, where we checked into our rented apartment in the walled old town. Then we had lunch at Scala Santa, of mussels in white wine, with Chardonnay barrique from Montenegro. We walked off our lunch excesses by climbing the one thousand three hundred and fifty steps to the top of the Kotor fortress. About halfway up, we passed a beautiful old church in which a service was being held, and at the top we had a beautiful view of the long Kotor bay.

On the 17th, we drove seven hours from Montenegro through Bosnia to Croatia. We stopped for lunch at a rest stop along the way, to feast on excellent local bread, cheese, ham, tomato with Chardonnay and pale pink Montenegrin rosé. The Hotel Plitvice, in the Jelena World Heritage National Park, is large and very communist in style, and we left it the next morning for a boat trip across a beautiful lake with waterfalls all around. The water was a beautiful blue – almost, but not quite as beautiful as our own Seven Mile beach. We hiked for about 6km, and returned to the hotel for dinner at the Lička Kuća restaurant, where we had lamb under an iron lid, with potatoes, a bottle of Dingač red wine, followed by dancing to local music. We drove a couple of hours to Zadar the next morning, and then into Krka National Park, where we parked our car and walked some 4km to the entrance. Unfortunately, the abundance of beautiful waterfalls was matched by the abundant crowds of visitors, so we took the boat back to the car and returned to Split. There, we checked into the Capogrosso Palace, where our apartment had somehow been double-booked with one Mrs Negri. After sorting that little matter out, we dined at the entirely appropriately named No Stress bistro in the square below.

The next morning, after breakfast, we went to the car to feed the meter and discovered we had incurred a 75 Kuna parking fine. We made up for this by having an excellent lunch of mussels with a big fresh salad and Pošip Cara white wine, and then climbed the St Domnius bell tower for a great view. At the top, we met a group of Australians and chatted about Sydney, where they were from. We then visited the museum for an outstanding history of Split, and went back to the Capogrosso Palace apartment, for nibbles and to catch up on work.

We went out for dinner at Konoba Matejuška – reputedly the best restaurant in Split – for excellent sea bream and shark with Dingač and Pošip wines. On 21st May, we packed up and drove to Split airport for our return to Heathrow and then Miami, where I visited Dr Miki so he could check how The Thumb was healing. I was delighted to hear him say all was proceeding well, and we flew to Cayman much relieved.

There, I began working out with Igor's new programme using Water Walkers, which he designed. They are large plastic oblong plates fixed to your feet with Velcro straps and which provide a great resistance workout in the pool, without impact.

On 25th May, CASE met at the Grand Old House, for the College of Fellows to induct Dr John Harvey into the college. The following day, I held a telephone conference with Shao Di from China Exim to discuss the progress on resolving the restart and completion of Baha Mar's construction.

I flew to Toronto on 1st June for a RLBC cocktail party the next day, with key guests from the Nationwide Appraisal Services (NAS). This is a standard appraisal service format that some of the Canadian Banks in the Caribbean used, and which we also used for those financial clients. On 3rd June we held our RLBC board meeting, followed by a directors' dinner.

Back in Cayman, I attended a UNESCO cultural virtual workshop on the 7th and 8th in an attempt to ensure we at CNCF availed ourselves of the best global cultural developments for Cayman. This was followed, on a much lighter note, with the performance of *Rundown* on 10th June.

On the 14th Viv and I travelled to Palma, Majorca, to celebrate my brother Rob's thirty-fifth wedding anniversary. We drove to Deià, often called Majorca's most beautiful village, to stay at Belmond's La Residencia Hotel. As we went to check in, the receptionist looked blank as we announced our name – understandably as, although we thought we had made a reservation, we had not. Luckily, they managed to find us a room, and we then enjoyed tapas, made with the freshest of ingredients, in typical Mallorcan style at El Barrigón, in Deià village.

On 17th June, we drove to the picturesque hill town of Valldemossa set in the Tramuntana mountain range and hiked a scenic loop trail, climbing some two thousand feet with great views down into Deià. That evening we had dinner at Sebastian's with Rob, Jenna, Anni and Nick. The next day we hiked to Sa Foradada from Son Marroig, finishing with an outstanding paella and well chilled rosé, and as we looked down into the harbour there was a Cayman Islands registered boat, making us feel very much at home. Returning to La Residencia for a refreshing swim and cocktails on the lawn, followed by a wonderful piano recital by Rob's good friend, Duncan, we celebrated Rob and Jenna's thirty fifth wedding anniversary with a spectacular dinner at the hotel's restaurant, El Olivio.

The next day we woke late, which had become a pattern, and drove to Fornalutx, through Sóller and Puerto de Sóller, and enjoyed a great lunch of Spanish omelette and red mullet at Ca N'Antuna. After a siesta back at the hotel, we had dinner with the family at Sa Vinya. On 20th June we drove to Banyalbufar, and hiked some two and a half hours to Port des Canonge with its tiny stone beach. We had an excellent lunch of garlic prawns, chicken salad and Ses Nines rosé, on the terrace of the charming family-run restaurant, C'an

Toni Moreno. Dinner was at the Grand Hotel Son Net in Puigpunyent, set in the Tramuntana mountains, and we were welcomed by a surprise bottle of champagne from Dottie, who knew the owner, served by Bjorn, the general manager. Getting there had been interesting as the road had many, many hairpin bends and one-lane sections. We purchased six bottles of the Son Net Syrah wine to take back to the Callaloo cellar and on 21st June we drove to Valldemossa for a final lunch at a typical Mallorcan restaurant, then reluctantly drove back to Palma to catch a (delayed) return flight to London.

Sadly, during our travels Cissy Delapenha had passed away. I was asked to write a eulogy, which I was honoured to do, recalling the many happy times we had spent both at the restaurant and their home, and noting Cissy's unique humour and welcoming hospitality. Unfortunately, Viv and I were unable to attend the funeral, as we left for London on 6th July to attend niece Charlotte and Bill's wedding.

This was at St John's Church in Baddingham, followed by a reception at nephew Richard's home, The Rectory, complete with dancing until 2.30am to nephew Jonnie Polyester's disco music. Given the previous night's excesses, we arose appropriately late, and drove to the White Horse pub in Sibton, where all the families were in attendance. There, Little Ed, as he is fondly known, held court and described how his family had to sell their ancestral home, Markree Castle, in County Sligo, Ireland, because it would have cost three million pounds to repair it.

We had a brief stopover in London before returning to Cayman, during which we saw Alan and Jenny Foster, did some shopping, and 'kidnapped' Maurice from St Wilfred's in Chelsea and enjoyed dinner together at the Coopers Arms before returning him, in his wheelchair, to his home – he really enjoyed these outings, as they took him back into the social realm and interaction within which his personality thrived.

With the construction of the further extension to the Esterly Tibbetts highway – originally the Harquail Bypass, and Mrs Harquail had never been too happy about the name change – CNCF were asked to provide access to the National Gallery via a road connecting the two properties. The prospect of such a physical connection was more than welcome, given our desire to see all the heritage and cultural entities located within a single campus. In fact, this had always been part of the masterplan while the highway extension was being constructed. We finalised the details of the connector road through CNCF to the National Gallery with the Ministry on 1st October.

I flew to Punta Cana on 1st August for a meeting with the owner's representative for Tropicalia and to visit the site in Miches. At the same time, I connected with Michell Vargas, who was helping appraise the local construction costs. The property is truly magnificent, with crystal clear blue water, a white, white sandy beach and mature coconut palms right down to the water's edge. I returned to Cayman on 3rd August to conduct a CNCF performance review for Henry and Marcia, and to catch up with the progress on claim assistance we were providing to Trinidad Contractors as part of the necessary remedial work they were completing to repair the damage caused by Hurricane Lenny to the shore works in St Kitts. Most importantly I arrived in time to enjoy the staging of the CNCF play, *Isabell* at the Harquail.

In late August I was preoccupied with several projects we were working on. These included the Outline Business Case for the Sunrise Adult Training Facility in Cayman, the Harbour Club, and the Landings in St Lucia. I then had two days of office meetings in Barbados and was back in Cayman on 2nd September.

On the 6th, I noted in my diary: 'the Gifts of Age as being Mature Perspective, Seasoned Creativity and Spiritual Vision'. I hope I have accumulated some, or even all of these, by this stage of my life. On 9th September, our office staff engaged in a team-building exercise called 'Locked In' at a new facility in George Town, during which we were locked into a room and given a number of clues to work on. The object was to collaborate to find the key to escape within a given time limit. Fortunately we were able to accomplish this, as we were hosting a cocktail party that evening at Callaloo for James Pollard, one of our senior valuers, to celebrate his engagement to Sana.

On 5th October, Viv and I flew to Miami, and then to London via Charlotte, North Carolina. The flight had had to be rerouted due to the passage of Hurricane Matthew. It was an ex-US Airways plane, with their US Airways crew, and sticks in our memory as one of the most miserable flights we have ever been on.

Once at QGM, we enjoyed a few days catching up with friends, and met with the St Kitts and Nevis Minister of Finance at a Caribbean Council event. Then we flew to Malta, where I was to represent Cayman at the IFACCA summit. Our good friend, Penny Cumber, very kindly allowed us to use her apartment in St Julians, and arranged for Ellen to pick us up from the airport and show us the ins and outs of the place. We enjoyed a great sea bream dinner at Lulu's restaurant, accompanied by Valetta red and white wine. The next day, another friend of Penny's, Mathew, drove me to pick up a hire car and then Viv and I drove across Malta to Ċirkewwa port to catch the ferry to Mġarr, on the island of Gozo, where we drove to Rabat (aka Victoria) and did a bit of sightseeing. We returned to Malta to enjoy a lunch of goat's cheese salad and bruschetta in St Georges Square, visited the Citadel, and then drove back to Portomasso Marina in St Julians, to enjoy dinner of pizza and samosas.

On 15th October, we drove to Mdina, a small, very ancient walled city, also called the 'City of Silence' because no cars are allowed within its walls. We walked through the narrow streets, then drove back to Valetta to check out the location of the Teatru Manoel, and to St Julians, to change before returning to Valetta. There are not many road signs, so way-finding was somewhat of a challenge, but we made it and enjoyed an excellent guitar recital by Simon Schembri with the Parisii Quartet at the Teatru Manoel. On 16th October we were treated to a Grand Harbour boat tour with Captain Morgan. Later we had drinks with Guy Cubitt, who had lived in Cayman in the early days, followed by dinner at the Blue Elephant.

The IFACCA summit commenced on the 17th with the CEO's conference. The next day we moved accommodation to the Excelsior Hotel for the IFACCA AGM and Grand Opening at St Elmo's Fort. On the 19th, whilst I attended the summit, Viv toured Mdina and Mosta, the Dingli Cliffs and St Johns Co-Cathedral. The next day, I attended summit meetings, followed by a gala dinner at Verdala Palace. There were more meetings on the 21st, after which we returned to London.

Back in Cayman a few days later, I flew to Kingston to attend bid meetings for the Special Economic Zone that was planned for the Caymanas area, on which we were partnering with Buro Happold. I also asked Mark Green to prepare invitations for the upcoming Gimistory performance on 27th November at Callaloo, and met with Heber Arch to review the CASE College of Fellows.

At the sixth iteration of CHICOS, held in San Juan, Puerto Rico, on 8th November, I moderated a discussion entitled 'Key Ingredients for Master-Planned Communities' with a great panel of seasoned experts, including Mark Durliat, of Grace Bay Resorts; Camilo Bolanos, of Hyatt International; Tim Peck, Chairman of OBM International; Dimitri Pekhterev, of Interval International, and Marta Molina, from Seal CPG Real Estate. As always, it was a great networking opportunity with some most informative exchanges about the state of the market.

On the 23rd we signed the construction contract with Alan Veeran's company, Smart Construction Management, for the Greenery self-storage facility. Because the building was to be over the rear car park of the Greenery, the first storage floor was over 19 feet above sea level, with concrete floors, walls and roof – in fact, it would be the proverbial 'bunker,' and in the event of a hurricane, probably one of the safest places to shelter on the island.

Ken Corsbie and his wife Beth arrived on the 25th to stay with us in readiness for our annual Gimistory festival. Each year we hosted a celebration at Callaloo for all Gimistory's sponsors, performers and our friends. This year, Gimistory took place on the 27th and the evening before we were treated to a performance by Dave Martins and the Tradewinds at Tiki Beach, under the stars on Seven Mile Beach.

On 7th December Viv and I left for our annual Alta ski week to celebrate our 21st wedding anniversary. This time we collected a 4-wheel drive hire car in Salt Lake City and, en route to Sugarplum, stopped by Whole Foods to buy groceries and wine at the State Liquor store. It was indeed interesting to see the excellent selection in the store, although these are the only places one may purchase alcoholic beverages in the state of Utah.

We then drove up the Canyon to Sugarplum Unit N, new to us but with the essential open log fire. The next day we skied for only half a day, after which Viv enjoyed her once-a-year Monster Burger at Rustler. On the 9th, I greeted Viv with an 'Ulster Fry' breakfast and a 'recycled' anniversary card, after which we skied six runs, followed by a concert at the Mormon Tabernacle Choir in Salt Lake City with Rolando Villazon as guest performer.

The 10th December was my seventy-first birthday, which was ushered in by eight inches of the best powder in the world, which we took the best advantage of during nine runs, after which we lunched at the Collins Grill, where we enjoyed our favourite arugula salad with a poached egg on top. The 11th was an absolutely perfect bluebird day which we enjoyed to the full, accomplishing 15,000 feet in nine runs. On 13th December we got out earlier than usual, which enabled us to lunch at Alta Lodge, where we met Mikey and caught up with his news. At Alta Lodge, one needed to get in early for lunch as the waiting staff were keen to get out for an afternoon's skiing. If you were somewhat late, you always got the 'bum's rush' to finish your meal and pay the tab. Rustler and Collins Grill were totally different and you could take your time over your meal.

It was Viv's custom to write Christmas cards during our December ski trips, and so on 15th December we drove up to the Alta post office to mail these. On 16th December, we experienced a major winter storm with twelve inches of new snow. We went out for three runs only, lunched at Rustler, and said goodbye to Cathy, Meg, and Vicky from Taiwan – she is a great artist, and her painting of the Goldminer's Daughter and mountain beyond hangs in our travel collection in the gym at Callaloo.

On 17th December, we thanked God that we had rented a 4-wheel drive Ford Escape. We got up at 2.30am and it was snowing so hard that we left in a total white-out. We slowly followed the car tracks in front of us down Little Cottonwood Canyon, gassed up the rental car, then drove to the airport and caught the 6am American flight to Cayman via Dallas. Home to Callaloo for a shower and change, and then up to Kaibo on Northside, for Dani Coleman and Darren Trickett's wedding. From snow to the beach in under twelve hours!

On 19th December I met with Ronnie Dunn, star accountant and friend, on the Special Needs project, and flew to Maimi on the 21st for a Tropicalia Four Seasons Project budget meeting, and back to Cayman that evening. As always, our traditional Christmas lunch at Callaloo was preceded by a game of croquet, and we rounded out the year with our traditional 'Do Drop In' party at Callaloo.

2017

'You can't go back and change the beginning, but you can start where you are and change the ending.' C.S. Lewis

Beginning the new year in an appropriate style, we cooked caviar eggs for Erik and Mary Monsen at Callaloo, after which we accepted Alasdair and Lisa's kind invitation to their traditional New Year's Day party at their home in the Yacht Club.

As Mark Green, wife Allie, and daughter Izy were in Cayman for a short visit, we enjoyed lunch with them on the 8th and caught up with all their developments down under, including Mark's rapidly growing insurance adjustment business, founded on his experience with us in Cayman after the passage of Hurricane Ivan.

The next day, there was another promising start to the new year as we signed the contract with the Ministry of Education, Employment and Gender Affairs to develop the Outline Business Case for the Sunrise Adult Training Facility (SATF), a tender we had won in November 2016. Like so many projects I have worked on, it was fascinating to get an insight into the functions and users of a very different type of building. The composition of the team members was key, particularly when the specialist skills needed to understand such specific and out-of-the-ordinary activities weren't available locally. These experts had to apply their specialist knowledge while also understanding our local culture and the relatively small size of our Caymanian community.

At the time, SATF's existing facility was housed in a converted duplex in West Bay, which was completely unfit for purpose. We developed the OBC using the UK Greenbook 5 case methodology, with an outstanding team that brought together key skills in specialised design, finance, costing and project management. It included Ronnie Dunn and Lidka Scott of Fincor for financial modelling, and Marcus Fox of First Fox Architecture and Design for specialist design information, while we provided lead consultancy, cost budgeting and management expertise. Once the OBC was complete, we presented our findings to Cabinet and were asked to consider alternative sites, which we did. One such site, near the airport, required us to employ noise technicians, as excessive noise can be problematic for people with certain special needs. After further analysis and presentations to government, it was concluded that the site in George Town was the most appropriate. The whole exercise took more than two years to complete. On 13th January we had our first SATF stakeholder meeting – the mapping and consultation of everyone affected by the construction of a new building is a key part of the Business Case preparation process.

I was in Phoenix to attend a RLBC board meeting at the head office of our American partners on 18th January, and was able to take advantage of the great hiking opportunities near Phoenix during this visit. I hiked the Pinnacle Peak trail the next day, with a vertical climb of about 1,000 ft. The summit offers wonderful panoramic views of the surrounding valleys and the McDowell and Camel Back mountains. I was to climb Camel Back the next day, and discovered why it's known as a 'real leg burner'. The trail rises 1,400 feet in a little over a mile, and once you reach the ridgeline it becomes a challenging and technical ascent, which I enjoyed negotiating – in fact, like a lot of climbs, the descent felt more difficult than the ascent, but I made it back to my car in good shape and then paid a visit to Cosanti's bell foundry, which Viv had visited on a previous trip to Phoenix. The foundry's buildings were constructed by carefully shaping dense mounds of sand, over which concrete was poured. Once the concrete had set, the sand was removed. Paolo Soleri, a student of Frank Lloyd Wright, was the designer, and Cosanti has earned a place on the Arizona Registry of Historic Places.

I got back to Cayman on the 22nd and found that John Brunner, a Harvard buddy with a condo in Cayman, was in town, and we enjoyed dinner together on 27th January. The balance of the month was taken up with further stakeholder meetings on SATF, Baha Mar costings, Tropicalia's budget discussions, and writing the CNCF Chairman's message for Cayfest.

February started out with an excellent conference, sponsored by Fidelity Bank, called the Cayman Economic Outlook. This provided a great foresight into the likely economic trends for the Cayman Islands economy for the upcoming year, with some excellent speakers both local and international. I made a quick day-trip to Miami on 3rd February to attend meetings on Tropicalia budget and finance, and the next day, back in Cayman, the shareholders of Gingerbread Limited met to decide how to distribute the remaining unsold apartments, following the completion of the Careenage condominium development. Gingerbread Limited had been an investor, and between us we held interests in both Careenage and Gingerbread. On 6th February, in view of Mortimer's reduced mobility, I invited Alan Veeran to join the board of RLBC in Mortimer's place, which was submitted to the board for their approval.

It was time for our Colorado ski infusion, and on the 9th Viv and I flew to Eagle Vail, to partake of the famous Nowery's all-inclusive service and to join the reunion with Boopie and George McInnis, and Alastair Moodie, who was visiting from South Africa.

The next day, the winds at Two Creeks at Snowmass were so high the upper lifts were closed, so we only made three runs before driving to Aspen to pick up Alastair from the airport. The next day we skied Aspen Highlands, and, as it snowed for most of the day, we enjoyed great powder conditions. We stopped for lunch in Cloud Nine, during which some of the wilder skiers danced on the tables and sprayed Veuve Clicquot, after which we made a cautious white-out descent to the base and back home.

On 13th February I was scheduled to speak at an Urban Land Institute Conference in Miami, so drove to Eagle Vail airport for my flight to Miami on the 12th. It arrived at 7pm, and I went straight from the airport to attend the cocktail reception at the Ritz Carlton in South Beach for some good networking, and then drove back to spend the night at Yacht Harbour. The next day I gave a talk at the Plenary Session on the state of the Caribbean market, which was very well received, and then drove back to Miami airport for my flight to JFK and to Eagle Vail, and the drive back to Aspen Glen – a long couple of days, but well worth it.

Valentine's day greeted us with beautiful snow and a sunny day, and George, Alastair and I skied at Snowmass, then celebrated over lunch with spaghetti with lemon rind, a touch of juice, and topped with caviar, which went down very well. Skiing was great on the 15th, and afterwards we celebrated Jimmy and Cynthia's 50th wedding anniversary over dinner at the golf club, followed by a champagne nightcap at Mariposa.

On the 16th, as we were leaving for Vail later that morning, I cooked our traditional caviar eggs to start the day. Cooking caviar eggs for Jimmy was always a challenge, as the timing to ensure the eggs are softly scrambled and then carefully put back into the egg shells, then topped with caviar, and garnished with a single chive is a delicate balancing act, especially for a table of seven. Invariably, just before serving, Jimmy will say, 'Why don't we have some bacon or sausage to go with it?' which naturally throws off the whole serving performance!

In Vail, Viv and I stayed at the Sonnenalp, enjoying room service in front of the fire in our room that evening. Another beautiful bluebird day greeted us the next morning, and after egg white omelettes and Mimosas, we went out to ski with Jerry and Sheila Katz on the front side of Vail, followed by lunch of fish tacos at our favourite Vail village restaurant, Sweet Basil. We enjoyed the next three days of skiing with much fresh powder and great lunches, and on 20th February, Jerry cooked up a storm at their home: seafood stew, apple pie and Veuve Clicquot – no trouble sleeping after a long day of powder skiing ending with such a meal!

We left Sonnenalp on the 21st and as Johannes, the owner, was bidding us farewell, we asked him where he would be spending time after the ski season. He replied, Mustique, where he owned a house. After all this time, we discovered he owned a house in our favourite destination! In Miami, we discussed various Caribbean construction opportunities we could work on together with Davide Mariane and Ricardo of contractors Rizzani de Eccher, then returned to Cayman on the evening flight.

Our work on SATF was very involved with stakeholders at this time; this project, coupled with advancements on funding for the Anguilla airport and its possible development, plus an RICS conference in Cayman, was keeping us busy during the latter part of February. Then on 1st March, I flew to Barbados for the RLBC board meeting the next day.

Viv loves to play tennis, usually very early in the morning, and on 14th March I received a call from her at 7.30am, saying she was at the hospital after having fallen backwards on the court, and that it was suspected she had broken her wrist. I rushed down to the hospital and met with Dr Hertzig, who confirmed this was indeed the case, and that she would require surgery to fix the fracture. Viv was in the hospital for most of the day but, thankfully, I was able to take her home that evening. Dr Hertzig did a great job, as she is now back on the court playing regular tennis.

In August the Cayman Islands were sending a large and varied cultural contingent to Barbados for Carifesta XIII and, on 15th March, we held a meeting at the Harquail to begin to cover the necessary extensive planning required to make this a success.

For some time, Viv and I had been talking about setting up a foundation to provide funds for those in need and, in particular, to assist artists and persons promoting and developing Caymanian culture. Accordingly, we had met with George Giglioli, our personal attorney, to discuss the legalities of such an entity. Following a series of meetings commencing in 2016 and continuing through 2017, we registered the foundation at the beginning of 2018. We already have made a number of grants covering a broad range of causes, and can honestly say we have secured as much joy out of it, as benefactors, as have our recipients.

As I noted earlier, as part of my participation as a shareholder in RLBC, commencing in 2007, I was required to commit to a ten-year term, at which time I would sell BCL's shares in RLBC. Fortunately, we had agreed on the formula to value them as part of the original agreement, this being a function of the profit. So, on 16th March, we continued the discussion that had begun during our board meeting earlier in the month to begin finalising the value. David Bucknall had never wanted to retire; however, given the widely held ownership of Bucknall Austin, the younger shareholders saw David's desire to remain in a senior position as an obstacle to their advancement in the company, and hence the ten-year threshold.

On 17th March, we held discussions with the Ministry of Education about Cayman's Special Needs School – the Lighthouse School – and how students leaving that school interfaced with the Sunrise Adult Training Facility. BCL has subsequently been retained to act as Lead Consultant on the expansion of the Lighthouse School, but more of that later.

On 23rd March CNCF were honoured to host the Jamaican National Dance Theatre Company in the Orchard at Callaloo for an outstanding performance, organised by choreographer and dancer Kirk Rowe.

Viv and I flew to London on the 24th, from where Viv travelled to Belfast to meet with her longtime friend, Dorothy Lynch, and I travelled to Warwick University, in the Midlands, to attend the RLB UK partners meeting there and give a presentation on RLBC's activities in the Caribbean. Back in QGM, we attended David Bridgeman's art show, and it was excellent to see Cayman's artistic talent on show in London. We held interviews for new staff for our Caribbean offices at RLB's London headquarters for two days, and on the 30th we had the pleasure of joining Jonathan and Zoey for dinner at Middle Temple. This was preceded by a moot, in which trainee barristers tested their skills in arguing their case.

We enjoyed pottering about in QGM for a few days before leaving for Dubai, where we arrived at 8.15am on 5th April and were met by the driver from the Taj Hotel. We had breakfast and then slept until the late afternoon, when I interviewed an RLB employee for potential work in our Caribbean offices. We had an excellent dinner afterwards with Rob Edgecombe and his wife Linda, from RLB Dubai, at La Serre restaurant in the La Vida Hotel. It was most interesting to learn about life in this vibrant city, and particularly about the size of projects here, and how they are resourced from a labour point of view.

Viv and I went to have lunch at the restaurant in the Burg Kalifa tower (the tallest building in the world) located on the 124th floor. Afterwards, in order to get our bearings of the city, we took a Big Bus tour. On 7th April we began the day with a swim at the Taj pool, followed by another Big Bus tour to Atlantis, in order to compare it with the Caribbean's own Atlantis, in Nassau.

The next day, we flew Emirates business class to Sri Lanka's Colombo airport, and had some of the best service ever enjoyed on a plane. We were met by the &Beyond driver, Suga, for the one-hour drive to the 100-year-old Horathapola Coconut Estate, where we enjoyed a homestay, with a magnificent dinner of Sri Lankan curries, potato, luffa, passion leaf, tuna fish with rice noodles on the terrace of our cottage. The friendly staff soon taught us a few words in Sinhalese, *Ayu Bo Wan* – hello/good morning, and *Bohama Sthuthi* – thank you very much. We were sad to leave the next day, after such a short stay in this most tranquil setting, but we had a four and a half hour drive to Dambulla, where we visited the Dambulla Cave Temple, a World Heritage Site dating back to the first century, with incredible Buddhist mural paintings and one hundred and fifty-seven statues of the Buddha.

We then drove to the Water Garden Sigiriya, where our accommodation was an elegant suite with a plunge pool, in which we cooled off while enjoying our welcome bottle of South African Tall Elephant Chardonnay. After a breakfast of excellent fresh fruits, we went to Sigiriya to visit the Lion's Rock Palace dating from the 5th century. The UNESCO World Heritage site is a massive, ancient stone fortress set on a huge rock, with a six hundred and fifty foot ascent to the top. As we climbed, we enjoyed the colourful frescos painted on the walls – an incredible place, as are the water gardens below. We then drove to the ancient city of Polonnaruwa and visited the ruins of the palace of King Parakramabahu, built in the 12th century. It was reputed to have had one thousand rooms, and is a reminder of just how great his kingdom was.

On the way back to the Water Garden, we stopped for an Ayurvedic oil massage and steam – most welcome after the steep climb in Sigiriya earlier in the day. While dining in our room that evening we saw water monitors – they look rather like our iguanas in Cayman – and spotted deer and numerous species of birds, about which Suga, our driver, was most knowledgeable and informative the next day.

On 11th April we drove to Kandy, and on the way stopped at a village house and saw the multiple products that come from the coconut palm. These include coconut milk, rope and coya (coir) – the fibres found between the coconut's inner hard shell and the outer, hard layer, and which is still used in the construction of mattresses. We stopped for lunch at an Ayurvedic spice garden, which also sold the herbs and spices grown there, and purchased several products to take home, including red oil tablets and red oil, which we have used for many years and swear by for aches and pains when applied in our steam room at Callaloo. We also purchased a banana leaf painting of a Sigiriyan lady for the gym at Callaloo. We continued to Kandy and checked into the Theva Residency, which was a bit 'modern' for our liking but nevertheless comfortable.

We visited the Royal Botanic Gardens of Peradeniya, accessed by a suspension bridge, where we saw flora very similar to that of Cayman, but larger, and unlike Cayman in that there were many playful monkeys and fruit bats (flying foxes). Back in Kandy, after lunch, during which we were served Lion beer in the largest bottle I have ever seen, we visited the Gem Museum. As we left, predictably, we were given a sales pitch to persuade us to purchase gems. Suga made up for this by buying us a book on Ceylon cooking. We then visited the Temple of the Sacred Tooth Relic – Sri Dalada Maligawa – containing one of Buddha's teeth, and the most sacred site in Sri Lanka since ancient times. It is believed that whoever holds the relic holds the governance of the country, and daily pujas and rituals are carried out there

We left Kandy on the 13th and drove to Colombo, stopping on the way at the elephant orphanage, where Viv learnt of a book called 'The Elephant Whisperer', an account about interacting with elephants. They did not have a copy for sale, but she did purchase a sapphire pendant, which she wears to this day. Viv subsequently found a copy of the book and thoroughly enjoyed reading it.

Before reaching Colombo, we took a slight detour to the Rosyth tea and rubber plantation, to see if Fantana and Neil, the owners of the plantation, were there. By pure coincidence, they also owned Gloucester Road Travel, just by QGM. Rosyth is also a wonderful boutique hotel and Fantana, after greeting us and inviting us (and Suga) for a very tasty lunch, admitted that on seeing our vehicle come up their driveway she had felt some dread as they were fully booked and she feared having forgotten a reservation! We caught up on all our news and then left and drove to Colombo and the Tintagel boutique hotel, where we checked into room #8 – the southwest royal suite, where Prince Charles had stayed with Camilla.

As it was the Sri Lankan New Year, no alcohol was available with dinner in their restaurant. So we had Perrier with our dinner of barramundi, and then had wine sent to the room This could be charged to our account on the next day, thereby avoiding any law-breaking by the hotel. On 14th April we left Tintagel; our driver was most accommodating and gave us a tour of the sites and buildings of Colombo's British Colonial period before taking us to the airport for Sri Lankan Airways 'Silk Route' business class service for our flight to Malé, in the Maldives.

We were hosted through the airport there, to our waiting boat for the forty-minute ride to Cocoa Island, by COMO who also manage Parrot Cay in the Turks & Caicos Islands, on which we had worked so many years before. Our overwater bungalow was just magnificent, and the manager's welcome cocktail party immediately made us feel at home. On the 15th, I began the day enjoying our patio overlooking the crystal-clear Maldives water while reading *Unleashing Demons*, Craig Oliver's excellent account of the Brexit story. Afterwards, we walked along the sand spit between the two Indian Oceans, followed by baby black-tip sharks. We had a lunch of giant prawns, rosé and Mâcon-Lugny, and dinner by the pool. The next day we relaxed some more, reading on our terrace, with lunch by the pool, and swimming in the crystal-clear ocean. That evening we were once again hosted for cocktails by Ben, the manager, and Sary, his Maldivian wife. This was rounded out with dinner of ravioli and excellent curry – a strange mix of national cooking, but nevertheless most enjoyable.

The vibe around this resort was truly relaxing and the next day followed suit, with a late breakfast, a walk to the end of the sand spit, followed by a cooking class featuring a dish of Kerala shrimp. We read our books and then had a Hatha Yoga class, and dinner of spicy noodles on our patio. It was difficult to leave on the 18th, though we managed to enjoy the hotel's breakfast in their restaurant. Then it was time to check out for the forty-minute boat ride directly into Malé airport to catch Qatar airlines to Doha.

We checked in at the Westin, where I interviewed a potential new staff member, followed by dinner with RLB local manager Sam Barakat and his wife Rita, at La Verandah restaurant. On the 19th, we enjoyed a visit to the museum of Islamic Art and a lunch of tasty hummus at Souq Wagif before leaving for London the next day.

Back in QGM, Viv refreshed our garden with a visit to Rassell's, our garden supplier, and in the evening we enjoyed a performance of *Jewels*, a ballet by George Balanchine, at the Royal Opera House, with our friend, Sarah Lamb, as lead. We enjoyed dinner in the Paul Hamlyn Hall, and Sarah joined us for a glass of champagne. On 22nd April, we were once again invited by Gordon, the new publican at the Queen's Arms in the Mews, for dinner of fish and chips as part of his excellent social interaction with the residents of the Mews.

Once back in Cayman, it was time for *Rundown* to open at the Harquail, and also for discussions with George Giglioli about the value of BCL shares in RLBC, the key issue being how 'profit' was interpreted and calculated.

With Robi Das we were still looking at the Park Hyatt in St Kitts, which was part of their Citizenship By Investment Programme that was offering three passports for the purchase of one key in the hotel. We were also looking at the Aman project in the Dominican Republic for Dolphin Capital. The 7th May was, of course, Viv's birthday and we celebrated at Callaloo with Alan and Claudia.

On 8th May I had an appointment with an optician – Dr Maeve – to be fitted with a pair of spectacles. Until now, I had been spectacles-free, but I guess, at seventy-one years of age, it was unreasonable not to expect time to begin catching up with me!

Pete Widmer's funeral took place on 16th May. It was a sad occasion, and it felt like only yesterday that Pete had interviewed with me on that cold day in Hasker Street, with Sue walking around outside shivering. By 22nd May, we were in the process of preparing a bid to manage the completion of the John Gray High School. This had been left only partially completed by a previous contractor, and we conducted several walk-throughs to view the state of completion and to examine the condition of the stacks of stored materials on site.

The Orchard at Callaloo was increasingly being used for functions. In early May, we had hosted an event for the National Gallery there to thank a group of artists, led by David Bridgeman, who had provided an art course at the Gallery. On 1st June, the Orchard hosted the Girl Guides celebration and performance.

A few days later, Viv and I flew to Miami for our RLBC board meeting on 7th June at The Mayfair Hotel. From there I flew to Nassau to meet with Simon Townsend, partner at KPMG, for a meeting with him and other senior consumers of appraisal services in the Bahamas, as we were promoting BCL's services with myself, Matt King and James Pollard as our senior RICS appraisers.

The 22nd June found us in Berlin, at the Hotel Adlon Kempinski by the Brandenburg Gate, where we took a walking tour of this fascinating city with a guide named Nick, from Austin, Texas. On the 23rd, after lunch – a massive Wienerschnitzel – at Aigner Gendarmenmarkt, we met Rob and family in the lobby of the Adlon. Viv and I then collected a rental car and drove to Gorlitz, where we enjoyed dinner at Patrizierhaus St Jonathan, finishing at 3am! The 24th was nephew Edward's fiftieth birthday, and we celebrated with a party to end all parties at Pałac Włosień, the Heldreich family's ancestral home, now in ruins, but which Edward is currently renovating. We all sang and danced to an Abba look-alike group until 3am – resulting in Viv losing her voice.

The next day we naturally breakfasted in bed, then enjoyed shrimp pasta for lunch at Casanova to celebrate Anni's 28th birthday, for which she received Tortuga Rum cake, a lime green T-shirt, and Fortnum and Mason's lotions as birthday presents. We once again had dinner at Patrizierhaus St Jonathan, and went to bed 'early' – at midnight! We returned to London on the 26th, and were back in Cayman and Callaloo with Puddie and our new cat, the stray Truffle, on the 29th.

However, after sorting out some selections for the new Greenery storage facility, working on the terms of sale of the RLBC shares, as well as discussing some construction dispute issues in St Kitts, Viv and I left Cayman on 8th July for Anchorage, Alaska, where we checked into the Hotel Captain Cook for the start of our Harvard reunion, organised by Ray and Rita Debenham.

It was good to catch up with Nancy Blake for dinner that evening. Her husband Otis, with whom I was very close at Harvard, had sadly passed, but it was great to see that Nancy felt very much at home with our group even though Otis was gone. Some thirty people were at this reunion, which spoke to the strength and bonding of our group some three decades after we had graduated. Viv and I started the day walking three miles along the Tony Knowles trail along the Anchorage waterfront, and then began the action-packed week planned for us.

It started with a white-water rafting trip in the afternoon from Lions Head, two hours' drive from Anchorage, for which we all donned full dry suits. After that wild adrenaline rush, we relaxed with dinner at the Quarter Deck at the Hotel Captain Cook, where we met up with Sally and George Falkiner, caught up with their news and Sally's jokes, and enjoyed a bottle of A to Z Oregon Chardonnay and a Malbec from Chile.

On Tuesday 11th July, we were off to Bird Creek trail head to enjoy a morning riding ATVs, followed by lunch on the coach to Crow Creek Mine, where we panned for gold in the creek – and indeed the gold fever set in, as we found some small (well, tiny actually) nuggets. We were then fortunate to drive through the Alaska Wildlife Conversation Centre, where we saw elk, bears, bald eagles and bison, followed by an excellent dinner at Ray and Rita's house, where the entrée was a freshly caught salmon, courtesy of George, who had been fishing earlier that day.

Next morning's start-up was very early – bags out at 6am, ready to go at 7am for the drive to Rust's Flying Service at Lake Hood, for the flight to Katmai to watch bears catching salmon on their annual run upstream to spawn. The bridge over the Brooks River was closed due to the number of bears on it, so we diverted to Brooks Lake, landed there, and sat down to enjoy our boxed lunch. Each lunch was marked with the intended consumer's name, and someone had taken Bob Mallett's lunch. He was not a happy camper! But worse was to follow: there was a porta-toilet along the trail to the bear-viewing spot, which one lady needed to use. Her husband, walking ahead of her on the trail, saw a bear in the middle distance walking straight towards him. He turned around and ran back, pounded on the locked porta-toilet door and announced his dangerous predicament – to which his wife announced from inside, 'A bear outside, and you want me to open the door? You must be crazy!' Fortunately, at the last moment she relented, letting her husband in as the bear walked by. It was an unbelievably exciting day being so close to nature. We relaxed later, enjoying a king crab dinner at the Bridge restaurant, and then took the coach to the Alyeska Resort for a well-earned sleep.

On 13th July, we took a coach to Seward after breakfast, where we boarded our boat for the day to view the beluga whales and do some salmon fishing. The next day was yet another exciting adventure: we took a helicopter to the glacier, for dogsledding. This was a truly magical and once-in-a-lifetime experience. There were sixteen dogs in each team; Nancy was seated as the passenger and Viv was on the front sled skis, while yours truly drove and acted as the brake man on the rear sled. We did make it around the course safely! Lunch at Alyeska consisted of steak frites, followed by a trip on the aerial tram to the top of the ski mountain, and then a coach to Anchorage airport for our red-eye flight via Dallas to Cayman and home. Quite the trip, and well done, Ray and Rita!

Jonathan Dingle arrived in Cayman on 16th July, but, unfortunately, I needed to go to Miami for Tropicalia meetings on 18th for the day. I returned the same evening, and we hosted a dinner party at Callaloo for J.D. on the 19th.

On the 21st, Derek and Dawn Evans arrived to stay with us at Callaloo, and we had a wonderful time catching up on the projects we had worked on jointly. For Viv and me, it was great to have the opportunity to repay the hospitality they had extended to us when we visited them at their various postings around the world. Derek had come to the end of his posting to Washington, and gave us a fascinating book which we treasure: *The Architecture of Diplomacy – The British Ambassador's Residence in Washington*. We had dined there at one of the CARE balls, and the author, Anthony Seldon, describes the Lutyens designed residence as a cross between an English country house and a neo-Palladian plantation.

I held a press conference a few days later to announce the upcoming Carifesta showcase, starting at the Harquail on 28th July, featuring all of the theatre, dance, music, fashion and visual arts that we were going to display in Barbados in August. Fortuitously, Michell and Beatriz were visiting us for a three-day stay and so were able to enjoy the Caymanian culture highlighted by the showcase. We, of course, also welcomed them with a BCL team cocktail party at Callaloo, and Alan kindly provided his boat to show them Stingray City.

Unfortunately for us, a 'roll over' law had been introduced in Cayman, whereby after eight years, non-Caymanian staff had to leave for a year, and could return after that. Our wonderful estate manager, Wayne, was now required to leave us under this rule, but suggested that his wife's nephew, Barrington, could substitute for him during his absence. Accordingly, Barrington came to visit us at Callaloo and fitted right in.

We were in London on 10th August, where in the evening we enjoyed a box at the Royal Albert Hall with Edward and Gillian to see Prom 33. The next day we picked up a rental car at Victoria and drove to Amberley Castle, in West Sussex at the foot of the South Downs, where we had dinner in their restaurant. On the 12th Viv and I began the day with a walk along the river, then drove to Pulborough for Claire and Ash's wedding at the village church, followed by a reception at their 'Country Pile'. What does one give a couple who have everything? Well, we thought of a farmhouse basket filled with Carabella wine complete with tasting notes, which they loved. We drove back to the 'Pile' from Amberley Castle the next morning for a Bloody Mary start to the day, which we followed with a six-mile walk on the South Downs, carrying a picnic of sandwiches and a well-chilled bottle of Pouilly-Fuissé. We followed this with a round on their 18-hole 'championship' putting golf course, and ended the day with a room service dinner at the castle. On the 14th we stopped at the magnificent Petworth House, set in a seven hundred-acre deer park, to see what is claimed to be one of the UK's finest art collections in the care of the National Trust, followed by fish and chips at a local pub.

On the 16th we arrived back in Cayman, and the next day we had a Mini Warehouse 2 board meeting, after which I flew to Barbados for the start of Carifesta, which had been postponed. But our own Swanky Kitchen Band were performing the next day at the Friday Fish Fry, in Oistins, and so, despite the postponement, all was well. On 19th August, we had the *Leviticus* book launch and Grand Market, with Swanky playing on the Esplanade, and on 20th August there was the Grand Parade in Queen's Park. Sadly, I developed a recurrence of my thumb nail infection, and therefore had to leave Carifesta early the next day to see Dr Miki, who once again removed my thumb nail, after which I returned to Cayman. The next day I reported to our family doctor, John Addleson, with an update, and then returned to Miami on 25th August to have Dr Miki review his surgery. He said the thumb was doing well, which was a relief.

On 28th August, and again ten days later, I met with Morgan DaCosta to discuss the funding options for work the Bould Foundation wished to accomplish in the coming year, as well as CNCF's strategic planning for a change in direction from the production company we had become, into a more focussed Arts Council organisation. On 29th August, I flew to Punta Cana to meet with Michell, returning two days later. Little did we know it, but life was now about to change dramatically. On 5th September, I met with George Giglioli and Nick Holland, who were tying up the key sales points of my and BCL's interest in RLBC. Part of our conversation, however, focused on Hurricane Maria, which had hit the BVI as a Category 5 hurricane, causing widespread damage.

We were working on a number of different regional projects at this time, including a dispute in St Kitts, but it was clear that help was going to be needed in BVI, Puerto Rico, USVI, St Martin and the Leewards generally. Then came the news that a second hurricane, Irma, had slammed into the area on 19th September, and had caused even more damage than Maria. We contacted our friends and associates in that part of the Caribbean and also got in touch with Mark Green in Australia, who said he would like to assist us in setting up a response team to help those who had suffered losses. So we met in Miami on 21st September, then flew to Punta Cana the next day, where Michell had assembled a team which we could mobilise to put on the ground in the Leeward Islands.

As it so happened, Mark instructed the team about the basics of loss adjusting, but then needed to return to Australia as he had won a major assignment there. I remained with Michell in Punta Cana, continuing with the organisation of our team, and on 25th September flew from Santo Domingo to Providenciales, which had also suffered significant damage. There I met with loss adjusters, property owners and insurance companies to offer our assistance, based very much on our extensive experience of catastrophic losses caused by hurricanes in the past.

I then flew back to Santo Domingo on the 27th to meet Michell in Punta Cana, where he had managed to charter a single-engine Piper Cherokee to fly us to Tortola, where the airport was closed due to hurricane damage. Nevertheless, we had managed to secure permission to land through the kind aegis of Percy Rhoden, a longtime associate of ours and a relative by marriage of the

Premier, Orlando Smith. Of course, there was little in the way of facilities such as vehicles, accommodation, office accommodation and Wi-Fi. Percy and his partner, Richard Starkey, were outstanding in the ways they assisted us with these essential services, which enabled us to set up our operation and apply the key knowledge we had acquired in 2004 during the aftermath of Hurricane Ivan, in Cayman.

Having set up our operation in BVI with Johmalvin and Ivan Montero from the Dominican Republic, I left BVI on 3rd October and flew back through Santo Domingo to Punta Cana, and on to Miami and Cayman to deal with pressing matters there. These included a Bould Foundation dinner, the construction dispute in St Kitts, a road compensation matter in Cayman, and corporate set-up requirements in BVI.

Viv and I then left Cayman for San Francisco on 7th October. I had been living in BVI since the hurricanes, once again collecting a bucket of water from the cistern each morning and showering by pouring water from a pan over my head, and with a limited electricity supply. It was time to revert to normalcy, and so a trip to Sonoma Valley was planned to provide this. On 8th October, Viv and I checked into the Ledson Hotel, on Sonoma Square, and we ventured over to the Girl & the Fig restaurant for a most relaxed lunch. We went back to the hotel for an afternoon nap, but slept through to the next morning. Going down to the lobby for breakfast, we found it deserted. The square outside was empty as well – then we heard that there were massive fires in the valley, spread by hurricane-force winds, and the only place for breakfast was the 7-Eleven.

We collected our bags from the Ledson and drove to Bodega Bay on the coast, where Alfred Hitchcock made the film *The Birds*. But this reminded us too much of Blackpool by the sea in the UK, so we drove back towards San Francisco to see if there was accommodation available in Sausalito. However, everything was full, and we finished up in Mill Valley, at the Mill Valley Inn, which was excellent. It was hard to believe we had attempted to achieve some normalcy away from the hurricane-caused chaos in the Caribbean, by travelling to the American West Coast almost three thousand miles away, only to be greeted by massive forest fires and a similar chaotic environment. On 10th October, we took the ferry from Sausalito to Pier One for a tapas lunch at Coqueta Pier 5. We had arrived early and the restaurant was empty, and we asked to be moved from the seat we had been given. The waiter who was helping us asked where we were from, and we told him the Cayman Islands. To our delight, he turned out to be John Graham-Taylor, the son of Richard and Sarah Graham-Taylor – longtime friends in Cayman – and brother to

Emma, who had set us up with Global Entry. It really seemed an improbably small world, particularly given the complicated and roundabout journey we had taken to arrive at this particular place for lunch.

We took the ferry back, and enjoyed dinner at the Café Balboa in Mill Valley. On 11th October, we drove to San Francisco airport for our flight to Portland and there met Jill McDonald, who, as always, was the epitome of hospitality. She hosted us at Inchinnan Farm, and Viv and I walked from there to Carabella the next day, enjoyed a great late lunch at the Ponzi vineyard, and returned for dinner at Inchinnan. We continued to relax with some wine tasting, as well as dinner, at the Speckled Hen, which was most enjoyable and then yours truly had to leave for an overnight flight from Portland to Miami, then San Juan. There, given the extent of devastation and more passengers than airplane seats, I spent all day trying to find a seat to Tortola without success.

Accordingly, I spent the night in San Juan, where I was fortunate to find a room at a charming boutique hotel. The next morning, I managed to nab an airline seat to Tortola, where I met up with Wellington, a new team member, as well as Johmalvin. Our office was probably the most densely populated bit of real estate on the island at the time, with up to five of us in a space measuring 8 × 10 feet, but it served us well. We had a rapidly expanding list of clients, all generally insured but who had limited knowledge of how to make a claim and even less understanding of what it meant to be underinsured – making them subject to having their claim reduced by 'average' or being the co-insurer for part of their loss. I was in Tortola for five days, and then returned to Miami to meet Viv, who was some miles short of making her Executive Platinum status, so we had arranged to fly to Buenos Aires overnight from Miami.

We arrived there at 7am and took a taxi to the Club Frances boutique hotel, in Recoleta, with a very nice quiet room. We ventured out for lunch at the Fervor Steakhouse, where we enjoyed a balcony table, and outstanding steak with Malbec, and then went to catch up on some sleep at the hotel. In the evening, we walked to the Park Hyatt, located in the Palacio Duhau, to have dinner in their Italian restaurant, Gioia Cocina Botanica – sounds great, doesn't it? However, as the next day – Sunday 22nd October – was election day in Buenos Aires, there was no wine. So we decided not to eat there and walked around for a while until we came across Brasero Atlantico. Although the front door was locked we could see it was buzzing inside, and we knocked to be let in. Once admitted, we enjoyed a simple, but delicious meal and a bottle of wine. Apparently, it was the only restaurant serving wine that evening – illegally. We met a great New Zealand air crew there, and made a party of the occasion.

On the 22nd, we walked up to the Japanese Garden, and enjoyed a simple lunch, walked along the Avenida de Mayo to look at the classical architecture of the buildings there, followed by dinner at the Park Hyatt Gioia Cocina Botanica – by now serving wine as the elections were completed. The next day we checked out of the Club Frances early, stored our baggage there, and walked to the Barolo Palace. This was now an office building, and the tallest building in Buenos Aires for more than a decade. Unbeknown to us, however, we were being followed by a thief, who grabbed and squeezed Viv's arm and in a flash undid the strap on Viv's Cartier Tank watch then jumped onto a waiting accomplice's motor bike and sped off. Viv was distraught, of course, but as a passerby said, we were both lucky not to have been injured in the incident. We continued to the Barolo Palace and took the elevator to the top floor with a view over Buenos Aires and took a picture of Viv – sans Cartier watch! We returned to the Club Frances hotel to pick up our luggage and took the night flight back to Miami, then to Grand Cayman. The quick trip gained Viv the remaining air miles needed for her Executive Platinum status with American Airlines, and we were able to source another Cartier Tank Française through a New York Estate House as Cartier no longer made that model.

For many years Neil Cruickshank, Denny Diedrick and I, through Equal Investments, had enjoyed good returns from our office building investments, but we had now decided to sell part of our holdings in the Cayman Financial Centre, so on 26th October we met to work out the closing of the sale.

Three days later I flew to Tortola, where I met clients and visited sites, as well as negotiating with various loss adjusters. Back in Cayman, Vivian's cousin Linda and her husband Jim had come to stay with us at Callaloo. I was of course embarrassed that I was away in Tortola while they were our guests. However, I managed to tie up business loose ends and returned to Cayman on 1st November, in time to host cocktails for them on the 2nd at Callaloo. Jim and Linda departed Cayman on 5th November, and Michell and I were busy finalising our arrangements to project-manage the rebuild of Guana Island resort, which lies offshore from Beef Island, BVI.

By 8th November, life was getting back more-or-less to normal and I spoke at the seventh CHICOS conference in Bermuda. This year, I moderated a panel entitled 'Caribbean Investment Opportunities', during which we discussed what types of projects were the most appealing to the Legacy Lenders – luxury, full service, limited service, boutique, all-inclusive, mixed use, and so on.

After two days there, I left to join Viv in London. A few relaxing days followed, with swim workouts at Imperial, walks in Hyde Park, and business meetings with British Expertise and the Caribbean Council, as well as joining Mort and Jan in Brightlingsea for lunch. On 17th November, we enjoyed an evening of ballet at the Royal Opera House, with Sarah Lamb dancing the lead in *Illustrated Farewell*. We had dinner on the balcony with Jonnie and great niece Emily, and Sarah joined us for a glass of fizz in the second interval.

During next few days, we relaxed at QGM, did some shopping, and bought our Christmas pudding at Fortnum and Mason. On the 22nd, we flew back to Cayman in time to greet Ken Corsbie and Beth, who were staying with us at Callaloo and performing in the Orchard for Gimistory, which was held on 26th November. Igor was also visiting Cayman and we were able to update our programme with him and Dottie, and also have the privilege of entertaining Igor and Irina for dinner on the 30th, as it was the day before Irina's birthday.

On 1st December, we enjoyed the National Gallery's Gala Dinner, and I left for Tortola the next morning to meet with our team and clients. We discussed the arrangements to manage the rebuild of Guana Island and other matters, including the insurance claim on Elizabeth Beach Resort, on the north coast of Tortola. I met Viv, who had all our ski gear, in Miami on the 7th, and we took off for Salt Lake City and Sugarplum. We got in a good seven runs the next day before driving to Salt Lake City for groceries. On the 9th, our twenty-second wedding anniversary, we had bacon and eggs for breakfast and lunch at Rustler.

For my seventy-second birthday the next day, Viv gave me a surprise present of a weekend in Little Cayman that she had won. On the 12th, we began thinking about our travel plans for 2018 as well as an OPM reunion in March 2019 with Sally in Tasmania.

That evening we drove into Salt Lake City, enjoyed dinner at Bambara, and were treated to *The Nutcracker* at the Capitol Theatre. As we came out, it was snowing, which meant that the next day's skiing would be on fresh powder! We posted our Christmas cards as usual from the post office in Alta Village, and enjoyed two more bluebird days of skiing in 'The Greatest Snow on Earth' before returning to Cayman.

On 19th December Henry Propper, Rick Murray and I met and agreed the distribution of the Gingerbread Ltd. assets, and then on 20th December I held a conference call to see how we could settle the insurance claim on the Elizabeth Beach property in Tortola. We were also closing out 2017 with the completion and promotion of the Greenery Self Service Storage, in the heart of Seven Mile Beach, following forty years of developing this essential business in the Cayman Islands.

We held our Christmas lunch at Callaloo, after playing croquet in the Orchard. There followed drinks with Bobby and Pat Nunes on Boxing Day, and, later that evening, Henry and Marcia's fabulous hospitality and cooking in their yard at Caribbean Paradise in South Sound. And finally, of course, we held our 'Do Drop In' at Callaloo on 31st December.

CHAPTER ELEVEN

Pandemics and Perspectives (2018–2021)

2018

The grass isn't always greener on the other side. It's greener where you water it.

As always, we spent New Year's Day at Alasdair and Lisa's, catching up on news and exchanging best wishes for 2018 with friends we hadn't seen in months. As the work year commenced the next day, we began planning a Chamber of Commerce 'Business After Hours' event to promote and celebrate the opening of our Greenery Self Storage facility. It was then time for me to return to Tortola to continue finalising our company status and complete our banking structure there. We also continued assessments of losses that had resulted from the combined impact of Hurricanes Maria and Irma in 2017.

We had a belated Cayman office Christmas lunch, and then Viv and I were off again, this time to London. There, we relaxed for a few days, rising late and reading the *Sunday Times* in bed, working out and taking long walks in Hyde Park. On 23rd January we saw *OVO*, by Cirque du Soleil, at the Royal Albert Hall, followed the next day by lunch at Middle Temple with Jonathan Dingle. During the next several days I carried out a series of staff interviews, after which I caught up with Oliver Cleghorn again about potential Caribbean opportunities.

On 25th January, with much sadness, we visited His Lordship Mortimer at his care home. It was distressing to see a man who had directed my business dealings for so many years and who was such a dear friend with whom I had shared so much, here at the end of his life. Viv left for Cayman on the 30th, but I remained in London one more day to make a presentation to a joint meeting of the Caribbean Council and British Expertise. The topic was the impact of hurricanes in the Caribbean, and how we might secure assistance from UK resources to ease the significant economic and social burdens these events created in our communities.

The big event for February, which we could not miss, was the wedding of our good friends Sir John Jenkinson and Louise James on 3rd February, at the Collins house in South Sound. It was super, and a very happy occasion. The next day, I flew to Tortola, where we were attempting to close out numerous claim settlements. This required lengthy negotiations with the adjusters representing the insurance companies. On the 10th I returned to Miami, where I met with Viv, Alan and Claudia to enjoy an excellent dinner at Zuma, followed by a concert featuring Andrea Bocelli at the American Airlines stadium downtown.

I spent the next week in Cayman, catching up with developments there. These included ongoing negotiations with BVI settlement matters, Tropicalia budget issues in the Dominican Republic, a residential insurance claim in Providenciales, as well as SATF stakeholder issues. I would be back a month later on 12th March for more site visits and meetings with clients about their claims. During this visit I attended a book launch at Tortola Pier Park. The book had been written by a relative of Dancia's, and described the tension of anticipating Hurricanes Maria and Irma's approach, the experience of having the roof torn off the house, and the realities of life afterwards. It was an impressive story – well told, and more than a little terrifying. I also had my second interview with Daniel Afoke, at which he accepted our offer to head up our team in BVI.

On 20th February, Viv and I flew to Eagle Vail, where we were met by Jim and Cynthia Nowery and George and Boopie McInnis. For the next four days we skied Ajax, Highlands and Snowmass, after which Viv and I left for Jackson Hole for another four days skiing, getting back to Cayman to celebrate Erik and Mary's anniversary on Sunday 4th March.

We had been summoned to make a presentation of the Business Case for SATF to Caucus, and on 5th March the day began with a rehearsal of this presentation with our team. There was much at stake, as this would be the point at which the government might approve funding to allow the project to go to the next stage. I also met with attorneys in connection with a further significant bequest by Mrs Harquail. We had been advised by the Executors that both CNCF and the Gallery were to receive further funds, but that there were a number of technicalities that needed to be resolved first. We were also talking with CIBC about the funding of a new Royalton Hotel in Antigua, for which BCL was being proposed as the Project Monitor.

During this time Viv and I paid a visit to George Town hospital. There, we received our vaccinations for an upcoming trip to Borneo at the month's end. Jonathan Dingle also arrived for a few day's stay, and of course we had a dinner party for him at Callaloo. A dinner with our good friend Charlie and Lori Adams at their house followed, and on 23rd March I attended the celebration party for OBMI's fiftieth anniversary at Hemmingway's restaurant on Seven Mile beach. It was indeed poignant that Bill Bissell, who had been so instrumental in building this business, was not there to enjoy the results of his considerable efforts.

Our ongoing efforts to rebuild the Guana Island Resort were being hampered by lack of structural and electrical detailing, added to the challenge of securing materials. These were in short supply because so much rebuilding was taking place in the islands following the passage of two hurricanes. The need to ship into Tortola, then trans-ship over to Guana, added an extra complication. Then there were what appeared to be minor challenges, but which in fact created difficulties. For example, there was not enough water on Guana to do the building crew's laundry, so it was sent back to Tortola for washing. But the items were often not properly tagged so items of clothing often went missing, which created morale issues. Alan Veeran went to support Johmalvin, even assisting with the physical painting work, to ensure scheduled completion dates were met. This was important, because it would enable repeat guests to book for similar periods to those they had booked during many past years.

We had a new Governor, Anwar Choudhury, in Cayman, and the cocktail party to welcome him was held at Government House on 27th March. Viv and I were invited, and we spent an excellent evening chatting with him about the work that CNCF and the NG were doing. He promised to meet with us, and support our efforts.

The next day Viv and I flew to Miami for a busy day shopping, a visit to the dentist, and then a flight to London. On 31st March, we received the devasting news that Viv's sister, Patricia, had passed away. Stunned, and somewhat at a loss what to do next, we lunched with Charlie Adams at Beach Blanket Babylon on Portobello Road, where we shared the news with him. In the evening we went to the Adelphi theatre to see the musical *Kinky Boots* in the hope it might relieve our gloom – the family had no idea when the funeral would take place and insisted we should not cancel our scheduled travel.

On 2nd April we boarded our 12-hour flight to Kuala Lumpur, during which we learned Malay for thank you – *terima kasih* and welcome – *selamat datang*. We had a one-hour drive to the Mandarin Oriental from the airport, where we checked in and then slept for eight hours. We had dinner at the Mandarin's Club when we woke, then visited the spectacular interlinked Petronas Twin Towers and looked at the shopping in their mall, capped off with an evening cocktail at the club. The next day we flew to Kuching Sarawak, Borneo, where we were met by Margaret, our guide. She took us to visit the Brooke Museum, highlighting the history of the White Rajahs of Sarawak, after which we checked into the Ranee Hotel. Then we had a walking tour of Kuching, including Fort Margherita, constructed in 1879 by Charles Brooke, the second Rajah, where we learned more about the Brooke dynasty. Afterwards we visited the Chinese Temple near Kuching's waterfront, followed by drinks at the Ranee Bar and a good night's sleep.

On 5th April our driver, Peter, met us for the drive to the Bako National Park, followed by a boat transfer to the shore of the South China Sea beach. No swimming is allowed there, because of the crocodiles, but we saw a proboscis monkey, green tree pit viper and many pitcher plants during a short, but steep hike through the rain forest to the plateau. We returned by boat and had tea and cake in a village house. Then it was back to the Ranee for a refreshing shower after a day of 95-degree weather. Another guide, Selvan, and James the driver (who was a member of the Iban tribe) met us on the 6th and drove us to the Semenggoh Orangutan Rehabilitation Centre, where we watched the orangutans being fed, and from there to the town market in Serlan to purchase food for our trip to a longhouse. We enjoyed lunch at Lachau Town, an Iban trading post, before boarding the low, narrow, wooden longboat on the Lemanak river for the hour-long trip to an Iban longhouse. There, we were greeted for tea and then had dinner with the Chief of this tribe of former head hunters. A traditional dance performance followed, after which we distributed gifts to the children and adults, including Tortuga Rum cakes for the adults.

After cleaning our teeth outside to the sounds of cockerels, ducks and children, we bedded down under mosquito nets in the long common room of the longhouse – a truly surreal experience, preparing for sleep in the home of head-hunters! On the way to the very basic bathroom facilities we spied little hanging bamboo baskets containing skulls – glad they don't do that anymore! The next morning, we awoke with our heads still on our shoulders, and I had a cold shave and shower outside. We then learned how to use a blowpipe to kill our enemies with poisoned barbs. The longhouse was home to some fifteen families, who divided the chores amongst themselves. Before sunrise, the women had already washed the clothes in the river and hung them out to dry, and although the river was brown the clothes came out looking clean, which was a bit of a miracle. We were taken on a tour of the plantation, where pepper, pineapple, rubber trees and various root vegetables were being cultivated. We departed the village in the longboat and were treated to a delicious lunch on the riverside, cooked in bamboo tubes over an open fire. Back in Kuching, a Chinese festive parade greeted us followed by dinner at the romantic restaurant, Bla Bla Bla. The food was excellent, but the portions were enormous – far too generous for our tastes.

By now the family had made arrangements for Patricia's funeral service, so we revised our itinerary and flew from Kuching to Kuala Lumpur, where we stayed overnight in the Sama Sama Hotel, which has a unique service: golf buggy service direct from the airport arrival hall to the hotel's check-in lobby. As our flight was not until the evening of 9th April, we took the KLIA Ekspres into Kuala Lumpur and then the Mass Rapid Transport into Merdeka Square. There we visited the market and enjoyed a delicious Chinese lunch, after which we visited the Royal Selangor Club, founded in 1884 by the British who ruled Malaya at the time. It fronted a cricket pitch and lawn – all very Colonial! We visited the Kuala Lumpur City Gallery, which had a great permanent exhibition of the Kuala Lumpur's history and a model of the city describing its development and plans for its future. We then returned to the hotel to collect our luggage, and catch our Malaysian Airlines flight to Heathrow.

On the 11th we flew to Miami, and then drove to Sebring. The 13th April was a sad, sad day. Patricia's five sons and their respective spouses were present, and for Viv, having a sister pass away – a sister who was, moreover, seven years younger – was absolutely devastating.

We were back in London the next day, meeting with Jonathan Dingle on the 17th to discuss mediation matters. We also had a delightful lunch with Mike Johnson at QGM, followed by drinks in the evening with Daniel Afoke and his wife Sarah. We dined at Da Mario, where we really should be shareholders given we eat there every time we're in London!

On 20th April, Viv and I travelled to Brightlingsea for Mortimer's funeral and wake. There, I spoke of the time we had spent together, and the long road we had travelled. Although I had been practicing my speech for this special friend, I broke up on several occasions while relating some unusual or amusing incident. Mortimer, coming from an age before computers, loved stationery and fine writing instruments and Jan gave me his beloved Mont Blanc pen which I still use every day, so he is never very far away. We spent most of the rest of the week at home, reflecting on these sudden losses of people so dear to us.

Back in Cayman, at the end of April, we held an SATF steering committee meeting. A few weeks later, in May, I would be meeting with Marcus Fox, who was our specialist architect on SATF, and Ronnie Dunn, who was the mastermind for the financial analysis of this key project.

On 27th April we held an Avata director's meeting, and on 1st May we were delighted to meet with Rita Estevanovich to confirm the Bould Foundation's sponsorship of her and the Cayman Islands Team for the World Championship of the Performing Arts, scheduled for 6th–14th July, 2018, in California.

I was back in Tortola on the 2nd, for another round of client meetings as the negotiation of their claims continued. I also met with Gus Jaspert, the newly appointed BVI Governor. We discussed the Vision 2008 Planning document we had developed specifically for Cayman and I promised to send him a copy of the Business Plan. On Saturday I took a break from work, and repeated one of my favourite climbs in BVI – Sage Mountain – which took three and a half hours. The next day, Daniel Afoke arrived to take up his position as head of the BCL office in BVI. Michell arrived on 7th May, so together we were able to establish key operational procedures. Further meetings followed with bankers and insurers and clients, and I then returned to Cayman on 9th May in time for our MW2 board meeting the next day.

For Mother's Day, Viv left to join the family in Florida from 9th–13th May. I met her for a few days in Miami, then I had to address some Harquail estate questions and there was a celebration marking Scotia Bank's opening of their branch at Camana Bay. On the 26th, our SATF team met, followed by a celebratory dinner at Callaloo for this outstanding and talented group of individuals.

On 1st June, I met with the new Governor of Cayman to present the credentials of CNCF, and the samples of our work over many years. The same day, I discussed the work of the Clinton Global Initiative and Marshall Hall with Jonathan Dingle,

On 3rd June, I flew to Tortola for meetings and to check on how Daniel Afoke was faring with life in BVI. I was delighted to see he was fitting in very well. He had secured accommodation with a longtime friend of mine – Michael Helm, an architect – in part of a house on a steep hillside facing the capital, Road Town. The house had a swimming pool, which literally hung on the side of the hill. On 7th June we attended a mediation on one of our client's cases. This resulted in an agreement, for which we were most grateful.

We celebrated a Cayman National Theatre Company performance at the Harquail on the 9th, at which I was privileged to speak, and then Viv and I flew to Panama City, Florida, for four days of fun with the Nowerys and the McInnises, where we cooked, partied, danced, boated and drank, returning to Cayman on the 14th.

More dancing followed the next day, with Miss Jackie's performance at the Harquail, where I once again was asked to speak. I believe that must have been something to do with knowing Jackie and her work for some forty-five years, or being the chairman of CNCF for so long. I must admit, I thoroughly enjoyed highlighting this continuously evolving talent in our community and its impact on our cultural development, so I said the following:

For all of us, life is a journey not a destination.

This is particularly true in the context of our cultural development in these blessed Cayman Islands.

It has been my privilege for many years, to know Jackie and her wonderful family as well as her extended family of dancers. I have quietly admired her accomplishments since she opened 'The Ballet School' in 1973, noting the disciplined development of her young artists and panache of her productions.

Her success and longevity in this demanding art form comes as no surprise, for she is a skilled and knowledgeable artist and teacher, as well as a tireless worker and strict disciplinarian.

Jackie's oeuvre is all the more important when we view it with the knowledge and understanding that human potential can only be fully developed when particular attention is paid to culture and its interpretation through the arts.

I chair an organisation, the Cayman National Cultural Foundation, which truly believes, and focuses its work on that premise.

Jackie, through the work she does in dance, is an integral cog in the wheel of cultural organisations that rotates, in this multicultural Caymanian society with one singular objective; to emancipate culture into the world of action through artistic endeavour, offering everyone a better physical and more informed moral, social and cultural perspective, to position themselves as bearers of a new world culture in the making.

I offer thanks to Miss Jackie for her tireless contribution to our cultural development over the past forty five years, and congratulate all the performers, volunteers and staff of Miss Jackie's School of Dance on this significant milestone. Let me assure you all that your work has not gone unnoticed or unappreciated.

Our health insurance company had come up with the brilliant idea of bringing Deepak Chopra to Cayman, to speak on his new book, *The Healing Self*, at the Ritz. He spoke for over two hours, and was truly inspirational. Afterwards, he signed copies of the new book. Attendees had been strictly instructed that he would only sign copies of this particular book – however I secretly brought along a copy of the very first book of his I had read and by which I have lived my life: *Ageless Body – Timeless Mind*, which Deepak willingly signed, and which I treasure.

On 5th July, Viv and I flew to Denver, and then drove to Aspen Glen to stay with Jimmy and Cynthia, where we had made arrangements with a guide, Heather Laferty, to climb Mount Sopris, with a summit height of 12,965 feet. We can see Mount Sopris clearly from Mariposa, where Jimmy and Cynthia's home is located, and for many years we had said we would like to climb it one day. We thought it might be a good idea to acclimatise ourselves to the altitude since we spent most of our time at sea level, so we drove to Independence Pass, on the Continental Divide near Aspen, at an elevation of 12,095 feet. From there we would climb up to Infinity Lake and enjoy a picnic lunch, and then descend back to the Nowery's for a dinner party, and Jimmy's seven-hour smoked ribs.

We were up at 3am to meet Heather in Carbondale, and we then drove to the Sopris trailhead to begin the eight-hour ascent to the summit. The scenery was magnificent and Heather did a great job of encouraging us when the shale underfoot made the ascent – and particularly the descent, which also took eight hours – hard-going. She was thoughtful enough to have brought a chilled bottle of champagne with which to celebrate our success at completion of our efforts. On getting back to Mariposa, we collapsed into bed and woke up the next morning with bodies aching, but feeling triumphant. We enjoyed brunch at the Village Smithy in Carbondale, followed by a soak and steam at the Aspen Glen Club to help our muscles recover. Later, we had dinner at Tempranillo in Basalt.

There had been a huge forest fire in the region, and the restaurant had kindly treated the firefighters to dinner. Afterwards, they gave an impressive performance of push-ups on the pavement outside the restaurant, to the cheers and applause of the patrons. On the 9th, we had caviar eggs and champagne with the Nowerys, and then drove to Denver to see Al Hallock, who was now in a hospice. We had a wonderful time and he was in great spirits, reminiscing about all the wonderful times we had spent together over so many years. Robin, Anne Hallock's daughter, was now engaged to Chris, and we celebrated this over dinner together before heading back to Denver for the flight back to Cayman the following day.

I was kept busy in Tortola for ten days in July, meeting with clients and insurers and taking side trips to Providenciales to look at a residential insurance claim, and Guana Island, where we had met the deadline to allow repeat guests to come and stay. On 3rd August, and back in Cayman, we were invited to Government House to meet Graham Brady from the UK Government, who was leading the All-Party Group for the Cayman Islands. This was a very useful exercise, as it allowed us to see how the UK Government viewed

Cayman from the 'on the ground' perspective as opposed to how we were regarded from Westminster.

The next day we held a fund-raising review at the National Gallery. The focus was on how to convey the message that supporting our work in the community was worthwhile, and part of the material that was presented has always stuck with me: it was a reputed quote by Winston Churchill during the Second World War, when it was suggested that the government should stop investing in the arts, to help pay for Britain's war effort. He was said to have responded, 'Then what would we be fighting for?'

On 7th August Viv and I attended the Clinton Global Initiative event in Miami, attended by President Bill Clinton and his wife, Hillary. The Initiative supported efforts to rebuild infrastructure damaged by the regional hurricanes, and so was directly aligned with what BCL was doing in the region at this time.

Earlier in the year Michael Treacy, who was running Avata, had suggested Alan and I sell our interest in the company to him. This we were willing to do subject, of course, to agreeing an appropriate price. We set about establishing this, essentially basing it on the contracts we had in place, which were then assembled for review.

Viv and I flew to Mauritius on 20th August. We settled into our hotel, the Four Seasons at Anahita, which is a beautiful property, and the next day were welcomed by the General Manager, Michael Volk, who had previously been the GM at The Four Seasons, Bora Bora. Lunch of langoustine with rosé followed at Île aux Cerfs, but then we spent a long and tedious time acquiring the Malarone anti-malarial tablets we needed to begin taking for our forthcoming visit to Tanzania. After an obligatory doctor's visit to our hotel room, we secured the necessary documentation and were able to buy the medication.

On the 24th, we hired a car so we could drive 250km to the south coast of Mauritius to see the Trou Aux Cerfs in Curepipe. This perfectly circular crater at the top of a 650-metre-high dormant cinder cone has a small lake in the middle. Then we drove to the lake of Grand Bassin and its Hindu temple, and on to the Black River Gorges National Park and the Rhumerie de Chamarel for an outstanding fish lunch with a Côtes de Provence rosé. We continued to Curious Corne, to view the Chamarel Seven Coloured Earth Geopark, and then to the village of Belle Ombre, along the south coast to Souillac and La Flora, and back to Four Seasons for room service while we packed for our pending safari.

We awoke at 4.45am to drive from the Four Seasons to catch our flight to Dar es Salaam, Tanzania, and then to Nairobi, Kenya, where we were met by the &Beyond representative with a supply of Malarone antimalarial pills. We drove to Hemingway's hotel in Karen, named after Karen Blixen, the Danish author better known as Isak Dinesen, and were accommodated in the Finch-Hatton suite.

We had so enjoyed the movie *Out of Africa*, based on Karen Blixen's memoir of her love affair with Denys Finch-Hatton, and the photographs of them which decorated the suite really brought it all to life. This was one of several trips we had taken with the &Beyond Company, and I must say their service was absolutely outstanding. We enjoyed a room service lunch served by the butler (or, rather, butleress) Lavinia, who bore a striking resemblance to Laurice Frazer, Viv's second-in-command at the Comstock International Bank and our good friend.

After an afternoon rest, we enjoyed dinner in the Bistro at Hemingway's, with delicious tomato and basil soup and truffled wild mushroom juice, followed by curried salmon for Viv and rack of lamb for me, served with an excellent bottle of South African Merlot.

We started 26th August with breakfast at Hemingway's, after which we were driven to Wilson airport in Nairobi to catch our Air Kenya flight to Kichwa Tembo Airstrip in Kenya's Maasai Mara, and the Bateleur tented camp. We were greeted with a glass of rosé champagne on the airstrip, followed by lunch and a game drive with Charity, our guide. We soon saw a pride of eight lions – with two males, four females and two cubs – a rhino, an elephant, a Thompson gazelle, impala, zebra, warthog and terrapins – which was certainly a good start to the safari!

Back at the camp, Joel, our butler, served us with glasses of Chardonnay and Merlot, and our room butler, Benson, had pre-warmed our beds with hot water bottles to take the chill off the night air. We enjoyed a dinner of roast lamb and rounded it out with a game of backgammon, then met Kataka, a Maasai warrior, and discussed the Maasai culture. Afterwards we practiced some Swahili words: *Asanti Sana* – thank you very much and *Karibu* – welcome. The Swahili name for callaloo is *Mchicha* and *Lala Salama* means sleep well! On the 27th, after breakfast, we went on another game drive with Charity, and saw baboons, topi (a kind of antelope), wildebeest, serval (a small wild cat), mongoose, hippos, eland, crocodile, waterbuck, zebra and terrapin. We saw literally thousands of animals, as August is when the great annual migrations begin. We were also lucky enough – if one can put it that way – to see a lion kill a wildebeest, and a crocodile catch a zebra at their river crossing.

After all this carnage, and the experience of life at its most basic form of survival, it felt good to stop for a salad lunch under an acacia tree with a glass of well chilled rosé. We returned to Bateleur Camp to soak after the day's adventures in a tub filled with warm water and rose petals. This was followed by a traditional Maasai jumping dance performance. The dance displays the young men's strength and grace, and when it's performed as part of courtship, the higher they jump, the more attractive they are considered to be. We also purchased a Maasai talking stick, which is hung with pride in our gym at Callaloo. In any Maasai village, it needed only to be raised by a male member of the tribe to command instant silence. Sadly, it seems to have lost its power, because Viv still talks as much as ever! We then watched the sun go down over the Savannah from our verandah to the theme music of the movie *Out of Africa* – Viv even got quite sentimental as she always looks at the romantic side of life.

After a dinner of snapper, we toured the incredible kitchen garden to see an extensive range of organic herbs and vegetable produce that fed the entire camp. On 28th August we arose to a bracing cup of coffee and a 6.30am game drive to look for rhino but saw only a jackal. We returned to camp for breakfast, followed by a visit to the local Maasai village, where on the way we saw the elusive rhino. The Chief's son showed us around the village and explained their culture – whereupon Viv joined the ladies of the tribe, with babies on their hips, for a rendition of the song *Hakuna Matata* – No Worries.

A 4pm game drive to look for a cheetah with Charity might have ended in disaster. We set off across the wide veldt and in a very short time our Land Rover got stuck – and it remained stuck despite Charity's sterling efforts to dislodge it. The key instruction we have always been given is not to step away from the vehicle. This is because as long as you remain in the vehicle, wild animals perceive you as part of it. Step away from the vehicle's mass, and you become a potential tasty meal. That said, we were clearly not going anywhere, so we and our fellow passengers, Alvin and Chauvani ventured from the safety of the vehicle and searched for stones and twigs to put under the jacked-up wheels of the Land Rover. We finally got it mobile again and made it back to camp and enjoyed our own dinner there.

We departed the Bateleur Camp after breakfast on the 29th and flew to Kichwa and then drove to the Tarime airstrip near the Tanzania border for a flight to Lobo airstrip in Serengeti National Park. Karapoi, our driver, and Franco, our tracker, collected us for a one and a half hour drive over very rough roads to Klein's Camp. We saw a leopard in a tree en route. After enjoying a late lunch, we went out on a game drive during which we saw a black-backed jackal, ostrich, Coke's hartebeest, ibis, blue monkey, and then two lions eating a wildebeest. The next day, after an early breakfast, we had an all-day game drive to the famous Mara river crossing, where during the Great Migration hundreds of wildebeest and zebra plunge into the river, hoping to cross without being eaten by the huge waiting crocodiles. We had our lunch in the bush and then drove back to the lodge, hopefully looking for cheetah en route, but none were to be found. We did have a great lion sighting though, followed by dinner at the lodge, where the chef was willing to buy Viv for twenty cows! But no deal was concluded, and we enjoyed a farewell party in the bar with Alvin and Chauvani.

On 31st August we drove to Lobo airport to catch our flight to Lake Manyara airstrip and then had a one and a half hour drive to Ngorongoro Crater Lodge. This was all very grand, with crystal chandeliers and vast windows overlooking the crater. We enjoyed duck breast for lunch then walked along the edge of the crater, with stunning views down into the valley below. Afterwards, a long hill climb felt good after so much safari food. The next day began with a 7.30am breakfast, followed by a full day crater floor safari, where we saw a Reed Buck, Grant's and Thompson Gazelles and a Bateleur Eagle (which is &Beyond's logo). Travelling in our jeep were Carmen and Dennis, from Hong Kong but now living in Auckland, New Zealand. We saw a golden jackal, black-backed Coke's hartebeest (kongoni), elephant, wildebeest, baboons, hippos and water buffalo. Returning to the lodge, the tub in our room was filled with a rose petal arrangement to perfume the water for soaking off the day's dust. Dao, our room butler, and Aziza, our guide and driver, greeted us at the door to our suite at dinner time, and said they wanted to show us an elephant in the grounds of the camp. But this was a decoy: instead, they guided us to the wine cellar, where a surprise dinner was laid on for just the two of us, complete with candles and a log fire, and the choice of anything we wanted to drink from the cellar. The menu was an outstanding thick vegetable soup, pork fillet and then cheese. The camp team came in and serenaded us with Swahili songs, accompanying themselves on an instrument called a *Zeze*, a kind of zither, made of a gourd with goatskin and two strings; an African drum (*Ngoma*), and a bead shaker (*Kayamba*). The set-up was incredibly similar to that of our Caymanian kitchen band – a bit of information which we shared with Swanky on our return to Cayman.

We enjoyed our final breakfast at the lodge on 2nd September, and then drove to Lake Manyara airstrip for our Auric Air flight to Kilimanjaro International Airport. I believe it was passing through this airport, that triggered my thoughts of climbing Mt Kilimanjaro, which I did in August 2019. We returned to London via Nairobi Wilson and Jomo Kenyatta airports, and stayed at QGM for a couple of days, where we entertained Rob for drinks. He brought along an associate of his, Roger Southam, who had just sold his property management company to one of the major players in the London market, and speaking with him gave us a guideline to help us assess the potential value of Avata.

Then, as the saying goes, it was again 'back to porridge'. We needed to promote our Greenery Climate Controlled storage building, to which end we were hosting another Chamber of Commerce 'Business After Hours' event on site on 13th September. These early evening events, held after working hours and with cocktails and canapés, gave members of the business community the chance to tour our new facility and see what we had to offer. The event was very successful for us, and continued the forty-year pattern of our business: a new facility is typically fully rented within six months of completion.

On 16th September, I flew to Providenciales to meet with the loss adjuster with regard to the residence insurance claim we were negotiating. The next day I flew to Tortola, where I stayed for five days. Each morning, I enjoyed the challenge of climbing Havers Hill from the apartment – a climb of eight hundred and ten vertical feet. This would set me up for the day of meetings and discussions about both insurance claims and the rebuild process.

The BVI Government had set up a Recovery and Development Agency to manage the procurement of rebuild and development projects, and during this time my good friend Dancia Penn introduced me to Paul Bailey, who had been hired to head up the agency, in part based on his experience overseeing rebuild efforts in Fiji after Cyclone Winston. Paul and his wife became good friends during his tenure in BVI. I spent a week at home in Cayman before returning to Tortola on 30th September for another week. I noted an improvement in my Havers Hill climb time – down to twenty-two minutes and forty-seven seconds.

I was then back in Cayman for various meetings on Avata until 16th October, when Viv and I flew to London. We went to the Royal Opera House with Jonnie and Vanessa to see Sarah Lamb dance the lead in *Mayerling* and were invited for a tour of the huge backstage area after the show, rounding off with dinner at Mr Chows. On 20th October, Rob and Jenna joined us for drinks at QGM, after which we walked over to the Royal Albert Hall to see a performance of *Guys and Dolls*, with dinner in our box. We also enjoyed a great catch-up lunch with Alan and Joan Scott at their home on 22nd October. I had a good meeting at the Foreign and Commonwealth Office about rebuilding projects in BVI, and Viv was able to pick up our Christmas Pudding at Fortnum and Mason.

We then returned to Miami and on the 27th drove up to Sebring for Halloween and Trick-or-Treat. All of Pat's boys, wives, girlfriends, grandnieces and nephews, and the young families of Pat's boys – even the dogs – were in fancy dress. On 28th October, after our four-mile walk, we went to a fishing tournament on the lake with Zac, followed by lunch at Gator Shack (there was more food on offer than alligator) and dinner at Joel and Danielle's home. It had been a tough year for the family, and it was good to be able to spend such a happy time with them.

On the 29th we returned to Cayman to attend the welcome reception at Government House for the new Governor, Martyn Roper, who had replaced the very short-tenured Governor Choudhury. The next day I left for Tortola, where I resumed my Havers Hill morning climbs, and reviewed sessions on the Lambert Beach Hotel claim we were negotiating. I also organised a presentation on the completion of Guana Island resort for the owners.

Viv and I had been delighted to be asked by the Plantana's Executive Committee to be part of a photo shoot there on 4th November, for the upgrade of their website. So, I returned for that, and a meeting with Caucus to present the latest Business Case for SATF on the 5th.

After enjoying CNCF's production of a wonderful piece of West Indian theatre: Errol John's play *Moon on a Rainbow Shawl*, I went to Bermuda to participate in CHICOS. The theme for 2018 was 'The Caribbean Market – Planning for the Future'. At this point, we had no idea COVID was around the corner! On the 9th we held a student session, where our younger generation tackled the seasoned professionals about where their future might lie. I would like to see more of this last.

On 2nd December I flew to Nassau, in company with Paul Bailey of the BVI RDA, to attend the third Caribbean Infrastructure Forum being held at Baha Mar. It was a great opportunity to catch up with Daniel Liu, and also to experience the ambiance of the resort and its rooms as a customer instead of an advisor!

Viv and I had planned to leave for Salt Lake City on 6th December, but our planned flight was cancelled, so we rebooked to fly through Charlotte, NC. After arriving in Salt Lake City, we picked up our car and drove to Alta, arriving at Sugarplum at 2am. Somehow, in spite of being in a daze, we managed to pick up bacon and eggs for breakfast en route, and we began our holiday by skiing some 14,000 vertical feet. The 9th was our twenty-third wedding anniversary, and we enjoyed a celebratory lunch at Sugarplum but still clocked up ten runs. The 10th December was my seventy-third birthday, which we celebrated by enjoying green Thai curry at Rustler and skiing fourteen runs.

We were submitting a bid to manage the completion of John Gray High School, to which end I had carried out several site tours. On 11th December, I needed to represent BCL at a presentation to the Cayman Islands Government, where we submitted our proposal for the project. So I flew to Cayman for the day, returning on the 12th, while Viv remained in Alta and had time to write our Christmas cards.

We enjoyed a long, lazy Christmas Day lunch for eleven guests at Callaloo, cooked by chef Carlos from Mise en Place, after playing croquet in the Orchard whilst partaking of hors d'oeuvres and champagne. I was given a copy of *The Oxygen Advantage*, by Patrick McKeown, as a Christmas present. This book teaches one how to breathe as part of a fitness regime, and what I learned would certainly change my daily workouts significantly from then on.

On the 27th, Viv and I were delighted that Arturo, one of my Harvard alumni, was in town. We were able to meet him and his wife and stepdaughter for dinner at Eric Ripert's 'Blue', at the Ritz, and catch up on his news.

Viv and I finished off a wonderful and active year with our traditional 'Do Drop In' at Callaloo.

2019

Know the Unknown, Hear the Unheard, See the Unseen.

As always, on New Year's Day we joined seldom-seen friends and neighbours at Alasdair and Lisa's home, where we were able to catch up on the previous year's news and happenings. Then, with only eight weeks to go before 1st March, Viv and I turned our minds to organising an appropriate celebration of my fifty years in the Caribbean. Mark Green came up with a brilliant logo of an immigration stamp with the two dates on it, as well as invitations in the format of boarding passes. This got us off to a great start, coupled with assembling our team for the event. This included Celebrations, Isaac Rankine, Henry Muttoo, Matt Brown, Michael Lemay, Rita, and Javee from Hopscotch for the lights, sound, and a projection screen for a slideshow of photographic highlights of the past decades.

On 8th January I flew to Tortola to meet with Michell and our team on the ground. We were working on the claim for damage at the sports club, which had been such a vital place immediately following the hurricanes, as it was one of the first places to open and serve food. We were also working on the claim for Lambert Beach Hotel, and I visited Virgin Gorda to complete a Reinstatement Cost Assessment on a luxury villa there. Our insured clients had experienced first-hand the problems of being underinsured, so we were now able to focus with them on appropriate coverage. We had also moved from our tiny offices in Meridian's building into more spacious premises, around the corner from Meridian yet still on Wickham's Cay.

On 17th January Viv and I left Cayman for Eagle Vail. There, Jimmy and Cynthia collected us and we drove to Glenwood Springs for lunch at Juicy Lucy's, followed by pasta and caviar (which we had ordered from Kelly's Katch, and shipped to Jimmy's home) for dinner at Mariposa. On 19th January, it was time to start our ski adventure, which we did at Snowmass, and at Aspen Highlands the next day

We awoke to fresh powder on the 21st and decided to test it out on Ajax Mountain, stopping for lunch at Little Nell's at Aspen base. The next day we were back to Snowmass after an overnight snowfall of eleven inches of new powder – what great conditions for us to enjoy! We then travelled to test out Vail and on the 24th, Johannes and Rosana Faessler, the owners of Sonnenalp, invited us to an outdoor picnic lunch at the 10th Mountain restaurant and welcome cocktails in the Kings Club back at the hotel, which we interspersed with some 12,000 vertical feet of great skiing.

On 25th, Viv decided it was time to chill out at the wonderful spa at Sonnenalp, whilst yours truly continued skiing, clocking up 20,000 vertical feet in thirteen runs. I stopped for a great lunch of bucatini pasta with black truffle at Sweet Basil in Vail Village, to which I introduced Viv the next day, followed by a cheese fondue dinner at the Swiss Chalet restaurant in the Sonnenalp. Between those two epicurean delights we skied 16,500 feet for our last ski day.

While Viv went to Cayman with our ski gear, I flew to San Juan to attend the Clinton Global Initiative summit at the Marriott before continuing to Tortola on 31st January, where I stayed until 6th February. Climbing Havers Hill every morning to start the day had become a routine, after which I would meet with Daniel, who provided detailed briefings of the progress the office was making on our various projects.

I have a note in my diary that on 13th November 2018, I began thinking about who might benefit from a sponsorship if I climbed Kilimanjaro in the summer of 2019. By February 2019, I had made the decision to undertake the climb. Viv and I then asked ourselves, where do we start with the training programme? Was it really a major undertaking or was it 'no big ting'.

We soon learnt that whilst it wasn't a technical climb, the altitude gain from the base to summit presented a significant challenge. Our judgement was based on our experiences during earlier climbs together in Bhutan, up to 16,000 feet, where Vivian suffered altitude sickness. We had also tackled the higher slopes in Colorado together, reaching 14,000 feet – all with guides as one has to know the terrain to master the summit. We decided that the Kilimanjaro summit of

19,000 feet was too high to attempt without significant technical preparation, and that I would need to make the climb on my own, though with Viv's wholehearted support.

During the next weeks we considered how we could use my upcoming Kilimanjaro climb to raise funds for a local charity. Having seen the work the Red Cross had done following hurricanes in the region, particularly following Ivan in Cayman and then Irma and Maria in BVI, I contacted Dani Coleman. I knew she had worked with the Red Cross, and she kindly put me in touch with Jondo Obi, who was the current director of the Cayman Islands Red Cross. After some discussion, it was agreed I would be representing the Red Cross of the Cayman Islands, and climbing to both raise funds and to parallel the preparation for the Mt Kilimanjaro climb with the preparation for the hurricane season in Cayman.

As I mentioned earlier, I had been given a copy of *The Oxygen Advantage*, which advocated a specific breathing method. Based on this, I began recording my Body Oxygen Level Test (BOLT) score. To get this, you breathe in, then breathe out, and count how long you can comfortably hold your breath. This provides a measure of your progress as you practice the method, and came to form a key part of my training for the Kilimanjaro climb, which was to take place in August.

On 21st February, CNCF held their 25th National Arts Awards, for which I presented the Chairman's Award, and shortly thereafter our guests began to arrive for the party to celebrate my fifty years in the Caribbean. George and Boopie, and Doreen and Alan, showed up on 27th February; Viv's cousin Linda and Jill McDonald on the 28th, and Jimmy and Cynthia and Nancy Blake just in time for the cocktail party on 1st March, which we held in the Orchard.

Matt Brown and Henry had written a great skit about my arrival at Palisadoes airport in Jamaica, using Patois to illustrate my difficulties in understanding what was being said. Music and a dance performance followed, with everyone saying what fun it was to reminisce about such a wonderful period of our lives together in the region. We followed with a formal black-tie dinner on 2nd March, and our North Sound Boat trip to Stingray City and Starfish Point the next day, with Carlos serving his classic paella on board. It was a great, three-day non-stop party.

By 7th March we were in Melbourne, Australia, to get ready for our Harvard OPM Tasmania reunion. We had arrived in the morning, and lunched at Il Bacaro, where we enjoyed lightly cooked calamari on arugula. Afterwards I had delicious agnolotti, while Viv relished pasta with Moreton Bay bugs. Viv, being a more traditional diner, had regarded these with some suspicion, but when she heard that Moreton Bay bugs are a kind of small lobster, she decided they were OK to eat!

After this feast, we returned to the Stamford Plaza and slept from 4pm to 4am! We flew to Hobart the next day, where we joined the group. On 11th March we left the hotel at 7.45am by bus to the Bruny Island Ferry terminal and took the yellow power boat for a tour of Australia's highest sea cliffs, deep sea caves and the Monument sea stack. We saw seals, bottlenose dolphins, and an albatross at the junction of the Tasman Sea and Southern Ocean, and we rounded out the day with dinner at the Drunken Admiral. On the 12th we walked around Hobart Harbour and took a five-hour bus trip to Cradle Mountain Lodge, enjoyed dinner with the alumni, then looked at a photograph of the 1986 OPM class to see how many names we could come up with of the group pictured therein. Sad to say, we could only come up with fifty, out of one hundred and twenty.

On 13th March we awoke to a beautiful morning in this World Heritage Site. We lit a log fire in our room, enjoyed breakfast in the lodge, and then took a two-hour walk around Dove Lake, which was absolutely beautiful, with great sunny (but chilly) weather. Afterwards we enjoyed room service in front of our log fire.

At 5pm we visited Devils @ Cradle, a conservation sanctuary dedicated to breeding and conserving Tasmanian Devils. We watched these incredible creatures, and the snarling, rather scary noises they made at each other. The next day we drove from Crater Mountain to Freycinet Lodge, stopping for lunch at the Devil's Corner Winery, where we purchased three bottles of excellent Pinot Noir for the Callaloo cellar. We checked into the magnificent twenty-room Saffire Freycinet Resort (built at a cost of US$31m) and then donned waders and walked out to the oyster beds for a tasting – one cannot get oysters any fresher than straight out of the sea, with champagne provided! We returned to the Saffire for dinner and a OPM meeting to discuss the next venue for our reunion. On the 15th we took a boat ride to Schouten Island to see the incredible rock formations there, and then had a 3km hike to see Wine Glass Bay, followed by a farewell dinner at Saffire. We started 16th March with a forty-five-minute helicopter ride to the Penal Colony at Port Arthur – it is now a museum, with no prisoners in attendance! – then transferred to Hobart airport for the flight to Sydney.

We flew on Qantas to Cairns the next day and checked into the Hilton, where we were upgraded to a spa room. Then, after eating a tapas lunch, we slept fifteen hours straight through. The next morning we walked along the

Cairns boardwalk to find the Coral Expeditions wharf, and after lunch we collected our luggage and boarded the *Coral Expeditions II* to commence our tour of the Great Barrier Reef. Unfortunately, because of Cyclone Trevor, our route had been changed to go south. We cruised overnight to Sudbury Cay, which is surrounded by a small, shallow reef. After breakfast John, one of the naturalists on board, gave a lecture on the Great Barrier Reef with a quiz to follow, which Viv won. She now wears her prize – a green Coral Expeditions hat – as part of her tennis gear. As the sea was still rough, we lazed around, had lunch and then took a glass-bottomed boat tour. Compared with Cayman there was very little to see. The water wasn't very clear, having been stirred up by the storm, so we declined snorkelling, which anyway involved donning a 'stinger suit' to avoid getting stung by the jelly fish in the water. On 20th March we cruised to Tongue Reef, but with the weather still overcast and the sea rough, we again declined snorkelling. Instead, we enjoyed a cultural lecture by Majik, a Torres Straits Islander, with some new words for us to learn: *Capu Migi* – good morning, *Esso* – thank you.

The bad weather continued, and the next day we were hosted by the captain for dinner on board. We then cruised back to Cairns and flew to Melbourne, where we visited our niece Charlotte and her husband Bill at their home in Heidelburg and met the new baby – named Baby Bill! On 23rd March, we drove to Bill and Charlotte's farm, where we relaxed for a few days and where, during a long walk, Viv finally saw kangaroos in the wild – something she had wanted to experience for years.

We then flew back to London, where we spent a few days and met Alan and Joan Scott for lunch at the Chesil Rectory, where we had excellent lamb and Château Cantemerle. Then we flew to Berlin, to meet Patrick McKeown. I had been so impressed with his book *The Oxygen Advantage*, that I emailed, saying I would like to meet him. He readily agreed, and I offered to go to Galway, where he lived, next time I was in UK. As it happened, right at the time we returned from Australia, he said he was going to be in Berlin, which was a whole heap easier to get to than Galway! So we drove to the Eden Centre in Pankow, outside Berlin. There we met Patrick, and nine other very fit-looking physical trainers, all in their twenties. Viv and I, in our seventies, felt at a slight disadvantage.

No matter! Patrick explained the theory of his course, a key aspect of which is that it is important to always breathe through your nose, as this improves the supply of oxygen to the blood far more than when you breathe through your mouth. To make sure the team practiced this, Patrick had a supply of paper tape to apply over our mouths just before going to bed. At first there was a slight feeling of claustrophobia, but we found one quickly gets used to the restriction. Viv was delighted, as it was an instant remedy for my snoring! After the theory, Patrick led us through the practical aspects of his programme. We all ran around the room holding our breath and then checking BOLT scores. Patrick asked Viv and me to take it a little easy! I think he was worried we might collapse, but we were fine. The next day there was more practice, and we thoroughly enjoyed the experience. Initially, I had been able to walk some twenty or so paces after exhaling and holding my breath, but before the Kilimanjaro climb I was able to walk ninety paces.

In the evening we took Patrick to dinner at Trattoria Rosini, where he shared how he had come to teach the Oxygen Advantage Method, originally developed by a Dr Konstantin Buteyko. As an asthma sufferer, Patrick had read about the technique and successfully applied it to himself. He subsequently gave up his stressful rental car business in Galway to teach Oxygen Advantage full-time instead. Around that time he met his future wife. When her father asked what he did, Patrick replied he was going to teach people how to breathe. Needless to say, his future father-in-law was not particularly impressed – but he would surely be impressed now, as Patrick's business has grown into a successful global enterprise.

On 1st April we caught a taxi to Tegel Airport, not being aware that the subway and bus services were on strike. Public transport was in chaos, and hordes of people were walking along the pavements with their rolling suitcases. The somewhat surreal sight made it appear as if the city was being abandoned.

Back in Cayman, we received a welcome enquiry from Kirk Freeport about securing retail space at the front of the Greenery shopping centre. We met on site with Kirk's representatives to see how we could accommodate their needs. Our new self-storage facility, located over the Greenery's rear car park, was filling up rapidly, so we had decided to convert part of the Greenery's original building into climate-controlled storage as well. This would be available in 2020, and could be easily administered through the office in the new facility. We would receive CPA approval for the conversion in November, which was as well because by then the new facility over the rear car park would be fully occupied.

On 13th April, Nick Holland came to Cayman make a presentation at a conference, and we had the delight of inviting him to dinner at Callaloo. Sadly, my longstanding friend and architect, Malcolm Stephenson, from the very early days in Cayman, had passed away earlier in April, and on the 17th many of his friends gathered at Morgan's restaurant in the Cayman Islands Yacht Club to give him an appropriate send off.

On 25th April, the architect Colin Lumsden, head of the George Town Revitalisation Project, made a lunchtime presentation at the George Town Yacht Club, updating those with business interests in our capital city with some ideas about what we could look forward to in the near future that would bring life back into the centre of Cayman's capital.

At this time I was developing a new course for key Project Management skills, basing it on the six key questions by which I have lived my professional life: 'What, Where, When, Why, Who and How' and that the answer had to be SMART, 'Specific, Measurable, Attainable, Relevant and Time bound' to achieve the objective.

Viv and I flew to Newark in mid-May for a Commodities Corporation fiftieth anniversary party. Commodities Corporation had been Viv's former employer before being acquired by Goldman Sachs in 1997 as part of Goldman Sachs's effort to expand its asset management business. According to DayTrading.com, at the time of the acquisition CC managed $1.8 billion in assets. The firm was subsequently renamed Goldman Sachs Princeton LLC, and is now known as Goldman Sachs Hedge Fund Strategy within Goldman Sachs Management. For Viv it was great to catch up with all her colleagues from the good old days as the bank had closed down with the takeover.

On 29th May, I was asked to attend a meeting at the Ministry of Culture. The Minister wanted CNCF to take over the running of Pirates Week, and we requested additional written information about the exact scope of this assignment to ensure we could meet the Ministry's expectations.

The Clinton Global Initiative conference took place on 3rd June, and the next day I took the ferry from Charlotte Amalie to Tortola and had meetings with Marvin Flax of OBMI, and then went to Scrub Island to meet with a potential client. On 6th June we inspected the extent of the damage and rebuild work on the Bougainvillea Clinic building in Road Town. It's a somewhat dominant building, given its purple colour as well as its elevated position in town. I was enjoying, as always, my early morning walks up Havers Hill as part of my Kilimanjaro training. At the same time, I began to assemble a detailed list of equipment required for my Kilimanjaro climb. As part of the suggested breath training, I was consuming a mixture of apple cider vinegar and bicarbonate of soda in the mornings. It was not a particularly pleasant way to start the day, but if it could improve my body's oxygen capacity on my climb, I was willing to give it a try. I note that on 12th May my blood pressure and heart rate were 122/73/67 with a BOLT score of 36, so my training was going in the right direction.

It was time for some more rigorous training at altitude, so we flew to Eagle Vail for some more challenging hiking. We hiked to Smuggler's Mountain and Hunter's Creek, affording us some 1,000 feet of vertical ascent. On 15th June we drove to Snowmass and hiked up to Elk Camp, enjoying a picnic by the lake, and gaining some 1,300 feet of altitude. The next day we had a lazy start at Mariposa, walked five miles around Aspen Glen, then drove into Aspen for an outstanding dinner. This set me up for the 3,160 foot climb of Ajax Mountain the next day. I reached the summit and the gondola just as a thunderstorm started. Viv had prepared a packed lunch for me and kissed me goodbye at Mariposa, and so I had to eat my picnic lunch in the gondola as it descended to the Ajax Tavern at the base, where there was a hailstorm. When I returned to Mariposa, I was greeted by a much-relieved Vivian, who had been tracking the weather with some unease. The next day we met our guide, Heather Lafferty, at Mushroom Rock overlooking Aspen Glen, and enjoyed a 900-foot climb followed by lunch at Smithy's in Carbondale.

Back in Cayman for only a few days, I was in the air again on 26th June, heading to Buenos Aires for the IFACCA Americas Summit, where I was representing Cayman. Once settled in the hotel, I decided to take a walk, but had failed to appreciate it was winter in Buenos Aires – I had to wear my airline sleeper suit under my clothes to keep warm! After clearing my head with a five-mile walk, we had an afternoon meeting at the Villa Ocampo, followed by drinks and hors d'oeuvres. The summit continued the next day at the Centro Culturo de la Ciencia (C3), in Godoy Cruz, with discussions on the topic of IT in cultural development, followed by the opening of the Argentine Creative Industries. On 29th June we had a workshop to establish policy, followed by the opening of the Figari Art Exhibition and a performance of Puccini's *Turandot* at the Buenos Aires Opera House.

I then took the night flight back to Miami and the afternoon flight to Tortola, where I spent the week working and continuing my training on Havers Hill. I achieved my best time yet: 21 minutes and 52 seconds, and a breath-hold of 90 seconds, with my weight now at 196 pounds. I returned to Cayman on 6th July, picking up the malaria pills I needed for Tanzania en route.

On 30th July Viv and I were back to London, with lunches at Da Mario with Charlene, and dim sum at Yauatcha, and swimming workouts at Imperial, and on 5th August I started my course of malaria pills. Then, on 7th August, I kissed Viv goodbye – it was time to start the Kilimanjaro adventure. My British Airways flight from Heathrow was delayed by one hour due to a computer malfunction, which meant I missed my Precision Air connection from Nairobi to Kilimanjaro, and had to overnight at the Crowne Plaza at the airport. This had the added complication that, as I was no longer simply transiting through Kenya, I had to obtain and pay for an entry visa.

Despite these challenges, on 9th August 2019, I joined twelve other climbers assembled at the Stella Maris Hotel in Moshi, Tanzania, for a briefing on what was required in order to successfully summit Mt Kilimanjaro which, at 19,341 feet, is the highest freestanding mountain (i.e., not part of a mountain range) in the world.

Among other things, the briefing covered the essential equipment for our daypacks and duffels – each climber was allowed 10kg in their daypack and 20kg in a duffel carried by the porters. To support our group of thirteen climbers, we needed six guides, two cooks and thirty-eight porters. These were all members of the Chagga tribe, who inhabit the land at the base of Kilimanjaro and speak Chagga, Swahili and some English.

Each day, the porters broke camp, packed the equipment and supplies and carried them to the next location, where they set up camp again. A critical part of the climb's success was water. This was sourced at each camp and treated with Aquatabs, and each climber needed to consume at least 4 litres a day. Gradual acclimatisation to the altitude was equally vital, so the choice of route to the summit was important. We chose the Lemosho route, one of eight possible paths to the summit, which provided a gradual ascent over six days and a two-day descent.

The danger of the Kilimanjaro climb is that as one continues to gain altitude the air pressure decreases and so does the oxygen level in the atmosphere. Consequently, there is less oxygen available in the air one breathes. Blood oxygen saturation, which is normally 100 per cent at sea level in a healthy person, drops to approximately 50 per cent at the summit. This can lead to altitude sickness or, more seriously, HAPE (High Altitude Pulmonary [O]Edema). This is a potentially fatal condition where fluid builds up in the brain and lungs. Diamox, a diuretic, is commonly used to mitigate the effects of altitude. Of our group only one other climber and I chose not to take the drug and rely on consuming the recommended quantities of water – fortunately, it worked for me!

Following the briefing, our group enjoyed a dinner together and a discussion on the adventure that awaited us all. Before beginning the climb, a medical check was required. Blood oxygen saturation (SPO2) and pulse rate were measured with an oximeter, and we were quizzed about our general physical condition: Did you sleep well? Do you feel nauseous? Did you eat well? Are you dizzy? etc. These checks were repeated twice a day, for the duration of the climb.

On Day One, 10th August, after breakfast at the Stella Maris Hotel, we set off in a minibus, stopping at a supermarket to acquire last minute supplies and to ensure all climbers had Nalgene water bottles (all plastics are banned in the Kilimanjaro National Park). Then we drove to Londorossi Gate, (elevation 7,742 feet) to register all the climbers, and where the equipment was weighed to ensure that each porter's load did not exceed the specified weight of 20kg in each waterproof duffel bag.

After a snack lunch, the climb commenced in earnest, with the guides exhorting each climber to take it slowly – 'pole, pole' – which became the chant from the beginning to the end of the climb. We started the climb at 2pm and hiked for two and three quarter hours, increasing our elevation by some 1,520 feet, to the camp at Mt Mkumba, at an elevation of some 9,500 feet above sea level.

The porters had set up camp by the time we arrived, with individual tents for sleeping and a communal mess tent for meals. A delicious dinner of pea soup, tilapia and roast potatoes and banana fritters reinvigorated us all. Dinner enabled our group to get to know each other better, as – with the exception of a group of four from Canada who knew each other from before the climb – this was the first time we had time to chat. We were indeed a diverse group, ranging from twenty-five to seventy-three years of age, from Scotland, Ireland, India, Canada, United States and Cayman. Once dinner was over, we retired to our tents for our first night under canvas. Although the day had been warm and sunny, the night was very cold, and we had to learn to manage the 'mummy' style sleeping bags, with a portion that fitted over your head. I found it to be somewhat claustrophobic, but the hood was essential if one wanted to stay warm.

Day Two, 11th August. No alarm was needed, as the white-tailed colobus monkeys began calling at 5.30am. Soon we were packing our sleeping bags and the porter's duffels, followed by breakfast in the mess tent. Again, it was a hearty meal, starting with warm porridge, then Spanish omelette and baked beans, and coffee or tea. The weather was very cold to start but soon warmed up as the sun rose higher in the sky.

The climb to the summit of Kilimanjaro passes through five distinct ecological climate zones: the cultivated zone, the rain forest zone, the heather/moorland zone, the alpine desert zone, and the arctic summit zone. That day our route was very steep and rocky as we walked through the rainforest and moorland zones for six hours, gaining some 2,800 feet in altitude from Mt Mkumba, to Shira 1 Camp, at an elevation of 11,500 feet and from where we could now see Kilimanjaro peak.

We arrived at around 2pm, and were treated to a lunch of leek soup, followed by veggie burgers and French fries. We rested after lunch, and around 5pm we met with all of the porters, who treated us to songs and dances from their region. We climbers happily participated, to the delight of both the guides and porters. 'Happy hour' followed at 5.30pm with popcorn and tea (no alcohol is allowed on the mountain). We enjoyed a hearty dinner of chicken stew, and then went to bed at 8pm. In the camp environment all is shared, including snores. Abhay from Toronto's tent was next to mine, and I know he slept well as he snored solidly from 9pm to 5am the next morning. If snoring is ever listed as an Olympic sport, Abhay will win a gold medal!

Day Three, 12th August. We climbed from Shira 1 Camp to Moir Hut at an elevation of 13,600 feet. There was a thick layer of ice on the outside of the tent when we woke at 5.30am, and it was bitterly cold. I had managed no more than two to three hours of sleep! Breakfast was hot porridge and bacon and eggs and green tea, and then we were on the trail by 7am. Our hike of six hours finished by lunch, which was spaghetti Bolognese. The food, as always, was good and plentiful – needed to fuel the physical exertion of the climb. After a rest of ninety minutes we had a two-hour acclimatisation hike up a steep slope, during which we gained some 1,200 feet to reach an elevation of more than 14,000 feet. The guides appeared happy with our ability as a group to accommodate this. Then we descended back to camp for a shave, a wash and a comb. The trail dust and dirt that permeated everywhere was becoming increasingly noticeable, and required gaiters to keep it out of our hiking boots. After happy hour, and a dinner of chicken soup and quiche, we turned in. Sleep was better for me than the previous nights, as I'd begun to master the art of sleeping in a mummy sleeping bag and to turn over in it without suffocation!

Day Four, 13th August. We climbed from Moir Hut to Lava Tower before lunch. Key that day was a long climb to an elevation of 15,190 feet, again as an acclimatisation exercise, during which we gained some 1,500 feet in elevation over a four-and-a-half-hour period, followed by a long three-hour descent to Lava Tower. There, the porters had erected the mess tent and we enjoyed a hot lunch of carrot soup, chicken and chips. Then we descended further to Barranco Camp, at an elevation of 13,000 feet, for a dinner of soup, macaroni meatballs and homemade chili. The principle of the exercise was to 'climb high and sleep low'. The day had commenced at 5.30am, with a breakfast of hot porridge and fresh fruit. Most of our climbing team were now suffering from headaches, nausea and lack of appetite, but I am delighted to say, having religiously followed the advice of drinking 4 litres of water daily, I felt fine and once again declined Diamox.

A climbers' meeting was held to discuss the tipping policy for our guides and porters. As might be imagined, with so many climbers and staff, this process was somewhat complex. Yours truly was elected to collect the funds! Bedtime followed at 8.30pm, and I enjoyed the best night's sleep since the climb began.

Day Five, 14th August. We awoke as usual and enjoyed breakfast, after which we scaled the Barranco Wall, an 800-foot near-vertical, sheer rock face, competing for footholds with the porters, who were scaling the wall at the same time. On reaching the top, you are treated to an unbelievable vista with all the clouds below you. The balance of the day's climb took us to Karanga Camp, at an elevation of 13,000 feet. Don't let that fool you into believing we did not have any altitude gain, we climbed 1,400 feet that day, which took some six hours. On arrival, we were treated to a hot lunch of potato soup and ugali (a kind of maize-meal porridge) and callaloo, which made me feel very much at home. It was a bright, sunny day and the scenery was outstanding as we worked our way around the base of the Kilimanjaro glacier. We were really blessed by the weather, and I cannot imagine doing this climb in the rainy season.

Abraham, the lead guide, treated us to a talk on the history of Tanzania and Kilimanjaro – the name means 'bright mountain' – at 5pm. Kilimanjaro is not only the highest freestanding mountain in the world and the highest point in Africa, it is also a volcano and has three peaks, Shira, Mawenzi and Kibo. Uhuru Peak is the highest summit on Kibo's crater rim. Kilimanjaro was first climbed in 1889, by Hans Meyer. Some 35,000 people each year attempt the climb, and there has been concern about the environmental damage and trash on the mountain. The guides appeared sensitive about this, defending the government's trash removal programme (which from personal observations appeared pretty ineffective). Dinner and 8pm bedtime followed.

Day Six, 15th August. At 8am we departed Karanga for Barafu Base Camp, at an elevation of 15,331 feet, which we reached after three and three quarter hours of climbing with a very steep rise at the end, gaining 2,000 feet in altitude. Following lunch, we were briefed on the summit climb, which was to commence at 11pm that evening. That day the meal schedule changed, so we had lunch around noon, dinner at 5pm, and breakfast at 10pm!

In addition to the six regular guides, two of the porters were also co-opted as guides, so that a total of eight staff would climb with us and encourage us at times of weakness. Clothing was discussed in detail. It was going to be very cold when we started, so multiple layers would be needed through the night, but it would become warm as we descended from the summit during the day.

As it was dark, all climbers wore a battery-powered headlamp – the strap of which should not be too tight as this can cause headaches at this altitude – and we would need to take spare batteries. We were lucky in that the moon was full that night. We would need ski gloves and liners, and any handwarmers would need to be activated at base camp as they need oxygen to function. The wind speed on the mountain was likely to be between 5km and 35km per hour, with a temperature of −6 to −15 degrees C at the summit. Hiking poles must be adjusted at base camp as the mechanism freezes at the summit. Drinking a lot of water was key, as always, but the tube from Camelbak water bags and bottles freezes at this altitude, so water bottles needed to be wrapped in socks and t-shirts in the daypack and carried upside down for the water to be accessible. All sugary foods for energy needed to be kept warm inside our jackets, to avoid freezing.

We enjoyed lunch of cucumber soup, rice, vegetables and shish kebab, and then slept. Dinner of soup, spaghetti and meat sauce was at 5.30pm and we napped again from 7pm to 10.30pm. We then awoke for 'breakfast' and were set to make the final 4,125 vertical ft ascent to the summit.

We assembled shortly before 11pm, all looking like 'Pillsbury doughboys', due to the number of layers we were wearing. I wore a Spyder ski jacket as a top layer, and quickly discovered I could not hold my hiking poles with my ski gloves and liners on. I quickly changed to a thinner pair of gloves, as the poles were essential gear to me for the climb. Starting uphill out of base camp, we could see people with headlamps in front and behind us, looking like a string of fairy lights at Christmas. It was bitterly cold and difficult to move due to the amount of clothing we were wearing, and we soon stopped to strip off some layers.

Day Seven, 16th August. We zigged and zagged up the mountain as our eight guides encouraged us to keep climbing. Particularly for me, Pungo (Joseph Nguma), was a great psychological help. At every turn the wind was biting cold, and almost threatened to blow us off the face of the mountain. During the seven and a half hour climb to the summit there were many times when I felt like giving up, as it was a very difficult ascent, either over large rocks or across slippery scree. What helped to keep me going was slow, deep breathing and all my training using the principles of the Oxygen Advantage programme, my commitment to raising funds for the Cayman Islands Red Cross, and the prospect of Vivian's welcome home party on Monday. How would the second two look if I didn't make it to the top!

Each time it seemed we had reached Stellar Point (the first sighting of the volcano's rim) we would round another corner, with another section to climb.

The last several hundred yards to Stellar Point were very slippery scree and particularly exhausting, as we had now been climbing through the night for more than six hours. We finally arrived at Stellar Point, and sheltered from the wind to enjoy a hot cup of tea and catch our breath – the sun was just rising in a spectacular display, lighting the volcanic basin and glacier. After tea we continued onto Uhuru Peak, which took a further hour of climbing. All thirteen of our team made it to the summit, but several had been very sick on the ascent. There was much mutual congratulation, and many photos were taken at the famous sign on the roof of Africa.

Then we immediately began the descent. As is often the case, this was almost more difficult than the ascent, as the sandy scree and dust made it very easy to lose your balance. The total descent time back to Barafu Base Camp was a little over two hours. After a short rest and then lunch, we continued for a further two and a half hours to Millennium Camp. After hiking all night to the summit and descending, this additional hike was both uninteresting and tiring, but was better than the original route. This would have taken us to Mweka camp, and would have taken more than twice as long. At Millennium Camp we were exactly at the point where the clouds below met the mountain, and whilst the ground was very dusty, the air was damp with moisture. We had a presentation from Abraham on the tipping ceremony and a team meeting to collect the cash, and I was asked to make a speech to thank all the porters and guides and present the tips the next day. Dinner followed and we all collapsed, exhausted by almost twenty-four hours of climbing.

Day Eight, 17th August. We awoke at 5.30am as usual and packed our daypacks and duffel bags for the last day on the trail. Breakfast and then the tipping ceremony followed, and afterwards much singing of Kilimanjaro songs and dancing. I thanked the guides and porters for moving the camp every day, and for sharing their culture with us, and getting us all to the summit and down again safely. We then broke camp and continued the descent to Mweka gate, with the vegetation changing dramatically as we descended through the moorland and re-entered the rain forest. The path became very muddy and slippery due to the wet conditions – at this point the steep descent was tough on the toenails! We finally arrived at Mweka gate, at an elevation of 5,380 feet, having descended 8,000 feet in just under five hours – a distance that had taken us several days to ascend. We signed out at the register at the gate, and drove back to the Stella Maris Hotel for a warm shower – what luxury!

At 3pm, we had an awards ceremony, during which each climber was presented with a certificate of their summit achievement. Grace, from Ultimate Kilimanjaro, questioned us about the quality of the climb and the service provided by the staff. I then enjoyed my first alcoholic drink in four months: an ice-cold Kilimanjaro beer! Chicken curry followed for dinner, some more celebratory drinks, and then a sleep in a bed – another luxury after eight nights spent sleeping on the ground!

Day Nine, 18th August. I awoke around 6am, looked at more than a week's worth of emails, and then breakfasted. We bade each other goodbye and finished packing. A driver collected me at noon from Stella Maris, and drove me to Kilimanjaro airport for my Kenya airways flight to Nairobi, and then to London.

On Day Ten, 19th August, I arrived in Heathrow to a fabulous surprise: Vivian was there in the arrival hall with a great big sign 'Congratulations, my darling – welcome home from Kilimanjaro. I love you'! Back to 62 QGM, followed by a welcome home party that evening with a further welcome surprise: a great gathering of friends to celebrate what had been 'the adventure of a lifetime'.

One thing that you come to realise about training for and then undertaking such an adventure is that it is somewhat selfish because, of course, for the duration you are focussing on what YOU want to do. Accordingly, I wanted to thank Viv for all her support and staunch encouragement, and so after a day spent relaxing at QGM we caught a flight from London City Airport to Florence, where we picked up a rental car and wound our way to Fonte de' Medici – one of Viv's favourite wines is Villa Antinori, and the family own the Fonte. There we enjoyed dinner after checking into our suite, which came complete with its own living room and kitchen that we were to make full use of during our stay.

On 22nd August we began our day with a five-mile walk around the vineyards, stopping for a rustic lunch at Casa Mia, and then at the local Co-op to purchase supplies for dinner. This we cooked in the suite's kitchen and then sat on our terrace overlooking the vineyards as we relaxed and enjoyed the meal. The next morning we were a little more adventurous, and took a seven-mile walk to Badia a Passignano. We were not sure if there was a loop return to the Fonte and so asked an incongruously suited gentleman if he knew the way back. He replied by saying he was a driver for someone visiting the local wine cellar for a tasting. He asked us where we were from and we said Cayman – to which he replied, 'That's amazing – I worked with the owner of Agua in Cayman.' Once again, we were reminded of what a small world it is.

We returned for lunch and then a cooking course at the Fonte, which focused on pasta-making techniques. Dinner at the Osteria di Passignano Antinori followed, including a tour of their wine caves. On the 24th we drove to Greve in Chianti for market day, which wasn't very impressive, then had a delicious late lunch of steak with black truffles at Ristoro L'Antica Scuderia in Badia di Passignano. On 25th we took a short two-mile walk, followed by lunch at the architecturally stunning Antinori winery in Bargino, designed as an 'invisible' building that merges with the hillside. Lunch included a tour of their cellars, with a tasting of their outstanding Chiantis. Later we drove back to Badia di Passignano and the Ristoro L'Antica for dinner of fresh pasta and black truffles. We were certainly sad to leave this relaxing part of the world the next day. After a few days in London we left for Miami, intending to stay for a few days. However, due to Hurricane Dorian, which looked as if it might affect Cayman, we made a last-minute decision to return to Callaloo to make preparations. Luckily, we were spared, for which we were thankful.

From 8th–13th September I was in Tortola, catching up on progress in the office after each morning's climb up Havers Hill. On returning to Miami, I met with Mick Stiksma of CRE Valuation Services. We would be speaking on the topic of 'Innovations, Challenges and Experience Sharing' at the 8th Annual RICS / IPTI Valuation and Construction Conference in Nassau, at the end of October. I was back in Cayman on the 16th for a RICS-sponsored presentation by London's Wilberforce Chambers on Beach Access Rights.

We were delighted to entertain the new Governor, Martyn Roper, and his wife Lissie for dinner at Callaloo on 2nd October, deliciously cooked by chef Keith Griffin. A few days later Viv and I flew to London, where we enjoyed meals with friends and family and I (once again) went to renew my UK passport. On the 16th I met Bob Dyson, a good friend of brother Rob's, at the Lansdowne Club to give him a detailed description of my Kilimanjaro climb as it was an ascent he very much wanted to do.

At the end of the month, after catching up with business developments in Cayman, I was off to Nassau on 30th October for meetings and then to Tortola for more meetings and to look at projects in Virgin Gorda. I was still improving my ascent times of Havers Hill, which led to the idea of climbing Pico Duarte in the Dominican Republic, with Michell and Beatriz, which we did in February of 2020.

As part of the Kilimanjaro 'Climb for Red' campaign with the Cayman Islands Red Cross, I had agreed to make presentations at schools and other venues, paralleling the preparations needed for strenuous and challenging mountain ascents with the preparedness necessary for coping with the impact of hurricanes on Cayman. On 12th November I met students at St Ignatius High School, accompanied by Michael from the Red Cross, and described my training and the climb, and the key safety protocols we had carried out. I had brought my rucksack and equipment with me, and judging by their questions, the students were interested and thoroughly enjoyed the talk. As it turned out, I was later humbled to be honoured for my work in fund raising and preparedness lectures for the 'Climb for Red' campaign at a Red Cross dinner in January 2020.

The next day I travelled to Kingston, collected a rental car and drove on the excellent new toll road to St Ann's Bay and along the north coast to Secrets Hotel in Montego Bay, where I was speaking at the 9th annual CHICOS conference on 'Hotel Design: focussed on Building to Satisfy the Ever-Changing Customer Demands and Weather Patterns.' Fellow panellists included designers, project managers, government representatives, hotel operators and contractors. Key talking points included the latest features and facilities of hotels, construction methodology options, and the reaction of the industry to the recent devastating hurricanes in the region. With a slowing of Revpar (revenue per available room) and ADR (average daily rate) in the Caribbean, there was keen interest in the global and regional economic cycle, measured against an increasing supply of rooms to the market. The dynamics of the market were also changing, as major brands entered the all-inclusive market for the first time, and lenders noted a ready supply of funding for new projects. As always, CHICOS provided a unique opportunity to gather government, operators, investors, developers, lenders and professional advisors – all the highly experienced players in the tourist industry – in one location.

The conference finished on 15th November, and I drove from Montego Bay to Strawberry Hill, where I met up with Viv, Fossie and Jen, and checked into 'Mountainview' one of our favourite villas facing Newcastle. There we cooked up a vast quantity of ratatouille sauce (affectionately referred to as 'Rat') and pasta, accompanied by a few glasses of wine, and great catch-up chat. For the next couple of days we breakfasted on fresh fruit, cooked up a storm for lunches and dinners, and relaxed. Sadly, on 18th November it was time for an early morning drive down from Strawberry Hill to Kingston, to catch our flight back to Cayman.

On 19th November we had the opening weekend of *Rundown* at the Harquail, which, as always, was most enthusiastically received; and on the 20th CASE convened a judging panel, of which I was a member, for the upcoming Governor's Award to be presented at Government House on 5th December.

On 23rd November, Barrington's work permit expired, and we were sad to see him go, but we were also very happy to welcome Wayne back as our estate manager after his one-year rollover in Jamaica. However, for Barrington, this marked the start of a great opportunity. We introduced him to the HR team at one of the Foster's Supermarkets, and we are pleased to say he has since worked his way through the ranks to a fairly senior management role there.

Changes were also happening in BCL's BVI operations, as Dan Afoke had decided to relocate with Sarah to the Bahamas (where she is from), and we were finalising a contact with Kishan Jessa, from South Africa, to take over Dan's position. We had also submitted what we felt was a very strong bid on the contract to manage the rebuild of the BVI Police Marine Facility that had been badly damaged in Hurricanes Irma and Maria.

In early December we flew to Miami, drove to Sebring and enjoyed dinner with Pat's family. The next morning, we took a walk in Hammock Park and made enquiries about having some kind of memorial there for Flo and Pat, who had both enjoyed walking through this vast natural landscape.

On our 24th wedding anniversary, we flew to Salt Lake City, picked up a rental car, and drove to Alta and Sugarplum via Whole Foods Market for supplies. Waking on 10th December, my seventy-fourth birthday, I was treated to breakfast in bed and then had a late start skiing, followed by a perfect birthday lunch at Rustler, where we were greeted as long-lost friends by Meg and Vicki. During lunch the news came from BCL's BVI office that we had won the BVI Police Marine project, which was a great birthday present and the real icing on the cake.

We topped this off by skiing 14,000 vertical feet in eight runs, and finished the evening with Viv's outstanding stuffed Portobello mushrooms at Sugarplum – a perfect birthday! During the next two days we enjoyed ideal skiing conditions, especially on the 12th, when six inches of powder fell overnight. After a day on the slopes, we had dinner at Snowpine Lodge and après ski at the Gulch Pub, after which we skied back in the dark to dig out our Nissan Maxima from the snow, with Viv ranting in my ear, 'Never again a two-wheel drive! Told you so!'

A week of fabulous skiing followed (though our attempts at exchanging the Nissan for a four-wheel drive vehicle failed) after which Viv returned to Cayman with our ski luggage while I went to Tortola for meetings and to sign the BVI Police Marine contract. I returned on 21st December, in time to greet my brother Rob and family, who were visiting Cayman for Christmas. We had a wonderful Christmas with family on the beach, took photos in Santa hats, enjoying sea, sand and sun, croquet on the lawn at Callaloo with bubbles and hors d'oeuvres before Christmas lunch. On the 28th, our good friend Gerhart took us on a North Sound boat trip, followed by lunch at the Calypso Grill. We rounded out 2019 with our 'Do Drop In' party at Callaloo, and Alasdair and Lisa's New Year's Day party at their home, to start the next decade in style.

2020

With the start of a new decade, my key focus was on qualities of the mind –

Perspective, Humility, Humour, and Acceptance,

and the heart –

Forgiveness, Gratitude, Compassion, and Generosity.

I committed to doing my best to live by these values in this new decade ahead.

Viv and I left for London and Geneva at the beginning of January, where we picked up a rental car and drove to Verbier. Despite heavy traffic on the A9, we arrived in time for dinner with Ray and Michèle at Fontenelle – a superb green Thai curry. The next day we headed up to Medran and skied Mont Fort – seven runs in total – followed by a lunch of rösti and mushrooms, then Dôle and Fendant back at La Rotonde, our hotel. On 12th January, after breakfast, Ray and Michèle kindly collected us for the drive to Crevacol, in Italy, where we enjoyed excellent skiing despite Viv injuring her knee in a fall on some ice. She was such a trooper, she just asked for an ice pack to treat her knee during our fabulous lunch at La Croix Blanche in Étroubles where, as always, we were warmly greeted by Mauro. We had veal Valdostana with ham and cheese, preceded by wafer-thin ham with chestnuts and honey, and tiramisu to finish, with coffee and Grappa with blueberries. Thankfully Ray drove us back, and on the 13th we returned to Geneva in our surprisingly fun Skoda Octavia for the return to London. That evening, we attended a most informative lecture on Haiti at the House of Lords, delivered by Lord Griffiths of Burry Port.

On 14th January, we had dinner with Annie and Nick at Fortnum and Mason. Partway through the evening, Viv went to the lady's bathroom – which was pretty dimly lit – and was unexpectedly greeted with a hug and the words 'Auntie Vivian!' from someone she didn't immediately recognise. It turned out to be Vanessa, Jonnie's friend, who had performed 'The Dying Swan' at our celebration at Callaloo some years earlier. Vanessa was dining with a colleague from Los Angeles, and they were discussing the choreography for her dance group's upcoming performance at the Royal Ballet – yet another reminder of just how small the world can be!

Also on the 14th, I had an important discussion with Sloane Rhulen, a talented real estate agent who had found a buyer for the BCQS office space in Genesis. The sale would result in a solid capital gain, while also reducing the ongoing costs of maintaining the space. Two days later, back in Cayman, Frank Reed kindly brought Bonfire, the government's procurement website, to our attention, where an RFP (request for proposal) had been issued for the preparation of an Outline Business Case for the redevelopment of the prisons in Cayman.

Whilst we had somewhat limited experience with building prisons, we did have the support of Fincor, along with Ronnie Dunn and Lidka Scott on the business case side, so had a solid foundation from which to begin the application process. For our bid on the prison redevelopment, we had identified architects HLM – rated as one of the world's leading prison designers – to be part of our team. Recognising the importance of local context, we requested HLM to enter into 'joint venture' discussions with Michael Meghoo of MJM, to cover the architectural aspects of this important project. To round out the team, we engaged Hydrock for ME&P and F (Mechanical, Electrical Plumbing and Fire services), partnering them with Reed Consulting Engineers to provide local context.

On 27th January I flew to Tortola for meetings with the stakeholders on the Police Marine project, and to look at the progress of a number of other projects we were managing. On the 31st, I met with Dancia Penn who, as always, provided sound commentary on what was happening in the BVI, both politically and socially, before my return to Cayman on 1st February.

Neil, Denny, and I had for some time been contemplating the future of Equal Investments Ltd., which owned the top floor of Genesis building, and we met on the 3rd with the tenants to discuss if they wished to purchase the space they were occupying – to which they agreed. I had also for some time been looking to sell part of Office Developments Ltd.'s holdings in the Genesis building, and based on an offer we had received for the second floor south, agreed to a sale, which closed in March 2020.

On the 6th, through Paul Bailey, we had an interesting request for an assignment for BCL's BVI office, on the basis of BCL's Caribbean-wide experience. The assignment was to assess the best location for a major regional insurance company's head office. This led to an in-depth review of political stability, ease of access, labour pool skills, currency and other factors, which made for a most fascinating assignment for our team.

The next day Viv and I flew to Punta Cana, where Michell met us and kindly accommodated us at his home, and we went on to dinner at the Meringa restaurant where, to complete the excellent meal, we enjoyed much singing and dancing with our friends Claudia and Oscar, and Ivan and Mariella. We were up late the next day, and after a shrimp and pasta lunch at Casa Vargas we watched the vibrant and colourful Punta Cana carnival from the Rica stand. This was followed by drinks at Cava Alta with Amil and Sabrina, and Sabrina's mother-in-law, Terry, from Israel. Viv had always been interested in life in Israel and Terry gave her a good account of everyday life there!

The next day we drove to the ecological park in Cap Cana and swam in a crystal-clear pond, had ceviche and wine at the beach club, and then drove back to Casa Vargas, where the chef cooked up paella and poor man's eggs. With the Tropicalia resort scheduled to move ahead on 10th February, we drove to Bavaro to see the model room the contractors had built there and visited the site in Miches to see the infrastructure work and view the incredible beachfront location. There, we were treated to a cooling drink of coconut water straight from the shell – one of life's great pleasures, available to even the poorest person – and the sight of a helicopter on the beach. The juxtaposition was a great illustration of the distinctions of wealth that exist in these islands.

Oscar and Claudia kindly hosted us for lunch in their home in Punta Cana – a delicious Lebanese sea bass dish with onions, garlic and tahini topped with roasted almonds, and a honey desert to follow. On 11th February we had a late start from Michell's house and drove to Santo Domingo, where the traffic was terrible. We stopped for a business meeting concerning a waste disposal plant with Fredy Pena and Van Heyningen, and then enjoyed wine and tapas at Cava Alta before checking into Hodelpa Nicolás de Ovando, in the colonial zone, which had formerly been the residence of the first Governor of the Americas. The next day we went sightseeing through the colonial zone, viewing the beautiful Santa Maria la Menor cathedral, the oldest cathedral in the Americas, completed in 1550.

Back at our hotel, we packed for the Pico Duarte climb – at 10,125 feet, Pico Duarte is the highest mountain in the Caribbean. We then had drinks at Lulu's wine bar with Michell, Beatriz and Edwin, and then went to Maraca, a wonderful eclectic restaurant with tapas, Cousiño-Macul Cabernet Sauvignon, and Baron Phillippe de Rothschild Chardonnay. David, Michell's father, joined us there as a welcome surprise. The next day Michell and I took an Uber to David Vargas's house where we left our spare luggage. Due to her ski injury in Switzerland in January, Viv had decided not to climb, and instead returned to Cayman to meet our nephew Richard Heldreich and his wife Claire, and their sons, George and Freddie, who were visiting as members of a touring cricket team. Michell and I drove to meet with Luis, our Pico Duarte guide, for the five-hour drive to the Edwin Gómez Ecolodge in the José Armando Bermúdez National Park. There, we were briefed on the climb and, of course, did some carbohydrate loading for energy in the form of spaghetti and salad. Then we went to sleep in the bunk bed dorms.

On 14th February we awoke at 5am for a 5.30am breakfast, and then drove to the base, where we began climbing in the dark. We climbed nine and a half hours that day, during which we gained almost 6,000 vertical feet in altitude. We stopped for ham and cheese sandwiches on the way, and arrived at La Compartición at 4.30pm. Mules had carried our additional gear, and we enjoyed the luxury of a hot shower, with water heated by a solar panel. Dinner was chicken and rice with corn, followed with some fun singing around the campfire, and then we slept. There were some twenty mattress pads on the floor and our slumbers were accompanied by much snoring, so after the day's exertions I did not get as much sleep as I would have expected. But I was snug in my fleece-lined sleeping bag, on top of the blow-up mattress from my Kilimanjaro climb.

The next day we awoke at 6am for the climb to the summit, which we reached at 11am. Ifrahim was my guide, and followed me both on the ascent and descent. This was comforting, given I was last in line. On the way down we stopped for lunch of tacos at Lilies, and continued back down to La Compartición, having climbed a total of 2,300 feet. We enjoyed another welcome hot shower, and planned the return to La Ciellaga, and Santo Domingo and Punta Cana, followed by an afternoon snooze and dinner of sancocho stew with rice, chicken caprese, and avocado, after which we sang celebratory songs around the campfire. Once again our sleep was disrupted by snoring, little abated by my non-effective ear plugs.

On 16th February we awoke at 5am for the 6.30am start of our descent. The sunrise was incredible, as it illuminated the mountain scenery with changing patterns of light. I rode a mule down to save my knees, which were hurting from the ascent, and arrived at the base at 1.30pm with a sore backside, but with knees well intact. On the ride back to Santo Domingo we stopped to savour arepa, a kind of typical stuffed corn flatbread, as well as cheese and crackers. My hosts certainly ensured I would not leave the Dominican Republic without enjoying all their typical food!

Then it was back to David Vargas's house to collect our spare luggage and I drove back to Punta Cana to stay with Michell and Beatriz, and see Amos and Mica. The next day was spent at the BCL DR office catching up on business and then returning to Cayman – what a great trip and climb it had been! I then relaxed with visiting family, and George and Freddie, both talented cricketers who had a wonderful time as part of the visiting team challenging our local sides.

On 20th February, CNCF held the 26th celebration of its Arts and Culture Awards, and I commented as follows:

There is always a profound joy in recognising and celebrating achievement in any field, but particularly that of Arts and Culture, as it lies at the true heart of who we really are as a people.

Tonight, as always, I am humbled by the expansive range of talent we identify and nurture in our comparatively small community.

CNCF's work covers a broad spectrum of activities of which we at CNCF are very proud and our Arts Awards recognise the efforts of a large number of people and organisations, without which our work would not be possible, both in front of our audiences and behind the scenes.

During the course of the last year, I would like to thank our hard-working CNCF Board, our dedicated staff, volunteers and performers who together have made huge strides in continuing our mission.

The Chairman's Award is given for outstanding long-term support of the work of CNCF.

Sandra Watler has been actively involved in all areas of volunteering with the National Cultural Foundation for the past four years. She sees the National Cultural Foundation as a fundamental and integral part of the Cayman Islands in the preservation and showcase of Caymanian culture, and delights in any opportunity to assist. To that extent, she has served as chaperone, driver, co-ordinator, assistant, box office attendant and stagehand. Though she does not identify herself as an artist, Mrs Watler actively demonstrates her love of the arts and inculcates this love in her children and others in her support of the work of CNCF over many years.

Please join me in applauding the work that Sandra has done to further the work of CNCF and for which I am delighted to present to her the Chairman's Award.

CNCF put on our annual celebration of all things cultural at the Harquail, on Saturday 27th February, with the Red Sky at Night celebration, starting at 4pm and running until midnight. This event gains more support from the general public every year, with all the performances, local crafted art, and of course the good local food, without which no Caymanian event would be complete.

On 2nd March it was time for me to visit Tortola again and meet with the RDA team, to work through our management process for the Police Marine facility and to ensure Kishan, who had now joined our team, was well settled in his new role as office manager. I returned to Cayman on 7th March, where we were delighted to have been invited to make a presentation to Caucus, the government's decision making body, on our proposal for the OBC for the prisons. This we did on the 9th, and it was very well received.

On 12th March Viv and I flew from Miami to Eagle Vail, where we were met by Jimmy and Cynthia, and drove to Mariposa for a welcome steak dinner. We started late the next day, managing only three runs – the memorable bottle of 2014 Gigondas we enjoyed with lunch may have had something to do with that – before returning to Mariposa for a pasta and caviar dinner and a catch-up on all the Nowerys' news. Since early 2020, there had been increasing concern about a rapidly spreading virus called COVID 19, first identified in Wuhan, China in late 2019. As we lightly touched on the subject, little did we appreciate just how quickly, and how profoundly, it would soon change everyone's lives.

Many of us had experienced an epidemic, but the word 'pandemic' was new. On 14th March, after a day's skiing, Jimmy suggested dining at Tempranillo, in Basalt. There, as she served us our tapas and Tempranillo wine, our waitress casually mentioned that Aspen and Vail had just closed due to COVID cases among some visiting Australian skiers. We started 15th March with our thirty-five-year tradition of caviar eggs and champagne, then rebooked our return to Cayman for 17th March. Much discussion then followed about what supplies might be needed to avoid spreading the new virus. We had been advised to get sanitising wipes and hand sanitiser, but Glenwood Springs and Carbondale had sold out of these, so we returned to Mariposa for the night. We were listed for an upgrade to first class on the return flight the next day, but when Viv and I boarded, we were not sitting together, and neither were several other couples. As we and our fellow passengers all swapped places, it was indeed surprising that so soon after the announcement of the spread of COVID, everyone was already busy wiping down the seats, arm rests and tables with sanitising wipes. In the end, we all finished up sitting together where we wanted.

In Cayman, Wayne picked us up from the airport. The government had decreed the previous day that all schools were to be closed and that travellers were required to self-quarantine for fourteen days. We asked Wayne to stay in his cottage, and asked our housekeeper, Hyacinth, to stay at her home and not come to work at Callaloo. There then followed an interesting change in the way we lived. We obviously needed food supplies for the house, given that we had been away for some days. So Viv would make up a list and leave it outside for Wayne, who would go to the supermarket and collect the requested items. The only challenge was that, as a Jamaican, Wayne's choice of 'chicken', for example, was decidedly different to ours, and would include frozen chicken parts including feet that we did not know what to do with (or want to eat). So, over time, we worked out that he would take a photograph of a particular item and email it back to the house from the supermarket for approval before putting it into his shopping cart and bringing it home.

I had not been back in Callaloo for more than three days when I began to feel very ill, with a high temperature and significant headaches. At the time, I described these as 'like someone sticking an ice pick in the side of my head'. I called our doctor and described the symptoms, and he was of the opinion that I had a bacterial infection, not COVID. As with all our illnesses and aches and pains, we also consulted with Igor. Based on his advice, we did several things to boost our immunity. These included taking finely chopped garlic in half a glass of warm water, and lemon and honey in hot tea, every three hours for a week. One of the only benefits of having COVID – which I was subsequently diagnosed with, and which I believed I caught on the plane from Eagle when we moved seats several times – was that I dropped 9 lbs in weight. Viv was in constant touch with our doctor, John Addleson, who did prescribe tablets, but he was taking small steps to control my condition based on his initial diagnosis. He told Viv she was to give me the tablets, adhering strictly to the time frame he had prescribed, and that if my temperature rose to over 102 degrees, the only way to bring it down was with a tepid bath, which Viv had filled to be at the ready.

The poor soul had not factored in the air conditioning, which was keeping the temperature cool enough that the bath water was icy cold, so when I had my first dip in the tub I nearly passed out! Alan and Claudia had a better remedy when their son Sasha was just a baby and running a very high fever: wet woollen socks worked well to lower his temperature, except that the socks had to be changed every few hours as they got bone dry. If my breathing rate rose to more than twenty breaths per minute, Viv would need to call the doctor, and once again my poor wife would not get a wink of sleep as she counted through the night and woke me to take my temperature or give me my tablets according to schedule. The government announced the closure of Cayman's borders on Sunday 22nd March, for what was initially intended to be a three-week period, but that was subsequently extended many times. 'Repatriation air bridge' flights were permitted, but arrivals were required to adhere to strictly monitored quarantine conditions, including body-tracking devices, and regular, government-monitored, physical inspections of quarantine conditions.

The government began daily televised briefings, with the Governor, Premier, Minister of Health, Chief Medical Officer, and Chief of Police providing updates on containment measures to prevent spread of the virus and updates on the infection numbers. Globally, COVID was spreading at an unprecedented rate. During a call on 21st March with Michell Vargas, he told me of a wedding in Cap Cana where thirty-four of the one hundred and twenty-two guests had contracted the virus.

There were an estimated 80 million COVID cases worldwide, and there had been 1.8 million deaths. By 26th March, BCL had published an operational release, confirming to our clients how we could operate given the restricted conditions. This would include seeking and receiving 'essential worker' status for our appraisers, so that economic progress would not be stymied by the lockdown conditions. Given the reduction in our operational activity, we had to take a serious look at our cash flow. At one point, we considered reducing staff salaries as part of a survival process. But, I am proud to say, we paid all our office and home staff on time, and in full, during the entire COVID lockdown.

On 28th March a curfew between 7pm and 5am was introduced across the island. Masks were mandatory, and public spaces such as supermarkets were restricted by 'name day', whereby the first letter of your surname determined on what day of the week you could visit. Despite all these measures, the first case of community transmission of COVID was announced on 31st March. On 7th April, one hundred and sixty-five thousand COVID test kits arrived in Cayman. These had been purchased in Korea, secured by the generosity of a Cayman resident, which, given the demand for these tests, was no mean feat. On 16th April the devastating news then came, via a telephone call from Dr Jenny Hobday, that Mikol Dise had died following a comparatively simple procedure that had required an epidural injection. The implications of not being able to move freely due to COVID restrictions now came into full focus, as due to my possible COVID diagnosis, I could not leave the house to assist physically with arrangements for my dear friend Mikol.

On 20th April, John Addleson suggested we drive down to his clinic, where he had erected a small freestanding cubicle with a raised floor in the car park. There he took blood tests and reiterated that in his opinion my condition was not COVID, a viral infection, but rather a bacterial infection, and prescribed antibiotics. Back at Callaloo, I returned to bed and did not feel any better.

Viv and I then went for a drive-through COVID test at Doctor's Hospital on 27th April, and after waiting some fifteen days for the result, were advised by our good friend, nurse Hazel Brown (who had been such an invaluable help with Flo, so many years before) that Viv was negative, but I was positive. Mikol's funeral was scheduled for that day, for which I was honoured to have been chosen as a pall bearer. I could not accept, and felt absolutely gutted that, given our many years of friendship, I would not be able to bid him a proper goodbye.

One game-changing result of COVID was the shift from in-person office work to virtual collaboration through platforms such as Teams and Zoom. I'm proud to note that the Cayman prison rebuild team used these tools to develop and complete the Outline Business Case entirely virtually, which speaks volumes for the cohesiveness of this newly assembled and highly talented team, which continues its work five years on for the essential rebuild of our prison.

Given the 'lockdown', the modus operandi of frequent flights to the BVI for Michell and me was obviously not possible. Moreover, business arrangements, including those for the leases of our domestic and business accommodations and office space, were being challenged, and we were fortunate that our landlords agreed to reduce the rent. However, we continued to be involved with the rebuild of the Police Marine Base, with Kishan based in Tortola and Michell and I holding frequent Teams calls to move the planning options of the project forward, and Johmalvin still based in the BVI, working on the fit-out of an office project.

On 15th May our office manager, Bernadine, and I discussed a recent press briefing detailing the various safety rules that needed to be in place for our office to re-open. These included wearing sanitary gloves and masks, tissues supplied on each desk, hand sanitisers available, and instructions to the cleaners that all surfaces needed to be cleaned and sanitised. During all of this focus on 'cleanliness', it was delightful to receive a call from friends like Isley from West Bay, saying she had 'plenty' mangoes for us to collect and enjoy.

As a relief from the relentless focus on COVID in Cayman, on 27th May I received a call from a contractor we had met in Grenada, about an arbitration pertaining to the construction of a residence hall at the St George's Medical School there. As it was a complicated matter that would require our combined talents to begin unravelling the pros and cons of the case, I contacted both Jerry Katz and Charles Leonard, and we assembled and provided a proposal to the contractor by 3rd June.

Given our home was now some fifteen years old, Viv and I had for some time discussed having Callaloo's exterior repainted. The walls and shutters, particularly, were beginning to look worn. Now, after spending more time there than usual, we decided it was time to bite the bullet. Given Viv's loving attention to the garden, the prospect provided some challenges: such as how we were going to cut back the landscaping to access the walls for painting. As always, Alan Veeran came to the rescue, which required some significant project management skills. Paint Pros eventually carried out the work of making Callaloo look brand new again most professionally under Alan Veeran's close supervision, completing the work by August.

In mid-June we installed a thermometer in the Genesis lobby, mounted on a stand, in front of which persons visiting the building stood with their faces close to a sensor which tested whether they were likely or not to have COVID. This precaution was coupled with a large notice fixed to the wall imploring people to maintain what was now being described as 'social distancing' – staying six feet apart. The floors were marked so people knew exactly how far apart six feet was, wearing masks was obligatory, and visitors were encouraged to wash their hands thoroughly and use the provided hand sanitiser dispenser – someone would usually take a fancy to this last item, so we had to replace it most days.

Other commercial opportunities arose in July, even during these difficult times, including a sales enquiry for one of the floors Office Developments owned in Genesis building. This was vacant, and its maintenance was a financial drain without any rental income. At BCL we continued to receive interesting opportunities, such as providing a proposal for the business case for improving the mains water supply in Bermuda, and an interesting provision for calculating the possible maximum loss for underwriters on a new condominium on Cable Beach in Nassau. We also continued our work on the best jurisdiction for the head office of the major insurance regional brokers. Also, BCL maintained its involvement with the Clinton Global Initiative through webinars. As mentioned throughout this story, a daily workout with Dottie started most days for me and just twice a week for Viv, as tennis and walking were part of her daily routine. Due to COVID this had obviously had to stop, so it was excellent news that certain restrictions would be lifted on 20th July, which meant we were able to resume our workouts.

I have always found myself fortunate in many serendipitous situations in my life, and certainly one of those was being introduced to Micky Webster, the wife of Doug Webster, the man in charge of the maintenance company that manages the landscaping at Callaloo. Micky is a real estate appraiser, with more than thirty years' experience in the USA. She had been in Cayman for about two years, working on her second career as an artist, when Doug mentioned to Viv that Micky was interested in starting work again as an appraiser. So, Micky came in for an initial interview on 24th July and commenced working for BCL in September. She remains with us today, heading up our residential appraisal business.

Our work on the Outline Business Case for the new prison continued and we were tasked, as part of the mandatory requirements of the methodology, to constantly challenge the conclusions we had reached. One of these, was to research if there was an alternate twenty-five-acre, government-owned parcel, that could be used instead of the prison's current location. We secured details of all such sites, and conducted detailed examinations of each, but found that none had the required capacity to accommodate the new prison and its appropriate security boundaries.

A further welcome release from the confines of COVID happened at the end of July, when we met on the Greenery site with representatives of Kirk Freeport, to review the progress toward completion of the vacant space, which they were to fit out as their new Rolex store and perfumery.

In our Tortola office, Johmalvin advised us he would be leaving to return to his home in the Dominican Republic. Shortly thereafter, Kishan advised us that his sister in South Africa had contracted COVID and he needed to return there at the end of the year to assist his family. So, our office in BVI faced significant staffing challenges and, given our travel restrictions, Michell and I reluctantly discussed the possibility of temporarily closing the office. In Cayman, as a result of the same travel restrictions, staycations were becoming very popular. Alan and Claudia started the trend for us by renting an apartment at Villas of the Galleon and hosting a party there on 29th August, which was a welcome relief from the constraints earlier in the year.

For Avata property management, we received an enquiry to provide facility management services for the recently completed Clifton Hunter High School. We carried out a site inspection on 23rd September and subsequently submitted a proposal that was accepted.

In late September, we hosted a dinner party at Callaloo for the Governor and Mrs Roper, for the Deputy Governor, Franz Manderson, and his wife, Nuvia, and Dani and Darren Trickett, to thank them for their part in all the work and leadership that had kept Cayman both safe and so well informed during the pandemic.

Around this time, Morgan and I met to continue our discussions on the ongoing development of the 2016 business plan for CNCF. With staff numbers reduced due to recent departures, and the need to meet with our Minister of Culture to address funding requirements to implement essential strategic changes, these discussions would continue into the following year. We focussed on developing detailed job descriptions for key members of staff, both those currently employed and those we would need for the revised plan.

On 26th September BCL was retained to prepare a Reinstatement Cost Assessment for the Kimpton Seafire Hotel and Residences. This was a considerable recognition of BCL's standing and knowledge of the requirements of the regional insurance industry, based on our experiences of so many major catastrophes in the Caribbean over the years.

Back in 2010, BCL had acted for many clients in negotiations with the Cayman Islands Government over compensation for land acquired through compulsory purchase – often tied to road building projects aimed at improving traffic flow for the ever-increasing number of vehicles. The process typically began with the publication of a gazette, setting a deadline for landowners to file a claim for the loss they had suffered. We were approached by such landowners due to our specialist knowledge of the property market and the various heads of claim under which compensation could be sought. Where agreement could not be reached, cases were referred to a Roads Assessment Committee, which reviewed written submissions, listened to oral arguments, and then issued rulings. In October, a new round of gazettals resulted in a new flow of work for BCL. Landowners sought help in structuring their claims to include comparable land values and in understanding the full range of compensable losses – some of which were quite complex. Fortunately my nephew, Richard, was a compensation case expert based in the UK, and was able to assist with some of the more technical aspects of certain claims.

On 3rd October, we entertained George Pappadakis and his wife at Callaloo. George's father, Nicky, was a good friend, and I had originally met him through the construction of the Beachcomber apartments on Seven Mile Beach. We'd had a memorable day skiing with Nicky in Europe, where he owned the gondola in Chamonix – more correctly, we had a very memorable day in the restaurant at the base, as the weather was so bad we were unable to ski. Instead, we had enjoyed many bottles of wine which, once consumed, had to be balanced on your head! Nicky had been born into a traditional shipping family with its roots on the Aegean Island of Kasos, and had begun his career with the family firm, A.G. Pappadakis & Co., back in 1961 before rising to head the company's ship chartering and operations. Nicky always felt that the Caymanian seafaring way of life closely resembled that of his birth island. It was now good to chat with the next generation of this interesting and talented family.

On 13th October, Mike Gibbs, head of Kensington Management Group, who owned space in the Genesis building, held his retirement party at Grand Old House. He seemed far too young to retire, but it might be unfair to compare my view of working and retiring with that of others. Approaching eighty myself, I have no intention of retiring as I thoroughly enjoy what I do far too much – moreover if I did retire, I would probably drive Vivian crazy being at home for long periods of time!

At Callaloo, a developer had purchased the vacant lot to the east of our orchard and was building a pretty monstrous duplex on it, which looked directly down into the orchard. We clearly needed to address this problem, as the orchard was our favourite place for performances, playing our Christmas croquet, and for leisurely lunches. Accordingly, we consulted with Viv's many landscaping experts. Together, we came up with a boundary wall and fence, and planned for two rows of coconut trees and fishtail palms, whose broad, fan-shaped fronds, growing densely from the base, provide excellent screening. This solution has worked magnificently, and we continue to enjoy privacy in the orchard. We feel that our new neighbours are happy as well to have such privacy, seeing dense greenery from their windows.

On 22nd October Viv and I, and our good friend Anita, were able to enjoy a piano recital at the George Town Library, put on by the Cayman Arts Festival. This festival was started in 2001 by Glen Inanga and Jennifer Micallef, after the public's overwhelmingly enthusiastic response to a piano duet they had performed. Since then, it attracts world class musicians and teaches in the schools, helping our young talent broaden their skills. Viv and I, through the Bould Foundation, sponsor various students to give them the opportunity to develop their talent, both here in Cayman and abroad.

We were once again in Cayman's hurricane season. On 6th October Hurricane Delta had passed close to us and caused significant wave action, but little damage. Nevertheless, due to COVID, the preparations for a possible direct hit were intensive and virtually shut down the island for forty-eight hours. From 24th–26th October, Hurricane Zeta caused heavy rains, rough seas and strong winds, and then in early November, Tropical Storm Eta bought heavy winds and tornados, causing the loss of power to some twenty thousand customers. With all this weather activity my good friend, Jimmy Powell, called the office and asked BCL to prepare Reinstatement Cost Assessments for his properties. The only problem was, that Jimmy owns so many properties that in spite of his descriptions of where they were located, it required some significant detective work to track them down. I clearly recall Micky returning to the office totally drenched, as the inspections had to be completed during the storm so the reports could be submitted to the insurance companies to secure increased cover.

Additional work arose for BCL's BVI office when we received a call from the NDA to submit a proposal to manage the rebuild of the West End Ferry Terminal. This was a complicated piece of work, given the site was constrained by the steep hill to the north of the terminal, resulting in limited parking and working space.

On 29th October we attended the launch of Graham Morse's book, *Fatal Fix*, at Fidelity Bank. It was a gripping crime thriller set in the world of Premier League football. Graham's father-in-law was the England team's manager, so he had great background information for his novel. Alan Veeran had built Graham's residence in Frank Sound and so knew him well, and Graham was a great resource to me as I set out to write this book.

Also, whilst on the subject of book launchings, on 3rd November Morgan called me in his role as head of CNCF's Grants and Awards Committee and asked if the Bould Foundation would assist in funding the publication of a book entitled *My Life in a Conch Shell* by Glenroy Lorenzo Bodden, affectionately known as Roy Bodden. Viv and I were delighted to assist.

November was indeed the month for book launches. On 25th November, Fidelity Bank hosted the launch of a new book by Derek Haines entitled, *Coast to Coast: a trundle along the Pyrenees*. Derek had raised significant amounts of money for local charities by running numerous marathons and his new book described his six hundred mile walk in 2019, with his friend Mike Burcombe, which raised $800,000 for the Special Needs Foundation. As a travel book released in the time of COVID, the book was particularly well received – an adventurous narrative about the wider world was welcome when our own travel ability was curtailed.

BCL were continuing our work on the Prison OBC, working closely with our local and global teams. We were modifying certain aspects of the business case in response to requirements brought to our attention by the prison director, Steve Barrett, who was an outstanding client to have, and passionate, as were we, about getting the new prison built. We also continued our work on the water supply project in Bermuda, as well as the conversion of the rear portion of the Greenery into self-storage units. In connection with the Greenery project, we had to prove posting to all neighbouring owners within a certain range. Due to COVID restrictions, we had to FEDEX the notices to the USA and have Pedro Gallinar, our director located in Miami, post them and obtain receipts as proof of posting.

On 4th December, we hosted the Girl Guides at Callaloo, where they all performed on the stage. It was a joyous time with everyone on the grass with their 'sit-upons'. Jimmy Powell and Isley's wedding took place the next day at Isley's home in West Bay, with former Premier, McKeeva Bush, as the marriage officer. I was honoured to be asked by Jimmy and Isley to give a speech following the ceremony. It was a very joyous occasion as Jimmy and Isley have known each other for many years.

The 9th December was our twenty-fifth wedding anniversary, followed by my seventy-fifth birthday. We celebrated with a fabulous black-tie dinner of scallops and rack of lamb at Callaloo, T-shirts and bookmarks with a brilliant dance logo with 'Peace and Love', designed by our goddaughter, Melanie Roddam. On 13th December we went out on the Allura, crewed by Alex and Shana and with chef Carlos cooking his famous paella on board. We cruised out to Stingray City and Starfish Point before returning to Callaloo. We missed our overseas friends for this joyful celebration, but travel restrictions meant it couldn't be otherwise.

On 19th December, Dance Unlimited presented their always-excellent dance performance at the Harquail, and on 21st December we hosted our Callaloo staff for celebratory Christmas drinks. For Christmas Day, we had our traditional croquet game before dinner at home, and of course finished the year with 'Do Drop In' party at Callaloo, followed by duck breasts for two on the cabana, cooked by yours truly, watching the fireworks.

2021

Transformation is the fire that fuels the soul's journey. Embrace the heat, trust the process, and let your light shine.

The year started with some good news: we had secured a new tenant for the vacated ground floor space that had started life as a deli, and then was let to a real estate company. This had closed due to the impact of COVID on their business, but now the space was to be a driving school. Quite a range of activities, but an ideal location in the centre of town, and a size that made the space affordable.

On the Greenery front, the conversion of part of the space occupied by the J. Michael store to a one hundred and ten unit self-storage facility, had met with an objection to the planning application. The owner of a beachfront condominium, located a significant distance from the Greenery, claimed that the conversion would create a nuisance, with trucks coming and going to drop off goods. Of course, the opposite was true. First, any deliveries would be to the access doors at the rear and, secondly, the amount of movement in and out of storage facilities is *de minimis*. However, a detailed response had to be drafted to the Planning Authority, and the objector had to be given the opportunity to address the Planning Board at a hearing to further explain their objection. In the event, the objector simply did not attend the meeting and our application was passed. Over the years the Greenery facility has been a great investment for us, with Foster's occupying the building as a supermarket until 1997, then the bowling alley, followed by J. Michael in 2005, and now self-storage and Kirk Freeport.

On 11th January I visited Arek Joseph's house, where Sandra kindly greeted me with coffee and lent me a copy of a book Arek had written about his life in Cayman, which provided a useful reference for me during the writing of this book. At this time I was also drafting my Chairman's remarks for the opening of Cayfest, now in its twenty-seventh year but which had been challenged by the restrictions relating to large gatherings due to COVID.

The new president of CASE, Dave Johnson, contacted me as a member of the College of Fellows, with the names of three persons who had been nominated for consideration to join the college. He asked me to make a presentation on behalf of the six current members, and I was, of course, delighted and honoured to be asked. The presentation was to take place on 20th May, and I would be addressing both my own career to date, as well as the award of CASE fellowships to the three new fellows: Cameron Graham, Sam Small and John Harvey. While doing my research, in addition to CASE's rules for such an award, I researched other organisations' considerations, to find that 'fellows are selected based on their potential to make long lasting contributions to their academic discipline' which indeed fitted the skills and approach of the three candidates.

At BCL we were in discussions with Dr Hart Porshe for the project management of his Balam Escape sustainable resort in Belize, with which we had been involved for many years. At home in Cayman, our prison team was overjoyed to be told that the prison project was to proceed from the OBC stage to full procurement drawings. The director, Steve Barrett, was equally delighted and we held meetings over a couple of days at the end of January, to ensure all details were clearly set out in the cabinet paper he was drafting to be presented on 1st February.

On 27th January, I met with Mervyn Cumber for lunch at Grand Old House to discuss some of the details in this book, and it was cathartic to relive the stories of more than fifty years ago when I first arrived in the Caribbean. The next day I attended the AGM of the Chamber of Commerce, of which Paul Harris, who had played a role in setting up our business in Cayman in 1969, had been an early president. At the Cayman Arts Festival some weeks later, there was a presentation on what it takes to write a book, with several authors including Graham Morse. This was particularly appropriate given the task I had set myself, and a book by Stephen King, entitled *On writing – a Memoir of the Craft* was recommended. This, of course, I purchased and read, to see how well (or otherwise) I was doing.

On the CNCF front, Morgan and I were interviewing new staff, as Henry and Marcia Muttoo would soon be retiring and the Leadership and

Organisational Development Plan was in the process of being implemented. Viv and I were delighted to join Rosie Twohey's friends to celebrate her sixtieth birthday at Luca on 6th February. Little did we know that, some four years later, Rosie would be appointed Managing Director of CNCF. The CNCF Arts Awards were held on the 18th, and I was privileged to greet the Governor and Lissie, and make a speech welcoming everyone to a special occasion given the restraints created by COVID. I said the following:

> What a year 2020 was! – the management of the COVID crisis once again illustrates Cayman's ability to rise to a global challenge and manage it.
>
> So many comments on New Year's Eve related to a better 2021, so what better way to start than by celebrating our culture – our culture is the way we live – and so it is with great pleasure that I welcome you back to Cayfest, now in its 27th year, showcasing the diversity of our cultural talents and demonstrating those things that make us uniquely Caymanian.
>
> More than thirty-five years on since the founding of the Foundation we see all around us evidence of the increasing importance and recognition of the celebration and development of our culture and we are proud to be playing our part in this.
>
> Recognizing those that have played an important part in the culture and heritage of the Cayman Islands we kick off Cayfest with the National Arts & Culture Awards tonight. These awards acknowledge twelve people in our community who have played a significant role in both cultural development and the recording thereof, arts and crafts, visual and theatre arts as well as music performance and management.
>
> From the awardees this evening you will see the broad range of activities being recognised: sliver thatch, storytelling, painting, acting, crafts, cooking which defines the way we live and what makes us uniquely Caymanian.
>
> I am delighted to present Captain Kem Jackson of the Cayman Catboat Club, with the Chairman's Award in recognition of his unstinting contribution as a volunteer in educating our youth at summer camp as to the importance of the catboat in Cayman's history.

On 19th February, Viv and I drove up to Rum Point with Patricia Bradley and checked into the new apartments at the Rum Point Club. For me, this was interesting because the Retreat, which I had developed so many years earlier, was next door. It was Beno Gillooly's wedding the next day, with the ceremony taking place on the beach. It was a most joyous occasion, and very good to greet several friends we had not seen for some time due to the restrictions.

Also in February, BCL were invited to lead a team to develop a new General Aviation Terminal at the Owen Roberts airport in Cayman. It was a great team, with handling agents CDS, Universal Aviation, Naco, Hydrock and Bouygues Construction, and we submitted our expression of interest on 9th March.

Government elections in Cayman were now in full swing, with election day set for 14th April. In early March we went to Bacaro, to meet Andre Ebanks, who was running in our district of West Bay South. We listened to his plans to improve the economy following the difficulties that had been suffered due to COVID. Andre was impressive, and we felt he had a good grasp of what was needed. I am pleased to say he was subsequently elected and secured a Ministerial position in finance. Election Day, on 14th April, saw a somewhat surprising election of a slate of independent candidates to form a new government, led by Wayne Panton, with 'Father of the House' McKeeva Bush as the Speaker.

On 12th March we left the island for the first time in over a year, and flew to Little Cayman with Alan and Claudia. We brought ample supplies of food and wine, and stayed at Neptune's Berth, in Sidney and Claire Coleman's apartment there. The next day we enjoyed a most relaxing chill-out, and in the evening went down to the dock for a sundowner. There, we were greeted by the sound of voices from 'Grand' that we knew well, including ALT, Bing Thompson, Everard Leacock and Robert Hurlstone, all looking to acquire property. On the 14th and 15th, we cooked up a storm and then took a BBQ to Point of Sand, even managing to make an expresso coffee on the BBQ despite a strong wind. We were enjoying ourselves so much we extended our stay by a day and flew back to Grand Cayman on the 17th.

Morgan and I met with Natalie from the National Gallery on the 27th, to discuss some of the key issues in the Reorganisation Plan. These included the finalisation of a national cultural policy, collaboration between all cultural entities, shared platforms, multiple agencies, cross-Ministry tourism/culture, value culture, an update of the CNCF law of 2013, the PA law, the appointment of a Managing Director, and the formation of a theatre company. Job positions were to be advertised through IFACCA, and we had identified a potential new artistic director to replace Henry, who was leaving at the end of August 2021.

At this time I was having some issues with my knee and, as you know, my 'go to' person is Igor, with whom I spoke on the 28th and noted the following advice: 'Move leg forward and back and side to side, loose ankle, hip and knee, good for circulation and safe stretching, stand up in office, work out more in water with cuffs, less land and more water, Topricin cream morning and night – the Japanese are healthiest, because they shower three times a day to reduce stress, and eat fresh food in small portions, and spend as much time as possible outside'. No pills or drugs, and his advice always works. We also purchased a 'red light' therapy device which is applied to the affected area, and speeds up healing by improving blood circulation.

On 29th March we received a most welcome enquiry for Avata, from the owner of the Britcay building on Eastern Avenue, who was looking for a property management company to take over its operation. We bid on the project and I am delighted to say we were successful, and continue to manage it to this day.

The accommodation for the J. Michael store was becoming a little like a game of musical chairs: Foster's Supermarket had moved out of the Greenery and into the Strand, and J. Michael had moved into their space in the Greenery after Hurricane Ivan. Now J. Michael were to move into the Strand where Foster's had been but who had now moved to new premises in Camana Bay. However, J. Michael's renovations at the Strand were not complete, so they extended their stay at the Greenery to 31st May.

For many years Viv has been a member of the Garden Club of Grand Cayman and, given the end result of our landscaping at Callaloo, which has been featured in magazines, this membership has certainly paid dividends. So we were delighted to be able to host the club's annual hat parade in the Orchard at Callaloo on 8th April.

One unexpected result of Cayman's closed borders during the COVID period was that we did not receive any mail, and so when mail was eventually delivered it was somewhat of a shock to receive a stack of demands from the Nyon police in Switzerland for a speeding fine, plus penalties for each month that it had not been paid. The incident had been recorded by a camera on the A9 freeway, on 13th January 2020, when we were driving from Geneva airport to Verbier to ski with Ray and Michèle. I contacted Ray, who kindly got in touch with the Nyon police and pleaded my case to pay the initial fine of 120 CHF, but to be let off from the late payment charges, given that mail had not been received for more than a year – to which the police agreed, thank goodness.

The 7th May was Viv's seventy-fifth birthday, and since it was a Friday we launched it with a great party in the Orchard, with Javee from Hopscotch providing light and sound technical management. Matt Brown was MC and performed a skit with Giselle Webb, Michael Lemay played the steel pan, and the Dream Chasers gave an excellent dance performance. We ate rotis and fish pie, with excellent service from a wonderful team of waiters from the Westin led by Edmundo. Edmundo was from the Philippines, was a trained butler, and provided impeccable service. We traditionally provided our guests with a bookmark and a scroll to keep as a souvenir of the event, and for Viv's birthday we included one of her mom's favourite pieces called 'The Brush' – particularly appropriate given Viv's dad's name was Joe:

> I am mother's only daughter
> That is what I am
> She says she would not let me marry any man
> I am courting one at present
> But mother doesn't know
> His Christian name I'll tell you
> His Christian name is Joe.
> One night when we were courting
> Mother passed us by
> The way she looked at poor old Joe
> With vengeance in her eye
> She asked him what he wanted
> And Joe began to blush
> Before he had time to answer
> She nailed him with the brush.
> Since that night it happened
> Joe never visits me
> Although he is afraid of mother
> He is very fond of me
> And when he's passing our house
> He does it in a rush
> He always looks behind him
> Because he minds the brush.

Thankfully my name is Martyn not Joe!!

As noted earlier, BCL's operations in the BVI had been seriously challenged by our inability to fly there, and we were in discussions with Percy Rhoden and Richard Starkey about our ongoing situation. One ray of hope about travel was the extensive commentary in the news about how soon a vaccine might be available to protect people from COVID, including one leading contender, AstraZeneca. The vaccination process was, of course, a serious matter, but there were some amusing side comments, not least of which was 'Rasta Zenica'.

Percy, who was from Jamaica, appreciated the humour. Viv and I debated for some time whether to have a COVID vaccination, but given it was a requirement for travel, we decided to go ahead and had our first jab with the Pfizer brand on 10th May.

On 28th April, Susan Olde, who chaired the National Gallery was appointed to the CNCF board. I asked Morgan, Lorna and Michael Meghoo to interview Natalie Coleman for the CEO position as part of the revised business plan for CNCF, given my earlier discussions I'd had with her about the role. On 12th May, I held a conference with Natalie about the CNCF Strategic Plan and to discuss her start date for working in a part-time capacity at CNCF, which could be impacted by a new venture, Cayman Art Week, scheduled for July. I also discussed her possible contract start date with Morgan on the 15th.

With new owners in the Genesis building, a meeting was requested to discuss updating the lobbies and central core of the building. The building has stood the test of time well, particularly given its hard-wearing ceramic tile exterior, and is considered to be a standout, iconic structure. So, we enlisted the services of architect John Doak to develop thoughts on the possible redesign and how any changes would fit into the Cayman Islands Government's revitalisation project for George Town. This was being considered in the context of a general business movement to the new town of Camana Bay. We held our first meeting on 13th May, which led to many follow-up meetings and thoughts and ideas.

On 16th May, we held our traditional North Sound trip for thirty guests on the Allura as part of Viv's birthday celebrations. Carlos cooked both seafood and vegetarian paella, and Edmundo provided his impeccable drinks service, which was preceded by champagne and hors d'oeuvres on the dock, with plenty of photographs taken.

We had by now become used to the 'staycation' idea, and so on 21st May we flew over to the Brac where, with Alan and Claudia, we had rented a house called Tides End. The house was located right on the beach and had a swimming pool, and two master suites directly facing the beach. Following our experience of our Little Cayman staycation, we had brought plenty of food and wine for the stay. Nevertheless, the next day we took a trip to Barry's Golden Jerk stand at the airport, where we chatted with him about a divorce he was sadly going through and for which he might need our assistance to prepare a valuation of a property he owned. A business opportunity often comes out of casual conversations in the strangest circumstances.

One of the great things about the Brac is the Bluff and the numerous walks that traverse it, of which we took great advantage. We walked the lighthouse trail on 23rd May where we saw dozens of Brown Booby birds nesting in the rocks, and in the evening, we had an excellent dinner at Le Soleil D'Or. On 24th May, I flew back to Grand Cayman to deal with some staff issues, returning to the Brac the same evening. The next day we walked the nature trail and the Bight Road up onto the Bluff, which has many caves where residents sheltered during the 1932 hurricane that devastated the Brac and caused significant loss of life. On the 27th we walked to Rebecca's Cave and the Salt Pond hike there, finishing our staycation with an East End beach walk on the 28th. We flew back to Grand Cayman in the evening, vowing to return soon, and arrived in time to celebrate Natalie's birthday at the National Gallery.

The next day, Morgan and I continued our discussions with Natalie and Susan Olde, as chairperson of the National Gallery, and in the evening went to see the Dream Chasers. They were putting on an exciting dance performance at Pedro's Castle, which provided a fabulous atmospheric backdrop for the talented performers. On 4th June, the board and staff of the National Gallery were invited, along with the staff of the Ministry, to a 'Meet and Greet' by the new Minister of Culture, the Hon. Bernie Bush, which was the first time such an event had taken place, and which was most welcome. On the 9th Morgan interviewed a potential candidate as future MD of the CNCF.

On 1st June it was time for our second Pfizer COVID injection, which was a strict requirement as part of our certification for future overseas travel.

When I climbed Kilimanjaro, in 2019, I had a guide called Pungo, who had been most helpful during the entire climb, and particularly on summit night, when, with a strong wind blowing and scree causing one's feet to slip backwards, he encouraged me to keep climbing. He contacted me out of the blue, by WhatsApp, telling me his mother was sick and needed treatment he couldn't afford. So I sent him some funds via Western Union – my first experience of this form of money transfer, which involves queuing at Foster's Supermarket for a significant amount of time. But the wait was worth it, and Pungo was eternally grateful as his mother is now fully recovered.

On 21st June we were approached by ABIS, an Aberdeen company, in connection with opportunities in Guyana, based on the discovery of huge oil reserves there, and we attended a virtual symposium the next day, known as the Guyana Gateway.

On 23rd June Morgan and I met at the Ministry of Culture to discuss our ongoing Strategic Planning Exercise. We made a Power Point presentation to them on 30th June and, in line with the development of our strategic plan, our interviews continued with potential staff for CNCF.

There was an interesting *Caymanian Compass* news release on 25th June, highlighting the inflation caused by the pandemic due to supply chain issues and its effects on the price of materials, and the fact that travel restrictions had slowed the supply of labour to Cayman. The headline read: 'Building Supply Shortage Fuelling New Cost of Living Concerns'.

CASE held a lunchtime meeting on 29th June, where I was asked to make a presentation on the differences between Mediation, Arbitration or Litigation in dispute resolution. The key here, in general terms, is the efficiency of mediation, where the mediator 'facilitates' a settlement as opposed to 'judging' it, while maintaining relationships between the parties. In contrast, during arbitration, the parties select their 'judge' and maintain privacy, but the length of time to settle and consequent costs can be significant. In litigation, which is conducted in the public domain, the judge may not be familiar with terminologies, the parties do not choose their judge, and potentially significant time and money are spent before the dispute is resolved.

On 14th July, Viv and I were privileged to be invited to a Bastille Day celebration at the Ritz, hosted by the French Ambassador in Cayman – who just happened to be Sebastien Guilbard, Cathy Delapenha's husband! We all managed to keep our heads on our shoulders, enjoyed conversation with friends, with great food and wine.

Fritz McPherson directed a performance of Frank McField's play *One White, One Black* at the Harquail Theatre a few days later. This had been a notable feature in Guyana's Carifesta, and was now being presented back in Cayman, with Fritz and Michael McLaughlin as the two actors. According to the report in the *Compass*, guests described the experience with superlatives ranging from 'amazing' and 'hilarious' to 'brilliant' and 'outstanding'. I must admit I feel great pride to hearing comments like this, given where we had come from and the planning we were now engaged in to move our cultural development forward.

As part of the Cayman Arts Festival, on 29th July there was music at the library, where we listened to Dequan Smith, an extremely talented cellist, and Annikki, a talented poet. Viv and I very much admired the work the Cayman Arts Festival was carrying out with Cayman's youth, and so we arranged to meet with Marius Gaina, their executive director, at Callaloo, and offered assistance for some of their students from the Bould Foundation,.

Also on the cultural front, I had the privilege of meeting and having discussions with Christopher Williams, the assistant professor of History, English and Philosophy at the University College of the Cayman Islands. In 2015 he had published *Defining the Caymanian Identity: The Effects of Globalisation, Economics, and Xenophobia on Caymanian Culture*. According to its introduction, the book analyses the factions and schisms surging through the multicultural, multi-ethnic and polarised Cayman Islands, to identify who, or what, is considered Caymanian. Having read the book, I felt it was a most informative study and analysis that could assist with our current Strategic Planning Exercise for CNCF, and so purchased a copy for each one of our CNCF board members.

Viv and I enjoyed a dinner with Jimmy Powell and Isley at Pappagallo restaurant. Although Jimmy and I talk over the phone weekly to catch up and discuss Cayman events, we all too rarely have a chance to spend time together face to face and for a longer time, which this evening provided.

On 17th August, with minimal warning, Cayman was hit by Tropical Storm Grace with almost hurricane force winds, which caused extensive damage as it passed. At Callaloo, about twenty trees were blown down, some of which we were able to raise back up and stake, but unfortunately we had to uproot and cart away quite a few. The copper pennant that adorned the roof of the folly was also blown off, and I searched both our property and those adjacent without success. We thought it was gone, but in a subsequent clear-up the gardeners found it, and we held an appropriate ceremony when it was reinstalled. As we had not closed our hurricane shutters, several of their hinges were damaged by the wind as it pulled them from the wall. We had purchased the shutters back in 2004, and so were not sure if we could locate the manufacturer, Poma, in Florida, to purchase replacements. We tried calling them, but without success. We did find the physical location of the company through a search on the website but could not find a telephone number. We contacted our nephew, Jason, in Florida, who is in the boat maintenance business, and it just so happened he was passing close to Poma's location and stopped in. Bingo! He found and purchased some replacement hinges, and FedExed them to us in Cayman.

We were soon busy replanting the trees in the Orchard that had blown down. This time we raised the level of soil within a circle made from round posts, to lift the roots of the trees away from potentially brackish water. We also worked on the fishtail palms and coconut trees along the screening boundary, with Giles from Paradise Landscaping. It was interesting to be working with the next generation, as Giles's father was Dennis Smith, whom I first met in Jamaica in the early 1970s and who shortly afterwards moved to Cayman and established a black coral jewellery shop on the waterfront, followed by a very successful store called the Diamond Mine.

On 21st August, we held a ceremony at the Harquail, to open a packing crate that contained three of Miss Lassie's paintings that had been purchased back in 1995 by our friends Gordon Jaynes and Lyle Lawson. They had made

– and kept – a promise that they would be donated to the CNCF when Gordon and Lyle decided to downsize their home, which they were now doing. The three paintings formed the centrepiece of an exhibition held at Miss Lassie's property on 4th November, welcoming them 'home', after more than a quarter of a century 'foreign'.

In September, Steve Barrett, the director of prisons with whom we had worked so closely on the OBC for the new prison, called me and said he was leaving Cayman. This absolutely stunned me, given the passion he had for ensuring that we build the new prison – sadly, he confirmed that the reason he was leaving was due to a medical condition that had been diagnosed as motor neuron disease – life can be tough.

On 20th October I had a call with Joan Bain, who was still in Haiti, to see how we could assist her, since Haiti had recently suffered a major earthquake and then had been hit by Hurricane Grace. Joan told me that where she lived was only accessible by mules, and that she needed rice and beans, tinned meat and tarpaulins. We were glad to be able to help her and the many children she looked after by sending funds for these items.

On 25th October we attended a caucus of the government with Steve Barrett, where we presented a revised phasing for the prison rebuild with a more palatable financing package likelier to find favour in the public domain – which, unfortunately, seemed to be one of the key driving forces.

From 1st–4th November, representing CNCF and the Cayman Islands, I attended the virtual meeting of the IFACCA Americas World Summit. It was a refreshing update on what our fellow agencies were doing in North and South America. The evening of the 4th I was called upon to provide an unexpected and impromptu speech at the exhibition of Miss Lassie's paintings, at Mind's Eye, in South Sound, which I was delighted to do after being part of the long journey to secure both the artwork and the property in which they were now being displayed. It was a great evening and it was good to see, as the centrepiece, the three paintings that Gordon and Lyle had gifted back to the people of the Cayman Islands.

By now, vaccination for COVID required a 'booster shot' to be considered effective, and so, on 6th November, Viv and I went along to the clinic at Camana Bay to receive ours.

I flew to Nassau on 9th November, to speak at the CHICOS conference being held at Baha Mar, and after working on its construction, it was indeed fascinating to be staying there. The day after my arrival I had to take a PCR test to make sure I was not COVID positive, which fortunately I was not! I have been a speaker at every one of the ten CHICOS events, and this year

I moderated a panel of experts discussing 'Hotel Design and Construction: Challenges and Opportunities in a Changing World'. Fellow panellists included designers, engineers and project managers, specialising in resorts and infrastructure provision, and particularly focussed on green technology, sustainability and flexibility in design. Noting the current trend in global fuel price increases and power shortages, the panel debated design recommendations to improve energy efficiencies, key risk management to deal with global supply chain issues, and design considerations to provide flexibility. It was of note that the pandemic meant potential guests had had more time to research destinations, amenities and experiences. In the panel, and throughout the conference, a common theme was that the COVID lockdown had given everyone time to think and reassess how project delivery and – most importantly – lifestyle changes, would be implemented as we emerged into a 'new normal'.

The mood of the conference was upbeat, and pent-up demand for travel following the lockdown saw many destinations showing forward bookings at higher levels than pre-pandemic. A key recommendation was to see if all regional countries might attempt to standardise COVID entry requirements, as the current plethora of differences in that regard led to confusion amongst travellers.

Flying back to Cayman directly from Nassau on 12th November, on arrival at the airport I was fitted with a wrist tracking device and was required to go into eight days of quarantine, while the taxi from the airport to Callaloo would have to return to the airport to be 'fumigated'. I stayed in our 'Annahavil' guest cottage, with an orange construction fence around it, and Viv would deliver meals to a table on the patio and then retreat, and I would come out to collect my food. After eating, I had to put the plates and utensils in a bucket of water treated with bleach to ensure anything coming out of the cottage was sanitised. I received several calls from the government officials tracking my whereabouts, as well as a couple of visits to the house to make sure I was appropriately quarantined. When 20th November arrived, I was delighted to be told I could drive myself down to the South Sound Community Centre at 8.50am to receive my PCR test, and even more delighted to hear a few hours later that I was now free to join the rest of the world.

On 23rd November, Morgan and I met with the Chief Officer at the Ministry of Culture to present our Strategic Plan. We began by noting that institutional memory can be short, and so we reminded her that, starting in 2016, we had worked to realign the operations of the CNCF with its legal mandate – that of an Arts Council – which was how it had been structured. We also acknowledged various HR issues that were linked to senior management that had been in place for over thirty-two years, and were now reaching retirement age. As part of the transition, we advertised for new posts, and Natalie had responded to one of these advertisements. However, we emphasised that the overriding focus of the Strategic Plan was about establishing a clear direction, not simply addressing resources.

The critical importance of building on the synergy of all cultural organisations was paramount and much had already been achieved in the 'cross pollination' of CNCF and the NG. We acknowledged Susan Olde's financial contribution to the Arts in Cayman, and my forty years' service to CNCF, as its only remaining founding board member. I had also been invited by Carole Owen and Monica Gore to serve as a founding board member of the National Gallery. Leslie Bigelman, a former CNCF board member, went on to become director of the National Gallery while Nancy Barnard, a former director of the National Gallery, later served on the CNCF board.

On 24th November, Viv and I left Cayman for Miami, having completed the extensive paperwork necessary to fly internationally. We arrived in Miami and saw #10E for the first time in twenty months and then celebrated with lunch at Strada in the Grove. Then we caught our flight to London, seated in first class and with great service, marred only by the need to wear masks. Back in QGM, we discovered the central heating was not working and it was bitterly cold, but no matter. We went to Da Mario with Charlene for our traditional lunch together, and with a lot of catching up to do after so long away. We then went to our local hardware store to purchase an electric fan heater to keep us warm in the house.

That evening we went to the theatre to see the musical called *Tina*, tickets for which Edward, our nephew had kindly arranged. The show was good, but we left at the intermission. Somehow, being in a public space with crowds of people, after so many months in only small groups, felt somewhat overwhelming.

For the next few days, we followed our traditional routine of walks in Hyde Park and Kensington Gardens, and then had our nephew, Jonnie, round for Sunday roast lamb with yours truly's special onion sauce. On 29th November, I had had an excellent conference call with Lord Cultural Resources and reviewed a draft proposal for their assistance with CNCF's Strategic Planning Exercise. On 30th November, being it was truffle season, Viv and I went to Lucio's to enjoy pasta and shaved truffle, and then in the evening went to J.D. and Zoey's new mews house in Artillery Close to enjoy an outstanding twelve-course dinner cooked by a private chef.

Viv and I wanted to catch up on all our favourite restaurants, and on 2nd December went to Scott's for a Dover sole lunch, followed by a shopping trip to

Fortnum and Mason, and then I attended the Caribbean Council AGM at the Caledonian Club, followed by Christmas drinks. It felt good to be catching up with so many of my business colleagues after a long COVID absence.

We held a CNCF board meeting by Zoom on the 4th, and then – a big surprise for me – Rob and Jen had arranged we should meet at Ham Yard Hotel for drinks and dinner, where we met Nick and Annie and Nick's parents, and then we were ushered up the road to the theatre, where the Bob Marley Musical, *Get Up Stand Up* was playing!

On 5th December, Gillian and Edward drove us down to see Jan Raath in Brightlingsea, where we enjoyed a great lunch and catch up. During the next few days we had Anni and Nick around for dinner, walked in the park and dined at Yauatcha for our favourite dim sum, held another remote CNCF board meeting, and then, for my seventy-sixth birthday, topped our stay with an outstanding lunch with Rob and Jen and Anni and Nick at Waterside Inn. With three Michelin stars for forty years it must be doing something right, and we had been dining there for almost that long. On the 12th, it was time to organize our COVID paperwork for the trip home, and so we went to Randox on Kensington High Street for our PCR test and certificate. We flew back to Miami on 13th December, where we had another PCR test for the flight back to Cayman.

On the 16th we held the CNCF Christmas lunch for the board and staff, and on 20th December Angela Morgan came to Callaloo and presented us with her traditional sprig of holly. We're never sure where she gets it from, but it always makes Christmas feel special. Our chef, Carlos, cooked Christmas lunch at Callaloo, for Viv and me, Norman and Jo (playing croquet for the first time and loving it), and Alan, Claudia and Sasha.

CHAPTER TWELVE

Beyond the Summit (2022–2025)

2022

Trust is the union of Intelligence & Integrity.

We started the working new year somewhat late, with caviar eggs at Callaloo with Alan and Claudia and Erik Monsen on 3rd January, followed by attending a meeting of the West Bay Action Committee at Pappagallo in West Bay, where the newly elected MP, André Ebanks, answered questions from the committee and the floor.

On the 26th, Michell called to tell me of some excellent work news to start the year: BCL were to be invited to respond to an RFP for the refurbishment of seven hotels in Barbados, comprising some five hundred and forty keys (rooms), which the Marriott Group had purchased in 2019 from the Elegant Group. Marriott had not entered the all-inclusive hotel market until 2018, and this acquisition allowed them to expand into that model across a wide range of targets, including luxury-, couples-, and family-focussed properties.

On 27th January, the Governor kindly hosted the Governor's Award for Architecture at Government House, after which we were invited to dinner at the Wharf by our long-standing friend, Penny Cumber.

It was about this time that Alan and Claudia suggested we look at hiking part of the Camino de Santiago and recommended an operator who appealed to all of us, perhaps because it was called 'Eat Northern Spain'. It provided an eight-day excursion walking through the most scenic parts of the Camino, with nights spent in luxury hotels and lunches at the finest restaurants. Transport would be in a luxury Mercedes van. This route varied significantly from the trek Derek Haines had undertaken in 2019, but was certainly more appealing. So, after further discussion with the owner, Elias, we booked to go in September.

The second week of February was one of celebratory dinners. Anita and her mother Meryl – at the grand age of ninety-eight – came to Callaloo on the

9th, Claudia visited to celebrate her sixty-fifth birthday on the 12th, and on the 14th, J.D. and Zoey came to play croquet in the orchard, followed by dinner.

On 17th it was time to go skiing again after the long COVID-caused hiatus. Viv and I flew to Denver, and then drove to Keystone Resort, Colorado, where we had not skied in a long time. We got settled into a one-room apartment in Buffalo Lodge, and the next day awoke to a beautiful bluebird day with perfect snow.

On the eighth and last run down, I stopped to make sure Viv was behind me, but she was nowhere to be seen. I called her from my cellphone, and she announced that she was stuck – her ski boot had disintegrated and consequently she could not ski. She asked me to go to the base and alert the ski patrol to her dilemma, which I did. But because Viv wasn't injured, the ski patrol were unable to assist. Fortunately, Viv managed to wave down a ski-doo, and after some significant persuasion, as the driver claimed he was not allowed to carry passengers due to liability issues, she convinced him to carry her down to the base. The driver had heard of Viv's dilemma on the radio, as I had to give a description of her to the ski patrol and mentioned her vibrant and distinctive pink ski suit. Along the line, someone had also added 'a fifty-year-old lady'. This, of course, delighted Viv no end.

Viv then caught the bus back to Buffalo Lodge, which in itself became another adventure. The driver, who appeared to be high as a kite, said 'Fasten your seat belts; we're taking off!' and when he passed the lodge, where Viv asked to be dropped off, he warned that Viv would not get her frequent flyer miles if she got off the bus. He finally conceded, and a relieved Viv limped back to the apartment, where I welcomed her with toasties and spaghetti Bolognese. What a first day skiing for Viv!

We started 20th February by getting Viv fitted with new ski boots and poles, and then tested out the new equipment with five runs in the afternoon. COVID had changed our typical skiing routine; instead of eating out twice a day, we now cooked almost all our meals in the apartment to avoid excessive contact with other people. It was interesting to be in Colorado, where almost no one wore masks, in stark contrast to Cayman and Florida, where everyone wore masks pretty much all the time. On the 21st we went shopping in Dillon for food and wine supplies, and also purchased a new set of ski poles for yours truly, testing them out skiing in Keystone during the next couple of days.

On the 23rd we drove to Edwards to ski with Jerry and Sheila Katz, where we enjoyed some fresh new overnight snow at Beaver Creek and Bachelor Gulch. We enjoyed a fabulous late lunch at the Ritz, where we were entertained by Jerry and Sheila's friend, Ken Ingram, who sang and played the guitar.

We checked out of Buffalo Lodge, which we would not rate as the best condo we have ever stayed in, but due to COVID it was all that had been available. We drove to Eagle Vail airport, where we met up with Jimmy and Cynthia and picked up George and Boopie. With all of our luggage and that of George and Boopie, even Jimmy's Ford Expedition was too small, so we kept our rental car and drove to Aspen Glen and Mariposa for dinner. During the subsequent week Viv and I drove to Two Creeks at Snowmass, where we skied a half day, and the next day George joined us there too and we had a great time. On the 27th we drove into Aspen and took the gondola to the top of Ajax Mountain, where we took a couple of runs to mid-station. Later we joined Jimmy and Cynthia at the Ajax Tavern, at the base, for truffle fries and Wiener Schnitzel, then finished the day with five more runs in fabulous snow.

During this ski trip, there had been many conference calls regarding our new Barbados assignment for Marriott. These fitted into our routine very nicely because of the time difference: in Colorado we were three hours behind Barbados, so business calls could be taken care of early in the morning, leaving the rest of the day free for skiing. We enjoyed Snowmass on 1st March, had lunch at the new restaurant at Elk Camp, and returned to Mariposa for dinner of pasta with caviar from Kelleys Katch. On 2nd March, we began the day with our traditional Nowerys breakfast of caviar eggs and champagne and then drove George and Boopie back to Eagle Vail to catch their flight home. Viv and I stopped at Beaver Creek to ski four runs there, with lunch at the Chophouse, sitting outside on a beautiful sunny day. Jimmy and Cynthia drove us to Eagle Vail to collect a rental car for our drive back to Denver the next day, where we met up with Anne, Christine, Robin and Chris for dinner, and then caught the 'red eye' flight back to Miami.

On 9th March at the Harquail, *Caymanian Proud: Memories of Her Majesty*, was held at the Harquail Theatre. The *Caymanian Compass* reported:

> What might have prompted The Queen to visit the Cayman Islands, not once but twice in just over a decade? What are some of the most engaging conversations Caymanians had with the Monarch? What are the public's lasting impressions about the Head of the Commonwealth following her visits? These questions and more were answered during 'Caymanian Proud: Memories of Her Majesty' at the Harquail Theatre on Wednesday 9 March 2022. The multigenerational event attracted mainly seniors and John A. Cumber Primary and the Lighthouse School students. Recollections by former government officials and by members of the public were shared at the Platinum Jubilee forum

organised by the Ministry of Youth, Sports, Culture & Heritage. Remarks from the Chairperson of the Platinum Jubilee Committee and Cabinet Secretary, Mr Samuel Rose and by Acting Minister for Youth, Sports, Culture & Heritage, Mr Issac Rankine were also part of the half-day event, which was also attended by His Excellency, the Governor Martyn Roper.

The Ministry and CNCF continued detailed and sensitive discussions about our proposed management changes, and the various conditions that had to be met to put them in place. These included budgets and cash flow, and the dialogues would continue throughout the balance of the year.

We were also asked to go to Miami to make a presentation to the Marriott team. I met with Michell and José, his architect partner, on the 17th and over dinner at Bellini's in the Grove, we discussed the presentations we were to make the next day. The Marriott team were very pleased with the presentations, which highlighted BCL's skills and experience in managing complex construction projects in difficult island locations to meet strict hotel operator requirements. We celebrated that evening with a drinks party at #10E and then enjoyed dinner at Caffe Abbracci, a traditional northern Italian restaurant in Coral Gables. On 20th March, Michell, Beatriz, and their son Amos, came to #10E for a Sunday brunch of caviar eggs, and Michell and I were able to discuss our resourcing for the Marriott project in a relaxing environment. BCL had also been invited to consider providing services in Guyana, in connection with a number of new projects linked to the recent discovery of major oil reserves there. So on the morning of 21st March, before returning to Cayman, we participated in a virtual conference between companies in Houston and Aberdeen, during which we highlighted our project management skills.

Back in Cayman on 22nd March, CNCF provided an update on the management handover we were processing.

On 31st March, BCL, acting as Lead Consultant on the prison redevelopment project, made a presentation to PWD and the Ministry of Home Affairs on our progress with the design. That afternoon, we held a feasibility conference for Asian Village, the major project in Antigua on which BCL had been working for a number of years. This project required expertise and staff we did not carry permanently, and so we called upon former employees to rejoin us on assignment, and contacted long-time contractors with whom we had worked over the years to provide up-to-date cost data from the field.

At this same time, BCL was also retained to advise on two residential projects: the construction of a luxury residence, where the owner felt he had overpaid the contractor relative to the work completed, and a modest house extension with a similar issue. Alan Veeran, with his extensive knowledge and experience of working with subcontractors, was a key member of our team. In both cases, the owners' concerns were justified. BCL prepared detailed reports identifying the overpayments, and negotiated a way forward to complete the works and resolve the disputes. Jerry Katz, our specialist construction attorney, played a key role in this process. At BCL we hold weekly team meetings with all staff so everyone is fully appraised of our active projects and can make suggestions for how we might improve. One such idea led to the launch of a customer survey, which returned very positive feedback.

Viv and I had decided to spend the Easter holiday in the UK. We arrived at QGM on 7th April, and over the next couple of days our nephews Edward and Jonnie joined us for a home-style dinner at QGM. On the 11th we renewed Viv's passport and were also able to discuss the publication of this book with Lord Ian Strathcarron of Unicorn. The following day we drove to Oxford to explore that 'city of dreaming spires', and then checked into Raymond Blanc's Manoir aux Quat'Saisons for the night and to dine on their tasting menu with a flight of wines. On 13th we drove to Blenheim Palace with the intention of touring this wonderful property, but it was simply too crowded so we returned to QGM. On Good Friday, the 15th, Viv and I went to a magnificent afternoon matinee performance of Handel's *Messiah* at the Royal Albert Hall – most appropriate given the day, and also because it is one of our favourite Easter performances.

On 16th April, Michell, Alan, and I discussed BCL's ongoing business plan, which now included a project-monitoring assignment for the rebuild of the Halcyon Cove resort in Antigua, for the Royalton Group. I have always found it interesting to see a hotel I have stayed in over many years transform into something completely different, as this one was about to do.

While we were in the UK, CNCF confirmed their intention to invite Lord Consultancy Services to draft a formal strategic plan, based on the recommendations already made. This would proceed, subject to the formal procurement process via the government's Bonfire portal.

We were enjoying the summery weather, and had begun using our Burdenko belts during the daily walks in Kensington Gardens. These fastened around our waist, and had elastic arm and leg tethers attached to provide resistance to all leg and arm movements. This significantly added to the exercise value of the walk while correcting any misalignment that can lead to joint issues. They also puzzled passersby, who looked at us rather strangely. I was still engaging in conference calls, particularly for the Marriott project in Barbados. Thanks to

COVID, we had become quite used to this way of discussing business matters, although I must admit that I still much prefer talking face-to-face.

On 26th April, I participated in the Guyana Investment seminar, and the next day Viv and I went to the House of Lords to meet with Ian Strathcarron, where we went over the details and publication scheduling of my book, for which I had written some 57,000 words at the time of our meeting. This was followed that evening by the Caribbean Council's Annual Cocktail Reception, also at the House of Lords, where I had the opportunity of meeting President Ali, of Guyana, which was fortuitous for the work BCL was considering there. Viv returned to Cayman on 3rd April, while I flew to Barbados with Michell, for Marriott meetings.

Barbados had launched a new app, called BimSafe, on which you were able list all your arrival information for Immigration and Customs as well as your COVID test results, which really sped up the arrival process in Barbados. The next three days were intense, with site visits to the Waves, Colony Club and Tamarind hotels. On 4th May we continued our hotel inspections, focussing on the room refurbishments – central to the Marriott rebrand – and also on the upgrading of common areas and services, which we believed required closer attention. In the afternoon, we met with Daniel Diaz to discuss our potential role as project monitor for the Royalton Halcyon Cove Antigua project. We also had important discussions about the effects of the Tourism Development Act in Barbados, including how duty-free concessions would be applied to materials we were purchasing for the Marriott hotel refurbishments. On the 5th, we met with attorneys to review the legal requirements of the Act. We also met with architectural firms about the assistance we felt would be needed to efficiently deliver the refurbishment objectives. BCL had been retained to look at the feasibility of a condominium development in Porters, and we met with our clients and their architect to review that project as well.

On 6th May, Michell and I returned to Miami en route to Cayman, and as we boarded the Cayman flight Michell received a call from Vivian – for some reason she could not get through on my phone – to say she had tested positive for COVID. So her birthday party dinner, catered by chef Keith Griffin, and planned for the next day, had to be cancelled at the last moment.

Before Viv went into quarantine for fourteen days in our Annahavil guest cottage on the Callaloo property, as I had done, she had rushed all around Callaloo gathering up everything she might need to take into quarantine. Once settled in, and getting ready for bed, she realised that the princess diamond from her engagement ring was missing. She leapt out of bed and ran into Callaloo to see if the diamond was on the bedroom floor, or the dressing room, or the bathroom floors – but it was not to be found anywhere. She returned to Annahavil very dejected, with the only recourse left to ask Hyacinth, the housekeeper, to keep her eyes open and not to vacuum any of the floors until the quarantine had been completed.

During the next two weeks I was delegated for supermarket and dinner duty. Michell, who was booked to stay with us, had to go and stay with Alan and Claudia for one evening whilst we made up the bed in the gym, where he then stayed. We made up for the cancelled dinner party by holding not one, but two lunches. One was on the 27th, catered by chef Keith, and a second on 29th May, catered by chef Dylan. I sourced a new diamond through Balaclava Jewelers; the original was never found. It may well be stuck between the cracks of our hardscape pavers in the garden.

On the CNCF front, I was asked to write a letter to the Ministry detailing the background to Henry Mutto's retirement, as part of the CNCF Strategic Plan. On 9th May I held discussions with Natalie about the process of employing Lord Cultural Services for the Strategic Planning Exercise. As mentioned earlier, this required the publication of an RFP on Bonfire, Cayman's public procurement vehicle, and I drafted the necessary document for publishing.

I was also in discussions with Tommy Bodden about his compensation case. By now, BCL had been working on this, and other compensation cases, for some nineteen months with little progress being made towards a negotiated settlement.

Both Michell Vargas and Alan Veeran had been closely involved in the work of BCL for several years. While their work and contributions had been recognised through professional fees, I considered it important that they should become shareholders in the company as part of our business planning. We had been discussing this for some time, and in mid-May we held more formal discussions, to fully acquaint them of the benefits and liabilities of ownership. We then commenced the process for each of them to acquire a 20 per cent share – a process that ultimately took over a year to complete.

On 2nd June Viv and I flew to London. It was Queen Elizabeth II's Platinum Jubilee. She was the first British Monarch to celebrate seventy years on the throne and so, most unusually, we sat glued to the TV on 4th June to enjoy footage of the festivities happening all around England. The next day, Sunday, we held a celebration lunch with Annie and Nick at QGM of tagliatelle and caviar, roast lamb and onion sauce, accompanied by a tasting of Carabella wines. Annie was undertaking an advanced sommelier's course and had become extremely good at judging the quality of wines, and so we were delighted to put our Carabella samples to the test. They passed with flying colours! As we were serving the lamb, Edward, our next-door neighbour, dropped by with his girlfriend Camille, and so with true Jamaican-style hospitality, we pulled up two extra chairs to the table and they joined us for lunch.

Conversation came around to what Camille did for a living, and she said she was an attorney in the States. In fact, she was currently representing the actor Johnny Depp, who was embroiled in a widely publicised defamation case involving his former wife, Amber Heard. A successful ruling had just been filed in his favour on 1st June – an interesting lunch table conversation!

We were back in Cayman on 20th June, and the 22nd saw the commencement of Cayman Arts Week. Cayman's burgeoning artistic talent was revealed, with exhibitions all over the island and free transport between the various venues, providing artists with a level of exposure that had never existed before.

In view of Mrs Harquail's ongoing, posthumous generosity toward Cayman's cultural development, I had for some time been thinking it would be only right for Mr Harquail's bust, currently languishing in a storage warehouse, to be returned to its appropriate, prominent position in the foyer of the theatre that bears his name. Sharon Roulstone, one of Mrs Harquail's executors, kindly advised me of the storage facility's location and gave me the key. On opening the door of the tiny warehouse, I found Mr Harquail, covered in dust, staring at me. Being on my own, I struggled to lift the weighty bronze bust of the gentleman whose generosity had ultimately been the catalyst for what the CNCF and the National Gallery had been able to achieve. I eventually got it into my Smart car and drove with the tailgate down along the Esterley Tibbetts highway. As noted earlier, Mrs Harquail had reportedly been very upset when the highway's name was changed from the Harquail bypass to the Esterley Tibbetts highway, but Mr Harquail, having escaped his dusty solitude, didn't seem to mind. Mr Harquail was soon welcomed into his rightful position, greeting all who enter the theatre and cultural centre.

By 24th June, we had complied with the public procurement requirements to advertise for and scrutinise all applicants, and subsequently selected Lord Cultural Resources to advise on our Strategic Planning Exercise, and we had also chosen the dates for their visit to the island to engage in stakeholder interviews.

Viv and I were delighted to attend the launch of Roy Bodden's book *My Life in a Conch Shell* at Miss Lassie's House, for which I had written the foreword:

> Glenroy Lorenzo Bodden's (fondly known as Roy Bodden) life
> story will make interesting reading for all lovers of Country and

Western music, not only here in the Cayman Islands but worldwide and, hopefully, will become a source of inspiration for our young Caymanian musicians to whom the book is dedicated, tracking as it does, Roy's development as a singer and musician and informs the current generation about a Caymanian's life in earlier and much more difficult times.

Roy's life story follows that of many Caymanians, with time living away from Cayman in both Jamaica and the United States, returning in more recent years to Cayman where his music and DJ skills found a welcome home on Radio Cayman for more than twelve years.

Given Caymanian's love of storytelling, our similar love of country and western music is perhaps easy to understand, with such music frequently telling a story of love and loss.

His skill and talent have been widely recognized by many, with him receiving numerous awards over some twenty years including in 1984 the Florida Country Music Association DJ of the Year Award, in 1989 an Award from the Society for the Preservation of Early Country and Western Music and for being the Founder of the Society, in 1997 the Medal of Honour and Certificate for Contribution to Caymanian Culture, in 1997 the Cayman National Cultural Foundation Heritage Award for Contributing to Caymanian Heritage-Music and in 1997 the Christian Male vocalist of the year Award.

Fortunately, in Cayman we are becoming increasingly aware of the critical importance of preserving our heritage and developing our culture in its many forms. My Life in a Conch Shell admirably adds to the growing volume of literature recording for prosperity what makes and enriches Cayman, the paradise we all enjoy.

Viv and I attended Dottie's birthday party at Renaissance at the end of June, and it was great to enjoy this event with so many of her friends. A day later, we attended a party held at Miss Lassie's House to congratulate Virginia Foster on her retirement from CNCF, where she had worked for many years and contributed so much to our projects.

At BCL, we had been advising a group of property owners for some months about windows that had been installed in their town houses. Ostensibly, they were hurricane-rated, bearing Dade County stickers to that effect. But it was suspected these stickers had been affixed later, and that these windows, in the event of a hurricane, might not perform as required. The dispute between the owners and the developer would continue for over a year, but was eventually resolved to the owner's satisfaction.

On 5th July we held a virtual meeting with David Aleman, the lead architect for Marriott, to discuss budgets for the seven Elegant hotels on Barbados, and our ongoing concern about divorcing the fit-out costs from the 'shell and core costs'. Simultaneously, back in Cayman, with BCL's expanding workload, we were exploring the possibility of redecorating the office and creating more desk space for additional staff.

On 7th July, Viv and I were invited to a reception at Government House, in honour of a visit from a representative of Stowe School. The institution was looking to set up a satellite school in Cayman, thereby offering first-class education to students while avoiding the need and expense of boarding such students far away from home.

On the 11th I wrote to the National Gallery, formally requesting an extension to Natalie's contract to work at CNCF, particularly in view of the pending arrival of the Lord Cultural Resources team to Cayman. Their representative, Brad King, arrived in Cayman on the 17th, and we welcomed him with a reception at Callaloo before they began their work on the Strategic Planning Exercise that had taken us so long to implement.

On 26th July, Viv and I began a significant walk – from Crested Butte (CB) to Maroon Bells (Aspen) – which we had been planning for a number of years. As Viv wrote at the time, 'Martyn has the travel bug again after COVID, and I have been very easily persuaded to be there for all the fun!' Working out the logistics and deciding which way we would hike (Crested Butte to Aspen or Aspen to Crested Butte) required research and we finally decided to do Crested Butte to Aspen. This was a good choice as our hosts, Cynthia and Jimmy, in Aspen Glen, drove us to Crested Butte with our guide, Heather, on 26th July. The drive is approximately ninety miles, and the idea was to arrive in time for Cynthia and Jimmy to have a noodle lunch with us at Ryce, before they turned around and drove the ninety miles back home – such super hosts!

After Jimmy and Cynthia left, we had a walk around the old town, which had been a camping ground for the silver mines in the 1870s, and later became a big coal mining town in the 1900s until 1950. We had wanted to have dinner at a lovely Italian Restaurant, Marchitelli's Gourmet Noodle, but it was fully booked, so we ended up in a lovely pizza place, Secret Stash. We had more salad on the pizza than naughty stuff, and the portions were so large that we had enough to take home for lunch on the trail the following day. Not the usual dinner or lunch for 'The Boulds' but really tasty. We overnighted at Crested Butte, then set out the next morning at 7.30am.

We were carrying large backpacks with clothing to cover all eventualities. Early mornings could be very cold and we would need thermal underwear, gloves, woolly hat and jacket. Also, as always in the mountains, the weather could be unpredictable, and thunder and lightning storms were prone to occur over the pass in the early afternoons. In the event, the weather was kind, and no changes of clothing were necessary except to peel off layers as we made our way up to the 12,500-foot pass. It took four hours to get there, plus a rest for an early lunch of cold pizza – anything at that altitude would taste good! The scenery was awesome, as were all the wildflowers. We were walking through fields of nature at her best, and everywhere we looked wildflowers painted the hillside in splendour.

At the pass we met up with other hikers of all ages, and we exchanged notes about where we were from. There was no one else from our little island – a mere sixty feet above sea level – so, as you can imagine, the climb to that altitude had been a greater challenge for us. I used the Oxygen Advantage breathing technique I had taught myself before I climbed Kilimanjaro – now I wished I had read the whole book! Once over the pass we had a good descent to the Maroon Bells trailhead, but it was twice as long as the ascent. Our guide, Heather, advised that we had to keep going without any stops along the way, or we would miss the last bus out of the trailhead at 4pm! Crossing streams and keeping our footing on this descent was not easy, so we applied caution. This slowed us down but kept us safe.

Eventually, Heather said she needed to rush on ahead to catch the last bus out from the trailhead in order to feed her horses. We had not known about feeding the horses until the last minute, but Heather said she would come back for us in her truck. We agreed, as we were not into rushing the hike we had waited so long to do. Heather then left, and as we continued on our way, we met people doing shorter loop hikes from Maroon Bells trailhead, or hiking into the area to camp overnight. We asked several of them how far it was to the trailhead. Almost all said three miles, and one said four miles, which was fairly soul-destroying. Along the way we spotted some wildlife – marmots, deer and even a bear with cubs. The last were on the other side of the lake, thank goodness! No moose, which we were happy about, as they're unpredictable and can charge at a moment's notice. We had our bear bells with us, but that wouldn't have done any good against a charging moose.

We eventually arrived at Maroon Bells Trailhead – there was no phone signal, but we were in civilisation, as there was a car park with people. We looked for Heather and her truck, but she was nowhere to be seen. Viv complimented me on being very observant, when I saw a van with 'Dolly's' written on the side driven by Todd from Crested Butte. He was letting off some hikers to pick up their car, so I asked him if he could drop us off at Highlands, another seven or eight miles down the Canyon. He agreed, to our considerable relief, and got the best tip we ever gave a driver!

We arrived in Highlands ski resort, where we skied many times in the winter, and walked into the carpeted lobby of the Ritz looking more than a little disheveled after eleven hours hiking. The only thing missing was straw coming out of our ears. I explained our situation and the lack of transport and the concierges, Dylan and Noor, very graciously suggested that we leave all our gear in the lobby and go to the bar and order some chilled wine and eats while waiting for our transport to arrive. It was the best chilled wine we have ever tasted!

Heather eventually arrived (with her dog) and enjoyed a glass of wine with us (with forbidden dog quietly hidden under the table). Then she drove us back to Aspen Glen, where she related her story to Jimmy and Cynthia, who had kindly made a big pot of southern black beans, rice and sausage. It had been a day to remember, with all the elements of adventure, and we had arrived back safe and sound after seeing Nature at her very best and meeting wonderful people – we felt very blessed.

On 29th July we left Eagle Vail for home, returning to Cayman and Callaloo and Puddie on the 30th. On 31st July, a tribute was held to honour the life of the late Maurice Stoppi, a fellow quantity surveyor and arbitrator from Jamaica, whom I had known since my arrival there. We had shared many discussions on all things arbitration, a field in which Maurice was widely regarded as the Caribbean expert and about which he had written many books. One of the truly special aspects about living and working in the Caribbean is the closeness of our professional community, which enables us to interact and exchange viewpoints with some of the region's great minds in so many fields – and Maurice had certainly been one of them.

During the first week of August, Fidelity, with whom we did a fair amount of business, announced that it would be realigning itself into a bank to be known as Proven, with its private wealth services to be handled by RF Bank & Trust (Cayman) Limited. We also held a pre-bid meeting for the prison OBC submission.

On 6th August, in Miami, I had dinner with Emilio Perez, the architectural lead on the Marriott projects, and the next day flew to Barbados for meetings with contractors, engineers, architects and hotel management, about the pre-construction work on the Elegant chain of hotels we were managing. We were also in business meetings about our corporate set-up, listing our services for various financial providers. Later that week, we held meetings on a luxury condominium project for which we were advising the developers on feasibility and planning, and the marketing and construction risks that needed analysis and management.

At the time of our first visit to Barbados on the Marriott project, the sea wall at the Tamarind Hotel had been compromised by storm action, as a result of which the foundation was being undermined. We were asked for our opinion on the proposed remedial work, which involved rebuilding a new seawall with poured concrete foundations in front of the hotel and the adjacent property. Designs had already been prepared for this solution, which would cost millions of dollars. We suggested simply placing large boulders along the waterfront, which would allow the waves to percolate through while breaking their force. This would be not only a cheaper but a far more aesthetic solution, and at a fraction of the cost. After much discussion, our suggested approach was followed.

I held a meeting at the National Gallery about Miss Lassie's paintings on the 11th, followed by a MW2 board meeting and an excellent lunch at the Foster's house at Cayman Kai, cooked by John Michael Foster, one of our directors, and the second generation of the family to be part of our leadership team.

For some time, I had been trying to persuade the Cayman Islands Government to host the CHICOS conference, given the significant exposure the conference would provide to our tourism product. On 17th August, I met with the Honorable Kenneth Bryan, our Minister of Tourism, and asked him to attend the planned November CHICOS conference in the Dominican Republic, so that he and his team could see first-hand the potential benefit to our islands. He said he would consider this invitation, and I am delighted to say he attended the conference and was suitably impressed. On 18th August we flew to Miami on the way to London, and held a virtual conference with David Marriott and his team in the Flagship lounge in Miami airport. We appraised him of the progress we were making on the Elegant hotels in Barbados, and in particular focused on the 'all-inclusive' services and the opportunities these provided, as well as the challenges of the ageing structures and services in the hotels they had acquired.

On 4th September, I flew to Barbados for another series of Marriott meetings. We met with the contractors and engineers for technical discussions. The focus was on the logistics of gaining access to the seafront to build the seawall in front of the Tamarind Hotel. On Barbados's west coast, nearly every inch of the seafront is built up, making access for heavy equipment and materials problematical, to say the least. In this case, we also had to ensure critical infrastructure, such as a septic tank, would not be damaged by equipment passing over it.

But as we say, 'So said so done'. We constructed a reinforced concrete slab over the septic tank, allowing safe passage for the heavy equipment to remove the debris from the demolished old reinforced concrete sea wall, and then replace it with large boulders. The operation required highly skilled equipment handling in the narrow walkway between the Tamarind and Treasure Beach hotel next door. I am delighted to report that when I last visited the site, there had been significant beach accretion. Guests could once again appreciate the full beachfront experience that they had come to Barbados to enjoy, with their feet in the sand and the Caribbean Sea at their doorstep. After three days of meetings, I returned to Miami for meetings with the food and beverage specialists at the interior designer's offices. There, we reviewed the range of culinary offerings that lie at the heart of the all-inclusive model, which were indeed impressive. Sadly, in the midst of the discussions, we heard the news that Queen Elizabeth II had died at Balmoral Castle at the age of ninety-six.

In Cayman, on 11th September, Viv and I attended the ceremony at Government House proclaiming the ascension of King Charles III to the throne. When singing the National Anthem, it was hard to remember to say 'King' as opposed to 'Queen' after seventy years! We spoke with the Governor, who admitted to having had the same problem while reading out the Proclamation.

We were in London on 19th September for the Queen's funeral. Jonnie and Charlene joined us for lunch, following which we walked to Cromwell Road to view the funeral procession as it made its way to Windsor Castle. Our timing was perfect; we were able to bow our heads to the late Queen. Such a remarkable woman, and the only Sovereign that Viv and I had ever known. The next day, we were invited by Jo and Norman to see their new Lords View apartment, and then we had a most enjoyable dinner at Oslo Court, with good English food served by waiters in tuxedos, in a very traditional setting. The meal began with Melba toast – one has to have been around a long time to remember Melba toast! Norman's mother and father dined there every Sunday evening for years, and many of the patrons there when we visited looked as if they had been doing the same.

On 22nd September we flew to Madrid, where we were to begin our 'Eat Northern Spain' Camino adventure with Alan and Claudia by staying overnight at the Palacio de los Duques Gran Meliá, enjoying the seasonal tasting menu, at Dos Cielos, located in the former stables of the hotel. The next morning, we drove to Madrid airport to meet Alan and Claudia and Elias (the owner of Eat Northern Spain), and our driver Alberto, who took us to Burgos. There, we stopped for lunch at Casa Ojeda, renowned for their specialty: slow-roasted lamb. The meal began with a partridge salad, and was accompanied by an excellent red Tempranillo – Pago de los Capellanes, from the Ribera del Duero.

After this delicious lunch, which set the tone for the upcoming journey, we visited the Catedral de Burgos, then checked into the Landa Palace Hotel. Now, this was a pilgrimage with a difference! I decided to brave the hotel pool, which was absolutely freezing – an appropriate reminder that we were on the Camino. We had dinner at the hotel, with a surprise visit from our friends Len and Rona from Turks & Caicos, now living in France. We enjoyed a special dinner of *foie gras* and *morcilla de Burgos* (black pudding), a Burgos specialty, followed by Dover sole – all accompanied by more of the Pago de los Capellanes. On 24th September, at 10am, we began our Camino de Santiago Compostela in earnest, walking some thirteen kilometres through fields and building up an appetite for lunch at Estrella del Bajo Carrión. We enjoyed an excellent tomato salad followed by steak with foie gras, paired with Viña Pedrosa Crianza, again from the Ribera del Duero wine region in northern Spain. 'Bon Appetit' – or as they say in Spain, '¡Que aproveche!'. It was a phrase we would repeat many times during our trip.

After lunch, we visited the Cathedral de Santa María in León. The next day, 25th September, we continued our Camino, covering another twelve kilometres before stopping for lunch at El Capricho, the famous wine cellar of José Gordón, located in a labyrinth of caves in Jiménez de Jamuz, with a huge selection of wine. The wine cellar was created by José's grandfather Segundo, but the vineyards had long been neglected. However, in 2016 José produced his first vintage of just two thousand bottles. Now, after meticulous care of the vines and additional acquisitions, José produces around thirty thousand bottles annually from twenty hectares of vineyards. I had a great time chatting with José about wine stories related to Carabella, but most importantly, the steak was superb – so much so that Alan nearly set a world record for the amount he consumed. Alan has always been rail-thin, so how he managed to put all that meat away remains a mystery. After such a commodious meal, we drove to Posada del Palacio de Canedo, a Swiss chalet-style hotel, in El Bierzo, once again surrounded by vineyards that have been harvested for centuries. We teased Elias that perhaps he should rename his company from 'Eat Northern Spain' to 'Eat and Drink Northern Spain'.

We awoke on the 26th to news of Hurricane Ian passing to the southwest of Grand Cayman as a Category 1 hurricane. Thankfully, we suffered only minor wind and storm damage, but Ian went on to strengthen and become one of the worst and costliest hurricanes to hit Florida since 1935. Each morning Alberto had to carefully pack our suitcases into the back of the Mercedes van – this was no easy feat, given it was luggage for all six of us. To our amazement, every morning Alberto was immaculately clad in a different three-piece suit, shirt and tie!

We enjoyed our breakfast at the Palacio, then began the eight-kilometre walk along the Camino Francés to Castillo de Villafranca del Bierzo, followed by a drive to Ribeira Sacra. There, we were escorted by a local guide, Anna, who gave us an overview of the area and in particular of the vineyards, planted on the very steep slopes along the river. Traditionally, once the grapes were picked, they would be transported by boat for crushing. We had lunch at Playa da Cova, then took a boat ride on the Ribeira before driving to the Monasterio de Santo Estevo, where we checked in for a two-night stay.

The next morning began with Anna guiding us through a famous local cheese factory, followed by an aperitivo at the bar before lunch at A Faragulla wine bar, located in the heart of the Ribera Sacra.

After lunch we drove to a vineyard, Finca Scintella, with Óscar, a new guide. Elías had told him (without our knowledge) of our interest in winemaking, and we were invited to step into a barrel and stomp the Mencía grapes, which we did with great laughter, holding onto the sides of the barrel to prevent ourselves falling in. Afterwards, we tasted the literal fruits of our labour. The experience continued with clams seasoned with rosemary and cooked in a dry grass fire – paired, of course, with local wine. Dinner at the winery followed, and concluded with a *queimada* – a traditional, highly alcoholic Galician ceremonial drink made from *orujo* (pomace brandy), sugar, lemon or orange peels and whole coffee beans. The drink is ignited and left to burn to 'ward off evil spirits' before drinking. We returned that night to the Monasterio de Santo Estevo, where we slept peacefully, secure in the knowledge that any evil spirits had been kept at bay. *Vale!*

On 28th September, we started the final six-kilometre stage of the Camino from Villamaior into the Praza do Obradoiro, Santiago de Compostela's main square, where we were greeted by the sound of Galician bagpipes – the area has strong Celtic roots. Hundreds of pilgrims were congratulating each other on completing the walk, a tradition over a thousand years old. I must admit, we felt a little bit like imposters, having walked only a few sections, but the spectacular food and wine more than made up for it! We stopped for lunch at A Curtidoria, a cosy restaurant in the old town, where we enjoyed *fideuà* – a paella-like dish made with pasta noodles instead of rice. Afterwards, we checked into the Parador de los Reyes Católicos – a fitting and historic end to our journey.

Alan was not feeling well and, after testing himself for COVID, found he was positive. So he stayed at the Parador while we went for a tasting-menu style dinner at La Radio – Pepe Solla, which was outstanding. The next day, we visited the market to see the freshest fish, cheeses and vegetables, followed by a tapas-style lunch at A Noiesa Casa de Comidas. We then did some souvenir shopping and enjoyed a farewell dinner with Elías at Casa Marcelo, known for its open kitchen and tasting menus. Sadly, Alan and Claudia couldn't join us after having shared so much of the great adventure. On 30th September we took a taxi to Santiago airport for our flight to Málaga, and then drove to Villa Karola to spend the week with Alan and Claudia. That evening we had a tasty dinner of Rogan Josh. Unfortunately, Claudia later tested positive for COVID, and we missed her company for the rest of our stay.

We started out 1st October with a three-mile walk along Marbella beach, but soon decided to keep our eyes pointed strictly forward and focussed on the middle distance – this particular stretch of the beach catered to nudists, and the sights were not exactly pleasing. We had lunch with Alan, then went shopping for wine in anticipation of drinks with Alan and Claudia's friends, Hans and Torsen, as well as Len and Rona who had come to stay with us. We had a dinner of paella on the beach at Las Flores. The next day we drove into Marbella old town with Len and Rona to explore what was on offer, returning to Villa Karola for a very spicy tomato pasta sauce. Yours truly had perhaps been a little too generous with the dried chilli flakes, but everyone said it was delicious.

During the next couple of days we alternated beach walks, lunches at local restaurants and dinners cooked at Villa Karola. On 5th October we took the taxi to Málaga airport and then flew to London and QGM.

The next day, we had banking meetings with our relationship manager, followed by shopping at Fortnum and Mason for Christmas puddings. The next evening, after dim sum at Yauatcha, we went to the Royal Opera House to once again enjoy Sarah Lamb's performance as principal dancer in *Mayerling* which we had first seen in 2018 and were then invited backstage to see Sarah and meet the cast, which was a truly memorable experience.

During this time I had continued 'swotting' for my loss adjusters exam, for the Chartered Institute of Loss Adjusters. I took the tube to Holborn to take the exam after lunch. It was unusual to be back in the realm of sitting exams, and security at the test centre to prevent cheating was tight to say the least. We were required to leave our cell phones, watch, and the contents of our pockets at security, and had to submit to a body search before sitting down at the desk to complete the exam papers.

On 11th October, we left for Cayman via Miami, and after overnighting at #10E, we returned to Puddie and Callaloo – shuttered up against possible damage from Hurricane Ian. Preparations for Gimistory at Callaloo had proceeded while we were away, and Hopscotch had scoped out their lighting and sound requirements on 7th October. We met with CNCF staff at Callaloo a week after we arrived, to review everything needed to ensure this would be a first-class show.

On 30th October I met with Michell in Tortola, where we reviewed the work Jasmine, a trainee quantity surveyor working with BCL, was doing for us. Michell and I then conducted a site visit to Antigua, where we inspected Halcyon Cove – the super all-inclusive CHIC resort Royalton was redeveloping, headed by their project manager, Rafael Navas. On 2nd November we flew to Barbados to meet with our corporate managers on our business structure, as well as Marriott, for discussions on the seven hotels we were refurbishing. The next day we met with Marriott's general manager to discuss the costs of the necessary renovations to the hotels' existing structures and services. It had been proposed these should be handled as part of the maintenance budget of each hotel and administered by their maintenance staff. BCL's opinion was that the costs were likely to be significantly greater than those envisaged and, further, that they would require complex scheduling interfaces with the contractors who would be carrying out the fit-out work of the rooms. This discussion would continue for many months.

A few days later I was back in Cayman for a meeting at the Kimpton Residences in connection with a Reinstatement Cost Assessment we were preparing for them, after which I discussed the Callaloo lighting and sound arrangements for the CNCF events in December with Hopscotch.

I was in Miami on the 8th, engaging in a virtual Marriott Capex call at 4pm, then attending a National Gallery Board meeting at 4.30pm. The next morning I flew to Punta Cana to meet Jose, Michell's architect partner, for lunch, and then drove to the Hilton La Romana for evening cocktails and the opening of the eleventh CHICOS conference. This time, I presented a discussion on 'Changes to the Caribbean Lodging Market Post–Pandemic' with a lively and distinguished panel. On the 11th I met Viv in Miami before we drove to Sebring to catch up with the Walkup family for the first time in three and a half years. For the next few days we simply relaxed with family again, enjoying dinners and long walks and admiring Joel and Danielle's new condo at the Sebring Country Club.

We were back in Cayman on the 15th, after which there followed a busy week of conference calls on the Marriott project in Barbados, the prison project in Cayman, the appraisal we were preparing on the Kimpton Residences, and the Lighthouse school proposal for which the submission deadline was 5pm on 21st November. Alan Veeran, who had spent the summer at his home in Spain, returned to Cayman, and it was good to have him back on the ground. Bernadine also returned – she had been on a hiking adventure to Everest Base Camp, so BCL was continuing to build on its reputation of climbing to new heights for its clients!

On 23rd November, Michael Meghoo, Alan Veeran and I visited Miss Lassie's duplex to inspect some termite damage there. CNCF benefitted greatly from the expert advisers who donated their time free of charge to address the properties' maintenance issues, which was very much appreciated. Sadly, Michael had resigned from the CNCF board on 29th July but continued to assist us with his knowledge and expertise. The National Gallery held its Fundraising Gala on the 25th, which was very successful.

The prison design team from HLM arrived on the island during the weekend of 26th November. We began their visit with a team lunch at Callaloo, after which we made a presentation at Northward Prison on the 28th, which was very well received. Meetings in Barbados to check on progress with the various contractors followed. Our brief for the initial phase of work was to complete three model rooms to reflect the different brand standards that Marriott were promoting as part of their all-inclusive vacation packages in three different hotels.

My hairdresser from Brazil, George Carvalho, had for some considerable time been talking to me about cooking a special, typically Brazilian fish dish at Callaloo. Sunday 4th December was the day, with Alan and Claudia joining us for a delicious and relaxed meal.

On 5th December CNCF received the report prepared by Lord Cultural Resources as a baseline for the Strategic Planning Exercise. As part of the regular board composition review, I had been asked to confirm my willingness to continue to serve on the CNCF board. This I had duly done. So I was surprised to receive a call from the Chief Officer in the Ministry of Culture, advising that my tenure on the board was not being renewed and asking if I had any comment. I, of course, expressed my disappointment, given my almost forty years of service and the Strategic Planning Exercise, of which I had been the instigator and architect. I was particularly keen to see this implemented, given the ground we had covered already. However, that was the decision, and I subsequently discovered Morgan's tenure had also been terminated. To this day, neither of us has received any explanation, letter of thanks, or acknowledgement of our accomplishments.

On 6th December Viv and I left for our annual ski trip to Alta, Utah, and on the 8th we were skiing on fresh powder in bluebird conditions. On the 9th we celebrated twenty-seven years of marriage, with Viv giving me a beautiful anniversary card. We had stopped giving each other presents years ago, as there was nothing we wanted or needed, but there was always the odd surprise we could give each other – usually some practical item. The following day was my seventy-seventh birthday – and yes, of course, I got another beautiful card from Viv and email greetings from friends. On the 11th we awoke to very high winds and snow, so we decided to stay home and enjoy a breakfast of scrambled eggs and bacon. Then we lit the fire, which formed a cosy backdrop as we caught up with emails.

After lunch, yours truly changed his mind about staying home and ventured out into fresh Utah powder to ski six runs and work up an appetite for dinner at Sugarplum. We were now locked down there, due to snow and avalanche danger. This resulted in a late start on the 12th, which Viv made the most of to finish writing her Christmas cards, which we then posted from the tiny Alta Post Office. This post office has served the Alta area for many decades, but now, in the email-order era, they have a problem with storing the many large Amazon boxes that arrive daily. Then we went out to ski, stopping for lunch at Rustler, where we saw Vicki from Taiwan. We skied seven runs, followed by a very slow drive back to Sugarplum due to the heavy snowfall. 13th December began with a trip to General Gritts at Snowbird to top up the cellar, after which we had lunch and then a short afternoon ski as it had been snowing all day. On the 14th we enjoyed lunch at the rebuilt Snowpine Lodge, where Viv had her once yearly burger.

A series of bluebird days with perfect snow followed, after which we drove to Salt Lake City. There, after a series of miscommunications between the Capitol Theatre, the Monaco Hotel and my cell phone service, we received our tickets for a wonderful performance of *The Nutcracker* with only thirty minutes to spare. We've never changed out of ski clothes so fast in our lives! We caught our flights to Cayman, Callaloo, and Puddie/Buster the next morning.

Viv and I were invited to Carols and Cocktails at Government House on the 20th, which got us straight into the Christmas mood, and was enhanced when we entertained Angela Morgan at Callaloo on the 22nd, as part of our Christmas tradition. On Christmas Day, we had lunch at Callaloo, preceded by croquet with Sir John and Louise, Alan and Claudia, and Sasha and Kristen. I was delighted when Viv gave me a Christmas present of an 'egg topper'. This wonderful device removes the top off an egg with a clean cut, which is ideal for my caviar eggs and far preferable aesthetically to the jagged cut made by using the pointed tip of a sharp knife, which is what I'd been doing for years.

Alan and Kathleen, our fellow wine makers who live in Vista del Mar opposite Callaloo, invited us for drinks and nibbles on 27th December to celebrate their daughter's wedding, rounding out the year except for our 'Do Drop In' on the last day of the old year.

2023

'Life is best lived by focusing on your goals and dancing through all other distractions.' Yogi Detox tea

2023 began with a kind invitation from Alaisdair and Lisa to their home in Cayman Islands Yacht Club, where we had a chance to catch up with friends we had not seen during the previous year. The working year began with several phone calls about the Barbados Marriott project, and discussions with a local engineer on a potential new project for a proposed Mandarin Oriental-branded mixed-use resort development. On the 7th there was a joyful break in the working routine to celebrate the wedding of John Michael and Zoe Foster's daughter at Luca, on the beach. Yet another great start to the year was chilling out with Morgan and Jocelyn at their home. There, Morgan displayed significant dexterity spinning the pizza dough to expand it to the correct size, before cooking it in his pride and joy: an outside, wood-fired pizza oven. It was all so delicious and such a great evening of laughter and discussing our goals for the new year.

The thought of climbing Aconcagua, in Argentina, had taken seed in my mind by then. It is the world's highest mountain outside Asia at 6,961 metres (22,838 feet), and I had been researching the climb's itinerary and the best time of year to undertake it. During this process I fortunately discovered a group of climbers from Cayman that had attempted the summit some years before. They had to abort the expedition due to COVID, but were able to give me some first-hand advice about climbing companies and the services they could provide.

On 10th January I flew to Barbados for meetings with contractors. We looked at key storage facilities for the materials we needed. These were being imported free of duty and therefore required bonded facilities. We also reviewed the three model rooms we were completing in preparation for a visit on 15th January by the Marriott team headed by Brian King, their President of Caribbean and Latin American operations. We then visited each of the seven hotels Marriott had acquired from Elegant: Turtle Beach, The Waves, Crystal Cove, The House, Tamarind, Treasure Beach and the Colony Club, as well as the Positano restaurant located between The House and Tamarind. We took many notes as we discussed the pros and cons of the existing structures, and the plans that had been suggested by the architects and interior designers for each property. The next day, back in Cayman, I met with the developer of the proposed Mandarin Oriental development to discuss our fees for an appraisal we were preparing for their financing package.

After our annual, most enjoyable twelve-day ski trip in Vail, I flew to Barbados on 20th February for Marriott hotel meetings. Marriott had appointed a client representative to work with us on the ground; this individual had hotel management and accounting experience, but little understanding of what it took to manage the risk of a complex refurbishment programme of aging hotel stock, so it took many, long discussions and considerable persuasion to get our recommendations implemented. We held another Marriott conference on 7th March, to discuss the kitchen designs. These were, of course, a key element in the refurbishment of their Barbados hotels, given the range of food outlets in the all-inclusive model.

Another challenge – among many – on the Marriott project was the fact that the floors in the rooms were finished with ceramic tiles in the traditional manner. These had seen the end of their useful life, and so needed replacing. However, removing and replacing them would be a messy and very noisy job, which would be problematic because the plan was to close only part of a particular hotel at any one time. We came up with the idea of covering the existing tile with a thin vinyl tile overlay. Initially the feeling was that this would look 'cheap', but we knew the manufacture of such tiles had come a long way. We met with Randy Stafford, a good friend from Bermuda, who was operating in Cayman and asked him for some samples to take to Barbados to compare with the colour of the selected tile. This we did, and it was extremely difficult to see any difference between the vinyl and the selected porcelain tiles.

In March we began looking at a barge trip in Ireland, where we would be joined by Alan and Jenny Foster. We got out the notes of our previous barge trip with Flo, but also looked at Barrowline Cruisers, based in Vicarstown, for cruises on the river Barrow and the Grand Canal to Dublin.

During this time I had a most interesting conference with Diane Dodd, a good friend from Spain, who was active at many of the IFACCA seminars I attended around the world on behalf of CNCF. She now headed up IGCAT, the international Institute of Gastronomy, Culture, Arts and Tourism, and we discussed the possibility of nominating Cayman as an International Region of Gastronomy. This aligned well with my love of food, as well as my passion for cultural preservation and development, and for linking both of these with tourism.

During the second week of March, we were kindly hosted by Brett Hill of RF bank, for their annual Cayman Economic Outlook, for which they brought together many talented speakers to review local and international economic changes, and forecast potential issues for the coming year.

One unusual, but extremely talented speaker, was Jeff Evans, who was a mountain guide. He spoke in particular about trust, and had written several books on this subject, including one called *Mountain Vision – Lessons Beyond the Summit.* In this, he described his adventures with Erik Weihenmayer, a blind adventurer who had competed in many gruelling and challenging races around the world and, alongside Jeff, was the only blind person to summit Everest. Jeff had mentioned climbing Aconcagua during his presentation, so I went to him afterwards and gained some useful tips about the climb to add to the information I was assembling in preparation for my own ascent, the plans for which were gradually beginning to take shape.

The 17th March was a tragic day for us. Puddie had been ailing for some time, and Viv was not getting anywhere with the current vet. By a serendipitous coincidence she was able to connect with Dr Colin, a wonderful, caring man who treated each animal as a precious being. On St Patrick's Day Viv called his surgery, Kman Vets, and his wife very kindly gave us an appointment. When Viv took Puddie in he was very lethargic and Dr Colin said he would do some tests and let us know the outcome. Unfortunately, we soon heard Puddie was not going to make it and, on a very rainy night, Wayne drove us through Friday traffic jams to say our goodbyes. It was a very sad day for everyone who dearly loved him and the joy he had brought to Callaloo. The following day Wayne picked up his little box, which we buried in the garden. We had a plaque made with the inscription: 'Puddie (Buster) Bould – Always in our Hearts' and a beautiful paw tile from the Adams family, who were real Puddie lovers. It was Viv who had always called him Puddie, which I had maintained was not a macho name for a male cat. For someone like me, with no prior experience with having a pet, it was one of Life's Lessons Well Learned.

On 19th March we entertained Jerry and Joanne Sibley for lunch at Callaloo, which was always an absolute delight, especially when Jerry told Jamaican stories and we heard of Joanne's latest art adventures, about which she was always so articulate. One funny Jamaican story they told us, was that when they closed up their country house in Chanteclair, on the north coast of Jamaica, they had to hide the WC as otherwise it was always missing on their return. They had no permanent staff in the house so the country folk quickly knew when the house was empty, and would just remove the 'pot' to install in their own homes!

Jonathan Dingle was in Cayman a few days later and came to Callaloo for dinner, where we discussed the idea of a new mediation course to be delivered here. On 25th March there was a celebration of life for Peter Kosa, held at the Cayman Drama Society. Peter was an extremely talented actor and had appeared in many plays both at CDS and also at CNCF. It was sad not to have him here with us anymore, but good to celebrate the life and talent he had bought to our shores and the skills he had so willingly shared.

On 26th March it was back to Barbados for a further inspection of all the model rooms with Brian King, Emilio Perez and Alex Fiz. We had by now entered into detailed conversations with sources in Miami about sourcing the FF&E (furniture, fixtures and equipment), but as we were buying product from around the world during our stay in Barbados, we held detailed conferences with the various suppliers. With Aconcagua in mind I was beginning each day with a new routine: first, the usual four-mile walk up Holders Hill, then once around the polo field part way up, and then to the top of the hill and back. The elevation gain, whilst not significant, was fairly steep and better training than any walks in flat Cayman. On the 31st, I dropped Michell at the airport, went for my three-mile walk around the Garrison, then flew back to Miami. There I met Vivian, and we entertained Emilio and his charming wife Teresa for dinner, coupled with a tasting of Carabella wines from our cellar at #10E.

Although I would not begin training for Aconcagua in earnest until August, in April I had begun walking around Cayman with a backpack loaded with 17 lbs of medicine balls. I also got in touch with a company that Ben Tonner had used for their climb, called Mountain Professionals, to ask how many would be climbing in the party, the use of porters on the climb, specifications for climbing boots, and also if they took the False Polish Route up the mountain, which Jeff Evans had recommended.

Earlier in the year, Viv and I had booked a hike in Corsica called 'From the Mountains to the Sea', through a company called The Natural Adventure. It was scheduled to begin on 16th April so we planned to leave for London on the 12th and spend a few days there en route. On the work front, we had a kickoff meeting scheduled for 17th April to begin the design work on the Lighthouse School extension, and Alan kindly agreed to lead this with Michell over Zoom, so Viv and I could continue with our hiking plans. In London, after the traditional lunch at Da Mario, yours truly was in the virtual business world, with conference calls running until 11.30pm. On 14th April we had a good walk through a drizzly Hyde Park, and then reviewed our plans for the Corsica hike, before I took more business calls – this time on the Prison and Marriott projects.

On 16th April we flew to Nice for our Air Corsica flight to Ajaccio. A driver from The Natural Adventure met us at Ajaccio airport and drove us to Corte – once the capital of Corsica, nestled in the mountains – for check-in at the Hôtel Duc de Padoue. Prinscilla, the hostess, was most helpful and recommended dinner at La Casuccia, where we had salad served in a bread bowl, large entrecôte steaks and an excellent red wine from Ajaccio. The next morning, Anna organised a delicious breakfast for us at the hotel, and recommended a walking route to Bocca d'Ominanda, which started just out of Corte on the Route de Saint-Pancrace. We climbed some seven hundred vertical feet over three and a half hours, then stopped for lunch – panini and Corse Figari red wine – before returning to the hotel. Dinner that evening was at Rivière des Vins, where we enjoyed excellent pork with mushrooms in cream sauce, a green salad, and demi-pichets of red and white wine.

On 18th April we began our hike in earnest. A taxi picked us up with our luggage, dropping us off at the Scala di Santa Regina Spring, the starting point of our trek. We carried only daypacks, while the taxi continued on with our bags to the hotel where we would finish that day's hike. The Natural Adventure had provided both a map and written directions, but we managed to get lost almost immediately by taking the wrong turning by the *Mairie* (town hall), before quickly finding the correct route. That day's trail was of great historical importance: it's the ancient path used by shepherds leading their herds into and out of the Niolu Valley. It leads upwards through a savage landscape of granite cliffs, along a dramatic balcony path, to a small Genoese bridge, Ponte D'Era, where we stopped for lunch.

The views soon opened up, and we continued through a very different landscape: the granite cliffs giving way to old chestnut groves and rolling forested hills. Yellow painted trail markers guided us down toward the lake at the base of the valley and onward to the village of Calacuccia, where our overnight stop – Hotel Acquaviva – was situated on the outskirts of the village. We were greeted by the owner, who was sitting in front of an open log fire, and welcomed us with a glass of wine. After having climbed roughly 2,600 vertical feet over seven hours, we headed into the village for dinner at Auberge U Fucaghjolu. The dinner was excellent, and it was obvious only the best local, seasonal ingredients had been used: Corsican cheese and salad, fresh pasta and veal, again with demi-pichets of local red and white wine. I must admit to a twinge of guilt – I had pitched this trip to Vivian as being from the mountain to the sea (which was, after all, its title) implying it would be pretty much downhill all the way. But after climbing 2,600 feet on day one, this clearly wasn't the case! We returned to the hotel and had no trouble sleeping.

On day three of our hike, we walked from Calacuccia to Évisa. After breakfast at Hôtel Acquaviva, where they also packed a baguette for our lunch, we took a short twenty-minute taxi transfer along a twisting mountain road to the vast Valdu Niellu, a Corsican pine forest. We were dropped off at Castel di Vergio, a small ski station near the Col de Vergio, the island's highest mountain road pass, where snow still lay on the ground. The pass marks the boundary between Corsica's two départements: Haute-Corse to the north and Corse-du-Sud to the south.

The views were majestic; the peaks were steep and loomed above. We studied both our map and the written route description, as well as the hikers' information board at the trailhead, to make sure we were setting off along the correct route, particularly after the previous day's bad start. The trail descended through the Aïtone pine forest and passed over the Pont de Casterica, where we stopped for lunch by the river and enjoyed a Clos d'Alezeto Ajaccio red with our baguettes. Afterwards we crossed a narrow suspension bridge – one hiker at a time – and entered the outskirts of Évisa. We passed the *piscine naturelle*, a large rock pool and local swimming spot, then continued down through the ancient chestnut woods that marked the approach to the village. We read that some of the trees with their thick, gnarled trunks had stood there for nearly two thousand years.

Évisa sits at around 2,700 feet in elevation. It's a vibrant mountain village with a healthy climate, unusually close to the sea for a village at this altitude, and is known locally as 'the pearl of the mountains'. We checked into Hotel Aïtone, at the top of the village, where our room had a tub – perfect for a long soak with Epsom salts! The hotel was full of Corsican character, and over dinner we watched the sunset over Porto – a beautiful sight.

We found that each section of the hike was taking us almost twice as long as the itinerary estimated – not a problem, but important to factor in when planning the day. Day four was a rest day, spent in Évisa. We started late, and stopped and chatted with two cyclists in the village – the steep hills in this area certainly provided them with a challenge. Then we had a beautiful walk through the chestnut forests along the 'Mare e Monti' trail. This path, once the only link between Évisa and the now-abandoned hamlet of Tassu, winds through the surrounding chestnut woods into dense maquis – Corsica's wild scrubland – a mix of oak, cistus, strawberry tree, rosemary and thyme, curry plant, blooming white tree heather and a multitude of other low evergreen plants, many endemic to the island. Corsicans say the scent of their maquis is unique, and that they can smell their island far out at sea. We stopped for lunch by the river, and enjoyed more of L' Aïtone's red wine, kindly given us by Jean

Pierre, the manager. We eventually arrived at Tassu, where we explored the ruins, including a small chapel that appeared to be still in use. That evening, we returned to spend the night at L' Aïtone, where we enjoyed a dinner of omelette Corse and, of course, some of their red wine.

On the fifth day of our hike, we walked from Évisa to Porto. After breakfast and making up sandwiches for lunch, we paid our bill – a very modest 170 Euros given our indulgences – and bid farewell to Jean Pierre. We set off on an old path which descended through the Spelunca Gorge, zig-zagging steeply into the depths of the valley. We soon noticed a dog trailing behind us – it had been chasing other dogs in the village earlier. Viv sternly commanded it to go home, which seemed to have the opposite effect, and despite repeated instructions from Viv (to whom I pointed out the dog probably understood French, not English) it continued to follow us.

We reached high arched Pont de Zeglia, a Genoese bridge, just as a herd of large-horned sheep were crossing. The dog seemed frightened, and backed away as Viv held it by the collar, leaving her holding the collar while the dog vanished into the bushes. The creature eventually came back to hide under the bushes and while Viv coaxed it out and tried to get the collar back on she noticed an embossed telephone number on the disc, which we resolved to call as soon as we reached Ota, the next village. We stopped for lunch by the river, attended by our new four-legged friend – the collar's disc unfortunately didn't give its name. The dog had a wonderful time running up the hill and down into the rock pools as if it had never seen so much water before, while we walked along the path that led alongside the torrent towards Ota.

This is a village where mountain architecture coexists with a hot Mediterranean climate and flora. Braying donkeys, hunting dogs, villagers working in their gardens, bright bougainvillea, lemon and fig trees all added to the colour. We stopped at Chez Marie restaurant for a well-earned glass of wine, still accompanied by the dog. One of the staff gave it a bowl of water, but it was not allowed into the restaurant area and looked very forlorn at having to stay outside. We called the number on the disc and spoke to the dog's owner, who was in Évisa and much distressed. Other guests in the restaurant helped her communicate that we should wait there, and that she, Mariedo, would drive over and collect Mira, as the dog was called, and which was only a six-month-old pup.

Can you imagine the adventure that Mira had that day and could only dream about, unable to tell a soul? As thanks for returning Mira, Mariedo drove us into Porto, as it was now dusk and our trail along the mountain path might not be safe. There we checked into Hotel Kalliste and had dinner at La Mer, by the harbour, of tossed green salad, paella and king prawns in cognac sauce, rounded out with mango and lemon sorbet. The last day of our Corsican hike would take us from Porto to Piana. We made lunch from our breakfast meats and had a chat with the manager of Kalliste about the impact of COVID on tourism. Then we crossed the bridge over the marina to the beach, climbing over the boulders and then along the oceanside road, looking down into the crystal clear blue sea.

After a short stretch of road walking we entered the maquis woodland, which provided welcome shade. We made the mistake of taking the off-road 'high option' over very mossy rocks, which led us on a very steep climb. Eventually we turned around to find the correct trail, marked with yellow trail blazes. We climbed for a long time to Fontaine d'Olivia Bona, and then descended through pine woods to Stade de Piana. From there, a long road led us to Hotel Scandola, where we rewarded ourselves for the seven-hour hike and 2,800 vertical feet of climbing with a well-deserved bottle of Domaine Casanova – a Corsican rosé. Dinner followed at Casa Corsa, in Piana, of veal brochette with a green salad, and lemon and mango sorbet – a great finish to a great day.

In total, we had walked eighty-four miles over the past six days of our hike. On 23rd April we had the best breakfast yet at the Scandola, made up our lunch baguettes, and were collected by the nephew of the proprietor of L'Aïtone in Évisa, who is a taxi driver. He drove us to Ajaccio airport, where we had booked a rental car from Sixt. The only problem: it was electric, a first for me. I spent a while figuring out how it started, even going so far as to hail a mechanic to complain it wouldn't move – only to be shown the lack of any engine noise was normal, albeit disconcerting. Once I got the hang of it, we drove to the prehistoric site of Filitosa, dating back almost eight thousand years, and saw the menhirs – a truly spectacular sight.

We then continued to Bonifacio, checked into the Hotel Caravelle overlooking the harbour, and had dinner. The next day, after breakfast, we took a tour of old Bonifacio, perched high on an undercut limestone cliff over the sea. We then drove to Porto Vecchio for lunch of linguine and a fine glass of rosé at Le Bistrot Maison Guiducci, and then back to the Caravelle for a rest and catch-up followed by dinner of filet de loup at L'Escale, on the harbour.

We left Bonifacio the next day and drove to Ajaccio airport to catch our Air Corsica flight to Marseilles, and from there to Heathrow and home to QGM to catch up on conference calls. The next few days we relaxed at QGM and enjoyed an early birthday dinner with Norman and Jo Linton, who entertained us at Hutong Chinese restaurant in the Shard and had bought Vivian a beautiful silver box for her collection when they were on holiday in Italy.

On 29th April we drove to Taplow, for a lunch at Roux to kick off Viv's birthday celebrations. Given our long-standing love of Alain Roux's cooking, we wanted to enjoy a meal at this French brasserie-style restaurant, and it did not disappoint. Alain was there, and we had a good conversation about the effect of COVID on tourism and his business.

We then drove to Cliveden and checked into the Lady Astor Suite, which is claimed to be the grandest in the UK, and it certainly lived up to its reputation. The next day Rob, Jen, Anni and Nick arrived at 11am for champagne. It was Nick's birthday as well, so a double celebration, which began with a buggy ride down to the Thames to board the *Suzy Ann* for a trip to the Waterside Inn with captain Wil, and champagne and hors d'oeuvres on the way. We were greeted there by maître d' Frederic, who had saved the best table facing the river for us. Anni was continuing her sommelier course, and so we had some great wine tasting and then a wonderful lunch of langoustine souffle, roast lamb, and rhubarb soufflé to finish.

On 3rd May we attended the Caribbean Council cocktail reception at the House of Lords, where Philip Davis, Prime Minister of the Bahamas, was the guest speaker. Washington Misick, now Prime Minister of Turks and Caicos, came up to me and asked if I remembered who he was – and of course I did. We then had a good laugh, remembering the time he (then nicknamed Washie) and Joe Anderson drove with the top down along the marl roads of Turks and Caicos, arriving at their destination transformed as 'white men' from the marl dust they were covered with.

The next day I attended a presentation at the Reform Club in Pall Mall, where investment opportunities in the Bahamas, including sea grass carbon credits, were being promoted. I met Thomas Hartley, the British High Commissioner based in Nassau there and discussed potential opportunities for BCL. I then left the presentation to meet with Ben Marston and Julie Désormiers, of architects Jestico and Whiles. They are architectural special needs school experts, and we discussed the potential challenges of the Lighthouse School project in Grand Cayman, for which BCL is the lead consultant.

Although Viv had already 'formally' celebrated her birthday, we celebrated again on the actual day with Jonnie and Charlene, and cousin Linda and Jim, beginning with a 'fizzy sharpener' at QGM, and a tasting menu at Launceston Place, followed by a 'Coronation' street party on Gloucester Road.

I had a lot of catching up in the office to do once we got back to Cayman on 10th May. On 19th May we left for Kingston, Jamaica for Cathy and Seb's COVID-delayed wedding, to be held at their home in Treasure Beach. The next day we drove to Tallawah Villa for their wedding ceremony, which was held on the beach, with Cayman's Chief Justice, Margaret Ramsay-Hale, Cathy's dear longtime friend, officiating. As you might imagine, there was 'plenty' music, dancing and drinking, with yours truly giving a toast and speech to the bride's mom and dad, Cissy and Bunny Delapenha. On 22nd May we enjoyed our breakfast of ackee and saltfish – a truly Jamaican, tasty breakfast – then drove to Norbrook in Kingston, arriving with a flat tyre at Alan and Jenny Foster's, where we were staying overnight. Alan suggested a walk around the Constant Spring Golf Course, which we did, passing mango trees more heavily laden with fruit than I had seen in a long time. Of course, Viv couldn't resist tasting them, with the juice running down her arms. Alan had, as usual, cooked up a storm, with dinner of baked pasta and a desert of – no surprise – mangoes!

Back in the office on the 24th, we received the bad news that the prison project in Cayman was not going ahead as planned, but that our presence was required in Antigua to review the site progress on Royalton's renovation of the Halcyon Cove project there. I made arrangements for the visit in conjunction with an upcoming trip to Barbados, leaving Cayman on 28th May.

After conducting the site tour of the Halcyon Cove Hotel, I returned to Barbados, where I paid a visit to the Barbados Immigration Department to secure my Barbados work permit. The department wanted proof of my professional qualifications, so I suggested they look online. This was not acceptable. They demanded to see my original professional certificates. I pointed out these were framed and hanging on the wall of my office, but they still needed to see them. Accordingly, I had them bubble-wrapped, hand carried them on my next visit over, and presented them to the immigration officer for his edification, after which my passport was duly stamped as the legal holder of a work permit.

During the next couple of days we continued with property inspections, including the less-than-glamourous inspection of a hotel sewage plant that was giving trouble, as well as a visit to the soon-to-open Sam Lord's Castle Hotel, a new all-inclusive hotel by Wyndham in the St Philip parish.

When I got back to Cayman on 3rd June, the entire Walkup family (fourteen in total) were in attendance and we chartered the catamaran *Allura* on 4th June, to collect everyone from Callaloo and take us out to Stingray City and Starfish Point, with lunch on board. I then had meetings about the Lighthouse School, lunch with Russell Day, the new MD of McAlpine, and on the 14th I took a call out of the blue from my good friend Raglan Roper, who invited me to lunch at Singh's Roti Shop, which I readily accepted. We had a great time catching up, and with many stories of 'the good old' early days in Cayman.

On the evening of Saturday 17th June, we had a welcome reception for Geoff Creswell at Ristorante Pappagallo. The Bould Foundation had sponsored him to return to Cayman, in part to celebrate Geoff's work as the catalyst for the Cayman National Theatre Company, beginning with the Inn Theatre Company almost forty years earlier. It was great to see so many of Geoff's students celebrating the gift he had provided by developing Cayman's cultural talent, and which had led to the formation of the Cayman National Cultural Foundation. On 21st June, Viv and I had the pleasure of attending the new hall at John Gray High School, to listen to one of our sponsored musicians perform as part of the Cayman Arts Festival. It was really heartwarming to see talent develop to this degree.

On 25th June I flew to Barbados to meet with the senior architect and client representative for Marriott. We were nearing completion of the pre-construction phase of the works, and were preparing to hand over to a local Bajan construction manager to carry out the physical construction on site. This required a significant amount of co-ordination, given we had been working closely on the project since 1st May 2022.

On 1st July, in Cayman, we enjoyed Morgan's daughter's wedding reception at Morgan and Jocelyn's home. The day was also one of celebration for BCL; to the delight of all parties, we formalised Alan and Michell's acquisition of 20 per cent shares each in Bould Consulting Limited. Alan was appointed a director, and Michell's appointment as managing director was reconfirmed, with Viv also joining the board as a director.

We had the pleasure of welcoming our new Governor in Cayman, Jane Owen, to the National Gallery on the 12th to meet our board and staff, and to familiarise herself with the extensive programmes the Gallery provided throughout the Cayman Islands. Also, I was now ready to commit to climbing Aconcagua in January 2024, and as the closing date for the next climbing season was 14th July, I applied, and was in!

For some time now, I had been in discussions with Suzy Soto, a good friend, about a book she had been writing for some twenty-four years, called *A History of Turtlers and Schooners of the Cayman Islands* and was delighted to attend its launch at the Cayman Turtle Centre. It was good to see so many supporters at the launch, as this was a book about our heritage that all Caymanians need to read.

On 16th July I worked out at Camana Bay in the morning, climbing the observation stair tower six times, and up and down the five storey car park once, before catching flights to Miami and Barbados. I began the next day on Holders Hill, as usual, followed by a design presentation by the Marriott architectural team. Then we visited the Colony Club, Crystal Cove and Turtle Beach, to ensure any defects in the model rooms and other works had been remedied, and for the hand-over of all contact information to the construction managers. Then I returned to Cayman for meetings on the Lighthouse School progress.

On 25th July Viv and I flew to London. As part of the Aconcagua summit gear list, I needed insulated double boots. Scarpa was the recommended brand, but no climbing shop stocked them for in-person fitting. Fortunately, Scarpa had a UK outlet in Manchester. The key point, was that feet tend to expand at altitude, but boots must also be snug without heel slippage. Being European-made, Scarpa boots were sized in millimetres, not UK sizes, which was a challenge. Scarpa's excellent customer service solved this: they sent both sizes 47 and 48 to our London home, where I chose the larger pair and returned the others. I also had to complete a multitude of forms relating to the Aconcagua climb – medical history, fitness level, medication and so forth, which I did.

We now began searching the web for gear. With the list in hand, I hoped to find crampons at Cotswold Outdoors, but the first store was out of stock. The next day, I managed to find a pair of Black Diamond brand crampons at another branch for £200 – pricey, but safety comes first. I also picked out a climbing helmet at Ellis Brigham. All this was new to me, so I had to trust I was making the right choices and just get started.

We flew to Dublin on 5th August, where we met Alan and Jenny and a taxi driven by Brian, the brother of the canal barge owner. Brian kindly stopped at the supermarket so we could shop for supplies, and then drove us on to Vicarstown, to meet Orla and Philip on board the *Finnery*, the forty-foot barge that would be home for the next few days.

After instruction from Philip on the boat's operation, we took a one-hour trip on the Grand Canal to Fishertown bridge, where we moored for the night. The Grand Canal was conceived in the 1700s as a way of connecting Dublin in the east to the River Shannon in the west. It was much used during the 19th century, especially for goods-transport, but with the advent of the railways and better roads in the early 20th century, it gradually fell into disuse. Now, people like us enjoy its quiet beauty.

We prepared a delicious dinner of lamb chops, carrots, turnips and broccoli, with Mâcon Lugny and Gigondas – sleep was no problem! We awoke on 6th August to a beautiful sunny day, and after breakfast started cruising from Fishertown Bridge to Moore's bridge, and our first lock – #25 – and a lifting bridge in Monasterevin. We travelled over the River Barrow on an aqueduct, astonished at this canal system's feats of engineering. On earlier barge trips on the

River Shannon, Viv and I had got used to operating the mechanised locks with a plastic card, but on the Grand Canal the locks were of a true, old-fashioned style, needing plenty of 'elbow grease' to turn the wheel that activated the sluice gates that drained and filled the locks. Alan was up to the task, though he sometimes needed to stand on the turn handle, to get it to move. We arrived at #24, a double lock, after Macartney Bridge.

The operator of both the locks and the lifting bridge was Joe Moore, for whom we bought a pint for his kind assistance. We motored along for a while and then stopped for lunch canal-side, after which we cruised to Rathangan Bridge to double lock #23, which is normally worked by operator P.J. Donegan, but he was off duty. It was here that Joe Moore's pint paid for itself, as he worked the lock in PJ's absence. I should add that when navigating the locks it was critical to use the engine to keep the barge centred. If the barge is too close to the rear of the lock by the gates when descending, the stern could get wedged on the cill at the end of the lock and only the bow of the boat will lower with the water level, so it can easily flood. After this lock we tied up for the night, then sought out dinner and found Darchini, a restaurant that offers both Indian and Italian meals from the same kitchen, both of which were good.

We went to the local pub, the Bridge Bar, where a band was playing and we sang along with the locals for more than an hour before going back to the barge to sleep. On the 7th, after breakfast, we set off towards Dublin and lock #22 at Glenaree Bridge, a fine and imposing stone feature over the canal. We were met by P.J. Donegan, who was back on duty after his Sunday off. He opened the lock for us, and then Fos jumped off and operated locks #21 and #20 under PJ's watchful eye. We then took the branch canal called the 'New Barrow Line' and moored for lunch, later setting off along the Shannon line to lock #20, where we passed under Downshire Bridge on the branch canal to Edenderry Harbour. There, we moored for the night, enjoying a chicken paillard dinner with a rice and vegetable stir fry, on board.

We had succeeded in breaking two wine glasses but found replacements in Edenderry, where we also stocked up on supplies. We set off again mid-morning, back through lock #20 on the Shannon Line, assisted by lock keeper James Conroy, and then tied up for a salad lunch under the Hamilton Bridge. Lock #19, just past the New Barrow Line fork, was next, after which we stopped in the very picturesque village of Robertstown for more supplies, then continued northeast on the Dublin Line towards Dublin. We moored for the night at lock #18, continuing to Sallins, our turn around point, the next day. On 9th August we had a late start, and while negotiating lock #18, caught the stern of the barge on the cill at the rear gate.

Fast action by Fos, who rapidly refilled the lock and freed us. Lock #17 provided our next adventure, as the rear gates were firmly stuck closed. Fos was assisted by a kind bystander called Brendan – who incidentally had Caymanian friends, Kathlyn and John Dunne, who owned Fidel Murphy's pub. Once the gates were opened, our next lock was #16, where we met a lady from Belarus who owned the Bridge Café at Digby Bridge, built in 1794 – they made things to last in those days! It featured a wonderful and somewhat incongruous espresso machine, with which she made us excellent coffees, and hot chocolate for Jen.

We then set off again using the Leinster Aqueduct to pass over the River Liffey to Sallins, where we once again stocked up on essential supplies at Lidl. After lunch we turned the barge to commence our return journey, but inadvertently ran the bow onto the opposite bank and once again broke the wine glasses! We cruised back to locks #16 and #17 and were assisted by Vinny, a fourth-generation lock keeper, who helped us with the 'stuck' gate and then back to lock #18. There, we purchased home-grown tomatoes from our Belarus lady at the Bridge Café, then went into Robertstown to top up the cellar. We moored for the night at the beginning of the Old Barrow Line Canal, where Fos took over the kitchen to cook a great spaghetti dinner complete with fresh tomato sauce.

On 10th August we had a fresh fruit breakfast prepared by Viv, and a very late 11.30am passage through lock #19, past Ballyteague Castle, through locks #20, #21 and #22 before Glenaree Bridge, arriving in Rathangan Bridge at 3pm. There, I went into the village to look for an internet connection, as I had a mediation conference with J.D. and the South African Arbitration Association. The pubs were all closed, so I connected by telephone aboard the *Finnery*. We then cruised a short distance to double lock #23, and moored for the night by Spencer Bridge. The next morning we awoke to a beautiful sunny day, made breakfast, and then Viv and I then took a four-mile walk along the towpath to Wilson Bridge, where we stopped two passing ladies and asked one of them, if she would mind taking a photo of us. She said it was no problem, and if we would step back two paces we would be standing in exactly the spot that the singer Bruce Springsteen had stood two months prior, when he had also stopped her and requested she take a photo of him. Apparently he was visiting the area to connect with distant relatives.

We returned to the barge and cast off, passing under the Umeras Bridge, negotiated double lock #24, passed under Macartney Bridge, and, out of the blue, were drenched by a torrential rain shower. So, we moored before the lifting bridge to put on dry clothes in Monasterevin. There, as it was lunchtime, we walked into town and stopped at Mooney's Pub for Viv's favourite half pint of Guiness and lunch. But there was no food, only potato crisps. Back to the barge, where our new-found friend, Joe, assisted with the operation of the lifting bridge, which stops the traffic, and we crossed the viaduct over the River Barrow, through lock #25, under both Moore's Bridge and Clogheen Bridge. We moored for a much-delayed meal of fried rice beautifully cooked by Jenny, then cruised to Fishertown Bridge, where we tied up for the night, and walked to the Fisherman's Thatched Inn for more Guiness and peanuts. Sean, the owner of the inn, insisted on giving us four wine glasses to replace those we had broken on board.

On 12th August we arose early for a change, so we could pack and tidy the barge, and after breakfast, cruised back to our starting point at Vicarstown, returning *Finnery* to Philip and Orla. It had been a great trip, and we felt the friendliness of the Irish never changed – it just gets better on every visit we make. After kisses and hugs all round with Alan and Jenny, and our sincere thanks to Alan for his great work in operating the locks, Brian then drove us back for our flight to Heathrow.

On the 15th we watched the musical *Aspects of Love* at the Lyric Theatre, with music and book by Andrew Lloyd Webber and lyrics by Don Black and Charles Hart. We have been followers of Andrew Lloyd Webber for many years, as his work is so enjoyable and entertaining. We followed this great performance with dinner at Mr Chow's, where we were warmly greeted by Dino, who walked us straight to our table even though there was a long queue of waiting clients – turned out it was Dino's 50th birthday.

The next few days we relaxed at QGM with beautiful summer weather, enjoying Hyde Park and our great facility at Imperial. Returning to Miami, I had ordered new Merrell hiking boots as part of my Aconcagua gear assembly, which were waiting for me to try on at #10E under Amazon's excellent 'Try before you Buy' service. These would be my second pair of Merrells, and I had ordered a size 13 (48 in European sizes). Unfortunately, when I tried them on the right boot fitted well, but the left one was too large and rubbed on my heel. So, back to Amazon they went.

Back in Cayman, we were kindly invited by Alasdair Robertson to his home, along with many of our neighbours in the Cayman Islands Yacht Club, to meet with our elected government representative, Hon André Ebanks MP. The get-together had been arranged to resolve a rather bizarre situation that had arisen: the government wanted to change the street numbering of our houses. This would require reinstalling street numbers on every house, reprinting stationery and, more importantly, where an address was a registered company address, a lot of administrative issues. After discussions with the group and the appropriate administrative powers, André was able to arrange for the street numbers to remain as they were.

On Monday 28th August, I met with Alan Markoff, who I have known for many years. He was now assisting the Cayman Arts Festival as a director, to raise funds for their activities, which the Bould Foundation was supporting. During our conversation, we did some brainstorming to come up with ideas for further involvement. This was also the starting day for my serious training for the Aconcagua climb, now booked with Mountain Professionals to commence on 15th January 2024. I made up a spreadsheet to monitor progress, with key information which included: Walk Distance, Pilates/Yoga, Swim Time, Weight, Blood Pressure, Pulse, SPO2, Breath Hold, Power Breathing, Body Oxygen Level Test, Alcohol, Days to Start of Climb, and Any Physio Issues. My weight that day was 215 lbs, and we were 140 days out from the start of the climb. Much as I love my glass of wine, as maybe you can tell by now, from then on I substituted it with my San Pellegrino cocktail, with ice, lime and a dash of Angostura bitters. I would not have another drink until I came down from Aconcagua, weighing 185 lbs. Monitoring physio issues was on the spreadsheet because I had developed plantar fasciitis, an annoying and painful problem, in my right foot. This was not a great start to my serious training campaign, but I was blessed in having spent years with Igor Burdenko and his water workout programme, which meant I could do a lot of leg strengthening exercises in the water without aggravating the issue.

At the beginning of September Alan, Claudia, Vivian and I discussed our next trip together. We wanted to continue the fun we enjoyed while travelling, beginning with the time we had a 'staycation' together during COVID restrictions and continuing with the Camino de Santiago. We had received a proposal from Elias at 'Eat Northern Spain' to walk a different section of the Camino, but we were looking at the alternative of renting a house in Tuscany, from which we could take walks in the mountains around that location. At about the same time, Jasmine Cayman's Palliative & Hospice Care Facility, one of the other charities we supported, gave a thank-you reception to which we were invited and were delighted to attend.

Our MW2 group had been invited to participate in a development on Walker's Road, almost opposite Cayman Court, where I had commenced my development career more than fifty years earlier. It would combine retail and office spaces and a large self-storage facility, and on sixth September, I met with the Foster's Group representative to discuss MW2's potential investment. In November, Lee Foster would provide me with additional information about the project.

On 7th September we conducted a site visit to the Lighthouse School with our team from Jestico & Whiles and local architects Chalmers Gibbs, to review the property and land constraints for the design that was being developed for the expansion of this key, much-needed facility. Stakeholder meetings were to follow during the week commencing 11th September. This was to ensure all involved parties were fully appraised of the design decisions and that their needs were incorporated as the project moved forward. Participants would include, amongst others, teachers and staff, government and the parent-teacher association. On the 12th, I attended a meeting at the George Town Public Library, to hear and see the plans for the revitalisation of Central George Town, which had become somewhat moribund with the development of Camana Bay. The next day, I commenced what would be regular visits to the physio to treat my plantar fasciitis, followed by a rather more pleasant occasion: enjoying dinner with John and Louise Jenkinson at Callaloo.

On 13th September Viv and I flew from Cayman to Miami, where we spent the night in #10E and picked up insoles for my shoes from Caresole, to help with my plantar fasciitis issue. The next day we arose at dawn to catch our early morning flights to Eagle Vail, where we were met by Jimmy and Cynthia. I wanted to complete a number of acclimatisation climbs at altitude as part of my Aconcagua training, and since Jimmy's house in Mariposa was already at an elevation of more 6,000 feet, it formed an ideal base.

A couple of days later, Viv and I drove into Aspen and took the gondola to the top of Ajax Mountain at 11,200 feet. From there we walked down part of the mountain and back up to the summit, where we had lunch in the summit restaurant. Afterwards, we ventured out for a further walk, the weather conditions varying from sunshine, to rain, to hail and back again. On the 16th, we drove to Snowmass Village, took the Elk Camp gondola and then the chair lift to the summit at 11,325 feet, overlooking Maroon Bells. We hiked down the summit trail and then took the chair lift down to Elk Camp restaurant for lunch. Afterwards we hiked the Rabbit Run and Sierra Loop trails before catching the gondola down and returning to Mariposa for pasta and caviar dinner.

We enjoyed avocado muffins for breakfast on the 17th before driving out to take the Elk Camp gondola to walk the Rabbit Run circuit to the picturesque lake, and then a second Rabbit Run circuit and part way up the Sierra Club Loop, before hunger set in. We then descended for a salad lunch at the Elk Camp restaurant, after which Viv sat by the lake while yours truly took a second one and a half hour hike up Rabbit Run and a full Sierra Club Loop. These hikes at altitude were good exercise for my lungs, and impossible to replicate at sea level. Sleeping at around 6,000 feet was also good acclimatisation. On the 18th we hiked Mushroom Rock and the Blue-Ribbon trail, which is close to Aspen Glen, and we had beautiful sunny weather until the early afternoon, when a thunderstorm moved in and we descended rapidly to the trail head and the safety of the car.

On 19th September I cooked our traditional caviar eggs and then we drove to Eagle Vail airport to catch our flights to Portland. We were kindly picked up from the airport by Jill McDonald, who was arriving at much the same time on a flight from the UK, where she had been attending a wedding. We were all starving by this time, but as it was late most restaurants were closed. We found one that served pizza, which we wolfed down with gusto, before driving onto Inchinnan for a great sleep. On the 20th I was up early for business calls, after which we walked up to the Carabella vineyard and back for a late lunch with Jill, then a snooze. Dinner of scallops was excellent, and finished with Marionberry ice cream and peach sorbet – life is good! The next day, I drove to Mount Hood to walk the Pacific Crest trail to Paradise Park, gaining some 1,000 feet of elevation in two and a half hours. Back at Inchinnan, we dressed for dinner at Jill's Town Club (for ladies only) and to meet Glen Holden, the ninety-six year-old American Ambassador to Jamaica from 1989 to 1992, during the time that Michael Manley was Prime Minister. Glen had also played polo until he was eighty-one, including matches with Prince Charles. Viv and I had a fascinating chat with him about my time in Jamaica and the work I did there over the years.

On 22nd September, a beautiful, sunny day, Viv, Jill and I drove to the Silver Falls State Park where we walked the Canyon trail and loop to the Rim Trail, stopping to enjoy lunch seated by the river before returning to Inchinnan for spaghetti Trapanese according to a recipe of Jamie Oliver's, ably cooked by Jill.

We wanted to participate in the vendage, and our wine maker, Mike, said there was one last block of Pinot Noir to be picked for a client from Walla Walla, Washington (where Gordon Jaynes hailed from). So Viv and I walked up to the vineyard the next day, but sadly they had just finished picking, so we walked back to Inchinnan and took Freddie, Jill's dog, for a walk along the Willamette River by the farm. That evening we lit the log fire in the living room at Inchinnan and enjoyed a beef Bourguignon dinner with David and Beth Lecki. On the 24th I took an early morning walk up to the vineyard – I should mention that it is a steep four-hundred foot climb, so good training – and then Jill's daughter Muffy and partner Doug, with their daughters Emma and Lily, came for afternoon tea. In the evening Mike and Cara invited us and their friends P.J. and Merrill for dinner with Mike, who is an excellent chef and made salmon faro risotto and salad. As we were in the home of our winemaker, there was much wine tasting to accompany this delicious food. When I announced I was in training, and hence not drinking, Mike said he would therefore need to return two bottles to the cellar!

We had to leave our home away from home, where we were always made to feel so very welcome, on the 25th. But first I did my early morning climb to the vineyard, and for the first time was able to make it to the top without stopping, so my fitness level was definitely improving. Jill kindly drove us to Portland Airport, and we were soon home at Callaloo after completing a trip which had included excellent training for Aconcagua, and had given me some confidence that the plantar fasciitis could be overcome in time for my climb.

On 28th September we had more Steering Committee meetings for the Lighthouse School project, which would be followed by a design progress meeting some days later. We also held the National Trust AGM at George Town Yacht Club that day, and finished the evening at the Harquail Theatre, with a performance of Matt Brown's *Wha Happening?* – the sequel to *Rundown*. I was still ordering gear for Aconcagua and found suitable gaiters from Pike Trail, ordered on Amazon, to keep pebbles and dust out of my boots.

Alan and I had continued to discuss options for renting a house in Tuscany in lieu of a second Camino walk, and by 1st October had settled on a house called Villa Pineta, offered through a great company called Friends of Tuscany, close to the small town of Ghivizzano about forty minutes north of Lucca.

On 2nd October we awoke early, as I had arranged a webinar with Patrick McKeown at 7am Cayman time as part of my breathing training for the Aconcagua climb. Also as part of my training programme, and as a way of dealing with my plantar fasciitis, I was using our steam room in conjunction with the red oil we purchased in Sri Lanka, which seemed to fix everything. The previous evening, I had noticed water all over the bamboo floor, so we appeared to be having problems with the steam-generating unit. As usual, Alan came to the rescue by lending us his dehumidifier, which rapidly dried out the floor. Trevor, our plumber, then checked on the steam unit, which we indeed needed to replace. Given it was almost twenty years old, it hadn't done a bad job.

On 3rd October I met with Jondo, the director of the Cayman Red Cross, to discuss the promotional plan to spread the word about my Aconcagua climb, and how we could maximise donations through social media, the press, promotional parties, and so on, to raise funds for the several projects being developed at this time. We also discussed how we could facilitate easier ways to make contributions online.

On the climbing gear front, I had purchased an insulated foam pad when we were in Aspen, which I would use under an inflatable mattress. The mattress had a clever inflation system: you connected its stuff sack – fitted with a non-return air valve – to the mattress, then rolled the bag opening over and downward to push its trapped air into the mattress. This meant that you did not need to use your own 'puff' to inflate it – a major plus at high altitude. The only issue was that the inflated mattress tended to gradually slide off the foam pad, especially on slight slopes, so I would often wake lying in a corner of the tent. Viv came up with a smart fix: she made two straps with quick-release buckles that kept the foam pad tightly rolled up while we were travelling, then at night, I used them to secure the pad and mattress together. We tested the set-up on the floor at Callaloo, which led to a few awkward explanations to arriving guests – no, I had not moved out of the matrimonial bedroom but was just testing the gear for the climb!

I continued to have some concerns about my foot issue and went to see a podiatrist, who examined it and said I should be OK to climb by the time the expedition began, provided I continued with my physio work and water workout routine. I began soaking my foot in hot water and Epsom salts to ease the pain somewhat, and used special insoles that Tenson, my physio, had recommended, to provide a lift to the arch of my foot. I was working out in the pool using water walkers, which I had first used in 2016 as part of Igor's programme. They offer excellent resistance and are great for strengthening leg muscles. It was now ninety-five days to the start of the climb, and my weight had dropped 11 lbs to 204 lbs – which was 11 lbs I no longer needed to carry up the mountain with me. Viv left for London on her own, most unusually, as a leak from the bathroom above our rear bedroom in QGM had caused some fairly significant damage. This required replacing the carpet, repainting and some electrical work, which she had kindly agreed to oversee.

The next day I attended Massive Equipment Rental's social gathering, held at their premises in the Airport Industrial Park, to celebrate their 25th year in business. This had been organised by the Cayman Islands Chamber of Commerce as part of their Business After Hours programme. These events, held in the evening after close of business, were very popular and were a good way for the host to promote their business while the attendees networked with the wider business community. At MW2 we used similar events when we completed a new building, to showcase the details and availability of our new products to the business community.

On 30th October, the developer of recently completed apartment complex managed by Avata, contacted BCL to seek advice on how to proceed toward resolving the issue of a contractor who had omitted to install the insulation to the exterior walls. Jerry Katz and I called for all the documentation so we could plan out the necessary steps to resolve this matter.

We had been visiting the Harquail Theatre regularly for performances of every kind. On 28th October, the Cayman Islands Folk Singers had provided wonderful entertainment, and on 8th November we had the pleasure of seeing a dramatic flamenco performance.

I consulted with the podiatrist again to review my progress before leaving for Miami on 10th November. There, we were able to host lunch at Bellinis for our travel agent, Dean Hoffman, to thank him in some small way for the excellent service he provided for both our personal and business travel. I then flew to St Thomas for the 12th edition of CHICOS, under the theme of 'Shining in the New Normal', celebrating the continuing improvement of the hotel industry following COVID. I would be moderating a discussion with the theme 'Opportunities in the Caribbean, Which Products and Which Islands' on 13th November with a great panel of distinguished, highly experienced and – most importantly – 'fun' people: Louis Alicea, Senior Director of Development, Caribbean – Wyndham Hotels & Resorts; Bill Clegg, Regional Director, Franchise Development – Best Western; Andrew Dickey, Managing Director – JLL Hotels & Hospitality; Alexandra Lalos Church, Managing Director – Hodges Ward Elliott; and Alex Mai, Regional VP of Development, LATAM & Caribbean – IHG. As always, the conference was informative, with good networking opportunities and the chance to catch up with long-standing friends.

On the 15th I met up with Michell, who was spending four days in Cayman to go over BCL's business plan development and to visit the sites of Lighthouse School and the prison, to discuss the monitoring of the new Royalton Hotel in Barbados, and to meet with our professional partners that formed the teams on our projects.

At the end of October, while reviewing the recommended equipment list for my climb, we noted that it included a number of freeze-dried dinners. We thought it a good idea to order some sample dinners through Amazon, to be delivered to #10E so we could test them to see what they tasted like and which, from an extensive choice, we liked the best.

I met with the Red Cross again to review the progress we were making on the fund-raising programme for my climb, and on 23rd November I contacted Ryan of Mountain Professionals for answers to the many questions I had about the climb itself. These included how many other climbers would be with me, and some details of their age and ability; the provision of porters and what was the limit to what they could carry; whether we would be met at the airport; recommendations for health insurance cover; whether a helicopter would be available in case of emergency; the likely weather; whether Ryan would be on the climb; the number of guides and suitable backpack size, and so on. I would be adding a supply of Compeed plasters to my gear, which we had discovered when we were in Ireland. These were padded, and could be applied over any heel or foot blisters where they would seem to 'blend' with your skin, providing pain-relieving cushioning while the skin healed underneath.

I began wearing my Scarpa insulated double boots for walks around the Cayman Islands Yacht Club, to break them in, and also flew to Miami for the day to purchase some additional equipment for the climb and collect items at #10E that had been delivered by Amazon. By 3rd December my weight had dropped to 197 lbs, and I started taking bicarbonate of soda and apple cider vinegar in the mornings as part of the Oxygen Advantage programme. This concoction had been reported to improve the oxygen absorption of the blood. I also began taking Arcoxia, which reduces pain and inflammation, for my fasciitis.

On 30th November I conducted a virtual interview with Patrick Stainton, a quantity surveyor who had been introduced to BCL by a UK recruitment agency. He seemed a promising candidate to help manage the growing workload in our practice.

On 6th December Viv and I flew to Salt Lake City, arriving at 11pm to find there was no one at Dollar Car Rental. So, we rented one from Alamo, which worked out to be $500 cheaper for the week, so a good start to the holiday. We drove up Little Cottonwood Canyon to Sugarplum and Unit N, unpacked and fell into bed at 4am, Cayman time.

On 7th December I awoke early due to the change in altitude and caught up with Ryan, who was leading a climb up Mount Vinson in Antarctica. He had some answers to my queries from November, including information about Global Rescue emergency and health insurance. He then told me I would be the only climber in the group and that there would be one guide, Juan P. Initially this caused me some concern, but the more I thought about it, the more I realised that it was a distinct advantage, as I would be able to climb at my own pace. Viv and I then went to Fresh Market for food supplies, then to REI in Salt Lake City to look at down parkas, which I needed for summit day on the Aconcagua climb. We stopped at General Grits for some Antinori red wine for Viv, then back to Unit N for toasties in front of the fire.

On the 8th there was a very heavy snowstorm outside, so we decided to stay home. The next day, our twenty-eighth wedding anniversary, there was a brilliant blue sky and masses of fresh snow. After a call with Patrick Stainton about his potential employment package with BCL, we went out onto the slopes to ski in wonderful conditions. We stopped for lunch at Rustler, where we saw Vicki and Tom – both the manager and the Mayor of Alta. We skied 14,000 vertical feet in seven runs, and afterwards drove to REI for another look at down parkas and other gear I needed. The 10th was my seventy-eighth birthday, and Viv treated me to avocado toast for breakfast in bed. We reached the ski base at noon, bought half-day tickets, and went for a couple of runs during which I tried out my new down parka. After lunch we went for five more runs before returning to Unit N for a soak in the tub with Epsom salts for our quads, and dinner at home.

11th December was another bluebird day of wonderful skiing, as was the 12th, when, after eight runs and lunch, I put on my Scarpa boots with crampons and climbed from the rope tow base to the Alta Lodge, and back down again, to get used to the feeling of them going both uphill and downhill in snow. We began the 13th with omelettes and emails with the Red Cross about fund-raising for my climb, followed by an Oxygen Advantage breath training seminar, and then skied seven runs. Back at Sugarplum, I donned my Scarpa boots and took a forty-five minute walk around the block, with liner and thick socks on, to check out what it felt like to walk at altitude on some steep inclines. The next morning I did the same, after which we went skiing. This routine – walking in my boots, then getting to the slopes for a half-day's skiing – continued for the next three days. The morning of our departure, after the morning routine, we drove in our ski gear to REI for some last-minute Aconcagua gear shopping, and then to Hotel Monaco to check into our suite. We showered and dressed, and went to see a great performance of *The Nutcracker* at the Capitol Theatre across the street. After a lazy day in the suite on the 17th, we left on the 18th for Cayman to get ready for Christmas at Callaloo.

As it always seems to happen, in that serendipitous way I have been blessed to experience so often, a good friend of Vivian's knew of a lady in Cayman who had climbed Aconcagua. Her name was Anoush Pal, and we asked her and her husband, Raoul, for drinks at Callaloo on 20th December. She was extremely generous with invaluable information and even lent me some of her equipment for the climb. One unusual piece of equipment, and one which I had not seen on gear lists, was the insulated cover required for Nalgene water bottles. Drinking enough water is key to avoiding altitude sickness, but due to the low temperatures at altitude, the water in Nalgene bottles and Camelbak water pouches tends to freeze.

At CHICOS in November, I had a good meeting with the owner of a partially developed resort in Abaco, in the Bahamas. He followed up on 21st December with additional information for us to review, and asked for a proposal outlining how BCL could assist with the next phase of the project's development.

On 22nd December we held our BCL team Christmas lunch – before Christmas, for a change, instead of well into the new year.

We enjoyed Christmas lunch at Callaloo, cooked by Chef Roman, with Alan and Claudia and Norman and Jo as our guests, and our usual croquet on the Orchard lawn.

At the end of December, BCL were asked to be part of a team to tender for the General Aviation Terminal at the Owen Roberts Airport in Cayman. Early in 2024, we would begin discussing the details of the bid with Jonathan of CDS, and Frank Reed. On 28th December I sent Patrick Stainton his employment contract for signature

Morgan and Jocelyn held an open house at their home on the 30th, to celebrate the announcement in the King's New Year's Honours list that Morgan had been awarded the King's Certificate and Badge of Honour. We were delighted to attend as I had nominated him for this richly-deserved award for all that he had done, and for his voluntary work in both the business and development arena and towards preserving Cayman's culture and traditions.

On 31st December I continued my Aconcagua training, working out at Camana Bay. I weighed 191 lbs, with blood pressure of 113/70 and a 59 BPM pulse rate. There were sixteen days left to the start of the climb – so I was getting there! We finished the year with our annual 'Do Drop In' at Callaloo with some thirty guests beginning their New Year celebrations, and later, Viv and I enjoyed our duck breasts on the pool patio while we watched the Seven Mile Beach fireworks.

2024

'Accept whatever comes to you, woven into the pattern of your destiny, for what could more aptly fit your needs.' Marcus Aurelius

On 2nd January, Anoush sent me a list of notes from a friend of hers who had recently climbed Aconcagua with Mountain Professionals, and on the 3rd, Reshma Ragoonath, a reporter from the *Compass* newspaper in Cayman, asked me to send her daily photos of the climb to publish, to raise awareness of the Red Cross fundraising aspect of my climb. On the 5th, I flew to Miami for the day to collect final items for my climb, including handwarmers, a neck buff,

Nalgene insulated covers, socks and iodine tablets – the last were necessary because all water supplies on the mountain are from melted snow, which might be contaminated.

We had now assembled all my climbing clothing and equipment on the bed in Annahavil, our guest cottage at Callaloo. Anoush kindly visited to check out what I had accumulated and, most importantly, lent me one black and one red waterproof duffel bag. She explained that the mules carrying these bags sometimes fell into the river, so it was also important to assemble different items of clothing in Ziplock bags, before putting them into the duffel bags. On the 8th I called Mark, our valet from Yacht Harbour, who had now retired but still had access to #10E, and asked him to bring to the airport the insulated covers for the Nalgene bottles. These had not been delivered when I was last in Miami, but had arrived in the meantime.

It was now time to leave Cayman for the long-anticipated climb. Viv was my greatest encouragement, and she said it had been fun putting the plan in motion but that she was glad she did not have to do the hard graft of all the disciplined training! And so, on 11th January, I left Cayman for Miami, where I met Mark at the airport for the Nalgene covers and some more water purification tablets.

On 12th January I arrived in Buenos Aires, about twenty minutes later than scheduled, and then caught a Tienda Leon shuttle bus to Aeroparque domestic terminal, where I caught the Aerolineas Argentina flight to Mendoza by the skin of my teeth. The reason for the tight connection was that the Tienda Leon bus had stopped some distance from the entrance to the terminal, leaving me with my backpack, laptop case and two heavy equipment duffels stranded on the pavement, and no luggage carts in view. Fortunately, the driver was kind enough to get out of the bus and go into the terminal to find me one. He richly deserved the $5 tip I offered him for saving me, though at first he refused to accept it.

At Mendoza I was met by a driver from Mountain Professionals, who took me to the Diplomatic Hotel, where I began to think about unpacking. Juan P, my guide, who was to meet me there, sent a message that he was delayed by twenty-four hours in Patagonia, but that he would meet me the next day at 6pm, for a gear check. I called Viv to let her know I had arrived safely, then took a walk around Independence Square, busy with people and which had a beautiful fountain. Based on a recommendation from the concierge in the hotel, I had dinner at Centauro, a farm-to-table Michelin starred restaurant, where I enjoyed an excellent starter of 'Desert Flower' zucchini with parmesan cheese and sriracha sauce, followed by tortellini in cream sauce. Afterwards, I returned to my room for a ten-hour sleep.

On 13th January, Juan P arrived at 7.30pm and we carried out the gear check, noting what needed to go into the red duffel bag, and what into the black duffel bag. The red bag would be loaded on the Plaza De Mulas mule, and the black bag would go on the Confluencia mule. After a long walk the next morning, I spent the next day reorganising my packing. It was like starting from scratch, as Viv and I had methodically placed all my clothes in the bags according to what we thought would be the ambient temperatures during the ascent. I also made up a list of what was in each bag, to make everything easy to find on the trail.

I then went for dinner at a highly recommended Italian restaurant, La Marchigiana, for what turned out to be the very worst ravioli I have ever eaten – or, more accurately, left on my plate. We were to begin the climb on 15th January, and I awoke at 5.30am for last minute preparations and emails, then had breakfast at 7am with Juan P. I left my laptop, a clean shirt and underwear in a bag at the Diplomatic Hotel to hold for my return. Our driver, Dario, from Grajales Expeditions, arrived at 8am for the drive to Los Penitentes, a small ski resort on the Argentine border close to Portillo, in Chile, where Viv and I had skied in the past. I dropped off the black and red duffel bags, then went to register at the park entrance and begin the climb to Confluencia Camp, which was some 1,800 vertical feet above the entrance. This took us two hours and fifty minutes in beautiful sunny weather. I had told Juan P about the fundraising nature of my climb and Reshma's request for photos, and he immediately transformed himself into both a guide and an ace photographer, insisting on action shots as opposed to posed ones. On arrival at Confluencia Camp we pitched two tents, setting up sleeping accommodation for the next three days.

Grajales Expeditions provided central mess tents and a shower tent, which was most welcome. Dinner was French onion soup, followed by steak and potatoes – not at all bad for a climbing camp! Now it was time for the first night on the insulated foam pad and blow-up mattress and down-filled sleeping bag. Viv's straps worked a treat, so there was no slippage into the corner of the tent, though I got little sleep, probably due to the altitude. On 16th January we were up at 7am for a breakfast of egg and avocado, and then did our first acclimatisation hike to Plaza de Francia, where we could see the south face and glacier of Aconcagua. It was a beautiful, sunny but windy, day. We climbed 2,240 vertical feet there and back, which took us six and three-quarter hours. Back at Confluencia Camp, we had medical exams at 6pm. The doctor was very pleased with my results and surprised at my low pulse rate of 59 BPM, given I was on no medications except for vitamins. My SPO2 was 86, which they also considered good, given the elevation.

The camp also had Wi-Fi, so I called Viv and updated her with my progress. She was very grateful to hear my voice, and I was able to send many photos Juan P had taken during the day, including ones in which I was wearing a Red Cross polo shirt I had been given. We had dinner of pumpkin soup, steak and sweet mashed potato, with tiramisu for dessert. Camping in the past was never like this – does anyone remember packages of Vesta curries, to which 'just add water'? Bedtime was at 9.30pm. The night was very cold in comparison with the day's heat, and again I got little sleep, this time due to a blocked nose.

The 17th January was a rest day at the camp, with breakfast at 8am, and the advice that today I needed to drink five litres of water, beginning with one litre at breakfast. After breakfast I decided to catch up on some sleep before it became too warm outside. I heard from J.D. about the mediation course the Bould Foundation was sponsoring, which was scheduled to commence on 29th January at the Cayman Arbitration Centre and hoped I would be back from the climb in time to attend, but that would depend on the weather. Lunch today was avocado on crispbread, chicken and polenta with mushroom sauce. Afterwards, I packed for tomorrow's 6am departure. A shower felt great, and dinner of potato soup and spaghetti Bolognese, with a brownie for dessert, was excellent. We bedded down at 9pm, and before going to sleep I had a great chat with Viv, who was in London overseeing the remedial work caused by the leak at QGM.

On 18th January the duffel was picked up for transport on the mule, and after breakfast we departed Confluencia Camp at 7am for the long trek to Plaza de Mulas, with the hardest climb at the end. We gained 3,500 feet during the ascent, which took us ten and a half hours. I was exhausted, but there was a warm welcome at the Grajales dining tent, with a great spread of hors d'oeuvres. I met Fernado Grajales, who kindly offered the use of their dormitory tent with bunk beds, as opposed to sleeping in a much smaller tent. We then enjoyed dinner of salad and spare ribs. Over dinner I met two climbers, Mohammed and Ali, doctors from Kuwait, together with their guide Ilan, who used to work in the Alta Lodge. So, of course, we shared stories about our time there. I slept much better that night, so perhaps I was getting used to the altitude, or maybe it was the more comfortable bunk.

The 19th was another rest day. After breakfast, Juan P left to carry supplies up to Camp 1, while I separated my gear to be weighed. It would be going up to Camps 1, 2 and 3 with the porters. Then I had a pleasant shower before lunch. Dinner was followed by a sound sleep in the dorm, in the company of new guests from Sweden. We had breakfast at 9am on 20th January and then set out for our first real mountain climb to Camp Canada (Camp 1). The trail began through the glacial snow just above Plaza de Mulas, then turned to shale that gave little traction – for each step forward, one slid half a step back. It was a stiff climb of 2,110 vertical feet, and the round trip from Plaza de Mulas and back took seven hours, during which Juan P took lots of photos. That day I was again aware of a very noticeable difference to the Kilimanjaro trail: on the Aconcagua trail, there was absolutely no litter. Once back at camp, I had a wonderful shower, and then dinner of soup, steak and chocolate dessert.

I awoke on 21st January having slept very well – not surprising given the preceding day's climb. Breakfast was at 9.30am that day. Although sunny in the mornings, it was always very cold, so as we gained altitude we tended to rise a little later and gave the sun time to warm things up. We underwent a medical exam at 11am, which showed my SPO2 as 87, and a blood pressure of 140/90 with a pulse of 58 BPM. The doctors felt these were excellent numbers, indicative of good heart condition. I then spent time sorting out which clothes were to remain at Plaza de Mulas, and which were to go to Camp 1. We had cannelloni for lunch, followed by a snooze in the afternoon, as today was another rest day. Wiener Schnitzel was enjoyed for dinner, but I slept badly that night. Having drunk the recommended five litres of water over the course of the day, I woke every half hour to pee, which was slightly embarrassing as well as a nuisance, given all the other climbers in the dormitory tent.

We began climbing again in earnest on the 22nd. Again, the weather was beautiful and sunny. After breakfast I delivered all the clothes and equipment I would need for the next six days to the porters and took the balance of my gear to be stored at Plaza de Mulas, to be collected on the way down.

Once again, we left Plaza de Mulas for Camp 1, this time climbing 2,140 vertical feet in four and three-quarter hours. A three-person tent was erected there for me to enjoy on my own, which was welcome after the dormitory experience of the last few days at Plaza de Mulas. I set up my sleeping bag and mattress, and asked Juan P if I could repeat the Nalgene hot water bottle experience I had enjoyed for the last few nights. No problem, and in the freezing cold at 16,500 feet it certainly felt luxurious to have a warm bottle for the feet in one's sleeping bag. Ali and Mohammed were also at Camp 1, but in the Grajales section. Juan P made excellent hamburgers with avocado for dinner, and I had a great sleep. We rested the next day, while Juan P climbed to Camp 2 with supplies for our stay there and returned to Camp 1, where I sat drinking water at regular intervals to come up to the five-litre recommended daily level. There was no internet in Camp 1, and I noted there had been a change from the published itinerary, which had me climbing to Camp 2 today. I took a test walk in my Scarpa boots and they felt good, particularly after all the test walks

I had done (though these had never been at this altitude) where I had been told your feet were likely to swell.

Juan P and I enjoyed cheese and salami for lunch and talked about summit day. I enjoyed a sleep in the afternoon and organised my packing for the porters to carry to Camp 2 tomorrow, and then we closed out the day with chicken and rice for dinner. On the 24th we had scrambled eggs with cheese and avocado for breakfast, and then climbed from Camp 1 to Camp 2. This was a tough climb of 1,855 vertical feet over scree, and which took us five and a half hours with the porters carrying most of the luggage. My tent had been erected by the time we arrived at Camp 2, (Nido de Condores) at an elevation of 18,200 feet. Over a dinner of lentils, Juan and I discussed summit day, which was looking promising from a weather point of view. The 25th January was another rest day, with porridge for breakfast, after which I donned my Scarpas for a second test walk, as the plan was to climb to Camp 3 tomorrow, which was at an altitude of 19,600 feet. There were many people on the trail, due to the excellent weather.

We started on the trail to Camp 3, with Juan P leading at a slow pace, but I found that suddenly, at each step, I needed to stop to catch my breath. There was obviously something wrong (what I didn't know, at this point, was that I had COVID). Then some bad news came to Juan P, passed down the mountain: a lady climber in the group climbing ahead of us had died due to high-altitude pulmonary oedema. Juan P took the decision that we should descend, and as quickly as we could. Descending was tough going and almost like skiing, with our feet sideways against the slope as we slid through the scree. We passed Camp 1, and on to Plaza de Mulas, where we were able to arrange a helicopter to take us down to the park entrance in the Horcones Valley, where a Grajales Expeditions van picked us up for the drive back to the Diplomatic Hotel. I was, of course, very disappointed, but there is wisdom in knowing when to turn back. It would have been foolish – even dangerous – to continue with the ascent, and the guide knew it. I awoke late on 27th January, had a coffee with Juan P, and then an excellent lunch of shrimp starter and roast lamb with a celebratory bottle of Cabernet Franc. After bidding goodbye to Juan P and thanking him for his great leadership, and making arrangements for my revised flight back to Cayman, I rested in the afternoon.

Viv met me when I arrived back in Cayman on 29th January, and immediately said I did not look well. She insisted we visit our doctor, John Addleson, without delay. He took one look at me and asked if I had tested for COVID, to which I replied no. He tested me, said I was positive, and so into isolation at Annahavil I went, weighing in at 185 lbs.

By 8th February I tested negative and was able to attend a meet-and-greet, hosted by the Ministry of Heritage, at the George Town Yacht Club. In a ministerial juggle, the government had split the ministries of culture and heritage – a move that I, and many others, failed to comprehend, given that the two are inextricably linked. To me, heritage is where you come from; it is that which guides our culture, which is constantly developing, but represents how we live, talk, eat and worship.

On 10th February I flew to Marsh Harbour, in Abaco, the Bahamas, for a site visit and to meet the resort owner whom we had first met at the CHICOS conference in November. I returned to Cayman on the 13th to collect our ski gear and the next morning we flew to Miami to overnight at #10E. On 15th February I had virtual meetings on the Eden Centre project – a 62,000 sq ft, mixed use development on which BCL were providing development and costing advice. Then Viv and I flew to Eagle Vail, where Jerry and Sheila picked us up. Jerry prepared a great dinner of halibut skewers and arugula salad – as well as being a highly accomplished construction attorney, he is a bold and innovative chef, with a kitchen full of tried and tested recipes from many sources, filed in ring binders. On 16th February we enjoyed five runs of fabulous new snow at Beaver Creek followed by après-ski drinks at the Ritz Carlton in Bachelor Gulf. As one review says: 'Bring your wallet packed with cash, and be prepared to wait for your drinks.' Back at Jerry and Sheila's, we finished the day with Jerry's rack of lamb.

The 17th and 18th February brought perfect bluebird conditions with new snow. After a delayed start on the 17th – Jerry had misplaced his money clip (later found in his pocket) – we skied Beaver Creek, Bachelor Gulch and Arrowhead, racking up some 10,000 vertical feet over seven runs. We returned for another half-day on the 18th, with après-ski at Jerry and Sheila's followed by dinner and dancing at Ollie's Route 6 with their friends Daniele and Greg, and Monty and Loniett. After a wonderful stay at Chez Katz with 'the hosts with the most' Jerry and Sheila drove us to Eagle Vail airport where we met Jimmy and Cynthia. We then had lunch at Juicy Lucy's, joined by their grandchildren Jayme, Mattie and Zoey, fresh from their own ski holiday with their grandparents.

The beds at the Nowery household barely have time to get cool! On 20th February we caught up on work, including a promising enquiry from a client in Tortola about preparing an appraisal of resort condos for sale. We had planned to ski, but discovered Cynthia had taken the Ford Expedition's key to Costco – so no skiing. I made spaghetti aglio e olio for dinner, and found a bottle of Lalo premium tequila, which we had purchased to welcome Boopie, arriving the next day.

On the 21st, I had conference calls about the Lighthouse School and the specialist furniture that would be required, and an enquiry into Caribbean hotel costs from my long-standing friend and architect, Steve Mendes. We then met Boopie and George at Aspen airport and drove to El Karita Mexican restaurant in Willetts, for late lunch. We finally hit the slopes on the 22nd, at Two Creeks, in Snowmass. We logged two runs, with George coached under my 'Springs and Wings Ski School' – bend the knees (springs) and arms up (wings). He fell a few times, but fresh snow softened the landings. That night, George had some live lobsters delivered to Mariposa – there was some debate over ethics and humaneness, but they were delicious.

I began the 23rd with a financing call for the Balam Escape resort in Belize. We had intended to begin skiing at noon, but parking at Two Creeks was impossible until the 'parking angel' intervened. In the evening, we dined in Carbondale at the Allegria. There, we spoke with Benoit de Francisco, the owner, who wanted to sell Carabella wine in the restaurant, so I put him in touch with Mike Hallock, our winemaker.

Sadly, departure loomed. On 26th February, we had our traditional caviar eggs and champagne for breakfast, and then skied Ajax. With the gondola closed due to wind, we ascended via Ruthie's and logged nine runs. We awoke on 27th February to a big snowstorm. Jayme kindly drove us to the airport, with Jimmy riding shotgun through Glenwood Canyon to Eagle Vail, where we caught our flight to Miami, and then home to Cayman the next day.

On 29th February, I held a site visit at the Greenery to resolve some issues in connection with the Kirk Freeport Rolex and La Parfumerie fit-out that was underway. Then I had a design development meeting on the Eden Centre. We were holding weekly development meetings on the project, and it was moving forward at a good pace. A few days later, BCL submitted a proposal to provide 'As and When' QS services to the Recovery and Development Agency in the British Virgin Islands.

The next day we held a reception at Callaloo to thank everyone who had kindly donated funds in support of my Climb for Red in support of the Red Cross, and the press for covering the climb so well. I produced a slide presentation about the Aconcagua training, climb and fundraising, which we were also going to share with some donors and friends in the UK. So, the day after flying to London on the 13th, Viv and I went out to buy the small but vital connection cable needed to show it on our TV in QGM.

On the 16th, a chauffeur picked us up at QGM for our drive to the Lansdowne Club for Rob's seventieth birthday party. A week earlier I had met with Raglan Roper – an excellent source for Cuban cigars with his contacts there – because I wanted to secure the best I could find for Rob's present. He was, quite rightfully, passionate about his after-dinner cigar! After checking in we went down to the Adam Room for tea and cakes, followed by a dynamic performance by two very athletic dancers. Cocktails then followed, and dinner of roast duck in memory of our dad, whose favourite dish it was, a short speech by yours truly, and then entertainment by a group of singers, topping off with a nightcap in the Adam room.

On the 17th, Patrick Stainton, who had accepted our offer to work with BCL, joined us for dinner at Da Mario. During the next few days Patrick and I met with Jestico and Whiles to discuss the Lighthouse School design work, Anni came round to QGM early for a rehabilitation conference with Igor, and we then had the Aconcagua thank-you party and presentation at QGM followed by a light supper.

On the 22nd we began the day with a conference with NACO airport consultants, and Reed Engineers in Cayman about the work to the General Aviation Terminal we were bidding on. In the evening Viv and I went to see the ABBA Voyage show at their purpose-built theatre, which was absolutely mesmerising. On the 26th we returned to Cayman and were no sooner back than I was off to a design meeting on the Eden Centre with architects MJM.

On 1st April, the twenty-eight-year-old Patrick Stainton arrived in Cayman to join BCL, and his enthusiasm and knowledge of quantity surveying was a perfect fit for the practice. Patrick had done an external degree, as I had, which meant he had some five years more practical experience than a typical full-time university graduate.

Since deciding to write this book, I have been particularly interested in other authors' experience in the craft, and so was delighted to be invited to Diane Siebens's book launch of *No Time for Fear* on 4th April at the George Town Yacht Club. The book describes Diane's fascinating life, and her near-death experience of being buried in an avalanche while helicopter backcountry skiing in Canada.

On 12th April Viv and I flew to Miami to spend the weekend, and whilst there I drafted a letter to our Minister of Culture, who had invited me to return as Chairman of CNCF. I met with him just over a week later, to discuss the direction CNCF was going in and how the Strategic Planning Exercise was being implemented, and whether I was prepared to take over the chairman's role again. I confirmed the contents of my earlier letter, saying I was prepared to return to this role once Heritage and Culture were combined under the same ministry again, given my concern over the wisdom of separating them.

Back in Cayman, I met with the consultant, Liberty, whom we had hired for the Eden Centre project. We wanted them to prepare an independent demand survey for the capacity of the self-storage business in Cayman as part of the risk-management process, both for our own knowledge and to demonstrate the need for a development such as ours in that particular location, to the Planning Authority.

At this time, Viv and I were considering a summer visit and hiking tour to Azerbaijan and Georgia. Katie Adams, an intrepid traveller who had visited both countries, kindly came to Callaloo on 17th April to discuss her experiences, places to stay and things to do.

On the 25th we enjoyed dinner with Angela and Orman Morgan at Blue Cilantro, and two days later we had drinks with Rafael and Patrick, and then dinner at Callaloo. Rafael was the nephew of Ray Lewis, and was working in Nassau for Pictet, the Swiss Bank. He was also a keen ultra-marathon runner, who had just completed a 100-kilometre run in Colorado. Pictet had an interesting division that advised charitable foundations on their formation and management, so we were able to discuss the Bould Foundation, and our goals and management, with him. We followed up a month later, when Viv and I had a conference with Christopher Courth, who was Pictet's expert on charitable foundations. He was most informative on key issues such as objectives, length of time of existence, management structures, and so on, as we continue to develop the Bould Foundation.

To thank Vivian and me for his first month in Cayman, Patrick subsequently invited us for dinner at Bacaro, which was certainly most enjoyable and unusual – the man has class. A few days later, I took Patrick to meet Jimmy Powell in West Bay. There, while Jimmy sat relaxed in his rocking chair on his patio, he related stories about building condos along Seven Mile Beach with me over the years. It was a great learning experience for Patrick; Jimmy was known all over Cayman as the 'Condo King' – a well-earned title.

On 2nd May we hosted the Garden Club of Grand Cayman's annual hat parade in the Orchard at Callaloo, with a large tent to keep everyone out of the sun as the guests sipped on glasses of champagne while watching the show. Three days later, we celebrated Viv's seventy-eighth birthday with a lunch at Callaloo prepared by Chef Roman. It began with hors d'oeuvres and Taittinger Brut Reserve champagne, diver scallops dynamite style with Carabella Dijon Clones Chardonnay 2021, roast lamb with Carabella Inchinnan Pinot Noir 2018, cheese with Gould Campbell Vintage Port 1994, lemon soufflé with raspberry sauce with Carabella Late Harvest Pinot Gris 2015. Our guests included Maureen and John Collins, John and Louise Jenkinson, Anita Hartwell and Patricia Bradley.

On 9th May I flew to Santo Domingo to meet with Hart Porsch, the developer of Balam Escape resort in Belize, who needed a solar power provider, and then drove to Punta Cana with Michell to meet with a team of alternative energy suppliers specialising in solar power, who had a highly sophisticated supply system which they provided to a large number of consumers. They had also developed the equivalent of a gas station, where one came to charge one's car and where, while waiting for the charge to complete, one could make use of an office work space, a playground for children, a fast food outlet and a car rental agency – there was even a retail sales centre for new vehicles. While we were sitting in the office and discussing the project in Belize, Michell received an email from PWD in Cayman stating BCL had been given the go-ahead to proceed with the detailed design on the prison after all. This was indeed exciting news, particularly given the length of time we had been working on this project. I returned to Cayman from Punta Cana via Miami on 12th May.

On 15th May I heard again from Pungo, my guide on Kilimanjaro who was in need of funds, this time to help his daughter. Viv kindly offered to go to Western Union this time, and the transfer only took three hours to process as I had given Viv all the due diligence information needed to prove what the funds were for.

We were kindly invited to the celebration of Sydney's eightieth birthday, and his and Claire Coleman's fiftieth wedding anniversary. The celebration was held at Morgan's in the Cayman Islands Yacht Club. At these events, it was always good to catch up with friends we had known for so many years but often did not see on a day-to-day basis. Somehow, it seems we met up with our friends much more easily in the 80s, when Cayman's population was only around twenty thousand people.

On the 21st, we attended a meeting at PWD to review the schedule for the prison design development and construction drawings. It was, of course, a complex project requiring a broad range of specialist skills and a team of around eighty experienced professionals, with BCL serving as the lead consultant. Two days later, I met with the Minister of Home Affairs and her Chief Officer to present in detail the Outline Business Case that we had developed for the prison and to explain how we were advancing this essential project closer to the construction stage. We also discussed the way we had developed the proposed phasing strategy, designed to make the project more politically appealing by avoiding a single, large-scale rollout.

Around this time we hosted a cocktail party at Callaloo for the Liberty team that were preparing our feasibility report for the Eden Centre self-storage facility. They had made great progress, and it was interesting to talk with them about the differences between the dynamics of the storage business in the USA versus that of Cayman, pioneered by MW2 forty years earlier.

On 22nd May, Cayman Art Week was launched at the National Gallery. This event has grown in stature each year and was becoming ever more popular as it exposed even more people to the broad range of artistic talent available in Cayman. That evening the BCL team attended a Business After Hours function, promoting a new form of storage which had been introduced to Cayman. Called UNITS, it featured a portable container that would be delivered to your site, where it could either remain or could be taken to a central facility and stored there.

We began our vacation in Tuscany and Marbella on 1st June, with a flight from Heathrow to Pisa, where we arrived at 7.30pm. We waited for Alan and Claudia to arrive from Málaga at 9.30pm, enjoying a pizza and glass of wine in the meantime. We then went to collect our rental car and drove to Villa Pineta. It was meant to be a one-hour drive, but although we followed the directions we had received, it took four and a half hours and many wrong turns before we finally arrived to find a fabulous villa with a large, but very cold, swimming pool. We rose late the next day, shopped for supplies, had lunch in Barga, and then made ourselves a welcome pasta carbonara for dinner. On the 3rd, after sorting out a Wi-Fi issue (thanks to Alan's engineering skills), we drove to the Orecchiella Natural Reserve for our first hike. It was a beautiful but steep climb in the Garfagnana Apennines of some 1,340 feet in four and a quarter hours. Our lunch baguettes were accompanied by a chilled rosé, kept cool by the insulated covers from my Aconcagua Nalgene bottles – a good boy scout is always prepared!

On the way back, we navigated using Alan's cell phone. But it ran out of charge just as we were making our way through a village. We stopped, and – serendipitously – looked up to discover we were right next to a shop selling charging cables. With maps working again, we drove back to Pineta, where we enjoyed tortellini with tomato sauce and leftover pizza in front of a roaring fire. On the 4th, after catching up with emails, we visited the walled city of Castelnuovo di Garfagnana to pick up some hiking maps from the tourist office there. That mission accomplished, we had an outstanding slow food lunch at Osteria al Ritrovo del Platano – ziti and vongole for Viv, wild boar for Alan, formaggi and jambon for Claudia, and pork and spinach for me, accompanied by rosé and Chardonnay. We all had tiramisu and panna cotta and coffees to finish – all for a mere €112.

On 5th June we walked five miles to the small town of Lucignana and back, then had a swim in the very cold pool. Viv prepared a salad lunch. Dinner was a Garfagnana tasting menu at Il Pozzo, in Pieve Fosciana, matched with their red and white wines. After breakfast on 6th June, we walked again to Lucignana. To our disappointment, we found it is a dry town mid-week, with no bars open. We returned for lunch, a nap, and dinner at Il Flamingo, by the bridge. We ended the evening by the log fire, chatting over a nightcap.

On 7th June, I began the day with the steep uphill walk to Lucignana, completing a six-mile round trip. After a lunch of frittata and a snooze, I took a few conference calls, then we enjoyed BBQ chicken paillard with new potatoes and broccoli, followed by a Magnum ice cream bar. We ended the evening around the log fire again – it was a delightful novelty for us, coming from Cayman. The 8th June was our travel day, but I managed another early morning six-mile walk through Lucignana admiring the exquisitely carved butterflies and animals lining the narrow streets.

After breakfast we drove through Lucca to Pisa airport for our Ryanair flight to Málaga where we were to spend a few days at Alan and Claudia's home in Marbella. Unfortunately, the flight was made horrible by a loud group of drunken men – easily the noisiest and rowdiest flight we have been on. The crew said nothing, and we just kept our heads down.

We arrived at Villa Karola (named after Claudia's mother) for lamb rogan josh and chicken tikka masala on the patio. On 9th June, we walked four miles along the beach to Albert's for an early lunch. We knew we had to pass the nudist beach, so Viv was forewarned not to look left! Burrata and tomatoes, chicken skewers, and Viña Sol and local rosé made a great meal. After an afternoon nap, we had tapas in Old Marbella Square and dinner at El Patio de Mariscal, where I enjoyed the white prawns and lamb shoulder and Viv had gambas pil pil, followed by Dorada. Mid-meal, the waiters burst into a rendition by the Three Tenors – they were very good, and the interlude was as entertaining as it was unexpected.

On 10th June, Viv and I had a one-hour workout with Alan and Claudia's personal trainer, Jamie from Columbia, followed by breakfast. I then had time to work on this book. That evening, we dined with Regina, a good friend, at Amanharvis, a magnificent boutique hotel in the hill town of Benahavís – food, wine and service were all excellent. On the 11th, we walked four miles along the beach to Albert's for lunch, then went out in the evening to Las Flores for paella and fish baked in salt. Along the beach, North African vendors were selling high-quality knock-off designer bags, and Viv purchased a few gifts for friends and family. The next day, it was time to leave. I took an early morning walk along the beach boardwalk, spotting rabbits and wild boar, too early to be disturbed by the crowds. Back to Karola, we had breakfast of avocado on toast, then took a taxi to Málaga airport and our flight back to Heathrow.

In London, Doreen and Alan arrived on the 14th to spend a long weekend with us. From our box at the Royal Albert Hall, we saw an incredible performance of *Swan Lake* in the round, by the English National Ballet, while enjoying Barolo, Chablis and hors d'oeuvres. The next day we went to the Royal Opera House to meet with Jonnie and Vanessa. Vanessa, being in the know, had arranged a backstage tour, after which we watched Fredrick Ashton's three-part ballet, *Les Rendezvous/ The Dream / Rhapsody*, performed by the Royal Ballet.

We finished with an anniversary lunch of dim sum at Yauatcha for Alan and Doreen. On the 16th, after a three-mile walk in Hyde Park, we went to Launceston Place for their excellent tasting menu. I took along a bottle of Carabella Chardonnay to taste against their Mâcon Villages, and a Dijon 113 Pinot Noir for the cheese course – leaving the surplus wine for the staff's enjoyment, of course. On 17th June, Alan and Doreen left to fly back to Belfast, after a really delightful weekend together.

On the 20th, Viv and I had the pleasure of being invited out for lunch by Chris Liddle and Mick Scherdel of HLM, our prison architects, at the Special Forces Club, where Chris is a member. It's always interesting to see how much tradition and history these private clubs display, making them a point of interest for members' guests. For dinner we were kindly invited to Oswald's Club, in Albemarle Street in Piccadilly, by Cullum and Amanda McAlpine – so it was a great day for socialising. Viv and I took our four mile walk in Hyde Park on the 23rd, then were picked up by our chauffeur, Tenvir, from Driven Worldwide, and dropped off at the River Café for an early lunch of scallops and langoustine, followed by veal loin, and – appropriately for a warm sunny day – a chilled Provençale rosé. Dining on the terrace of the River Café is a great place to be, with a really international group of patrons. Tenvir then drove us to Queen's Tennis Club, to watch the men's finals between Musetti and Paul – an excellent match and warm-up for Wimbledon – and then back to QGM for a light supper.

On 26th June we were driven to Heathrow for our flights to Cayman, where it was back to work on the 28th with a morning meeting with PWD and the prison heads of department, to ensure their key stakeholder input was captured as the design progressed. Patrick was now very much involved in the prison project and had the opportunity to tour the prison and enjoy lunch there. On 17th July we would meet at the Governor's office to present the current stage of the redesign and discuss any assistance they could provide as a stakeholder, given the prison's oversight under UK standards.

We enjoyed an outstanding performance of Cayman Dance on 30th June, at the Harquail and, three days later, we felt very fortunate to be in Cayman instead of travelling – although it was very early in the season, Hurricane Beryl, a rare and powerful early-season Category 3 storm, skirted the islands. It brought heavy rain and storm surge that caused pockets of serious damage but left the majority of the islands largely unscathed. Fortunately we had little damage at Callaloo, because we had been prepared with the hurricane shutters installed on the windows and doors. These would remain in place until the end of the hurricane season in November, making Callaloo feel like the Black Hole of Calcutta.

On 8th July I met with Deputy Premier André Ebanks, our MP, to see what ideas he might have about promoting a Mediation Course, headed by my good friend Jonathan Dingle, that the Bould Foundation was sponsoring in November. He gladly embraced the endeavour, noting that there were several newly qualified Caymanian attorneys who were finding it difficult to secure articles with law firms, and that the additional item of mediation skills on their CVs might well improve their chances. He kindly agreed to put such candidates in touch with me and the Cayman Arbitration Centre, that were hosting the event, headed by Megan Paget-Brown.

Viv had now agreed to our trip to Georgia and Azerbaijan, which she had carefully researched relative to terrorist activities, weather problems, and how 'Third World' they were. So I applied for our tourist visas and began to look at hiking companies, hotels and flights.

On 10th July BCL had a very interesting enquiry from a US client, asking if we could prepare an insurance reinstatement cost assessment on a residence in Barbuda, to which I replied in the affirmative. In several subsequent email and telephone exchanges, we were provided with further details of this interesting project. The residence was a beach villa still under construction, with the roof on, costing around $60 million. Given that it had been under construction during COVID, the insurers did not want to renew the Contractors All Risk Insurance. Instead, they wanted the house owners to take out property cover, with the thought that, in the event of a catastrophe, replacing the house might in fact be less expensive than its cost, given the inefficiencies caused by supply chain issues during COVID. We submitted a proposal to visit the site and examine the work to date, provide an estimate of the cost to complete, as well as our opinion of the replacement cost when completed. We were also continuing our discussions with Hart Porsch, the developer of the Balam Escape resort project in Belize, concerning sources of financing and what key information was needed in order to move the negotiations of an offer package forward.

On 19th July we held discussions with a representative of Tui Global Hospitality Fund, who were interested in purchasing a hotel in Discovery Bay on the north coast of Jamaica. They wanted BCL to carry out a due diligence exercise, which we were delighted to do along with our ME&P consultant friends AdeB (Attas Defor Bengiat). It was rewarding to be working with a company with whom I had worked for more than fifty years – on my arrival in Jamaica in 1969, I had worked with Jack Attas and Freddie Bengiat. The fact that we were now working with their MD, Martell Lee, illustrates how companies thrive and survive when you do your job well.

On 20th July, Patrick and I flew to Miami to overnight there en route to Tortola, and enjoyed a fine dinner at Bellinis in Coconut Grove. The next morning, before catching our Tortola flight, I was able to show Patrick some of the tricks and shortcuts of moving through the vast expanse of Miami airport to save time. We had been asked to look at an insurance claim for storm water runoff damage to a sea wall at a beachfront home in Virgin Gorda. We were also able to make a site visit with the owner to look at a home on Havers Hill, damaged during Hurricane Irma in 2017. No remedial work had been carried out on the house since then, and it was heavily overgrown with vegetation. It was so dense, that the owner couldn't see the rotten wooden lid covering a rainwater storage cistern. This collapsed when he stepped on it, dropping his leg into the stagnant water. Fortunately, he wasn't seriously injured. I then walked under the eaves where there was an infestation of Jack Spaniard wasps, and I suddenly felt sharp stings to the end of my nose and on the side of my cheek. Sure enough, I had come too close to their nest and been attacked. As you can see, quantity surveying is a dangerous occupation.

We drove our client to the north coast where he was staying, and then went into town to Pusser's pub for some vinegar to treat the wasp stings. An English Pub that sells fish and chips was sure to have vinegar – which of course they did. Pusser's is also famous for their rum punches, known as Pain Killers, and which come in various strengths. The two guys at the bar were testing out the strength of each one, and needless to say they were feeling no pain at all by the late afternoon.

We enjoyed dinner that evening with Percy Rhoden, our partner, who had provided such great assistance following Hurricane Irma. We caught the morning ferry to Virgin Gorda to meet with the contractor for the insurance claim and visit the site to examine the damage. It was a good example of the havoc that can result when high volumes of runoff from heavy rainstorms or hurricanes aren't properly managed. The water had flowed down the side of the hill, inundated one house where the floors needed to be replaced, and undermined the seawall of two beachfront homes. We caught the ferry back to Tortola and met with the Recovery and Development Agency about a bid we had submitted, and then met with our good friend, Dancia Penn, at her office. I took a telephone call there from the airline on which we were booked to fly from Antigua to Barbuda the following day. The flight was cancelled as they had no fuel, but they had booked us on the ferry instead – life in the Caribbean!

The next day we did a quick site inspection of Dancia's hurricane-damaged office building, then went out to the airport to catch our flight to Antigua. The check-in counter was already closed, as we were late, but after sufficient and appropriate grovelling we talked a security guard into finding an agent and caught the plane by the skin of our teeth. Arriving in Antigua, we hired a car and went to visit the Royalton CHIC hotel, the rebuild of which we had monitored, and there we were treated to lunch by a most hospitable general manager. Arising early on 24th July we caught the 6.30am ferry and after a very rough, wet ride arrived in Barbuda. We went to the site of the partially-built residence, which was located on a magnificent stretch of the whitest sand you have ever seen, and proceeded to measure and photograph it.

The Barbuda Ocean Club and clubhouse are part of a development by a company called PLH, which delightfully and very appropriately stands for 'Peace Love and Happiness'. It is owned in part by the founder of the Patron tequila brand. That evening, after some issues with an apartment we had rented for the night, we found a place for Patrick to rest his head and went out for dinner. After a long day we were looking forward to a nice glass of wine and drove to a restaurant that had been recommended in Codrington for its wine – but the only brand they had was a sweet red – so it was Heineken for us with our fish and chips. On 25th July we returned to Antigua from Barbuda and overnighted in St John's, where a street carnival was well underway at typical high volume. We returned to Cayman on the next day, in good time to meet with the HLM architectural team who were visiting for stakeholder meetings for the prison.

On Sunday 28th July we hosted the prison team for lunch at Callaloo to set a welcoming tone for a busy week of meetings, and the next day visited both the male prison at Northward and the female prison at Fairbanks, followed by stakeholder discussions and presentations throughout the week. We wrapped up on Friday 2nd August, with the HLM team flying back to UK that evening. Lunch was kindly provided by the prison kitchen, and I joked with Patrick that he had witnessed the Caribbean's full range of dining options over a two-week period, having eaten both in the Billionaires Club in Barbuda and the prison in Cayman.

We were in London a few days later, where on 10th August Erika, who was a member of the Groucho Club, invited us for dinner there with nephew the performance of traditional Georgian singing and dance really excellent. On 27th August we had a three-mile walk before driving to the airport – this time in the hotel car, for our flight to Baku on Azerbaijan Airlines. I should mention at this point that Viv had agreed to travel on what was assumed to be a 'Third World' airline for this leg of the journey as it was only one hour.

Well – check-in for business class at the Azerbaijan Airlines was efficient, they had an excellent First-Class Prime lounge, a brand new A320 plane with proper First-Class seats, a choice of champagne and wines, and a meal of different types of bread and humus – so much for preconceptions! In Baku, we took a London-style black cab to the Shah Palace Hotel, where we waited about an hour and a half for our room to be available. After unpacking we took a walk through the Old Town to the Art Club – rated as the #3 restaurant in Baku, with great décor and service – for pre-dinner Qutab, which were thin pancakes with duck filling, accompanied by a glass of Sauvignon Blanc for me and a glass of red for Viv. Dinner at another restaurant was indifferent, so back at the Shah Palace we had biscuits and a glass of red wine and tea and booked a walking tour of old and new Baku before heading upstairs for a sound sleep.

On 28th August, after breakfast and a walk around old Baku, where the quality of the restoration work was impressive, we stopped for lunch at the Old Garden restaurant, Qadim Bağ. There, we had a delicious tomato salad before beginning our walking tour with Nikan, an exceptionally informative guide and also an industrial engineering student. Our first stop was the Heydar Aliyev Center, a dramatic cultural complex designed by Zaha Hadid, showing the history and culture of Azerbaijan. We then visited Highland Park, which offered sweeping views of the city and is home to the graves of some one hundred and forty-seven victims of Black January, in 1990, when Soviet troops suppressed the Azerbaijan independence movement. They are commemorated in the Alley of Martyrs and by a perpetual flame. Then we returned to the Old City to visit the Maiden Tower and Double Gates.

Dinner that evening was at the Art Club. Viv had Kutabi, a thin pancake filled with greens and herbs, while I had tomato soup. We then shared a chicken sadj, served on a round domed iron griddle and accompanied by the freshest vegetables and herbs.

The next morning we were collected by Sabina, our guide from Bug Baku, and Ali our driver, for the two-hour drive to Quba for our hiking excursion. This had originally been planned as a three-day trek with homestays in the mountains, but we changed it to a series of day hikes due to the forced revision to our travel plans. In Quba, we transferred to a 4 × 4 Russian-built Lada driven by Xalid, with a carpet draped over the rear seat to make up for the

Jonnie. Afterwards, we chatted with the security guard, who insisted on giving us a beautiful coffee-table book on the club's history. I had developed a chesty cough and called John Addleson, our doctor in Cayman, that evening for advice. During the next few days Viv also began feeling unwell, and on 12th August she tested positive for COVID. We tracked down a private doctor or the internet, who interviewed Viv on a conference call and recommended a antiviral drug called Paxlovid, and where it could be purchased.

We then called John Addleson, who emphatically vetoed the suggestio of Paxlovid due to its possible side effects. We arranged for John to prescri an alternative, which turned out not to be available in the UK. Then I beg rescheduling the flights, hotels and hiking trips we had booked for our trip Georgia and Azerbaijan. In the event, we were able to change only some of hotel bookings which we had made on Expedia. Bernadine kindly arrange pick up the medications Doc John had prescribed for Viv and FedExed th to us in London.

The FedExed medications did not turn up at QGM, and we discovered postal code had been incorrectly entered – they were now resting in the F distribution centre in Bermondsey. So I travelled there by Tube, and a long search they found them. Now, with luck, Viv would recover fully fc rescheduled trip.

On 24th August, we flew Lufthansa to Tbilisi, in Georgia, where we a at 5.30am after a pretty grim flight, all things considered. We took a taxi, charged us twice the going rate to our hotel, the Tiflis Palace. We fell in figuring things could only get better. We slept until 3pm the next day, ar out for dinner at a restaurant called OtsY. Large portions of excellent c avocado, goats cheese and walnut salad and then a shared dish of ch a cream sauce, accompanied by excellent Georgian red and white wi much to make us feel more positive.

Our table on the patio of OtsY overlooked the crooked clock Tbilisi's puppet theatre. It leans at a crazy, precarious angle, and on a series of mechanical characters run out of open doors and back ir the delight of the audience that gathers in anticipation of every per After a deep sleep, we took a guided walking tour through the Old next day, complete with wine tasting and a cable car up to the Old looking the city. We then went for lunch at Terrace 21, of delicio (Georgian dumplings) with cheese salad, Qisi white wine (Georgia nay) followed by the biggest fruit plate we have ever seen, ice cream For dinner we took a cab to Tbilisi's old district for a dinner show rant called 'In the Shadow of Metekhi', where the local food was re the performance of traditional Georgian singing and dance really excellent. On 27th August we had a three-mile walk before driving to the airport – this time in the hotel car, for our flight to Baku on Azerbaijan Airlines. I should mention at this point that Viv had agreed to travel on what was assumed to be a 'Third World' airline for this leg of the journey as it was only one hour.

Well – check-in for business class at the Azerbaijan Airlines was efficient, they had an excellent First-Class Prime lounge, a brand new A320 plane with proper First-Class seats, a choice of champagne and wines, and a meal of different types of bread and humus – so much for preconceptions! In Baku, we took a London-style black cab to the Shah Palace Hotel, where we waited about an hour and a half for our room to be available. After unpacking we took a walk through the Old Town to the Art Club – rated as the #3 restaurant in Baku, with great décor and service – for pre-dinner Qutab, which were thin pancakes with duck filling, accompanied by a glass of Sauvignon Blanc for me and a glass of red for Viv. Dinner at another restaurant was indifferent, so back at the Shah Palace we had biscuits and a glass of red wine and tea and booked a walking tour of old and new Baku before heading upstairs for a sound sleep.

On 28th August, after breakfast and a walk around old Baku, where the quality of the restoration work was impressive, we stopped for lunch at the Old Garden restaurant, Qadim Bağ. There, we had a delicious tomato salad before beginning our walking tour with Nikan, an exceptionally informative guide and also an industrial engineering student. Our first stop was the Heydar Aliyev Center, a dramatic cultural complex designed by Zaha Hadid, showing the history and culture of Azerbaijan. We then visited Highland Park, which offered sweeping views of the city and is home to the graves of some one hundred and forty-seven victims of Black January, in 1990, when Soviet troops suppressed the Azerbaijan independence movement. They are commemorated in the Alley of Martyrs and by a perpetual flame. Then we returned to the Old City to visit the Maiden Tower and Double Gates.

Dinner that evening was at the Art Club. Viv had Kutabi, a thin pancake filled with greens and herbs, while I had tomato soup. We then shared a chicken sadj, served on a round domed iron griddle and accompanied by the freshest vegetables and herbs.

The next morning we were collected by Sabina, our guide from Bug Baku, and Ali our driver, for the two-hour drive to Quba for our hiking excursion. This had originally been planned as a three-day trek with homestays in the mountains, but we changed it to a series of day hikes due to the forced revision to our travel plans. In Quba, we transferred to a 4 × 4 Russian-built Lada driven by Xalid, with a carpet draped over the rear seat to make up for the

Jonnie. Afterwards, we chatted with the security guard, who insisted on giving us a beautiful coffee-table book on the club's history. I had developed a chesty cough and called John Addleson, our doctor in Cayman, that evening for advice. During the next few days Viv also began feeling unwell, and on 12th August she tested positive for COVID. We tracked down a private doctor on the internet, who interviewed Viv on a conference call and recommended an antiviral drug called Paxlovid, and where it could be purchased.

We then called John Addleson, who emphatically vetoed the suggestion of Paxlovid due to its possible side effects. We arranged for John to prescribe an alternative, which turned out not to be available in the UK. Then I began rescheduling the flights, hotels and hiking trips we had booked for our trip to Georgia and Azerbaijan. In the event, we were able to change only some of our hotel bookings which we had made on Expedia. Bernadine kindly arranged to pick up the medications Doc John had prescribed for Viv and FedExed them to us in London.

The FedExed medications did not turn up at QGM, and we discovered the postal code had been incorrectly entered – they were now resting in the FedEx distribution centre in Bermondsey. So I travelled there by Tube, and after a long search they found them. Now, with luck, Viv would recover fully for our rescheduled trip.

On 24th August, we flew Lufthansa to Tbilisi, in Georgia, where we arrived at 5.30am after a pretty grim flight, all things considered. We took a taxi, which charged us twice the going rate to our hotel, the Tiflis Palace. We fell into bed, figuring things could only get better. We slept until 3pm the next day, and went out for dinner at a restaurant called OtsY. Large portions of excellent crab and avocado, goats cheese and walnut salad and then a shared dish of chicken in a cream sauce, accompanied by excellent Georgian red and white wines, did much to make us feel more positive.

Our table on the patio of OtsY overlooked the crooked clock tower of Tbilisi's puppet theatre. It leans at a crazy, precarious angle, and on the hour a series of mechanical characters run out of open doors and back in again, to the delight of the audience that gathers in anticipation of every performance. After a deep sleep, we took a guided walking tour through the Old Town the next day, complete with wine tasting and a cable car up to the Old Fort overlooking the city. We then went for lunch at Terrace 21, of delicious *khinkali* (Georgian dumplings) with cheese salad, Qisi white wine (Georgian Chardonnay) followed by the biggest fruit plate we have ever seen, ice cream and coffee. For dinner we took a cab to Tbilisi's old district for a dinner show at a restaurant called 'In the Shadow of Metekhi', where the local food was reasonable and lack of upholstery. Before departing, Xalid stopped for fuel, filled up, and then became quite agitated when someone pulled up behind him – he needed space to jump-start the Lada by rolling backward down the sloped forecourt!

We set off on the road to Griz village, stopping on the way to take pictures of the dramatic mountain scenery. To start the Lada this time, Xalid had Sabina turn the ignition key whilst he poked the starter motor with a piece of rebar – a technique he seemed to have used many times before, as it was successful. The final approach to Griz was along an extremely rough secondary road with a precipitous drop on one side. As we bounced along, Viv began to feel quite sick, so we got out and hiked the last stretch up to the village in the fresh air. Lunch was cooked by a local couple in their home. Our host was Gulbala, whose wife was very much in the background – she did not want to be photographed and did not join us at table. We were served a delicious, hearty soup made with lamb meatballs and potatoes, served with kutab bread, an all-organic salad with fresh herbs, and grilled chicken and potatoes. As we would find throughout Azerbaijan, the portions were enormous.

After lunch we hiked some 2,000 vertical feet to a most dramatic waterfall inside a cave – frozen solid in winter. The round trip took four and a half hours. Xalid then drove us back to Quba extremely slowly down a steep but paved road, as the Lada's brake pads had become dangerously hot – hot enough, I pointed out, to light his cigarette. We freewheeled down with the engine off to conserve fuel, and the dashboard gauges showed an empty gas tank and no temperature. We then encountered herds of sheep and cattle, through which Xalid drove with reckless abandon and with many near-misses. Once back in Quba, we tipped Xalid 20 Manat, and told him the day's entertainment had been worth far more. We switched back to Ali's car for the drive back to the Shah Palace and a room service dinner to round out a perfect day.

On 30th August we began the morning with a late breakfast and a walk to the Maiden Tower Museum, climbing to its rooftop through its various floors. We then toured the Yeralti Hamam and Anthropological Museums, followed by a relaxing room service lunch in our hotel room. We spent the afternoon organising a hiking tour with Sabina for the next day, to Laza, in the Qusar District.

We then ventured out for dinner of delicious buttery shrimp and chicken sadj on the terrace at the Museum Inn, back in the Old City. We returned to our hotel room for tea and dessert and a glass of Maxmari Qirmizi Quru, a premium red wine, then called it a night. The next day, after breakfast at the Shah Palace, we took the three-hour drive to the Qusar/Laza ski resort, accompanied by our guide Sabina, her three-year-old daughter Miriam, and her husband Elimir (from whom she was separated) as driver. Life does get interesting! Not far from our destination, we encountered army troops walking in single file along both sides of the road, while armoured vehicles headed in the opposite direction. Viv's eyes looked ready to pop out of her head and she was convinced we were witnessing the start of World War Three.

However, Sabina advised that we were coming up to an army base on the border with Iran. It is worth noting that Azerbaijan borders four countries: Russia, Georgia, Armenia and Iran. It also shares a long eastern coastline with the Caspian Sea to the east. Despite these land borders, there is effectively no cross-border traffic by road for foreigners, and one can only fly into and out of the country. That day we hiked some 1,100 vertical feet to the three Laza waterfalls and a viewpoint from which to look out over the magnificent mountain scenery. We returned to Laza Kafe for lunch – once again, far too much food but all of it delicious. We had ashgara chicken and rice, *tskän* (a layered, fried meat and potatoes dish resembling lasagne) and special Laza bread.

After lunch, we hiked back down the valley, trying to work off at least some of the substantial lunch, before beginning the three-hour drive back to Baku in heavy Saturday afternoon traffic. That evening we kept it simple, with a room service dinner of omelette with fresh cucumber and tomato salad.

We attended to our packing on 1st September, and returned once more to the Art Club for lunch. We had Gutab duck-filled pancakes and *suzme plov*, a pilaf-style rice dish with lamb, served wrapped in a thin naan-like bread formed into a dome, and ceremoniously broken open at table and served. The waiters in the Art Club were as interesting as the food itself. Our waiter that day was Vladimir, a Jewish/Azerbaijani man who offered us a fascinating insight into the history of his religion in Azerbaijan. After lunch we took a short walk to the Palace of the Shirvanshahs, a beautifully preserved medieval complex, which gave us a further insight into the history of this intriguing city. In a stark contrast, we witnessed the preparations of the road network for the upcoming Baku Grand Prix. We returned to the Shah Palace to rest and prepare for our 4.30am flight from Azerbaijan to Frankfurt and then London on 'First World' airline Lufthansa, which as far as we were concerned had earned the title of 'Not the World's Favourite Airline.'

Our alarm woke us at 1.30am for a 2am pickup. It was interesting to see that Baku was still very much alive at that hour – with people out partying in the streets. The drive to the airport was somewhat disconcerting, as our driver stayed on WhatsApp the entire time.

On 8th September, back in Cayman, we attended a Celebration of Life for Dave Martins at the Harquail. I was reminded how fortunate I have been throughout my life with the extraordinarily talented people I have met and worked with, and how they have enriched my existence – Dave had certainly been one of these people.

On the 9th, I attended a site meeting at Cayman Islands Further Education Centre (CIFEC), where BCL had been retained to provide project management oversight and quantity surveying services. Later the same day, I held a virtual conference with Jonathan Dingle regarding details of the mediation course the Bould Foundation was sponsoring, scheduled for November in Cayman.

Rafael had been invited to make a presentation on his training and achievements in the ultra-marathon field at the Windsor school in the Bahamas. For this, he was to receive a stipend, and in turn had agreed to donate this stipend directly to a charity of our choosing as the Bould Foundation does not accept donations from outside sources. We suggested the Lighthouse School, which we visited with Rafael on the 17th. There, the principal, Denise Williams, gave us a most informative tour of the school and its facilities.

We were continuing our discussions with our client, as well as the engineers, on the Jamaica Jewel acquisition. At BCL, we had been working for several years to assist landowners whose property had been compulsorily acquired by the government. Appropriate compensation was meant to be paid; however, progress in arriving at an equitable settlement was painstakingly slow, so in late September we met with the office of the Ombudsman to see how they might be able to assist with negotiating settlements.

On 26th September it was time for another Cayman Arts Festival piano concert at the library, followed by a side-splitting performance of *Wha Happening?* at the Harquail. I had been invited by my good friend, Miles Weekes, to speak at the Caribbean branch of the Chartered Institute of Arbitrators in Trinidad on 16th October, and so that evening he and I, along with our fellow panellists, discussed the format of the presentation we were to make.

On 28th September we attended the funeral mass of J.C. Calhoun, a longstanding friend and pioneer of the real estate business in the Cayman Islands – suddenly, it seemed so many friends and associates were simply not with us anymore.

And then came a hammer blow. On Sunday morning, 29th September, the news came that Morgan DaCosta had passed away suddenly at home at the age of fifty-seven. It was hard to believe that my good friend and fellow cultural advocate was gone. We had shared so much, working on preserving all that was best in Caymanian culture, and on how we could carry it to the next level of strategic development.

At his funeral a month later, at the Baptist Church in Savannah, I presented a eulogy for this great man and friend – though it was not easy to remain composed. In part, I said the following:

> Morgan DaCosta was a Caymanian business owner who throughout his career provided not only outstanding service to his community but also gave freely of his time on an extensive and voluntary basis in assisting and guiding numerous organisations in the Cayman Islands. The Cayman National Cultural Foundation is one of those.
>
> Morgan joined the board of the Cayman National Cultural Foundation ('CNCF') in 1997, almost thirty years ago. and served as my Deputy Chair for many years. Morgan spent countless hours of support as we steered the forty-year-old foundation, through a complex and challenging strategic planning process, for more than six years, to realign the organisation into an overall Arts Council model as opposed to the production organisation it had become, which we felt essential for the efficient onward recognition of Cayman's heritage and the continuing development of its culture. The finalisation of that strategic plan is now being implemented …

and

> Morgan DaCosta was far more than a very successful Caymanian businessman. He was one of a breed of people who believed it was his duty to help and assist others, from whatever background or walk of life, who are beset with problems or challenges. A natural facilitator, he resolved disputes using his natural understanding, his experience, and his mediator's skills so that solutions can happen. He combined an eye for detail with an interest in people, and a passion for Cayman and the Caribbean that was regional and not insular.
>
> So that his work for CNCF will always be remembered, Vivian and I, through the Bould Foundation, are endowing The Morgan DaCosta Arts Award for Excellence to be awarded annually.

On 29th September Hyacinth (our housekeeper for the last 13 years) gave me a copy of the plans for her and Ken's house in Golden Grove Jamaica, and asked if I could help move its construction forward, particularly given that I was to be in Jamaica in October – which I was delighted to do. I left Cayman on 1st October and flew to Kingston, picking up a rental car at Island Car Rentals. I met Georgie at the exit ramp to Golden Grove, whom I then followed to the site of Hyacinth and Ken's partially built house. There, I met 'Six Pack', their contractor. The contractor's name comes from his side-gig as a DJ when not engaged in the building trade – he uses it as a stage name to disguise his identity. We measured the house as built against the original plans and identified several variations. Then we discussed what he needed in order to move on with construction. I took a series of photos, and had a much clearer sense of what Hyacinth and Ken were aiming to achieve.

I then drove on in very heavy rain to arrive at the Rose Hall Hilton in Montego Bay, where the 11th RICS/IPTI conference on valuation and construction was being held. There, I checked in and attended the welcome cocktail party. On 2nd October, in the afternoon, I presented 'Risks in the Procurement Process in the Caribbean' along with my fellow presenter, Jamaican quantity surveyor Michael Robinson, who enlightened the audience on 'Charting the Future – the Construction Industry Policy of Jamaica' all very ably moderated by Alexandra Faciu. That evening we enjoyed dinner with Chris Smith, the RICS Americas World Regional Board Chair, and Justin Sullivan, the new President of the RICS. On 3rd and 4th October, I had a fabulous early morning walk around the Cinnamon Hill golf course adjoining the hotel, with beautiful views, vegetation and wildlife, and then drove back to Kingston to catch the afternoon flight to Cayman.

On 8th October Rafael introduced Vivan and me to several of his colleagues at Pictet when we had a meeting about the Bould Foundation at Callaloo. The 9th October was a busy day – I was invited for breakfast by Russell Day, the McAlpine MD, to meet Hector McAlpine, Cullum McAlpine's son. Later in the morning I discussed a project in Nevis with my brother Rob, and finally held a conference with my fellow panellists about the thirteenth CHICOS conference, which would be held in Barbados on 14th November.

During the afternoon of 11th October, BCL was privileged to make a presentation on our credentials and leading market skills in the preparation of appraisals to the lending officer at Proven Bank. In the evening, the National Gallery and CNCF held a joint board meeting to continue exploring our joint objectives as part of the Strategic Planning Exercise. The real sadness, was that Morgan was not there to see the long years of our efforts and work finally beginning to bear fruit.

On 15th October, I flew to Port of Spain to present at the Chartered Institute of Arbitrators Caribbean Branch Conference, entitled 'Pathways to Peace – Evolving Trends in Dispute Resolution' held at the University of the West Indies Campus. The next morning, I was able to start my day by driving from the downtown Hyatt hotel to the Queen's Park Savannah, where I walked several circuits and watched all of life waking up to greet the day. Later, I headed out to the St Augustine Campus of UWI to join my fellow presenters – Nigel Aqui, Derek Outridge and Shardon Haye – for our session, titled 'Revisiting Construction Arbitration', ably moderated by Miles Weekes. The presentation was followed by cocktails that evening, and there, for reasons still unclear to me, I won a prize as one of the best dancers, 'winding down' to Carnival music. Viv and I had had a fortuitous meeting with Steve and Debbie Mendes in Miami airport some weeks before, so while I was in Trinidad they invited me to their home, where over dinner we had a long conversation about the many people we had met over the more than fifty years we have known each other.

On 2nd November, Viv and I were invited to a cultural fashion presentation at the National Gallery, showing the work of Jawara Alleyne. It was a memorable evening, as Jawara had been one of the emerging talents first recognised some years earlier, when CNCF began to feature fashion as part of our cultural development with the FRESH presentation. Returning from the event, I slipped on a step in front of Callaloo and fell heavily, landing on my back and hip, with additional cuts to my knee and lip. Viv bandaged me up, but by Sunday morning it was clear I needed more detailed medical examination. We went to Doctors Hospital, where – fortuitously for a Sunday – Matthais Hertzig, their orthopedic surgeon, was on duty. A physical examination and comprehensive X-rays revealed there was no fracture, I would need a walker and some medication. Naturally, I consulted Igor for advice on treating the bruising. No surprise – he recommended water workouts and physiotherapy, which I began with physiotherapist Tenson, one of his trained practitioners who knew his methods well.

We had planned a long-overdue visit to Mustique – Viv's all-time favourite island – in November, before heading to Barbados for the CHICOS conference, where I was scheduled to moderate a panel. But after my fall we decided to postpone the trip. Then as if the stars were aligned against us, Hurricane Rafael passed by Cayman the next day – an unusually late storm, following the early-season Hurricane Beryl.

On 11th November, Viv and I left Cayman for Barbados. The 13th edition of CHICOS had the theme 'Riding the Wave', and was being held at Sam Lords Castle, a Wyndham hotel which had recently opened. I was of course still feeling a little tender from my tumble and Viv had thoughtfully brought a cushion, which eased the pain in my back when I sat for long periods of time.

As always, I had a most interesting panel. This time we covered a very broad spectrum of subjects, 'Key Considerations of Developing and Operating in the Caribbean: Insurance, Training, Shipping & Energy' with an outstanding group of panellists to explore these topics: Bill Brown, Executive Vice President

– DCK; Daniela Correia, CEO & Founder – DC Global Talent; Juan Mosseri, Sales Manager – E-Finity Distributed Generation; David Beckley, SVP, Real Estate & Hospitality Team – McGriff; and Marvin Flax, Managing Director – OBMI. As always it was a great opportunity to share experience, information and knowledge and to network amongst our peers in the Caribbean region.

When Viv and I returned to Cayman on 17th November, we were in time for the week-long mediation course with Jonathan Dingle at the Cayman Islands Arbitration Centre, kindly hosted by Megan Paget-Brown, with a participation group that had now grown to eighteen.

On 19th November an interesting opportunity arose for BCL with an invitation to bid on the expansion of the Faith hospital in Cayman Brac. We assembled a multi-talented team of specialists, and held our first conference to align our bid. The following day, a dinner at Callaloo with Johnathan Dingle was an opportunity to discuss progress on the mediation training. We were joined by Jerry Grad and his wife, from the International Property Tax Institute, who with RICS had co-hosted the joint conference we had recently completed in Montego Bay.

Tenson was working diligently during our physiotherapy sessions to get me back into shape so I could enjoy our planned ski trip to Utah. In the meantime I also had a bone density test at Doctors Hospital, with good results,

Michell arrived in Cayman on the afternoon of the 22nd, to participate in a BCL business planning meeting. The same day we received a promising enquiry from a client seeking project management services for a new house in the Cayman Islands Yacht Club, not far from Callaloo – so business continued to look up. That evening, we hosted a cocktail reception at Callaloo for all eighteen graduates of the mediation course. While they relaxed after a rigorous week of study and exercises, André Ebanks MP, kindly greeted and congratulated all graduates.

On 25th November I began the day with a short early morning water work out, followed by a midday physio session. Later, Frank Reed and his team kindly hosted a casual meet-and-greet for Michell to meet their team. We had been working with them on a growing number of projects, and this was an opportunity to strengthen the relationship before Michell's departure for Punta Cana the next day.

Two days later, we held a meeting with our planning consultant on the Eden Centre project. A potential condition for planning approval had revealed itself: the Central Planning Authority was considering a request to realign Walkers Road in front of our property. The proposed change seemed designed to benefit a residence on the opposite side of the road, owned by a family linked to a civil servant who was part of the National Roads Authority. The Eden

Centre shareholder team attended the Central Planning Authority meeting on 4th December to present our application, which was based on the questions asked by the panel members, and our responses appeared to be well received.

On 1st December Viv and I entertained Patricia Bradley, an accomplished author, for lunch at Callaloo, and discussed this book. Patricia gave me some useful insights as to what had yet to be done.

On 2nd December we held a conference with the appointed cost consultants on the prison about their schedule for the delivery of the cost plan, and later that evening, thanks to the difference in time zones, we were able to meet with Carabella Partners to discuss some changes in our corporate Articles.

Now it was time to ski, and Viv and I had picked up our rental car in Salt Lake City and driven to Alta and Sugarplum. On this occasion we were staying in Unit G, a modern but comfortable apartment very different from our usual unit. The next morning, after a conference call about the Eden Centre budget, we drove down into Salt Lake City to go shopping and to the State Liquor Store. Luckily, I had remembered that, in addition to my driving licence ID, I also needed my passport to prove I was over twenty-one years of age – I suppose it's a measure of my senior years that I'm now pleased to be asked!

We settled in that evening with a simple dinner of chicken stew, Côtes du Rhône and Mâcon Villages. The next morning, after breakfast, we dealt with some business emails then ventured out to ski at 12.30pm. In spite of the late start, we managed three runs and 5,000 vertical feet – my first real test post-injury. The next day we had another late start, after stopping first for lunch at Rustler to avoid a 'bum's rush'. We made only one run afterward, but it was a pleasant day nonetheless.

9th December was our twenty-ninth wedding anniversary. We enjoyed scrambled eggs and smoked salmon for breakfast, and new powder had fallen so the skiing would be fine. Visibility wasn't so great, however, so we had a celebratory lunch of fish tacos at Snowpine, where our server, Sarah, surprised us with complimentary dessert and coffee. Then it was out for a couple of runs of 3,500 feet, and dinner at home. The 10th December was my seventy-ninth birthday, and one year closer to free skiing on my eightieth! We began the day with a celebratory bacon and egg Ulster Fry, followed by business calls, and three runs, and another lunch at Snowpine.

The next day brought a bluebird sky and excellent snow. After breakfast and business calls, we skied the backside of the mountain and had lunch at Rustler, where we met the manager, Tom. This year, after many years of trying, we had finally secured four lottery tickets to the Morman Tabernacle Christmas Concert. Sadly, the performance was scheduled for 19th December, after our planned return to Cayman. We passed the tickets on to Tom, to share with the Rustler staff.

The next day, we had two good runs totalling 4,000 vertical feet, then decided to call it a day. On 13th December we awoke to a huge snowfall, and I was tied up with various conference calls. Later, we drove through very deep snow (by now we knew enough to always hire a four-wheel drive car) to the Alta post office, to send Viv's handwritten Christmas cards, then slowly made our way back to spend a lazy, relaxed afternoon and evening at Sugarplum. On 14th December we were up at 1.30am to drive to Salt Lake City Airport for our early flight to Dallas and then Cayman. As Viv checked in at Dallas for our direct flight back to Cayman, she returned with two First Class boarding passes – her smile said it all.

On 15th December, we sadly paid our final respects to Bobby Nunes, our longtime friend who had achieved the grand age of ninety. At this celebration of his life, he was truly acknowledged for the wonderful, unselfish work he had performed throughout his life, and his many contributions to sport, including cycling and the Olympics. I was delighted to have been asked to say a few words in celebration.

The year ended, as always, with croquet and Christmas lunch at Callaloo, and our 'Do Drop In' on 31st December.

2025

'Life is a series of natural and spontaneous changes. Don't resist them; that only creates sorrow. Let reality be reality. Let things flow naturally forward in whatever way they like.' Lao Tzu

For the past several years, I have enjoyed writing this cathartic review of my life of almost eighty years and, in January 2025, I was both humbled and delighted to be honoured by the Cayman Islands Government, on National Hero's Day, as a 'Legacy Builder', which was announced with the following release:

> Bould Consulting Limited Chairman, Martyn Bould was honoured on Monday 27th January 2025 with the Award as a 'Legacy Builder' for laying the groundwork for future economic development, while shaping the social and cultural landscape of the Cayman Islands for generations. Individuals in this category founded or opened businesses in the Cayman Islands prior to 1970, with those businesses contributing to the local economy, community and culture for twenty years or longer. These individuals demonstrated leadership in building

the foundations of an enduring Caymanian business culture, helping to set standards for future generations.

In announcing Cayman Hero's Day 2025, the Premier, the Honorable Juliana O'Connor-Connolly, highlighted the theme 'Celebrating the Icons of Business and Entrepreneurship: A Tribute to Caymanian Business Ingenuity, Creativity, Successes, Hard Work and Innovation and Leadership', we recognise those who have built and shaped our nation's economic landscape. These individuals and businesses have demonstrated remarkable resilience, creativity and vision, transforming their ideas into thriving enterprises that not only contribute to our economy but also inspire future generations of entrepreneurs. Through their hard work and leadership, they have paved the way for progress, showcasing the best of Caymanian determination and ambition.

As we celebrate their achievements, we are reminded of the vital role that innovation, creativity and leadership play in our growth as a nation. By acknowledging these icons of business and entrepreneurship, we reaffirm our commitment to fostering an environment where ingenuity and enterprise can continue to flourish.

Which seems to be an appropriate place to pause – not end – this story, as we plan to visit Tibet, Taiwan, South Korea and Japan, and I plan to climb Mount Fuji to raise funds for the Cayman Islands Red Cross. My beloved Viv will be at the base of Mount Fuji, awaiting my descent, and ready for our next adventure together.

As the late David Niven loved to say:

'Go Slowly, Come Back Quickly.'

Regarding Baha Mar, where this story began, it is worth noting that during construction there had been murmurs of some form of 'conspiracy' by the contractor to delay completion.

After the developers filed for Chapter 11 bankruptcy, and the property's subsequent liquidation and sale, the developers – BML Properties – represented by Sarkis Izmirlian, filed a suit for fraud in the New York Courts. The claim centred on the contractor's failure to meet the agreed completion date. After protracted hearings the court awarded US$1.6 billion in damages against the contractor, CCA Americas. As of May 2025, CCA Americas has filed an appeal against the award, which is waiting to be heard.

As for my beloved Cayman Islands, Roy Bodden released his latest book *De-Constructing Development – Immigration, Society and Economy in Early 21st Century Cayman* in July 2025. In it, he provides a well-researched and thought-provoking examination of the duality of 'paradise' and 'the plantation' and the challenges of balancing our life and growth here.

For me, these islands have been neither paradise nor plantation, but home – a home that also has its tensions and unspoken truths about history and identity. Living here, I have always tried to help preserve and develop what is distinctly Caymanian – not out of nostalgia, but for the sake of coherence, and also to narrow the space between what some imagine this place to be and what it truly is for those who have always lived here. I have tried, and will continue to try, to do my level best to narrow the gap between 'paradise' and 'the plantation' because I believe that by paying attention to each other's needs and taking care, being willing to act honestly, with eyes open and heart engaged, our society will be able to progress toward unity without forgetting who we are.

And so, after almost eighty years on this earth and the many thousands of words in this book describing my journey, what are the Life's Lessons Well Learned for me?

I have tried to live my life by the values and expressed sentiments in the poem *If*, which my mother gave me on my 21st birthday, and by the aphorisms linked to the beginning of each year in this book. At the heart of it all is a simple goal: to find happiness, and to feel that my life has been well spent and that I have done my level best to leave the world a better place than I found it.

None of this would have been possible without the support of so many people who have enriched my life in ways beyond measure. Unsurprisingly, leading that group is Viv – still and always my teenager in spirit and energy – with whom I've been fortunate to share a fabulous marriage. At our wedding, Reverend Baillie offered us a piece of advice we've adhered to ever since: look after each other's needs before your own. Viv often shares that line with newlyweds, and after being tried and tested for thirty years, we can say with confidence – it holds up.

Marriage came to me late in life, and in that timing I found the right partner. Being of a similar age, background and outlook gave us a shared sense of direction and focus – tempered by Viv's grounding influence. Her banker's training to 'follow the rules' helped keep my entrepreneurial spirit on the right track!

For the rest – in work, as in life, I've learned a few principles worth repeating:

Look after your health; maintain your fitness.
Listen more than you speak. We continue to learn.
There are no stupid questions.
Treat everyone fairly and with respect – and Keep Climbing.

TO BE CONTINUED

The Cayman Islands: Significant Dates

1503 – Columbus sights the Sister Islands and names them Las Tortugas. Over the next 100 years, the name Caymanas or Cayman becomes common.

1586 – Sir Francis Drake's fleet of 23 ships stops for two days at Grand Cayman. The island is not inhabited, but crocodiles, alligators, iguanas and numerous turtles are recorded.

1655 – England captures Jamaica from the Spanish.

1670 – Under the Treaty of Madrid, Spain recognises England's sovereignty over Jamaica and various other Caribbean islands, including Cayman.

1700 – Permanent settlement has probably begun by this time with a few families, notably Boddens, living on Grand Cayman.

1734–42 – Five land grants in Grand Cayman are made by the Governor of Jamaica. Mahogany and logwood are being exported to Jamaica. Population perhaps 100–150.

1773 – First survey or 'map' of Cayman made by the Royal Navy. The population is 400, approximately half of which are slaves.

1798 – First record of a magistrate in Cayman being appointed by the Governor of Jamaica.

1820s – Local laws are passed by a self-appointed group of 'principal inhabitants'.

1831 – Decision to form an elected assembly is taken at Pedro Castle on 5th December. Elections follow five days later and the new Assembly passes first legislation on 31st December. The population is approximately 2,000.

1835 – Governor Sligo of Jamaica lands in Cayman to declare all slaves free in accordance with the Emancipation Act of 1833.

1863 – Act of the Imperial Parliament in London makes Cayman a dependency of Jamaica (although Cayman had been loosely 'governed' as such from 1670).

1898 – Frederick Sanguinetti, an official in the Jamaican Government, is appointed as the first Commissioner of the Cayman Islands. Cayman will be governed by Commissioners until 1962.

1920 – A major Education Act provides for government schools in all districts.

1953 – An airfield is opened in Grand Cayman, eventually replacing the seaplane service which had operated since the 1940s. The George Town Hospital is opened. Cayman's first commercial bank, Barclays, opens.

1959 – Cayman receives its first written constitution, which grants the vote to women. Cayman ceases to be a dependency of Jamaica.

1961 – The Hon. Annie Huldah Bodden, OBE, became the first woman nominated as a Member of the Legislative Assembly. The following year, National Hero, The Hon. Mary Evelyn Wood, Cert. Hon. was the first woman elected as a Member of the Legislative Assembly.

1962 – Following Jamaica's independence from Great Britain, Cayman chooses to remain a Crown Colony, governed by an administrator who reports directly to Westminster.

1965 – The Mosquito Research Control Unit (MRCU) begins operating. The Chamber of Commerce is formed.

1966 – Landmark legislation is introduced to encourage the banking industry.

1968 – Cayman Airways begins service.

1970 – The population of the Cayman Islands is 10,249, with only 403 visitors.

1972 – A new Constitution is introduced under which Cayman is governed by a Legislative Assembly, Executive Council and a Governor. Cayman introduces its own currency. The census reports the population of the Cayman Islands is 16,677.

1979 – Cayman Islands National Museum established, but only opened to the public in 1990.

1981 – Northward Prison opens.

1982 – The Islands celebrate the 150th Anniversary of Parliamentary Government.

1983 – Her Majesty Queen Elizabeth II visits the Cayman Islands for the first time. The Cayman Islands Audit Office is established. The Auditor-General is appointed by the Governor and is independent of the Executive and Legislative branches.

1984 – Cayman National Cultural Foundation is formed.

1987 – The National Trust for the Cayman Islands Law is passed and the Trust begins operation the next year.

1989 – The census reports the population of the Cayman Islands is 25,355.

1991 – Mrs Sybil McLaughlin, who became the first Clerk of the Legislative Assembly and woman to hold that post in the entire Commonwealth in 1959, becomes the first Speaker of the Legislative Assembly.

1991-5 – The 'Cuban Crisis' sees a trickle of asylum-seekers and economic migrants become hundreds, and then thousands. Government resources (Immigration, Social Services, Police, Public Works and Health) are stretched thin. Almost 1,100 Cubans arrive between 1st August and 16th September 1994. A residential camp, later known as Tent City, allows for long-term management. Groups from the UN, UK and USA visit and are involved in resolving the problem. Most of the refugees eventually are allowed into the US; some go to other Latin American countries; a few qualify for, and are granted, political asylum in Cayman. Tent City closes in June 1995.

1992 – Membership in the Legislative Assembly increases from 12 elected members to 15 elected members, with the districts of George Town, Bodden Town and West Bay each gaining a seat.

1993 – The National Heroes Law is passed and the next year Mr James Manoah Bodden (d. 1988) becomes the country's first National Hero. The Cayman Islands' Coat of Arms, Flag and National Song Law is passed. The Department of Environment is created, incorporating the environmental health section from Public Health, the MRCU, and the Natural Resources Unit from the Ministry. The Financial Services Supervision Department is formed by amalgamating the Banking Supervision and Insurance departments.

1994 – Her Majesty Queen Elizabeth II pays her second visit, knights the former Financial Secretary, Sir Vassel Johnson, and opens the Queen Elizabeth II Botanic Park. After several years of operation, the National Archive officially opens. Constitutional amendments come into force including: Executive Council (ExCo) members are now to be called 'ministers' and a fifth minister is to be added to ExCo; provisions are to be made for paying public service pensions, holding referenda, establishing a register of interests for LA members and appointing a speaker and deputy speaker for the LA, adding a Bill of Rights to the Constitution, and appointing a Complaints Commissioner.

1996 – Residents of all ages are polled, and the National Symbols Law make their choices official: the Cayman Parrot is the National Bird; the Banana Orchid is the National Flower; the Silver Thatch is the National Tree. Mrs Sybil McLaughlin, the first Caymanian speaker of the Legislative Assembly, is designated the country's second National Hero. Split from the Department of Environment, Environmental Health becomes a separate department. National Gallery of the Cayman Islands is established

1997 – The Cayman Islands Monetary Authority begins operating. The Cayman Islands Stock Exchange opens. The Hon. Juliana O'Connor-Connolly becomes the first female Minister appointed to the Executive Council. The Women's Resource Centre is opened.

1998 – National Health Insurance Law comes into effect. National Pensions Law is passed.

1999 – Government establishes a Financial Services Secretariat under the Portfolio of Finance and Economic Development. A Memorandum of Understanding is signed with Cuba for the repatriation of illegal Cuban migrants. The census reports the population of the Cayman Islands is 39,410.

2001 – The United Democratic Party (UDP) is formed. The UDP brings and wins a vote of no confidence against Leader of Government Business, the Hon. Kurt Tibbetts. Mr Tibbetts and The Hon. Edna Moyle are removed from Executive Council.

2002 – The People's Progressive Movement (PPM) is formed.

2003 – A year-long celebration marks the country's Quincentennial. The Constitution is amended to provide for the appointment of a Leader of Government Business, a Leader of the Opposition, and an Electoral Boundary Commission. The Executive Council is renamed Executive Cabinet. The Complaints Commissioner Law is passed. Cabinet grants Caymanian status to 2,850 residents.

2004 – A new Immigration Law goes into effect; the Immigration Board is replaced with three boards: the Work Permit Board, the Caymanian Status and Permanent Residency Board, and the Business Staffing Plan Board. Hurricane Ivan hits Grand Cayman in September. There are two deaths and CI$2.8 billion in damage.

2006 – The Turtle Farm is redeveloped and turned into a major tourism attraction dubbed Boatswain Bay.

2009 – The current Constitution comes into effect. The Hon. McKeeva Bush is appointed as the first Premier of the Cayman Islands and the Hon. Donovan Ebanks is appointed as the first Deputy Governor of the Cayman Islands.

2012 – The Hon. Juliana O'Connor-Connolly is appointed the first woman Premier of the Cayman Islands.

2020 – Following amendments to the 2009 Constitution, the Legislative Assembly of the Cayman Islands is renamed the Parliament of the Cayman Islands.

For a short history of Cayman's interesting architectural development, see: https://www.johndoak.com/wp-content/uploads/2018/05/2011-Grand-Cayman-magazine-Top-Ten-Milestones.pdf

Bibliography

Bodden, Roy. *De-Constructing Development – Immigration, Society and Economy in Early 21st Century Cayman*. Kingston: Ian Randle Publishers, 2025.

Bodden, Roy L. *My Life in a Conch Shell*. Grand Cayman: Cayman National Cultural Foundation, 2022.

Bodden, Roy. *Patronage, Personalities, and Parties: The Caymanian Politics from 1950–2000*. Kingston: Ian Randle Publishers, 2010.

Bodden, Roy. *Stories My Grandfather Never Told Me*. Grand Cayman: Cayman National Cultural Foundation, 2007.

Bodden, Roy. *The Cayman Islands in Transition: The Politics, History, and Sociology of a Changing Society*. Kingston: Ian Randle Publishers, 2007.

Cayman Maritime Heritage Foundation. *A History of Turtlers and Schooners of the Cayman Islands*. George Town: CLM Publishing, 2021.

Chopra, Deepak. *Ageless Body – Timeless Mind*. UK: Rider & Co., 1993.

Chopra, Deepak & Rudolph Tanzi. *The Healing Self – A Revolutionary New Plan to Supercharge Your Immunity and Stay Well for Life: A Longevity Book*. USA: Harmony/Rodale/Convergent, 2018.

Davies, John. *Kosen*. Leica, 2016.

Dilbert, Leonard. *Grown from This Ground*. Grand Cayman: Cayman National Cultural Foundation, 2003.

Ebanks, Consuelo, and Carol Winker. *The Southwell Years: Recollections of Caymanian Seamen and Those Who Served at Home*. Grand Cayman: Cayman National Cultural Foundation, 2003.

Epstein, Edward Jay. *Dossier: The Secret History of Armand Hammer*. New York: Random House, 1996.

Evans, Jeff. *Mountain Vision: Lessons Beyond the Summit*. MountainVision Inc., 2007.

Fisher, Roger, and William Ury. *Getting to Yes: Negotiating Agreement Without Giving In*. Boston: Houghton Mifflin, 1981.

Ashwell, Margaret. *Five Shillings and a Bicycle*. Publisher unknown, date unknown.

Greene, Graham. *The Comedians*. London: Bodley Head, 1966.

Haines, Derek, MBE. *Coast to Coast: A Trundle Along the Pyrenees*. Brisbane: Printing Brisbane, 2020.

Kelly, Terence R. *The Carib Sands*. London: Macmillan & Co. Ltd., 1963.

Kidd, Billy. *Ski in Six Days*. New York: McGraw-Hill Contemporary, 1975.

Kieran, Brian L. *The Lawless Caymanas: A Story of Slavery, Freedom, and the West India Regiment*. 1992.

King, Stephen. *On Writing: A Memoir of the Craft.* New York: Charles Scribner's Sons, 2000.

Latham, Sir Michael. *Constructing the Team: Joint Review of Procurement and Contractual Arrangements in the United Kingdom Construction Industry—Final Report.* London: HM Stationery Office, 1994.

Lovelace, Earl. *The Dragon Can't Dance.* London: André Deutsch, 1979.

Mahvi, Pascal. *Deadly Secrets of Iranian Princes: Audacity to Act.* Victoria, BC: FriesenPress, 2010.

Masouri, John. *Wailing Blues: The Story of Bob Marley's Wailers.* London: Omnibus Press, 2008.

McKeown, Patrick. *The Oxygen Advantage.* London: Platkus, 2015.

Miller, Olive H., MBE. *Cayman Rhyme Time with Miss Olive.* 2011.

Morse, Graham. *Fatal Fix.* Nottingham: Shipstone Publishing, 2020.

Muttoo, Henry D., and Karl 'Jerry' Craig. *My Markings: The Art of Gladwyn K. Bush.* Grand Cayman: Cayman National Cultural Foundation, 1994.

Netherlands Antilles National Commission for UNESCO. *Carib Art: Contemporary Art of the Caribbean.* Paris: UNESCO, 1993.

Norton, Janette. *Walking in Provence: 42 Walks in the Alpes Maritime, Var, Vaucluse, and Northern Provence.* Milnthorpe: Cicerone Press, 2008.

Oliver, Craig. *Unleashing Demons: The Inside Story of Brexit.* London: Hodder & Stoughton, 2016.

Scott, Joan Hall. *The Governor's Lady: Entertainment and Recipes at Government House, The Cayman Islands, 1987–1992.* 2007.

Seldon, Anthony, and Daniel Collings. *The Architecture of Diplomacy: The British Ambassador's Residence in Washington.* Paris: Flammarion, 2014.

Sherwood, Shirley, with Ivan Fallon. *Shirley: The Life of a Botanical Adventurer.* London: Unicorn Publishing Group, 2024.

Siebens, Diane. *No Time for Fear: My Path to Awakening.* Bloomington, IN: Balboa Press, 2022.

Slesin, Suzanne, Stafford Cliff, and Gilles de Chabaneix. *Caribbean Style.* New York: Crown Publishing Group, T.H.E., 1985.

Thomson, Ian. *The Dead Yard: Tales of Modern Jamaica.* London: Faber & Faber, 2009.

Tolle, Eckhart. *Stillness Speaks.* Novato, CA: New World Library, 2003.

Turen, Teppo. *The Tuntsa.* Chicago: Henry Regnery Company, 1961.

Walcott, Derek. *Omeros.* London: Faber & Faber, 2002.

Walker, John, (ed). *The Armand Hammer Collection: Five Centuries of Masterpieces.* New York: Abrams, 1980.

White, Paul F., and Philip Wright. *Exploring Jamaica: A Guide for Motorists.* London: André Deutsch, 1969.

Williams, Christopher A. *Defining the Caymanian Identity: The Effects of Globalization, Economics, and Xenophobia on Caymanian Culture.* Lanham, MD: Lexington Books, 2015.

Williams, Neville. *A History of the Cayman Islands.* George Town: The Government of the Cayman Islands, 1970.

Index

Adams, Charles, 31, 32, 39, 48, 55, 75, 76, 92, 178, 198–9, 352, 353
Adams, Lori, 92, 352
Afoke, Daniel, 352, 355, 356, 366, 382
Alaska, 342–3
Alleyne, Jawara, 478
Alma (canoe), 6
Alta, Utah, 139–40, 151, 159, 166–7, 204, 216, 231, 265, 276, 296, 302, 316–17, 332–3, 349, 364, 382, 430, 452–3, 480–1
Altman, Ruth, 167
Ambrose, John, 20, 29, 36, 38–9, 41, 165
Ambrose, Val, 165
American Football, 59, 70
Amin, Sanjay, 114, 128, 134
Andrew, Duke of York, 141, 171
Anguilla, 245, 306, 319, 336
Antigua, 130–1, 141, 352, 470
  Royalton Halcyon Cove, 414, 415, 416, 428, 440
Arch, David, 35, 42
Argentina, 347–8, 371, 431, 455–9
Ashwell, Harold, 38–9
Ashwell, Margaret, 39, 135–6
Aspen, Colorado, 61, 85, 169–70, 218, 257, 267, 279, 304–5, 313, 335–6, 352, 358, 366, 370–1, 388, 413, 447–8, 460–1
Athenaeum Club, Kingston, 16–17, 28
Australia, 219–21, 319–20, 367–9
Austria, 143
Avata, 355, 359, 363, 393, 401, 450
Azerbaijan, 463, 468, 471–4

Baha Mar, Bahamas
  bankruptcy filing, 3, 310–11, 482
  Bould as Project Monitor, 1–2, 264, 271–2
  China Exim funding for, 1–2, 248, 310
  fee proposal, 249–50, 252
  groundbreaking, 258
  hotels, 285
  next steps, post-bankruptcy declaration, 318, 319, 324, 328
  project delays and cost overruns, 1–3, 247–8, 270, 271–2, 274, 278, 297, 299, 309–10
  RLBC's involvement in, 244–5, 253, 255, 260, 261, 266, 273
  update meetings and site visits, 272, 273, 278, 296–7, 301, 304, 306, 307
Baha Mar Ltd., 1, 2, 3
Bailey, Jill, 133
Bailey, Roger, 133, 205
Bain, Joan, 138, 169, 407
Bali, 262
Balls, Jackie, 158–9, 165, 356–7
Bank of Butterfield, 79, 134, 153, 179, 193, 239, 260, 286, 306, 307
Barbados, 95–6, 141–2, 156, 170, 416
  horse racing, 232
  Marriott hotel refurbishment, 411, 413, 414, 415, 416, 419, 422–4, 428, 429, 431–2, 434, 441–2
  Newton Business Park, 203, 204–5, 212, 216
Barbuda, 470
Barclays Property Holdings, 103, 106, 109, 112–13, 119, 123, 124, 125–6, 129, 130, 138, 156
Barnard, Ian, 152, 161
Barnard, Nancy, 161, 223, 228, 409
Barnes, Pat, 27
Barnes, Spencer, 27, 41
Barnett, John, 48
Barrett, Steve, 407
Basdeo, Mrs Joy, 127
BCM Cape Ltd., 95–6, 97, 105, 108
BCQS International, 90
BCQS Property Management Ltd., 91, 114, 121, 133, 153, 163

Index

Beachcomber development, 46, 47, 57, 78, 394
Behrman, Basil, 114, 150, 196, 219, 256, 261, 308
Behrman, Sammy, 150, 196, 219, 256, 261, 308
Belize, 159, 275, 398, 461, 464, 468
Bell, Mike, 132, 138, 142, 153, 169, 180, 182, 197, 208
Bennett, Cathy, 280, 299, 325
Benson & Clegg, 79
Bentley, Ann, 190, 191
Bermuda, 105
Bevan, Garth, 130
BGW Cawston & Partners, 13–14, 22
Bhutan, 145–50
Big Sky, Montana, 54, 84, 93, 97, 120, 139
Bigelman, Leslie, 94, 107, 129, 142, 212, 409
Birchall, Simon, 198, 206, 209, 222
Bishop Vesey Grammar School, 5, 80, 200, 259, 275, 280–1
Bissell, Bill, 30–1, 39, 45, 46, 47, 50, 54, 58, 61, 67, 101, 112, 113, 215–16, 228, 266, 353
Bissell, Edna, 30–1, 215, 228
Blake, Nancy, 142, 182, 256, 342, 367
Blake, Otis, 142, 182, 256, 342
Bloomfield, Valerie, 41
Bodden, Atlee, 145
Bodden, Ethyl, 42, 46
Bodden, Eversley, 46
Bodden, Jewel, 42
Bodden, Jim, 36, 54
Bodden, Naul, 129, 161
Bodden, Norman, 230
Bodden, Roland, 197
Bodden, Roy, 171, 172, 173, 208, 213, 252, 418–19, 482–3
Bodden, Tommy, 106
Bodini, Daniele, 74, 76
Borneo, 352, 353–4
Bould, Ann, 234
Bould, Annabelle, 88, 89–90
Bould, Carole Patricia, 5, 62, 76
Bould, Fredrick Charles
  death of, 66
  joinery factory, 4, 6–7, 47
  love of fine suits, 7, 62
  visit to Cayman, 62–3, 66
Bould, Jenna, 53, 88, 200, 251, 306, 328, 363, 410
Bould, Martyn
  authorship, 398, 415, 416, 481

award from the CNCF, 83
award of an MBE, 270–1, 279
21st birthday, 9
30th birthday, 40–1
40th birthday, 71
50th birthday, 113, 114
60th birthday, 195–6
65th birthday, 254, 256, 259
69th birthday, 302
70th birthday, 303, 312, 315, 316
75th birthday, 396–7
broken pelvis, 317, 319
cars, 8, 38, 45, 72, 81, 123, 132, 142, 143, 154, 169, 170, 173, 184, 185, 187, 189, 297, 319
caught speeding, 66, 401
caviar eggs, 83, 286, 333, 335–6, 358, 388, 411, 413, 414, 430, 448, 461
Caymanian Status, 50, 230, 238
as Chairman of RLB, 209–10, 226
Cleveland Clinic physical tests, 187–8, 189, 230, 258
on the CNCF board, 429, 462
commercial pilot work, 35
COVID 19, 389, 459, 471
cracked coccyx, 126
croquet, 130–1
cross-country running, 80
in the Cubs and Scouts, 4–5
early career as a quantity surveyor, 10–11
early life in Birmingham, 4–5, 280
education, 4, 5–6
50 years in the Caribbean, 365, 367
first job at D.F.J. Henri & Partners, 8
flights, 29–30
godchildren, 10, 91
Gold Heritage Cross Award, 245
Harvard reunions, 82–3, 109–10, 128–9, 134, 180–1, 200–1, 220, 226–7, 254, 272–3, 290–2, 300, 342–3, 349, 367
health, 4, 45
inauguration at Buckingham Palace, 274–5, 279
Joy Brandon award, 112
kidney stones, 45
Legacy Builder award, 481–2
Life's Lessons, 483
loss adjusters exam, 427
love of cooking, 61
love of fine suits, 7, 79, 129
marriage to Vivian, 483

491

mediation and dispute resolution work, 130, 133, 145, 153, 158, 202, 264, 267, 269, 270, 284, 286, 405, 468, 475, 479
Owner President Management Programme, Harvard, 67–70, 71, 74, 76–7
Oxygen Advantage method, 365, 367, 369–70, 371, 449, 452, 453
pilates, 155
pilot training, 18–19, 20
plantar fasciitis, 446, 447, 449, 450, 451, 452
as President of CASE, 43
proposal to Vivian, 100
quantity surveying training, 7–9
quits smoking, 41, 219
rugby playing, 5, 10, 20
secretaries, 41–2
shares in BCQS Ltd., 162, 167
silver bars, 198–9, 239, 284
skiing, 52, 55, 57, 61, 66, 84, 85–6, 93, 97, 98, 102, 114–15, 120, 125, 126, 133, 137, 139–40, 141, 151, 159, 166–7, 169–70, 179, 204, 205, 208, 216, 218, 231, 237, 247, 249, 257, 261, 265, 267, 276, 279, 296, 302, 316–17, 324, 332–3, 335–6, 349, 364, 366, 382, 383, 388, 412–13, 430, 432, 452–3, 460–1, 480–1
sobriety, 94, 108, 113
spectacles, 341
squash playing, 20, 36, 38
steps down from BCQS, 167, 168
thumb infections, 324–5, 344–5
'12 Bore' side-hustle, 10
US visa, 191–2
10th wedding anniversary, 195–6
15th wedding anniversary, 254, 256, 259
19th wedding anniversary, 302
20th wedding anniversary, 303, 312, 315, 316
25th wedding anniversary, 396–7
wedding to Vivian, 109, 111, 112, 113, 114, 115
will and grave plot, 266–7
yoga, 118, 262, 291, 304, 318, 319, 340
see also climbing and hiking
Bould, Phyllis Margaret, 4, 46–7, 66
Bould, Robert John, 5, 38, 53, 88, 89, 102, 113, 179, 196, 200, 234, 251, 259, 274, 275, 290, 306, 328, 362–3, 382, 410, 461–2
Bould, Vivian
 40th birthday, 71, 72–3
 54th birthday, 143
 60th birthday, 200
 70th birthday, 325–6
 75th birthday, 401–2, 403
 78th birthday, 462
 Bould as a non-smoker, 41, 219
 at Buckingham Palace, 274
 at Commodities Corporation, 278, 371
 COVID 19, 416–17, 471
 engagement ring, 100, 416
 godchildren, 10, 91
 London life, 79–80
 love of cooking, 61
 love of gardening, 156, 162, 182–3, 281, 302
 love of travel, 61
 Martyn's proposal, 100
 relationship with Martyn, 61
 at Royal Ascot, 284
 sister Patricia's death, 353, 355
 skiing, 61, 86, 102, 114–15, 120
 surprise party for Bould's 40th birthday, 71
 tennis playing, 336
 10th wedding anniversary, 195–6
 15th wedding anniversary, 254, 256, 259
 19th wedding anniversary, 302
 20th wedding anniversary, 303, 312, 315, 316, 396–7
 wedding to Martyn, 109, 111, 112, 113, 114, 115
 will and grave plot, 266–7
 and Winnie Mandela, 240
Bould Chartered Quantity Surveyors (BCQS)
 30th anniversary, 134, 137
 in the British Virgin Islands, 91, 116, 168
 Hyatt Britannia, 65
 as limited liability company, 103, 162, 167
 London alliances, 122
 pan-Caribbean business model, 96–7, 106, 119–20, 131, 134
 promotional strategies, 101, 115
 seminars, 105–6, 115, 158
 sponsorship of running events, 50, 115
 strategic planning, 71–2
 in Tortola, 106, 114, 116, 119–20, 128
 in the Turks & Caicos, 85, 89, 91, 96, 114, 128, 168
 see also Genesis development; Plantana
Bould Construction Economists Ltd., 37
Bould Consulting Limited (BCL)
 arrangement with Bucknall Austin, 209, 249, 337

Index

Barbados hotel refurbishment, 411, 413, 414, 415, 416, 419, 422–4, 428, 429, 431–2, 434, 441–2
Eden Centre, 369, 460, 461, 462, 464–5, 479–80
Gazettals, 394
General Aviation Terminal, 400, 454, 462
Kimpton Seafire Hotel and Residences, 393–4
Kirk Freeport, 370, 393, 461
Lighthouse School, 337, 413, 434, 439, 440, 442, 446, 447, 449, 451, 461, 462, 475
prison rebuilding programme, 207, 384, 388, 391, 392–3, 396, 398, 407, 414, 422, 428–9, 434, 440, 464, 467, 470
residential appraisal business, 392
residential projects, 414–15
and Rider Levett Bucknall, 279
Royalton Halcyon Cove, 414, 415, 416, 428, 440
shares in, 417, 441
valuation services, 213, 260
see also Careenage (Cayman Grand Harbour development)
Bould Foundation, 267, 336–7, 345, 346, 355, 396, 398, 441, 446, 477
Bowers, John, 253
Bozman, Ruthie, 84
Brac, 403–4
Bradley, Patricia, 303, 317, 399, 480
Brandon, Karl, 26
Brazil, 175–7
Breakspeare, Cindy, 40
Bridgeman, David, 94, 337, 341
British Executive Services Overseas (BESO), 71–2
British Virgin Islands
 BCQS in, 91, 116, 168
 Police Marine Facility, 382, 383, 384, 387–8
 The World (cruise ship), 277–8
 see also Tortola
Britton, Gordon, 7, 8
Brown, Flo, 72, 73, 92, 100–1, 109, 113, 120, 121, 140, 142–3, 157, 165, 170, 175, 177, 178, 188, 196, 212, 230, 241, 246, 382
Brown, Joe, 72, 73, 100–1, 109, 113, 120, 121, 140, 142–3, 157, 165, 382
Brown, Matt, 367, 449, 475
Bruce D. Campbell & Co., 22
Bucknall, David, 180, 187, 190, 191, 197, 200, 205, 213, 219, 230, 249, 271, 315, 337

Bucknall Austin Caribbean Ltd., 190, 191, 197, 198, 200, 205–6, 209, 213
Bueno, Edson, 70, 175–6, 292
Bueno, Solange, 176, 292
Bully, Alwin, 124
Burdenko, Igor, 155, 170, 174, 177, 189, 196, 247, 271, 276, 283–4, 300, 304, 311, 317, 325, 327, 400–1, 446, 450, 478
Burdenko, Irina, 300, 311
Burdenko belts, 415
Burland, Alan, 95, 108–9
Burma, 322
Burrowes, Dr Jimmy, 14, 15
Bush, Gladwyn K., 'Miss Lassie'
 house saved by CNCF, 217–18, 225, 226, 228, 238, 242, 248, 252, 255–6, 257, 258, 267, 268, 275, 287, 288, 298
 life and artworks, 94, 103, 107, 114, 121, 123, 129, 132, 406–7
 My Markings, 94, 103, 107, 114, 138, 174
Bush, McKeeva, 136–7
Butcher, Jo, 31, 57, 65, 79, 81, 87
Butler, Don, 42, 46–7
Butz, Bobby, 40, 59

Cable & Wireless, 26
Café Cayman, 153
Callaloo, 110, 119
 'Arts in the Orchard,' 315, 316
 Christmas croquet, 131, 224, 231, 303, 365, 395, 410, 481
 construction, 168–9, 173, 177–8, 179, 182–3, 187, 190, 195, 196–7, 225
 'Culture Meets Tourism' event, 202
 design, 157, 159–60
 'Do Drop In' New Years Eve celebrations, 265, 276, 289, 303, 317, 333, 350, 365, 382, 397, 431, 454, 481
 first party, 195–6
 flooding, 265, 266, 269, 278
 gardens, 162, 182–3, 304, 391–2, 395, 401, 406
 Gimistory, 275, 288, 331, 332, 349, 428
 housekeepers/estate managers, 233, 254, 275, 344, 381, 388–9
 magazine articles, 204, 256, 401
 Orchard, 224, 312, 315, 316, 319, 337, 395, 406, 462
 Persian rugs, 265, 266, 278
 plot, 156
 Puddie/Buster the cat, 242, 342, 422, 428, 430, 433

493

repainting, 391–2
sculptures and art works, 132, 173–4, 188, 332, 339
serpentine louvres, 172, 178, 183
swimming pool, 174, 185
tennis court, 213, 223, 231
Tropical Storm Grace, 406
Callaloo, Villa Sorrento, 116, 122, 128, 152, 156
Calvert, John, 83–4
Camana Bay, 160
Cambodia, 150, 291–3
Came, Mike, 18
Campbell, Bruce, 22, 32
Candy & Candy, 215, 218–19, 281
Canyon Ranch Spa, 304, 318–19
Carabella vineyard, 108, 121, 155, 163–4, 174–5, 204, 208, 212, 240, 253, 257, 259, 261, 313–14, 347, 417–18, 448–9, 480
Careenage (Cayman Grand Harbour development), 132, 138, 142, 153, 180, 182, 190, 192, 195, 197, 199, 203, 208, 232, 242, 244, 335
Caribartel Cayman, 27, 28
Caribbean
  Chinese investment in, 258, 267, 269, 270, 273, 274, 282–3, 284, 288
  history, 21
  see also individual islands
Caribbean Club, 71
Caribbean Construction Advisory Services (CCAS), 105, 158, 161, 162, 164, 165, 168, 170, 172, 174, 175, 180, 186, 187, 189, 193, 194, 195, 197, 199, 201, 203, 205, 209, 229, 238
Caribbean Construction Magazine, 238, 242, 258
Caribbean Council, 282, 306, 311, 325, 330, 351, 410, 439
Caribbean Hotel and Resort Investment Summit, 282, 297, 306–7
Caribbean Hotel and Tourism Investment Conference, 141–2, 270
Caribbean Hotel Investment Conference, 224
Caribbean Intelligence, 197, 242, 249, 252, 253, 269, 279, 295, 314
Carifesta, 144, 172, 173, 202, 227, 336, 344, 405
catboats, 222, 250, 399
Cawston, Basil, 11–12, 15, 16, 29, 219
Cawston, Kitty, 16
Cawston, Sandra, 34

Cayfest, 115, 122–3, 128, 153, 179, 190, 199, 208, 222, 305, 398
Cayman Airways, 62, 67
Cayman Arts Festival, 395, 398, 405, 441, 446, 475
Cayman Arts Week, 418, 465
Cayman Court development, 35–6, 38
Cayman Court Limited, 28–9
Cayman Court Owners Association Limited (CCOA), 28
Cayman Dance, 467–8
Cayman Economic Outlook, 433
Cayman Islands
  arts in, 22, 93–4, 107, 112, 115, 119, 122–3, 129–30, 133, 159, 163, 188, 267, 337, 341
  backing sand, 288
  banking, 22–3, 31, 33, 37, 87
  Beach Club Colony, 25–6
  Bould's first visit to, 20, 22
  catboats, 222, 250, 399
  Caymanian culture, 21, 22, 39
  construction contracts, 43
  COVID 19, 389–91, 395, 399
  crime youth report, 206–7
  The Firm (film), 99
  history, 50
  mosquitos, 23, 25, 26
  National Cultural Policy, 160, 315
  Pirates Week, 82, 83, 88
  prison rebuilding programme, 207, 384, 388, 391, 392–3, 396, 398, 407, 414, 422, 428–9, 434, 440, 464, 467, 470
  quincentennial celebrations, 168, 171, 177
  social life, 26–7
  tax status, 22
  tourism, 34
  townhouse development, 28–9
  unique history, 20, 21
  Vision 2008 (National Strategic Plan), 127–8, 136, 356
  WTC&P's offices, 27, 36
Cayman Islands Folk Singers, 252, 254, 255, 256, 258, 316, 451
Cayman Islands Yacht Club, 100, 110, 122, 156, 179, 445
Cayman Kai, 47, 52, 65, 66, 125, 185
Cayman National Cultural Foundation (CNCF)
  25th anniversary, 240, 243–4, 245
  30th anniversary, 300, 305

494

Index

'Art at Governors,' 160
Arts Awards, 224–5, 239, 267–8, 279, 305, 367, 386–7, 399
award for Bould, 83
Batabano, 169
board members, 121
Bould as Chairman, 429, 462
Carib Art exhibition, 93–4, 107
Caribbean Film showcase, 212
CNCF Law, 233, 252
cruise ship industry, 287, 290
'Culture meets Tourism' programme, 202, 228
'Dos Visiones' exhibition, 171
formation, 60
Foundation, 157–8, 163, 177, 198
FRESH (fashion programme), 208, 254, 264, 478
Gimistory, 138–9, 151, 159, 188, 195, 213, 259
Miss Lassie's collection acquired by, 129, 139
Miss Lassie's House saved by, 217–18, 225, 226, 228, 238, 242, 248, 252, 255–6, 257, 258, 267, 268, 275, 287, 288, 298
One White, One Black, 227–8
Playwriting Competition, 154
Red Sky at Night celebrations, 305, 387
Rundown (musical review), 93, 126, 134, 179, 255, 270, 328, 341, 381
Seafarer's Association, 175
site for, 60, 70
Sitting in Limbo, 136
Strategic Planning Exercise, 120–1, 403, 404, 406, 408–9, 414, 415, 417, 418, 429, 462
Young Image Makers, 260–1, 270, 310
see also National Gallery
Cayman National Theatre Company, 61, 83, 441
Cayman Quadrille, 112, 240, 254–5
Cayman Society of Architects, Surveyors and Engineers (CASE), 35, 43, 258, 271, 275, 285, 398, 405
Cayman Triangle (film), 34, 44, 166
CERN's Large Hadron Collider (LHC), 133, 205
Chalmers Gibbs, 16, 34, 63
Chalmers Gibbs Martin Foster, 17, 49
Charles III, 424
Chartered Institute of Arbitrators Caribbean Branch Conference, 477–8
Chi Ho Law (George), 297, 298
CHICOS conferences, 264, 267, 270, 274, 288, 301, 315, 331, 348, 364, 381, 407–8, 423, 428, 451, 454, 460, 478–9
Chile, 289–90
China
   Bould's tourist visits to, 104–5
   Hong Kong, 104, 221, 290, 294
   investment in the Caribbean, 258, 267, 269, 270, 273, 274, 282–3, 284, 288
   see also Baha Mar, Bahamas
China Construction America (CCA), 1, 260
China Exim (Export Import Bank of China), 1, 244, 247, 249, 260, 269, 270, 297, 306, 307
China Harbour, 269
China International Fair for Trade and Services (CIFTIS), 283
China State Construction and Engineering Corporation, 206, 248, 250, 271–2
China State, 270
Chopra, Deepak, 357
Choudhury, Anwar, 353, 364
Chow, Michael, 10
CHRIS, 306
Christopher Columbus development, 45–6
Civil & Structural Engineering Limited, 131, 157
Claridges, London, 72, 82, 86, 87
Clarke, Leroy, 194, 195, 202
Cliff, Jimmy, 10, 33, 157
Clifton Hunter High School, 393
climbing and hiking
   Aconcagua, 431, 433, 434, 442, 446, 447, 449–50, 451–2, 453, 454, 454–9, 461
   Aspen, Colorado, 370–1, 447–8
   Blue Mountain Peak, 111–12, 161–2
   Camino de Santiago, 411, 424–7, 446, 449
   in Chile, 290
   Corsica, 435–8
   Crested Butte to Aspen, 420–2
   Dragon's Back, Hong Kong, 294
   Georgia and Azerbaijan, 471–4
   Gorges du Verdon, 211, 259
   Havers Hill, 363, 364, 366, 371, 380, 434
   Hawaii, 294–5
   Hunter Creek Smugglers Loop, 313
   Italy, 298
   Jomolhari trek, 145, 147–50
   Majorca, 328
   Mont Blanc, 190, 192, 193
   Mount Hood, 163, 175, 314
   Mount Sporis, 358

495

Mt Kilimanjaro, 362, 366–7, 370, 371–9, 380–1, 404, 463
Perito Moreno Glacier, 176–7
Phoenix, 334
Pico Duarte, 385–6
Sage Mountain, 356
Sydney Harbour Bridge, 220–1
Table Mountain, 134
Tongariro Crossing, 233
Tour de Mont Blanc, 193
Clinton, Bill, 205, 359
Clinton, Hilary, 269, 359
Clinton Global Initiative, 205, 278, 356, 359, 366, 371, 392
Coleman, Natalie, 403, 404, 417, 419, 429
Coley, Maureen, 53
Concorde, 86, 87
Corsbie, Beth, 332, 349
Corsbie, Ken, 224, 332, 349
Corsica, 434–8
COVID 19, 388–91, 392, 393, 395, 399, 402–3, 407, 408
Coxe, Catherine, 55
Crater, Dwight, 42
Cresswell, Geoff, 56–7, 83, 177, 243, 441
Cresswell, Sir Peter, 284, 286
Croatia, 326–7
croquet, 130–1, 224, 231, 303, 365, 395, 410, 481
Cruickshank, Neil, 58, 112, 113, 348
Cruise, Tom, 99
Cuba, 121, 171, 196, 225
   Monte Barreto hotel project, 231–2, 233, 239, 249, 311
Cullen, Maurice, 63, 64, 65, 79, 281, 312, 314, 329
Cumber, Mervyn, 20, 108, 398
Cumber, Penny, 20, 330
Cumber, Sir John, 20

Da Mario restaurant, 355, 371, 372, 409, 462
DaCosta, Cardinal, 240, 255
DaCosta, Jocelyn, 441
DaCosta, Morgan, 93, 134, 345, 398, 400, 403, 404, 408–9, 441, 475–6
Dance Unlimited, 74, 137, 177, 202, 238, 255, 316, 397
Davidson, Art, 92
Davidson, Faye, 92
Davies, John, 235, 236, 271, 290
Day, Graeme, 225

Day, Liam, 90
Day, Russell, 440, 477
Delapenha, Bunny, 224
Delapenha, Cathy, 39, 157, 405, 439–40
Delapenha, Cicely ('Cissy'), 39–40, 53, 71, 81, 112, 144, 303, 329
Delapenha, Richard, 144
Denmark, 226
Department For International Development, 246
Design Collaborative, 34, 36
D.F.J. Henri & Partners, 8
Diedrick, Denny, 40, 58, 73, 348
Dilbert, Leonard, 163, 172, 240, 255
Dingle, Jonathan, 264, 267, 269, 278, 343, 352, 355, 434, 468, 475, 479
Dinwiddy, Bruce, 162–3, 171, 179, 238, 253
Dinwiddy, Emma, 238
Dinwiddy, Sylvia (née Bould), 163, 179
Dise, Don, 52, 65, 66, 138, 172
Dise, Margaret, 94, 212, 265
Dise, Mikol, 47, 51, 65, 67, 94–5, 142, 182, 187, 251, 265, 282, 390, 391
Doak, John, 61, 124, 156, 159, 160, 180, 182, 195, 204, 208, 213, 217, 223, 303, 312, 403
Dodd, Dianne, 432
Dominican Republic, 301, 329–30, 384–5
   Tropicalia project, 264, 297, 329, 333, 334, 335, 343, 352, 385
Donaldson, Rodrick, 50–1
Dot, Miss, 7
Doucet, Jean, 22–3
Dubai, 337–8
Dunlap, Tom, 253, 296, 298, 304, 306, 307

Eastern and Oriental Express, 320–1
Ebanks, Al, 119, 134, 255
Ebanks, André, 400, 411, 445–6, 468, 479
Ebanks, Anita, 56, 395, 411
Ebanks, Dalmain ('DD'), 29, 36
Ebanks, Isley, 396, 406
Ecuador, 201
Edward, Duke of Edinburgh, 171, 188
Egypt, 254
Elegant Hotels chain, 156
Elizabeth II, 60, 102, 274–5, 284, 413–14, 417, 424
Elmslie Church, 102–3, 112, 117, 141, 275
Equal Investments Ltd., 58, 348, 384
Evans, Betty, 42, 114

Index

Evans, Dawn, 210, 343
Evans, Derek, 114, 154, 210, 343
Evans, Jeff, 433, 434

Falkiner, George, 220, 290, 291, 342
Falkiner, Sally, 220, 290, 291, 342, 349
FIDIC Contract, 145, 189, 192, 193
First Caribbean International Bank (FCIB), 157, 165
Forde, Yolande, 206–7
Foreign and Commonwealth Office (FCO), 96–7, 103, 106, 108, 109, 114, 129
Foster, Alan, 17, 34, 65–6, 101, 103, 111, 163, 172, 183, 191, 204, 214, 215, 256, 269, 325–6, 329, 432, 440, 442–5
Foster, Chi Chi, 25, 26, 125, 140, 151
Foster, David, 26, 51, 125, 140, 151, 169, 192
Foster, Jenny, 17, 101, 103, 163, 191, 204, 214, 215, 256, 269, 325–6, 329, 432, 440, 442–5
Foster, Steve, 51, 169
Foster, Virginia, 419
Fosters Food Fair/Supermarkets, 65–6, 108, 122, 397, 401, 404
France, 123, 129, 132, 175, 181, 193, 200, 210–11, 212, 213, 259
Frasier, Cathy, 116
Frasier, Jerry, 116
Fredricks, Keith, 16
Freytag, Gil, 156, 223

Galapagos Islands, 201
Galleon Beach Hotel, 35, 40, 45, 49, 60, 106
Garden Club of Grand Cayman, 228
Gates, Judith, 133
Genesis development, 59, 70, 73, 74, 81, 95, 114, 130, 192, 252–3, 257, 383, 392, 403
George, Sheila, 106, 162, 191
Georgia, 463, 468, 471–4
Germany, 341–2
Gibbs, Ian, 16, 35
Giglioli, George, 337, 341, 345
Gill, Casey, 58, 59
Gingerbread complex, 101, 180
Gingerbread Ltd., 101, 182, 192, 335, 349
Glen, Gordon, 253, 272, 297, 306, 309
Glen, Jude, 272
golf course development, 63–5
Gordon Britton, 315
Graham-Taylor, Emma, 280, 347
Graham-Taylor, John, 346–7

Graham-Taylor, Richard, 346
Graham-Taylor, Sarah, 346
Grand Cayman Company, 75–6
Grand Palazzo Hotel arbitration, 95–6, 97, 98, 99, 100, 105, 108, 130
Grant, Bunny, 16
Great House Ltd., 78–9, 80–1, 85, 89, 90, 99, 112
Greece, 254
Green, Mark, 189, 303, 331, 333, 345, 365
Green, Stan, 26
Greenery Self Storage facility, 303, 306, 307, 313, 331, 342, 349, 351, 397
Greenery Shopping Centre, 65–6, 122, 397, 401
Grenada, 190, 215, 244, 265, 266, 391
Ground, Dace, 80
Guana Island Resort, 348, 353, 358
Guerard, Michel, 55, 81, 83
Guilbard, Sebastien, 405
Guillaume, Claude, 224
Gunzburg, Baron Jean-Louis de, 87, 88
Gunzburg, Dagmar, 87
Guyana, 404, 416

Hailie Selassie I, 21, 25, 33
Haines, Derek, 396
Haiti, 23–4, 58, 102–3, 137–8, 169, 407
Haladay, Ed, 64, 76, 85, 100, 106, 110, 156, 174
Hallock, Al, 79, 98, 108, 137, 179, 240
Hallock, Jane, 240
Hallock, Mike, 108, 164–5, 313, 314, 448–9
Hamaty, Carlene, 172
Hamaty, Robbie, 18, 19, 41, 172, 219
hammams (bath houses), 110
Hammer, Michael, 106–7
Hammer, Pru, 106–7
Hare, John, 265, 266
Harquail, Helen, 60, 73, 83, 120, 129, 132, 141, 162, 165, 245, 285, 310, 329, 352, 418
Harquail Theatre
  bust of Mr Harquail, 166, 418
  Caymanian Proud: Memories of Her Majesty, 413–14
  design and construction, 56–7, 60, 70–1
  Helen Harquail's donations, 56, 60, 73
  hurricane damage, 198, 205
  local dance performance, 158–9, 166
  Moonshine Tonight, 107

497

One White, One Black, 405
opening, 73–4
Wha Happening?, 449, 475
Harris, Paul, 22
Harvard reunions, 82–3, 109–10, 128–9, 134, 180–1, 200–1, 220, 226–7, 254, 272–3, 290–2, 300, 342–3, 349, 367
Harvard University, 67–70, 71, 74, 76–7, 82–3, 109–10
Hash House Harriers, 46, 50
Hatch, John, 25–6
Hawaii, 294–5
Heathman Hotel, 122
Heldreich, Edward, 183–5, 196, 253, 273, 288, 341–2, 409, 415
Heldreich, Graeme, 5
Heldreich, Jonnie, 196, 253, 273, 288, 329, 409, 415
Heldreich, Richard, 275, 385
Henning, Amy, 42
Henriques, Dossie, 17
Hepburn, Tim, 91, 163
Higgs & Hill, 14
hiking *see* climbing and hiking
Hildalgo, Rafael, 428, 463, 475, 477
Historic Advisory Committee, 116–17, 124, 132–3
Hoffberger, Rebecca, 174
Honduras, 287–8
Hong Kong, 104, 221, 290, 294
Howieson, Rex, 30
Howland, Andrew, 88
Hubert, René, 231, 239
Hudson, Amy, 4
Hudson, Jim, 4
Hungary, 272–3
Hunte, Daphne, 191, 193
Hunte, Robin, 191, 193
Hurricane Gilbert, 81
Hurricane Irma, 345, 367
Hurricane Ivan, 183–7, 188, 190, 209, 218, 219, 222, 226, 229, 245–6, 367
Hurricane Paloma, 230
Hyatt Britania, 64–5
Hyatt Regency, 85–6
Hydes, Bendel, 56, 74, 94, 119, 255

India, 117, 118–19, 262–4
Inn Theatre Company, 56–7, 60, 61, 441; *see also* Harquail Theatre
Institute of Directors, London, 103

International Federation of Arts Councils and Cultural Agencies (IFACCA), 151, 200, 219–20, 240, 241, 242, 243, 245, 261–2, 289, 331, 371, 400, 407, 432
Ireland, 432, 442–5
Italy, 123, 180–1, 193, 250–1, 298–9, 379–80, 383, 446, 449, 465–6
Izmirlian, Sarkis, 2, 3, 309, 311

J. Michael store, 182, 183, 397, 401
Jack, Stuart, 194–5, 198, 248
Jamaica
air transport around, 19, 31–2, 35, 38, 39
Blue Mountain Peak, 111–12, 161–2
Bould's arrival in, 13–14, 15
on Bould's RICS Appointments Register, 11
The Dead Yard, 281–2
foreign-exchange controls, 35
Jamaica-Cayman commutes, 34, 35, 39
jerk pork, 84
Maroons, 17–18
National Dance Theatre Company of Jamaica, 120, 141
political situation, 33, 35, 41
Rastafarianism, 21, 33
Reggae, 37, 40
social life in, 15, 16, 19–20, 22, 30, 34
Jamaica Flying Club, 18
Jamaica Investment Forum, 268–9, 306
Japan, 235–7, 323–4
Jaynes, Gordon, 64–5, 65, 109, 113, 114, 115, 145, 202, 406–7
Jenkinson, Louise, 352, 430
Jenkinson, Sir John, 352, 430
Jennings, Brenda, 14
Jennings, L.D. 'Jenks,' 14, 15
Jessa, Kishan, 382, 391, 393
John Gray High School, 182, 224, 239, 364–5
Johnson, Chris, 41, 62
Johnson, Dave, 398
Johnson, Doreen, 10, 91, 100, 315, 325
Johnson, Hannah, 10, 91
Johnson, Karen, 247, 248
Johnson, Lisa, 238
Johnson, Michael, 10, 71, 91, 100, 315, 325
Jones, Andrew, 204, 208, 248, 284
Jones, Felicity, 204, 208, 248
Jones, Felix, 284
Jones, Richard, 52, 78
Joseph, Arek, 34–5, 43, 398
Julia, Miss (drummer), 240, 255, 257, 267, 316

Index

Katz, Jerry, 2, 98, 101, 105–6, 158, 161, 162, 180, 189, 190–1, 196, 197, 205, 238, 245, 261, 297–8, 304, 309, 336, 391, 412, 415, 451, 460
Katz, Sheila, 98, 190–1, 196, 336, 412, 460
Kelly, C.T.R. (Terence), 14–15
Kelly, Donna, 204
Kelly, Mike, 204
Kelly, Mr, 92–3
Kempadoo, Val, 202, 203
Kenya, 359–61
Kieran, Brian, 104
Kieran, Sylvie, 104
Kilpatrick, Helen, 286
Kipling, Rudyard, 'If—', 9–10
Kirk Freeport, 370, 393, 461
Kirkconnell, Moses, 287, 290
Klopfer, Ellie, 277, 278
Klopfer, George, 180, 231, 254, 276, 277–8
Kosa, Peter, 434

La Bouscatière, Moustiers-Sainte-Marie, 210–11, 213, 246–7, 259
Langer, Marshall, 22
Lassie, Miss *see* Bush, Gladwyn K. 'Miss Lassie'
Lawson, Lyle, 64, 65, 109, 113, 114, 145, 406–7
Lea, Maurice, 280
Leonard, Charles, 106, 192, 245, 256, 271, 272, 391
Lewis, Michèle, 125, 133, 141, 205, 247, 257, 325, 383
Lewis, Ray, 124, 125, 133, 141, 205, 247, 257, 325, 383, 401
Liguanea Club, 15–16, 18, 20
Lime Tree Bay development, 42
Little Cayman, 400
Liu, Daniel, 304, 364
Lloyd, Peter, 73
Lo, Cindy, 247, 249–50
Lobster Pot restaurant, 27, 30, 41
London *see* 62 Queen's Gate Mews (The Doll's House)
Lord Cultural Resources, 409, 418, 419, 429
Lovelace, Earl, 179
Ludwig, Daniel, 40
Lustig, Phil, 35

Macdonald, Jim, 23
MACO magazine, 204, 256
Mahvi, Pascal, 228–9
Majorca, 328–9
Malaysia, 320–1, 353, 354
Maldives, 340
Manley, Michael, 33, 35, 41
Mann, Freddie, 27–8
Marais, Pierre, 154–5
Markoff, Alan, 446
Marley, Bob, 13, 18, 21, 37, 40, 52, 251, 410
Martin, Brian, 302
Martin, David, 22, 40, 255
Martins, Dave, 84, 93, 112, 115, 245, 332, 474–5
Marzouca, Patrick, 19
Matthew Bolton Technical College, 7–8
Mauritius, 359
McAlpine, Cullum, 90, 92
McAlpine, Sir Robin, 59–60
McAlpine Ltd., 31, 35, 42, 43, 49, 54, 63, 71, 81, 95, 108–9, 171, 173
McDonald, Jill, 212, 251, 253, 256, 261, 313, 314, 347, 367, 448, 449
McDonald, Peter, 212, 251, 253, 256, 261
McField, Frank, 56, 227, 240, 245, 255, 405
McInnis, Boopie, 270, 335, 352, 356, 367, 413, 460, 461
McInnis, George, 270, 335, 352, 356, 367, 413, 461
McKeown, Patrick, 365, 367, 369–70, 449
McLaughlin, Alden, 75, 218, 228, 306
Medical Associates Hospital, Kingston, 14, 24
Meghoo, Michael, 403, 429
Meister, Claudine, 52, 53, 66, 81, 84–5, 86, 114, 123, 124, 140, 151, 192, 193, 257
Meister, René, 52–3, 66, 81, 84–5, 86, 112, 113, 114, 123, 124, 132, 140, 151, 192, 193, 257
Melody Lane duplex, Cayman, 34–5, 43, 46, 92
Mendes, Steve, 33, 34, 158
Messick, Don, 47–8, 52, 53–4, 67
Mills, Norman, 7, 315
Mini Warehouse Ltd., 51, 54, 115–16, 131–2, 142, 168, 184, 194, 197, 200
Mini Warehouse Two Ltd., 51, 65, 131, 177, 179, 303, 306, 307, 344
 Greenery self-storage facility, 303, 306, 307, 313, 331
Minshall, Peter, 126–7, 260
Miss World competition, 40, 49
Misick, Washington, 153–4, 439
Mitchell, Jim, 32
Monsen, Erik, 303, 333, 411
Monsen, Mary, 303, 323, 333
Montserrat, 123, 142, 144–5, 152, 156, 160

More Than Just The Climb

Moodie, Alastair, 134
Moodie, Frances, 134
Moore, Wendy, 143–4
Morgan, Angela, 302–3, 410, 430, 462
Morgan, John, 190, 191, 192, 197, 198
Mormon Tabernacle Choir, 139–40, 159, 167, 216, 302, 332, 480–1
Morse, Graham, 396
Mottley, Mia, 205
Mr Chow's, Knightsbridge, 10, 230, 282, 306, 363, 445
Murrain, Bernadine, 248
Mustique, 77, 96, 100, 113, 229, 336, 478
Muttoo, Henry, 84, 94, 124, 144, 170–1, 172, 173, 188, 202, 245, 260, 287, 303, 312, 316, 330, 365, 398, 417
Muttoo, Marcia, 303, 315, 330, 398
MW2, 356, 423, 447, 450
My Markings (Miss Lassie), 94, 103, 107, 114, 138, 174
Myanmar, 322–3

Napa Valley wineries, 307–8
National Gallery, 22, 107, 115, 120, 124, 126, 129, 132, 161, 195, 204, 223, 226, 265, 275, 329, 400, 409, 419
National Trust for the Cayman Islands, 80, 116, 132–3, 136–7, 138, 141, 143–4, 151, 165, 208
  cricket competition, 163
  Fish Tea, 152
  Mission House renovation, 152–3, 154, 163, 171–2, 208–9, 218
  sustainable development, 155
  wine tasting and auction, 155–6
Native Sons Art Collective, 112, 119, 133
Naylor, Sallie, 174, 196, 204, 304
Nepal, 117–18
Nettleford, Rex, 120, 124, 153, 177, 248
New Zealand, 233–5
Nicklaus, Jack, 63
Northern Ireland, 92, 100–1, 109, 121, 142–3, 157, 165, 175, 188
Nowery, Cynthia, 70, 83, 85, 135, 169–70, 210, 218, 220, 257, 279, 285–6, 304–5, 310, 313, 335, 352, 356, 358, 366, 367, 388, 413, 420, 422, 447, 460
Nowery, Jimmy, 70, 83, 135, 160, 169–70, 175, 210, 218, 220, 227, 257, 279, 285–6, 304–5, 310, 313, 335, 352, 356, 358, 366, 367, 388, 413, 420, 422, 447, 460

Nunes, Bobby, 17, 81, 88, 89, 120, 168, 208, 303, 481

O'Connell, Jack, 35
Office Developments Ltd., 55, 58–9
Olde, Susan, 403, 404, 409
Oliver, Ed, 29
O'Neal, Hon Ralph, 106, 116, 128
Owen, Carole, 107, 115, 120, 124, 126, 129, 275, 409
Owen, Jane, 441
Owen, John, 115, 126, 275

Pacotto, Paul, 132
Pal, Anoush, 453, 454, 455
Palladio, Andrea, 123
Pan Am's Clipper Club, 92–3
Panama, 315
  Casi Cielo project, 297, 299, 301–2, 304, 306–7, 308, 310, 311, 312–13, 319, 324
Panton, Marjorie, 172
Pappadakis, George, 394
Pappadakis, Nicky, 394
Parker, Bruce, 53–4
Parker, Jeffrey, 75–6
Paterson, Jim, 24
Pedrick-Moyle, Stephen, 91, 114
Peru, 200–1
Peyton, Roger, 7
Philip, Duke of Edinburgh, 102
Plantana, 48, 49–50, 52, 53, 54, 55, 57, 59, 67, 364
  #26 Plantana, 58, 61, 62, 88, 113, 156, 183
Polynesia, 308–9
Powell, Jimmy, 42, 45, 46, 54, 396, 406, 462
Powery, Miguel, 129–30
PRAG construction, 42–3, 45
Priestnell, Willy, 17, 19
Privateers Rugby Club, 20
Property Mediation Council, 270
Propper, Henry, 35, 36, 171, 173, 196, 349
Purton, Neil, 109, 114

Qatar, 340
Quappe, Barrie, 151
62 Queen's Gate Mews (The Doll's House), 80, 90, 163, 229–30, 239, 250, 253, 258, 274, 280, 281, 282, 285–6, 288, 298, 299–300, 306, 330, 340, 348–9, 351, 362–3, 409, 415, 450

500

Index

Raath, Jan, 288, 305, 312, 355, 410
Raath, Mortimer, 72, 87–8, 93, 103, 119, 121, 122, 124, 138, 238, 249, 251, 274, 282, 288, 305, 312, 351, 355
Racquet Club, Cayman, 38, 40, 43, 44–5, 46, 49, 54, 61
Rankine, Oswell, 83, 84
Rau, Dottie, 155, 170, 196, 247, 271, 276, 299, 317, 419
Red Cross of the Cayman Islands, 367, 380–1, 449, 451, 454, 461
Reggae, 33, 37, 40
Reid, Lorna, 177
Remony, Lisa, 165
Rider Levett Bucknall (RLB), 209–10, 213, 226, 279
Rigol, Isabel, 226
RLB, 219, 221, 222, 223, 224, 231, 233, 244–5, 257, 262, 269, 320
RLBC, 242, 246, 247, 248, 249, 252, 257, 258–9, 261, 281, 304, 337
  Caribbean Intelligence, 197, 242, 249, 252, 253, 269, 279, 295, 314
Robert Mondavi vineyard, California, 54–5
Robertson, Alasdair, 333, 351, 365, 382, 431, 445
Robertson, Barbara, 128–9, 300
Robertson, John, 128–9, 300
Robertson, Lisa, 333, 351, 365, 382, 431, 445
Rome, 86
Roosevelt, Theodore, 160
Roper, Lissie, 380, 399
Roper, Martyn, 364, 380, 393, 399
Roper, Raglan, 440, 461–2
Ross, Nick, 275
Royal Institution of Chartered Surveyors, 5, 7, 9
RP Developments Ltd., 54
Rum Point Club, 54, 399–400
Rum Point Club's Retreat, 66, 67
Rundown (musical review), 93, 126, 134, 179, 255, 270, 328, 341, 381
Russia, 154, 227

Sanchez, Vincente, 200–1
Saraç, Hasan, 109–10
Scott, Alan, 5, 80, 81, 82–3, 89, 90, 154, 175, 181, 194, 205, 251, 256, 275, 284, 367, 467
Scott, Dave, 157
Scott, Denise, 157
Scott, Doreen, 190, 194, 205, 251, 256, 282, 367, 467

Scott, Edmund, 245
Scott, Joan, 80, 81, 82, 89, 90, 154, 175, 181, 215, 284
Scout movement, 4–5
Seaview bar, 50–1
Sermoneta, Giorgio, 82, 86, 180, 181, 281, 286
Serrant, George, 131, 182
Seven Mile Beach development, 46, 47–50, 53
Shakeshaft, Hannah, 104
Shakeshaft, Trevor, 104
Shao Di, 247, 249–50, 266, 297, 298, 304, 328
Shervington, Alison, 14
Shervington, Pluto, 14
Sherwood, Sir James, 320, 321
Sibley, Jerry, 31, 34, 208, 253, 433
Sibley, Joanne, 94, 208, 253, 433
Simpson Miller, Portia, 268–9
Singapore, 320
Slattery, Jim, 78, 85, 88, 91, 103, 124
Slattery, Margaret, 88
Slaughter, Terry, 59
Smith, Franklin, 39
Smith, Peter, 136, 137, 160–1
Soto, Juan, 301–2, 306, 310, 313
Soto, Suzy, 441
South Africa, 134–6, 240–1, 242
Spain, 465, 466
Spanish Court nightclub, 36–7
Spencer, Jeremy, 57–8, 71
Spencer, Rupert, 191, 192
Spraggon, Ken, 26–7
Spry, Ivor, 13, 14
Sri Lanka, 281, 338–40
'St Andrew Housewives Set,' 14
St John, George Bernard 'Monty,' 112–13
St Kitts, 23, 27, 203, 304, 311, 330, 341, 345
St Lucia, 24, 224, 226, 228–9
St Thomas, 95–6, 97
Stainton, Patrick, 462, 469–70
staycations, 393, 403
Sternberg, George, 178
Stoppi, Maurice, 422
Stowe School, 419
Strata Titles Registration Law, 51, 54
Strathcarron, Lord Ian, 415, 416
Stuart, Mitch, 48, 245
Sunrise Adult Training Facility (SATF), 333–4, 337, 352, 355, 364
Suriname, 173–4, 272
Swaby, Ingrid, 223, 254
Swaby, Wayne, 223, 254, 344, 381, 388–9

Swanky Kitchen Band, 202, 238, 240, 255, 256, 258, 316, 344

Tanzania, 361–2, 371–2
Tarquynn Manor development, 42–3
Tasmania, 349, 367–8
Taylor, Duncan, 248–9, 253, 265, 270–1
Taylor, Lance, 222
Taylor, Marie Beatrice, 248
Thailand, 145–6, 221, 321–2
The World (cruise ship), 277–8, 281, 300
Theatre Projects, 57, 60, 70
Thomson, Ian, 281–2
Thorpe, Cathy, 42
Tiernan, Rob, 55, 61
Tortola, 106, 112–13, 124
   BCQS in, 106, 114, 116, 119–20, 128, 153
   hurricane damage, 345–6, 347, 348, 349, 352, 353, 356, 358, 363, 364, 365, 366, 371, 380, 469–70
Towns, Anne-Marie, 302, 303
Trafalgar House, Jamaica, 97, 103–4, 108, 111, 114, 115
travel agents, 55, 247
Trinidad, 158, 161, 162, 163, 170, 172, 179, 202
   Brian Lara Cricket Academy, 198, 206, 212, 217
   Carnival, 24–5, 127, 260
   UDeCOTT, 198, 202, 203, 204, 205, 206, 210, 212
Tropical Storm Grace, 406
Turkey, 109–11
Turks & Caicos, 62, 81, 152
   BCQS in, 85, 89, 91, 96, 114, 128, 153, 168
   Bould Construction Economists Ltd., 37
Twiss, Dave, 33–4, 37, 38, 39, 188, 202
Twiss, Noreen, 33–4, 188
Twohey, Rosie, 399

Udenhout, Jhunry, 173
Uff, Professor John, 229, 258
Ugland, Andreas, 129, 142, 161
University of Reading, 6, 7

Vargas, Beatriz, 344
Vargas, David, 386
Vargas, Michell, 301, 330, 344, 345–6, 384, 386, 391, 393, 411, 414, 415, 416, 417, 428, 434, 441, 451, 463, 479
Veeran, Alan, 197, 216, 228, 232, 233, 245, 250, 266, 272, 297, 301, 303, 331, 352, 353, 391–2, 393, 400, 403, 410, 411, 415, 417, 424–7, 429, 430, 441, 446, 449, 465–6
Veeran, Claudia, 216, 272, 299, 352, 393, 400, 403, 410, 411, 412, 424–7, 429, 430, 446, 465–6
Verbier, Switzerland, 66, 86, 125, 133, 141, 152, 205, 247, 257, 269, 279, 326, 383, 401
Vietnam, 290–1, 292–3
Villa Sorrento, 128, 152

Wadell, Rod, 233, 238
Wakeman Trower, Cawston and Partners (WTC&P), 22, 23, 36
Walcott, Sir Derek, 56, 170, 229
Walker, Hal, 61, 63, 64, 92
Walker, Janet, 22
Walker, William (Bill) S., 22, 31, 38
Washington, 97, 98
Waterside Inn, Bray, 200, 275, 282, 439
Webster, Burnett, 47, 48, 75–6, 78
Webster, Desmond, 75–6, 78
Webster, Micky, 392, 395
Welch, Mark, 280, 299, 311
Western, Dr Cliff, 16–17
Westin Casuarina hotel, 106
Wettstein, Wieland, 63, 64, 253
Wheaton, Nita, 179
Whitelock, Colin, 172
Whitelock, Michael, 129, 153
Widmer, Pete, 57, 65, 78, 103, 341
Widmer, Sue, 341
Williams, Christopher, 405–6
Williams, Evan, 36–7, 39
Wills and Hingley, 10
Wilson, Canute (Ken), 275
Wilson, Hyacinth, 275, 476–7
Wilson, Ken, 476–7
Wu, Adam, 258, 267, 269, 273, 282, 288, 290, 297, 301
Wu, Lucinda, 290
Wu, Tiger, 2, 260, 278, 288, 297, 301, 304, 306, 307, 309

Y2K bug, 140
yoga, 118, 262, 291, 304, 318, 319, 340
Young, Sir Colville, 159

Zander, Benjamin, 300–1
Zephaniah, Benjamin, 281–2